Greece

Fodor's 91
Greece

FODOR'S TRAVEL PUBLICATIONS, INC.
New York & London

Fodor's Greece

Editor: Andrew E. Beresky
Area Editor: Frances Arnold
Editorial Contributors: Carolyn Price, Robert Liddell, Peter Sheldon
Drawings: Lorraine Calaora
Maps: Swanston Graphics, Brian Stimson
Cover Photograph: Marc S. Dubin/Wheeler Pictures

Cover Design: Vignelli Associates

Special Sales

Fodor's Travel Publications are available at special discounts for bulk purchases (100 copies or more) for sales promotions or premiums. Special editions, including personalized covers, excerpts of existing guides, and corporate imprints, can be created in large quantities for special needs. For more information, write to Special Marketing, Fodor's Travel Publications, 201 East 50th Street, New York, NY 10022. Inquiries from the United Kingdom should be sent to Fodors' Travel Publications, 20 Vauxhall Bridge Rd., London, England SWIV 2SA.

MANUFACTURED IN THE UNITED STATES OF AMERICA
10 9 8 7 6 5 4 3 2 1

CONTENTS

CONTENTS

SUPPLEMENTS

FOREWORD

Greece has a great deal to offer—sun and sand, art and history or just a good time. And prices are still reasonable within a vast range of holiday possibilities, from inexpensive to luxury; there is, however, a general lack of solid comfort and outstanding food.

It is a land of contrasts where the influences of all the waves of invaders which flowed and ebbed across Greek soil can still be seen. There are Byzantine towns, Venetian fortresses and Frankish monuments, as well as the glorious remains of ancient Greece itself, or the ruins of the Minoan era on Crete. It is not necessary to be a scholar of history or archeology to feel the closeness of ancient Greece.

The islands have gained in importance as tourist centers, especially Corfu, Crete and Rhodes, which feature prominently in mass tourism, with the inevitable hotel-elephantiasis that has spread along most shores of the Mediterranean. Huge and sadly undistinguished hotels line the ever longer and broader track beaten by tourism. Package tours now blanket the whole of Greece. Happily the lesser islands and mainland beaches are sufficiently numerous for some to remain the sweet-scented peaceful havens they always were. But even they are in danger of being engulfed in the tide of concrete. Moreover, Greece has become one of Europe's leading centers for sailing and yachting besides providing all traditional and recent nautical sports.

In this Guide, we have naturally devoted considerable space to the history and mythology of ancient Greece and to the world-renowned sites where European civilization first flourished. But we also have included practical information for the yachtsman who wants to cruise the Aegean, the sportsman who wants to swim, fish, play golf or ski, or just the easygoing wanderer who wants nothing more than a pleasant spot with the sunshine by day and congenial cafes by night. The English-speaking tourist should find no difficulty in making himself understood, even in outlying villages.

*

We wish especially to acknowledge the help of Frances Arnold in preparing this edition, and also to extend our sincere thanks to the many individuals and organizations who helped in collecting material contained in this book. Our gratitude goes especially to the Greek National Tourist Organization in Athens, together with the Director of the London and New York offices and their staffs.

*

While every care has been taken to assure the accuracy of the information in this guide, the passage of time will always bring change, and consequently the publisher cannot accept responsibility for errors that may occur.

All prices and opening times quoted in this guide are based on information available to us at press time. Hours and admission fees may change, however, and the prudent traveler will avoid inconvenience by calling ahead.

Fodor's wants to hear about your travel experiences, both pleasant and unpleasant. When a hotel or restaurant fails to live up to its billing, let us know and we will investigate the complaint and revise our entries where the facts warrant it.

Send your letters to the editors of Fodor's Travel Publications, 201 E. 50th Street, New York, NY 10022.

FACTS AT YOUR FINGERTIPS

Planning Your Trip

MONEY. The Greek monetary unit is the *drachme*. There are 1, 2, 5, 10, 20 and 50 drachmes coins and banknotes of 50, 100, 500, 1,000 and 5,000 drachmes.

At time of going to press there were 156 dr. to the U.S. $ and 255 dr. to the £ sterling. Daily exchange rates are prominently displayed at all banks. You'll get a better exchange rate at banks than from hotels or stores.

WHAT IT WILL COST. Continuing high inflation in Greece, and periodic devaluations and fluctuations in currencies make accurate budgeting long in advance an impossibility. Prices mentioned throughout this book are indicative only of costs at the time of going to press. Keep a weather eye open for fluctuations in exchange rates, both when planning your trip and while on it.

Inflation continues to be high, but the dollar exchange rate hasn't varied as much as elsewhere. (There *are* regional price differences: Santorini, for instance, is more expensive than Athens). Judicious choosing and advance booking can still ensure good value even for limited budgets.

We give details of hotels and restaurant costs later in this section. There are no regional price differences, variations within each of the five hotel categories depend on location—part of town; near or far from a beach—as well as on the extras—airconditioning, swimming pool, sauna, etc. Groups invariably receive substantial discounts. The better-class resort hotels insist on half board.

Off-season rates are 15–20% lower from April 15 to May 31, and from September 15 to October 31; they are up to 40% lower in the few seaside hotels which stay open from November 1 to April 15—excluding, of course, Christmas and Easter holidays.

A word of warning: seaside taverns, despite their deceptively simple appearance, are often classified A or B, charging accordingly. Make sure of the category, which must be prominently indicated, and in the lowlier places follow the Greek custom—go into the kitchen to select the fish, have it weighed and priced. By far the most economic meals are the set menus in A to C hotels—there are none in outside restaurants—but they are of the dreary international variety which wrongly calls itself French.

For those who are budget minded, the package tour, bought through a travel agency or airline company, normally takes care of your transportation, accommodation, meals, tips. It may, or may not, include excursions and entertainment, so check carefully on this. Outside of your quoted tour fare then, your only expenses are likely to be for postage, drinks, gifts and personal shopping.

Some Miscellaneous Costs. An *ouzo* costs from 100 to 240 dr., a small bottle of beer 100 to 300 dr., a bottle of local wine 300 to 1,000 dr., a half liter of *retsina* from 120 to 200 dr., a coke from 80 to 200 dr., American coffee (or *nes* as it's commonly called) 180 to 300 dr., and Greek coffee

80 to 170 dr. A haircut costs from 700 dr. at the most basic barber to 1,800 dr. in a luxury hotel. Hairdressers charge from 1,000 to 3,500 dr.

WHEN TO GO. The main tourist season in Greece runs from about the beginning of April to the end of October, with the peak coming in July and August. For most British and American holiday-seekers the country is at its best from April to June and from September through October. Some of the islands, like Rhodes, Corfu and Crete cater for tourists all year round, but on the many rainy days offer little entertainment; it is pleasant but hardly sufficient that the daily average temperature through the year is about 22°C (71°F). Athens, in July and August, can make sightseeing hard work, but winter is pleasant.

July and August are not only the hottest months, but also the most tourist-ridden and expensive. On the other hand, for sun-worshippers the coast of Attica and the Aegean islands are quite bearable—a northerly wind, the *meltémi,* attenuates the midsummer heat. This is also the liveliest season, when Athenians flee their badly polluted city and crowd such fashionable spots as Corfu, Crete, Mýkonos, Rhodes, etc. Therefore, if you intend to take your Greek vacation at the height of summer, plan well in advance to avoid disappointment. Count also on paying much higher prices during July and August.

Average afternoon daily temperatures in degrees Fahrenheit and centigrade:

Athens	Jan.	Feb.	Mar.	Apr.	May	June	July	Aug.	Sept.	Oct.	Nov.	Dec.
F°	54	55	60	67	77	85	90	90	83	74	64	57
C°	12	13	16	19	25	29	32	32	28	23	18	14

Off-Season Travel. This has become more popular in recent years as visitors have come to appreciate the advantages of avoiding the crowded periods. Transatlantic sea and air fares are cheaper and so are hotel rates. Even more important, you have a wider choice of accommodation in the tourist centers and more attentive service. Moreover, the Greeks are friendlier when not swamped by tourists. Spring is particularly delightful for nature lovers, fall is best for bathing, the sea being warm and the beaches empty; both seasons are the least exhausting for sightseeing. Winters are cold inland but fairly mild by the sea; except in Athens and Thessaloníki, there is little entertainment on the many rainy days.

SEASONAL EVENTS that attract foreign visitors to Greece include open-air festivals of music and drama during the summer, folklore events and a few international sports contests. Many of the innumerable minor local festivities are indicated in the regional chapters.

Religious ceremonies play a major role in Greek life and, fittingly, the new year commences with the feast of St. Basil *(Ágios Vassílis)* when, according to an old Byzantine custom, the *Vassilópita,* a cake containing a lucky coin, is sliced and distributed. A more solemn note is struck on **January 6,** when the Blessing of the Water at the celebration of Epiphany is especially impressive at Piraeus, the port of Athens. Carnival starts ten Sundays before the date fixed for Easter, gathering momentum through **February.** The Pátra carnival processions are held on the two Sundays before Lent, usually early in **March.** On Shrove Monday, a holiday, there is a general exodus into the country; Thebes stages an amusing parody of a highland (Vlach) wedding. Military parades commemorate the outbreak of the War of Independence, on the Feast of the Annunciation, March 25, 1821. On Palm Sunday, Messolóngi commemorates the heroic sortie of its defenders in 1826, during the War of Liberation.

To the Orthodox faith Easter is more important than Christmas, and Greek and Western Easter only rarely coincide. It is usually in **April,** but can be as late as May. Good Friday is kept as a day of mourning throughout the nation and in Athens the highest church dignitaries and members of the Government participate in the funeral procession. During Saturday midnight service, held in all churches, the light of resurrection is passed by candle from one to the other. General jubilation commences and continues on Easter Sunday. The traditional lamb-roasting takes place outdoors, followed by dancing, quite often in regional costumes. Visitors are welcomed in the country, where the most typical festivities are held at Aráhova and Livadiá not far from Delphi. Monday is a nationwide holiday, and is mainly dedicated to recovering from overeating.

The Sound and Light spectacle at the Acropolis of Athens, at the Old Venetian Castle in Corfu, and at the Palace of the Grand Masters in Rhodes is presented nightly in Greek, English, French or German from April through October.

The traditional *trata* is performed at Mégara, near Athens, on Tuesday after Easter. The same custom survives on the nearby island of Sálamis. During the second half of **May** Macedonia enters the picture: Édessa holds a two week Flower Festival—a delayed action carnival. Langadas, near Thessaloníki, and Agía Eleni, near Séres, perform on May 21, feast of St. Constantine and St. Helen, the heretical Byzantine ceremony of the *anastenarides.* Its outstanding feature is the barefooted dancing on burning embers, holding icons.

In late **June** some special artistic events usually provided by renowned foreign orchestras and performers, are the curtain raiser to the least expensive of the world's acclaimed artistic manifestations, the Athens Festival, which lasts well into September. It provides suprisingly good value with performances of orchestral and chamber music, operas, ballets, as well as classical tragedies and comedies in the ancient Herodes Atticus open-air theater, on the slopes of the Acropolis.

The Epidaurus Festival presents ancient drama every weekend from late **June** through August. During the summer performances take place in the ancient theaters of Dodóni in Epirus, Philíppi and Thássos in Macedonia, though to call them festivals (like the Ólympos Festival, divided between the castle of Platamónas and the ancient theater of Dío), seems an overstatement. Navy Week in early July is celebrated in various ports, most originally at Agriá near Vólos and Plómari on Lésbos.

From early July to early September a Wine Festival is held near the Byzantine monastery of Daphni, on the outskirts of Athens. For a modest entrance fee you can taste dozens of wines from all parts of Greece. Deafening orchestras enliven several outdoor tavernas. There are similar festivals at Thessaloníki and Alexandróupoli in northern Greece, Rethymnon (Crete), and on Rhodes and Euboea.

A miscellany of expositions, musical and theatrical performances, lectures and folkloric events characterize the Epirotika at Ioánina, the Prose and Art Festival at Lefkáda, and the Hippokratia at Kos, in **August.** This is also a month of religious festivity. On the 6th, the Feast of the Savior, the Corfiots make their annual pilgrimage to the islet of Pontikonissi, where a fair is held afterwards. The hundreds of small boats converging upon it offer a sight to remember. Five days later on the same Corfu island, St. Spyridon is honored by a sumptuous procession, followed by festivities. The spotlight moves to the Aegean: there is a nationwide pilgrimage to Tinos (Cyclades) on August 15, to the miraculous icon of the Holy Virgin. The celebration at Páros is also impressive. A picturesque procession on Ionian Zákynthos commemorates its patron saint, St. Dionysios, on August 24.

An international Sailsurfing competition is held in the Halkidikí and the International Fair at Thessaloníki opens in **September** for two weeks, accompanied by a Song Festival and followed first by a Greek Film Festival, then by the Dimitria Festival of Byzantine Music and Drama to October 26, St. Dimitrios' Day, while the second National Day on the 28th brings President and government to Thessaloníki for a big military parade.

National Holidays. Jan.1 (New Year's Day); Jan. 6 (Epiphany); Feb. 18; Mar. 25 (Independence); Apr. 5–8 (Greek Easter); May 27 (Pentecost); Aug. 15 (Assumption); Oct. 28 (Ochi); Dec. 25, 26.

SOURCES OF INFORMATION. For information on all aspects of travel to and in Greece, the Greek National Tourist Organization (G.N.T.O.) is useful. Their addresses are:

In the U.S.: 645 Fifth Avenue, Olympic Tower, New York, N.Y. 10022 (tel. 212–421–5777); 611 West 6th St., Suite 2198, Los Angeles, CA 90017 (tel. 213–626–6696); 168 North Michigan Ave., Chicago, IL 60601 (tel. 312–782–1084).

In Canada: 1233 Rue de la Montagne, Suite 101, Montreal, Quebec H3G 1Z2 (tel. 514–871–1535); 1300 Bay St., Toronto, Ont. M5R 3K8 (tel. 416–968–2200).

In the U.K.: 4 Conduit St., London W1R 0DJ (tel. 071–734 5997).

TOUR OPERATORS. There are dozens of firms organizing holidays to Greece, ranging from luxurious art cruises to package camp-outs. The National Tourist Organization of Greece annually publishes *Travel Agent's Manual,* giving an itinerary, list of representatives in the U.S. and Greece, and all the major tour operators sending tours to Greece, and, for each, their tours for that particular year. (The manual is not available to the general public; ask your travel agent to order.) The itineraries and prices listed here are representative of those offered by established operators; while specifics may vary from year to year, similar tours can always be found.

Globus-Gateway/Cosmos, 150 S. Los Roblos Ave., Suite 860, Pasadena, CA 91101, tel. 818–449–0919 or 800–556–5454. combines Athens and Classical Greece with a four-day Aegean cruise for a total of 11 days, beginning at $600 (land only). *American Express,* Box 5014, Atlanta, GA 30302, tel. 800–241–1700 or, in Georgia, 800–637–6200. has several tours.

From the U.K. *Timsway Holidays,* Nightingales Corner, Little Chalfont, Bucks. HP7 9QS (tel. 02404 5541), specializes in wide-ranging Greek holiday packages, with accommodations from 1st-class hotels to bed and breakfasts and self-catering villas.

Sunmed "Go Greek," 4–6 Manor Mount, London, SE23 3PZ (tel. 081–699 8833), also offer a very comprehensive program.

Laskarina Holidays, St Marys Gate, Wirksworth, Derby DE4 4DQ (tel. 0629–822203), is a good specialist operator, with holidays mostly to the Dodecanese and the Sporades islands.

Cox and Kings, St James Court, 45 Buckingham Gate, London SW1E 6AF (tel. 071–931 9106), offers guided botanical tours of Crete from £995 for 15 days, of the Peloponnese from £895 for 12 days, and of Rhodes from £925 for 15 days.

Among the classically-oriented tour operators are *Swan Hellenic,* 77 New Oxford St., London WC1A 1PP (tel. 071–831 1234). They run various 14-day cruises throughout the Aegean, visiting the main archaeological sites, from £1,280, accompanied by guest lecturers who give talks both on board the ship and on site. Book well in advance as these tours sell like hot cakes.

Olympic Holidays, Olympic House, 30–32 Cross St., London N1 (tel. 071–359 3500), offer a huge variety of holidays in all parts of Greece.

ROUGHING IT. The Greek National Tourist Organization, the Hellenic Touring Club, municipalities and companies have set up over 100 camping sites in some of the most attractive parts of the country. Those of the G.N.T.O. are usually the best sited and equipped. Prices vary according to the facilities offered but generally fees are from 540 dr. per person and 660–850 dr. for tent or caravan.

Camping and Caravaning in Europe is published in the U.K. by A.A. Publications and is available in the U.S. through Rand McNally. It contains much useful information.

The *Greek Youth Hostels Association,* Dragatsaniou 4, Athens, is affiliated to the International Youth Hostel Federation and members are admitted to its 16 hostels throughout the country. The fee for joining in Greece is 1,200 dr. Members may stay at a hostel for three consecutive nights, but this rule is not rigid; bed 450–600 dr., sheets extra. To join in North America write to: *American Youth Hostels Inc.,* P.O. Box 37613, Washington, D.C. 20013-7613; or *Canadian Hosteling Assoc.,* 18 Dyward Market, Ottawa, Ontario K1N 71A. In Britain, contact the *Youth Hostels Assoc.,* 14 Southampton St., London WC2.

More comfortable are the *Y.M.C.A.,* Omirou 28, Athens and the *Y.W.C.A.,* Amerikas 11, Athens and Agias Sofias 11, Thessaloníki, summer only.

In many parts of the country simple accommodation is available in private houses. The charges range from 1,500 dr. for a double room without bath up to 3,000 dr. for a double room with bath. Inquire of the Tourist Police in the area concerned.

WHAT TO TAKE. Airline baggage allowances to most countries are figured by size rather than by weight. In First Class, two pieces, each up to an overall measure of 62 inches (length, width and height added together); in Economy Class, two pieces, neither one over 62 inches and both together not over 106 inches. Carry-on, underseat baggage up to 45 inches for either class. Extra charges for oversize can be very high. Some airlines make special provision for bicycles and skis, so inquire separately. Within Europe, many bus lines and international trains restrict the free baggage allowance to 55 pounds and porters are increasingly scarce these days.

Travel simply: Greece is an informal country, where one rarely dresses for dinner outside Athens and bikinis may be worn at any beach. In summer men wear lightweight slacks, open-neck shirts and sandals. Women prefer simple cotton dresses or slacks. Sunglasses, a flashlight for grottos, camping and monasteries; a pocket knife, thermos bottle, roll-up beach mat, and a towel or two will come in handy, as well as a hat with a visor or broad brim against the sun in summer. All hotels down to C category offer laundry facilities, but results vary greatly. Dry cleaning in all towns and resorts. Pharmacies and supermarkets stock a wide range of American and European drugs, cosmetics and suntan lotions. For roughing you'll need your own soap and a roll of toilet paper (small country or island hotels don't supply them).

Baggage by Air. The very first thing is to make sure your baggage is distinctive. If you have bought one of the mass-produced varieties, put some colored tape or other very easily spotted marking on it. You'll be amazed how many suitcases exactly like yours roll along that conveyor belt.

Don't pack valuables—jewelry, important papers, money and travelers checks—in your checked baggage. They should be close to you at all times.

Lock each item and put name and address labels both inside and outside.

Ensure that the check-in clerk puts the correct destination on the baggage tag and fixes it on properly.

Check that he or she puts the correct destination on the baggage claim tag attached to your passenger ticket.

If your baggage doesn't appear on arrival, tell the airline representative immediately, so they have the details necessary to start their tracing system straightaway.

PASSPORTS. Americans. Major post offices and many county courthouses process passport applications, as do U.S. Passport Agency offices in various cities. The cost is $42 when applying in person. You may renew your passport by mail for $35 provided your previous passport is less than 12 years old. ($27 for under-18s.) Adult passports are valid for 10 years, others for five years. Also needed: a birth certificate/proof of citizenship; two identical photographs 2-inches square, full face and black and white or color; and proof of identity, such as a driver's license or any other document with your photograph and signature. Allow at least six to eight weeks for processing, unless it is urgent. However, the Passport Office only consider applications "emergency" if you are leaving in 24 to 48 hours from the time you apply, and you must have proof of your departure date.

Canadians. Canadian citizens apply in person to regional passport offices or post offices, or by mail to the Bureau of Passports, External Affairs, Ottawa, Ontario, K1A 0G3. A $25 fee, two photographs, a guarantor, and evidence of citizenship are required. Canadian passports are valid for five years; you must reapply for a new one.

British Subjects. You must apply for passports on special forms obtainable from main post offices or a travel agent. The application should be sent or taken to the Passport Office according to residential area (as indicated on the guidance form) or lodged with them through a travel agent. Apply at least five weeks before the passport is required. The regional Passport Offices are located in London, Liverpool, Peterborough, Glasgow and Newport. The application must be countersigned by your bank manager or by a solicitor, barrister, doctor, clergyman or justice of the peace who knows you personally. You will need two full-face photos. The fee is £15: passport valid for ten years.

British Visitor's Passport. This simplified form of passport has advantages for the once-in-a-while tourist to most European countries (Yugoslavia and Eastern European countries presently excepted). Valid for one year and not renewable, it costs £7.50. Application may be made at main post offices in England, Scotland and Wales and at the Ministry of Health and Social Security offices in Northern Ireland. Birth certificate or medical card for identification and two passport photographs are required—no other formalities.

Visas. Not required for nationals of the U.S., Canada, the U.K. and other Western European states; however, those wishing to stay longer than three months must apply for a residence permit, once in Greece.

Health Certificate. Not required for entry into Greece.

Warning. The Greek Government has warned that visitors with *Turkish Republic of Cyprus* or *The Turkish State of Cyprus* stamps in their passports would not be admitted to Greece.

Getting to Greece

FROM NORTH AMERICA

BY AIR. The Greek national carrier, *Olympic Airways,* operates flights to Athens, daily from New York in peak season and twice weekly from Montreal and Toronto; *Pan Am's* New York–Athens direct flight operates twice a day. *Olympic*'s lowest fare is a bargain mid-week return fare of $605 (to be booked 30 days in advance), but the most economic fare from the U.S. is either a direct charter or a regularly scheduled APEX flight to London and a further passage booked from there. There are many package tours to choose from out of London—often at prices much lower than those available in the U.S.

Tour operators who have booked entire blocks of seats on scheduled flights offer economy-fare passage even for those not buying an entire package, and these can be as cheap as charter travel. Unless you want stopovers, which can only be got by taking one of the much more expensive regular flights, you will save greatly by picking one of the various types of excursion or package fares.

BY SHIP. Of the almost extinct liner services, *Cunard's QE 2,* sailing to northern Europe has first- and tourist-class accommodation. You can also arrange for a fly/sail combination (flying one direction and going by ship the other). Opportunities for transatlantic travel on modern container ships are on the increase, but return fares start at around $2,000, so it isn't a cheap alternative.

The most popular alternative for travelers to Greece seeking to spend time on the water is to take a short Mediterranean cruise around various Greek ports and/or one that takes in, say, Greece, Turkey, Israel and Egypt. Among those offering such cruises are *Sun Line Cruises,* 1 Rockefeller Plaza, Suite 315, New York, N.Y. 10020 and *Royal Viking,* 2 Alhambra Plaza, Coral Gables, FL 33134. In the latter instance, cruises begin from Fort Lauderdale, Florida, before continuing across the Atlantic.

P & O Cruises also operate cruises calling at various Greek ports including Piraeus and many islands, both sailing direct from the U.K. (Southampton). There is also a fly-cruise program starting at various Mediterranean ports including Piraeus. Details of 1991 program from travel agencies.

FROM GREAT BRITAIN

BY AIR. Athens has a service of at least four flights daily from London Heathrow airport operated jointly by *British Airways* and *Olympic Airways.* The flying time is around 3 hours 45 minutes. During the summer there is also a direct flight from Manchester on a couple of days a week. Fares for the scheduled services are high. The return fare in Club Class works out at around £560, with the lowest ranging from around £180 to £219 for a British Airways PEX saver return (no booking in advance necessary) in high summer.

A large number of charter operators sell seats on flights from London Gatwick airport to a wide range of destinations in Greece including: Athens, Thessaloníki, Corfu, Kefalonía, Zákynthos, Rhodes, Kos, Iráklio, Mýkonos, Skíathos, Lésbos, Sámos, Mytilíni (Lésbos), and Kavála. These services only operate on a couple of days a week, usually from May to October. Fares are usually slightly cheaper than PEX tickets. There are also flights from regional airports including Birmingham, Luton, Manchester and Glasgow to the more important holiday centers. To get round the flight regulations all include minimal accommodation—you are not expected to use it!

In many cases it is cheaper to book a fully inclusive holiday and then use the pre-booked accommodation for only part of the time. Or to wait until the last minute and try to find a bargain. However these are becoming increasingly rare as the demand for holidays in Greece from all over Europe rapidly increases: check the classified columns of papers such as the *Times, Standard, Mail on Sunday, Sunday Times* and the *Observer.* Alternatively, go to a travel agent and get them to use their Prestel system to check the late availability from the larger operators.

BY TRAIN. There are two main routes to choose from if you wish to go to Greece by train from the U.K.: the overland route via Yugoslavia; and the route down through Italy, then by ferry from Brindisi to Pátra on the Peloponnese.

The best choice of trains on the Yugoslav route is as follows. Catch the evening boat train from London Liverpool Street to connect with the overnight sailing to the Hook of Holland, which is reached early the next morning. Change trains there and go as far as Köln (Cologne), where a connecting train to Athens will depart in the afternoon, allowing a good two hours to have a meal and see the famous cathedral. The train runs to München (Munich), which is reached early evening. Switch again there and then travel overnight via Salzburg and Ljubljana to Zagreb. The next day is spent crossing Yugoslavia, and the train finally pulls into Athens around noon on the following day. Second-class day carriages and couchettes run throughout the route, with 1st- and 2nd-class sleeping-cars available from Munich to Athens on certain days. Reservation is obligatory on this service. It is well worth traveling 1st class.

Traveling via Italy offers a much higher standard of comfort and is more relaxing, with a mini-cruise at the end. In high summer catch the train from London Victoria to Dover for the crossing to Calais and the connecting service to Paris Gare du Nord. From there, transfer to the Gare de Lyon for the train which runs via Switzerland to Milan. Switch there and travel through to Brindisi Maritime station. The train connects with the ferry direct to Pátra, which is reached the following day. From Pátra there is a special bus service to Athens; alternatively, rail buffs can catch one of the quaint narrow-gauge trains to Athens/Piraeus. On the train from Paris, 1st- and 2nd-class sleepers and couchettes are available. Refreshment facilities are provided only between Paris and Dijon.

For planning your rail journey to Greece the *Thomas Cook European Timetable* is essential. It is available in the U.K. from Thomas Cook, Timetable Publishing Office, P.O. Box 36, Thorpe Wood, Peterborough, Cambridgeshire PE3 6SB; in the U.S.A. from Forsyth Travel Library, P.O. Box 2975, Shawnee Mission, Kansas, 66201-1375. In the U.S. call toll-free 1–800–FORSYTH.

Fares are quite high. For travelers 26 and older, the best bet is a Eurail Flexipass ($198), which gives you 5 days of unlimited first-class travel over a period of 15 days. Under 26s should automatically buy an *Inter-Rail* card if going overland at £160, or an *Inter-Rail + Boat* card at £180 if going by sea from Brindisi. The cards are both valid for one month and give unlimited rail travel throughout Western Europe, and half fare in the U.K. and on cross-Channel services. (Unless you're going for more than a month it's not worth buying a discount youth ticket from *Transalpino* or *Eurotrain*).

BY BUS. In the U.K. the most reputable coach services to Greece are now promoted under the banner of *International Express*. As with the trains there is a choice of routes—either overland via Yugoslavia or via Italy and then by sea. Both are operated by *Eurolines,* 52 Grosvenor Gardens, London SW1W OAU (tel. 071–730 0202). First, overland. During the summer there is a thrice-weekly service to Thessaloníki and Athens. The journey to Athens (via Munich, where you change coaches) occupies the best part of four days of virtually continuous traveling. The adult return fare works out at around £155 with slight reductions for students. Travelers from the U.S.A. must obtain a transit visa for Yugoslavia.

Secondly, overland via Paris and Rome to Brindisi, then by ferry to Pátra, and finally by coach to Athens. On this route there are two departures a week and it takes only a few hours longer than the route via Munich. Fares are also similar. Please note that luggage space is severely restricted. Details of International Express services can be obtained from *Eurolines* or any of their appointed travel agents.

Hellenic State Railways operate regular bus services from Paris and Dortmund to Thessaloníki and Athens. Details can be obtained from the Greek National Tourist Organization. Buses from Paris can be used in conjunction with the *Hoverspeed Citylink* service from London Victoria Coach Station—full details in the International Express timetables. There are other operators who run buses to destinations in Greece, especially from France, Italy, and West Germany, but many of these companies operate poorly maintained vehicles and do not obey the regulations on drivers' hours—they may be cheaper but . . .

BY CAR. The shortest route from Britain, if you want to drive all the way, is from Ostend via Frankfurt, Munich, Salzburg and Klagenfurt to Ljubljana in Yugoslavia, then along that country's only through highway to Beograd and Skopje, connecting with the Greek road system (there are no motorways as such in Greece, only sections of toll road) at the border station of Evzoni. The scenically lovelier Adriatic highway turns inland before Albania and connects with the Greek roads at Niki. Both routes are about 3,058 km. (1,900 miles) long.

Car-Sleeper Expresses. Some 1,328 km. (825 miles) and two or three days of driving can be saved by crossing from Dover to Ostend and boarding the summer express from Brussels to Ljubljana (Yugoslavia). Driving may be greatly reduced by using the Paris–Milan and Milan–Brindisi car-sleeper and then a car-ferry to Corfu, Igoumenitsa or Pátra. While the car-sleeper is apparently expensive, it whittles down somewhat when set off against the expenses of gasoline and hotels. It is obviously more advantageous for a party of four than two. The R.A.C. and A.A. provide bookings and information.

Car Ferries. Greek and Italian shipping lines provide very frequent sailings between Italy and Greece. In summer there are at least 7 a day from Brindisi, 2 each from Bari and Ancona, 1 from Otranto, and 2–3 a week from Trieste; all to Corfu and/or Igoumenítsa, and Pátra (3 a week call at Kefaloniá). There is also about 1 a week from Venice to Piraeus. The shipping lines include the *Adriatic Ferries, Adriatica, Anek, Fragline, Hellenic Mediterranean, Karageorgis, Marlines, Minoan, Strintzis* and *Ventouris.* Some ferries also continue on to Crete, Cyprus, and Rhodes and from there, on to Alexandria and Port Said in Egypt, Haifa in Israel, and even one to Odessa in the U.S.S.R. These last few destinations are also all served by weekly car ferries from Piraeus.

In summer there are twice-weekly sailings from ports in Yugoslavia to Corfu and Igoumenítsa.

British Ferries operate a weekly service from Venice to Athens using their luxury car ferry *Orient Express* from May to October. Details from *Orient Express,* Suite 200, Hudson's Place, Victoria Station, London SW1V 1JL. (tel. 071–834 8122). Details of the *Adriatica Lines* services from Brindisi to Igoumenítsa, and Pátra; and from Venice to Piraeus can be obtained from the *Sealink Travel Centre,* opposite Platform 2, Victoria Station, London SW1V 1JT (tel. 01–828 1940). For information on the Minoan Lines car ferries between Ancona and Igoumenítsa and Pátra contact *P&O European Ferries,* Channel House, Channel View Road, Dover CT17 9TJ (tel. 0304 203388). Always ask about through booking discounts from Britain to Greece.

Four car ferries ply every week between the ports of Vólos in Thessaly on the east coast of Greece and Tartoush in Syria.

Most boats are airconditioned and have three cabin classes as well as a large number of aircraft-type seats in the observation saloon, besides restaurant, bar and swimming pool. Bookings for the summer months should be made well in advance and reconfirmed shortly before sailing.

Arriving in Greece

CUSTOMS. The dual flow Green and Red System operates at most customs posts; Green if nothing to declare, Red even if in doubt. Duty free for passengers arriving from an E.E.C. country are 300 cigarettes or 75 cigars, 1.50 liters of alcoholic beverages or 5 liters of wine, 75 gr. perfume; gifts up to a total value of 55,000 dr. or a single gift up to a value of 44,500 dr. Passengers from any other countries can bring in 200 cigarettes or 50 cigars, 1 liter of alcoholic beverages or 2 liters of wine, 50 gr. perfume and gifts up to a total value of 7,000 dr.

Cats and dogs require a health and rabies inoculation certificate issued by a veterinary authority in the country of origin stating that inoculations took place not more than 12 months (for cats 6 months) and not less than 6 days prior to arrival. Health clearance at port of entry.

Foreign banknotes in excess of $1,000 (about £575) must be declared for re-export. There is no restriction on travelers' checks. Only 20,000 drachmas may be imported or exported.

At the end of your stay you may take out, duty free, almost any amount of souvenirs and gifts. For purchases of archeological items etc., you will have to obtain an export license.

Staying in Greece

HOTELS. The six official categories of graded hotels, L, A, B, C, D, and E (a star system is envisaged), are supposedly defined according to the level of comfort and service offered, but, in fact, standards within any one grade vary enormously. This variation is reflected in the prices—there are some "L" hotels cheaper than some "B", and there are "C" hotels more expensive than some "A". So prices have been our main criterion in classifying hotels as (L) Deluxe, (E) Expensive, (M) Moderate, (I) Inexpensive. The Deluxe grading is generally below the equivalent grading in other western countries, though above its Balkan counterparts, and usually not what most of our readers would expect from Luxury establishments; the international chains are notable and creditable exceptions to this generalization. The lower gradings are mostly of strictly utilitarian sameness, lacking any individual features or atmosphere. The official E, the rockbottom grading, exists mostly in remote areas and, though clean, is probably better avoided, and does not figure in our own listings.

All (L) and (E), most (M), even some (I) listed are airconditioned. All listed have been constructed or completely renovated subsequent to 1965, with private baths or showers, but few (I)s have their own restaurant. All prices in the table below are for high season and include 15% service charges, taxes, airconditioning in the top categories, and heating (but not breakfast).

	(L)	(E)	(M)	(I)
Single	15,000–35,000	7,000–15,000	4,000–7,000	2,000–4,000
Double	20,000–45,000	10,000–20,000	5,000–10,000	2,500–5,000

Hotels are open all year round in the towns, though most close from November to April 15 in the beach resorts. T.V. and radio are available in the top two categories.

The few pensions are not distinguishable with the naked eye; by some quirk of officialdom they are graded one category above the price they are authorized to charge. Some will be listed together with the (I) hotels, while the rather expensive service flats mainly join the (E)s. At the lower end are almost 50,000 rooms in authorized private houses. These village guest houses, usually in a separate annex, are divided into three categories, with prices ranging from 1,500 to 4,000 dr. for a double room. The roughly one half in A and B categories are often grandiloquently advertised as flats or apartments. They differ from hotels mainly in providing cooking facilities, but little or no service. In the high season they are popular with Greek families. Because of the smallness of the units, no lists are available. Careful inspection is indicated; even more so for C category and the 150,000 unauthorized rooms, which are sometimes even cheaper, but rarely cleaner. In view of the unpredictable side effects, being a paying guest in a Mediterranean household should be by choice and not as a last resort.

Most (E) and (M) resort hotels insist on half board, with full board available on demand. (I) hotels are rarely referred to by travel agencies, yet those listed are adequate for basic needs; they have restaurants only when specifically stated.

Reservations for the summer season should be made well in advance. A confirmation is necessary, especially if any deposit has been paid. As few hotels bother to answer individual letters, it is advisable to make arrangements through a travel agency. Overbooking is a major problem in the summer—be sure you have a written confirmation of your reservation.

Picturesque villages have been dolled up by the G.N.T.O. as traditional settlements. On the islands of Híos, Kefaloniá and Thíra, in the Peloponnese and on Mount Pílio, otherwise largely abandoned villages have been restored and modern conveniences installed. Rooms are rented at (M) category prices. Local craftsmen are encouraged and a local village atmosphere is maintained. A different program has been named *Agrotourism*—this is an organized system of accommodating visitors in village houses, in various areas including Aráhova, and the islands of Híos and Lésvos (Petra). Ask at any tourist information office for the brochure.

Credit Cards. The initials AE, DC, MC, and V in our listings refer to the credit cards that establishments will accept—American Express, Diners Club, MasterCard (Access), and Visa (Barclaycard).

Villas. Renting a villa or apartment may be pleasant and economical for a long vacation, but it is chancy to rely on the uniformly glamorous advertisement photos. Only reputable agencies should be used. Among those in the U.S., try *Villas International,* 71 W. 23rd St., New York, N.Y. 10010. In addition, the G.N.T.O., 645 Fifth Ave., New York, N.Y. 10022, publishes a list of Greek agents with whom you may deal directly.

In the U.K.: *Meon Villa Holidays,* Meon House, Petersfield, Hants GU32 3JN (tel. 0730 66561) and the *Greek Islands Club,* 66 High Street, Walton on Thames, Surrey KT12 1BU (tel. 0932 220416). Another specialist is *C.V. Travel,* with villas on Corfu and Paxos, 43 Cadogan St., London SW3 2PR (tel. 01–581 0851). Again the G.N.T.O. can advise.

HOLIDAY CLUBS AND VILLAGES. These are on commercial lines, catering mostly to foreign visitors. Some of them offer package holidays, including charter flights from various points of Western Europe or boat from Italy. Accommodation is in hotels, bungalows, bamboo huts or tents. They have their private beach, dance band and other entertainment and they offer organized excursions, sailing, underwater fishing, etc. Rates range from 2,000 dr. for two, bed and breakfast in a bamboo village to over 30,000 dr. for two, full board, including wine, per day in the luxury hotels of the Club Méditerranée.

Angistri, island off Égina. Apply: STS Ltd., Filellinon 1, Athens 118.

Club Méditerranée, at Corfu (two sites), Euboea (Gregolímano), Égio-Lambiri, 29 km. (18 miles) east of Pátra, Skafídia (Pýrgos), and Kéfalos, Kos. Apply: Club Méditerranée, 8 Rue de la Bourse, Paris; 106–108 Brompton Rd., London SW3; *Club Mediterranee Hellas S.A.,* Mesogeion 2–4, Athens 115 27, or *Manos Travel System,* Panepistimiou 39, Athens 106 79.

Club Poseidon, Loutráki, 80 km. (50 miles) from Athens. Apply direct.

Engazi—Z. Plage (Bungo huts), Diakoftó, Peloponnese, 177 km. (110 miles) from Athens. Apply direct.

Eros Beach, Petalídi Messinias, south coast of the Peloponnese, between Kalámata and Koróni. Apply Ippokratous 71, Athens 144.

Hercules Beach, Póros, Kefalonía, 43 km. (27 miles) from Argostóli. Apply: Kalamáki Beach, Filellinon 4, Athens 118.

Kalogria Beach, 40 km. (25 miles) beyond Pátra. Apply Arvanitis, Kalogria, Metóhi.

Lassi Holiday Center (only for youths under 25) on Kefalonía; eight-bed bungalows. Apply at Argostóli.

Libero Camping, eight km. (five miles) before the Corinth Canal. Apply: Libero Tours, Ag. Konstantinou 2, Athens.

Pirgi Village, 16 km. (ten miles) north of Corfu town. Apply: Mastoras Travel, Sophocleous 23, Athens.

Sikyon Beach, Xylókastro, 120 km. (75 miles) from Athens. Apply direct.

RESTAURANTS. There are many worthwhile eating places, but locating them among the hundreds of inexpensive—and expensive—tavernas, can be difficult. The standard, decent Greek taverna will serve good, basic fare in fairly unprepossessing, though clean and comfortable, surroundings; there are few top-class restaurants outside Athens. But at least in the capital there is an adequate number of restaurants in the Deluxe (L), Expensive (E) price category as well as in the Moderate (M) and Inexpensive (I) categories, though it should be remembered that standards are lower than in most other European countries. Prices are for one person, inclusive of taxes and tips, but exclusive of beverages.

	(L)	(E)	(M)	(I)
Breakfast	1,000–1,400	600–1,000	400–600	300–400
Lunch/Dinner	above 5,000	3,500–5,000	1,500–3,500	800–1,500

Only hotels offer set menus; they are unimaginative, except for the buffet lunches round the pools in the top categories, but at the lower end of the relevant price range. At the seaside try the open-air tavernas, where you walk into the kitchen and choose your own dishes. Breakfast is served continental style.

Service is sometimes slow and uncertain in the lesser places.

Credit Cards. The initials AE, DC, MC, and V in our listings refer to the credit cards that establishments will accept—American Express, Diners Club, MasterCard (Access), and Visa (Barclaycard).

TIPPING. Hotel bills include a service charge of 15%. For a longer stay, an extra 10% might be divided among chambermaid, porter and room service. Except for the hotel menus, restaurants list somewhat confusingly two prices for each dish, without and with the added 12–15% service charge; the former for taking away the food. In better-class establishments it is customary to leave an extra 5% to 10% when you pay, but you must leave something on the table for the junior, say 20–50 dr. per person. Where there is definitely only one person serving, as in many tavernas, leave your tip on the table. In cafes and bars service is included in the price of drinks; leave an extra 5%. On cruises, cabin and dining room stewards are tipped at the rate of about 300 dr. per day.

Barbers and hairdressers expect 20 to 30%. Strangely enough one does not usually tip taxi-drivers. Check what the meter indicates (30 dr. on the clock then 26 dr. per km., minimum charge 180 dr., 200 dr. in Athens), and round off the amount shown to the next multiple of 20, or even 50. There are additional charges for luggage, after midnight and at Christmas and Easter. Porters, if you can find any, charge according to a fixed scale, usually 50 dr. per bag; hotel porters and bellhops expect 50 dr. per bag. Ushers at cinemas, theaters and concerts expect 20–40 dr. for showing you to your seat. Hat-check attendants expect 70 dr. or more, depending on the type of place you are in and the number in your party. Washroom attendants receive 20 to 50 dr. according to the use you make of the facilities.

MAIL, TELEPHONES. Airmail letters within Europe, 70 dr. for 20 grams, 60 dr. for small postcards. To the U.S. and Canada, 80 dr. for 20 grams, 70 dr. for small postcards. Liable to increase. A letter from England or the U.S. may reach Athens in 48 and 72 hours respectively, but might take up to a week to some out-of-the-way island.

Public telephones, some coin operated, are at all the numerous newspaper kiosks. Local calls cost 8 dr., long distance calls within the country from 25 dr. to 150 dr. for three minutes. Calls 8 P.M. to 8 A.M. and at weekends are 30% cheaper. To phone to New York through the operator you will have to pay 1,159 dr. for three minutes, and 386 dr. for each additional minute; to London 402 dr. for three minutes and 134 dr. for each additional minute. No special night rates. Hotels charge unreasonably for putting through calls: it is much more economical to do so from public telephone centers (OTE).

The main Post Office in Athens is at Eolou 100, branch offices on Platía Sýntagma and Omónia subway station and, for parcels only, in the courtyard at Stadiou 4. Central Cable Office: 28 Oktovríou 85; Central Telephone Exchange: Stadiou 15.

CLOSING TIMES. The principal national and religious holidays are: January 1, New Year's Day; January 6, Epiphany; February 18, Lent Monday; March 25, Greek Revolution (1821) Memorial Day; April 5–8, Good Friday to Easter Monday; May 1, May Day; May 27, Whit Monday; August 15, Assumption; October 28, Ohi Day; December 25–26, Christmas.

Clocks go forward one hour from the first Sunday in April to the last Sunday in September. The G.N.T.O. supplies a list of banks which remain open afternoons and Sundays. Business hours vary from season to season and from district to district; furthermore, the traditional midday break is being progressively abolished, but a satisfactory summer timetable for shops has not yet been agreed on. Many shops in the towns and villages away from resort areas are open from 8.30 A.M. to 1.30 P.M., and from 5.30 P.M. to 9. P.M. on Tues., Thurs., and Fri. The rest of the week they are open from 8.30 A.M. to 2 P.M. only. However, Athens summer hours are approximately as follows:

banks...............	8 A.M. to 2 P.M. (Mon.–Fri.)
travel agencies	8.30 or 9 A.M. to 4.30 or 5 P.M. (closed Sat. afternoons)

restaurants	noon to 3.30 P.M. and 7.30 P.M. to midnight
cafes.	8 A.M. to well after midnight
nightclubs	9 P.M. to 3 A.M.
cinemas	5 P.M. to midnight (open-air, 8 to mid-night.)
shops	the summer timetable for 1990 will only be announced in spring. For the rest of the year shops are open: Mon. 1 to 7 P.M.; Tues. through Fri. 9.30 A.M. to 7 P.M.; Sat. 9 A.M. to 3 P.M.

MEDICAL SERVICES. The *I.A.M.A.T.* (International Assoc. for Medical Assistance to Travelers) offers you a list of approved English-speaking doctors who have had postgraduate training in the U.S., Canada or Gt. Britain. Membership is free; the scheme is world-wide with many European countries participating. For information apply in the U.S. to 417 Center St., Lewiston, N.Y. 14092; in Canada, 188 Nicklin Rd., Guelph, Ontario N1H 7L5; in Europe, 57 Viorets, 1212 Grand-Lancy-Geneva, Switzerland.

A similar service is provided by *Travel Assistance International,* the American arm of Europ Assistance; they both offer a comprehensive program of immediate, on-the-spot medical, personal and financial help. Trip protection ranges from $35 for an individual for up to eight days to $250 for an entire family for a six-month period. In the U.K., these costs in mid-1990 were £16.50 and £160 respectively. (These figures may be revised before 1991.) For full details, contact your travel agent or insurance broker, or write Europ Assistance Worldwide Services Inc., 1133 15th St., N.W., Suite 400, Washington, D.C. 20005 (800–821–2828). In the U.K., contact Europ Assistance Ltd., 252 High St., Croydon, Surrey (tel. 01–680 1234).

LAUNDRY. Relatively cheap and quick in all hotels down to C category, though ironing is often careless. Laundromats in all major towns. In Athens: two in the center, Angelou Yeronda 10 and Xenofontos 10, and two in the Exarchia area: *Zanussi,* Ippokratous 121, and *Kokkinis,* Didotou 46, where they also undertake ironing. Dry cleaners are innumerable.

CONVENIENT CONVENIENCES. Except at air terminals and railway stations there are hardly any. The one on Platía Sýntagma in Athens is not signposted. You can use the facilities in the better cafés; in the simpler places it's very often of the no-seat variety.

NEWSPAPERS. English and Paris-published American papers are on sale toward late afternoon on the day of their publication. The daily English-language *Athens News* is useful for happenings in towns; also the *Week in Athens,* available free at the G.N.T.O. offices and the better hotels, and the monthly *Athenian* (325 dr.). *Greece's Weekly* (200 dr.) deals with the economic and political scene.

PHOTOGRAPHY. Greece is the perfect f22 country, and indeed the bright sunlight and endless color and variety of the landscape seem to cry aloud to be photographed or filmed. You can buy Kodak and Agfa-Gevaert film in all the better photo-shops. Black and white film can be developed and printed practically everywhere in Greece, and one-hour developing of color film is common in larger towns and cities. Motion picture footage can also be processed in Athens but may take too long for you.

It is somewhat less than wise to photograph to seaward on border islands, or wherever it is expressly forbidden. Care should be taken in this regard.

MUSEUMS AND ARCHAEOLOGICAL SITES. Ever since Johann Winckelmann laid the basis of archeology with his *History of The Art of Antiquity* in 1764, hardly a week has passed in Greece without important archeological finds coming to light. But however thrilling pre-historic, antique or medieval foundations, potsherds and fragments may be to the expert excavator, they hold little interest for the layman. A careful selection of sites has, therefore, been made in this book, restricted to those where there is actually something to see. Almost every town features a museum of antique and folkloric miscellany good for a rainy day, but only those warranting a visit in any weather are mentioned. It is, of course, impossible to foresee when and for how long monuments or churches may be closed for repairs, especially after earthquakes. Strikes by guards occur with even greater frequency.

Opening hours for museums are: summer (April 1 to October 15)— weekdays 8 or 9 to 4 or later; Sundays, holidays, and in winter they open later and/or close earlier. Closed on Mondays (except Benaki, Cycladic Arts, and Natural History museums in Athens; check the listings for opening times), Christmas, New Year, March 25, Orthodox Easter Sunday. Admission 200–500 dr.

Archeological sites are open from 7.30, 8 or 9 in the summer to 7. In winter, they mostly close at 5. There are quite considerable variations.

Please note that all these times are liable to change—so be sure to check.

ARCHAEOLOGICAL OUTLINE. The pre-Hellenic period is characterized by the supremacy of the Minoan civilization of the Bronze Age (2400–1200 B.C.) Minos, legendary king of Crete, built the palaces of Knossós and Phaestós which date from about 2000 B.C. Cretan hegemony spread to the mainland (Peloponnese) to be succeeded by Mycenae which became the political and cultural center of the Aegean between 1400 and 1200 B.C. after the destruction of Knossós. The Mycenaean civilization disappeared with the arrival of the Dorians whose architecture was born of a combination of solemn Nordic inspiration, measured Mycenaean outlay and of Oriental influences in decoration. The Doric style predominant till the end of the 5th century B.C. was characterized by severe simplicity; the flowering of the Ionic style lasted until the period of Macedonian hegemony (338 B.C.), when it was superseded by the more florid Corinthian style of the Hellenistic and Roman domination.

Greek sculpture played an important role in the ornamentation of temples but it was also an independent art. The most important periods of its evolution were: the *Archaic* (8th to 6th century B.C.), characterized by a column-like rigidity of its subjects; the *Classic* period, attaining the summit of corporeal harmony (500 to 340 B.C.). The most outstanding artists of this epoch were Pheidias and Praxiteles. Alexander the Great and his armies introduced Greek art to the eastern Mediterranean and this era (334 to 150 B.C.), typified by an opulent anatomy and by Asiatic influences, is known as the *Hellenistic* period.

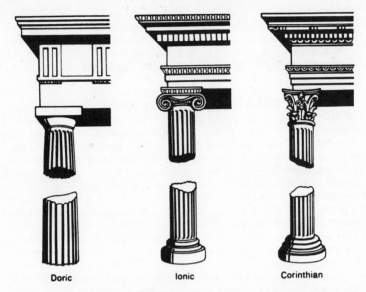

Doric   Ionic   Corinthian

The Greek temple, open mainly to priests but sometimes to prominent citizens, was the home of the Divinity, and more often than not it was of small proportions. A rare exception to the oblong, rectangular outlay is the *tholos,* a round temple with circular colonnade. Ictinus, Callicrates and Mnesicles were among the most outstanding architects.

Secular architecture consisted of open-air theaters, stadiums, and of the *agora,* the city's commercial and civic center. The *acropolis,* a citadel, usually enclosed all the sanctuaries. The Greek cities were surrounded by ramparts, the walls of which varied with the epoch (Cyclopean, Pelasgic, Trapezoidal, etc.).

Important archaeological work has been carried out by the American School of Classical Studies in Athens as well as several American universities: in Athens (the Agora), in the Peloponnese (Corinth, Neméa, Pýlos), in Macedonia and on the island of Samothrace. British excavation work was most notable at Megalopolis and later at Mycenae in the Peloponnese, in Thessaly and, of course, in Crete (Knossós, Phaestós). The French unearthed the sanctuaries of Delphi and Delos. Germany's contribution is mainly Mycenae and Olýmpia. In recent years, the Greeks themselves have made important finds at Brauron, Díon, Pélla, Thíra, and Vergína, and there are other foreign archaeological teams at work.

Current archaeological terms, with their meanings, are:

Amphora vase, jug
Apse semicircular part of an edifice
Basilica rectangular, oblong edifice
Bouleuterion senate house
Capital uppermost part of a column, usually decorated
Caryatid sculpture of maiden, replacing a column
Hieron sacred enclosure

Megaron reception hall in Mycenaean place
Metope plain or carved panel on temple's frieze
Naos sanctuary of temple
Odeon roofed edifice for artistic performances
Peristyle inner or outer colonnade
Pinacotheca picture gallery

Plinth rectangular base of a column
Pronaos vestibule of sanctuary
Propylaea pillared gate to monumental sites
Stele upright, decorated tombstones

Stereobate substructure of a temple
Stoa roofed building, supported by frontal columns, usually a business center
Stylobate foundation platform of a temple

POLLUTION REPORT. Much of the long, indented coast of the mainland and the innumerable islands is unpolluted, owing to a stringent enforcement of the international conventions by spotter planes of the harbor police, which impartially impose heavy fines for any violation on Greek and foreign shipping alike. Yet, like anywhere else in the Mediterranean, tar is washed ashore even on the most remote beaches.

The bigger island towns, especially Corfu, pour out a seemingly disproportionate amount of sewage, luckily restricted to the town seafront. Bathing is prohibited in all the major ports—not that anyone would want to. Greater Athens' shores are washed by a chemical mixture of which H^2O is only a part. The effluent of four million people and the bulk of the country's industry give the Homeric wine dark sea a wholly new connotation. The same holds good for Thessaloníki, where the Aretsóu beach had to be closed, and Vólos. Near these industrial zones air pollution is sometimes above what W.H.O. considers safe. Athens is increasingly under a "chemical cloud," a euphemistic term for obnoxious pollution which is as harmful to man as it is to the antique marbles. As cars undoubtedly contribute to this, there are now severe restrictions in central Athens to reduce the total amount of traffic. Some sections are closed to traffic, in others only half the cars may circulate on any one day.

SEA SPORTS. Along 15,020 km. (9,333 miles) of coastline water sports are, of course, by far the most important. Swimming is safe everywhere—though sharks have been known to bite—there being neither currents nor tides. Organized beaches, mainly under the aegis of the G.N.T.O., as well as all larger beach hotels, provide water skiing and wind surfing. No eyebrow, official or otherwise, is raised over toplessness; nude bathing is not officially allowed but is unofficially practised even on open beaches on several islands. Windsurfers can be hired at most coastal resorts; for details of windsurfing competitions, contact the *Greek Windsurfing Assocation,* Filellinon 7, Athens (tel. 323 2877).

Submarine fishing without breathing apparatus is permitted, except in ports or at organized beaches.

Submarine fishing with breathing apparatus is forbidden; gogglers, however, may explore the underwater abysses for entertainment only in certain specific areas, like the Cyclades, the Ionian Islands and the Halkidikí peninsula. Check with the local G.N.T.O. or the tourist police.

Swimming and diving lessons at the *Hellenic Federation of Submarine Activities,* Agios Kosmas (13 km., eight miles from Athens), tel. 981 9961, and at several organized beaches.

Fishing tackle and boats can be hired at most coastal towns and villages. Charge for a pedal boat is about 500 dr. per hour, for a motorboat from 1,500 to 2,500 dr. *Amateur Anglers and Maritime Sports Club,* Akti Moutsopoulou, Zéa Harbor, Piraeus, tel. 451 5731.

Sweetwater fishing is free all over Greece and its principal catch is the mountain trout. The best regions are: Epirus (rivers Voidomatis, Thiamis,

Louros, Aoos and the artificial lakes); Central Greece (Sperhios, Tavropos and Acheloos); Peloponnese (Vouraïkos, Alfios and Ladonas).

SAILING AND YACHTING. The jagged coasts and innumerable islands offer a unique blend of archeology, folklore, fishing, skin diving or just lazing in the sun. At the height of summer, the Aegean can be a great deal rougher than most people think, especially in August when the *meltémi,* the north wind, is a regular visitor to these waters. Yachting is a year-round sport in Greece and the water is fine for swimming from May to the end of October. Zéa harbor in Piraeus offers the most extensive mooring and wintering facilities. Among the remaining 100 yacht supply stations, Vouliagméni, Gouvia (Corfu), Pátra, Rhodes, Sýros and Thessaloníki are best equipped. For information, contact: *Hellenic Yachting Federation,* Akti Navarchou Kountourioti 7, Piraeus (tel. 413 7351).

From April through November the Yacht Club of Greece organizes a series of international sailing races under the I.Y.R.U. rules.

Renting a Yacht. Yacht rental agencies and travel agents have over 1,000 yachts of all sizes and at all prices for hire, but in high season it is necessary to book well in advance. Complaints are frequent, even on the luxury vessels.

In the U.S.: The G.N.T.O. offices supply lists of brokers and agencies.

In Great Britain:*Crestar Yacht Charters,* Colette Court, 125/126 Sloane St., London SW1X 9AU (tel. 071–730 9962); *Halsey Marine International Ltd.,* 22 Boston Place, Dorset Sq., London NW1 6HZ (tel. 071–724 1303); *Sunsail International Ltd.,* The Port House, Port Solent, Portsmouth, Hants. PO6 4TH (tel. 0705–210345); *Worldwide Yachting Holidays,* c/o Liz Fenner, 35 Fairfax Pl., London NW6 4EJ (tel. 071–328 1033/4). *Falcon Sailing,* 33 Notting Hill Gate, London W11 3JQ (tel. 071–727 0232) and *Flotilla Sailing Holidays Ltd.,* 2 St Johns Terrace, Harrow Rd., London W10 4RB (tel. 081–969 5423) offer organized sailing holidays round the Greek mainland coast and islands.

In Greece: Contact the G.N.T.O. for their listing, or the *Greek Yacht Brokers,* Alkyonis 36, Old Phaleron 17561 (tel. 981 6582).

It is essential to give the following information in your first letter when you write to reserve a yacht: desired date and period of charter; the number of passengers; with or without crew; the type of craft you want—auxiliary sailing yacht, motor yacht or caique.

What Will It Cost? There is something for every budget—on condition that your budget is not too tight! The cost of chartering obviously depends on the size and age of the yacht, the accommodations, the degree of comfort, the facilities aboard, and, of course, the season you choose for your trip. The basic price will cover the wages and expenses of any crew, insurance, sometimes fuel (for a maximum of eight hours' sailing every day) and all other expenses connected with the charter.

Crewed yachts, generally over 15 meters (50 feet), include sailing yachts, motor sailers, and motor caiques (skiffs); the larger yachts tend to be deluxe, with Cordon Bleu chefs, splendid accommodations, and prices to match. If you wish to rent in Greece, contact the *Greek Yacht Brokers* (address above) for price details.

Bareboats, auxiliary sailing yachts up to 15 meters (49 feet), can be chartered without a crew, provided two of the charterers hold a certificate from a recognized yacht club. Again, prices for rental from Greece, can be obtained from the *Greek Yacht Brokers.*

However, yachts can of course be chartered in advance from the U.S. or the U.K. The U.K. prices quoted are approximate and range from low to high season: a large sailing yacht of 15 meters (50 feet), without crew, from £4,600 to £6,300, for 14 days for 10 to 12 passengers; a smaller sailing yacht of 9.75 meters (32 feet), without crew, from £920 to £1,650, for 14 days for four to six passengers.

If you want to take all your meals on board, 2,000 to 4,000 dr. per person per day (for three meals) should be added. A cook can also be hired and his wages will be additional to the charges mentioned. It's hard to cook aboard a small craft where there is just about enough room to prepare breakfast and nothing else. This, however, is no serious disadvantage because nothing prevents you from going ashore at meal times to have a reasonably priced lunch or dinner at one of the tavernas you are bound to find there.

Flotilla cruising at 16 knots is an elegant form of Follow My Leader among the islands or along the shores. Power boating in twin-engined boats that handle like cars require no previous experience. Two weeks in a six-berth vessel comes to about £525 per person, including flight from the U.K.

If you have two weeks or so for your cruise, then you will have no problem in planning your itinerary. But if you only have a week, the question becomes somewhat more delicate. Here we offer two alternatives, allowing, however, for only the briefest visits ashore.

	Trip No. 1.	*Trip No. 2.*
1st Day	Aegina–Ğdra	Sóunio–Sérifos
2nd Day	Mílos	Íos–Thíra
3rd Day	Iráklio (Crete)	Astypaléa
4th Day	Thíra–Íos	Rhodes
5th Day	Páros	Kos–Kálymnos
6th Day	Délos–Mýkonos	Mýkonos–Délos
7th Day	Tínos–Sýros	Tínos–Kýthnos
8th Day	Zéa Marina, Piraeus	Zéa Marina, Piraeus

GOLF. The 18-hole *Glifada Golf Course (tel. 894 6820)* is near the airport, 13 km. (eight miles) from Athens. Entrance fee up to 11 A.M., 3,000 dr., then 4,000 dr. per day, 6,000 dr. weekends. Golf clubs 1,200 dr., push-cart 350 dr., electric 2,200 dr. There are three other 18-hole courses, on Corfu, Rhodes, and Pórto Carrás, Halkidikí; the first two are international standard, but the latter has been poorly maintained. There is a 9-hole course on Skíathos.

RIDING. *Riding Club of Greece,* Paradissou 18, Amaroussi (tel. 682 6128), 13 km. (8 miles) from Athens; *Riding Club of Athens,* Gerakas, Agia Paraskevi (tel. 661 1088), eight km. (5 miles). Non-members are admitted. *Northern Greece Riding Club,* Mikro Emvolo, Thessaloníki (tel. 031–432 895); *Scholi Philippon,* Thermi, Thessaloníki (tel. 031–462 991).

TENNIS. Greek National Tourist Organization beaches near Athens offer, among other facilities, several tennis courts. The *Athens Tennis Club,*

Vassilissis Olgas 2, is nearly always booked out by members. Courts also at most resorts and organized beaches.

GAMBLING. Casinos near Athens (Mount Parnis), on Corfu and Rhodes, also at Pórto Carrás (hotel guests only); baccarat, chemin-de-fer and roulette.

MOUNTAINEERING. *The Hellenic Federation of Mountaineering Clubs (E.O.S.),* Karageorgi Servias 7, Athens 126 (tel. 323 4555) operates some 40 mountain refuges (Olýmpos, Parnassós, Taygetos, White Mountains, etc.). Cost is 700 dr. per night, reduced for members of foreign alpine clubs. Pack animals with guide cost around 4,000 dr. per day. Points of departure: for the Olýmpos range, Litóhoro (sub-section of the Federation); for Mount Vérmio, Seli. There are sections of the Federation at other important starting points, such as Ioánina and Iráklio (Crete). Climbers who are visiting Northern Greece should contact the Thessaloníki section, Karolou Deal 15. All guides have a rudimentary inkling of English, French or German.

SKIING. The main ski centers in order of importance are: Mount Parnassós, Mount Vérmio, Métsovo, Mount Falakro and Mount Pílio. Skilifts operate on ten other mountains. Contact *The Hellenic Federation of Skiing Clubs (E.O.H.),* Agia Konstantinou 34, Athens (tel. 524 0057), for further information.

Traveling in Greece

BY AIR. Divided by mountain ranges and sea, Greece has developed a comprehensive network of internal air services operated by *Olympic Airways*. This network is like a giant cartwheel centered on Athens: from there you can fly to Áktio, Alexandróupoli, Ioánina, Kastoriá, Kavála, Kozáni, Lárissa and Thessaloníki, all on the mainland; Kalamáta, in the Peloponnese; to the islands: Kýthira, Crete (Haniá and Iráklio), Híos, Kos, Léros, Lésbos, Límnos, Mílos, Mýkonos, Paros, Rhodes, Sámos, Skiáthos, Skýros and Thíra, in the Aegean Sea; Corfu, Kefaloniá and Zákynthos, in the Ionian Sea. Mýkonos, Rhodes and Thessaloníki are secondary hubs. Regional connections, especially between the islands, are mentioned in the appropriate chapters.

The frequency varies greatly according to the time of year, and it is essential to book well in advance during high summer or before festivals and holidays. Fares are quite low and there is a 25% discount for students on nearly all international flights. In early 1990 the single fare from Athens to Thessaloníki was 8,300 dr.; to Rhodes, 10,900 dr.; to Corfu, 9,700 dr.; and to Iráklio, 8,700 dr. Return fares are double. There are also bargain night fares to Crete, Corfu, Rhodes and Thessaloníki.

The free baggage allowance is 15 kilos (33 lbs.) per passenger. There is a 90% reduction for infants, and children from 2 to 12 years pay half fare.

Details and timetables in the U.S. from Olympic Airways, 647 Fifth Avenue, New York, NY 10022 (tel. 212–735–0200). They also have offices in Houston, Los Angeles, Miami, Philadelphia, and Washington. In the U.K. from Olympic Airways, Trafalgar House, 2 Chalk Hill Road, London W6 8SB. (tel. 081–846 9966). Regional offices in Birmingham, Manchester and Glasgow. Strikes occasionally cause cancellations or postponements.

Airports. Athens Airport Elliniko is divided into the East Terminal used by all foreign airlines, and the West Terminal exclusive to Olympic Airways international as well as domestic flights. A new blue and yellow coach service connects the two air terminals, Syntagma Square, bus and train stations, and Piraeus. They run every 15 minutes from 6 A.M. to midnight (fare: 100 dr.) and every 90 minutes from midnight to 6 A.M. (fare: 150 dr.). A taxi into the center of Athens should cost no more than 700 dr. (unless a particularly roundabout route is followed, which is not improbable).

International airports are at Athens, Corfu, Ioánina, Iráklio (Crete), Kavála, Rhodes and Thessaloníki. Duty free shops sell mainly Greek folk art, liquor and cigarettes. Olympic Airways provide buses to both international and provincial airports, which are adequate if simple.

BY TRAIN. Greece is not particularly well endowed with railroads. The only main line runs from Athens to Thessaloníki on the standard gauge network, with new twice-daily "high-speed" express trains which take about 6½ hours for the 590-km. (366-mile) run. There are also four other trains daily, as well as four overnight trains (sleeping cars and couchettes), all taking around 7½ hours; daytime trains have either a restaurant car or refreshment services. There are also services to Vólos and Kalambáka and to Flórina and Alexandróupoli (from Thessaloníki).

Even more basic is the narrow gauge system, twisting and turning, burrowing and soaring on its course round the Peloponnese. Except for the tiresome hooting at the numerous unguarded crossings, it might please rail buffs, besides being a quaint way to see the country and meet the people. Departing from Athens, the line serves all the main centers on the Peloponnese. At Corinth, one branch leads west to Pátra, Kylíni, Pýrgos (Olýmpia) and then south to Kalamáta, and the other south to Árgos (Náfplio), Trípoli and Megalópolis, also ending at Kalamáta.

Trains are slow and advance planning is essential. Use the *Thomas Cook Continental Timetable*, or contact the G.N.T.O. who will send photocopies of the timetable on request. The railroads of Greece are covered by the *InterRail* ticket (for Europeans under 26 and over 65 for men and 60 for women), and by the *Eurailpass/Youthpass* tickets (for visitors living outside Western Europe). These tickets are worth buying only if the visit to Greece is part of a rail-based tour of Europe. If you intend to fly to Greece and then travel around by rail, remember that train fares are cheap. Hellenic State Railways offer a 20% discount on return tickets, and touring cards are available in 2nd class, giving unlimited travel; the price varies according to the number of people using the card (details from the G.N.T.O.). In summer it is well worth paying the extra and traveling 1st class—for comfort's sake and to avoid the crush. The following examples of fares may be useful.

Fares in Drachmes

	1st Class	2nd Class
Athens–Alexandróupoli	3,620	2,410
Athens–Corinth	480	320
Athens–Pátra	950	630
Athens–Thessaloníki	2,280	1,520

BY SHIP. Island hopping had been a necessity for millennia, when the Athenian *Triremes* made it less hazardous in the fifth century B.C. The full-size model that joined the Greek navy in 1987 is no more a thing of the past than the discipline that once embarked 170 oarsmen in a scramble so that all sat in the right places. The summer crowds still embark in a scramble, the right places are more doubtful, and luckily they are not required to pull together. As there are daily ferries to most islands, and regular inter-island services, a general plan can be made well in advance, allowing some leeway for side trips and delays. Unlike on international services, advance bookings from abroad are chancy on domestic lines and have to be confirmed close to the sailing date. Accidents and incidents, not to mention Acts of God and strikes, will happen.

Our ferry map shows the lines operating the year round, naturally less frequent in winter. The following examples of 1990 fares (excluding meals) may be useful. First class fares vary from one vessel to another.

Fares in Drachmes from Piraeus

	Cars	2nd	Tourist	3rd
Iráklio	7,475–9,775	3,535	2,853	2,115
Mýkonos	7,016–9,334	2,269	1,756	1,448
Mytilíni	8,413–11,109	3,590	2,635	2,116
Náxos	6,945–9,261	2,306	1,792	1,505
Rhodes	9,044–11,868	5,031	3,816	2,914
Thíra	9,551–12,448	2,839	2,244	1,856

Tourist and third are redolent with local atmosphere (which often means transport of livestock). Embarkation Tax (included in the ticket price): from Piraeus 114 dr.; from all other ports 114 dr. plus 5% of the fare.

There are also hydrofoil services (passengers only) to Égina, Póros, Ýdra, Spétses, Pórto Héli, Monemvasía and Kýthira.

Thomas Cook Continental Timetable and the monthly *Greek Travel Pages,* published at Dimotikou Stadiou 12, Kallithea, Athens, and available in the U.K. through *Timsway Holidays,* list international and domestic lines.

Accommodation on some ferries is fairly simple. All have varying forms of refreshment facilities. Longer routes have cabins at additional cost.

AEGEAN CRUISES. The effortless way of touring the Greek islands (but not of meeting the Greeks, as at least two-thirds of the passengers are foreigners), is by cruise ships, operating mostly out of Piraeus but also out of some Adriatic ports. These cruises usually consist of full-day stopovers and conducted sightseeing at such places as Corfu, Rhodes, Crete, Mýkonos (and Delos), Athens (two days); some include visits to Istanbul, Izmir, Ephesus and Halicarnassus in Turkey, others combine with a stay at attractive resorts. Occasionally Israeli or Egyptian ports are substituted for the Turkish ones on the longer cruises.

From April through October, there are many cruises of the Greek Islands out of Piraeus (Athens). Among the lines offering one-day to seven-day Greek Island cruises (combined with Turkey or Yugoslavia) are *Blue Aegean Sea Line, Cycladic Cruises, Epirotiki, Hellenic Cruises, Hellenic Mediterranean, K Lines, Oceanic Sun Line* and *Saronic Cruises.* Other cruise lines call at Piraeus and other Greek ports. They include the *Chandris, Mediterranean Sun Cruises, Royal Viking Line* and *Royal Cruise Line.*

BY BUS. Organized tours by bus from one to five days can be safely booked together with hotel reservations at any travel agent, though it is hardly necessary. Several efficient operators compete out of major tourist resorts, always able to add an extra bus if needed. *American Express,* Platia Syntagma; *CHAT,* Stadiou 4; *Hellas Tours,* Stadiou 7; *Key Tours,* Ermou 2, etc. have their own fleet of luxury buses (Pullmans) for a wide-ranging choice of tours. The G.N.T.O. information sheets give an indication of the routes' frequency, times, and fares, as well as the departure points within Athens. However all information must be checked locally on arrival as, this being Greece, schedules are liable to change at short notice—but this is all part of the fun of being unpackaged! Always get to the bus depot in plenty of time, especially if you want a good seat. Travel by bus in

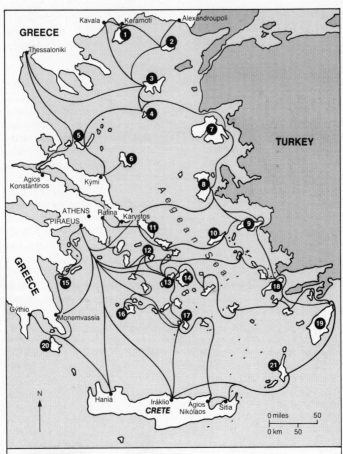

GREEK ISLAND FERRIES

This map shows the main ferry routes serving the Greek Islands. Ferry services are subject to change so this map should be used for general guidance only.

Greek Islands

1 Thassos
2 Samothrace
3 Límnos
4 Ágios Efstratios
5 Skópelos
6 Skýros (Linaria)
7 Lesvos (Mytilini)
8 Híos
9 Sámos (Sámos/Karlóvassi)
10 Ikaria (Agios Kírykos)
11 Andros (Gávrio)

12 Sýros
13 Paros
14 Naxos
15 Spetses
16 Milos
17 Thira/Santorini
18 Kos
19 Rhodes
20 Kythira (Agía Pelagía)
21 Kárpathos

Greece is inexpensive (about half what it is in the U.K.). For example, the single fare from Athens to Thessaloníki was 3,000 dr. in early 1990.

The network of bus services extends to even the smallest villages—frequencies vary, but once daily is a minimum. The two main overland-bus terminals in Athens are at Kifissou 100, for the Peloponnese, Western Greece, the Ionian Islands and Northern Greece, and at Liossion 260, for Euboea, Central and Eastern Greece. Other major towns are hubs for their respective regions.

BY CAR. Ordinary registration papers and an international third party insurance (green card) are required as well as a driving license (American, EC, or international) for those who are to drive the vehicle within Greece. A free entry card is issued, valid for four months. The car may circulate for a further eight months without payment of import duty, provided a guarantee for duty payment is given by a Greek national and provided it can be proved (with receipts of foreign currency transactions) that the car driver is a tourist and not working in Greece. Greek road tax must also then be paid (only about 1,500 dr. a month). You are recommended to take out full insurance, including coverage against collision with an uninsured motorist—not just third-party insurance. Greek law requires an accident to be reported, which Greek motorists often fail to do, before the insurance companies consider claims. Redress at court, even with witnesses, takes a very long time.

Current price of gasoline (petrol) is 85 dr. per liter for regular, 90 dr. for super, 40 dr. for diesel, in the main centers, slightly more in remote areas. Motor oils from 200 to 260 dr. Unleaded fuel is sold at gas stations along the toll roads and in the main towns. Toll roads are part of the European road system and are numbered accordingly.

Car Rental. There is a well developed rental system in Athens, as well as in the major resorts. Cars are delivered to the airport, harbor or railroad station. Rates include public liability, third party, passenger and fire risks, oil and greasing. Charges are higher between June and October, ranging from 2,500 dr. per day plus 36 dr. per km. to 8,800 dr. plus 79 dr. per km. Always add 16% for tax and service. Unlimited mileage, in high season, ranges from 47,000 dr. to 125,000 dr. for seven days. Prices indicated do not include luxury cars. *Ansa International,* Syngrou 33; *Avis,* Leoforos Amalias 48; *Budget,* Syngrou 8; *Hellascar,* Syngrou 148 and Stadiou 7; *Hertz,* Syngrou 12, and Vouliagmenis Ave. 567A; Athens. All have branches in Corfu, Iráklio, Rhodes, Thessaloníki.

Transit Cars. Several firms on Leoforos Syngrou and Leoforos Alexandras are authorized to buy and sell cars in transit. The largest and most experienced in cutting through the red tape are *Boomerang,* Heiden 17, and *Kokkinos,* Frantzi 9.

Automobile Associations. The *Automobile & Touring Club of Greece* [E.L.P.A.], Athens Tower, Messogion 2, tel. 174, for tourist information.

Rules of the Road. International road signs are in use throughout Greece. You drive on the right, pass on the left, and yield right of way to all vehicles approaching from the right (except on posted main highways). Speed limits are visibly marked, keep to 30–50 km/h (18–31 mph) in built-up areas. In many streets parking alternates, even months right, odd months left. Though illegal, pavement parking is common; fines are 12,000 dr., and being a foreigner doesn't help. The ways of the police are unpredictable. Appalling road manners alternate with utmost helpfulness. The use of the triangular danger warning is compulsory if you have a breakdown. Roving repair trucks, manned by skilled E.L.P.A. mechanics, patrol the major highways; services free of charge, but a commensurate tip is expected. Police are empowered to impose on-the-spot fines for offenses, but do so rarely. It should be noted that there are severe restrictions on the circulation of cars in central Athens in order to lessen congestion and pollution. Cars with registration numbers ending in odd numbers are excluded on one day, those with even numbers on the following day. However, this regulation applies to visiting motorists only after they have been in Greece for forty days.

Car-Ferry Services. In addition to the ferries from Italy to Greek ports, there are numerous domestic services which can shorten a journey by many hours. The local ferry boat between Corfu and Igoumenítsa runs many times daily in each direction. The coastal highway leads directly to Préveza and the ferry to Aktio every half hour from 6 A.M. to 10 P.M., every hour during the night, and via Messolóngi to the Río–Antírio ferry which connects Epirus with the N.W. Peloponnese; every 15 minutes from both sides, 7 A.M. to 11 P.M.; every half hour during the night. Daily ferry from Astakós to Itháki; and Kefalonía; from Pátra to Sámi, Kefalonía, and Itháki. Lefkáda is connected by a drawbridge across the narrow canal separating it from the mainland. Zákynthos and Kefalonía can be reached several times daily from Kylíni on the Western Peloponnese.

The Aegean island of Euboea is connected with the mainland: south, Rafína to Marmári and Kárystos twice or three times daily; Agía Marína (Marathon) central, to Néa Stýra, four times daily; Oropós to Erétria and vice versa every half hour from daybreak to 10 P.M.; in the north, Arkítsa to Edipsós, seven to 12 times daily; Glyfá 13 km. (eight miles) off the Lamía–Vólos road, to Agiókambos, north of Edipsós, five to eight times daily; from Kými (East Euboea) to Skýros, Alonissos, Skópelos; Skíathos, once daily. From Ágios Konstantínos and Vólos to Skíathos, Skópelos, Alonissos, twice daily. From Kavála to Thássos, 15 times daily; more frequent on holidays.

From Piraeus to Aegina, 12 to 35 times daily; to Méthana, and Póros, six times daily; to the Cyclades at least twice daily. Piraeus to Haniá or Iráklio once or twice daily. The shortest crossing to the Cyclades is from Rafína in Attica, once or twice daily, and from Lávrio to Kéa and Kýthnos. About eight times weekly; Piraeus–Kos–Rhodes; Piraeus–Híos–Lésbos; Piraeus–Samos. Crossings to Turkey are from Lesbos to Dikeli; Híos to Cesme; and Samos to Kusadasi.

Speed Limits. The maximum speed allowed on the Pátra–Corinth–Athens–Thessaloníki–Evzóni (Yugoslav border) toll road is 110 km.p.h. (68 m.p.h.); on all other roads 100 km.p.h. (63 m.p.h.) unless lower limits are indicated.

Spare Parts. These are readily available in all Greek towns, but not always on transit through Yugoslavia. Before leaving home, ask your dealer for a kit of vital spares; if you find you don't have to open it on your trip, you can usually return it. Make sure your spare wheel is in good shape. As for mechanical repairs, there are garages with competent mechanics even in the smallest towns. Most of the leading American and European automobile manufacturers have agents in the main cities of Greece. Here is a list of dealers you can contact in an emergency: *British Leyland,* Leofóros Syngrou 116; *Citroën,* Leofóros Syngrou 100; *Ford,* Kondellis, Plapouta 10, Argyróupoli; *General Motors, Talbot, Renault, Volvo,* Leofóros Athinon 71; *Fiat,* Evdoxon 73; *Volkswagen,* Iera Odos 131; *Mercedes, Auto Union,* Fosteropoulos, Leofóros Athinon 40. All in Athens.

Leaving Greece

CUSTOMS ON RETURNING HOME. If you propose to take on your holiday any *foreign-made* articles, such as cameras, binoculars, expensive time-pieces, and the like, it is wise to put with your travel documents the receipt from the retailer or some other evidence that the item was bought in your home country. If you bought the article on a previous holiday abroad and have already paid duty on it, carry with you the receipt for this.

U.S. Residents. You may bring in $400 worth of foreign merchandise as gifts or for personal use without having to pay duty, provided you have been out of the country more than 48 hours and provided you have not claimed a similar exemption within the previous 30 days. Every member of a family is entitled to the same exemption, regardless of age, and the exemptions can be pooled. For the next $1,000 worth of goods a flat 10% rate is assessed.

The $400 figure is based on the fair retail value of the goods in the country where acquired. Included for travelers over the age of 21 are one liter of alcohol, 100 cigars (non-Cuban) and 200 cigarettes. Any amount in excess of those limits will be taxed at the port of entry, and may additionally be taxed in the traveler's home state. Only one bottle of perfume trademarked in the U.S. may be brought in. Unlimited amounts of goods from certain specially designated "developing" countries may also be brought in duty-free; check with U.S. Customs Service, 1301 Constitution Ave., NW, Washington, DC 20044. Write to the same address for information regarding importation of automobiles and/or motorcycles. You may not bring home meats, fruits, plants, soil or other agricultural items.

Gifts valued at under $50 may be mailed to friends or relatives at home, but not more than one per day (of receipt) to any one addressee. These gifts must not include tobacco (other than cigars) or liquor.

Military personnel returning from abroad should check with the nearest American Embassy for special regulations pertaining to them.

Canadian Residents. In addition to personal effects, the following articles may be brought in duty free: a maximum of 50 cigars, 200 cigarettes, 2.2 pounds of tobacco and 40 ounces of liquor, provided these are declared in writing to customs on arrival and accompany the traveler in hand or checked-through baggage. These are included in the basic exemption of $300 a year. Personal gifts should be mailed as "Unsolicited Gift—Value Under $40." Canadian customs regulations are strictly enforced: you are recommended to check what your allowances are and to make sure you have kept receipts for whatever you have bought abroad. For details ask for the Canada Customs brochure, "I Declare."

British Residents except those under the age of 17 years, may import duty-free from *any* country the following: 200 cigarettes or 100 cigarillos or 50 cigars or 250 grams of tobacco; 1 liter of alcoholic drink over 22% volume (i.e. whiskey and other hard liquor), *or* 2 liters of alcoholic drink (including still, fortified or sparkling wine) under 22% vol. plus 2 liters of still table wine. Also 60 milliliters of perfume, ¼ liter of toilet water and £32 worth of other normally dutiable goods (not to include more than 50 liters of beer).

Returning from any *European Community* (and remember that Greece is now in the EC.), you may, *instead* of the above exemptions, bring in the following, provided you can prove they were *not* bought in a duty-free shop: 300 cigarettes or 150 cigarillos or 75 cigars or 400 grams of tobacco; 1½ liters of alcoholic drink over 22% volume, *or* 3 liters under 22% vol. (including still, fortified or sparkling wine) plus 5 liters of still table wine (it would be wise to check the latest position regarding wine allowance); 90 milliliters of perfume and ⅜ liter of toilet water; 1,000 grams of coffee or 375 grams of coffee extract; and £250 worth of other normally dutiable goods (again, not more than 50 liters of beer).

MADE IN MAN'S IMAGE

A Chronicle of Gods and Heroes

Ancient Greece was happily free from the religious fanaticism of later ages for the Greek attitude toward their gods was remarkably eclectic and never hidebound by rigid tradition. Gods from many parts of the Ancient world were assimilated into the Olympian family. This extremely tolerant and open attitude toward their gods accounts to a very large degree for the development of the great Greek philosophic systems side by side with popular religion.

Like most Mediterraneans the original inhabitants of Greece worshipped the Great Triple Goddess. Her celestial symbol was the moon, whose three phases recalled the change from the maiden into the woman and finally into a crone. Ever since, three has remained a sacred number, playing a mystical part in religion.

In the pre-Hellenic matriarchal organization the tribes were ruled by a queen, whose annual lover was sacrificed at the end of the year and his blood sprinkled on trees and crops. His flesh was devoured by the priestesses disguised as mares, sows or bitches. The frenzied followers of Dionysos indulged in this cannibalistic practice down to the 6th century, with Orpheus as their most famous victim.

Successive invasions of Hellenic tribes undermined the authority of the terrible Great Goddess, and introduced male supremacy and succession towards the close of the 2nd millennium B.C. Yet the goddesses were never completely stripped of all influence, thanks to the great poets, especially Homer, who had clearly defined their spheres of action.

Religion was an imaginative comment on natural phenomena, without any rigid creed. As the moral consciousness developed, the notion of reward and punishment based on ethical conduct gained strength, and by the 6th century B.C. hell, purgatory and paradise had become established concepts. But the gods were not exempt from passions and faults, they simply acted on a grander scale. Even their immortality depended on the divine food and drink of ambrosia and nectar. They were conceived as an upper class of very superior nobles, above the humans, yet essentially human.

Feasts and ceremonies followed largely older local traditions, while rules were concerned with pleasing the gods, not with regulating the belief of the worshipper. Impiety was a crime only when it led to a neglect of ritual determining the daily life. This close connection makes some familiarity with mythology essential for the better understanding of the Greek mind.

Owing to the different poetical interpretations, the gods were endowed with a bewildering assortment of vices and virtues to satisfy everybody's taste. Greek sense of humor, moreover, was stronger than blind respect for the immortals. The Olympians' amorous misadventures or their far from harmonious family life were discussed with relish.

The Creation Myth

At the beginning was Chaos, from which Gaea (Earth) emerged—though how successfully has remained a point of dispute. All by herself she bore a son, Uranos (Heaven), who was ashamed of his naked mother. His tears of indignation must have been copious, as rivers and seas, flowers and trees, and even animals sprang up where they had fallen. The earth became divided into two equal parts by the Mediterranean and the Black Sea, with the river Okeanos encircling the disc. Greece occupied the central position, while far north, in the inaccessible British Isles, lived the blameless Hyperboreans in perpetual springtide. (It is pleasant to reflect that Britain once enjoyed such a reputation.) They were often visited by the gods, like their southern counterpart, the equally virtuous Ethiopians.

Incest was a practical necessity for the first gods and men alike, in both cases with singularly unprepossessing results. Heaven's union with Mother Earth produced three 100-handed giants, followed by three hardly more attractive one-eyed Cyclopes. It is not surprising that the exasperated father flung his hideous brood into Tartaros, the remotest and gloomiest part of the underworld. Yet Uranos must have been fond of children, as he proceeded to father the seven Titans, more pleasing in appearance, but far more dangerous to their luckless progenitor. Urged on by their mother, who pined for her exiled Cyclopes, the Titans attacked their sleeping father with a flint sickle and castrated him.

The Titans divided the world among themselves under the leadership of the youngest, Kronos (Time). Mother Earth, however, failed in her attempt to set the beloved Cyclopes free. After one look Kronos confined them and their 100-handed brothers again to Tartaros; and in revenge the frustrated mother prophesied that he too would be dethroned by one of his own sons.

Kronos married his sister Rhea but, mindful of the prophecy, swallowed the children his wife bore him, a parable of Time annihilating all creation. On Mother Earth's advice Rhea substituted for her sixth child a stone wrapped in swaddling clothes which Kronos promptly devoured. It says a lot for his excellent digestion that he never noticed the fraud.

The infant Zeus was hidden in the cave of Dicte in Crete, under the care of the goat Amalthea, whose milk he drank together with his foster-brother Goat-Pan. Zeus showed his gratitude to his nurse by setting her image among the stars as Capricorn. Around the infant's cradle Rhea's priests performed wild dances, clashing shields and uttering piercing screams to drown the noise of his wailing. He grew up among the shepherds of Mount Ida, and with his mother's assistance was made cupbearer to his unsuspecting father. Rhea provided Zeus with a mixture so potent that even Kronos could not stomach it. He vomited up first the stone—venerated throughout antiquity in Delphi—and then disgorged his elder children.

After deposing their father, Zeus, Poseidon and Hades drew lots for the division of the world. Zeus won the heaven, Poseidon the sea, and Hades the underworld. The earth was left common to all the gods under the vague sovereignty of Zeus, who only succeeded in controlling his quarrelsome family by the threat of the thunderbolts he alone might wield. And it was the thunderbolts—forged by the Cyclopes at last released—that give the third generation victory over those Titans who refused to acknowledge Zeus as their master. For ten years a terrible war raged in Thessaly, the rebels piling mountain upon mountain to reach the abode of the gods, before Kronos was defeated and banished to the British Isles. According to another version, he was allowed to withdraw to Italy, where he ruled a prosperous kingdom, until in his dotage he was compensated with the Elysian Fields. Atlas, his second-in-command, was set to hold up the sky, while the lesser Titans took the Cyclopes' place in Tartaros.

Having successfully disposed of his uncles, Zeus settled down to enjoy his unlawfully obtained power. But Mother Earth changed sides, and, never averse to bringing forth a monster, now created the worst abomination of all, called Typhon.

To a hundred dragon heads spouting flames were added arms reaching a hundred leagues in either direction, while instead of legs he featured the coils of a serpent. One glance at Gaea's youngest sent the gods in headlong flight to Egypt, a favorite refuge for divinity in distress. For greater safeguard Zeus assumed the form of a ram, Hera became a cow, Artemis a cat, each god choosing the animal shape of his Egyptian counterpart.

But Zeus soon grew ashamed of his cowardice and resuming his true form pursued Typhon with thunderbolts, finally hurling Mount Aetna at him. Buried beneath the Sicilian mountain the monster still belches forth fire and flame, and when he occasionally changes his position an earthquake ensues.

The Story of Man

Prometheus (Forethought), the wisest of the Titans, had foreseen the outcome of Kronos' rebellion and loyally fought on the Olympians' side. As a reward he was entrusted with the creation of man. From a lump of clay kneaded with water Prometheus fashioned a creature in the image of the gods, and bestowed on man the supreme gift of fire, lighting a torch at the sun itself.

During the Age of Gold men lived without care and without women. After Zeus had fathered the seasons life became harder for men, who had to seek refuge from wind and cold in caves. No more could they live on fruit, milk and honey, but had to work for their food. Contrary to expectation, work and sin went hand in hand, and as punishment Zeus extinguished the fire. Prometheus once again came to the rescue and brought a torch to earth hidden in the pithy hollow of a giant fennel stalk. But the gods took a terrible vengeance on both Prometheus and mankind. The Titan was chained to a peak in the Caucasian mountains, where an eagle tore at his liver all day; and there was no end to his pain, because every night the liver grew whole again and the ghastly process was resumed the next morning.

To men was meted out a fate hardly less atrocious. Haephaestos fashioned a woman, Aphrodite taking care of the sex appeal. This gift of all the gods, Pandora, was sent to Epimetheus (Afterthought), who in spite of his brother Prometheus' warnings was enslaved by her charms. As dowry Pandora had received a jeweled box, which Zeus had exhorted her never to open, realizing full well that disobedience and curiosity would distinguish the female. Before long Pandora did indeed open the box, and out flew all the mental and bodily diseases that have plagued mankind ever since. But caught under the lid remained Hope, which alone makes men's lives bearable.

Mankind degenerated so intolerably that Zeus resolved to destroy it in a flood. But there was one righteous man, Deukalion, who with his wife Pyrrha had been warned to take refuge in an ark, which floated about for nine days, before at last coming to rest on Mount Parnassós. When the flood receded a divine voice ordered them to fling the bones of their mother behind. This they rightly interpreted as meaning the bones of Mother Earth, the rocks. Those thrown by Deukalion became men, and those by Pyrrha women. Thus humanity was renewed, though the couple also produced one son in the orthodox way. He was called Hellen, who gave his name to the Hellenic race, and his sons Aelos and Doros, and grandsons Ion and Achaius, became the ancestors of the tribes bearing their names.

The Olympians—Zeus and Hera

Having thus connected the tribes, Greek love of systematization likewise wrought the principal gods into one great family, regardless of their varied origins.

Zeus fixed the abode of the gods in Mount Olympos, whence he decreed laws and controlled the heavenly bodies. When his mother Rhea forbade him to marry, he violated her and proceeded to court his sister Hera—unsuccessfully, until he transformed himself into a bedraggled cuckoo, which the merciful goddess warmed against her bosom. Resuming his true shape, Zeus ravished her, shaming her into marriage.

Mother, now grandmother, Earth gave Hera a tree with golden apples as a wedding present. The newlyweds spent the wedding night, lasting 300 years, on Samos, but in spite of the birth of two sons and one daughter, Ares, Hephaestos and Hebe, the marriage could hardly be called happy. There was constant bickering over Zeus' numerous infidelities, which Hera proved utterly incapable of preventing, though she occasionally took terrible revenge on her rivals or their children.

She only rarely succeeded in arousing her husband's passion, even though she sometimes borrowed Aphrodite's girdle; perhaps the wedding night had been too prolonged. Their family, however, increased to 12, partly by children born in wedlock, partly through extra-marital affairs with nymphs or mortals, a yield of four supplemented by two miraculous births.

Zeus grew increasingly overbearing, and at last the Olympians revolted, binding him, as he lay asleep, with rawhide thongs tied in a hundred knots. While the gods were quarreling over his succession, the sea nymph Thetis, fearing a civil war, set one of the 100-handed uncles to untie the knots all at once. No sooner was Zeus free than he hung Hera, the ringleader, in golden chains from heaven, with heavy anvils weighing down her ankles. She was only released after her fellow conspirators had taken an oath of loyalty.

Poseidon

Poseidon too had taken a prominent part in the rebellion, and was condemned to serve King Laomedon for one year, for whom he built with Apollo's assistance the city of Troy. He equaled his brother Zeus in dignity, though not in power, which was all for the good considering his perpetual bad temper.

In the best family tradition he raped his sister Demeter, then had a son, a most objectionable giant, by his grandmother Earth, before he began courting the sea nymph Thetis, to have a spouse who would feel at home in the depth of the sea. Zeus was his rival for Thetis' hand, but both desisted when it was prophesied that her son would outshine his father. They forthwith encouraged her to wed an innocuous mortal, King Peleus, the future father of Achilles.

Another sea nymph, Amphitrite, became his consort and though rather insignificant herself, she could rise to fits of jealousy worthy of Hera. Needless to say she had plenty of provocation. Her children were singularly undistinguished, with the exception of Triton, the dangerous and touchy merman.

Not content with the seas, Poseidon was exceedingly greedy for earthly kingdoms, quarreling fiercely with Dionysos over Náxos, with Hera over Árgos, and especially with Athena over Athens.

Hestia and Demeter

Though both unmarried, these two sisters of Zeus were unlike in character. Hestia, alone of all Olympians was never connected with any scandal, and it was probably her very purity that made her lose her place to the orgiastic Dionysos. The ancient Greeks were too fond of love and intrigue to honor greatly so placid, mild and charitable a goddess as this protectress of the hearth.

Demeter, on the other hand, shared fully the stormy life of the Olympians. She did not escape Zeus' amorous advances and bore him Persephone. After a passing affair with a Titan, she was raped by brother Poseidon.

But this dallying came to a sudden stop when Hades abducted young Persephone while she was picking flowers. The disconsolate mother searched in vain, until she reached Eleusis, where the king's elder son had news of the vanished Persephone. He had seen a chariot drawn by black horses racing down a bottomless chasm. And then the earth closed again over the driver who was clasping a struggling girl. There could be no doubt as to the charioteer's identity.

Demeter instantly forbade all trees to bear fruit and all grain to grow, until life on earth was threatened with extinction. She only relented after a compromise was reached thanks to mother Rhea's intervention. Persephone was to spend the three winter months with Hades, and the rest of the year with her mother. Demeter lifted the curse, instructed the king's son in her mysteries and rewarded him with seed corn and a wooden plow to teach mankind the art of agriculture.

Aphrodite and Eros

The goddess of love rose naked from the sea. Though originally an orgiastic Oriental, her cult, if not her conduct, improved in comformity with the Greek moral code. Only in Corinth, the trading center most exposed to foreign influences, did temple harlots serve her in the Syrian fashion.

Aphrodite was exceedingly fickle and capricious, but worst of all, she hardly ever lent her magic girdle, which made its wearer irresistible. As punishment she was married off to Hephaestos, physically the least attractive Olympian. Yet this match was harder on the husband than on the wife, who had fallen for the virility of Ares. Hephaestos surprised the lovers in bed, and throwing an unbreakable net over them summoned the gods to witness their shame. The immortals were merely amused, while Poseidon and Hermes greatly appreciated Aphrodite's provocative helplessness. As reward for Hermes' flattering remarks she spent a night with him and bore double-sexed Hermaphroditos. Then she could not but do likewise with Poseidon, and, after rounding off a hectic season with Dionysos, she retired to Cyprus renewing her virginity in the sea, to the pained envy of mortals and immortals.

Woe to anyone who offended the goddess of love. Her main instrument of vengeance was her son Eros, whose progenitor could never be ascertained owing to the mother's promiscuity. Eros wantonly kindled passions with his golden arrows shot at random, yet he himself did not escape the fate he had meted out to countless victims.

He had been instructed by his jealous mother to make Psyche (Soul) fall in love. For once handling the fateful arrows clumsily, he wounded himself, while Psyche remained untouched. Aphrodite was enraged that his own weapon had been turned against her son. She set the desperate maiden some seemingly impossible tasks which Psyche nevertheless accomplished, sustained by Eros' invisible assistance. As supreme trial she was bidden to fetch some of Persephone's beauty from the underworld, as Aphrodite had lost some of hers tending her love-sick son. Psyche was on her way back with the priceless gift wrapped in a box, when she bethought herself that a touch of divine beauty might not come amiss to restore any possible ravages caused by her sorrow. Pandora's heritage of disobedience and curiosity undid Psyche for a second time. Yet thanks to the power of love and Eros' fervent pleading, Psyche was made immortal and married her lover. Spiritual and bodily love were united and blessed with a child called Delight.

Athena

Some cannibalistic tendencies still persisted among the gods, especially within the close family circle. After having got his aunt, the wise Titaness Metis, with child, Zeus swallowed her. Surprisingly enough this did not cause indigestion, but a raging headache. As a drastic, though unusual remedy Zeus ordered Hephaestos to cleave his skull open with an axe. The fruit of this heroic midwifery was Athena, who sprang full-grown and fully armed from her father's head.

Though excelling in the domestic arts, she was a formidable warrior, but only supported just causes and, unlike Ares, did not love war for its own sake. She inherited her luckless mother's wisdom, which kept her from the petty jealousies so common on Olympos. Only once did the boast of Princess Arachne (Spider) that she wove more skillfully than the goddess, drive Athena to cruel revenge. Defeated in a competition, Arachne hanged herself and was changed into a spider weaving for all eternity.

Apollo

Leto was vainly seeking for a place to bear Zeus' child, abandoned by her lover to his wife's vindictiveness. Hera forbade Mother Earth to grant Leto hospitality and sent a monstrous serpent, Python, in pursuit. At last Poseidon took pity, and on the floating island of Délos, Leto gave birth to a son and a daughter.

In the land of the Hyperboreans Apollo grew into a skillful archer, ready to avenge his mother on the Python, who had been rewarded with the guardianship of the sacred cave in Delphi. To commemorate his slaying of the monster, Apollo instituted the Pythian games, culminating in a race from Delphi to Thessaly—what a pleasant stroll the Marathon seems in comparison!

The victor returned crowned with laurels, which recalled one of Apollo's many misadventures. In spite of his great beauty he was singularly unlucky in love, as Eros was determined to prove the superiority of his own bow and arrow: Apollo chased Daphne, Peneus' daughter, through the forest. In answer to the terrified maiden's prayers, Peneus, a river god, changed her into a laurel tree on the banks of his stream. In his grief Apollo decreed that laurel wreaths should thenceforward be the reward of athletes and artists.

A flower, too, bears witness to the god's misfortune. He loved a handsome youth named Hyacinthos, who was also coveted by Zephiros, god of the west wind. Apollo and the boy were throwing the discus at Amyclae, near Sparta, when Zephiros blew Apollo's discus so violently aside that it wounded Hyacinthos mortally. The drops of blood were changed into a cluster of hyacinths.

Apollo usurped the place of the sun god Helios whose statue, the famous Colossus, stood astride the harbor of Rhodes. Heralded by his attendant Eos (Dawn), Helios drove the sun chariot daily from his splendid palace in the east to the far western sea. After pasturing his horses in the Fortunate Isles, he sailed back on the ocean stream which encircles the world. Because of the similarity of attributes and youthful beauty, Helios became identified with Phoebus Apollo, and the myths attaching to them merged into one cycle.

Artemis

Like her twin brother Apollo, Artemis usurped the place of the older goddess Selene, mistress of the moon. Artemis was a great huntress, and, when she had finished driving the moon chariot she spent the rest of the night in the woods with her attendant nymphs. From a silver bow she shot her unfailing arrows indiscriminately at beasts and those unlucky huntsmen who accidentally saw her bathing in the nude. Her inordinate irritability and morbid insistence on chastity make her an obvious case of acute frustration. Yet there were ugly rumors in connection with a handsome shepherd, Endymion, whom Zeus put to perpetual sleep for the sake of his daughter's reputation. Even more serious was her infatuation with Orion, a fellow-hunter. Apollo, aware that amorous Eros had already fallen for Orion's charms, thought it necessary to intervene. Playing on his sister's prejudice, he tricked her into shooting the object of her affection. That he was subsequently placed with his faithful dog Sirius among the stars seemed but little consolation.

Ares, Hephaestos and Hebe

The impetuous god of war was exceedingly unpopular on Olympos, even with his own parents, though his mother Hera often used him for her own ends. Always spoiling for a fight he was not consistently victorious. Athena twice worsted him in battle, and Heracles sent him running back to Olympos. Ares was among the numerous claimants to paternity of Eros, but his ascertained progeny was hardly less formidable: Eris (Discord), Phobos (Fear) and Pallor (Terror).

His brother Hephaestos presented a startling contrast to the general run of Olympian good looks. He was such an ugly baby that his disgusted mother dropped him from Olympos and forgot all about him. Kind Thetis brought him up, and the child became exceedingly clever with his hands. It was only when Hera inquired where Thetis' lovely jewelry came from that she learned of her son's matchless skill and promptly fetched him home. Hephaestos was of a forgiving nature and became strongly attached to his mother. He even dared to draw up the chains by which she was hanging in punishment for her abortive rebellion. It was now Zeus' turn to hurl his son from heaven. Striking the earth at the island of Lemnos he broke both his legs and was permanently lamed. Zeus became reconciled to Hera, but neither thought of recalling Hephaestos.

Hebe, the third legitimate child and personification of youth, was never admitted into the inner council of the big twelve. She was her father's cupbearer, until she was ousted even from this minor position by Ganymede. Zeus had taken a passionate fancy to the boy and abducted him in the disguise of an eagle. Despite Hera's violent protests, Ganymede was constantly at Zeus' side. Hebe was married off to Heracles.

Hermes

One of Zeus' innumerable extra-marital relations was with Maia, Atlas' daughter. Luckier than Leto, she met with no particular difficulty in bringing Hermes into the world in an Arcadian cave. No sooner had the mother turned her back than the child prodigy left his cradle, strangled a tortoise and from its shell made the first lyre, with which he lulled Maia to sleep. He then went in search of adventures to Macedonia, stole 50 cows belonging to Apollo and drove them backwards to Pylos, so that their hoofmarks pointed in the opposite direction. He made sacrifice to the 12 Olympians, among whom he modestly included himself, and returned to his cradle. When Apollo came looking for his cattle, Maia indignantly pointed at the child still wrapped in swaddling bands and feigning sleep. But Apollo was not deceived and hauled the culprit before their father, who was rather proud of his youngest's cunning and bade them be reconciled. This was effected by exchanging the lyre against the cattle, and the two half-brothers became friends.

For his ingenuity Hermes was chosen the herald and messenger of the gods. His duties included the making of treaties, the promotion of commerce and the protection of travelers. But in memory of his promising beginnings he was also the god of thieves, and it must have happened many a time that a robber and his victim both invoked Hermes' help for opposite ends.

Dionysos

Semele, daughter of King Cadmus of Thebes, was proud of Zeus' love. Rumors reached Hera, who assumed the shape of Semele's old nurse and pretended to doubt the lover's divine nature. So Semele pestered Zeus to reveal himself in all his splendor, but when he finally consented she had a miscarriage and died. The infant was sewn up in the father's thigh and delivered three months later. That is why Dionysos was called twice-born and became immortal. When he grew up he discovered how to make wine, and went roaming about the world, accompanied by a wild army of Satyrs and Maenads.

Dionysos propagated the cult of the vine, and the resistance to this innovation is the clue to his bitter struggles from Asia Minor to India. The new intoxicant met with particularly strong opposition in Thrace, where beer had long been established as the national drink. Only after the Thracian king had gone mad and believing his son to be a vine, started pruning the poor boy's nose, ears and fingers, did Dionysos triumph.

No better fate awaited the king of Thebes, who wanted to arrest his cousin for disorderly conduct. The raving Maenads rent the king limb from limb, led by his own mother who wrenched off his head. The constant recurrence of the madness theme in these myths shows the devastating effect of wine at its first appearance.

When all Boetia had acknowledged Dionysos' divinity, he made a tour of the Aegean islands, during which he was kidnapped by pirates. But his bonds fell off, vine and ivy grew about the mast and rigging and to the sound of flutes, lions and tigers played round the god's feet. The terrified pirates leaped overboard and were turned into dolphins. Dionysos steered the ship to Náxos, where he married Cretan Ariadne, abandoned by Theseus.

The Underworld

To Hades, Kronos' eldest son, had been allotted the underworld, a gloomy, though vague concept trying to reconcile conflicting views of the afterlife.

The souls of the dead were ferried across the river Styx by Charon, who demanded the coin laid under their tongue before the burial. Yet why they should be so anxious to enter the underworld, instead of dallying with the penniless souls on the near bank, is hard to understand. The three-headed dog Kerberos guarded the entrance to the Asphodel Fields, a kind of purgatory for minor transgressions. In front of Hades' palace lay the twin pools of Forgetfulness and Memory, from which the souls might drink at their choice.

Though Hades only rarely visited the upperworld, being less amorous than his brothers, he delegated the judgment of the souls to the wise kings Minos, Radamanthys and Aeakos; the second was competent for Asiatics, the third for Europeans, while Minos held a court of appeal. The evil-doers were sent to Tartaros to undergo eternal punishment, as for instance Sisyphos, who had to roll a heavy stone up a hill only to see it crash down again.

Virtuous souls were allowed to enter the Elysian Fields, over which Hades had no power, but which formed the domain of old Kronos. In that paradise there was constant feasting, games, music and dancing. Yet one grade superior were the Fortunate Isles, reserved for the privileged though underserving few, like Achilles and Helen of Troy, who just failed to make Olympos.

Minor Deities

But there were also several divinities who never attained Olympian status. Zeus' foster-brother, goat-footed Pan, was content to live in Arcadia. When he was not guarding his numerous flocks, he was busy seducing nymphs, and boasted of having possessed all the drunken Maenads. An unusually chaste nymph preferred turning into a reed to his embrace. Unable to distinguish her from all the rest, he cut several reeds at random and made them into a pan-pipe, which was afterwards copied by Hermes and claimed as his own invention.

The Thessalian Princess Koronis was with child by Apollo. The correct behavior for a mortal pregnant by a god was to remain faithful till the child was born. But Koronis did not comply with this reasonable rule of conduct. Artemis avenged this insult by killing her with an arrow, but as she lay on the funeral pyre Apollo rescued the unborn baby and entrusted it to Chiron, the wise Centaur.

Under his tuition young Asklepios grew marvelously proficient in medicine, so that he not only cured the sick, but even restored a dead man to life. Zeus was annoyed at this interference with the normal course of events and hurled a thunderbolt at the culprit. Yet later Zeus himself repeated Asklepios' transgression and resurrected him as god of healing. Asklepios became increasingly popular, and at his shrines, especially at Epidaurus, medical science came into being.

Aeolos ruled the seven islands in the Tyrrhenian sea, which bore his name. Hera had entrusted him with the guardianship over the Winds, which were confined in deep caverns. At his own discretion or at the request of some Olympian, Aeolos would thrust his spear into the cliff and the appropriate wind would stream out of the hole, until he sealed it again.

Halfway between the Aeolian islands and the underworld lay the kingdom of Hypnos (Sleep), surrounded by the waters of Lethe (Oblivion). Round the entrance to his palace grew poppies and other plants that induce dreams.

The relationship between Zeus and the Moirai (Fates) always remained uncertain. Some held that Zeus determined destiny, while others believed that Zeus himself was subject to the Fates. The three sisters assigned to each newborn child his lot by spinning, measuring and cutting the thread of life.

Apollo as patron of the arts was assisted by the nine Muses, the daughters of Zeus and Mnemosyne, goddess of memory. Each presided over a separate artistic or scientific sector, but they met regularly in the divinely inspired academy on Mount Helicon, to discuss the latest intellectual movement.

The Heroic Legends

The great cycles of legends which originated in Mycenaean times were grouped principally round two families: the descendants of Tantalos, and those of Io.

King Tantalos of Phrygia was the progenitor of the most intolerably tragic family ever known, each generation adding new, hateful crimes and punishments to an unparalleled record. Tantalos had been favored by the Olympians and even been admitted to their banquets. Yet in return he set before the gods the roasted flesh of his own son Pelops, as a test of their omniscience. The immortals were not deceived; only Demeter, distraught with grief over the loss of Persephone, helped herself to a tender shoulder. Tantalos was thrown into the underworld, eternally thirsting for the water in which he stood up to his neck, while Pelops was restored to life, complete with a miraculous ivory shoulder that healed all disease at a touch.

Unlike his sister Niobe, Pelops prospered and became Poseidon's lover. He left his native country for that part of Greece which was named after him, the Peloponnese, and with the god's help won the daughter of Oenomaos, king of Pisa. Oenomaos, who was in control of the Olympic games, had been forewarned that his son-in-law would cause his death. Confident in his superb horses, he stipulated that every suitor should compete with him in a chariot race, and pay with his life if defeated. Thirteen princes had already suffered this fate when Pelops appeared in a golden chariot, drawn by Poseidon's own horses. Yet Pelops did not rely entirely on his divine protector, but to be on the safe side bribed the king's charioteer to replace the linch-pins of his master's chariot with wax. The wheels fell off, the king was killed, and so was the charioteer on claiming his reward.

But not before he had cursed Pelops and his sons, Atreus and Thyestes, who later led the Achaeans to the conquest of Mycenae. Atreus succeeded to the dynasty founded by Perseus, but the gruesome family habits did not improve. Thyestes seduced his brother's wife, and in revenge Atreus followed their grandfather's example by serving up Thyestes' children at a banquet. One son however escaped, Aegisthos, who was instrumental in fulfilling the old curses, while becoming the cause of new blood-guilt. Atreus' son Agamemnon extended his hegemony over the entire Peloponnese, and was thus the natural leader of the Greek expedition against Troy, to recover his brother Menelaus' wife, Helen.

An adverse wind kept the fleet at Aulis, and Artemis demanded the sacrifice of Iphigenia, Agamemnon's daughter. Iphigenia and her mother Clytemnestra were lured to Aulis under the pretext of the girl's betrothal to Achilles, the most attractive of the Greek heroes. Clytemnestra never forgave her husband, even though the goddess relented in the last moment and substituted a hind for the victim kneeling at the altar. The inconsolable mother withdrew to Mycenae, where Aegisthos became her lover. On Agamemnon's return from Troy ten years later, she murdered her victorious husband in his bath.

Their daughter Electra, in her turn, nagged her brother Orestes into avenging the beloved father. For his matricide Orestes was pursued by the

Furies, till he rescued Iphigenia from Artemis' sanctuary in savage Tauris. The ancient curses were at last lifted and a double marriage provided an unexpected happy end: Electra to Pylades, her brother's companion in the Taurian adventure, and Orestes to his cousin Hermione, daughter of Menelaos and Helen. Their descendants ruled over Mycenae till the coming of the Dorians in the 12th century B.C.

Menelaos was king of Sparta, but his main claim to fame was his marriage with Helen. She and her brother Polydeuces (Pollux) were Leda's children by Zeus, disguised as a swan, while Castor and Clytemnestra were fathered by Tyndareus, the lawful husband.

Helen's incomparable beauty attracted numerous suitors. To avoid quarrels Tyndareus made them swear to respect Helen's choice and to champion the cause of her future husband. She chose Menelaos, and when she eloped with Paris the rejected suitors kept their oath and followed Agamemnon to the war against Troy.

The Loves of Zeus

A considerable share of Zeus's amorous intrigues fell to one mortal family, which not only produced a corresponding number of heroes, but was also singularly geographically minded, naming seas, continents and countries.

It all started with Io, daughter of the river god Inarchos of Argos. Although Zeus changed her into a heifer at the approach of his jealous spouse, long and bitter experience had made Hera distrustful and she set 100-eyed Argos to watch over the suspect. Hermes lulled Argos to sleep and slew him. Thereupon Hera placed her faithful servant's eyes in the tail of the peacock, and sent a gadfly to sting poor Io, who, maddened by pain, plunged into the sea, later called in her honor the Ionian Sea. After what must have been a record swim for a cow, Io came ashore in Egypt where Zeus, by a touch, restored her to human form. She bore him a son, Epaphos (him of the touch), whose daughter Libya became by Poseidon the mother of Agenor and Belos, the biblical Baal.

Zeus now lusted for Agenor's daughter Europa and approached her in the form of a gentle white bull. The misguided maiden jumped upon his broad back, to be carried away to Crete, where she gave birth to Minos, Rhadamanthys and Sarpedon. Minos founded the Cretan dynasty and after his death became, together with his second brother, judge in the underworld. The love for bulls was pathological in the family and Minos' queen, Pasiphae, followed in Europa's footsteps but with less satisfying results, as her offspring, the Minotaur, was a most unprepossessing monster.

Agenor sent his sons Phoenix, Cilix and Cadmos in search of their sister. Far and wide did they travel, until Phoenix and Cilix, weary of the hopeless quest, settled in the fertile countries they had reached named Phoenicia and Cilicia respectively. Cadmos consulted the Delphic oracle, and following a cow as bidden, built the Theban Acropolis, the Cadmea, where the beast lay down. He married Harmonia, daughter of Ares and Aphrodite, and one of their children was Semele. Oedipos likewise traced his descent from Cadmos.

Neither did Belus lack in progeny. His eldest, Pygmalion, fell in love with the statue he had fashioned and prayed to Aphrodite to make the smooth marble come to life. The goddess gladly acquiesced as Pygmalion had hitherto not been among her devotees. Galatea proved even more enchanting as a woman than she had been as a work of art.

The younger twins Aegyptos and Danaus quarreled over their inheritance, and the latter fled with his 50 daughters to Argos, which accepted him as king. The 50 sons of Aegyptos followed their cousins, and Danaus feigned agreement to a mass marriage, but secretly advised the brides to kill their husbands on their wedding night. All obeyed except Hypermnestra, who helped her husband to escape. He later returned, slew Danaus, and became the ancestor of a line of famous Argive kings. The murderous 49 Danaids were condemned to eternal frustration in Tartaros, carrying water in sieves to fill a cask with a hole in the bottom.

Hypermnestra's grandson Acrisios had been warned that his own grandson was fated to kill him. To prevent this he imprisoned his only daughter Danaë in a tower of bronze, a vain precaution against Zeus, who came upon the maiden as a shower of gold. When the distraught king was told of the birth of a grandson, he locked Danaë and the infant Perseus into a chest, which was cast into the sea. Washed ashore at the island of Seriphos, they were kindly received by King Polydectes, who fell in love with the appealing outcast. Wanting to rid himself of the brawny youth, he cajoled Perseus into fetching the head of the Gorgon Medusa, whose glance turned every living creature to stone. Medusa was the only mortal of three wildly unattractive sisters, who featured snakes instead of hair, and had faces to match.

Never could Perseus hope to carry out his rash enterprise unaided, but the gods gave a helping hand. Hades lent his helmet of invisibility, Hermes his winged sandals, and Athena her brightly polished shield, so that Perseus might cut off Medusa's head, looking at her reflection.

Triumphantly holding his hideous booty, Perseus on his return flight turned the inhospitable Titan Atlas into a mountain. Somewhat off his course, he saw the Ethiopian Princess Andromeda chained to a rock, waiting to be devoured by a sea monster. A display of the head, and Perseus was at leisure to cut Andromeda's chains and take her back to Seriphos. There was more work for Medusa's head, as Polydectes had been bothering Danaë. The king and his courtiers were promptly turned to stone; the circle of boulders is still shown on the island.

Perseus returned the magic objects to their kind owners, trimming Athena's shield with the fatal head. Soon afterwards he fulfilled the prophecy by accidentally killing his grandfather with a discus. Ashamed to succeed his victim at Argos, the hero founded Mycenae and a new royal line.

Untiring Heracles

It was now his granddaughter Alcmene's turn to be favored by Zeus, who showed great constancy in his inconstancies. Their son Heracles gave from his birth undeniable proof that he was destined to grow into the greatest of all the heroes, but also the object of Hera's unrelenting hatred. Not unnaturally the Queen of Heaven wanted at last to get even with the family that had caused her so much matrimonial unhappiness. She sent two huge serpents, but the amazing child in the cradle strangled them. Brought up like all the best people by the wise Centaur Chiron—tutor of Asklepios, Jason and Achilles, to name but three—Heracles married the Theban Princess Megara, whom he killed together with their children in a fit of madness. To expiate the crime, the Delphic oracle decreed that

Heracles should perform 12 labors for his uncle Euristheus, king of Mycenae.

These labors included some useful work, as for example the killing of the Nemean lion and the Lernean Hydra, and above all the cleansing of the Augean stables by diverting the river Alpheus. But there were also some utterly futile enterprises, like the abduction of the hellbound Kerberos.

On that visit to the underworld, Heracles had to compete with the river god Achelous, who assumed the form of a bull. One of his horns was broken off and was presented by the victor to the goddess of plenty. Filled with fruits and grain, it is known as Cornucopia, the fabled Horn of Abundance.

Zeus caught him up to Olympos, where he was received among the immortals. Even Hera at last relented and gave the hero her daughter Hebe in marriage and the couple lived happily ever after. . . .

Divine IDs

The 12 chief gods formed the elite of Olympos. Each represented one of the forces of nature and also a human characteristic, interpreted by sculptors in their statues of the gods. They also had attributes, by which they can often be identified. The Romans, influenced by the arts and letters of Greece, largely identified their own gods with those of Greece, with the result that Greek gods had Latin names as well, by which they are known today.

| *Name* | | *Natural and human* | *Attributes* |
Greek	*Latin*	*characteristics*	
Zeus	Jupiter	sky, supreme god	scepter, thunder
Hera	Juno	sky, queen, marriage	peacock
Athena	Minerva	wisdom	owl, olive
Artemis	Diana	moon, chastity	stag
Aphrodite	Venus	love, beauty	dove
Demeter	Ceres	earth, fecundity	sheaf, sickle
Hestia	Vesta	hearth, domestic virtues	eternal fire
Apollo	Phoebus	sun, music and poetry	bow, lyre
Ares	Mars	tumult, war	spear, helmet
Hephaestos	Vulcan	fire, industry	hammer, anvil
Hermes	Mercury	trade, eloquence	caduceus, wings
Poseidon	Neptune	sea, earthquake	trident

ARMS AND MAN

A Surfeit of History

by
PETER SHELDON

A resident of Greece for many years and a past director of the British School *on Crete, Peter Sheldon has traveled extensively in every part of the country. Besides lecturing on English literature, he has written several books on Greece and contributed most of the chapters in this volume.*

Ancient history has been the most widely taught period in western education, for the very good reason that within 1,000 years, all possible—and several impossible—forms of government were tried and found wanting. Tribal, feudal, absolute and constitutional monarchy; landed and commercial oligarchy; tyranny—which was not half as bad as it sounds, being more often than not benevolent dictatorship of an ambitious aristocrat; totalitarian racism with a sprinkling of communism; democracy with its concomitant demagogic abuses; and ephemeral empires . . . all had their moments of glory and all failed in turn, less because of any inherent faults in the systems themselves, but rather because of the one weak point they all shared, the human factor.

While failure may have been inevitable when a system made its first appearance—democracy had its world première in Athens—this cycle of failures became progressively less excusable. Politicians the world over seem determined to ignore the lessons of the past, though the dreary repetition of mistakes has brought about the same dire consequences for almost 3,000 years of recorded history, not to mention another millennium of pre-history, when legends tell the same tale of disasters.

From the Bull of Minos to the Trojan Horse

Europe's oldest state—as opposed to mere tribal groupings—arose in Crete. It was a theocracy founded by an Asiatic people which invaded that island before 3000 B.C., developed an astounding culture and extended its dominion over the South-Aegean islands and parts of the mainland coast, before coming to a dramatic end in about 1450 B.C. Myths and theories for its downfall abound, ranging from a devastating earthquake accompanied by a tidal wave to an Achaean invasion, perhaps from Athens.

On the mainland the original Celtic inhabitants experienced—but hardly enjoyed—successive waves of invaders, starting in about 1900 B.C. with the Pelasgians, followed by the Achaeans, Aeolians and Ionians till the Dorians began to destroy the kingdoms of their precursors from 1200 B.C. on. The invaders were all Indo-European and came from the north; which is a vague enough statement to leave room for endless scientific disputes. Whether the Pelasgians were Greek or not is another favorite guessing game among academics, but the rest certainly were, though they could hardly have differed more in appearance and mentality; the earlier tribes were remarkably short, dark, brown-eyed and quickwitted; the Dorians were somewhat taller, blond, blue-eyed and slow, a racial divergence which explains much of 1,000 years of incompatibility.

Paradox is a Greek word and highly applicable to Greek history. Since the rehabilitation of Homer by Schliemann's excavations, Agamemnon, Great King of Mycenae, and his subject Achaean princes have moved from legend into history and the remote 13th century B.C. is more familiar than most of Greek happenings in better documented later periods. Not that subsequent ages were any duller, the one epithet that is utterly unsuitable in Greece, but they lacked the master-touch of the great epic poet. This is true even of the 5th century B.C., which produced the world's greatest journalist, Herodotus, and the first unbiased historian, Thucydides.

As Homer has proved so remarkably accurate in geographic descriptions, why should we spurn his poetic version that the Trojan War was caused by Helen's elopement with Paris, and insist instead that it was brought about by the economic necessity of keeping the Hellespont open for trade? The Trojans did ask a toll from passing ships and Troy was destroyed quite often enough—some eight times—to leave room for the dialectic interpretation. Be that as it may, the Trojan War was the starting point in the never-ending ding-dong match between Europe and Asia, which was to lead the Persians to Athens, Alexander the Great to India, and the Turks to Vienna, to mention only the rounds fought across the Hellespont. The first round went to Europe, but the Achaean princes had little time left to enjoy their victory, as soon after the destruction of Troy in about 1220 B.C. their brilliant Bronze-Age civilization went down before the iron weapons of the barbaric Dorians.

Laying the Foundations

The Dark Ages descended, almost 400 years of which next to nothing is known. The Greek renaissance of the 9th century B.C. was centered on the city-states of Ionia on the coast of Asia Minor, founded by the refugees from the Dorians, who had subjugated most of the Peloponnese and the mainland. The quest for better government spread more rapidly westwards across the Aegean islands than did philosophy or the arts, which remained an Ionian preserve for some 200 years. Monarchies tottered and were overthrown by the landed aristocracy, which, since Homeric times, alone possessed the horses essential for warfare. The military revolution of the 8th century heralded 1,000 years of infantry predominance, first manifested in the hoplite formation, with the citizen-soldier supplying his own short spear, sword, shield and armor. This participation in defense tilted the balance of power in favor of the merchants and wealthy artisans, and broke the monopoly of the landowners. Tyrants supported by this new middle class formed the necessary link between oligarchy and democracy, and, dependent on popular support, carried out largescale land reforms, public works and, on the whole, peaceful foreign policies. They acquired their bad present-day reputation only through Aristotle, who wrote in the 4th century about the ruthless military dictators of his own time. Semilegendary Lykourgos laid the foundation of Spartan totalitarianism; approximately 100 years later Dracon promulgated his harsh laws in Athens, where revolution was only averted by the reforms of Solon in 593. For over 200 years Athenian public life was dominated by Europe's first political family, the Alcmaeonids.

In the 8th century B.C. the Olympic Games assumed a Panhellenic character, sacred peace prevailed while they were in progress, a uniform reckoning of time was based on their quadrennial celebration, and participation meant recognition as part of Hellenism.

Threat from the East

In the middle of the 6th century Persia became the dominant near-Eastern power and, by the conquest of Lydia, the master of the Greek cities of Ionia. When these revolted in 499, Athens rashly intervened where Sparta, Greece's leading military state, feared to tread. An Athenian contingent advanced as far as Sardis, the Lydian capital, burnt it down, but was then decisively beaten and forced to sail home. A slave ruined every dinner for Darius, the Great King, by reminding him of the Athenian misdeeds. The promptings bore fruit for, after a first expedition had been wrecked in a storm off Mount Áthos, some 25,000 Persians sailed across the Aegean in 490.

After sacking Náxos and occupying Euboea they landed at Márathon, on the advice of Hippias, the former tyrant of Athens who accompanied the Persian force. Only 1,000 Plataeans fought on the side of the 10,000 Athenians—"serves them right" seemed the consensus of Greek public opinion—but the brilliant strategy of Miltiades, one of the ten generals who took turns as field commander for one day, won a decisive victory. In gratitude the democratic but hardly efficient shared-command was abandoned and Miltiades led a punitive expedition against the island of Páros, which had aided and abetted the Persians. Miltiades failed, got entangled with a priestess of Hera, and was wounded jumping over her garden wall. Accused of mismanagement by the Alcmaeonid Xanthippus, Miltiades was condemned to an enormous fine. He was unable to pay and died in prison.

Xerxes, the new Great King, hesitated for a long time whether to avenge his father's defeat. Urged by exiles from all the leading Greek states and the rulers of some of the minor ones, he decided not on a mere punishment of Athens but on total subjugation of Greece. An alliance was concluded with Carthage, to attack the Greeks in Sicily, thus bringing about the first world war; a canal was dug across the isthmus of the Áthos peninsula and the two-mile-wide Hellespont was bridged; supply depots were established in Thrace and Macedonia for the largest army Europe had ever seen, some 180,000 combatants—though hardly the 5,000,000 mentioned by Herodotus.

To face that monstrous horde 31 Greek states temporarily patched up their feuds and under Spartan leadership formed an alliance, the largest since the Trojan war. But when the first natural defense barrier in the Vale of Témpe was turned early in 480 the alliance was deprived of the Thessalian cavalry. The second natural defense, the Pass of Thermopylae, was held by a totally insufficient force—the main Spartan army being once again delayed by a religious festival—exposing Sparta's chief rival, Athens. The heroic sacrifice of King Leonidas and his 300 men was in vain, and most of Boeotia defected to the Persians. The Spartans began the construction of a wall across the Isthmus of Corinth, abandoning mainland Greece to the enemy.

Themistocles

The political genius and patriotism of a great Athenian, Themistocles, foiled the Asian invader and triumphantly re-established Europe in Asia Minor. Though not above accepting a bribe from the Euboeans to defend them in the sea battle of Artemision, and sharing it with his Spartan commander-in-chief, he probably used part of the remainder to bribe the oracle of Delphi, which for once had abandoned its customary ambiguity and foretold a Persian victory. A complete reversal of so defeatist a stance would have lacked credibility, but Themistocles ingeniously used obscure references to "wooden walls would be the salvation" to persuade the Athenians to evacuate the town by ship, and "divine Sálamis" as a prediction of a Greek victory. This somewhat thin religious argument was reinforced by the tactical fact that the narrow straits of Sálamis provided the smaller Greek ships with the required advantage of maneuver. To this was added both the threat that the Athenian contingent would sail to Italy in case the Spartans withdrew, and even apparent treason, by advising Xerxes to bottle up the Allied fleet.

The end justified the means, the unwilling Allies won a resounding victory and Xerxes returned to Asia, but left a large army behind. Defeating the Persians proved a lesser problem than keeping the Allies together; Themistocles, for instance, was unable to destroy the demoralized Persian fleet, for fear of losing the blackmail lever of indispensable Athenian maritime power. Aware of Allied disunity, the Persians offered generous terms to Athens in a diplomatic turnabout which at last shocked the Spartans out of their prevarications. By the battle of Plataea Greece was finally freed from the Asian threat.

Every Man has His Price

Sensationalism makes Herodotus place another great Allied victory, on the promontory of Mykale, on the same day in August 479. The Spartans wished to forestall involvement in a second Ionian revolt by proposing the evacuation of the entire Greek population of Asia Minor, a dramatic solution which was actually imposed some 2,400 years later in another turn of the wheel. Athens succeeded in reopening the vital Hellespont alone, which aroused Spartan jealousy sufficiently to send King Leotichydas, victor of Mykale, to Thessaly, and Pausanias, victor of Plataea, to Byzantium. The former was bribed by pro-Persian local rulers, condemned to death, but allowed to escape; the latter conspired with Xerxes to make him "Ruler of Hellas," was recalled but only fined. He was finally stoned to death, his mother reportedly throwing the first stone, when he tried to raise the helots in revolt.

The recurrent bribery of Spartan leaders—who, though condemned to death were usually allowed to escape, remain kings and sometimes were even recalled—is matched by an equal laxity in democratic Athens, where politicians rarely escaped trial for an astounding variety of misdemeanors. Even high treason was not the end to a distinguished career, as was demonstrated by the most brilliant of the Alcmaeonids, Alcibiades, who decisively influenced the policies of Athens, Sparta and Persia, betrayed each and was condemned to death in each. Though bringing about the greatest military disaster suffered by Athens, he was wooed by all political parties, deserted the oligarchs he had just raised to power, and was given the greatest triumph ever accorded an elected commander-in-chief.

Sparta's discomfiture was Athens' finest hour. It assumed leadership of an Aegean confederacy based on Apollo's sacred island of Delos. But when the Persian danger receded, due to the brilliant victories of Miltiades' son Kimon, the Delian League was transformed into an Athenian empire, the member states were brought under Athenian jurisdiction and the treasury moved from Delos to Athens in 454. Only the deeply rooted belief in the *polis* (city) as the ideal unit of government prevented the formation of a unified Aegean state.

Kimon's foreign policy as leader of the conservatives was coexistence with Sparta and extension of the maritime dominions. After Themistocles' ostracism and death sentence—albeit passed *in absentia,* as the great man mistrusted the democracy he had saved, and fled to Persia where he was given the governorship of three towns—Kimon went too far in his basically correct limitation of spheres of influence between Greece's main maritime and territorial powers. He was ostracized in turn, though acquitted on a bribery charge brought by the Alcmaeonid Pericles, in a replica of their fathers' confrontation.

Pericles and the Golden Age

The stage was now set for the Golden Age of Pericles, who dominated Athens, and through it Greece, for some 30 years. He was exceedingly lucky in coming to the fore when Athens had been raised to the zenith of its power by the political genius of Themistocles and the military genius of Kimon. Moreover, after Kimon's ostracism and the murder of his fellow democrat, Ephialtes, Pericles was without any serious rival from the very outset of his career. A complete change of policy led to a head-on collision with Sparta, from which Pericles could only extricate himself by bribing King Pleistoanax. Condemned to death, the king found asylum in the sanctuary of Zeus in the Arcadian mountains and 19 years later was restored on the command of the Delphic oracle, to which the Athenian bribe finally passed.

War with Persia came to an end in 448. Pericles showed once again his astuteness as party politician by sending Kimon's brother-in-law as ambassador, thus forestalling any conservative criticism of a treaty which left Cyprus to the Persians, but confirmed Athenian dominance in the Aegean, from which the Persian fleet was excluded. After a royal betrayal the Spartans were always ready to conclude peace, and this rare commodity came to Greece in 445. Officially intended for 30 years—which seemed all that could be conceded—though in reality it lasted only half that time, it was sufficient to make Athens the unrivaled cultural center and most beautiful town of antiquity, due to the most glorious misuse of public money in world history. The contributions of member states of the Delian League, by then rightly renamed "tribute of subjects," was employed in the rebuilding of the Acropolis and of temples throughout Attica.

In 435 Pericles resumed a policy of brinkmanship which, after several lucky escapes, led to the Peloponnesian War. Even his eulogist, Plutarch, could not decide if Pericles acted "inspired by the highest motives and a clear conception of Athens' advantage or whether by arrogance, contentiousness and a desire to display his own power." He died of the plague in 429, together with about one half of his fellow citizens.

But for a short interval of peace, patched up by the conservative leader Nicias and the restored Pleistoanax, the war continued amidst increasing atrocities, destructive, demoralizing, to be finally decided by Persian gold and the mistakes of Athens, where demagogues again and again prevented favorable peace. True to form, the worst of these excrescences of a decaying democracy was discovered to have evaded his military service and was executed.

Alas, too late. Athens was stripped of all its possessions, the walls were pulled down and the fleet surrendered. But the very greatness of the Spartan victory united such inveterate enemies as Athens, Corinth and Thebes in opposition. The ephemeral Spartan empire collapsed in 394 and the Greek towns of Asia Minor once more fell under Persian sway. A weak Persia, racked by dissensions and rebellions, became the arbiter of Greece, due to the judicious use of gold needed for the hiring of mercenaries.

The hitherto invincible Spartan hoplite army was shattered by the Thebans in 371 at the battle of Leuctra, but, with the death of Epaminondas in the battle of Mantinea ten years later, Theban federalism proved as impotent as Athenian and Spartan coercion had before.

Enter Alexander the Great

The power vacuum was filled by Philip II of Macedon, as great a diplomat as he was a general. The Athenian orator, Demosthenes, still championed the obsolete city-state, but in 338 Philip crushed the uncommonly united Greeks at Chaeronea. Macedonians garrisoned the main towns and at a Panhellenic congress at Isthmía, Philip was "elected" leader with full executive power and commander of a crusade against Persia in which the Greeks felt no desire to take part.

Philip's murder in 336 was joyfully received throughout Greece, but his 20-year-old son, Alexander, showed the lightning decisiveness which was to make him master of the greatest empire the world had yet seen. He executed the rival Macedonian claimants to the throne; cowed the Greek cities—which were busy passing votes of thanks to Philip's murderers—into electing him their leader; subdued the barbaric tribes beyond the Danube as well as the Illyrians north of Epirus; marched back to Greece and razed rebellious Thebes to the ground, sparing only the house of the poet Pindar. The incipient Greek revolt collapsed.

In spring 334 Alexander crossed the Hellespont into Asia and, with some 40,000 men—of whom less than a third were Hellenes—marched out of Greek history. But in the ensuing 11 years of unparalleled triumphs he spread Greek culture from the Nile to the Indus by founding 30 towns which bore his name. Passing beyond his tutor Aristotle's political philosophy, he attempted to merge the Macedonians and Persians into a new master race, but when he died in Babylon in 323 his revolutionary concept, as well as his family, were sacrificed to the unscrupulous rapacity of his generals. In the merciless struggle for the succession, Antigonus almost reconstituted the empire; his brilliant but unstable son, Demetrius Poliorketes (the Besieger) nearly established a Macedonian kingdom, which was realized on a diminished scale by the grandson, Antigonus Gonatas, in 276.

The able monarchs of the Antigonid dynasty imposed their rule on turbulent Greece in competition with the Seleucids of Syria and the Ptolemies of Egypt, both houses founded by Alexander's generals. But rebellion was endemic and once again the shifting leagues and confederacies called in a foreign power. Rome "liberated" with fire and sword, and finally annexed Macedonia as well as Greece in 146. The cultural conquest-in-reverse and the *Pax Romana* compensated for the loss of a much abused independence.

Rome's University

In the three decisive battles for the mastery of Rome the Greeks consistently backed the wrong side. In 48 Pompey's vastly superior army was annihilated by Julius Caesar at Pharsala in Thessaly. In 42 Brutus kept his fatal appointment with Caesar's ghost at Philippi in Macedonia; Brutus and Cassius committed suicide; Mark Antony and Octavian divided the empire and prepared for the final contest. In 31 Mark Antony abandoned his army at Actium in Epirus, breaking off the naval engagement to follow Cleopatra in her flight; Octavian became Augustus and the first Roman emperor.

Successive emperors favored their classical province which was renamed Achaia. Nero won the chariot races in all the venerable Games—which had to be celebrated in the year of his visit, A.D. 67—and also the singing competitions introduced for his benefit, though hardly that of his sophisticated audience. He also carted off hundreds of statues. Hadrian carried out a grandiose scheme of embellishment of towns and sanctuaries around A.D. 125.

The Roman jeunesse dorée studied rhetoric at the academies of Athens and Rhodes; tourists flocked to the monuments and battlefields, using Pausanias' excellent guidebook, published in the 2nd century A.D.; but Greece remained a political backwater, even after the transfer of the capital to Byzantium, renamed Constantinople, by Constantine the Great (324–337). His adoption of Christianity as the state religion, leading to the suppression of the Olympic Games and of the Delphic oracle by Theodosius the Great (379–395), started the decline which was hastened by Justinian's closure of the Academy of Philosophy in Athens in 529.

Slavs, Schisms and Serbians

Ruin was consummated by disastrous raids of Goths, Huns, Vandals and Avars. But only the Slavs settled permanently and, according to no less an authority than the Emperor Constantine Porphyrogenitus, the country districts became entirely Slavonic after the great plague of 747. The Macedonian dynasty, especially Basil II (the Bulgar-slayer, 976–1025), re-established effective imperial rule, which continued under the Comneni and Angeli dynasties (1081–1204), despite frequent raids by the Sicilian Normans.

But the schism of 1054 between the Greek and the Roman Churches was to lead to the shameful Fourth Crusade, diverted by Venetian greed from the reconquest of the Holy Land to the occupation of the Christian bulwark against the eastern Moslems. Powerless Latin emperors from 1204 to 1261 claimed suzerainty over feudal lords, but not over the large Venetian part of the spoils, mainly islands. Marquis Bonifacio of Montferrat, King of Thessaloniki, married the widow of Isaac II Angelus in an attempt to unite Greeks and Franks. With his stepson Manuel, who had a good claim to the imperial crown, he conquered Thessaly, where he captured the ignoble Alexius III Angelus and the imperial regalia. Bestowing Athens and Thebes on the Burgundian Othon de la Roche, Bonifacio consented to the occupation of the Peloponnese by Guillaume de Champlitte and Geoffroy de Villehardouin. The threat to his capital by the Despot Michael Angelus of Epirus and Bulgarian raids called Bonifacio north. He was killed in an ambush and his severed head was sent to the Bulgarian king, who had previously imprisoned and murdered the first Latin emperor, Baldwin of Flanders. With the death of Bonifacio in 1207 all hope for a Frankish-Greek reconciliation disappeared.

From 1222 onwards, the Byzantines regained some territories at the expense of the Frankish principalities. Michael Palaeologus reestablished an emaciated Byzantine Empire in Constantinople in 1261, but the Serbian Empire extended deep into Greece by the middle of the 14th century, while Catalan mercenaries no one could afford to hire established lawless soldier-republics.

Turkish Domination

By the close of the century, the Turks had occupied Macedonia and Thessaly. The dying Byzantine Empire achieved a final triumph by conquering the Frankish Peloponnese in 1430, but 30 years later the last emperor's brothers, who shared the rule of this province which had outlived the empire, quarreled and called in the Turks.

Mohammed II, the Conqueror, preserved the feudal system of military fiefs, but Turkish veterans replaced the Frankish and Greek nobles. The Greek peasants remained serfs paying, beside tithes, a poll-tax and a blood tribute of a fifth of their male children. Brought up as Moslems, the most gifted boys entered the imperial administration, especially the corps of Janissaries, the elite of the Turkish army.

The Orthodox Church remained as the sole Christian organization and the Patriarch of Constantinople became the representative of the Greek nation. Ecclesiastical tribunals judged most cases in which only Christians were involved. The parochial clergy was mainly responsible for the survival of the subject races during centuries of ruthless suppression, while the bishops assumed temporal as well as spiritual guidance.

The Struggle for Independence

War continued intermittently between the Turks and the Venetians, but though the latter lost all their Aegean possessions in the course of the 17th century, the decline of the Ottoman Empire became apparent not long after. The sultans cared little about what happened in their vast domains as long as tribute flowed into the imperial treasury. Inherited feuds, frequent rebellions and constant brigandage reduced the country to near anarchy. The enterprising sailors of the islands of Híos, Ýdra, Spétses and Psara benefited, however, from the breakdown of the central administration and their merchant navies played a decisive part in the War of Independence.

In 1770 Prince Orloff, favorite of Catherine the Great, attempted to establish a Greek principality, relying on the common bond of religion. The appearance of a Russian fleet was the signal for a rising in the Peloponnese, which was bloodily suppressed. Continued resistance by the outlaws in the mountains was complemented by a cultural revival in Greek communities. Literary and political societies were founded by wealthy Greek merchants in Europe, the most important being the *Philiki Hetairia* (Friendly Society), which eventually included 200,000 adherents.

Where Orloff failed, a Moslem Albanian adventurer briefly succeeded. By unscrupulous treachery combined with merciless cruelty Ali of Tepelen, Pasha of Trikala, extended his rule over the western Greek mainland and most of Albania. Yet, after his surrender in 1822, he himself fell victim to Turkish treachery and was murdered.

Turkish preoccupation with Ali Pasha provided an opportunity for revolts throughout the Balkans. Alexander Ypsilanti raised Moldavia, which his ancestors had ruled under Turkish suzerainty, but failed in 1821. On March 25 of the same year, the feast of the Annunciation, Archbishop Germanos of Patras proclaimed Greek independence at the monastery of Agia Lavra in the Peloponnese. The Turks retaliated with massacres of Greeks in Macedonia and Constantinople, where the Patriarch was hanged on Easter Sunday.

The War of Independence started with daring exploits of the *klepht* (outlaw) leaders, Botzaris and Kolokotronis on land, Kanaris and Miaoulis at sea, soon marred by fratricidal quarrels and even fighting. The intervention by an Egyptian force under Ibrahim Pasha in 1825 led to a Triple Alliance of Great Britain, France and Russia to mediate. Lord Byron's stint as Greek commander-in-chief had been too brief to change the course of the war and as he had been chosen mainly for his financial contribution and European reputation his authority was by no means generally recognized. However, the appointment of Sir Richard Church and Lord Cochrane as commanders of the insurgent army and navy added the badly needed professional touch.

In 1827 Count Capodistrias, former foreign secretary of Tsar Alexander I of Russia, was elected first President of Greece, but Ibrahim Pasha reconquered a large part of the Peloponnese and Athens fell to the Turks. An ill-advised Turkish shot precipitated the destruction of the Turkish-Egyptian fleet in the harbor of Navarino by the Allies, despite their orders to abstain from any active intervention. But in accordance with the rules of ancient tragedy it was Demetrius Ypsilanti, Alexander's brother, who defeated the Turks in the last engagement in 1829.

Jockeying for a Throne

In the same year Greek independence was recognized by the Treaty of Adrianople. The frontiers were drawn rather haphazardly from the Gulf of Arta to the Gulf of Volos by the Protocol of London in 1832. This left the majority of Greeks under Turkish rule, but the new state was guaranteed by the three main European powers. The assassination of Capodistrias by a Peloponnesian clan led to near-anarchy. In the first of the alternations between republic and monarchy, which have been so remarkably constant an element in modern Greece, the throne was offered to Prince Leopold of Saxe-Coburg, widower of Princess Charlotte, King George IV's only child. In an age when thrones and not their occupants went begging, Leopold could afford to decline, and became King of the Belgians instead.

The choice then fell on the younger son of King Ludwig I of Bavaria, 17-year-old Prince Otho. Neither the Bavarian Council of Regency nor the young King, who transferred the capital to Athens, showed sufficient regard for Greek nationalist feelings, trying too hard to equate Greece with a central European kingdom. The foundation of Athens University as a center of Hellenic culture only added students to the other discontented sectors of the population. The bloodless revolution of 1843 obtained a constitution and sent the multitude of Bavarian dignitaries packing. During the Crimean War the King patriotically but unwisely gave voice to the pro-Russian sympathies of his subjects. An Anglo-French fleet occupied the Piraeus, Otho lost face and Russia lost the war. Greece was beset by brigandage, bankruptcy and disaffection, Queen Amalia failed to produce an heir, and the army forced Otho's abdication in 1863.

The Protocol of London excluded dynasts of the Protecting Powers from the Greek throne. Never taking no for an answer and eager to regain British support, the Greeks voted overwhelmingly for the Duke of Edinburgh, Queen Victoria's second son, in the first in the long series of constitutional plebiscites. An ideal substitute was found in Prince William George of Denmark, who was brother-in-law to both Edward, Prince of Wales and the Russian Tsarevich Alexander. To sweeten acceptance, Great Britain ceded the Ionian Islands on the accession of the new king.

Like his predecessor, George I was 17 years old, but he soon learned to keep out of the grueling party strife by adhering to the spirit of the 1864 constitution, which restricted the royal prerogative. The adoption of the title "King of the Hellenes" signified not only willingness to follow the French and Belgian model, but also the aspiration to include the unredeemed Greeks in the kingdom.

A Cretan rebellion in 1866 nearly led to war with Turkey; British support at the Conference of Constantinople in 1881 gained Thessaly and further concessions in Crete. The Cretan revolt of 1897 led to war, Crown Prince Constantine's army was driven out of Thessaly, George I almost lost his throne and only Gladstone's intervention halted the victorious Turkish forces.

Venizelos and the First World War

In exchange for the loss of a northern Thessalian district, Crete was granted autonomy, with Prince George of Greece as High Commissioner under nominal Turkish suzerainty. In 1906 the Prince was forced to resign by the up-and-coming Cretan politician, Eleutherios Venizelos, to be succeeded by Alexander Zaïmis, who had proved his diplomatic subtlety as prime minister at the peace negotiations in 1897. His final score after 40 years in public life amounted to: High Commissioner of Crete, Governor of the Bank of Greece, ten times Prime Minister and once President of the Republic.

The defeat in the recent war brought about a Military League of some 500 officers, who forced the King to exclude the royal princes from all commands, remove the discredited politicians from office and appoint Venizelos, who in Zaïmis' absence had proclaimed union with Greece.

After a false start with a Revisionary National Assembly, Venizelos obtained a sufficient majority to introduce badly needed administrative, agricultural and educational reforms. A British naval and a French military mission reorganized the armed forces, while for the sake of national unity Crown Prince Constantine was reinstated as Inspector-General of the Army. Venizelos' greatest achievement was, however, the formation of a Balkan League of hereditary enemies against Turkey. While the latter was resisting Italian aggression in Libya, disturbances in Macedonia led in 1912 to the First Balkan War. The League was victorious on all fronts, but dissensions quickly became apparent and Crown Prince Constantine's army occupied Thessaloniki only hours before the arrival of a Bulgarian division. George I triumphantly entered the Macedonian capital, where he was murdered by a lunatic early in 1913.

Turkey ceded all European territory to the League, and in the ensuring quarrel over the spoils Greece joined Serbia and Romania in the Second Balkan War against Bulgaria. The Turks regained eastern Thrace, Bulgaria surrendered, and the Treaty of Bucharest doubled the area of Greece. The Dodecanese was provisionally assigned to Italy and retained in violation of formal obligations.

Greek sympathies lay with the reunited Protecting Powers in World War I. But after two bloody wars Greece desperately needed time to recover, while King Constantine, who lacked his father's political wisdom, firmly believed in the superiority of Germany, where he had received his military training. The ancient conflict between Themistocles and the conservatives, representing maritime and landed interest, was revived in the King and his Prime Minister. Queen Sophia and the pro-German General Staff prevented any reconciliation, Venizelos resigned and Zaïmis tried to preserve strict neutrality. Cyprus was refused as the price of Greek support for the Allies; Venizelos formed a government in Thessaloníki in October 1916; the King was forced by the Allies to leave the country, and was succeeded by his second son Alexander.

Venizelos, once more Prime Minister of a united Greece, wholeheartedly supported the Allied army in Macedonia, where the decisive penetration of fortress Europe in September 1918 sealed the fate of the Central Powers. With the Treaty of Sèvres in 1920 the Kingdom of the Hellenes became a reality, by assigning Thrace and the Province of Smyrna, ancient Ionia, to Greece.

In the same year King Alexander died of blood-poisoning from a monkey bite, leaving only a daughter from a morganatic marriage.

A plebiscite declared overwhelmingly in favor of King Constantine, and it was Venizelos' turn in the modern form of ostracism.

Between the Wars

Turkey's revival under Mustapha Kemal was assisted by France and Italy, while Great Britain ceased to support Greece on the return of King Constantine. Initial victories hardened Greek pretensions at a time when the commander-in-chief thought himself literally possessed of a pair of glass feet, on which he lavished greater care than on the over-extended troops.

Lunacy on top of incompetence brought about disastrous defeat. The Greek army was driven back to the coast and in a typical irrational reversion of popular feeling a military Revolutionary Committee of the few efficient officers forced King Constantine's abdication in favor of his eldest son, George II. Venizelos declined to return, but represented Greece at the Lausanne Peace Conference. Even Zaïmis refused the premiership, as the army insisted on the execution of three royalist prime ministers, two ministers and the commander-in-chief of glass-feet fame.

In July 1923 Greece ceded to Turkey the Thracian districts east of the Evros river as well as all claims in Asia Minor, and agreed to a hitherto unprecedented wholesale exchange of population, almost 2,000,000 Greeks against 370,000 Moslems. The resettlement of refugees numbering almost one half of the existing population led to untold misery which, however, only exacerbated petty politicking. Zaïmis failed to reconcile monarchists and republicans; King George II left the country; Venizelos resigned and the Armed Forces proclaimed the Republic on March 25, 1924, anniversary of the Revolution. By a coup within the coup General Pangalos became Premier-President, brought some order into chaos, but was laughed out of office on decreeing that women's skirts must rise no higher than a maximum 14 centimeters from the ground. The police spent a busy time on their knees with measuring rods. Pangalos was overthrown in 1926, Zaïmis formed a coalition government and Venizelos returned in 1928. He abolished proportional representation, which had made the country ungovernable, while Pangalos was imprisoned for corruption.

Thanks to English and American loans the economy recovered, brigandage was suppressed, relations with Turkey improved and involvement in the Cyprus rebellion of 1931 was avoided. The monarchists won the election of 1935, Venizelos resigned and a 97% majority voted for the King's restoration in yet another plebiscite.

George II insisted on including Venizelos in a general amnesty, but the elections in 1936 gave 15 Communist deputies the balance of power. The old party leaders, who had been playing musical chairs far too long for the good of the nation, died opportunely though naturally, opening the way for General Metaxas to assume dictatorial powers to deal with a Communist-inspired general strike. He alone, among all contemporary Balkan regimes, changed from the execution of political opponents to the traditional Byzantine device of exile to remote islands. He also laid the basis of social welfare, and on the whole followed the example of antique paternalistic tyrants.

World War II and After

World War II found the Greeks for once united in their desire to remain neutral, despite Italy's annexation of Albania and the torpedoing of the cruiser *Helle* by an Italian submarine during the celebration of the Assumption of the Virgin at the island of Tinos. Metaxas' historic "No" was vindicated by the occupation of nearly one third of Albania by the Greek army, inferior in numbers and equipment, but brilliantly led by General Papagos according to the strategy of Metaxas, the only foreigner to graduate top of his class in the Imperial Military Academy of pre-World War I Germany.

Metaxas died on January 29, 1941; on April 6 the Germans invaded Yugoslavia and Greece. Anglo-Hellenic forces fought Hitler's war machine heroically against a background of defeatism, intrigue and incipient treason till the inevitable evacuation. The determined courage of King George II after the suicide of his Prime Minister prolonged resistance sufficiently to delay the German aggression against Russia, thus probably altering the course of the war. But when the royal government had to abandon Crete for exile in Cairo, the squabbles among the politicians there equaled those within the puppet governments in Athens. Greek troops, however, participated on the side of their British allies in the campaigns of Africa and Italy.

Under the German, Italian and Bulgarian occupation famine claimed innumerable victims, while the Communist-dominated guerrilla faction soon ceased fighting the invader and prepared for a takeover. Their moment seemed to have come when the small Anglo-Hellenic force, which had entered Athens on October 13, 1944, held little less than the center of the capital and a corridor to the airport. In December the Communists massacred 10,000 hostages on their retreat to the mountains.

This retreat was due to Churchill's decisive intervention on his visit with Eden, the Foreign Secretary, when the vacillating Papandreou was dismissed and Plastiras, the surviving leader of the Revolutionary Committee of 1922, was installed as Prime Minister under the regency of Archbishop Damaskinos, who had valiantly opposed the Germans.

The plebiscite of 1946 declared overwhelmingly in favor of George II, who returned to face a second Communist rebellion, actively supported by Greece's northern neighbors. Only after Yugoslavia's break with Russia, the displacement of over 700,000 villagers, the abduction of 25,000 children to be indoctrinated behind the Iron Curtain, destruction and murder of their fellow-Greeks by the partisans far surpassing those committed by the enemy, and after the reorganization of the armed forces first by a British and then by an American military mission, did General Papagos defeat the Communists in late 1949.

King, Colonels and the Return of Democracy

On April 1, 1947 King George II died childless and was succeeded by his brother Paul. Political instability and unscrupulous jockeying for power retarded economic rehabilitation, despite massive American aid, till General Papagos' newly founded party swept the poll in 1952. Confidence returned, industrialization gathered momentum, and Greece joined N.A.T.O. Yet the gods were as jealous as ever; when it was not the politicians, Nature herself disturbed the peace. Three major earthquakes devastated the Ionian Islands, Central Thessaly and the Pelion region, before Papagos died in 1955.

Karamanlis, the popular Minister of Public Works, was appointed Prime Minister, and in the approved Greek fashion formed a new party,

winning three successive elections, unparalleled in modern Greece. During
this period of relative political serenity, the standard of living rose spectacularly and economic recovery culminated in acceptance as first associate
member of the E.C. But in June 1963 Karamanlis resigned and went into
self-imposed exile in Paris. Three caretaker governments and two elections
later, Papandreous returned to the political fore and formed a government.
King Paul died in March 1964 and was succeeded by his son Constantine
who, however, was not called "the Second" because of the ill-defined yet
inviolable pretense that the Greek kings continued the line of Byzantine
emperors among which there had been eleven Constantines. The young
King's popularity as winner of the sailing competition in the Olympic
Games—the only gold medal ever for royalty in an international race of
that prestige—was further enhanced by his marriage to Princess Anna
Maria of Denmark, but the fall of the Papandreou government heralded
a period of acute instability.

Governments rose and fell every few weeks till the Colonel's Revolution
of April 21, 1967. On December 13 the King, supported by his Prime Minister and the army high command, attempted a counter coup, but the
armed forces obeyed the colonels. The King left the country, one of the
generals who had sided with the colonels was appointed regent, and Papadopoulos, who emerged as the regime's strong man, became Prime Minister and eventually also regent.

A plebiscite in 1968 confirmed the constitutional monarchy, while another in 1973 declared for a republic. Papadopoulos became President,
martial law was lifted and an elder statesman appointed Prime Minister
to prepare elections.

A few days before the state visit of the Romanian President, a proof
that ideological differences were no hindrance to peaceful coexistence in
the Balkans, riots at the Polytechnic University were suppressed by the
army with some loss of life, more among innocent bystanders than students and activists. But the Romanian state visit was canceled.

Within days the hard core of young officers staged another coup under
the leadership of Brigadier Ioannides, commander of the military police
which had been built up to considerable strength. Papadopoulos became
a non-person, though left free, another general was appointed President,
a Greek-American lawyer became Prime Minister, but real power lay with
Ioannides.

Ever since 1954 the problem of Cyprus had bedeviled foreign relations,
first with Great Britain, then bringing Greece, on several occasions, to the
brink of war with Turkey. Never closer than in summer 1974, when a coup
overthrew the Cypriot President, Archbishop Makarios, who sought refuge in the British military base. Turkish troops landed in Cyprus. Faced
with war the Greek high command forced Ioannides to resign; Karamanlis
returned in triumph. Makarios was reinstated but died in 1977, with the
Turks still holding almost half of the island.

In the subsequent election Karamanlis' renamed party obtained the
largest parliamentary majority in Europe and yet another plebiscite in December 1974 confirmed the republic by a two-to-one vote.

The constitution of 1975 was an emaciated presidential democracy,
where much depended on the respective personalities of president and
prime minister, by giving the former the right to appeal directly to the
people. The leaders of the military regime, who had not availed themselves

of the ample opportunities to leave the country, were tried but their death sentences were commuted to life imprisonment.

The restoration of democracy was achieved in a conspicuously painless way and the Karamanlis government could rightly claim that never before had Greece been more democratic and prosperous. Unemployment remained well below the E.C. average while income rose spectacularly above the per capita threshold for developed countries. Yet the largest number of newspapers in any capital, representing every shade of political opinion—but not unbiased reporting—has kept political passions at an unhealthy fever pitch with sensational stories as lurid as they are unfounded.

Greece Today

Karamanlis claimed Greece's entry as a full member of the European Community as his crowning achievement, and in 1980 he was elected by the required two thirds of the single Chamber's 300 deputies as President of the Republic for a five-year term. He was succeeded as Prime Minister by George Rallis, whose father and grandfather had held the same office. Political leadership is as hereditary in modern as in ancient Greek democracy, in the Republican no less than the Royalist party, and confined to a few families, with Karamanlis being the outstanding exception. The Socialist victory in the election of October 1981 brought to power the son of another former prime minister, and to continue the dynasty a grandson was elected Greece's youngest deputy and became a junior minister after the following election. Andreas Papandreou, once a Professor at Berkeley and a U.S. citizen, reneged on his campaign slogan of withdrawal from the EC and NATO but became increasingly at odds with his partners over loosening traditional ties with the West.

The generally expected reelection of the widely respected President Karamanlis in 1985 was at the last moment opposed by the Socialist Prime Minister. A Supreme Court judge was chosen instead by a disputed margin of one. Parliamentary elections in the same year reduced Papandreou's majority. In 1986 he adopted more stringent austerity measures than those he had so vehemently opposed when in opposition; these were to some extent relaxed in 1988.

Late 1988 and early 1989 saw corruption and disarray in the government. Issues of considerable controversy—Papandreou's affair with the 35-year-old Ms. Liani, now his wife, scandals involving government officials in fraud and embezzlement and the Greek treatment of middle-Eastern terrorists—caused a political crisis for Papandreou. However, in spite of all this, the opposition, the conservative New Democracy party, failed to win an absolute majority in either of the 1989 elections although they did have a definite lead in the popular vote. At press time, the Greek communist parties, in an attempt to survive the major crisis over recent developments in Eastern Europe, have moved from an alliance with the conservative party to side with Papandreou. Such an alliance could once again block a conservative victory in the forthcoming 1990 elections and lead to yet another right-left coalition government and more political uncertainty.

Greece's economic situation has rapidly deteriorated in the last few years, with increased inflation (three times higher than the E.C. average) and increased total debt, 47% of the Gross Domestic Product in 1989. Over-consumption is rampant; for example, the number of cars being purchased rises steadily despite import duties that more than double the cost. In early 1990, the country was fast approaching bankruptcy. The escalating economic difficulties were unlikely to be reduced unless the national economic policy became more balanced, with less public sector and more private enterprise. Major banks are state-controlled, and the public sector accounts for about 30% of industrial production, much above the EC average. Yet the most successful industry is privately owned, usually by one family or even one individual, those fabulous Greek shipowners. Although the Greek-flag fleet has fallen to just under 2,000 ships totaling about 21,000,000 tons, the Greek-owned fleet, including ships under flags of convenience, holds first place in the world, at 80,000,000 tons. The country's second-largest industry is still the second-largest foreign exchange earner, after tourism, despite the continuing lay-up of millions of tons, as Greek shipping firms have ridden out the storm better than many foreign competitors. But the shipyards, which are mainly repair yards, largely occupied in maintaining the aging fleet, have begun to feel the crisis.

Tourism is the largest industry, earning 2.4 billion dollars from over 8,200,000 visitors in 1989. But the very rapidity of totting up million upon million has created serious problems, and the country's 15,000 km. (9,333 miles) of coast are becoming as crowded as the western European Mediterranean shore. Hotel capacity stands at over 400,000 beds, the shipowners once again having secured a very prominent position. The Chandris group owns a large chain, connected with its cruise operations; Carras has built the biggest luxury holiday complex, even producing its own excellent wine, in the Halkidikí.

The Public Power Corporation has completed its rural electrification program and supplies 99% of the population with 18,000 million K.W.H., a per capita consumption of 1,780 K.W.H. 70% of the electricity is produced from indigenous lignite and waterpower, the rest from imported oil. Production from the offshore Prinos field near Thássos covers about 10% of oil consumption. Drilling is in progress in many parts of the country, and promising uranium deposits have been discovered in Macedonia.

Agriculture still employs about 20% of the labor force, achieving self-sufficiency in cereals and exporting large quantities of fruit, olive oil and, above all, tobacco. Greece is Europe's largest cement exporter, and a well-established textile producer based on homegrown cotton and wool; other industries enjoy a constantly lengthened period for the necessary adjustments within the E.C., from which Greece has reaped considerable benefits.

PROMETHEUS UNBOUND

The Spring of Western Civilization

In *Prometheus Bound* Aeschylus dramatized the legend of the defiant titan, the first symbol of revolution, who stole fire from the gods and taught men the crafts of Athena and Hephaestos, thus giving them wisdom to stay alive. For this act he was terribly punished by Zeus.

But according to the philosopher Protagoras, the creator of tragedy conceived a happy ending in a sequel, the lost play *Prometheus Unbound,* in which Zeus became reconciled to Prometheus and added political wisdom, justice and reverence, so that man might lead a civilized life. Yet progress was man's own task.

This progress reached its first European flowering in Minoan Crete, where, by the middle of the 2nd millennium B.C., rudimentary Egyptian elements had been developed to sophisticated perfection. This splendor was reflected, but not equaled, by the Mycenean Bronze-Age civilization, which perished in the Dorian invasion of the 12th century B.C.

Dawn in the East

The Greek awakening dawned on the shores of Asia Minor and the nearby islands, to which numerous Ionians had fled during the Dark Ages. Phoenician traders taught the humble refugee settlements the alphabet and commerce, which enabled them to turn from the crude struggle for survival to things spiritual.

The offshore island of Chios claimed Homer and the wandering minstrels of the 9th and 8th centuries B.C., who celebrated in epic strains a cycle of stories revolving round the Siege of Thebes, the Trojan War and the return of the heroes. Homer fashioned gods in the likeness of man in two great epic poems, the *Iliad* and the *Odyssey*—if indeed both were composed by the same poet or either by one man. By depicting gods endowed with the virtues and vices of mankind, the Greeks stressed man's responsibility and dignity, thus putting man in the center of the universe where the Israelites had placed God. Despite the cogent unity in Achilles' impulsive emotionalism and Odysseus' continuous low cunning, some literary experts insist that these epics must have been conceived in the Greeks' exuberant youth, but completed only in full artistic maturity. Yet during all the centuries in which they constituted the basis of education in Greece and Rome, they were ascribed to one Homer.

Hesiod was born around 700 B.C. in Asia Minor where his father had traded before returning to a farm in Boeotia. His *Works and Days* is an impassioned appeal for divine and human justice against being cheated out of his farm inheritance by his brothers, besides enumerating all the favorable and unfavorable omens for agriculture. Homer praised the glory of heroic death, while Hesiod extolled the joys of simple life. His *Theogeny* remained the standard genealogy of the Olympians.

In the 7th and 6th centuries the Aeolians substituted varied metrical forms for the epic hexameter. In short songs, accompanied by a lyre or flute, the gods and heroes were abandoned for the passions the poets felt and the deeds of their contemporaries. Time and Christian prejudice destroyed most of this lyric poetry which, however, immortalized an aristocratic society in rare fragments.

Alcaeus of Lésbos showed his disdain for the rising merchant class and delighted in the pleasures of wine. Another Lesbian, Burning Sappho, brought lyric poetry to its passionate perfection. Priestess of a sanctuary of Aphrodite, the goddess of love seems to have inspired her violent and searing poems addressed to various girls, which connects Lésbos forever with a particular form of love.

Abandoning his native Ionia for the courts of Polycrates at Sámos and of Hipparchus at Athens, Anacreon described his love for boys in no uncertain words. Nor could his epitaph, composed by no less a poet than Simonides, be called squeamish.

The last of these lyric poets belongs to Greece-in-Europe, Pindar of Thebes, who wrote odes for tyrants and nobles, or glorified the victors at the great Panhellenic games.

The Nature of Man

Greece-in-Asia likewise gave birth to philosophy, which originated in a cosmic mythology. Yet Greek creativeness was no less impressive for incorporating alien ideas and achievements. Thales of Miletus, most ancient of the sages, answered in about 600 the question "What is God?" by "That which has no beginning and no end," thus taking the decisive step from myth to rational thought. His disciples Anaximander and Anaximenes were astoundingly modern in their attempt to reduce the material world to a common principle in a philosophical system where the infinite, animated and eternal, albeit impersonal, was none other than the One God. The Greek version of the universal tradition of the Great Flood—where Deukalion, cast in the role of Noah but landing in considerably more places, created a new race of men from rocks and dragons' teeth—

was elaborated into a scientific theory of origin from the wet element. Spontaneous generation, caused by the action of warmth on mud, produced thin womb-like membranes from which life emerged.

Pythagoras (572–500 B.C.) invented the term Philosophy, which he combined with strict moral rules and mathematics. Stating that "the body is a tomb" led to such peculiar prohibitions as beans, bed linen and white cocks. Leaving the brilliant court of the Tyrant Polycrates on his native Samos, Pythagoras was one of the rare foreigners ever to be initiated into the Egyptian mysteries before founding and governing Croton in southern Italy.

Heracleitus of Ephesus (d. 500 B.C.) started the unphilosophical but very common contempt for his predecessors and contemporaries, yet he found enthusiastic admirers from the Stoics to Nietzsche. He believed in a governing principle of the universe, yet also in eternal change, summed up in his famous saying: "All is in flux, nothing abides." Harmony is the final aim, but it consists in the union of opposites. That is why "War is the father of all things."

Hecataeus from Miletus provided history and geography with a rational basis, being the first to use *historia* in the meaning of "research." Hellanicus of Lésbos reconstructed early history through chronological lists of kings and officials, to which later historians are indebted.

Another significant attempt at rational thinking was in the field of medicine, where the human individual was the object to be treated. Hippocrates was born in about 460 into the family of the Asklepiads, whose name indicates a connection with the god of healing, but more as practitioners of medicine than as priests of Asklepios. Hippocrates freed medicine from magic and founded a medical school on his native island of Kos. Clinical observation was collected in the 58 books of the *Corpus Hippocraticum,* but the outstanding document is the Hippocratic oath, a code of behavior of very high ethical standards.

In a mere 150 years the Asian Greeks advanced from primitive simplicity to mature awareness and even disillusionment before the Persian conquest scattered philosophers, poets, musicians and artists westwards to teach their tardier European brothers profounder thought and greater perfection.

Go West, Young Man

Anaxagoras, Protagoras and Herodotus provide the link with Athens where all the beauty and wisdom of antiquity was to gather. Anaxagoras of Clazomenae (c. 500–c. 428) deserted from Xerxes' army and became a resident of Athens, where he was chosen as Pericles' tutor and evolved the doctrine that *nous,* the mind, dominated the universe. Pericles' political opponents accused him of impiety for stating that the sun was a ball of fire and there were mountains in the moon. Pericles could not obtain his acquittal, but arranged his escape to Lampsacus on the Hellespont, where an altar was set up to Mind and Truth, flanked by the phallic pillars of Priapus, who possessed many devotees in that versatile community.

The sophists were not a school of philosophy but individual teachers giving lessons for pay to the sons of the wealthy. Man was the central subject of their teaching, which consisted mainly of political education, with special emphasis on rhetoric as essential in a democracy. The earliest and greatest of the sophists was Protagoras of Abdera (c. 485–c. 415), who repeatedly visited Athens where he was admitted to Pericles' inner circle. His "Man is the measure of all things" and "As to the gods, I have no possibility of knowing that they are, nor that they are not" brilliantly summed up the scepticism of his time.

What Herodotus of Halicarnassus (c. 484–c. 420) had observed or heard of his extensive travels he described in his *History* in an astonishing blend of the supernatural, sensationalism and common sense. Ranging from Babylon to Egypt, his main theme is the Persian empire under Xerxes, who had committed *hubris,* excessive pride inevitably punished by the jealous gods.

The School of Hellas

By the middle of the 5th century B.C., Athens had become the leading cultural center of Greece, attracting the great names in philosophy and literature from abroad. Then suddenly there happened a flowering of native talent in every field of intellect and art as has never been surpassed and only once been equaled, though more diffused, in the Italy of the Renaissance.

While Herodotus described with exuberant optimism the victory of freedom, Thucydides witnessed with profound disillusionment the decay of freedom into demagogy and licentiousness. Born in Athens in 471, he served in the siege of Sámos in 442, together with Herodotus, Sophocles and Socrates under the command of Pericles, who then made the deeply melancholic remark: "The spring has gone out of the year." It was indeed high-summer for Athens, and though the creative genius outlasted military and political disaster, the youthful zest had gone forever. Exiled for failing to relieve Amphipolis, to which the fleet he commanded was ordered too late, Thucydides records with admirable impartiality the decline into brutality and treachery in his *History of the Peloponnesian War,* which ends with the folly of the Sicilian campaign.

Xenophon continues in his *Hellenica* the tragic history of Greek dissent to the battle of Mantinea in 362 in which his son was killed. His inevitable exile by the decaying Athenian democracy had embittered him sufficiently to write with a strong pro-Spartan bias, which is particularly noticeable in his praise of Lykourgos in the *Republic of the Lacedaimonians.* On the country estate near Olympia which his former commander, King Agesilaus of Sparta, had put at his disposal, Xenophon was at leisure to recount in the *Anabasis* his own brilliant exploits as leader of 10,000 Greek mercenaries on their retreat across Asia Minor. Not only had he played a prominent part in the rebellion of Cyrus the Younger against his brother King Artaxerxes but, like so many Greek intellectuals, Xenophon was fascinated by the great power in the east, whose origin he traces in *The Education of Cyrus.* Beside this historical romance, he ventured into economics in his *Ways and Means,* in which he advocated income tax, a nationalized merchant-fleet and hotels. In his *Memorabilia,* Socrates is depicted as a virtuous and rather commonplace philistine.

The Aim of Man

Socrates, the greatest and yet least known among the intellectual giants of that unique period, was born in 470 son of a stone mason, a profession he followed in a somewhat lackadaisical manner. Much more consistently he practised his mother's calling, midwifery, by bringing men's hidden thoughts to life. He soon turned to teaching, but unlike the sophists he charged no fee, to the vitriolic chagrin of his wife Xanthippe. He founded no school or philosophical system, yet changed the direction of human thought by simply talking to pupils and opponents in a city he never left except on military service. His didactic method has been immortalized in a series of dialogues by his most famous disciple, Plato. But, as they were written several years after Socrates' death, it can never be established where the master ends and Plato begins. Aristotle ascribes to him inductive reasoning and universal definition.

In a head-on collision with the sophists, Socrates derided their endeavor of "making the weaker case the stronger one." He declared rhetoric a useless study, because "if a case has merit it does not require artful advocacy, and if it has not such art may prove harmful," a prophetic warning, as demagogues have all too often brought disaster on Greece. Not that his views were popular in the restored Athenian democracy. His outspoken criticism as well as his contempt for public opinion led inevitably to the time-honored accusation of impiety coupled with an up-to-date one of corrupting youth.

In a typical Socratic cross-examination he embroiled the official accuser in contradictory charges of atheism and of introducing new gods. Condemned to death by a majority of 60 from the 501 angry judges, he was, according to Athenian law, entitled to propose an alternative penalty. Instead of an acceptable sentence of exile, Socrates suggested free meals at state expense. Refusing to escape and stressing his loyalty to the laws of the state, he drank the cup of hemlock. A people's court put to death the man who taught the freedom of the individual.

Despairing of the excesses of democracy, Plato (428–347) journeyed three times to Syracuse in Sicily to make the young tyrant Dionysius II into the philosopher-king of his *Republic,* a dismal failure ending in flight. Unable to turn a ruler into a philosopher, Plato taught philosophers how to rule—or at least to advise rulers—in the Academy, established in a grove sacred to the hero Academus outside Athens in 387. Plato emphasized the importance of the soul, incorporeal and immortal, which from previous incarnations retains memories mistakenly thought to be new discoveries hitherto unknown. Though the creator of idealist philosophy, Plato remained concerned with practical political and moral problems, and his pupils spread his theories throughout distraught Hellas.

None with greater success than Aristotle of Stagiros (384–322), who studied and taught at the Academy from 366 to Plato's death, but failed to be appointed the latter's successor. Instead he became tutor of young Alexander of Macedonia, in another attempt at forming a philosopher-king, in accordance with the *Treatise on Monarchy.* On his return to Athens in 336, Aristotle founded a rival to the Academy, the Lyceum, complete with an extensive library and a museum. In an unparalleled universality of research, he created the sciences of meteorology, zoology, embryology and botany, beside teaching literature and eloquence in his *Poetics* and *Rhetorics,* establishing a new terminology in the *Physics,* expounding the theoretical sciences in the *Metaphysics,* moral and political theories in the *Nichomachean Ethics* and the *Politics,* and, most important, providing in the *Organon* a system of thought which dominated the Middle Ages down to St. Thomas Aquinas.

Charged with impiety in 323, Aristotle fled to Chalkis, declaring that "he would not allow Athens to sin twice against philosophy." The probably apocryphal story of his suicide the following year for failing to discover the cause of the Euripus' constantly changing current is, nevertheless, well in keeping with an inquisitive mind irked beyond endurance by an inexplicable phenomenon.

Spontaneous originality had discovered everything that was worth knowing and the philosophers, poets, scientists and artists of the Hellenistic Age only elaborated what had already been created.

The Birth of Dramatic Art

The Greek theater was constructed under the open sky. Its tiers of seats were laid out in the shape of an enormous fan. On the stage an all-male cast struggled in vain against an inexorable destiny. For tragedy as for comedy the actors wore masks with a mouthpiece of copper designed to amplify the voice.

Before the appearance of the great tragic Athenian poets, there were a few obscure playwrights. It was apparently the success of the resistance against the Persians which gave the stimulus necessary for changing from the religious spectacle of choral singing and dancing with interspersed speeches into true drama, where the suffering of man became that of an individual hero.

Aeschylus endowed Greek tragedy with its classic form and instituted its major theme: the conflict between thought which strives to liberate itself, and traditional belief. The *Oresteia* trilogy, which dates from 450 B.C., is the masterpiece of the Greek theater and perhaps of all times. The chorus pleads in favor of a new belief, one which knows forgiveness. Religious feeling has profound overtones with Aeschylus, who was a thinker as well as a great poet. The qualities which characterize the seven that survive of his 90 or so tragedies—imaginative power, amplitude of dramatic development, depth of characterization, beauty of style—are not found in combination again until the time of Shakespeare. Yet contrary to Elizabethan custom, the *Persians* presents Xerxes' insolent pride and his punishment by the Greeks far from the scene of battle and action. With mysterious fate playing so prominent a part, it is not unfitting that Aeschylus' death seems to have been caused by a tortoise dropped on his bald head by an eagle searching for a rock to crack the shell.

Of 125 plays written by Sophocles, 24 won first prize, but only seven are extant today. With this poet, tragic language takes on a more natural tone. His psychological perspicacity makes him seem like a relative of our modern dramatists. He opposes hope to fatality: if the moral order of the world is too subtle for us to understand it, it exists nonetheless, and justice will triumph in the end. In his Theban trilogy, *Oedipus Rex, Oedipus at Colonus* and *Antigone,* Aristotle's dictum that "the function of tragedy is to rouse pity and fear" is most closely realized as Oedipus moves with heroic grandeur to his tragic death at Colonus, Sophocles' own birthplace in 495.

Aeschylus had shown the way and fixed the form of tragedy in austere verses which express his grave philosophy. Sophocles models his art with proportion, harmony and serene wisdom. Euripides completes antique tragedy in works that overflow with pathos and passionate feeling. One can compare Aeschylus to a preacher as rigorous as the prophets of Israel:

Sophocles to a classic artist. As for Euripides, he never wrote a perfect tragedy because of the irregularity of his dramatic action and the length of his philosophical tirades, but of the three he is the most human. He also surpasses the others in the depiction of characters and in psychological skill. He represents that generation which scoffed at the old myths and cherished the dream of a new order in which man would not be exploited by man and all men by the state. Certain of his plays have modern accents, and the battle of the sexes is brought up, as in the plays of Ibsen. In the *Trojan Women* he exposed the ignominy of revenge and the hollowness of victory, an unequivocal condemnation of contemporary Athenian atrocities. In the *Bacchae* he shows the evil of excessive emotionalism; while *Medea* is equally critical of the barbarian lacking the restraint of Greek civilization as of the prim husband Jason. No wonder that only four of his 90 plays won him first prize.

Comedy originated in fertility rites, which accounts for obscenity being an integral part of the plays, which first flourished in the Greek towns of Sicily. But ancient comedy has become synonymous with the work of the Athenian Aristophanes.

He was still a young man at the outbreak of the Peloponnesian War in 431, a conflict which provided him with bitter raw material for his work. Denouncing this hateful internecine war and the Greeks who massacred each other, he turned his comedies into spirited please for peace. In *Lysistrata* the wives refuse their matrimonial duties to blackmail their menfolk into stopping the struggle; in the *Peace* a clown rides on a beetle of Ólympus to ask Zeus to stop the war which only politicians and profiteers still desired; in the *Birds* an exemplary citizen leaves Athens to escape from politics and violence; the anti-hero makes its first appearance with the god Dionysos disguised as Heracles in the *Frogs,* which is a sly attack on Euripides; while the *Clouds* ridiculed Socrates so effectively that it permanently prejudiced the Athenians.

For him the weakened state of public life in Athens came from two evils: the decadence of democracy and the irreligious spirit. His art is a mixture of wisdom, poetic fantasy and scurrilous language. He let himself go to such an extent in lampooning his contemporaries that a law was passed forbidding all satire aimed at living persons. Subsequent playwrights like Menander and Philemon had to play it safer; their comedies of manners and imagination, known as the New Comedy, are more concerned with elaborate plots and happy endings than with social criticism.

The Cult of Harmony

Greek art did not spring in a blinding flash like Athena fully modeled from the brain of Zeus. The earliest ceramic cup, said by legend to have been moulded after the breast of Helen of Troy, is a libel on that siren's reputation; it is much older, coarse, clumsy and rough, typical of the Cycladic civilization, whose anonymous artists and artisans worked in the 3rd millennium B.C. Promoted from a German archeologist's first appreciation in 1891, "a repulsively ugly head," to Henry Moore's "the Cycladic sculpture's unbelievably pure sense of style, of unity of form," this primitive beginning provided the pioneers of modern sculpture with starkly simple models.

Less controversial are the Minoans, who took the relay torch in Crete in about 2000 B.C. and who before their decline and fall 600 years later accomplished several European firsts: in colorful and comfortable architecture, in delightful impressionist frescos, and in an astonishing variety of superb pottery. The torch passed to the less sophisticated Mycenaeans who, nevertheless, introduced naturalism into vase painting before succumbing to the Dorian barbarians.

Like philosophy and poetry, the plastic arts emerged from the Dark Ages in the more propitious atmosphere of Greece-in-Asia, where the abstract designs of the geometric style developed in the 8th century B.C. Subsequent centuries saw the perfection of the black-figured, red-figured and polychrome vases, in all of which Athens achieved supreme artistry.

Before attacking stone, Greek sculptors worked in wood. The earliest temples were made of wood and plaster or brick; the use of stone only developed as the country prospered. The architectural concepts are an exact reflection of the personality of the peoples who composed the Greek world. Thus the Doric order is all mathematics; the Ionian and Corinthian, all poetry. The first is northern; the others are essentially southern and Oriental. The first expresses the proud reserve, massive strength and severe simplicity of the Dorians. The other two represent suppleness, sensitivity, elegance and a love of fine detail. No matter what the order, however, the Greek column exerted such a sway over all subsequent architecture that even the modern architect has difficulty in freeing himself from it. This phenomenon is explained by the fact that Greek art is the absolute incarnation of reason in form. The tradition asserts itself everywhere: in the logic of a line in painting, in the cult of symmetry in sculpture, in the geometric harmony of architecture. The Archaic and Classical Greeks did not propose to represent reality with its clutter of uncoordinated details; their aim was to seize the essence of things and let its light shine forth. And here again Athens achieved the architectural masterpiece, the Acropolis, where the most perfect Doric and Ionic temples stand side by side. The great architects and sculptors of the Golden Age, Ictinus, Callicrates, Mnesicles and Pheidias, worked in close cooperation on this shrine of Classical art. The climax of idealized refinement was achieved by Praxiteles in the following century.

But it would be false to conclude, as certain romantic spirits have done, that the Greeks were effeminate aesthetes, lost in ecstasy before abstract beauty and subordinating their lives to it. Quite the reverse: it was the art of living which, for the Greeks, was the supreme art. A healthy utilitarian inclination combined with their worship of beauty to such an extent that art within their homes was not an idle ornament, but had a functional quality related to everyday life. Nourished by such a society, the artist was not an isolated man expressing himself in a language incomprehensible to the ordinary citizen.

The Inheritors

Alexander the Great and the Macedonian conquest of the Persian Empire changed not only the face of history but the face of art. Far from having worn itself out after 150 years of glory, the Greek creative genius gained another lease of life by turning from simplifying Classicism to the novel directness and emotional impact of Baroque Hellenistic realism. The artistic lead had come full circle even earlier, when Greece-in-Asia resumed its pioneering role with the grandiose tomb of Mausolus at Halicarnassus. Begun by the Hellenized king before his death in 353, it was finished by his widow Artemisia to rank among the Seven Wonders of the World. The founding fathers of the new School, Bryaxis, Leochares, Scopas and Timotheos, used the fashionable dramatic diagonals and twisted leanings, deliberately indicating a distinctive foreignness. More important, they created sculptural portraiture in individualized marbles and bronzes, while retaining a delicate balance between the old idealism and the new realism. The most famous surviving originals are the *Venus of Milo,* generally attributed to Scopas, and Lysippus' and/or Leochares' *Winged Victory of Samothrace,* both in the Louvre in Paris. Lysippus, Alexander the Great's favorite artist, truly captured the king's virile, leonine features, which greatly influenced coin portraiture. Imaginative with Alexander's good looks, the ruthless fidelity in depicting later remarkably ugly monarchs is astounding.

The most flamboyant concentration of colossal Hellenistic statuary was sponsored by the Attalid dynasty at Pergamum. Attalus I, one of the earliest art collectors, bought classical masterpieces in Athens, linked to his capital by a common divine patron, Athena. In about 200 B.C. he celebrated his victory over the Galatians in what must have been one of the most ambitious sculptural monuments ever attempted. Only marble Roman copies are left of the bronze circle of the half-recumbent vanquished, among whom was the *Dying Gaul,* now at the Capitoline Museum in Rome. The *Barberini Faun,* at Munich, stood in the royal palace, as did *Laocoon and His Sons* struggling in the deadly embrace of snakes, by Polydorus of Rhodes, a climax of dynamic art, now in the Vatican Museum. Attalus I dedicated an ex-voto on the Acropolis and laid out the Academy gardens in Athens, where his successors, Eumenes II and Attalus II, built two splendid stoas. In his capital, Eumenes II commissioned the frieze round the Altar of Zeus, depicting the *Gigantomachy,* the Battle of the Gods against the Giants, more than 1,200 figures in bas reliefs running in a continuous band for 130 meters (425 ft.) round the outer wall of ancient Greece's largest and most tempestuous work still in existence, at the Pergamum Museum in East Berlin. The bronze *Colossus* of Chares of Lindos—Greece's tallest statue—bestrode the harbor of Rhodes for only about 70 years before it was felled by an earthquake in 227 B.C. Size began to rival beauty in importance.

Alexander's court painter Apelles also enjoyed the favor of Antigonus I and Ptolemy I. The greatest Hellenistic portraitist, he was a revolutionary innovator, using mixed instead of pure colors, and exploiting foreshortening and *trompe l'oeil* effects. None of his pictures survived, but they were reproduced in countless large pebble mosaics, as, for example, the hunts and battles of Alexander, at Pélla, or Antigonus in three-quarter view to hide his empty eye-socket.

The luxurious courts of Alexandria, Antioch and Pergamum took the place of Athens, which gradually assumed the role of a university town where the rulers of the empires of the world sent their sons to study the precepts of the greater empire of the spirit. Thanks to the diffusion of Greek as a common language, a cultural unity was established which lasted in the eastern Mediterranean for nearly 1,000 years. Eleven hundred Hellenistic writers wrote for a public impregnated by Greek art and thought. Attalus I broadened the religious link with Athens to include philosophy by engaging teachers from the Platonic Academy, which he had generously endowed, as well as from the Aristotelian Lyceum. The Lyceum of Pergamum became the nucleus of a great library, soon imitated and rivaled. In the library of Alexandria toward the end of the reign of Ptolemy Philadelphus in the 3rd century B.C., there were no less than 532,000 scrolls, the equivalent of 100,000 modern books. Among those drawn to the court of this king, a patron of the arts, was Theocritus, creator of pastoral poetry. The library had grown to some 700,000 papyri and parchments by A.D. 641, when the Caliph Omar I ordered them to be burned.

But in the older Greek centers, research and discovery continued. Aristarchus of Sámos even formulated the hypothesis that the earth revolved around the sun and that the sun was the center of the system to which the earth belonged. It took mankind 17 centuries to rediscover this explanation of the world, in the time of Copernicus. Euclid formulated the first principles of plane geometry. Hipparchus of Nicaea created the science of trigonometry. Apollonius anticipated analytical geometry, made possible the theory of projectiles, and exerted incalculable influence on mechanics, navigation and astronomy. Archimedes, without knowing the decimal system, conceived infinitesimal calculi and opened immense horizons to physics and mechanics by finding the means of determining the specific gravity of bodies. Eratosthenes measured the surface of the earth and drew the first comprehensive map. Philosophical schools flourished. Pyrrho, first of the sceptics, declared that all certainty is impossible, that all is relative, a pattern of thinking very congenial to the 20th century. Epicurus based his doctrine of moderation and good sense on the enjoyment of life, while the stoics preached austerity.

The last of the great historians, Plutarch, was born at historical Chaironeia in A.D. 46. In appreciation for his *Parallel Lives,* a biographical comparison of eminent Greeks and Romans, he was given priesthood at Delphi as a sinecure, though he mostly resided in Rome.

The ancient Greeks, by virtue of having cultivated science and the science of ideas to their highest point, continued, long after the decline of their civilization, to be the teachers of the world. Among the problems which occupy us today, there are hardly any which they did not tackle with freedom of spirit and matchless ardor, and it is to their language, 2,000 years after the fall of Athens, that scientists of all countries turn to designate the instruments and the ideas of a new world.

The Greek Message

The classical culture which was the grandeur of the Greek world died, for civilizations are mortal. But it left indelible marks in all domains, bearing witness to its universal radiance. Through the intermediary of Rome, it was spread throughout the world. The Roman state took over the laws of Greek cities as a basis for its own legislation. The writers of Rome pillaged the literature of Greece, helping themselves to an inexhaustible treasure of lyric poetry, odes, stories, essays, orations, biographies, and above all of tragedy and comedy. Plautus and Terence borrowed plots from Menander and Philemon, thus making them accessible centuries later to Ben Jonson and Molière, who found in them the source material for their comic masterpieces. Roman painters and sculptors copied for centuries the great Classical and Hellenistic models; and their only original inspiration, Hadrian's Greek favorite Antinous, produced little more than an amalgam of these two styles in the last flash of beauty before the descent into the ugliness of primitivity that brought antique art full circle.

From the cultural point of view Roman expansion is nothing more than the propagation throughout Europe of the Greek artistic and intellectual inheritance. Greek thought was concentrated in Byzantium, the adopted daughter of antique Greece. From this city the great ideas which form the basis of our civilization were dispersed throughout the world. Greek works, translated into Latin, were the sparks that lit the fires of the Italian Renaissance. From then on, schools, universities, theaters and stadiums are marked with the seal of Greece. Classical architecture lives again in public buildings, palaces and academies which rise in the greatest cities of Europe and America. The basis of our musical scale and many of our instruments are bequests from ancient Greece. Modern mathematics would be inconceivable without reference to Pythagoras and Euclid. And even our daily vocabulary, from atom to zoology, from psychoanalysis to stratosphere, is a lexicon of Greek words.

Why does this ancient civilization continue to correspond to our daily needs? Why does its universality continue to encompass our epoch, dominated as it is by a technical progress unimaginable in antique Greece? The answer is simple: while the sages of Egypt and Babylon evolved empirical formulas, the Greek masterminds extracted pure science from the formulas. Eager to explain everything—nature, society, the soul—the Greek genius represented, in all domains and for the first time, the liberation of the human spirit.

As ancient Greek literature achieved a last, if somewhat decadent, flowering in the Alexandria of the Macedonian Ptolemies, so the first internationally recognized modern Greek literary figure was Kavafis, an Alexandrian poet influenced by the cosmopolitan decadence prevailing under another dynasty originating in Macedonia. With George Seferis and Odysseus Elytis, Literature Nobel Prize winners in 1963 and 1980, poetry returned to its European homeland.

FOOD AND DRINK

Greece "à la Carte"

Although the cuisines of Greece and Britain are so very different, a number of generalizations will apply to them both. In neither country would a gourmet travel for the sake of the food, as he might in France or parts of Italy; the general level of cooking is undistinguished, and there can hardly be said to be any significant regional differences between one province and another. In both countries, the food has been exaggeratedly condemned by travelers who have had bad luck, or have not known what to order; in Greece it has also been patriotically or romantically overpraised by nationals or foreigners. Overpraise is, ultimately, as much a disservice as exaggerated condemnation. A balanced verdict on Greece would be this: the food is never good enough to travel for, and not bad enough to keep anyone away. A prudent traveler will not expect "European" food (at least, he will not expect it to be excellent) outside deluxe establishments, and he will be well advised to avoid second-rate imitations in the provinces. He will eat the dishes of the country, or he will order a plain grill or fried eggs; if he shows a little interest, the restaurateur is more likely to think him worth pleasing, and he should not fare too badly—he may even have an occasional pleasant surprise.

Now for the specific character of Greek food. It is a variant of the food of the Eastern Mediterranean, found all over those countries (Turkey, Syria and Egypt) which once formed part of the Ottoman Empire. It will probably never be known if any dishes were specifically Greek, what dishes were introduced by the Turks, and what came from further east—for Persia influenced both Byzantium and the Ottoman Turks. Olive oil is its basis, nearly always well-refined, but in the cheaper eating-places there is simply too much of it, more often than not as a lukewarm, oily tomato sauce; stick to boiled or grilled food. Those who are unused to eating food cooked in oil will do well to take some simple precautions against the slight upsets which may result from the change in diet.

Lunch can generally be obtained from one o'clock, or even a little earlier, dinner from about eight o'clock, though the Greeks prefer to have their evening meal considerably later. In private houses, the Greeks will generally have their midday meal often as late as three o'clock, and they will sup when they like, off odds and ends. Peasants are frugal and live cheerfully for days on little more than bread, sheep's cheese, tomatoes and olives, but on a feastday, they put away quantities of food (such as sheep's heads and roast pork) that would astonish a western visitor. The "nothing too much" of the ancients is not the rule.

It is a great convenience for the traveler—especially if he does not know the language—that it is a habit in all *tavernas*, and in most provincial restaurants, for the customer to go into the kitchen and look into the pots, rather than to choose his food from a menu. You know what you are getting, and what you can face. If the eye is sometimes deceived by the brightness of the colors, the nose may be relied on as a guide.

Apéritifs and Appetizers

The traditional apéritif is *oúzo,* a spirit with an aniseed flavor. In the provinces it is generally served neat in thimblefuls; in the towns you get larger quantities, and most people prefer to add water, which clouds it. There are good Greek vermouths, but you will be rather lucky if one is served to you in a cafe. Another apéritif, sweeter and more scented than *oúzo,* is *mastíka,* and in the islands you may sometimes find *Kítro* (sweet, and with a citrus flavor), which is made in Náxos.

They are usually accompanied by a *mezes,* some form of appetizer, or *mezedes,* a selection. In the simplest form this will consist of a small bit of cheese and an olive, and a slice of tomato or cucumber, but it can be very elaborate indeed. Perhaps the best known of all Greek appetizers is the spread known as *taramasaláta* (a delicious preparation of fish roes). Other good appetizers are *dzadzíki* (cucumber with yogurt and garlic), *melitzanasalata* (an eggplant and garlic dip), or small *keftédes* or *dolmádes.* Olives of various sorts may be sampled, green or black (the oval olive of Delphi, or the pointed olive of Kalamáta). If you are sitting at a cafe pedlars will probably pass and you can supplement your *mezé* by buying pistachio nuts or almonds. A more substantial snack is the *tyrópitta* or cheese pie. This may be filled with egg and cheese, or with just a piece of dryish white cheese. In the country, made of local cheese and marjoram, it can be very tasty.

There are two main types of soup: a chicken broth with rice thickened with an egg and lemon (*avgolémono*) mixture, or a fish broth, *(psarósoupa)* generally served with pieces of boiled fish and vegetables in it.

Seafood

Standards for freshness of fish are high; inland, it is of the frozen variety, often even dried Atlantic cod. It is usually eaten for the main course of a meal (indeed, outside tourist hotels, Greece knows nothing of the table d'hôte; one or two dishes are ordered à la carte, and are served in generous portions). However, although fish is excellent, especially if eaten along the shore, it *is* expensive. Pollution and overfishing have between them reduced the availability of fish in the Mediterranean and consequently forced prices up.

Of shellfish and their like: prawns *(garídes)*, langoustines *(karavídes)* and crayfish, frequently misnamed lobster *(astakó)*, are usually served boiled, with a simple sauce of oil and lemon juice *(ladolémono sálsa)*.

Octopus *(oktapódi)* and squid *(kalamarákia)* which may be new to many Western visitors are often stewed in wine; they have an interesting and individual flavor, but are apt to be tough. A greater favorite with foreigners is the young cuttlefish *(soupiá)*; if very small and crisply fried, they seldom fail to please.

Of the larger fishes, various types of sea bream *(lithríni, synagrída, tsipoúra)* are served, either whole or in slices, fried or grilled. Squares of swordfish *(xifías)* are grilled on skewers with tomato, onion and bayleaf between the pieces—a delicious dish. Red mullet *(barboúnia)* is generally very good, and sometimes one gets an excellent sole *(glóssa)*. Delicious trout *(péstropha)* can be found, but unfortunately it's only fresh near the rivers and streams of northern Greece. Bogue, a small sea bream *(gópa)*, are rather bony but a tasty and cheap alternative to other more expensive fish. Fish should be chosen personally, and it will be gladly brought out for your inspection. Whitebait *(marídes)* are good in season, but are not worth eating once they are too large. Mussels *(mydia)* are also good, particularly when served in a hot, spicy soup.

Meat Courses

Meat is of poorer quality, but there are two honorable exceptions. Lamb *(arnáki)* is killed very young in the spring, and sucking-pigs *(gourounópoulo)* in the late summer; both of these are best when roasted whole over charcoal. At any time of the year, lamb cutlets are safe, but in summer avoid pork (*chirinó*) except in expensive restaurants. A favorite dish in any sort of eating-place is *souvlákia*, kebabs of meat grilled on a skewer, and often dusted with marjoram. *Giuvetsi* (roast lamb with pasta) is a specialty of many an Athens taverna, cooked and served in an earthenware dish.

Dishes made of minced meat are better avoided in a restaurant in which you have little confidence, though they are excellent when conscientiously prepared, and of good materials. They include *keftédes* (meat-balls); *soutzoukákia* (oval-shaped balls of meat and rice, served either on their own or in a tomato or egg and lemon sauce); *moussaká* (a pie made of minced meat and aubergines); and a number of dishes made of stuffed vegetables, such as tomatoes, courgettes, green peppers and aubergines, or *dolmádes* (vine or cabbage leaves, folded round a stuffing of mince and rice). Rice, which is generally well cooked in Greece, occurs in combination with minced meat, in the above-mentioned dishes; one may also find a variety of vegetables, sometimes stuffed with currants, pine nut kernels, and herbs, cooked in oil and served cold *(laderá)*. These are often excellent—the *dolmádes* of vine leaves *(yaprák dolmádes)* are specially to be commended. Moreover a rice pilaff is a wholesome and satisfying dish, whether served with a tomato sauce, or with one of the many possible garnishes, such as prawns (very good in Thessaloníki), glazed tomatoes—a Smyrniot touch—or kidneys. Macaroni is often overboiled.

Ragouts are best inspected in their pots. There are many stews of meat and vegetables, in tomato or in egg-and-lemon sauce, which, while they lack subtlety, can be excellent if well prepared, and make a welcome change in a limited diet. In spring, the fricassée of lamb with lettuce or with artichokes, or of pork with celery can be delicious, and at any time of the year *styphádo,* a stew of Italian origin, made of veal or tongue or (best) of hare, with oil and wine and small onions, is often very good indeed. The ubiquity of tomato sauce, fresh in summer and preserved in winter, is apt to be monotonous: try and manage not to have too much of it.

In season, game is good, especially hare, woodcock and wild pigeons; poultry is tasty: try chicken *(kotópoulo)* grilled or roasted on a spit over charcoal. Turkeys, stuffed with chestnuts and raisins or olives *(galópoulo yemistó)* are also very good in winter.

Restaurants make good use of the vegetables in season; in spring one finds peapods *(bisélia),* cabbage *(láchano),* French beans *(fasólia fréska),* lettuce *(maroúli)* and broccoli *(brókola)* on the menu. Artichokes *(angináres)* and broad beans *(yígantes),* mixed or separate, make an excellent dish served cold in oil, with a touch of dill and lemon. Beetroot *(pandzári)* is a common and tasty side dish when boiled and served with oil and vinegar. Courgettes *(kolokithákia)* and eggplants *(melintzánes),* the main vegetables in summer, are good when sliced and fried; they can be eaten—by those who can put up with the smell—with a strong garlic sauce *(skordaliá).* Eggplant stuffed with tomato and onion must have been the Turkish clergy's favorite, judging by its name: *imám bayildí* ("the priest fainted"). Dandelions *(radíkia)* and other wild mountain leaves, such as *vlíta,* and *hortá,* are boiled, and served cold with oil and lemon.

Desserts

Fruit is plentiful and good all the year round, from the first strawberries *(fráoules)* and cherries *(kerássia)* to the last oranges *(portokália)* in April. Specially to be commended are the yellow peaches *(rodákina),* nectarines *(nektarínia),* yellow-fleshed melons *(pepónia)* of Argos, and the small seedless grapes *(stafída),* black or white.

There are now lots of good local cheeses including quite successful attempts at Gruyére types called *graviéra*—especially *Corfu, Séres, Naxos.* Other varieties include *kaséri,* a hard cheese, and *féta,* a soft cheese made of sheep's milk—these being the most popular and good when not too salty—as well as *Metsovo kapnistó* (smoked). The white soft cheeses, the Cretan goat's cheese, *manóuri* and *myzíthra* are very good in the spring; they are sometimes eaten with honey. Féta, mashed with butter sauce and baked makes a tasty cheese pie called *tyrópitta.* Don't miss yoghourt *(yaoúrti),* but insist on *próveio,* made from sheep's milk; with honey it is one of the highlights of the Greek menu.

Desserts and coffee are not usually served in restaurants or tavernas unless they are first-class establishments. Most people move on to a sweetshop *(zacharoplasteío* or *patisseria)* to be tempted by all sorts of pastries, cakes, cookies, ice creams, and chocolates. Most of these shops-cum-eating places serve the sticky Turkish cakes, made of flaky pastry, honey and nuts combined in various ways—such are *baklavá, kataífi,* and *galaktoboúreko* (with a custard filling), and *copenhái* (so called because created in honor of the election of Prince William of Denmark as George I of Greece).

These are all called *glyká toú tapsióu* (sweets of the dish or pan, for they are baked in large shallow pans, and afterwards cut up). Sadly, though, such traditional pastries are fast being replaced by standardized factory products.

Cafes, except the with-it western-style establishments, provide what used to be known as Turkish, but has chauvinistically been renamed Greek coffee, served in tiny cups, (*skéto*—without sugar; *métrio*—with a moderate amount of sugar; *glykó*—sweet: and these distinctions may be further qualified by *vrastó*—well boiled, or *varí*—heavy) or a "sweet of the spoon" *(glykó tou koutalióu)*, a spoonful of syrupy jam dissolved in water, or a preserved fruit; *vísina* (black cherries); *nerántzi* (slices of orange peel) or *nerantzakia* (tiny green oranges); *fráoula* (strawberry-flavored grapes); *ypovríchion* (a spoonful of white mastic jam, served in a glass of water); *ánthos* (lemon blossom); *triantáfillo* (rose petal); *melintzanáki* (a tiny eggplant) and many more. In the country they are a symbol of the proverbial Greek hospitality: the stranger is immediately offered a spoonful of preserved fruit and a glass of cold water.

Drinks

Beer is served well-iced; *Henninger* and *Amstel*, light lagers, are best. Coca-Cola and Pepsi-Cola are available everywhere as are cartons of fresh juice, the excellent *IVI* orange and lemon squash (and other makes), and fizzy orange soda. Other soft drinks include *visináda* (a syrup made of black cherries, diluted with water), and a wide choice of orangeades and lemonades, nearly always too sweet to quench the thirst. There are a number of good mineral waters: *Loutráki, Nigríta, Sáriza* and others.

Many tourists are at first taken aback by the most characteristic wines of Greece, those rugged white wines mixed with resin *(retsína)* an inheritance from the ancients. *Kokkinéli* (rosé) generally contains less resin, and is more palatable to those who have not got used to the taste. *Retsína*, though a few like it from the first, is an acquired taste, except that most never acquire it. There is, of course, retsina and retsina—the best from the barrels of one of the taverns in the plain of Attica, or, if bottled, *Hyméttos* or *Kourtákis*. An addition of mineral water is refreshing, and reduces the taste of the resin.

The better restaurants have their own unresinated wine on draught (red or white), but everywhere bottled unresinated wine is available. Reliable are the red, rosé and white *Calligas* from Kefaloniá, *Porto Carras* from the Halkidikí, and the white *Tsantali* from the nearby Holy Mountain. The red *Aharnes* from Crete won a prize at the European Wine Exhibition, and the red and white *Minos* and *Mirabello* from the same island are also quite drinkable. Likewise the white Attic *Kava Camba, Cellar, Elisar, Apelia,* and rather more expensive *Chateau Matsa; St. Helena,* from the Peloponnese. *Kaviros, Castel Danieli,* and *Igoumenitsa* (rather cheaper) are good reds; *Náoussa,* the pleasant, full-bodied red wine from Macedonia is named after its place of origin; the best is produced by *Boutaris,* which also bottles the pleasant white *Lac des Roches*. The ubiquitous *Demestica* lacks character, both red and white.

Several Athenian taverns specialize in the products of the various regions; the very drinkable red and white wines are kept in the barrel. A discerning Athenian friend may guide you to these; the directions would be too complicated to give here—nor are the wines so good as to justify it. It may be said, however, that good, light, drinkable wine is nearly every-where obtainable.

Sweet wines are those of Achaia *(Mavrodáphne)*, Santoríni *(Vino Santo)* and the *Moscháto* of Samos (Byron: "Fill high the bowl with Samian wine!"). In those islands, and in Patra, these wines may be had at their best; a glass brought to you in Athens may well be disappointing. *Campari,* and *Cinzano* vermouth are locally produced, as is *Martini.* Brandy, if you take what a provincial cafe will give you, may easily taste of hair oil or cheap scent; but goodish Greek brandy exists, and if you order a *Botrys* you will find it enjoyable but different from what you have been accus-tomed to. Greek liqueurs, based on synthetic fruit syrups, delight the eye by their deep and unconvincing colors, but hardly please the palate with their cloying sweetness.

It is safe to drink the water; in Athens, it is purified by an unpleasant surfeit of chloride of lime. In the country, especially in the mountains, the water can be exceptionally pure and delicious. The Castalian spring of Del-phi has, rightly, been famous since ancient times.

Many cafes and snackbars serve breakfast with *croissants* or *brioches.* The standard bread is good when fresh—the local butter is indifferent. Fortunately instant coffee (usually called *Nes*) is provided everywhere and is much more palatable than the attempts made at French coffee, or than the Greek coffee served with hot milk. Honey is always delicious—that of Mount Hymettus is very likely the best in the world. Honey will, if you ask for it, be served with a hotel breakfast, and in many places in the prov-inces you will find a café that advertises "Butter and honey" *(voútyro-méli).*

EXPLORING GREECE

ANCIENT ATHENS

Birthplace of Democracy

It was called "the violet-crowned" by the ancients because, just before sunset, the flanks of Ymitós (Mount Hymettus), running like a backbone between the Attic plain and the vine country of the Mesógia, often glow with a curiously warm violet-tinted light which is reflected on the buildings of the city below. Then, suddenly, as though a switch had been worked by the unseen hand of some Olympian deity, everything turns dun-gray and Athens and its encircling mountains are engulfed in the shadows. This remarkable sight may now be observed only by courtesy of the north wind, blowing away the noxious mixture of carbon monoxide, sulphur dioxide and lead particles, forming the notorious chemical cloud, and temporarily restoring the unrivaled clarity and brilliance of the Athenian atmosphere.

Many millennia ago, according to the legend, Kekrops, a Phoenician, came to Attica, where he founded a city on the great rock near the sea. Two of the most powerful gods of Ólympos, Poseidon and Athena, contended for the patronage of the new strategically-placed city, ringed round by a semicircle of protective mountains and possessing the excellent harbors of the Saronikós (Saronic) Gulf at the seaward end of the plain. Poseidon, to prove the justice of his claim to divine overlordship struck the earth with his trident, and instantly a magnificent horse sprang forth, symbolizing all the manly qualities for which the marine god was famous. But the astute Athena, goddess of wisdom, in her attempt to outbid Poseidon, merely produced an olive tree from the ground. This, she explained, represented the qualities of peace and prosperity which would serve mankind to better purpose than the arts of war personified by Poseidon's fiery steed.

The council of gods decided in her favor, and the city of Kekrops, where European culture was destined to be born, was accordingly named Athens. Henceforth its inhabitants regarded the goddess of wisdom as their tutelary deity.

Handicapped by the natural aridity of the soil—little else but the vine and the olive have ever been successfully cultivated in Attica—Athens is nevertheless admirably situated; and the practical convenience of its position marks it out as the obvious capital of the country. Facing the Saronikós Gulf, with its good anchorages, on the main trade routes between Italy and the coast of Asia Minor on the one hand, and the Black Sea and the Straits of Gibraltar on the other, the modern city is built around the Acropolis (as the ancient one was) and the pinnacled crag of Mount Lycabettus, which the goddess Athena was said to have dropped on a spot north-east of the Acropolis, where it could serve as a bulwark to defend the city. With the increase in population and building activity since the late 1950s, the suburbs have covered the barren plain in all directions, in some places actually climbing the foothills of the mountains.

A Leader in Political Fashion

The historical origins are, of course, enveloped in the mists of mythology. Built by Kekrops in the remote Pelasgian Age, the city was enlarged by Erechtheus, who, half-man, half-serpent, was buried in a temple on the Acropolis afterwards known as the Erechtheion. Later, the legendary hero, Theseus, united the independent states of Attica into a single body, making Athens the capital of the state.

In the age of recorded history, what Athens did one day Greece did the next and Europe did two and a half millennia later. In 593 B.C., the ruling oligarchy appointed Solon, one of the Seven Wise Men of Antiquity, to carry out the necessary reforms to stave off tyranny, which had been prevented in 628 B.C. only by the decisive, if sacrilegious, action of the Alcmaeonid Megacles. Solon cancelled all debts, freed citizens enslaved for debts and prohibited future enslavement, bought back those sold abroad at state expense, limited landholdings, gave citizenship to foreign artisans, introduced pensions for war widows and orphans, introduced trial by jury and changed the coinage. But by basing himself on the maxim, "nothing in excess" he displeased all the social classes and there ensued 50 years of civil strife, till a successful general, Peisistratus, firmly established tyranny and the tradition of military interference in politics.

In a typical Greek paradox, he imposed the Solonian reforms, which had been intended to prevent tyranny. A sound economist and administrator, he raised Athens from the status of a country town to that of a city of international importance. He also erected temples and public buildings, and encouraged the development of poetry and drama, which revived public interest in the epics of Homer.

His son and successor Hippias, appointed his brother Hipparchos as a singularly successful Minister of Culture. To Athens flocked all the great names in Ionian intelligentsia till Hipparchos' murder in 514 B.C.

The first political family in Europe, the Alcmaeonids, in exile for the third time and experts in propaganda, turned a lovers' quarrel into the heroic deed of tyrannicides. But they failed to rouse the Athenians and had to use their influence over the Delphic oracle to bring about the overthrow of Hippias by Spartan intervention in 510 B.C. The Alcmaeonid

Cleisthenes completed the Solonian reforms by what is generally termed the "first democratic constitution in world history," which retained sufficient checks and balances to make it workable.

Athenian intervention in the Ionian Revolt in 499 B.C. had made Persian retaliation inevitable. The campaigns of 490 and 480 B.C., culminating in the defeat of the Persian invaders at Márathon, Sálamis and Plataea, inaugurated a new era in the history of Athens which had been reduced to ashes by Xerxes, the Persian king, on the eve of the destruction of his own fleet at Sálamis. The prestige of Athens which had resisted and routed the Asiatic hordes, now naturally stood very high in the Greek world. Under Themistocles, celebrated for his unrivaled statesmanship in keeping the Greek alliance together, the security of the city was ensured by surrounding it with fortified walls, and its chief port was transferred from the open roadstead of Phaleron to the security of the admirable harbors of the Piraeus. The process of construction and embellishment continued under Kimon.

The Golden Age

For its architectural splendor, however, Athens is chiefly indebted to Pericles. It was indeed in the golden Periclean age of Athenian democracy that the Parthenon, the Erechtheion and the Propylaea of the Acropolis were built. The rapid development of Athens as a maritime power, begun under Themistocles, continued, and a virtual Athenian empire was soon established over the Aegean.

The Peloponnesian War, in which Athens and Sparta fought for the supremacy of Greece, and in which Athens was finally defeated in 404 B.C., brought an end to the Classical Age. But during those miraculous years, the little state had produced an unparalleled succession of geniuses. To name only a few: statesmen such as Themistocles, Pericles and the glamorous though utterly unscrupulous Alcibiades; Aeschylus, Sophocles and Euripides among the dramatists, and Pheidias and Myron, masters of the art of sculpture; historians of the caliber of Herodotus, Thucydides and Xenophon; as well as an entire galaxy of architects, poets and comic writers. As for the philosophers—Socrates, Plato and Aristotle, above all—their teachings have never ceased to influence Western thought and civilization to this day.

Little more than ten years after its defeat, however, Athens won a naval victory over the Spartans off Cnidos, under the Athenian admiral Conon, turned commander of the Persian navy in one of those kaleidoscopic changes of alliance so frequent in Greece. This enabled the Athenians to turn their thoughts once more to the improvement of their city. Persian gold started the rebuilding of the fortifications and the theater of Dionysus and the Stadium were eventually completed.

In the second half of the 4th century B.C., the Macedonians, led by Philip, invaded Greece, and Athens and its allies suffered a crushing defeat at the battle of Chaironéia. This spelt the end of Greek democracy, for Philip, and his son, Alexander the Great, who succeeded him, imposed a rigid rule over the conquered city states. After 200 years of uneasy acquiescence to Macedonian overlordship, the stage was set for the Roman conquest. Materially Athens suffered disastrously when Sulla, the Roman general, captured the city in 86 B.C., after which commerce and maritime power declined rapidly.

The Romans, Goths, and Turks

Nevertheless, under the Romans, Athens continued to be the cultural capital of the Graeco-Roman world, and was much frequented by Romans as a seat of learning and refinement, becoming, in fact, a kind of "finishing school" for elegant and educated patricians. Numerous public buildings were erected and embellishments made by the Roman emperors, especially by Hadrian. During the reign of the Antonines, imperial munificence was emulated by a rich banker, Herodes Atticus, the first of many public benefactors to whom Athens, even in modern times, owes much of its municipal architecture.

The city remained intact until the 4th century A.D., after which public buildings fell into disrepair and a general decay set in. Paganism was now gradually being stamped out and Christianity beginning to flourish triumphantly in Constantinople, the new capital of the civilized world.

The curtain had thus come down on the violet-crowned city. At the end of the 4th century Greece suffered the appalling visitation of Alaric and his Goths. Athens was sacked, ravaged, and henceforth left to moulder away in total insignificance. In the 13th century, when the great feudal barons of Western Europe, descending upon the eastern Mediterranean on the pretext of liberating the Holy City from the Infidel, began to carve out principalities for themselves out of the Christian Byzantine Empire, Athens came under the suzerainty of Florentine bankers, the Acciajuolis. In 1455, two years after the fall of Constantinople, the city was captured by a general of the triumphant Turkish Sultan, and henceforth remained, for nearly two centuries, little more than a dilapidated oriental village, a group of houses clustered round the dismantled Acropolis.

One episode during the dark centuries of Ottoman occupation is, however, worth recording. In 1687, the Venetians, under Francesco Morosini, later to become Doge, tried to wrest Athens from the Turks. The Acropolis underwent a sustained bombardment, and a Venetian shell, bursting on the Parthenon, where the Turks had placed their gunpowder magazine, caused a terrific explosion which reduced a considerable part of the temple to a heap of ruins. It was largely from the debris left by this explosion that Lord Elgin later recovered several statues and fragments of the frieze and metopes, now in the British Museum.

Exploring Ancient Athens

Although Athens, together with its suburbs and port, the Piraeus, sprawls across the plain for more than 150 square miles, most of the ancient monuments cluster round the Acropolis, which rises like a massive sentinel, white and beautiful, out of the center of the city. Sightseeing is therefore confined to a fairly limited area and is not likely to prove too tiring. Nor do the Byzantine churches of the Middle Ages lie far off.

The history of Athens falls into three sharply defined chronological periods—ancient, Byzantine and modern: a fact naturally reflected in the existing monuments, most of which actually belong to the first and most famous of these periods. The gap of nearly 400 years of Ottoman domination, between the Byzantine and modern eras, when the "dead hand of the Turk" lay heavy on the Greek lands, has left no architectural legacy worth speaking of.

The Acropolis—the Glory that was Greece

In mountainous Greece, most ancient towns were backed up by an acropolis, an easily defensible upper town (which is what the word means), but when spelt with a capital "A" it can only refer to antiquity's most splendid group of buildings—the Acropolis of Athens.

The square precipitous rock of limestone, 270 meters (886 ft.) at its greatest length and 156 meters (512 ft.) broad, rising over 60 meters (200 ft.) above the surrounding plain, served both as a fortress and as the sacred sanctuary of Athena, its tutelary goddess, whose festival, the Panathenaea, was celebrated every four years when an embroidered crocus-colored robe, woven by the upper-class maidens of Athens, was carried in great pomp to the holiest of her shrines in the Erechtheion. Today it is crowned by the ruins of three temples and an entrance way, the architectural perfection of which has not been surpassed in 2,500 years.

Despite the efforts of U.N.E.S.C.O. and the Greek government to protect monuments from pollution, especially from rains acid with sulphur, an international symposium of archeologists and architects has despairingly concluded that among all known methods for the protection of marbles, there exists none harmless and efficient enough that they could recommend. During the restorations, the equilibrium of the monuments was strengthened and the iron clamps of the previous major works dating from the turn of the century and the 30s, which held the teetering marble blocks together, were replaced by titanium; the buildings have been closed to the thousands of daily visitors; but all these measures are mere palliatives.

Starting from Platía Sýntagma (Constitution Square), center of modern Athens and following Leofóros Amalias and Dionysiou Areopagitou, the approaches to the Acropolis are reached in about five minutes by car or 15 on foot. The first ancient monument on the southern slope of the Acropolis is Peisistratus' 6th-century B.C. theater of Dionysus. Here, for several days in the early summer of each year, 15,000 Athenians would gather to witness a succession of tragedies, dealing with the awful fate that befell the Atreids or some other doomed family, by Aeschylus, Sophocles and Euripides. These performances, livened by the satirical sallies and witty obscenities of Aristophanes, were attended by the entire population of the capital and lasted from daybreak to sunset. They were known as the festival of the Dionysia and combined plays and bacchanalian feasts.

Repeatedly enlarged and embellished, the theater is scheduled to be restored for performances of ancient drama. The circular stage and bas-relief frieze, depicting the exploits of the winegod, which supported the proscenium, date from the Roman period. The crouching figure of that famous old satyr, Silenus, is worth noting. The front row of 67 seats, more ample and comfortable than the rest, was intended for V.I.P.s, and the one in the center was occupied by the officiating priest at the festival. From the holes in the pavement, supports held up an awning to protect the complexion of this dignitary from the bright spring sunshine.

Above the last tier of seats, perched on the southern side of the rock, will be seen a grotto converted in the 4th century B.C. into a little temple by Thrasyllus the Choragus (the ancient counterpart of a modern impresario). Beside the grotto, and immediately below the great southern wall of the Acropolis, rise two delicate Corinthian columns of the Roman period.

Continuing in a westerly direction, along Leofóros Dionysiou Areopagitou, and below the ruins of a colonnade intended as a foyer, one reaches

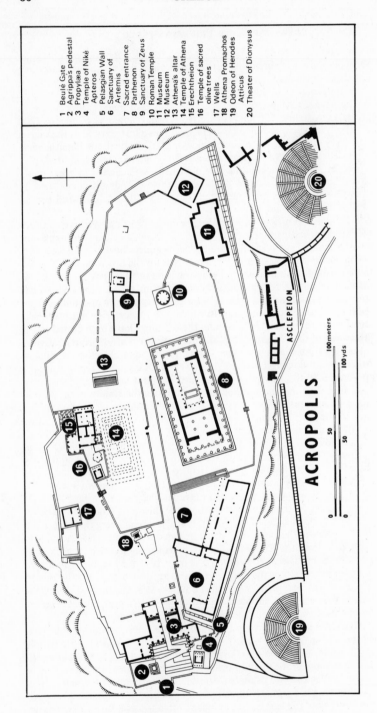

1 Beulé Gate
2 Agrippa's pedestal
3 Propylaea
4 Temple of Niké Apteros
5 Pelasgian Wall
6 Sanctuary of Artemis
7 Sacred entrance
8 Parthenon
9 Sanctuary of Zeus
10 Roman Temple
11 Museum
12 Museum
13 Athena's altar
14 Temple of Athena
15 Erechtheion
16 Temple of sacred olive trees
17 Wells
18 Athena Promachos
19 Odeon of Herodes Atticus
20 Theater of Dionysus

ACROPOLIS

ASCLEPEION

100 meters
100 yds

another theater: that of Herodes Atticus, built by that opulent public bene-factor of the 2nd century A.D. as a memorial to his deceased wife. Once roofed with cedar wood, with a seating capacity of 5,000, it still remains in a good state of preservation, although the roof has long since vanished. The mellowed brick facade, with its arched niches where statues were once placed, looks particularly dramatic when floodlit.

Here the Athens Festival of Music and Drama is held every summer, and the ancient tragedies and Attic comedies performed in modern Greek in their original incomparable setting.

Motor coaches disgorge unending streams of sightseers, who should wear sensible shoes for the ascent of the ramp and staircase. Tourist can-teens, at the top of the steep climb, below the ticket office, provide refresh-ments. The first monument, an eight-meter (27-ft.) high pedestal on the left, originally bore a Hellenistic king. Never ones to let a good pedestal go to waste, the eminently practical Athenians, having backed once again the losing side, replaced him in 27 B.C. with a statue showing the Roman general Agrippa, victor of Actium, erect in a bronze chariot.

The Propylaea, one of the masterpieces of Classical architecture, serves as a magnificent entrance way to the buildings of the "upper city." With the defeat of the Persian fleet at Sálamis and the decisive Greek victory at Plataea in the following year, the Persian menace had been finally re-moved, and Athens, under Kimon and Pericles rose to the heights of power and creative achievement. The adornment of the Acropolis with imperishable works of art was one of the main preoccupations of Pericles. He entrusted the building of the Propylaea to Mnesicles, a fashionable ar-chitect of the time, who completed it in five years. Built entirely of Pentelic marble, it extends 45 meters (150 ft.) across the whole western front of the Acropolis, which was, and still is, the only means of access to the sum-mit. It thus formed a vestibule to the five gates through which the Acropo-lis was entered, and the marks of the chariot wheels may still be seen on the age-worn rock. The porticos consist of six massive fluted Doric col-umns on the outside, doubled by graceful Ionic inside; the large north wing, the *Pinakotheke,* where pictures, mostly by Polygnotus, were exhib-ited, became the residence of the Orthodox archbishops, and later of the Frankish dukes, when a huge fortified tower was added. The Acciajuoli dynasty was replaced by the Turkish commander, who kept his powder dry in the portico till it was struck by lightning in 1645. The Turks placed their guns in the shattered walls. The German archeologist Schliemann paid for the removal of the Frankish tower in the 19th century, when the successful reconstruction, even of parts of the roof with its marble beams and decorated coffers, was begun.

The one room of the south wing might have served as a waiting room for the adjoining temple of Athena Nike, sometimes called Nike Apteros (Wingless Victory), because the crafty Athenians depicted Nike wingless, to prevent Nike from flying away. This little temple (only eight meters (27 ft.) long and five and a half meters (18 ft.) broad), its eight delicate Ionic columns glistening in the sun, stands on a western bastion of the Acropolis, commanding a superb prospect of the plain, sea and islands of the Saronikós Gulf, with the backcloth of the crenelated ridges of the Méthana Peninsula and the mountains of the Peloponnese beyond. To the south-west, Egáleo tapers off into the sea, where the hump of the Kastella headland and the sprawling conglomeration of houses, docks and smoking factories of the Piraeus extend against the background of the off-shore island of Salamis.

According to legend, King Aegeus flung himself from this bastion into the sea—no mean achievement considering the six-mile distance—to which he has given his name. His son, Theseus, had forgotten to hoist the white sails proclaiming his slaying of the Minotaur, a strange omission as he had also rid himself of his protectress, Ariadne, and on seeing the black sails, the aggrieved father committed the somewhat acrobatic suicide. The bas-reliefs of the Frieze of Victories on the surrounding parapet, now closed to the public, must have been of exceptional workmanship, judging from "Nike unfastening her sandal" in the Acropolis museum.

The temple of Nike Apteros was built to commemorate the Greek victories over the Persians in the 5th century B.C. Completely demolished by the Turks in order to provide building material for a gun battery, the fragments were reconstructed during the 19th century into a perfect replica of the original. After this temporary respite for victorious Athena, the foundations gave way in 1936 because of unsuspected Turkish cisterns. The strengthening of the base led to the discovery of the foundations of Peisistratus' temple of Artemis, below the once again rebuilt home of Victory. The frieze, extending all 26 meters (86 ft.) round the building, represented scenes from mythology and battles.

The Parthenon

Returning to the Propylaea, and passing through one of its five gates onto a rocky plateau, one is confronted with a staggering view of the western front of the Parthenon, its honey-colored columns of Pentelic marble rising from a massive limestone base which extends across the highest part of the Acropolis. The Sacred Way from the Propylaea to the Parthenon was once lined with statues, ex-votos and foundations of more ancient temples. Here, too, was Pheidias's colossal statue of Athena Promachos (all traces of which have now vanished), whose raised spear and plumed helmet could be seen flashing in the sunlight by sailors approaching the coast. Today the approach to the Parthenon, littered with slabs of marble and broken drums, is crowded with sightseers talking a dozen different languages, with garrulous guides and leech-like photographers. But neither they, nor all the evidence of the wanton destruction caused as much by man and his rapacity as by time and the elements, can detract from the awe felt at that first prospect of the ruins of the Parthenon. But the hard marble is slowly being dissolved by the sulphuric acid in the polluted air, which has stripped off the age-old patina and exposed new white stone.

The Parthenon, the "Virgin's Chamber," was built on the site of earlier temples also dedicated to the worship of the virgin goddess, Athena. Standing on the highest part of the plateau, its base was on a level with the roof of the Propylaea. It was under construction for nine years, and the design was drawn up by Ictinus, while Pheidias, the greatest sculptor of the age was entrusted with the sculptural decoration. But both Ictinus and Pheidias were responsible to Pericles, who took a keen personal interest in the completion of what was destined to be the most perfect example of Doric architecture in existence.

The temple had eight fluted columns at either end and 17 on each side, and was entirely built of Pentelic marble, which, with age, has taken on a warm golden tint of astonishing beauty. The genius of Ictinus and his collaborators is revealed in the fact that the structure does not possess a single straight line of any length, the shafts of the columns inclining slightly inwards, the lines of the cornices of the gables being oblique, and the entablature rising gradually to a point three inches higher in the middle: all these gentle deflections creating an unusually pleasing and tranquil effect. The subtle convexity of the columns can be seen best from either end of the two great colonnades. At every point, moreover, the simplicity, grandeur and complete harmony of design and execution astonishes and delights.

The exterior sculptural decorations, all of which were originally brightly colored, and commemorated the history of the goddess Athena, were of a fabulous quality and richness—92 sculptured metopes, 44 statues ornamenting the gables, and a frieze 160 meters (523 ft.) long: all the work of Pheidias and his pupils. Most of the sculptural ornaments which escaped destruction from the Venetian siege of 1687 were taken down in 1801 by Lord Elgin, British Ambassador in Constantinople and, with the Sultan's permission, shipped to England, where they now form one of the showpieces of the British Museum. Those remaining became so badly damaged by pollution that they had to be removed to the Acropolis Museum.

In the eminently practical way of the Athenians, the Parthenon was a place of worship and, at the same time, a national treasury. It contained bullion as well as priceless ornaments and it stood as a symbol of Athenian imperialistic pride. Even Pheidias' huge chryselephantine statue of the goddess Athena, in her detachable dress of solid gold formed part of the bullion reserve. When the sculptor was charged with embezzlement, the robe was found to weigh the full 40 talents' worth of gold. Pheidias had to be acquitted only to be rearrested on a charge of impiety, in the relentless way with which the Athenian democracy persecuted all its great men, as he had depicted himself and Pericles upon Athena's shield. He either died in prison or, helped by Pericles to escape, was killed in an anti-Athenian riot at Olympia. The spot occupied by the statue can be identified by a paving of dark-colored limestone.

The subsequent history of the Parthenon is eventful. Alexander the Great dedicated the gilded shields taken from the Persians to Athena, but one of his successors, Demetrius Poliorketes, installed his mistress in the Virgin's Chamber. Athena eventually took her revenge when Demetrius came to a bad end, but could not prevent the removal of her jewels when the Athenian commander absconded with the temple treasure during Demetrius' siege of Athens in 298 B.C. Pheidias' statue was taken to Constantinople by the Emperor Theodosius II in A.D. 426, when the Parthenon became the Church of Holy Wisdom. Some 100 years later, the Emperor Justinian dedicated the church to the Virgin of another faith, perhaps because he resented so glorious a rival to his own Saint Sophia. In 1206, the Franks changed the rite but kept the patroness and Saint Marie of Athens was worshipped till the conversion into a mosque in 1460. A minaret was attached, but nothing could prevent the Turks from storing ammunition in inappropriate places, with the obvious disastrous consequences.

The hazards of war returned in 1944, when British paratroops chased the Communists out of besieged Athens, after siting their bazookas between the Parthenon's columns. Since then, a more insidious enemy has been added to 2,400 years of warfare—pollution—so that intense effort, time and money have now to be devoted to preservation.

The Erechtheion

More than any other ancient monument, the Erechtheion, which lies north of the Parthenon, has its roots in the legendary origins of Athens. Here it was that the contest between Poseidon and Athena took place for the possession of the city. Here grew the olive tree which Athena had called forth from the ground, and the fountain, which had sprung up where Poseidon struck the earth with his trident, trickled. Here was buried Kekrops, the founder of Athens, and Erechtheus, Athena's ward, after whom the shrine was named, and at the first sight of whose serpent tail some of the royal attendants went mad with fright and hurled themselves from the top of the Acropolis. And here finally was venerated the ancient olive-wood statue of Athena Polias, which was said to have fallen from heaven.

Burnt by the Persians on the eve of the battle of Sálamis, the Erechtheion was rebuilt on its original site after the outbreak of the Peloponnesian War. If the Parthenon is the masterpiece of Doric architecture, the Erechtheion is undoubtedly that of the more graceful and feminine Ionic order. A considerably smaller edifice than the Parthenon, for sheer elegance and refinement of design and execution, it cannot be matched by any other monument of antiquity. Extensive restoration, criticized in some quarters as excessive, was completed in 1988. Possibly this sanctuary of Athena, Poseidon, and Erechtheus is now more like its original self, completely different in style from any other known Greek temple. Irregular in shape and built on different levels, it has three porticos of different dimensions. The six slender columns of the exquisitely proportioned northern portico framed the richly ornamented doorway which led into the chamber of Erechtheus. The southern portico, equally famous though less beautiful, is that of the Caryatids—six larger-than-lifesize maidens (replaced by cement casts, while five of the originals are in the Acropolis Museum and one in the British Museum), supporting a heavy roof of over two tons of Pentelic marble. Taking into account the enormous burden which these impassive maidens are carrying, their uniformly complacent, almost simpering expressions seem a little out of place.

If, during the Turkish occupation, the Parthenon suffered the indignity of being converted into a gunpowder dump, a fate of a quite different kind befell the Erechtheion. For here, in these holiest of ancient Athenian precincts, the Turkish governor, who himself resided in the Propylaea, housed the plump oriental beauties of his extensive harem.

East of the Erechtheion, there is a belvedere from which the modern city can be seen sprawling around Lycabettus and over the suburban plain rolling eastwards towards the foothills of Mount Hymettus.

The contents of the Acropolis Museum—they will in due course be moving to the new museum down below—are described in the section on museums.

If asked what is the best time to see the Acropolis, one might be hard put to find an answer. Such is the beauty of the monuments and the grandeur of the setting that a visit in all weathers and at all hours is rewarding. In winter if there are clouds trailing across the mountains, and shafts of sun occasionally lighting up the marble columns, which glisten with added brilliance after a shower of rain or a thunderstorm, the setting takes on an even more dramatic quality. In summer the heat is blistering at noontime, and the reflection of the light thrown back by the rock and marble ruins almost blinding; morning and late afternoon are preferable.

Sites near the Acropolis

After the Acropolis all will at first seem to be an anti-climax. But there is still much that is well worth seeing, especially the sites on the periphery of the Acropolis. A few low hills face its main entrance. The hill of the Muses is crowned with the funeral monument of Philopappos, the last descendant of the Commagene kings (Asia Minor), who was an important personage in the Roman administration. In the central upper niche of the ruined marble memorial, erected in about A.D. 116, are the remains of the statue of Philopappos.

This hill, now a favorite haunt of couples at sundown, is honey-combed with caves, one of which is commonly known as (but not proved to be) the prison of Socrates. And here, it is said, the greatest of ancient philosophers, condemned for the alleged corruption of Athenian youth by his advanced ideas on religion, drained the fatal cup of hemlock as the sun set fierily behind Sálamis, its last rays liquefying the columns of the Parthenon into gold.

Northwest of the hill of Philopappos rises the low, rocky Pnyx. The semi-circular terrace on its summit was the place of assembly of the Athenian people; and in the middle of a wall of rock projects a solid rectangular block, identified as the tribune from which the great orators of antiquity— Solon, Themistocles, Pericles, Aristides and Demosthenes—addressed the national assemblies. It must have been an ideal spot on which to arouse patriotic fervor, with the imposing entrance way of the Propylaea above, and the city below studded with all the public edifices attesting to the glory of Athens.

Every evening (April to October) audiences gather on the Pnyx to watch the impressive floodlighting effects on the rock and temples of the Acropolis, accompanied by an overly-dramatic commentary in English, French, and German in an effective sound and light performance.

Northeast of the Pnyx is the Areopagus, the "hill of Ares," so-called because it was here that the god of war was brought to trial before the council of gods by Poseidon for the willful killing of one of his sons. Being the first judgment ever to be pronounced in a murder trial, it made legal history and after a distinguished record of some thousand years in antiquity the name Areopagus was revived for the Supreme Court of modern Greece.

The Areopagus has two other associations: one mythological and the other historical. A dark cavern in a chasm of the rock corresponds to the sanctuary of the Eumenides, the restless Furies who hounded Orestes from the Lion Gate of Mycenae to Delphi and Athens. On the Areopagus too St. Paul made his famous sermon to the Athenians, in the course of which the senator Dionysos was converted to Christianity and subsequently canonized by the Orthodox Church for being the first Athenian to adopt the Christian faith. As St. Denis the Areopagite he was declared patron saint of the city; but the veneration which the Athenians once felt for their pagan tutelary deity does not seem to have been extended to her Christian successor, who remains a worthy but dim figure in the annals of Athenian history.

Between the Pnyx and the Areopagus, Apostolou Pavlou descends, leaving to the left the hill of the Nymphs, crowned by the observatory, designed, like so many of the 19th-century public buildings, by Hansen and paid for by Baron Sina. It is scheduled to become the Museum of Old Instruments. The flat area below the northwestern bastions of the Acropolis was the center of the antique town, now mainly unrecognizable ruins.

On the right of Apostolou Pavlou is the Hephaestion, the best-preserved temple in Greece, which has erroneously been styled the Theseion for many centuries, because the sculptures of the frieze depict the exploits of Theseus and Heracles. It was, however, dedicated to Hephaestos, the god of artisans and blacksmiths, whose shops and forges, from antiquity to the present day, have echoed with the hammering of metal on anvil in this part of the town.

Designed by Ictinus, the architect of the Parthenon, it is, likewise, a Doric temple, surrounded by 34 columns, and 32 meters (104 ft.) in length. The porticos were once filled with sculptures, but today the only remaining adornment is the mutilated frieze and a few metopes. These, like those of the Parthenon, were painted, and still preserve remains of the colors when carefully examined.

The Hephaestion's chief claim to fame rests in its excellent state of preservation. Although conceived and executed in the best of 5th-century B.C. workmanship, it is likely to leave the spectator rather cold, and even to recall some of those commonplace replicas of Doric temples much favored by municipal architecture in Western Europe during the 19th century. The reason for the failure of the Hephaestion to create an impact similar to that made by the Parthenon or the Propylaea may also be due to the fact that it lacks a noble site. Its ample enclosure is surrounded by the houses of a poorish, densely-populated quarter, criss-crossed with crowded suburban bus routes to the Piraeus and the Athens–Piraeus electric railway line.

The Agora—Commercial Hub of Ancient Athens

The remains of the ancient Agora, the marketplace, extend southeastwards, dominated by the restored Stoa of Attalus. The Classical scholar and archeologist may well find the exploration of the Agora and the identification of the ancient municipal buildings—thoroughly destroyed by successive invaders—an occupation of absorbing interest. The scene, however, as it strikes the layman, is one of sprawling confusion, since none of the buildings are standing, and it is not always easy to identify the foundations among the rubble of stones and broken slabs of marble.

The Agora was the center of public life, and all the principal urban roads and country highways traversed it. The procession of the great Panathenaea Festival, composed of chariots, magistrates, virgins, priests and sacrificial animals, also crossed the Agora on its way from the Dipylon gate to the Acropolis. Six stoas, long colonnades closed on three sides, offered shade in summer and protection from rain in winter to the throng of people who transacted the day-to-day business of the city. Here taught a succession of philosophers including the stoics (named after the stoas), whose master Zeno preached serene endurance; here, too, several centuries later, St. Paul went about his missionary task. It was indeed the heart of the city and a general meeting place, where news was exchanged and bargains transacted, alive with all the rumors and gossip of the market place.

In 1981 the American School of Classical Studies celebrated its centenary and the 50th anniversary of the Agora excavations, a major archeological event, by the discovery of the Stoa Poikile (Painted Stoa). A whole quarter had to be torn down to remove layer after layer of older buildings, finally revealing the antique foundations. The northwest corner was only recently expropriated, so that the first important building to rise from the ashes of the Persian invasion of 480 B.C. was the last to come to light. The Stoa Poikile received its name from the murals depicting mythical and historical battles, executed by the greatest painters of around 460 B.C.; it served thus as an art gallery as well as a war memorial.

The foundations of some of the main buildings which may be most easily distinguished include the Tholos, the principal seat of executive power in the city, the Bouleuterion, where the 400 senators met, the Metroon, a vast building of complicated structure, in which the state archives were kept, and the Stoa of Zeus, where Socrates lectured and incited the youth of Athens to adopt his progressive ideas on morality.

The reconstructed Stoa of Attalus, which cost the Rockefeller Foundation $1,500,000 in the 1950s, is of course the showpiece of the Agora. The two superimposed colonnades of 134 columns, of which the lower are Doric and the upper Ionic, gleam white and all too obviously new above the ruins of the Agora. The original Stoa, built by Attalus, King of Pergamum, in the 2nd century B.C., as a tribute and memorial to Greek culture, was lined with statues and expensive shops, and soon became the favorite strolling ground of fashionable Athenians. In the principal hall of the reconstructed Stoa may be seen the vases and sculptures found on the site. Two statues, a headless Apollo and a Winged Victory, have been placed on either side of the Stoa.

Keramikos Cemetery

Leaving the Hephaestion on the right and continuing along Apostolou Pavlou, you reach the Keramikos. This, from the 7th century B.C. onwards, was the smart cemetery of ancient Athens. During succeeding ages cemeteries were superimposed on the ancient one until the latter was discovered in 1861 during the construction of Odós Pireos, the main road linking the capital with its port.

Situated in one of the noisiest and shoddiest parts of modern Athens, the setting of the Keramikos is not inspiring, although the gasworks that have for a century deposited soot on this archaeological site are scheduled to be replaced by a park. An alley bordered by sculptured memorials to the dead includes several 6th-century B.C. bas-reliefs of exceptional artistic value, depicting horsemen and wild animals. Some are in the small museum on the site, but the finest *steles* (funerary tablets) have been taken to the National Archaeological Museum. Beyond the Sacred Gate, a hotchpotch of masonry of successive periods, is the Dipylon, built in the 4th century B.C. into a section of Themistocles' earlier wall. This rectangular court with two gateways facing northwest and southeast (hence the name Dipylon: the two doors), led from the inner into the outer Keramikos and was the most used of all the city's gates. It was also the favorite huntingground of prostitutes of antiquity, who lurked in its shadow, offering the solace of their charms to the weary traveler entering Athens.

The Tower of the Winds

Behind the Stoa of Attalus, the broken marbles of the small Roman Agora serve in summer as a setting for performances of antique plays.

Slightly higher up, the Tower of the Winds is surrounded by a cluster of old houses on the western slope of the Acropolis.

This edifice—more precisely, an hydraulic clock—was built in the shape of an octagonal tower in the 1st century B.C. in order to serve as a public clock and weather-vane. Its eight sides face the direction of the eight winds into which the compass was divided. The weathercock, long since vanished, consisted of a bronze Triton turning on a pivot on the summit of the tower. The frieze is sculptured with the inscriptions and figures of the eight winds.

Below the Tower of the Winds, a glance at the few remaining columns of the library of the Emperor Hadrian, once a vast quadrilateral edifice, with 100 Corinthian columns, will complete the tour of the periphery of the Acropolis.

The City of Hadrian

Starting from Sýntagma, follow Leofóros Amalias, which skirts the National Gardens until reaching the Arch of Hadrian, a conspicuous landmark. Built by the Emperor Hadrian to define the limits of the original "city of Theseus"—all that lay beyond was the "city of Hadrian"—this monument consists of a Roman archway, with a Greek superstructure of Corinthian pilasters topped by an architrave and pediment. Visiting heads of states are officially welcomed at this rather ungainly combination of Greek and Roman styles.

Across Leofóros Amalias is Lysikratous, leading to the Choragic Monument of Lysicrates amid a jumble of antique foundations below the eastern walls of the Acropolis. A small circular marble edifice, covered by a cupola, supported by six Corinthian columns, it dates from the 4th century B.C. and has a delightfully elegant appearance. The frieze depicts the rout of the Tyrrhenian pirates by Dionysos. It was elevated in honor of a group of young musicians who won a contest at the neighboring theater of Dionysos. The adjacent street of the Tripods (Tripodon) was once bordered by a series of similar monuments, surmounted by bronze tripods awarded as prizes to contestants in the Dionysiac festivals.

At the end of the 17th century, the monument of Lysicrates was incorporated in the grounds of a French Capuchin monastery and formed part of the monk's library. Here Byron stayed during his first visit to Athens, and met Theresa Makris, the "Maid of Athens" of his famous poem, who lived in a house overlooking the monastery garden where the English lord would sometimes amuse himself by joining in the games of a group of convent-reared boys.

Returning to the Arch of Hadrian, one enters the vast precincts of the temple of Olympian Zeus. This famous temple, begun by Peisistratus in the 6th century B.C., was only completed 700 years, and two styles, later. Exceeding in magnitude all other temples in Greece, Aristotle, who could only have seen the incomplete Ionic version, described it as being in the same class as the Pyramids of Egypt. It was finally consecrated, in the Corinthian style, by the Emperor Hadrian, who had already done so much to embellish Athens. Beside the statue of Zeus, father of the gods, he placed one of himself and probably one of his ubiquitous favorite, Antinous, whose subsequent death by drowning in the Nile caused the grief-stricken Emperor to enrol him among the gods. The destruction of the temple dates from the invasion of Alaric's Goths, and during the Middle

Ages its massive masonry and the drums of its columns, the largest of any marble temple of antiquity in Europe, supplied the Athenians and their successive conquerors with building materials. During this period also a Byzantine anchorite perched his eyrie on a piece of lonely architrave above two columns which had been completely detached from the rest.

Although inferior in conception and execution to the temples of the Acropolis, the immense scale of the temple's design (it is almost 108 meters, 354 ft., long and 41 meters, 135 ft. broad) and the majesty of the towering sun-browned columns, with their decorative acanthus leaf capitals, makes a deep impression. It is thrilling also, when approaching Athens from the sea (and the airport), to see two of the 16 remaining columns standing like sentinels on either side of Leofóros Syngrou before it curves round by the Arch of Hadrian into the center of the town.

The Stadium

From the temple of Olympian Zeus, Leofóros Ólgas, flanked on one side by the Zapio Gardens, leads to the last important monument of ancient Athens, the Stadium, now completely restored, and situated in a fold of the pineclad Ardittos Hill. Laid out in the 4th century B.C., it was embellished by the public-spirited Herodes Atticus four centuries later, and completely restored by George Averoff, a 20th-century Herodes Atticus, among whose various other works of public benefaction was the defrayment of the cost of a battleship to the nation.

The Stadium, when completed in 1896, was the scene of the revived Olympic Games. A vast structure of white Pentelic marble, set against the surrounding green of dwarf-pines, it is an accurate replica of the ancient Roman stadium, and can seat 70,000 spectators, but the track area is too restricted for large international sporting events, which are held in the Olympic Stadium in the northern Kalogresa suburb. The tunnel of rock at the end of the arena may have been used, it is thought, as an exit for animals in the course of wild beast shows during Roman times. It is very much hoped that Greece will be the venue for the "Golden Olympics," the Centenary Games of 1996.

Byzantine Athens—Decay and Oblivion

During the 1,000 years of the Byzantine Empire, Athens declined in power and influence in inverse ratio to the growth and development of Constantinople as the capital of the Greek world. The paucity and modest proportions of such Byzantine monuments as may now be seen in Athens are proof of the insignificant status to which the city of Pericles had been reduced.

At no point, and at no time, does Athens, with its ruined Classical temples, and its present feverish tempo of life, conjure up any of the usual concepts associated with Byzantium. The word "Byzantine" recalls an atmosphere of slow-moving, semi-Eastern ritual, redolent of incense, echoing with solemn liturgies chanted in chapels glowing with elaborate frescos. The beauty of Athens lies in the open—in the sun: that of Byzantium in dim mysterious interiors. Athens is Europe; Constantinople is already the Orient—or, at least, the beginning of it.

Three Byzantine churches, architectural gems of their kind, however, will be found tucked away in one of the busiest quarters of the modern town. Small in size, built in the traditional Greek Cross plan of "cross in square," their exteriors (brickwork in the case of the first two and marble in that of the third), crowned by a dome resting on the arches of an octagonal drum, are very arresting.

The oldest and best preserved is that of Agii Theodori, which may be seen from Stadíou, surrounded on three sides by tall buildings, at the lower righthand corner of Platía Klafthmonos ("square of weeping"), so called because it was here that a group of dismissed civil servants once assembled to bemoan their fate; this, it seems, they did so loudly and persistently that the authorities were compelled to rescind their decision and restore them to their former jobs.

Not far off, in the middle of a minute square, halfway down the incline of crowded Ermóu, is the coquettish little Kapnikarea, hemmed in by drapers' shops. Turning to the left into Mitropoleos, the smallest and loveliest of these churches of the 12th and 13th centuries, the Old Metropolis, nestles below the vast structure of the 19th-century cathedral of Athens. The latter is an incongruous mixture of non-styles constructed from the debris of 70 churches to furnish an object-lesson in the decline of good taste in the course of six centuries!

The Old Metropolis, built of Pentelic marble which has matured to a warm ocher hue, is distinguished by an exterior decoration of exquisite variety and refinement. All four sides are embellished with bas-reliefs of symbolic beasts, as well as with ancient fragments of Classical friezes depicting the principal feasts of the calendar, and various heraldic or purely ornamental designs, all of extreme elegance.

Wandering in the tortuous ways of the Plaka—the little that is left of the 19th-century Athens which Byron knew—on the northern slope of the Acropolis, one does occasionally stumble upon a pretty little chapel. These, although probably of later construction than the three churches already described, present some of the best qualities of Byzantine church architecture in miniature.

Of the strange interlude of Frankish occupation, which resulted from that most sordid of all politico-religious mockeries, the Fourth Crusade, no architectural trace remains. The brief sojourn of the feudal barons of the West, who virtually ruled Athens from Thebes, left no mark on the city. Their rapacity and chivalry, their jousting and heraldry seem strangely out of place under the blazing sky of Attica. As for the four long centuries of Ottoman domination, so low had the fortunes of Athens then sunk that only one mosque was constructed, in 1759, by an Athenian Moslem governor, who obtained good lime by burning a marble column of the temple of Olympian Zeus. Now housing an exposition of Greek handicrafts, but badly in need of repairs, the mosque of Tzistarákis adds an oriental touch to Platía Monastiráki.

MODERN ATHINA

Progress and the Pick-Axe

The recent change from the prehistoric name *Athine* to demotic *Athina* stresses the lack of historical continuity, more apparent than in any other important European capital. After the sack of the city by the Goths no building of importance was erected, with the exception of a few Byzantine shrines, until it became the capital of the new kingdom in 1834, when it was little more than an oriental village.

The first sovereign of the independent state, the Bavarian King Otho, brought with him in the second quarter of the 19th century, a group of German architects, who planned and built much of the city which existed until the 1950s. Othonian Athens was of course planned as the modest capital of a small Mediterranean state, whose main thoroughfares had only to accommodate horse-drawn traffic and pedestrian strollers (Greek pedestrians prefer to walk in the middle of the street, whether bent on business or pleasure). Long after most of the imported German architects had left Greece or died, Othonian architecture continued to flourish as the domestic style: rows of stuccoed facades, heavy wrought-iron balconies, ornamental balustrades, little porches of Ionic columns. Now it has all—or practically all—been engulfed in the maw of Progress.

The pick-axe has done its work, and the cement mixer has engendered the Athens-Piraeus conurbation, a vast capital city—choked with traffic—of apartment buildings up to 24 stories high. But there is hardly a monument to attest to the city's history for the past 18 centuries.

The centuries of decay, neglect and even oblivion reduced Athens to a village of 5,000 souls centered on a group of marble columns. But after

97

the Greek War of Independence against the Turks (1821–30) and the choice of Athens as the capital of the independent state, the village rapidly became the focus of all the reawakened social, political and commercial forces in the country. In 1834, the population of Athens, together with its port, the Piraeus, was under 10,000. It has now risen to over 4,000,000, including the outlying suburbs, which fill the entire plain from the sea to the mountains. After the evacuation of Asia Minor in 1922 and during the Communist rebellion of 1946–49, waves of refugees swamped the city resulting in the emergence of large new quarters.

Since the rapid industrialization of the 1960s, and 70s, some 100,000 country people have been settling annually in the ever-increasing circle of unplanned suburbs adding to the general overcrowding and stifling pollution.

Exploring Modern Athens

Modern Athens is centered around the twin hills of the Acropolis and Lykavitós (Lycabettus). Skirting their bases, it spreads untidily in every direction, but the center and heart of the city is Platía Sýntagma (Constitution Square, or simply Sýntagma), about midway between the two. Built on an incline, bordered with hotels and travel agencies, the central expanse of asphalt is brightened by orange trees, a fountain and several cafes, where customers sit till late at night.

Above the square are the marble and bronze bas-reliefs of the dignified Tomb of the Unknown Warrior on the marble ramp leading to a large 19th-century building, sometimes likened to a barracks: the former palace of the kings of Greece, built by Bavarian architects for King Otho. It was paid for by his father, King Ludwig I of Bavaria, who luckily vetoed the plans for a royal residence on the Acropolis, using one end of the Parthenon as the entrance and blowing up the rest. The palace was finished just in time for Otho to grant the constitution of 1843, which gave the name to the square. After the revolution of 1923, the palace served as shelter for refugees from Asia Minor, and since 1933 has housed the parliament or some substitute.

The Heart of the City

Though traffic is one-way in the center of Athens, 900,000 cars plus a startling number of buses, emitting the blackest diesel smoke imaginable, cause horrendous traffic jams, and parking is as difficult as driving. The two chief thoroughfares of the city, Stadíou, the main shopping street, and Panepistimíou, very rarely called by its "new" name, Venizelou, run northwestwards, and parallel to each other, from Sýntagma. Both streets terminate in Platía Omónias (Omónia Square), a bedlam of touts and pedlars of unambiguously ambiguous charms centered by a pool and fountain which spouts water above the underground station of the Piraeus–Athens–Kifíssia electric railway.

Halfway down Panepistimíou, an imposing group of marble buildings conjures up an illusion of Classical antiquity. They consist of the 19th-century neo-Classic structures of the Academy, adorned with a colonnade and pediment, the University, which has a colored colonnade, and the National Library, faced with a Doric portico. Statues of Athena and Apollo, on tall columns, flank either side of the Academy. Paid for by the Austro-

Greek Baron Sina, the Academy is a copy of the Parliament in Vienna. The architects were the Danish Hansen brothers, who also designed the neo-Byzantine Eye Hospital next door, adjoining the Catholic Cathedral of St. Denis. The German archeologist Schliemann's mansion, distinguished by a loggia, has been restored and is scheduled to become the Numismatic Museum. The graceful Othonian building behind the University houses the Theater Museum.

North of Omónia extends a residential area on either side of Íkosiokto (28) Oktovríou, usually called by its former name, Patissíon, leading to the Patíssia district, below the distant barrier of Párnitha (Mount Parnis). Past the neo-Classic Polytechnic and the Archaeological Museum, at the junction with Leofóros Alexandras, is one of the very few parks, resounding in summer to the tunes played by the band of a popular cabaret of distinctive *Merry Widow* flavor. One of the alleys is bordered by marble busts of the heroes of the War of Independence, and above the wispy eucalyptus treetops, rises a memorial to British Commonwealth servicemen killed in Greece in the last war, consisting of a helmeted Britannia precariously placed on top of a column, at the foot of which crouches the British lion. Britannia's hand, struck and severed by lightning, has been replaced.

Returning to Sýntagma, Leofóros Vassilíssis (Queen) Sofías, known as millionaires' row, leads past embassies, museums, the long-unfinished concert hall and the Venizelos monument to the Olympic Stadium, inaugurated for the 1982 European Games, and the northern residential suburbs of Psihikó, Filothéi and Kifissia at the foot of Pentéli, whose sides are scarred with marble quarries, both ancient and modern.

An Oasis of Parks

Leofóros Amalías runs south from Sýntagma to the Arch of Hadrian. Immediately on the left, after Parliament House, extend the National Gardens: an oasis of green in the desert of cement and marble. This delightfully informal park was laid out by a German landscape gardener at the request of Queen Amalia, in the middle of the 19th century. Its cool shady alleys are a welcome refuge from the glare and bustle of the main streets.

The National Gardens adjoin the wide walks of the Zapio Gardens, named after the benefactor who built the semi-circular edifice with a Corinthian portico. Renovated for the E.C. summit in 1983, the Zapio has since been used as a conference center. There is a good view of the Acropolis and the columns of the temple of Olympian Zeus from the gardens, a favorite strolling ground of Athenians on summer evenings when the cafe next to the exhibition hall presents musical programs.

Southeast of the Zapio lies the Stadium, from which shady Irodou Attikou (not to be confused with the theater of Herodes Atticus situated at the foot of the Acropolis) runs northward, with the National Gardens on the left. On the right the pseudo-Renaissance palace built for the first Crown Prince Constantine in the 1880s became the royal residence after the restoration in 1935. It now houses the President of the Republic; outside the gates the colorful kilted Evzones (the Presidential Guard) stand on duty: sturdy and impassive, as the tourists' cameras click.

The Evzones barracks at the corner of Leofóros Vassilíssis Sofías face the Benaki Museum at the corner of Koumbari. From there Kolonaki, the fashionable residential quarter, climbs the slopes of Mount Lycabettus. Two streets further along, at Neofitou Douka 4, is the Museum of Cycladic

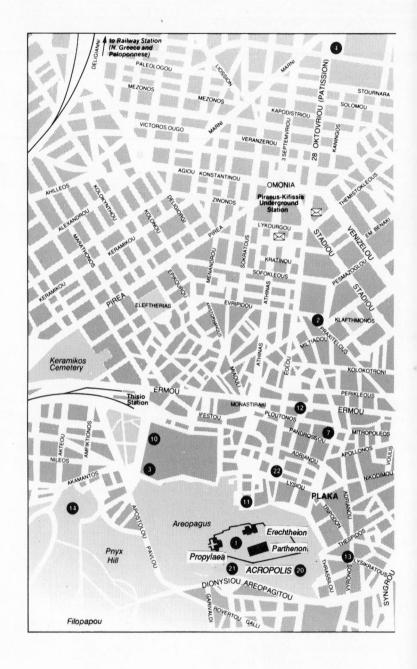

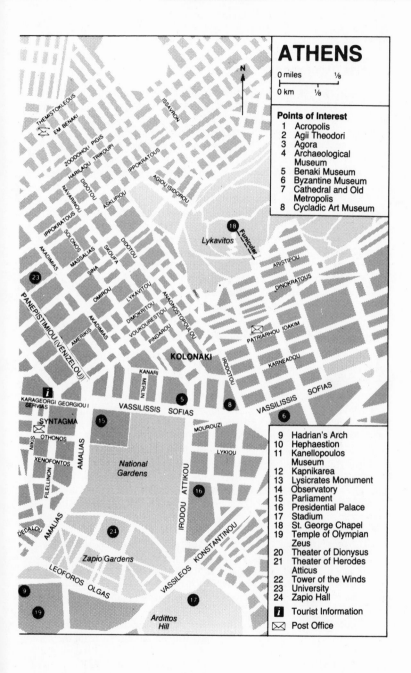

ATHENS

0 miles   1/8
0 km   1/8

Points of Interest
1 Acropolis
2 Agii Theodori
3 Agora
4 Archaeological
   Museum
5 Benaki Museum
6 Byzantine Museum
7 Cathedral and Old
   Metropolis
8 Cycladic Art Museum

9   Hadrian's Arch
10 Hephaestion
11 Kanellopoulos
    Museum
12 Kapnikarea
13 Lysicrates Monument
14 Observatory
15 Parliament
16 Presidential Palace
17 Stadium
18 St. George Chapel
19 Temple of Olympian
    Zeus
20 Theater of Dionysus
21 Theater of Herodes
    Atticus
22 Tower of the Winds
23 University
24 Zapio Hall

ℹ Tourist Information
✉ Post Office

and Ancient Greek Art. In the relentless sea of cement rising to the fringe of pines in the upper reaches, the pretty gardens in which the British and American archeological schools are set provide a pleasant break.

A Fine Panorama

The ascent of Mount Lycabettus, nearly three times the height of the Acropolis, can be made by funicular fron Aristipou Street, Kolonaki. The summit of this crag, rising sheer above the city, is crowned by the little chapel of St. George and a restaurant, but the open-air theater in a crater below is accessible by car. The view from the terrace of the chapel not only embraces all Athens filling the plain of Attica, but may include, pollution permitting, Aegina, Sálamis and the distant mountains of the Peloponnese in the west.

The last remains of 19th-century Athens are in the Plaka, a quarter climbing the northern slope of the Acropolis. This maze of narrow, winding streets and steps, small, color-washed houses with upper wooden stories, miniature Byzantine chapels, dank cellars filled with wine vats, narrow stairways lined with tavernas, and occasionally a court or tiny garden, has been partly restored. Numerous small shops display antiques, most of doubtful provenance, tourist souvenirs of equally doubtful taste and handicrafts and leather work along the pedestrian zone. Only the quieter nightspots have survived the recent clean up.

The Piraeus—Yachts, Wharves and Factories

Pireás (The Piraeus), separated from the center of Athens by ten km. (six miles) of lesser suburbia, is at once one of the great emporiums of the Levant and the main port and industrial center of Greece. The port and famous Long Walls, protecting the approach from Athens, were begun by Themistocles, the victor of Sálamis and creator of Athenian maritime power, and were finished by Pericles, who employed Greece's foremost town-planner, Hippodamus of Miletus, to lay out a new town on the gridiron system, just finished at the outbreak of the Peloponnesian War in 431 B.C. The Attic farmers sheltered behind the Long Walls, but the overcrowding rapidly spread the plague which killed more than half of the population. The victorious Spartan general Lysander ordered the Long Walls to be demolished, according to Xenophon, to the sound of flutes (though how these rather delicate instruments could have been heard over the unavoidable din is not specified). A mere ten years later, after Conon's victory over the Spartans, they rose again together with elaborate port fortifications, soon to be occupied by the Macedonians for 100 years. After Athens had yet again backed the losing side in the Roman wars, the Piraeus was destroyed so thoroughly by Sulla in 86 B.C. that recovery took almost two millennia, until after the establishment of the Greek kingdom in the 19th century.

The relentless urge to cover the entire Attic plain with concrete has spread wharves and dockyards, mills, factories and foundries from the sea to the barren ridge of Mount Egáleo. The main harbor, one of the busiest in the Mediterranean, is crowded with ships flying the flags of all nations; from the central quay, the numerous island ferries bound for the different archipelagos, sail at all hours of the day. On Epiphany, January 6, the "Blessing of the Waters" is celebrated by the Archbishop of Athens and

All Greece in the presence of the government with great solemnity. Church bells clang and sirens hoot deafeningly as the cross is thrown into the sea, more often than not to be hauled up by a rope as on a cold day youths no longer dive after it into the chilly waters.

But the small vessels of antiquity anchored in the infinitely more attractive two semi-circular basins facing south towards Aegina. From the extreme tip of the Piraeus promontory a coastal road runs parallel to the foundations of Conon's fortifications to the larger basin, the well-equipped port of Zéa, with mooring and wintering facilities for yachts. The waterfront is bordered with open-air cafes, extending to the Naval Museum at the further end below the meager remains of a Hellenistic theater next to the Archaeological Museum. The road winds round the steep headland of Kastélla, which is topped by the Bowling Center and the Veákio open-air amphitheater. This amphitheater greatly improves on the ancient models by providing backrests, so that the performances of ancient dramas and folk dances can be enjoyed to the full against the superb backdrop of the Saronikós Gulf and Mount Hymettus. Below the Yacht Club, smaller, crescent-shaped Mikrolímano—until recently Turkolímano—is crowded with sailing craft and lined with fish restaurants to the fill-in that extends across the wide Bay of Fáliro (Phaleron), the most ancient roadstead of Athens, where visiting warships and very large cruise liners still anchor. At Néo (New) Fáliro is the Palais des Sports, which officials insist on calling the Stadium of Peace and Friendship, and which is claimed to be Europe's largest covered arena. Besides sport, this concrete excrescence is used for political gatherings and rock concerts. The surrounding installations, including a circular open-air theater, are no more aesthetic but at least smaller. A very fancy concrete-bordered canal is perhaps intended to divert attention from the brown slime at the mouth of the Ilissos, whose banks were once favorite walks of Socrates and his disciples, but which has been degraded into a partly open sewer.

But then even sewers may have unexpected uses. Repairing one some 30 years ago, workmen discovered a number of ancient statues of great archaeological value imbedded in the soil. Among these were a superb *kouros* (young man) in perfect condition (now known as the *Apollo of Pireus*), a helmeted Athena in a beautifully draped full-length robe, an Artemis with quiver and bolt, and a handsome Hellenistic maiden. These bronze statues were probably stored by the Romans after Sulla's sack of Athens in 86 B.C., with the intention of shipping them to Rome. Why the shipment was never made can only remain a matter of conjecture.

In Greece the past is omnipresent. When a bus hit the olive tree under which Plato supposedly lectured at his academy on the sacred way to Eleusis, the Greek atomic commission obligingly certified the tree's age by carbon dating as 2,500 years. The remaining roots sprouted a new olive bush beside the mangled trunk. After this propitious reanimation, the Academy grounds were made into a park.

PRACTICAL INFORMATION FOR ATHENS

WHEN TO COME. As in most places, spring and early fall are best. In May, when it is warm without being too hot, Athens is at its best; the beaches are not yet overcrowded and the countryside around the city has not yet been parched by months of blazing sunshine. But October and early November are also good, with days of mellow sunshine, and are an ideal period for sightseeing. July-August-September is the peak of the tourist season. The heat is sometimes intense, and the nearer bathing beaches are always overcrowded and often badly polluted. In winter, though the rains rarely last more than a few days and snow makes only one or two appearances, the city has less appeal than in the other seasons.

TOURIST OFFICES. There are tourist information (G.N.T.O.) offices in the bank at Karageorgi Servias 2 (tel. 322 2545); at East Elleniko airport (tel. 970 2395); and at Piraeus, Marina Zeas (tel. 413 5716).

HOTELS. Athens hotels are, on the whole, adequate in each price range, but remember that the Greek word for hotel is *xenodochion,* meaning container for strangers. And, with some notable exceptions, this is exactly what they are: adequate for a rest and a wash, but not to spend any time in. The Greeks are an outdoor people and they rarely spend much time at home, let alone in an hotel. Where there are public rooms, besides restaurants and mini-bars, they are dark and forbidding.

Try to avoid rooms fronting the street, as they tend to be noisy. Go instead for those overlooking the courtyard. Reserve well in advance, especially from June to September.

All listed Moderate hotels have restaurants and are airconditioned, unless otherwise stated, but there is very little to distinguish one from another other than location. Inexpensive hotels do not have either restaurants or airconditioning unless stated. Most better hotels provide baby sitters. If not, consult the daily *Athens News* or *Athens Star.*

Deluxe

Athenaeum Intercontinental, Syngrou 89 (tel. 902 3666). 580 rooms, 20 suites. This large hotel is about a 15-minute walk down Syngrou from Hadrian's Arch. *La Rôtisserie* has a French chef; *Kubla Khan* offers Mongolian specialties; *Première,* on the 9th floor, and with a fabulous view of the Acropolis, serves all kinds of kebabs; *Café Pergola* looks out over the small ground floor pool and serves Sunday brunch; *Club Labyrinthos* disco; *Kava Bar* open to 2 A.M.; night club, roofgarden pool. AE, DC, MC, V.

Athens Hilton, Vassilíssis Sofías 46 (tel. 722 0201/10). 473 rooms, 3 main and several junior suites; 83 rooms plus 4 suites set apart on the two executive top floors. Slightly off-center in luxurious residential district near the U.S. Embassy. Oldest of the international chain hotels, but updated in 1985. *Ta Nissia* is a Greek-style taverna; *Kellari* specializes in wines and snacks. The *Byzantine Café* also serves a few specialties; while more pleasant is eating at the large pool in summer. Roofgarden *Galaxy* does lunches and is a piano bar at night. AE, DC, MC, V.

Caravel, Vassiléos Alexandrou 2 (tel. 729 0721/60). 450 rooms, 25 suites. This earthquake-proofed hotel near the Hilton has an Italian restaurant, bouzouki tavern; piano bar and roofgarden pool; inhouse mosque. AE, DC, MC.

Grande Bretagne, Syntagma (tel. 323 0251/10). Maintains its great tradition in enlarged and modernized premises in the heart of the city. The restaurant and bar are favorite meeting places. AE, DC, MC, V.

Ledra Marriott, Syngrou 113 (tel. 934 7711). 258 rooms, 20 suites. Rooms facing noisy Syngrou are soundproofed. Like the other American chain representatives, out of the center, but this is also the best for food and service. *Bali Lounge* and *Kona Kai* Polynesian restaurant—expensive but worth it—complete with waterfall; *Ledra Grill, Zephyros Cafe,* meals and refreshments at all hours, and outstanding Sunday buffet brunch. Roofgarden barbecue round pool. AE, DC, MC, V.

N.J.V. Meridien, Syntagma (tel. 325 5301/9). 170 rooms, 12 suites. A member of the French luxury chain, so special attention is paid to the orig-
● inal *Brasserie des Arts* with its French cuisine and superb service. *The Athenian Bistro* serves Greek snacks and a buffet every evening. Same fine view as its neighbor, the Grande Bretagne. AE, DC, MC, V.

Expensive

Athens Chandris, Syngrou 385 (tel. 941 4824/6). 386 rooms. Pool, roofgarden. A fair way out of town towards the sea.

Delice, Vassileos Alexandrou 3 (tel. 723 8311/3). Service flats, next to Caravel Hotel; 20 suites. AE, DC, MC, V.

Divani Palace Acropolis, Parthenonos 19 (tel. 922 2945/9). 253 rooms. Near the Plaka district; pool. AE, DC, MC, V.

Electra Palace, Nikodimou 18 (tel. 324 1401/7). 106 rooms, 5 suites. On the quiet fringe of the Plaka; roofgarden pool. AE, DC, MC, V.

Golden Age, Mihalakopoulou 57 (tel. 724 0861/9). 122 rooms. More than adequate hotel near the Holiday Inn; disco. AE, DC, V.

Herodion, Rovertou Galli 4 (tel. 923 6832/6). 90 rooms. This place is clean, cool and close to the Acropolis; roofgarden. AE, DC, MC, V.

Holiday Inn, Mihalakopoulou 50 (tel. 724 8322/9). 200 rooms, 8 suites. Near the Hilton, with bowling alley, disco, and 24-hour coffee shop. The recently renovated *Bistro Greek* is a creditable restaurant. AE, DC, MC, V.

Park, Leofóros Alexandras 10 (tel. 883 2711/19). 145 rooms. Restaurant *Latina,* nightclub. Very reasonable for what it offers.

President, Kifissias 43 (tel. 692 4600). 513 rooms. Largest and furthest from the center in this category, but in good residential district; night club, roofgarden, pool. AE, DC, MC, V.

Riva, Mihalakopoulou 114 (tel. 770 6611/5). 56 rooms, 19 studios, 7 apartments. The Riva has an outstanding restaurant that is worth visiting; near the Hilton. AE, DC, V.

St. George Lycabettus, Kleomenous 2 (tel. 729 0710/19). 150 rooms, in a lovely position above central Athens, in the Kolonaki district. Excellent rooftop restaurant, *Le Grand Balcon,* with marvelous view.

Zafolia, Leofóros Alexandras 87 (tel. 644 9012). 191 rooms, 8 suites. A little far from the center, but good value; roofgarden pool and minigolf. AE, DC, MC, V.

Moderate

Alexandros, Timoleontos Vassou 8 (tel. 643 0464/10). 96 rooms. Near the U.S. Embassy; garage. AE, DC, V.

Alfa, Halkokondyli 17 (tel. 524 3584). 88 rooms. Near Omonia. DC, V.

Arethusa, Mitropoleos 6 (tel. 322 9431/9). 87 rooms. Just off Syntagma; roofgarden. AE, DC, MC, V.

Athens Gate, Leofóros Syngrou 10 (tel. 923 8302/9). 106 rooms. Opposite Hadrian's Arch, but the price for the fine view is the noise from the major thoroughfare, though back rooms are quiet. Clean, modern decor. AE, DC, MC, V.

Athinaïs, Vassilíssis Sofias 99 (tel. 643 1133). 84 rooms. Conveniently placed near the U.S. Embassy, this hotel has a roofgarden. AE, DC, MC, V.

Candia, Deliyanni 40 (tel. 524 6112/7). 142 rooms. Near Omonia; small roofgarden pool. AE, DC.

Christina, Petmeza 15 (tel. 921 5353). 93 rooms. Fairly near the Acropolis. V.

Clare's House, Sorvolou 24 (tel. 922 2288). 20 rooms. This spotless pension is in a quiet location up steep Sorvolou. It's an excellent value in an up-market area.

Dorian Inn, 15–19 Pireos (tel. 523 9782). 146 rooms. Swimming pool on roof.

Hera, Falirou 9 (tel. 923 6682). 49 rooms. It's good situation, near the Acroplis, makes up for the small rooms. Roofgarden and garage. AE, DC.

Lycabette, Valaoritou 6 (tel. 363 3514/8). 39 rooms. Only hotel in the tiny, quiet pedestrian zone off Leofóros Venizelou, with good view from the topfloor rooms with balconies; no restaurant. AE, DC, MC, V.

La Mirage, M. Kotopouli 3, Omonia (tel. 523 4071/3). 208 rooms, partly soundproofed. New.

Marathon, Karolou 23 (tel. 523 1865/8). 93 rooms. Near Omonia. AE, DC.

Minoa, Karolou 12 (tel. 523 4622/4). 42 rooms. Near Omonia. AE, DC, V.

Myrto, Nikis 40 (tel. 322 7237). 12 rooms. Just off Syntagma; this hotel is worth the price. AE, V.

Omiros, Appollonos 15 (tel. 323 5486). 37 rooms. On the fringe of the Plaka. AE, DC, V.

Oscar, Samou 25 (tel. 883 4215/9). 124 rooms. Near railway station; disco, roofgarden. AE, DC.

Pan, Mitropleos 11 (tel. 323 7816/9). 48 rooms. Near Syntagma; no restaurant. AE, DC, MC, V.

Stanley, Platia Karaiskaki (tel. 524 1611/8). 395 rooms. Near Omonia; small roofgarden pool. AE, V.

Inexpensive

Acropolis House, Kodhrou 6 (tel. 322 2344). 19 rooms. Located in the Plaka; this small place is a good value. AE, DC, V.

Alkistis, Platia Theatrou 18 (tel. 321 9811/9). 120 rooms. Near Omonia; roofgarden restaurant. AE, DC, MC, V.

Art Gallery Pension, Erehtheou 3 (tel. 923 1933). 19 pleasantly furnished rooms. In the center of the Plaka.

Athens Connection Hostel, Ioulianou 20 (tel. 821 3940). 26 rooms, with singles and doubles as well as 4-bed dorms. At present, this is the most comfortable of several hostels near the rail station.

Athinea, Vilara 9 (tel. 524 3884/5). 42 rooms. Airconditioned. Near Omonia.

Austria, Mouson 7 (tel. 923 5151). 40 rooms. Below the Hill of the Muses, opposite the Acropolis. AE, DC, V.

Capri, Psaromilingou 6 (tel. 325 2085). 44 rooms. Airconditioned, roofgarden restaurant.

Erechthion, Flammarion 8 (tel. 345 9606). 22 rooms; in this Thission area. Near the Acropolis.

Filoxenia, Aharnon 50 (tel. 882 8611/5). 51 rooms. Airconditioned, restaurant. V.

Ionis, Halkokondyli 41 (tel. 523 2311/4). 102 rooms. Airconditioned, restaurant.

King Jason, Kolonou 26 (tel. 523 4721). 114 rooms. Restaurant.

Museum, Bouboulinas 16 (tel. 360 5611/3). 58 rooms. Nicely situated, near the Acropolis, park, and the Archaeological Museum. AE, DC.

Omonia, Platia Omonias 4 (tel. 523 7210/20). 260 rooms. Restaurant, bar. AE.

Paradise Hostel, Mezonos 28 (tel. 522 0084). Rooms with 2 to 6 beds. Close to railroad station.

Plaza, Aharnon 78 (tel. 822 5111/6). 116 rooms. Airconditioned, restaurant.

Theoxenia, Gladstonos 6 (tel. 360 0250). 59 rooms. Restaurant. AE, V.

In Piraeus

Moderate

Castella, Vassileos Pavlou 75 (tel. 411 4735). 33 rooms. On the Kastella headland with a lovely view over the Saronic Gulf.

Cavo d'Oro, Vassiléos Pavlou 19 (tel. 411 3742). 74 rooms. Disco and roofgarden; similar fine position as hotel above. AE, DC, MC, V.

Diogenis, Vassiléos Georgiou 27 (tel. 412 5471/5). 78 rooms. Disco and small roofgarden pool; near harbor. AE, DC, MC, V.

Omiridion, Harliaou Trikoupi 32 (tel. 451 9811/5). 59 rooms. Disco and roofgarden; near harbor. AE, DC, MC, V.

Park, Kolokotroni 103 (tel. 452 4611/5). 80 rooms. Disco and roofgarden; near harbor. AE, DC, MC, V.

Savoy, Vassiléos Konstantinou 93 (tel. 413 1102/8). 71 rooms. Roofgarden; near harbor. AE, DC, MC, V.

Inexpensive

Anemoni, Karaoli Dimitriou 65 (tel. 411 1768). 45 rooms. V.

Atlantis, Notara 138 (tel. 452 6871/4). 54 rooms.

Capitol, Filonos 147 (tel. 452 4911/4). 56 rooms.

Cavo, Filonos 79 (tel. 411 6134/5). 47 rooms. Near harbor. DC.

Diana, Filellinon 11 (tel. 452 5020). 41 rooms.

Lilia, Zeas 131 (tel. 417 9108). 17 rooms. Facing the yacht harbor.

RESTAURANTS. Athens has a number of expensive (and some very expensive) restaurants aiming at French or international cuisine, not always successfully. Lesser places perhaps do not provide culinary experiences, but at least they don't cost much.

Outside the deluxe hotels, the international restaurants are grouped around the Hilton Hotel, Sýntagma or the central Kolonaki quarter. The Plaka district below the Acropolis hill features the largest number of tavernas. These are listed separately below, as are the seafood restaurants in Piraeus and on Syngrou, which connects Athens with the sea.

Expensive

L'Abreuvoir, Xenokratous 51 (tel. 722 9061). One of the most popular and expensive French restaurants in Kolonaki, this place is elegant and romantic. Two specialties here are the steak tartare and spinach tart. Closed Mon. AE, DC, MC, V.

Athenaeum, Amerikis 8 (tel. 363 1125). Off Panepistimiou. This rather grand restaurant (*the Bistrot*) serves fresh Scotch salmon for lunch and dinner accompanied by piano music. The *Kellari* basement tavern, dinner only, is a little less expensive. DC.

Avance, Xenokratous 43 (tel. 723 8687). Kolonaki. Specialty esçalope Parisienne, vol-au-vent Cardinal; piano and singer at night. Top of its category.

Bajazzo, Ploutarhou 35 (tel. 729 1420). Excellent service in converted Kolonaki mansion, with fancy and expensive cuisine by Austrian chef. Specialities include vine leaves stuffed with sea bass mousse and swordfish stuffed with mussells in a saffron sauce. AE, DC.

Balalaika, Antinoros 36 (tel. 724 6287). Russian restaurant with French cuisine and a nostalgic muscial program. Very expensive. Closed Sun. AE, DC.

Blue Bayou, Meandrou 15 (tel. 724 8676). Opposite Holiday Inn. Continental cuisine plus Creole and Cajun specialties. AE, DC, MC, V.

Chang's House, Doiranis 15 (tel. 959 5179). Chefs from Taipei and Hong Kong. Dinner and business lunch, except Sunday. AE, DC.

Le Calvados, Alkmanos 5 (tel. 722 6291). Another French effort; closed Sun. AE, DC, V.

China, Efroniou 72 (tel. 723 3200). Probably the best of several Chinese spots in town. AE, DC.

Al Convento, Anapiron Polemou 4 (tel. 723 9163). This good Italian spot serves pasta and scalloppine. closed Sun. DC.

Da Walter, adjoining above, same management but more expensive (tel. 724 8726). DC.

Dionyssos, Robertou Galli 43 (tel. 923 3182). Fine view of the Acropolis opposite. Moderate-priced version on Lycabettus; good for charcoal-broiled shrimps. Closed Sun. DC.

Fatsios, Efroniou 5 (tel. 721 7421). Good selection of Greek and Middle East specialties; lunch only. DC.

Gerofinikas, Pindarou 10 (tel. 362 2719). Slightly pretentious restaurant skillfully hidden; selection of Greek and Turkish specialties. Cosmopolitan atmosphere. AE, DC, MC, V.

Grande Bretagne Corner, Grande Bretagne Hotel (tel. 323 0251). Outstanding for atmosphere and service at very reasonable prices; less a part of the hotel than the other restaurants due to its direct entrance from Panepistimiou. AE, DC, MC, V.

Je Reviens, Xenokratus 49 (tel. 721 1174). Good French restaurant in Kolonaki, with piano music. AE, DC, MC, V.

Maralinas, Vrassida 11 (tel. 723 5425). Behind the Hilton. Lebanese specialties with an Oriental *plat du jour;* and at dinner Oriental song and dance. Pricewise at the top of its category. AE, DC, MC, V.

Michel, Filellinon 15 (tel. 323 1315). Near Syntagma. Dinner only, with musical program and dancing. Closed Sun. AE, DC.

Michiko, Kidathineon 27 (tel. 322 0980). Unusual but nonetheless pleasantly situated top-class Japanese restaurant in the largest surviving mansion in the Plaka, with small garden; closed Sun. AE, DC, V.

Nautilus, Fthiotidos 6 (tel. 693 0089). Unusual, varied Continental and Greek dishes by Mýkonos' best-known chef. Elegant Cycladic building with seagoing ambience. Dinner only. AE, DC.

L'Orangerie, Efroniou 55 (tel. 724 2735). Opposite the Caravel Hotel. French food to piano music at dinner in a charming decor. AE, DC.

Prince of Wales, Sinopis 14 (tel. 777 8008). Steakhouse and pub. Good at all times, especially for business lunch. The speciality here is steak in burgundy sauce. Closed Sat., Sun. AE, DC.

Prunier, Ipsilantou 63 (tel. 722 7379). No connection with its famous Parisian namesake, but still fairly French; a speciality is Wellington fillet. Closed Sun. AE, DC, V.

Stage Coach, Leoforos Kifissias 18 (tel. 671 0091). This popular steak house has relocated to the northern suburb, Paradiso. Steaks are broiled to your order and the service is good. AE, DC.

Steak Room, Eginitou 6 (tel. 721 7445). The best of the steak houses, excellent meat from own supply; charcoal broils and genuine French snails; closed Sun. AE, DC, MC, V.

Tabula, Pondou 40 (tel. 771 0824). Behind the Riva Hotel, and with a wide choice and well-stocked bar; closed Sun. DC.

Vengera, Aristippou 34 (tel. 724 4327). Good variety and near the funicular; closed Sun. AE, DC.

Seafood Restaurants

The choicest concentration among the hundreds of fish taverns along the Attic coasts are in Piraeus on Akti Koumoundourou in the picturesque fishing port of Mikrolímano below the Yacht Club. For much of the year food is served on the water's edge, especially at lunch time. They can be very crowded on summer evenings, particularly at weekends, and hover between upper-Moderate and Expensive.

Aglamair, Akti Koumoundourou 54 (tel. 411 5511). The most expensive of the bunch, with the accent on lobsters. AE, DC, MC, V.

Bouillabaisse, Zisimopoulou 28 (tel. 941 9082). Behind the Planetarium on Syngrou, but any resemblance to the Marseilles original is purely accidental; nonetheless good fresh fish and shell fish.

El Greco, Akti Koumoundourou 24 (tel. 412 7324). Excellent shrimps. AE, DC, MC, V.

Kranai, Akti Koumoundourou 34 (tel. 417 0156). The speciality here is prawns in cheese and tomato sauce. AE, DC, MC, V.

Red Boat, Akti Koumoundourou 18 (tel. 417 5853). One of the oldest and still fairly reasonable.

Zorbas, Akti Koumoundourou 14 (tel. 411 1663). Stuffed mussels. AE, DC.

Moderate

Dionyssos, on top of Lycabettus (tel. 722 6374). Cheaper version of the one opposite the Acropolis. Reached by funicular railway starting on top of Ploutarhou. Commands sweeping view of the whole town. Cafe and snack bar beside restaurant open 9 A.M. to 11:45 P.M. AE, DC, MC, V.

Drugstore, Korai St., in the passage, (tel. 352 6464). Restaurant, *ouzeri* and cafe.

Flame Steak House, Hatziyanni Mexi 9 (tel. 723 8540). Charcoal broiled steaks and chops; bar. AE, DC.

Hermion, Pandrossou 15 (tel. 324 6725). Has a charming garden court. Also has fixed priced menu. AE, DC, MC, V.

Ideal, Panepistimíou 46 (tel. 361 4604). Exceptionally large menu, always busy but with excellent service. DC.

Jimmy's Cooking, Peace and Friendship Stadium (tel. 489 3275). Great for the price. AE, V.

Juicy, Loukianou 34 (tel. 722 4817). This is a vegetarian restaurant with a wide selection of exotic fruits and juices, served in generous portions and mixed with excellent ingredients.

Miltons, Adrianou 91 (tel. 324 9129). This delightful oasis of overhanging trees and white umbrellas in the busy Plaka specializes in seafood and an unusual Greek salad. Good for both business lunches and evenings. AE, DC, V.

Orient, Lekka 26 (tel. 322 1992). Near Syntagma. Korean specialties like oyster and mussel soup.

Othello's, Mihalakopoulou 45 (tel. 729 1481). International cuisine. Very reasonable for a place of its type. AE, DC, MC, V.

Ploughman, Iridanou 26 (tel. 721 2623). English food; dartboard.

Possidon, corner of Adrianou and Kapnikareas (tel. 322 3822). Cuisine not remarkable, but the situation compensates.

Inexpensive

American Coffee Shop and Restaurant, Karageorgi Servias 1 (tel. 324 8673). A very good place to know, excellent for a snack or a proper meal, and quick. Closed Sun.

American Restaurant, Mitropoleos 3 (tel. 322 8155), in the passage. A bit basic, but good value.

Delfi, Nikis 13 (tel. 323 4869). Extremely popular, often crowded with locals. Excellent Greek and other dishes.

Diros, Xenofondos 10 (tel. 323 2392). Also very near Syntagma. Geared to tourists (in a good sense).

Eden, Flessa 3 (tel. 324 8858). Vegetarian restaurant with a range of excellent dishes, in a charming old house in Plaka. Closed Wed.

Floca, Emm. Benaki 16 (tel. 363 3550). Immediate self-service restaurant. Closed Sat. evening and Sun.

Kentrikon, Kolokotroni 3 (tel. 323 2482). Standard, reliable, but somewhat uninspiring. Not open at night or on Sat., Sun.

Nea Olympia, Emm. Benaki 3 (tel. 321 7972). Another favorite place especially for a good midday meal. Closed Sat. evening and Sun.

Sidrivani, Filellinon 5 (tel. 323 8662). Good, mainly Greek, food in a charming small garden.

Informal Eating

Fast Food. These are now to be found all over Athens and elsewhere, and vary enormously, from small places with Greek-type food to large American-style establishments. Among the best are: **Mr. Trip,** Mihalakopoulou and Iridanou corner; **Galleria,** Venizelou 52; **Goody's,** Solonos 108; **Spyro's Gyro,** Alexandras 118.

Snack-bars. Again a fairly new development. Most have fresh juices. **Si,** Venizelou 9b; **Jimmy's Coffeeshop,** Valaoritou 7; **Mövenpick,** Akadimias 28. There is a quiet cafeteria open to the public at the Y.W.C.A., Amerikas 11, and the **Bretannia,** Omonia, apart from having traditional Greek sweets, does fried eggs etc. at all hours.

Psistaria (charcoal grills) abound in the small pedestrian zone off Omonia. No, you won't get a steak—which in any case should only be ordered in top-grade establishments—but try *doner kebab,* a huge hunk of pressed and seasoned meat turning outside on a spit. Also available in grillrooms are chicken, *souvlakia, keftedakia* (usually with salad) and *tiri feta* (goat's cheese) which is tasty but salty. Rather more humble are the *souvlaki* shops, selling freshly grilled pieces of meat on a skewer, with pieces of *pitta* or bread.

Pizzerias now abound, and may be full-scale restaurants or stand-up places on the street. Choose the most crowded! There are several excellent pie shops near Kolonaki Square, on Skoufa, Irakleitou and Tsakalof.

Local Color

Tavernas. The moderately priced and more genuinely Greek tavernas the tourist is likely to sample are mostly in the Plaka. An orchestra of three guitarists is common; without them the food improves. In winter they are frequented by Greeks, but in the summer the small gardens and tables on the pavements are almost entirely taken over by tourists. If, like the Athenians, you don't mind braving the chaotic traffic, drive to the open-air tavernas and nightclubs stretching along the coast from Faliro to Sounio. But you will need a car as the buses in the evening are infrequent and crowded.

Aerides, M. Avrilou 3, Plaka (tel. 322 6266). Looks onto the Tower of the Winds. Inexpensive fixed price menus.

Bakaliarakia, Kydathineon 41 (tel. 332 5084). Specializes in cod, as the name indicates, best with garlic mash; in the classical Plaka basement.

Kostoyannis, Zaimi 37 (tel. 821 2496). Near the Archeological Museum. Excellent selection, from expensive *mezedes* and fresh seafood to desserts; closed Sun.

O Platanos, Diogenous 4 (tel. 322 0666). One of the oldest Plaka tavernas; no music so prices are low for what is offered in the large garden.

Palia Taverna Stamatopoulou, Lysiou 26 (tel. 322 8722). As lively and typical a place as you will find.

Psarra, Erehtheou 16 (tel. 325 0285). Specialty here is swordfish kebab; casual, friendly place—sometimes has music. Closed in winter.

Socrates' Prison, Mitseon 20 (tel. 671 3997). Named not after the philosopher but after the owner of the taverna; opposite the Acropolis. Speciality here is rolled pork with carrots and celery; closed Sun.

Theophilos, Vakhou 1 (tel. 322 3901). Above average food and good open rosé; closed Sun.

Vassilena, Etolikou 72 (tel. 461 2457). The only fish tavern to be highly recommended; in Piraeus (to the right facing the main harbor). You don't order, but are served some 20 seafood *hors d'oeuvres* before soup, chicken and fruit, with unlimited retsina; and all for an astoundingly low price. Perhaps the cheapest meal in town for quality and quantity.

Xynou, Angelou Geronta 4 (tel. 322 1065). Large but fairly quiet and perhaps the best truly Greek taverna in Athens, thus Greek customers all the year round. It's a little difficult to find, but worth asking the way. Food more pleasing than decor.

Zafiris, Thespidos 4 (tel. 322 5460). *The* place for game (chosen from colorful cards presented by the owner) and unchanged since 1918, and hence deceptively simple. Reservations essential; closed Sun.

Tourist Tavernas. Concentrated in the Plaka, these places have a local color which is all too obviously artificial. They are fairly expensive nightclubs and have floor shows but call themselves tavernas nonetheless (and indeed stress their Greekness not only in the nature of their shows but in their very indifferent food). Among the best are:

Dionyssos, Lysiou 7 (tel. 322 7589). DC, MC, V.

Kalokerinos, Kekropos 10 (tel. 323 2054). DC.

Mostrou, Minisikleous 22 (tel. 324 2441). Can usually be relied upon for a good show. AE, DC, MC.

Palia Athena, Flessa 4 (tel. 322 2000). The closest of all to a cabaret, but with a strong Greek element. AE, DC, MC, V.

Stratos, Eilellinon 15 (tel. 323 1315), near Syntagma. Perhaps more strictly Greek than the others.

Vrahos, Adrianou 101 (tel. 324 7575). DC, V.

Cafes, Sweetshops. Though still the social center of remoter villages, the traditional *kafenío,* in which a goodly proportion of the male population spent hours over tiny cups of Turkish (now Greek) coffee, playing backgammon or more often just lounging about, has almost vanished from the towns. Its place has been taken by western-style cafes, tea houses, and *zaharoplastia* (sweetshops), which, wherever possible, extend over the sidewalk or take up entire squares. Athenians keep late hours, sitting over ices and rich cream cakes summer and winter alike. Most cafes and sweetshops fall into the Moderate price range.

There are many large cafes on Syntagma, very agreeable to sit at when it isn't too hot. The best are **Dionyssos** and **Papaspyrou** (which also has a self-service restaurant); **Everyday,** on Stadiou and Voukourestiou corner, and **Zonar's** (which also has a restaurant) are a cut above the Syntagma places. There are very pleasant, slightly quieter, cafes round Kolonaki Square; some offer light meals. Good indoor cafes are the **Drugstore,** Korai passage, **Ermis,** Ermou 56, and upstairs at Pandrossou 36, a fascinating place full of handicrafts. The **Filomousa,** Platia Filomouson 1, has everything, except meals, in a fine old house on a small Plaka square. Also in the Plaka is **To Tristato,** on the corner of Dedhalou and Angelou Yeronda, with coffee, cakes and salads; quaint and comfortable if rather expensive. **De Profundis,** in an old mansion at Hatzimichali 1, serves herb teas, homemade pastries, and quiches. It's reasonable despite being trendy.

The large hotels mostly have excellent coffee shops—the most popular is the **Byzantine Cafe** at the Hilton.

Ouzerí. These drinking establishments, named after the national aperitif, are the only genuine local bars, but there are very few anywhere in the country as drinking is nearly always accompanied by a meal (which helps account for the remarkably small number of drunks).

Apotsos, Venizelou 10 (tel. 363 7046). The capital's oldest and most original *ouzerí,* with amusing old posters, and a favorite of resident Anglo Saxons. Wide selection of ouzo from all over Greece accompanied by appropriate mezedes.

Drugstore, in the passage off Korai Street (tel. 352 6464). A very good place to know.

Salamandra, Matzarou 3, in Kolonaki (tel. 364 2990). The most elegant Athens *ouzerí,* in neo-classical mansion. *Mezedes* of mushrooms with bacon. Closed Sun.

Yialí Kafenis, Ploutarhou 13, Kolonaki (tel. 722 5846). Small and elegant.

Piano Bar Restaurants. These newcomers on the Athens scene usually have a singer or two and are lively, enjoyable, and sometimes expensive. Bar-hopping presents no problems, given the geography of the main concentrations, which are around the Hilton and in Kolonaki.

Entre Nous, Alopekis 9 (tel. 729 1669). Piano bar. AE, V.

Fame Club, Levendi 3 (tel. 723 0507). Drinks and snacks.

Mets, Markou Mousouri 14 (tel. 922 9494). This fashionable French-style brasserie serves food and wine; the latter very expensive.

Mike's, Vassileos Alexandrou 5 (tel. 729 1689). Fashionable and quite expensive.

Montparnasse, Haritos 32 (tel. 729 0746). Three-level bar restaurant favored by the theater crowd. DC.

Public, Hadjiyanni Mexi 6 (tel. 721 6258). Located in the Hilton area; this restaurant has a pub-like atmosphere.

Remezzo, Haritos 6 (tel. 722 8950). Intimate, and very chic. Closed Sun. AE, DC.

NIGHTLIFE. In all nightspots, 3 A.M. closing has been decreed, though it is not always observed, especially in summer when the scene moves to the coast. Classification of the various establishments is not easy as several nightclubs double their dance orchestras with bouzoukia orchestras, or alternatively might suddenly restrict themselves to one of the two, or even convert themselves to discos or cabarets. Staying power and consistency of individual spots must, therefore, be a decisive factor in the determination of our listings.

Cabarets. Unlike the tourist tavernas in the Plaka, the main accent, in Athens cabaret spots, is on the international as opposed to the local. They are all expensive, though fairly cheap in every other respect by western standards. All are in the center.

Among them are:

Copacabana, Kallirois 4, opposite the Temple of Olympian Zeus (tel. 923 2648). Striptease, among the other pleasures offered, mainly English dancers.

Maxim, Othonos 6, Syntagma (tel. 323 4831). Hungarian dancers and oriental striptease.

Mocambo, Mihalakopoulou 23 (tel. 724 8052), near the Hilton. Similar but less expensive.

Bouzoukia. Greece's contribution to nightlife was introduced in the 1920s by refugees from Asia Minor, who danced to a large clanging Oriental version of the mandoline in numerous humble taverns in the suburbs, especially in the Piraeus area. In the '50s, the odd rhythms of this popular music were taken up by the Athenian smart set as the true expression of Greek entertainment, displaying a fine disregard of its obvious Anatolian and Balkan influences. It thus became established as the genuine local noise; tourists should have one go, few will desire a second. Food in the *bouzoukia* is sinfully expensive for what is offered, and if you have fruit only you don't get away with paying any less. In the larger *bouzoukia,* orchestras often feature a female vocalist generously amplified by loudspeakers.

Unlike in the tourist tavernas, the dances are not performed by professionals but by the customers. The nostalgic *zeimbékiko* is a solo dance for men, with the dancer bending down to run his hand piously across the ground. Likewise dealing with exile, the faithlessness of women, death and similar popular themes, the *hassápiko,* the butcher's dance, originated in Constantinople. It is performed by two or three people, and increasingly by women these days—hissing and snapping their fingers to a rhythm clearly marked by footbeats. The steps are precise and intricate, with graceful bending and stretching of the knees. The only joyful tunes and refrains are those that accompany the *sérviko,* which, as its name declares, is of Serbian antecedence, quick, lively, almost acrobatic. The *tsiftetéli* is a debased oriental belly dance performed by a man. Because of the noise and shouting, several of the most popular are along the motorway, out of reach for the average tourist. The most fashionable, largest and loudest are on Leofóros Syngrou, and there are more scattered along Leofóros Posidonos, the coastal road of Néo Fáliro.

Athina, Leofóros Syngrou 165 (tel. 934 3485). AE.

Athinaia, Leofóros Posidonos 63 (tel. 942 3089). Highly prized and priced.

Babis Kifissia, Othonos 26 (tel. 801 3926). Closed Mon.

Diogenes, Leofóros Syngrou 255 (tel. 942 4267). Not purely *bouzouki.* Expensive and ritzy. Closed Tues. AE.

Hryso Vareli, Leofóros Posidonos 33 (tel. 942 2858). Closed Thurs.

Iphigenia, Leofóros Syngrou 201 (tel. 934 9444).

Lido, Zoodohou Pigis 3 (tel. 362 3933). In the center.

Pavillion, Mesogeion 329 (tel. 671 4362). Closed Tues.

Regina, Leofóros Syngrou 140 (tel. 922 8902). The cheapest. Closed Sun.

Boites. Their number has been greatly reduced since the closing of numerous low-ceilinged, dark, smoky and rather claustrophobic nightspots in the Plaka. Some folk and revolutionary songs are still strummed out, mainly in the Exarhia district, but other places have gone up in the world and feature top singers. The admission price includes one drink and ranges from about 600 dr. to 2,000 dr.

Esperides, Thoulou 6, Plaka (tel. 322 5482).

Klotho, Ippokratous 56 (tel. 360 5790). No cultural claptrap.

Snob, Anapiron Polemou 10, Kolonaki (tel. 721 492 9). Closed Tues.

Zoom, or **Seirios,** Kydathinaion 37, Plaka (tel. 322 5920). Here, whatever the name, you are likely to hear the top performers.

Discos. Very much "in." They are divided here, but not very strictly, into **disco restaurants** (E) and plain **discos** (M), with cold plates and drinks. It's difficult to say which come and go more rapidly. The largest and noisiest are either on Leoforos Syngrou or out of town, at Kifissia or Glyfada. Among the disco restaurants:

Athinea, Panepistimíou (tel. 362 0777). Conveniently central; continues long tradition at present with dinner dances and cabaret, but might easily resume its earlier disco incarnation; closed Sun. DC.

Barbarella, Leofóros Syngrou 253 (tel. 942 5602). Three dance floors. Barbarella girls.

Jazz-Blue-Swing Bar, Tsakalof 10, Kolonaki (tel. 360 5889). Surprisingly good food!

9 + 9 (Ennea Syn Ennea), Agras 5, Platia Stadiou 5 (tel. 722 2258). Right next to the Stadium, so grand that it doesn't even advertise its name as everyone is supposed to know and, judging by the attendance, does; good restaurant; closed July–Aug.

Papagayo, Patriarhou Ioakim 37, Kolonaki (tel. 724 0736). Dining on ground floor, dancing in basement. AE, DC.

Rock'n Roll Cafe, Loukianou 6, Kolonaki. Inexpensive food, loud music especially after 12, and very "in" with the young—not for dancing.

Among the discos:
A.B.C., Patission 177 (tel. 861 7922).
Aerobic, Leofóros Syngrou 137 (tel. 932 0206).
Aftokinisi, Leoforos Kifissias 7 (tel. 681 2360). Out at Kifissia; sophisticated.
Disco 14, Kolonaki 14 (tel. 724 5938). For the younger generation.
Make Up, Panepistimíou 10 (tel. 364 2160). Most central.
Rescue, Akademias 43 (tel. 364 8027).
Retro, Mihalakopoulou 206 (tel. 770 1618). Behind the Hilton.
Rigel, Mihalakopoulou 39 (tel. 724 1418). Also near the Hilton.

Beware of the several "Nightclub open all day" clubs in Nikis, off Syntagma. These clip joints do indeed open before midday, but they are not subject to any price controls. But if the hostesses that loom there and, with even less inhibition though also less expensively, in some bars around Omonia, should leave any doubts as to their hospitable intentions, these doubts vanish in the cabarets (using the term very loosely, that is) in those clubs near the main port in Piraeus, where neither prices nor holds are barred.

GETTING AROUND. By Train. Electric trains, underground through the town center, run from Piraeus via Néo Fáliro, Thisio, Monastiráki, Platía Omónias, Platía Viktorias and the northern suburbs to Kifissia.

By Bus and Trolleybus. Buses, and the more comfortable yellow trolleybuses, run until midnight; at rush hours they are dangerously overcrowded and one has literally to fight one's way through a seething crowd. Green buses from Filellinon, near Platía Syntagma, go to Piraeus; blue buses from Leofóros Ólgas, below the Zapio Gardens, go to the beaches of the southern coast.

There are conducted motor coach tours of the city by day and night, organized by *American Express,* Syntagma, *CHAT,* Stadiou 4 and *Key Tours,* Ermou 2, among others.

By Taxi. It is quite immaterial whether the signs on the 17,000 yellow cabs are lit or unlit. The drivers are choosy about directions and passengers, adding to the latter at will, and generally charge each passenger the full fare on the meter. For utter frustration try for one in the rush hours, which seem to stretch longer and longer, or when it rains. According to a recent poll, the Athenian cabbie tops all lists for rudeness, avarice, cheating and incompetence. Indeed, drivers appear to have arrived in town simultaneously with the tourists, judging by the ignorance of any but the main streets, which, to add to the confusion, are renamed more frequently than seems justifiable. Insist on having the car radio turned off, unless you really enjoy long speeches in Greek or weird music. A show of authority might even get you to your destination by a less round-about route. The fare from the airport or Piraeus harbor to the town center is about 600 dr., though the unwary may be stung for five times as much.

MUSEUMS. For opening times, see Museums in *Facts at Your Fingertips,* but they vary and change, quite apart from being frequently affected by strikes. As this is one aspect the omniscient hotel porters are likely to ignore, better ring for a last-minute check.

Acropolis Museum, (tel. 323 6665). Full of rare objects of Attic art found on the Acropolis. Its show piece is the unrivaled collection of archaic statues of women of the 6th century B.C., notable for the delicacy and intricacy of their head-dress, their enigmatic expressions and faintly mocking smiles. These young women, known as *korai,* are strangely impersonal, though they most likely represent priestesses. Here also are the Caryatids, who had to carry the Erechtheion to long; acid rain had reduced them to leprous anonymity before they were lodged in special glass cases to prevent further deterioration, hard though it would be for the unfortunate maidens to lose even more face. Noteworthy are the sculptures of a bull devoured by a lion, the struggle of Heracles against the Triton (a monster with three bodies), the famous statue of a man carrying a calf across his shoulders, and the bas-relief of Athena leaning on her lance. Open Tues.–Fri. 8–7; weekends and holidays 8:30–3; closed Mon. Admission 600 dr.

Archaeological Museum of Piraeus, Harilaou Trikoupi 31 (tel. 452 1598). Exhibits of local finds mainly, but also has a fine Hermes from Kifissia. Open 8:30–3; closed Mon. Admission 200 dr.

Benaki Museum, Koumbari 1 (tel. 361 1617). Well-arranged and interesting museum, containing a hotch-potch of objects from different countries and periods, acquired largely from private collections. There are Byzantine icons and a rare collection of Byzantine jewelry as well as Ottoman ceramics, Coptic textiles and, above all and not to be missed, a stunning collection of genuine Greek national costumes, remarkable for their color, variety and opulence. Open 8:30–2; closed Tues. Admission 200 dr.

Byzantine and Christian Museum, Vassilíssis Sofias 22 (tel. 721 1027). Housed in the attractive 19th-century town residence of the Duchesse de Plaisance, who lived in Athens during the reign of King Otho. A visit to this museum gives one an idea of what to expect at the principal Byzantine sites outside Athens: Daphni, Óssios Loukás and Mystrás. There are exhibits of early Byzantine decorative sculpture and a large collection of icons. The most beautiful single exhibit is the famous Epitaphios of Thessaloníki, a masterpiece of 14th-century Byzantine embroidery in gold, silver, yellow and green. It represents the body of Christ laid out on a bier. Open 8–7; weekends and holidays 8:30–3; closed Mon. Admission 300 dr.

Center for Folk Art and Traditions, Hadzimihali 6, Plaka (tel. 324 3987). What its name implies. Open Tues., Thurs. 9–9; Wed., Fri., and Sat. 9–1, 5–9; closed Sun. afternoon and Mon. Admission free.

Epigraphical Museum, (tel. 821 7637). Attached to the Archeological Museum; an extensive collection of valuable historical inscriptions (of interest mainly to scholars). Open 8:30–3; closed Mon. Admission free.

Historical and Ethnological Museum, in the Old Parliament, Stadiou (tel. 323 7617). Items from 1453 to World War II, with main emphasis on the Greek War of Independence. Open 9–2; weekends and holidays 9–1; closed Mon. Admission 100 dr.

Jewish Museum, Amalias 36, third floor (tel. 323 1577). Small but expanding collection of art and artifacts from local Jewish communities. Open Sun. to Fri. 9–1.

Kanellopoulos Museum, corner of Theorias and Panos (tel. 321 2313). In the Plaka, a private collection of pre-Christian and later exhibits, including some remarkable Tanagra figurines and Byzantine icons and jewelry. Open 8:45–3; weekends and holidays 9:30–2:30; closed Mon. Admission 200 dr.

Keramikos Museum, Ermóu 148 (tel. 346 3552). Finds from the ancient cemetery. Open (including site) 8:30–3; closed Mon. Admission 300 dr.

Museum of the City of Athens, Paparigopoulou 7 (tel. 323 0168). King Otho's first Athenian residence; still has most of the original furniture and a number of interesting contemporary prints. Open Mon., Wed. and Fri. 9–1.30 only. Admission 100 dr. (free on Wed.).

Museum of Cycladic and Ancient Greek Art, Neofytou Douka 4 (tel. 723 4931). The Goulandris collection spans 5,000 years. Unique are the 230 exhibits of the Cycladic civilization (3000–2000 B.C.) in an interesting comparison with modern primitives. Artistic copies on sale in museum shop. Open 10–4, Sat. 10–3; closed Tues. and Sun. Admission 200 dr., Sat. free.

Museum of Greek Popular Art, Kydathineon 17 (tel. 321 3018). Contains 6,000 examples of traditional folk art, a collection of pottery from Rhodes, clerical robes, costumes and embroideries. Open 10–2; closed Mon. Admission 200 dr.

National Archaeological Museum, Tossitsa 1, off 28 Oktovriou (tel. 821 7717). By far the most important museum in Athens. The well-arranged exhibits illustrate every period of ancient Greek civilization, complemented by an interesting Byzantine collection. New finds are constantly added, though on occasion they remain only till the construction of a local museum.

But by far the most sensational finds are those made by Schliemann in the course of his excavations of the royal tombs on the Homeric site of Mycenae in the 1870s. This treasure-trove has thrown a new light on the hitherto unsuspected standard of artistic refinement achieved in the prehistoric Bronze Age. There are priceless gold vessels, exquisitely designed gold dishes, gold balances and masks of gold which covered the faces of the dead. Many of the gold ornaments are based on maritime subjects, such as shellfish and seaweed, and the bases are beautifully shaped and ornamented. Further treasures found in another series of royal tombs, including gold cups, diadems, and a delightful crystal bowl with a handle shaped like a duck's head are also on display, as are the superb 15th-century B.C. frescos unearthed in 1972–3 on the island of Thíra.

Other exhibits of later periods, particularly the classical period, which should not be missed, include the enormous head of a *kouros* (young man) found in the Keramikos; a 5th-century tombstone depicting a young man followed by his servitor; the famous Eleusinian bas-relief of Demeter, goddess of plenty, handing the first ear of corn to the youthful Triptolemus, the inventor of the plough; and the tombstone of a young hunter, his father at his side and his little servant at his feet. The latter is believed to be the work of Scopas.

The most famous individual statues are: Kalamis' majestic bronze Poseidon about to throw a trident (surely one of the greatest statues in the world), a colossal archaic Apollo, a lovely marble head of the goddess Hygenia, also attributed to Scopas, and the bronze jockey boy (a masterpiece of movement). These, and other magnificent bronze statues, were, for the most part, found in the sea off the coasts and islands of Greece. The museum also contains numerous painted vases and the delightful little statuettes from Tanagra. Open 8–7; weekends and holidays 8:30–3; closed Mon. mornings. Admission 500 dr.

National Picture Gallery, Vassileos Konstantinou 50 (tel. 721 1010). Contains some works by El Greco, but the bulk of the collection is of 19th-century Greek pictures. Open 9–3, Sun. and holidays 10–2; closed Mon. Admission 30 dr.

Numismatic Museum, same building as the National Archeological Museum (tel. 821 7769). Contains 250,000 ancient Greek, Hellenistic, Roman and Byzantine coins. The most interesting and unique are those from the Ptolemaic period. Scheduled for transfer to the Schliemann mansion in Venizelou, presently undergoing restoration, where the archeologist's remarkable collection will be added. Open 8:30–1:30; Sun. and holidays 9–2; closed Mon.

Piraeus Naval Museum, Akti Themistokleous (tel. 451 6822). Model ships from ancient to modern times and naval memorabilia. Open 9–12:30; Sun. and holidays 10–1, 5–8; (free on Tues. and Fri.). closed Mon. Admission 50 dr.

Stoa of Attalos Museum, (tel. 321 0185). At the ancient Agora; displays the excavation finds of the American School of Classical Studies. Open 8:30–3; closed Mon. Admission 400 dr.

War Museum, Vassilíssis Sofias 24 (tel. 729 0543). Weapons, flags and uniforms. Open 9–2; closed Mon. Admission free.

SHOPPING. Though the *National Organization of Greek Handicrafts,* the leading jewelers and top boutiques have branches in the main tourist centers, and while souvenir shops are all-too-prevalent wherever a tourist might venture, Athens still overshadows the rest of the country for a serious shopping spree. We start, therefore, with an indication of where to look for what in the capital. This is no great problem, as the two main shopping streets branch off central Syntagma.

Stadíou is the more elegant street, ending in bigger, though not necessarily better, stores near Omónia. The whole area from Syntagma to Kolonaki Square, including Voukourestiou and side streets, and Upper Panepistimíou, is full of high-class, chic, expensive shops of all kinds. Voukourestiou pedestrian arcade, off Panepistimiou, has small shops selling imports, such as relatively cheap tailor-made clothes in suede and leather.

More popular Ermóu runs west to Monastiráki. Along Ermóu, you will find women's fashions, furs, shoes, fabrics, and large shops selling everything from household appliances to art objects. Towards Monastiraki, despite all price labeling and other modern business procedures, a lot of purchasing is based on bargaining. It is difficult to explain where bargaining is in place, but roughly, the further you proceed from Sýntagma, the more you come into bargaining areas. The heart of Haggledom is Monastiráki and its vicinity. Food and commercial products, imported as well as local, are usually dealt with by the fixed-price system; antiques, second-hand objects and handicrafts by the bargaining system. It must be left very much to the individual's flair to know where he can play the pleasurable game of bargaining, so as to acquire some handsome object at a reasonable price.

Antiquities and Handicrafts. Antiques and local handicrafts are the items that are special to Greece and you can buy them at a commensurate price. Antique dealers are concentrated in the Monastiráki area, with the top echelon in Pandróssou, running parallel to lower Ermóu.

Remember that antiquities are governed by special laws. Customs officers will prevent you from taking out of Greece any object from the Greco-Roman or Byzantine period, but will, instead, take you to jail, unless you have written permission from the Greek Ministry of Culture. Any genuine antique dealer will assist in obtaining it.

The shopkeepers usually know some English, but their willingness to bargain stands in inverse ratio to their knowledge. If, however, you are not an expert, or accompanied by one, you may easily be buying a fake at too high a price. Admittedly this is a real problem, but considering that a permanent flow of genuine old pottery and ancient coins finds its way into Pandróssou, falsification, in many instances, would just not pay.

Articles belonging from all periods can be found in the antique shops in Pandróssou: *Martinos* (no. 50), the most reliable and expensive, with the biggest choice; *Adam's* (no. 47); *Vitalis* (no. 75). Equally interesting are *Antika*, Amalias 4; *Stoa*, Kolokotroni 3 (in the court); *Dora Lambrou*, Nikodimou 7—especially for silver. In the Kolonaki district, *Rodi*, Neofytou Douka 5, and *Vasiliadis*, Voukourestiou 36.

On the shadier side (no mean achievement) of Monastiráki, next to the underground train station, is Ifestou (Hephaestos). The name is most fitting, for here are the picturesque workshops of many copper- and black-smiths, interspersed with some of the more dubious antique shops.

The Athens Flea Market functions only on Sunday mornings. All along Ifestou you can get anything from a used toothbrush to broken auto spare parts and from old pants to an obsolete dentist's chair. Shops are closed, but the sellers spread out all their wares on the ground and an occasional villager will sell an ancient copper jug, a nicely-worked ring, or a rug.

If you have not the time and occasion to travel all over the country, a representative selection of this type of work can be found in Athens itself. The best quality can be found in the *Arts and Crafts* shops of the National Welfare Organization, Voukourestiou 24 and Ypatias 6, near the Cathedral, (especially for rugs). For embroidery, visit the *Greek Lyceum*, Dimokritou 17, and the *Greek Women's Institution*, Kolokotroni 3 (in the courtyard). *Eommex* sells carpets and rugs on several floors at Mitropoleos 9, and upstairs are handicrafts from village cooperatives.

You might also try Pandróssou 36 (upstairs), where, as well as a large selection of handicrafts, there is a pleasant cafe-snack bar. *Flokati* and *Kokkinos*, both Mitropoleos 3, specialize in traditional rugs, especially *flokates*, long-haired woolen rugs, sometimes brightly dyed, found also at *Karamichos*, Voulis 31–3, and on Mitropoleos and Pendelis corner. *Tanagraia*, slightly higher up Mitropoleos, has lovely ceramics.

Objects of Greek craftsmanship will also be found in many tourist shops. They should, however, be strictly distinguished from the products of the souvenir industry which, despite any merits they may or may not have, are certainly not representative of Greek handicraft. These tourist shops, often called just that, are numerous in the first part of the Plaka area. Adrianou is a very good street for most of these things. The more expensive tourist and gift shops are in the Syntagma area: *Greek Arts,* Panepistimíou 6; *Kalokerinos,* Panepistimíou 3a and Voukourestiou 8; *Knossos,* Stadiou 4; one or two are in the passage between Stadiou and Karageorgi Servias, and at Nikis 10.

In the passage off Valaoritou is a gallery of modern Greek art, *Nées Morphes,* with paintings, ceramics, sculpture and other signed items by leading contemporary artists.

Jewels and Furs. *Lalaounis Elias* and *Zolotas* at Panepistimíou 8 and 10 offer the original jewelry based on antique models at cheaper prices than at their international branches. *Athiniotakis, Vourakis, Xnathopoulos* and *Michalis* are other leading jewelers, all in Voukourestiou.

The famous fur coats from Kastoria consist of every imaginable kind of fur scrap, including mink, sent to that picturesque old town in Macedonia from all over the world. They are pieced together by workers with a skill acquired through a centuries-old tradition and made up into rolls like woven textiles and eventually into somewhat heavy coats. Still, this is a chance to buy a fur coat at a price lower-income brackets can afford. Naturally, you can also get coats made of whole skins.

The most important furriers in Athens are: *Sistovaris,* Ermou 4, Voulis 14, and Panepistimíou 9; *Mylonas,* Nikodimou 2; *Fur House,* Filellinon 7; *Voula Mitsakou* and *Maris,* Mitropoleos 7; *Alexandros,* Mitropoléos 10; and several more at no. 12; *Canada Furs,* Karagéorgi Servíás 1.

Albums and Books. For records of Greek music, *bouzoukia* and others, visit *Iho,* Korai 2; *Discophile,* Voukourestiou 17; *Ikaros,* Voulis 4; *Music Box,* Nikis 2; *Neodisk,* Panepistimíou 25, in the passage; *Pop 11,* Pindarou 38, Kolonaki. You will find the greatest selection of books on Greece and also modern novels, at *Eleftheroudakis,* Nikis 4, *Pantelides,* Amerikis 11, *American* at no. 21 and *Kaufmann,* Stadíou 28 and Voukourestiou 11. *Compendium,* Nikis 28, sells second-hand as well as new books.

Street Corner Kiosks. The little *períptera* (kiosks) at street corners are open from morning to night. In addition to cigarettes, matches, periodicals and newspapers from all over the world, you will be able to buy aspirins, batteries, shoe laces and almost anything you might urgently need.

Should you need something more complicated than an aspirin, try one of the following chemists' shops, at all of which English is spoken: *Pitsinos,* Voulis 23, Syntagma; *Bakakos,* Triti Septembriou and Marnis, Omónia; *Marinopoulos,* corner of Patission and Venizélou, Omónia, and at Kanaris 23; *Vyzas,* Kanaris 10c (Kolonaki); *Damvergis,* Venizélou 6.

Helpful Hints. The National Tourist Organization card pasted on some shop windows indicate membership of the Foreign Visitors Service organizations and affords a certain guarantee as to quality and price.

But what is the good of knowing all about shopping in Athens if you find the shops closed? Opening hours have always been changeable; the progressive abolition of the midday break has made them more so. The timetable for summer 1991 will be announced in spring. For the rest of the year shops will be open: Mon. 1 to 7, Sat. 9 to 3, all other days 9 to 7. Food stores: Mon. and Sat. 9 to 2:30, other days 9 to 4 (later on Fridays).

Barbers: Mon., Wed., Sat. 8 to 2, other days 8 to 1 and 4 to 8. Hairdressers open at 9, close Mon., Wed. at 2, Sat. at 4, other days at 6.

Parcels and registered letters must be handed in at post offices open so that the contents can be inspected.

Major hotels are entitled to change money, but do so at disadvantageous rates. Some U.K. and U.S. banks have branches near Sýntagma, (*Bank of America, Barclays, Citibank, National Westminster* and others), but only some Greek banks in the same area stay open on Saturdays, Sunday mornings and holidays to exchange money and travelers' checks.

No need to lose contact with Wall Street: *Merrill Lynch* has an office at Valaoritou 17, and there's also *Droulia & Co.* at Stadíou 4.

MUSIC AND THEATER. The Athens Festival of Music and Drama is held each year from July to September in the theater of Herodes Atticus, the ocher-colored Roman building which glows in a brilliant floodlit scene that includes the Acropolis, the monument of Philopappos and the temple of Olympian Zeus. The festival is a revival of the Dionysia instituted by the tyrant Peisistratus in the 6th century B.C. The programs include symphony concerts by the Athens State Orchestra, as well as by foreign orchestras. There are also performances of opera and ballet by Greek and foreign companies.

One of the highlights of the festival is the cycle of ancient Greek tragedies and Attic comedies put on by the National Theater. In an incomparable setting at the foot of the Acropolis, these productions have done much to revive interest in ancient drama. The familiar old legends are retold in the noble verse of Aeschylus, the brilliant plots of Sophocles, and the moving choruses of Euripides. The performances are all in modern Greek. Ancient drama and other performances are also presented at the Lycabettus theater, provincial troupes perform on the Roman Agora, while the Philopappas theater is given over to folk dancing from May through September. Tickets for the festival should be obtained in advance from the ticket office in Spirou Miliou Arcade, off Stadíou 4 (tel. 322 1459), 500 dr. to 4,000 dr. for most performances.

Otherwise, there is opera at the Olympia Theater, Akadimias 59, but it is of very uneven quality. Numerous theaters have plays and shows to offer, but they are, of course, in Greek. There are symphony concerts every Monday evening in winter at the Rex, Venizelou, and the ancient theater of Herodes Atticus in summer. Check the *Athenian* for up-to-date listings of piano and chamber-music recitals, jazz concerts and other musical performances.

SON ET LUMIÈRE. From the start of April through October the National Tourist Organization presents a rather over-dramatic Sound and Light pageant in the setting of the Acropolis. The public on the Pnyx may watch the changing lighting of the monuments while listening to historical texts accompanied by music and sound effects. Every night a performance in English is given, at 9 to 9:45 Seats cost 500 dr. Tickets can be obtained at Stadiou 4 (tel. 322 1459) or at the Pnyx before the performance. To reach the Pnyx you take the Thisio–Thon bus—or a taxi. Flower festival in Kifissia on May 1.

SPECIAL EVENTS. Easter is the most solemnly observed of all Greek religious holidays. It also falls at one of the loveliest times of the year.

Nobody should miss the Good Friday procession, in the course of which a bier, supporting an effigy of the body of Christ, is borne through the streets between 9 and 10 P.M. The procession is followed by the Archbishop of Athens and all Greece and other high dignitaries of the Church in colorful robes, by members of the government and contingents of the Army, Navy and Air Force, while military bands crash out solemn funeral marches. At the conclusion of the Resurrection service on the following night, church bells toll and pious churchgoers finally wind their way home, carrying lighted candles cupped in their hands. The fairylike procession of candles zigzagging down the path from the chapel of St. George on the top of Mount Lycabettus is something worth seeing.

In keeping with the Dionysian origin, a Wine Festival is held from mid-July to early September at the monastery of Daphni (Dafní) on the southwestern outskirts. A small entrance fee entitles you to unlimited consumption of all sorts of wine.

Greek folk dances are performed from May to September by the Dora Stratou Group, at the open-air Philopappou Theatre, a short walk from the Pnyx. Here you will see up to six different styles, authentically presented. The program takes place nightly at 10:15, except on Wed. and Sun., when the Group performs at 8:15 as well. Tickets can usually be bought at the door for 750 dr.–950 dr. (tel. 324 4395 for information).

SPORTS. Swimming. The west and east coasts of Attica are fringed with beaches and coves, with pine trees often stretching down to the water's edge. Nearer to Athens on the southeast coast are the popular G.N.T.O. (Greek National Tourist Office) beaches at Vóula, Vouliagméni and Varkiza. All are well under an hour's drive from Athens. However, they become very crowded on Sundays. Vouliagméni in particular is an enchanting spot, with a deeply indented shore, red cliffs, pine trees, a freshwater lake with mineral baths and, apart from the G.N.T.O. beach, another more exclusive one (the Astir beach), which, like the other Astir beach at Glyfáda (a little nearer to Athens) is well provided with bars, restaurants and sports facilities.

Closer still to Athens is another G.N.T.O. beach at Alimos, near the Ágios Kosmas Athletic Club, which provides swimming and diving instruction, but is badly polluted and cannot be recommended. Another diving school operates at Vouliagméni.

There are windsurfing and water skiing centers at Vouliagméni and three sailing clubs at Mikrolímano in Piraeus.

Tennis. There are tennis courts at all the G.N.T.O. beaches, as well as at the Glyfáda Athletic Club and the Ágios Kosmas Athletic Club. The Athens Tennis Club is at Leofóros Olgas 2.

Riding. There are riding clubs at Paradissou 18, Maroussi, and Gerakas, Agía Paraskeví, both some miles outside Athens. There are horse races at the Fáliro Race Course every Wednesday and Saturday.

Golf. There is an 18-hole golf course at Glyfáda, near the airport, tel. 894 6820 (see *Facts at Your Fingertips* for fees).

Winter Sports. While Greece is hardly renowned for its winter sports, there is nonetheless skiing to be had, including on Mount Párnitha, little more than an hour's drive from the capital. However, it is limited to January and February, and then only if it snows.

USEFUL ADDRESSES. Consulates. *Australia,* Dimitriou Soutsou 37 (tel. 644 7303); *Canada,* Ioannou Gennadiou 4 (tel. 723 9511); *Great*

Britain, Ploutarhou 1 (tel. 723 6211); *Ireland,* Vassileos Konstantinou 7 (tel. 723 2771); *United States,* Vassilíssis Sofias 91 (tel. 721 2951).

Airlines. The terminals of all the major airlines are on or near Syntagma, as is the ticket office of *Olympic Airways,* Othonos 6 (tel. 961 6161 for reservations), the Greek national airline. Their head office and terminal, however, is at Syngrou 96. *British Airways,* Othonos 10 (tel. 322 2521); *Pan Am,* Othonos 4 (tel. 323 5242); *T.W.A.,* Xenofontos 8 (tel. 323 6837); *Air France,* Karageorgi Servias 4 (tel. 323 0501); and *Lufthansa,* Vassilíssis Sofias (tel. 369 2411).

Travel Agencies. *American Express,* Ermou 2 and at the Hilton; *C.H.A.T.,* Stadiou 4; *HellasTours,* Stadiou 7; *Key Tours,* Ermou 2; *Wagon Lits/Tourisme,* Skoufou 6 and Stadiou 5.

Car Hire. *Ansa International,* Syngrou 33; *Avis,* Amalias 48; *Budget,* Syngrou 8; *Hellascars,* Stadiou 7; *Hertz,* Syngrou 12 and Vouliagmenis 576A.

Touring. *Automobile & Touring Club of Greece,* (E.L.P.A.), Tower of Athens, Mesogeion 2 (tel. 779 1615); road assistance, tel. 104; tourist guidance, tel. 174.

Emergencies. City Police, tel. 100; Traffic Police, tel. 523 0111; Tourist Police, tel. 171. First aid Center, tel. 166.

Churches. St. Paul's Anglican Church is at Filellinon 29; St. Andrew's (Interdenominational) Church at Sina 66; Church of Christ at Kifíssia 24. The Roman Catholic Cathedral of St. Denis is at Panepistimíou 24. There is a Synagogue at Meltioni 5, off Ermóu.

ATTICA

Industry, Antiquity and Beaches

The history of Attikí (Attica) is the history of Athens: a mountainous country, bounded on three sides by sea and an indented coastline fringed with beaches. On the stony foothills the soil is so poor that only a few pungently aromatic shrubs grow: thyme, myrtle and lentisk. Higher up, the feathery pine of Attica is supplanted by dark fir trees. The plains yield little but the olive and the grape. How the immemorial beehives of Ymitós (Hymettus) produce ever-greater quantities of the popular clear honey is a mystery. The quarries of Mount Penteli are no longer worked for the famed white marble that weathers to a warm golden tint. The remoter parts are still blessed with the purest of lights, sharply delineating the mountains, sea and plain, though not the capital, round which most of the Greek industry is concentrated. If anything was ever truly classical, it is the landscape of Attica.

Exploring Attica

The bare undulating foothills of Hymettus, the closest to the capital of the mountains ringed round Athens, are dotted with Byzantine shrines. Six km. (four miles) east of Athens, beyond the working-class suburb of Kessarianí (Kaisariani), is the charming monastery of Kaisariani, built on a sanctuary of Aphrodite, and partly restored on the tree-planted slope of the mountain. The spring, shaded by a large plane tree, is reputed to have retained its remarkable powers of fertility, despite the change of religion.

The church, parts of which date from the 11th century, is in the best Byzantine style of architecture, and some of the decorative work indicates a harmonious blending of different classical styles. The frescos date from the 16th and 17th centuries. Worth nothing are those of the Virgin seated between the Archangels in the apse, and the portraits of the Apostles on the north wall of the narthex. The monastery, with its shady trees and spring, is a favorite haunt of holiday-makers on Sundays.

From Kaisariani the road winds up to the airforce installations on the bleak summit of Hymettus, from which there is an incomparable view of the whole of Attica, the Saronikós Gulf, southern Euboea and some of the Cyclades in the east. About half way between the monastery of Kaisariani and the saddle of Hymettus, the Byzantine chapel of Asteri may be seen from the road.

Along the lower foothills, covered with bushes of thyme and origan—in early spring they are carpeted with delicate pink, white and mauve anemones—one can easily spot the church of St. John the Theologian, and, on a ridge farther north, that of St. John the Hunter. The urban periphery has crept ominously close to this rolling, shrub-scented heathland, under the shadow of violet Hymettus.

The Monastery of Dafní (Daphni)

The main exit from Athens to the west and the Peloponnese is by Leofóros Athinas, a broad highway running roughly parallel to the ancient Sacred Way from Athens to Elefsína (Eleusis). After mounting the rocky slopes of Mount Egáleo, the road enters a wide pass, long barred by the Emperor Justinian's fortified monastery of Daphni, enclosed within tall battlemented walls.

In turn sacked by Crusaders, reconsecrated by Cistercian monks and desecrated by Turks, Daphni remains one of the most splendid Byzantine monuments in Greece. Dating from the 11th century, the Golden Age of Byzantine art, the squat dome and drum are supported by four pendentives forming the four arms of the Greek Cross plan. The iconographic disposition is strictly liturgical and symbolical. There is a series of mosaics without parallel in the legacy of Byzantium: portraits of austere prophets, venerable saints and ephebe-like archangels, as well as compositions of scenes from the life of Christ, colored in the loveliest of pinks, greens, and blues against gold backgrounds. In the dome lowers the great Christ Pantocrator: a formidable Messiah, with eyes that transfix and with the power to inspire terror. Note the long index finger crooked over the jeweled Book of Judgment; and the thin-lipped almost predatory mouth turning down at the sides. This is a Christ of Nemesis; all the austerity of Byzantium, the death-fixation of Greek folk songs, the savage dirge-like measures of Greek popular music, are represented in this astonishing portrait. The last Acciajuoli Duke strangled his usurping aunt before the altar, which led Sultan Mohammed II to occupy Athens, murder the Duke and drive out the Cistercians. The ducal sarcophagi with their fleurs-de-lis and Latin crosses still stand in the Gothic cloister. The grove beyond the crenelated walls is from the beginning of July to early September the site of the Athens Wine Festival, and offers pleasant walks the year round.

The Shores of the Saronikós

From Daphni, the road descends towards the Bay of Eleusis, where many laid-up ships reflect the world recession. Beyond is the island of Sálamis, and in the narrow straits to the left occurred the momentous sea battle in 480 B.C. which decided the fate of Europe. To the right, the road runs between the sea and the dammed up salt springs of Rheiti, sacred to Demeter, and across the Thriasian plain, where, according to legend, corn was grown for the first time. At the end of the plain lies Eleusis, now a center of heavy industry and thus the least attractive of Greece's ancient sites. Hemmed in by factories are the marble blocks of the Great Propylaea, a gift of Antoninus Pius, one of the eight Roman emperors to be initiated; the foundations of a temple of Demeter, once the largest in Greece; and of the Telesterium, the great Hall of the Mysteries, where the most famous of all ancient religious rites was celebrated annually. For millenia the initiates kept the oath of secrecy as to what had occurred after they had drunk the sacred kykeom, a mixture based on opium. The story of Demeter, the goddess of fertility, and of Persephone, the offspring of her incestuous relationship with her brother Zeus, was probably reenacted. The performance of the Mysteries was accompanied by orgiastic dances, the singing of obscene songs on the fertility theme, (no doubt to relieve emotional tension) and spectacular torchlight processions which proceeded from the Hall of the Mysteries to the temples of Demeter and Persephone.

The toll motorway by-passes Eleusis. The branch to the right just beyond the town is the old road to Thebes and Delphi, while the highway links up with the Thessaloníki–Athens motorway and continues along the coast of the Saronikós (Saronic Gulf), scarred by shipyards and refineries, parallel to the island of Sálamis, towards Corinth and the Peloponnese.

After by-passing Mégara—a quiet country town—Sálamis and a group of islets seemingly floating on the sea and guarding the western entrance to the narrow bay, are lost to sight. The scenery becomes more spectacular and the Scironian Rocks, once the lair of Sciron, a mythological bandit who used to compel travelers to halt and wash his feet on the brink of the precipice, rise sheer out of the aquamarine-colored sea. While his unfortunate victims were obeying his orders, he would kick them over into the depths below, where a gigantic turtle lurked in readiness to devour them. Theseus alone, on his way from Trizína (Troezene) to Athens defied Sciron and hurled him into the sea, where he too was swallowed up in the maw of the omnivorous turtle. The descent from the Scironian Rocks leads to a wooded coastal belt with a strand of fine shingle several miles long, fringed with pines. The whole of this shore, known as Kinétta, is dotted with roadhouses and taverns, and is a favorite resort of campers and picnickers. The sea, owing to a number of cross-currents, is always cool, with a sparkling quality, even on the hottest day of August.

Beyond the by-passed village of Ágii Theódori extends the Isthmus of Corinth, a bleak and windswept stretch of land. Here Theseus slew that other dreaded scourge, Sinis the pine-bender, whose favorite pastime was to bend the tops of two pine trees until they met, tie the arms of innocent travelers to each and then loosen his hold, thus causing the victims to be ripped asunder as the trees were released. Before reaching the bridge that spans the canal, a branch road leads to the spa of Loutráki—a string of hotels and thermal stations. Two submersible bridges also cross the canal.

Twelve km. (eight miles) west, Perahóra was destroyed in the devastating earthquake of February 1981, which hit Corinth, Kiáto, Mégara and Thebes. Beyond the pine-fringed inlet, the tip of a rocky headland divides the Gulf of Corinth from the sweep of the Halcyonic Gulf. Little remains of the buildings of the archaic Sanctuary of Hera, the Iréo, except foundations. But there is a feeling of magnificent isolation, with the snowcapped peaks of Zíria towering above the wooded Achaian coast and the waters of the inland sea lit at night by the beams of the lighthouse above the Sacred Harbor. Near Hera's shrine stood the sanctuary in memory of the children of Medea, whom the Colchian sorceress slaughtered with her own hands in order to spite their faithless father, Jason.

Returning along the enchanting lagoon-like inlet, past seafood taverns, continue up through the village of Perahóra to Píssia. From there it is six km. (four miles) through an idyllic pine forest down to Shinós on the deep Halcyonic Gulf, which can be followed eastward on an unpaved but scenically lovely road to Alepohóri. Till this up-and-coming beach resort, the excursion is far off the beaten tourist track, which is joined by turning inland to Mégara.

Cape Sóunio

Another excursion along the shores of the Saronikós Gulf is in the opposite direction, south-east of Athens. Leofóros Syngróu, Athens' widest avenue, descends to the racecourse in the center of the Fáliro Bay, called the Delta (though the Ilissós deposits its filth further to the right, at Néo Fáliro). To the left, the coastal road skirts the blocks of apartments of Paleó Fáliro, the British and Commonwealth War Cemetery and the Ellinikó airport to Glyfáda, with its 18-hole, 150-acre golf course, the smart Asteria beach and nightclub.

Beyond Glyfáda, where the foothills of Hymettus descend gently to the sea, the road passes the pine-clad promontories of Kavóuri and Vouliagméni. Hotels and blocks of flats crowd less densely, pollution recedes and bathing becomes enjoyable on the beaches below the red rocks. Set off dramatically by great gray granite cliffs from Hymettus' last spur, the theatrical potentialities of the tiny Vouliagméni Lake are, indeed, used occasionally for performances on a floating stage. In the excitement of a rock concert a good part of the orchestra once slid into the warm mineral waters, less involuntarily frequented by rheumatic sufferers.

From the next headland, the male nudists that frequent its tip enjoy a fine view over the inlets to the long sand beach of Várkiza, the best along this stretch of coast, now a resort only slightly less crowded than Glyfada despite the extra distance from Athens, Here, one of the frequent reimpositions of the ancient names, the infinitely more euphonic Alianthos, has been quietly dropped, except on the buses from Athens. The game of causing maximum confusion with a minimum of effort has, however, been vastly successful, especially with tourists. The corniche winds in and out of rush-bordered coves and strips of sand and shingle, fringed with islets shimmering in the sun-dazzled sea. Beyond the sweep of the bay of Anávyssos rises the rocky promontory of Sóunio, the southernmost tip of Attica. A 5th-century B.C. temple of Poseidon, of which 12 Doric columns remain erect, crowns the cliff rising perpendicularly from the sea. The circuit of ancient walls can still be traced and on one of the slender columns, whose gleaming whiteness stands out like a beacon to ships approaching the

Saronikós Gulf, Byron carved his ubiquitous signature. The panorama of sea and islands from this airy platform on Attica's southernmost cape is spectacular. At the foot of the temple is a tourist pavilion, plus a hotel on the beach below.

After Sóunio the road follows the coast north beneath curiously metallic-colored hills facing Makroníssi (Long Island), where communist rebels were exiled during the Civil War of 1946–49. At Lávrio, a shoddy little town celebrated in antiquity for its silver mines, huge slag heaps point to the continued exploitation of the local metallurgical deposits. At Thóriko, antiquity's only purely industrial town, an ancient theater is being restored. The road turns inland through rolling vineyards, olive orchards and rich red earth, known as the Mesógia (Middle Land), dotted with archaic necropolises and numerous villages. From Keratéa it is eight km. (five miles) east to the convent of the *Palaioemerologitae* (followers of the Julian calendar) looking like the stage set for a Russian ballet, high above the beach of Kakí Thálassa. The most interesting of several prosperous villages is Peanía, birthplace of Demosthenes, because of the Vorres Museum. Three restored village houses and a stable accommodate folklore items collected by a Greek-Canadian. In a striking modern wing is the largest collection of contemporary Greek art—over 300 paintings and 60 sculptures, donated to the nation. The Vorres Museum is open Saturday and Sunday, 10–2. The frescos in the largest church were painted in the best derivative Byzantine style, by Kontoglou, a fashionable contemporary painter. Two miles along the eastern slope of Mount Hymettus is the large stalactite Koutóuki cave, open from 9:30 to 4:30. At the road fork, six km. (four miles) north, the right prong leads to the Márathon coast, the left back to Athens, eight km. (five miles) through the Agía Paraskeví suburb.

The Márathon Coast

A series of pine-girt beaches, reached from the various villages of the Mesógia, dotted with remains of Mycenaean castles, beehive tombs, archaic and classical shrines, Hellenistic fortresses and Frankish towers, extends along the east coast of Attica. The coastal road begins at Pórto Ráfti, where the entrance to the bay is guarded by a gaunt islet in the shape of a pyramid, crowned with the remains of a Roman statue representing a seated man, alleged to be a tailor: hence the name Pórto Ráfti, "the port of the tailor." At Vravróna, ancient Brauron, divine confusion reigned, after the local divinity of fertility, Iphigenia, became somewhat surprisingly identified with the most determined of virgins, Artemis. The plot thickened when another Iphigenia, supposedly sacrificed to Artemis at Aulis, further up the coast, but, in fact, spirited away to savage Taurus in the Crimea, landed with her brother Orestes at Brauron. She became High Priestess and was deified. The good women of Athens, who walked every fourth year in solemn procession all the 37 km. (23 miles) from town, might well have wondered whom they were asking for fertility, especially as the curious bear cult belonged to the first, only dimly remembered, Iphigenia.

The well-arranged local museum, open from 8:30 to 3, (closed Mon.), houses the bas-reliefs, statues, jewels and unique wooden vases dug out of the mud of the Erasinos. The large temple of Artemis has been partly reconstructed, but only foundations remain of the 5th-century B.C. stoa, where the daughters of the best Athenian families were initiated in the ritual dances. Close by are the foundations of an early Christian basilica and, about halfway between Vravróna and the village of Markópoulo, a Frankish tower stands sentinel on a lonely eminence, dominating the rolling vine country.

Beyond the pine-shaded sandy shore of Lóutsa and the small port of Rafína extend more beaches and coves until the crescent-shaped Bay of Márathon is reached. Here, in 490 B.C., took place the famous battle in which the greatly outnumbered Athenian *hoplites* broke the onslaught of the Persion hordes in the swampy ground between the sea and Mount Pentéli. From the shepherd god Pan's intervention on the side of the Greeks derives the word panic, while the runner who expired after having announced the news of the victory added the term, a "Marathon race" (a test of endurance). Amid fields and orchards of almond trees rises the 12-meter (39-ft.) high tumulus erected over the ashes of the 192 Athenians who fell in battle. Some five km. (three miles) inland, the graves of their only allies, the Plataeans, can be seen within a recently discovered mound on the actual battlefield. Nearby are a museum and a prehistoric graveyard of tiny men and horses protected by a concrete shell.

Just before the village of Marathónas (Márathon), a road branches right to the lovely beach of Shinias, a long pine-fringed sandy bay very popular with windsurfers. The road then turns north to ancient Ramnóus, facing the majestic mountain chain of Euboea across the channel. In this secluded spot rise the platforms of two Doric temples, supported by marble walls. The smaller 6th-century B.C. temple of Themis, the blindfolded goddess of justice, having been destroyed when the Persians attacked a nearby Athenian fortress, the larger one was erected in honor of Nemesis, goddess of divine vengeance. Though the London Society of Dilettanti shipped part of the goddess' head to the British Museum in 1813, the innumerable fragments of the marble statue by Agorakritos—Pheidias' favorite pupil—have been painstakingly put together. This is the only surviving cult statue of the golden age. A new museum houses finds, mostly from the Sacred Way, which leads north to the relatively well-preserved 5th-century citadel. The site and the museum are open from 8:30 to 3 (closed Mon.).

The whole place has an atmosphere of awe and desolation, well suited to a sanctuary of the most implacable of ancient deities. A path lined by monumental tombs leads to the white marble walls of the Acropolis, choked in undergrowth; below is the port that guarded the entrance to the Euboean Channel. After Marathónas the road rises, affording splendid views over the bay; at Kapandríti it joins the Kalamos branch from the motorway.

In the Interior

After passing the suburban villas of Psyhikó and Halándri, about a third of the way up Mount Pentéli, the most symmetrical of the mountains surrounding the Attic plain, there is a large prosperous monastery, enclosed within white-washed walls and shaded with poplars and plane trees under which cool streams trickle. The monastery contains the skull, enriched with jewels, of its 16th-century founder. A little farther up, to the right, stands the Gothic-revival country house built by the eccentric French philhellene, the Duchesse de Plaisance, in the mid-19th century. This eccentric daughter of a French diplomat (who negotiated the Louisiana Purchase) and of an American mother, became tired of the sophisticated life of Parisian literary and political salons, left her husband, a statesman under Napoleon III, and settled in Greece. She preferred the friendship of semi-literate but colorful revolutionary leaders to that of King Otho's courtiers. Nearby is the tomb of her daughter, surrounded by cypresses. A strange relationship, alternating between extremes of affection and rivalry, apparently existed between mother and daughter, both of whom entertained the tenderest feelings for a bandit dwelling in a neighboring cave supposedly connected by an underground passage with the Duchesse's residence. Restored in the 1960s, the mansion is not open to the public, but the courtyard is the setting for a Chamber Music Festival in July.

A track climbs from the bus terminal to the summit of Pentéli, past disused marble quarries inhabited by herds of baleful-eyed goats. The view from the summit embraces the whole of Attica, the sea on three sides and the distant Cyclades. Access to the sea view is reached more comfortably from the road along Pentéli's eastern slope, through pine forests where fires rage every summer, but there are still pleasant walks. The Dionyssos branch road is joined at the north slope.

The villas, hotels, restaurants and clubs of the American colony spread over Pentéli's western foothills at Kifíssia, birthplace of Menander, the ancient comic writer. The Goulandri Natural History Museum, Levidou 13, (open 9–1 and 5–8, closed Fri.), combines botanical, zoological and paleontological exhibits. The two most elegant suburbs, Kastrí, family seat of the Papandreou political family, and Ekáli, further on, provide the easiest, though not quickest, access to the motorway north, which converges on Mount Pentéli with four widely-spaced branch roads to the right (east). The first leads to Diónyssos, at the foot of huge marble quarries: the site of ancient Icaria, where Dionysos, the god of wine, when visiting Attica for the first time, was entertained by Icarius whom he afterwards instructed to spread the blessings of the grape to mankind. The road descends to Néa Mákri on the east coast.

The second branch leads to the Márathon dam, an artificial lake for Athens' water supply. The dam, entirely faced with marble, was completed in the late 1920s by a firm of American engineers and serves as a barrage against the escape of waters through a deep glen into the Marathonian plain. The reservoir is fed by pipelines from Lake Ylíki and since 1980 from the Mórnos River, over a 100 miles northwest.

The third branch runs between gently undulating hills to the fishing village of Ágii Apóstoli and the Amfiáreo (Amphiaraion) bright with oleanders, above the Euboean channel. The sheltered sanctuary is dedicated to Amphiáraos, a prophet-general, who was swallowed up by the earth together with his chariot. An interpreter of dreams, he was raised to divinity and his sanctuary became a popular dream-oracle. Close to a stream said to possess curative properties, there are ruins of a theater, a Doric temple, a large hospital and the 109-meter (120-yard) long portico, in which pilgrims, lying on the skin of a sacrificial ram, were visited by revelatory dreams. A final branch leads to the little port of Oropós, whence there is a half-hourly ferry boat across the blue streak of the channel to Erétria, on the opposite coast of Euboea. A secondary road hugs the mainland coast from Oropós to Halkída, passing Avlída, where Iphigenia was sacrificed to secure favorable winds for the Greek expedition against Troy. The motorway by-passes Avlóna which has a museum of embroideries, and

Tanagra with a small museum of antiquities, then skirts Lake Ylíki, the main reservoir of Athens, before turning again to the sea.

On Mount Parnís

West of Mount Pentéli, the barrier of Párnitha (Mount Parnís), the highest mountain in Attica, extends across the plain. After the military airport, the road climbs the foothills of Dekélia through luxuriant woods to the private estate of the royal family. The lovely park with the royal tombs, including those of the Duke of Edinburgh's parents, can be entered just below the Leonidas Restaurant at Varybóbi; no signpost. The drive continues to Ágios Merkóuris, whence a very rough road descends through the scattered oak forests to the motorway at the Oropós branch.

Another road, leading through the village of Aharnés whose farmlands were constantly ravaged during the Peloponnesian War by the Spartan infantry entrenched in the fortified camp of Dekélia—climbs Mount Parnís in a long series of hairpin bends. Towards the top, fir trees replace the eternal pines of Attica and the air becomes more alpine and rarified. A funicular railway provides an easier approach, rising in four minutes to the hotel casino at 915 meters (3,000 ft.) with a splendid view over the Attic plain. The road continues past several restaurants to the military installations shortly before the summit.

A third road leads through the village of Fýli to the convent of Moní Klistón (Our Lady of the Defile) into an austere mountain landscape gashed with precipitous defiles and spiky crevasses. The branch left leads to the ruins of the 4th-century B.C. fortress of Phyle, one round and two square towers dramatically perched on a little plateau guarding the shortest route into Attica from Thebes.

The Byzantine monastery of Ossios Melétis in the northwestern foothills is reached by turning right at Inoï, 48 km. (30 miles) along the inland road to Thebes from Athens. Scattered pines and fir trees cling to the slate-gray mountain sides—in ancient times a preserve of wild boar, lions and wolves. Just before entering the pass between Attica and Boeotia, a road branches left, passes the village of Vília, shaded with plane trees, and descends from the impressive bare uplands and passes through deserted pine groves and olive orchards into a placid inlet of the Halcyonic Gulf. Here rise the ruins of towers and posterns, as well as a massive enceinte of walls, of the 4th-century B.C. fortress of Egósthena. On the shingle beach of Pórto Germenó are several taverns and, in late summer, plagues of horse-flies. Except at week-ends, the beach is practically deserted.

PRACTICAL INFORMATION FOR ATTICA

WHEN TO COME. Preferably in spring, early summer or fall. In spring an extraordinary variety of wild flowers carpet the arid hillsides of Attica (particularly around Hymettus, Parnís and the Marathonian plain and hills leading to Ramnóus). The beaches, of course, are most enjoyable in high summer; but then you have to put up with the crowds. The smartest are the Astir beaches at Glyfáda and Vouliagméni. Sailing continues all year round.

SPECIAL EVENTS. July. Pentéli Festival, consisting of concerts given in the courtyard of the Duchesse de Plaisance's country house. The Athens Wine Festival, still held at the Daphni Monastery from early July to early Sept., has long been scheduled for transfer to a village among the Mesógia vineyards.

HOTELS AND RESTAURANTS. The southeast coast from Fáliro to Sóunio is studded with hotels on or facing the sea. Deluxe, Expensive and Moderate hotels in our listings are all airconditioned, unless otherwise stated. Most charge halfboard. Distances in km. and miles from Athens are shown in brackets after the name of the town or resort.

Southeast Coast

Anávyssos (50/31). *Alexander Beach* (M), tel. 5 3461. 105 rooms. Disco, pool. *Akti Apollon* (M), tel. 3 6493. 91 rooms. Disco. *Eden Beach* (M), tel. 5 2761/5. 286 rooms. Disco, pool, minigolf, roofgarden, no airconditioning. DC. *Silver Beach* (I), tel. 3 6203. 28 rooms.

Glyfáda (18/11). Largest concentration of hotels, despite proximity to noisy airport; marina. *Astir* (E), tel. 894 6461/5. 128 aging bungalows. Pool, tennis, minigolf, nightclub; the only one with private beach, but sea not as clean as it should be. AE, DC, MC. *Atrium* (E), tel. 894 0971/5. 56 rooms. Roofgarden. AE, MC, V. *Congo Palace* (E), tel. 894 6711/5. 91 rooms. Roofgarden, pool and tennis nearby. AE, DC, V. *Emmantina* (E), tel. 898 0683. 95 rooms. Roofgarden, pool. AE, DC, MC, V. *Filissia* (E), tel. 894 1552. 20 suites. One of several sets of unjustifiably expensive furnished apartments. *Oasis* (E), tel. 894 1662. 70 suites. Pool. AE, DC, V.

Fenix (M), tel. 894 7229. 143 rooms. Roofgarden, disco, pool, but not by beach. AE, DC, MC, V. *Four Seasons* (M), tel. 894 2211/3. 78 rooms. AE, DC, V. *Golden Sun* (M), tel. 895 5218/9. 60 rooms. AE, DC, MC, V. *Gripsholm* (M), tel. 894 4911/4. 67 rooms. AE, DC, MC, V. *John's* (M), tel. 894 6837. 68 rooms. AE. *Palace* (M), tel. 894 8361. 75 rooms. Renovated 1988. Pool. *Regina Maris* (M), tel. 894 5050. 72 rooms. Pool. AE, DC, MC. *Sea View* (M), tel. 894 7681. 74 rooms. Tennis and pool nearby. AE. *Beau Rivage* (I), tel. 894 9292. 82 rooms. Roofgarden, airconditioned. AE, DC, MC, V. *Glyfada* (I), tel. 894 1137. 52 rooms. Pool, tennis. *Oceanis* (I), tel. 894 4038. 73 rooms. Pool.

Restaurants. *Antonopoulos* (E), tel. 894 5636. Renowned seafood restaurant opposite the marina. *Athenaia* (E), Akti Astiros (tel. 894 6898). Emphasis on seafood; dancing to live orchestra; where visiting celebrities are entertained. AE. *Churrasco* (E), tel. 844 1252. Less expensive, with elaborate steak tartare. AE, DC. *Psaropoulos* (E), tel. 894 5677. Opposite marina, well-known for seafood. *Quo Vadis* (E), tel. 894 4905. French and international cuisine, also piano bar. AE, DC, V.

Antonis (M), tel. 894 7423. For shrimp ragout and wild boar. *Entre-Nous Sivilla* (M), tel. 894 5954. Specializes in French cuisine; shrimp and bacon, tournedos. *La Boussola* (M), tel. 894 2605. Scampi and other Italian dishes. *Dovinos* (M), tel. 894 4229. Fish baked and grilled. *El Greco* (M), tel. 899 4249. Also strong on baked and grilled fish. *Kowloon* (M), tel. 894 4528. Wide choice of Chinese dishes. AE, DC. *Loxandra* (M), tel. 893 1400. A mainly Greek menu is offered here, with dishes like *bourekakia* (cheese pies), stuffed veal, and *gouvetsi loxandra* (pork on a spit). *Plaza Garden* (M), tel. 894 3880. Large terrace in the shopping center; piano accompaniment. AE.

Barba Petros (I), tel. 891 4937. Cheese pies, kid, grills. AE. *Kanatakia* (I), corner Metaxas and Pandoros tel. 895 1843. Pies and short orders, wine from the barrel. AE.

Entertainment. Nightspots are as numerous as restaurants. *Dilina* (E), tel. 894 0205. Features well-known names in Greek and international show biz. Closed Mon. AE. *B.B.G. Disco* (M), tel. 893 1933. *Esperides* (M), tel. 894 8179. Disco. *Oui* (M), tel. 894 1456. Dance to retro music.

Kalamáki (13/8). *Marina Alimos* (E), tel. 982 8911/7. 47 suites. No restaurant; next to the airport. AE, DC. *Albatross* (M), tel. 982 4981/3. 80 rooms. Airconditioned; restaurant; beach across coastal road. MC. *Hellenikon* (M), tel. 981 7227. 52 rooms. On coastal road; airconditioned; mini-golf, restaurant. *Galaxy* (I), tel. 981 8603. 44 rooms; beach across coastal road; airconditioned; restaurant. AE, DC. *Tropical* (I), tel. 981 3993. 46 rooms. Also on coastal road; airconditioned; minigolf, restaurant. DC, MC.

Restaurants. All on or near coastal road. *Curry Palace* (M), tel. 983 8889. Indian specialties. AE. *La Fontanina* (M), tel. 983 0738. Italian pasta dishes with seafood. *Sta Kavourakia* (M), tel. 981 0093. Specializes in crabs, as its name indicates; other seafood too. Dinner only.

Entertainment. *Anabella* (M), tel. 981 1124. Dinner dancing, in summer only.

For moderately good shows based on *bouzouki* music in a very lively atmosphere, try the following. *Fantasia,* tel. 982 0300. *Neraida,* tel. 981 2004. AE, DC. *Stork,* tel. 982 9865.

Kavóuri (21/13). *Amarilia* (E), tel. 899 0391/5. 100 rooms. Pool. *Pine Hill* (M), tel. 896 0871. 83 rooms. 90 meters (100 yards) from beach. Roofgarden, tennis, pool. AE. *Sunrise* (M), tel. 895 6178. 60 rooms. AE, DC, MC, V.

Restaurants. Seafood restaurants on the coast. *Fulya* (E), tel. 895 8603. One of the most varied seafood places. AE, DC, MC, V. *Imbros* (M), tel. 895 1139. Features international cuisine with both meat and fish. *Mythos* (M), tel. 895 5214. DC. *Nirides* (M), tel. 896 1560. Also cafeteria. Piano and terraces.

Lagoníssi (38/24). *Xenia Lagonissi* (E), tel. 8 3911/25. 357 rooms and deluxe bungalows. Several restaurants, nightclub, cinema, 2 pools, tennis, mini-golf. DC, MC, V.

Legrená (64/40). *Minos* (I), tel. 3 9321/3. 38 rooms. Restaurant.

Páleo (Old) Fáliro (8/5). Sea too polluted for bathing. *Coral* (M), tel. 981 6441. 89 rooms. Some rooms air-conditioned; pool, roof garden; on noisy coastal road. AE, DC, MC, V. *Nestorian* (M), tel. 942 5010. 29 rooms. Roofgarden. *Possidon* (M), tel. 982 2086. 90 rooms. Like Coral, on noisy coastal road, with pool and roofgarden. AE, DC, MC, V.

Restaurants. Most restaurants are on the coastal road. *Bistrot 1900* (E), tel. 981 6245. Successfully nostalgic. *Botsares* (M), Zisimopoulou 24 (tel. 941 3022). Further inland, well known for seafood. DC. *Bouillabessa* (M), Zisimopoulou 28 (tel. 941 9082). Not quite the French ideal, but still tasty.

Camino (M), tel. 982 9647. Pastas, pizzas, and scalloppini Camino. Not as expensive as other Italians restaurants. *Gaskon Toma* (M), tel. 982 1114. Evenings only, with music. Ouzo and wine free. *Il Fungo* (M), tel. 981 6765. Pizzas and pastas, evenings only, except for Sun. lunch. AE. *Hickory Grill* (M), tel. 982 1972. *Kapri* (M), tel. 981 6379. Cafeteria. DC. *Pontos* (M), tel. 983 1963. Mussels and shrimps specialties.

Saronída (48/30). *Saronic Gate* (E), tel. 5 3711/5. 105 rooms. Beach, pool, tennis, minigolf. DC.

Sóunio (71/44). *Cape Sounion Beach* (M), tel. 3 9391/4. 200 bungalows. Not airconditioned, but not really necessary as very windy. Pool, disco. AE, DC. *Egeon* (M), tel. 3 9200. 44 rooms. On beach below temple; not airconditioned. AE, DC. *Surf Beach Club* (M), tel. 2 2363/4. 265 rooms in central block and bungalows. Pool, tennis, disco.

Várkiza (Alianthos) (32/20). All hotels are across busy coastal road from the large G.N.T.O. beach. None are airconditioned. *Glaros* (M), tel. 897 1217/8. 48 rooms. *Stefanakis* (M), tel. 897 0528. 41 rooms. Gym, sauna. *Varkiza* (M), tel. 897 0927/9. 30 rooms. *Holidays* (I), tel. 897 0915/7. 34 rooms.

Restaurant. *Petros* (E), tel. 897 3700. Outstanding for seafood; dining terrace over the sea just before the village. *Varkiza* (M), tel. 897 0789. All sorts of steaks are offered in this garden restaurant.

Voula (18/11). *Voula Beach* (E), tel. 895 3851/4. 54 rooms. Not airconditioned; beach, disco. *Noufara* (M), tel. 895 3450. 22 rooms.

Restaurants. *Bo* (E), tel. 895 9645. Recommended *caprice du chef. Epicure* (M), tel. 895 3544. Excellent for hamburgers. *Rive* (M), tel. 895 6061. AE.

Vouliagméni (25/16). *Astir Palace* (L), tel. 896 0211/9. 422 rooms in three hotels, each with pool; and 77 bungalows. The three hotels are *Aphrodite,* new and most simple, *Arion,* the luxurious and elegant, and *Nafsika,* the chic and modern. On pine-clad promontory with private beach, tennis, minigolf, nightclub, in a self-contained complex. AE, DC, MC, V. *Armonia* (E), tel. 896 0030. 105 rooms. Pool. roof garden. AE, DC, V. *Greek Coast* (E), tel. 896 0401. 55 rooms. Pool, roofgarden. DC, V. *Margi House* (E), tel. 896 2061/5. 110 rooms. Pool roof garden. AE, DC, V. *Blue Spell* (M), tel. 896 0131/2. 38 rooms. Pool, roofgarden. AE, DC, MC, V. *Paradise* (M), tel. 896 3304/7. 61 rooms. Small pool. DC, V. *Strand* (M), tel. 896 0705/7. 72 rooms. Disco. AE.

Restaurants. The Astir Palace's *Club House, Grill Room, Jason, Kymata, Pegasus, Pergola* and *Spilia,* all (E). *Mooring's* (E), tel. 896 1113. Equally international; above Greece's most elegant marina; speciality is lobster flambé. AE, DC, MC. *Oceanis* (E), tel. 896 1133. On the G.N.T.O. beach, for French cuisine. AE, DC. *Psarofili* (M), tel. 896 1887. Seafood. *Toscana* (M), tel. 896 2497. Italian cuisine, further inland. AE, DC. There are several Moderate fish taverns near the Astir Beach which frequently change owner and name. AE, V.

East Coast

Ágii Apóstoli (50/31). *Kalamos Beach* (M), tel. 8 1465/7. 177 rooms. Not airconditioned; pool, tennis, minigolf, disco. *The Dolphins* (I), tel. 8 1202. 138 rooms. Pool, roofgarden, disco.
Restaurants. There are numerous Moderate fish taverns.

Márathon (42/26). *Golden Coast* (M), tel. 9 2102. 241 rooms. Pool, tennis, minigolf, disco. Near the tumulus. The coast is anything but golden till the Shinas beach half a mile away. AE, DC, V.

Máti (30/19). *Attica Beach* (M), tel. 7 1711. 94 rooms. AE. Pool. *Máti* (M), tel. 7 1511. 70 rooms, 5 suites. Pool, roof garden, disco. *Myrto* (I), tel. 7 1431. 800 yards from beach.

Néa Makrí (34/21). *Márathon Beach* (M), tel. 9 1255. 166 rooms. Pool, tennis, minigolf, disco; on beach. AE. *Nereus* (I), tel. 9 1214. 127 rooms. Close to beach. *Zouberi* (I), tel. 7 1920/4. 128 rooms. Roof garden, pool, disco; on beach.
Restaurants. *Limanaki* (M), tel. 9 1330. Fresh fish.

Oropós (53/33). *Alkyonis* (I), tel. 3 2490. 91 rooms. On waterfront. *Flisvos* (I), tel. 3 2480. 60 rooms. Disco. Like Alkyonis, on waterfront and close to not very inviting beach.
Restaurants. Numerous Moderate fish taverns on waterfront.

Pórto Ráfti (39/24). *Artemis* (E), tel. 7 2000. 32 apartments; 600 yards from beach. *Korali* (I), tel. 7 2602. 16 rooms. Close to fish taverns and beach.

Rafína (30/19). Outstanding town for seafood, no good for bathing. *Avra* (I), tel. 2 2781. 96 rooms. *Ina Marina* (I), tel. 2 2215. 79 rooms.

Vravróna (37/23). *Vravróna Bay* (M), tel. 8 2591/5. 352 rooms in large central block and bungalows on vestigial beach. Pool, tennis, minigolf, disco. AE.

West Coast

Ágii Theódori (74/46). *Hanikian Beach* (E), tel. 6 7151/60. 271 rooms. On beach, minigolf, tennis, exceptionally well-run. *Siagas Beach* (M), tel. 6 7501/3. 101 rooms. Near beach, minigolf, disco.

Kinétta (58/36). *Kinétta Beach* (M), tel. 6 2512/4. 181 bungalows on beach. Pool, tennis, disco. *Sun* (I), tel. 6 2243. 51 rooms. Near beach; restaurant. AE.

Néa Péramos (34/21). *Megalo Pefko* (I), tel. 3 3205. 70 rooms. Restaurant.
Restaurants. There are a number of (M) fish taverns on the seafront.

On Gulf of Corinth

Loutráki (87/54). Most of the some 40 hotels ranged along the seafront and round the springs in Greece's most popular spa date from the early 1960s. Only those with private baths or showers to all rooms have been listed. For the most part, they are frequented by Greek rather than foreign visitors. The locally much-appreciated roofgardens are a common feature. None is airconditioned.

Angelopoulos Holidays (M), tel. 4 1662. 50 furnished apartments. No restaurant. *Marinos* (M), tel. 4 2575. 51 rooms. Pool, roofgarden, disco. v. *Paolo* (M), tel. 4 8742. 80 rooms. Roofgarden. Close to mediocre beach. AE, DC, v. *Pappas* (M), tel. 4 3936/8. 84 rooms. on Pefkaki Beach. Disco. AE, DC. *Excelsior* (I), tel. 4 2254. 33 rooms. DC. *Galaxy* (I), tel. 4 8282. On the town fringe. MC. *Marion* (I), tel. 4 2346. 45 rooms. DC, MC, v. Disco. *Mitzithra* (I), tel. 4 2316. 43 rooms. v.

A little further west are the comfortable bungalows of *Club Poseidon* (M). (See under *Holiday Villages,* p. 13).

Restaurants. Most hotels operate their own restaurants, but they are as indifferent as the few in the main street.

Pórto Germenó (53/33). *Egosthenion* (I), tel. 4 1226. 80 rooms. 275 meters (300 yards) from shingle beach. Roofgarden.

Restaurants. There are several (M) fish taverns on the seafront.

Inland

Most villages possess at least one Inexpensive hotel, mostly quite modern, but not likely to be suitable for tourists; these are not listed.

Halándri (10/6). *Acropole* (I), tel. 682 6221. 55 rooms.

Restaurants. *Dido* (M), tel. 682 2209, piano bar. *Erato* (M), tel. 683 1864, pleasant evening outing.

Kifíssia (16/10). Garden suburb of Athens and summer resort, very lively in the evening. The hotels cater mainly to a Greek clientele. Because of the relative coolness, airconditioning is unnecessary.

Pentelikon (L), tel. 801 2837. 43 rooms, airconditioned. *Vardis* restaurant, pool, gym. Reopened 1987. *Semiramis* (M), tel. 801 2587. 42 rooms. Nightclub, pool, roofgarden; halfboard only. AE, v. *Theoxenia* (M), tel. 801 2751. 65 rooms. Pool; halfboard only. Renovated 1988. *Pines* (I), tel. 807 2402. 69 rooms. On the national road.

Restaurants. *Blue Pine* (E), tel. 807 7722. Fine assortment of hors d'oeuvres and charcoal broils, dinners only and country-club atmosphere with discreet music. AE, DC. *La Belle Helène* (E), tel. 807 7994. French cuisine. including fillet with Greek Madeira sauce and chicken crepes. Average service. *Chevalier* (E), tel. 801 0162. Top-class French restaurant. *Cozy* (E), tel. 813 3342. Steak with mushrooms to piano music. DC. *Piccolo Mondo* (E), tel. 802 0437. Coquilles St. Jacques, with piano and singer. DC. *Le Sommelier* (E), tel. 801 2871. Wine bar and bistro in a charming old house. *Symposium House* (E), tel. 801 6707. International cuisine; in Politeia Sq. AE.

Aztec (M), tel. 801 5335. Mexican food with a helpful glossary of dishes. *Bokaris* (M), tel. 801 2589. Just below the electric train station, unusually large selection, rabbit stew, wild boar, wine from the barrel. DC. *Moustakas* (M), tel. 801 4584. Baked kid with oil and origan, shrimp sauce, guitars in the evening, open Sun, lunch. AE, DC. *O Nikos* (M), tel. 801 5537. Likewise kid with oil and origan, evenings and Sun. lunch. *Red Dragon* (M), tel. 801 7034. One of several branches; good Cantonese restaurant.

Mesógia Region. Restaurants. There are numerous taverns along the roads through the wine villages of the Mesógia, such as Liópesi and Koropí. The food is generally at least acceptable, the local retsina from the barrel is excellent. Those given below are not necessarily better, but more established.

Peanía. Restaurants. *Glaros* (M), tel. 664 2546. Dinners and Sun. lunches. Veal in wine sauce, kid in lemon sauce, washed down with rosé retsina in a pleasant garden. *Lagos* (M), tel. 664 2740. Not only hare, as the name indicates, but quail, woodcock and all kinds of game.

Pikermi. Restaurant. *Tou Skordou* (M), tel. 667 7240. The Garlic Inn, best known for game; opposite the bus stop; open daily 1 P.M.–2 A.M.

Mount Párnitha/Parnis (32/20). Reached by road or funicular. *Mont Parnes* (L), tel. 246 9111/5. 106 double rooms, 16 suites. The accommodation is surprisingly cheap, so is (M). Everything else is (E) to (L). Casino, nightclub, pool, tennis, spectacular view. AE, DC.
Several Inexpensive taverns at the fringe of the fir forest.

Varybóbi (19/12). *Auberge Tatoï* (M), tel. 801 4537. 9 rooms, tennis, the only reason to stay in the not particularly attractive surroundings is the excellent food. DC.
Restaurant. Just above the entrance to the royal estate, *Leonidas* (M), tel. 801 0000. Perhaps the best restaurant in Attica for the price; large outside terrace, but insufficient for the noisy weekend crowd.

GETTING AROUND. By Car. This is the preferable means of travel. With a little planning several interesting spots can be visited in a few hours, perhaps with a swim and a seaside meal thrown in. But signposting is poor.

By Bus. All the beaches and villages mentioned, but not all archaeological sites, can be reached by bus. Buses for most destinations in Attica leave from the Mavromateon terminal near the National Archaeological Museum (Mavromateon 14), but check for details at your hotel.

By Cablecar. There is a cableway to the Casino on Mount Parnís. The starting point at Metohí is not served by public transport.

DELPHI AND THE PARNASSÓS

"Navel of the Earth"

The "Parnassós (Parnassus) Country" is a term frequently applied to the area on either side of the spine of mountains extending northwest from the borders of Attica. Rising between the Boeotian plains and the sparsely inhabited northern shores of the Gulf of Corinth, most of this highland region is rich in mythological and historical allusion. One of the great courtesans of ancient times, Phryne—mistress of statesmen and soldiers— was born here. The rugged slopes of Kitherónas (Mount Kitheron) are associated with the haunts of Pan, the god of shepherds, and his goat-like satyrs; and the sacred grove where the nine muses dwelt, lay in a secluded valley of Elikónas (Mount Helikon). The caves and crevasses of Parnassós itself, towering above its neighbors, were the scene of five-yearly bacchanalian revels and nocturnal dances performed by Boeotian women dressed in animal skins; and, clinging to the side of one of its spurs, Delphi, the most celebrated oracle of antiquity, rose, terrace upon terrace, above what the ancients called the "navel of the earth."

Recorded history begins with the growth of the towns in the plains of Boeotia. The most important of these was Thebes, which, according to legend, was founded by Cadmus and subsequently ruled by the Labdacides, one of whom, the luckless Oedipus, was destined to kill his father and marry his mother. During the Persian Wars, Thebes, out of jealousy of Athens, allied itself to the Persians, whose decisive defeat at Plataea it shared in 479 B.C. Yet 100 years later, the Thebans were allied to the Athenians and for a brief ten years, from 371 to 362 B.C., dominated Greece due to the introduction of a revolutionary fighting formation, the phalanx.

Young Philip of Macedon, in those years a hostage in Thebes, later perfected the phalanx sufficiently to crush the Thebans and Athenians at Chaironéia in 338 B.C. In the Middle Ages, Thebes was successively overrun by Bulgars, Normans, Franks and Lombards, and the Turkish conquerors finally moved the seat of the capital of Boeotia to Livadiá. The latter, situated at the foot of Mount Helikon, had grown in importance and the Catalans built a castle, the ruins of which still dominate the town. Under Turkish rule, Livadiá became the second town of Greece after Athens.

Beyond Parnassós, at the foot of the mountainous mass of the Panetolikó and Vardóussia, lies the port of Náfpaktos on the northern shore of the Gulf of Corinth. Náfpaktos, like Livadiá, only gained prominence in the Middle Ages, and its possession was keenly disputed by Venetians and Turks, both of whom understood the strategic importance of its position guarding the narrows of the Gulf of Corinth. It was known as Lepanto when the Turkish fleet sailed out to be decisively defeated by a Spanish-Italian fleet under Don Juan of Austria in 1571. This was the end of Turkish naval supremacy in the Mediterranean and the turning point in Turkish history.

About midway between Thebes in the east and Náfpaktos in the west, lies Delphi: in the very heart of the Parnassós country. The origins of the history of Delphi go back to the first mysterious exhalations which issued out of a cave below the giant cliffs of the Phaedriades. At first the spot was dedicated to the cult of the earth-goddess, but, in time, Apollo came to be regarded as the presiding deity, worshipped in the guise of a dolphin *(delphos)*. The mysterious prophecies of a pythoness were associated with the earth's exhalations, and a sacred city grew up around the oracle. Games, dedicated to the worship of the Pythian Apollo, were held in the stadium, and the oracular pronouncements, now made through the lips of a priestess, not only gained renown throughout the ancient world, but influenced the actions of great politicians as well as humble people who flocked to Delphi to consult the oracle. Her utterances decided the fate of men and nations.

Greek art and literature are steeped in the legend of the oracle, and there are few tragedies of Aeschylus, Sophocles and Euripides, the plot of which does not hinge on some dramatic and often ambiguous pronouncement of the priestess.

Exploring the Parnassós Country

The quickest approach is by the motorway, from which Thíva (Thebes) is visible on a slight eminence in the center of the Boeotian plain to the west. The equidistant 70 km. (44 miles) mountainous inland road enters the narrow pass separating Attica from Boeotia just after the branch to Vília, passing below the ruins of the 4th-century B.C. fortress of Elefthére, with its seven gateways and several two-story towers. The road rises till a panoramic view is obtained of the Boeotian plains, with the mountain chain of the island of Euboea in the north. To the west stretches the backbone of Kitherónas, the crenellated range of Elikónas with the towering mass of Parnassós (often capped with snow until May or even June).

In the plain below, the first village is Erithrés, from where a branch road left six km. (four miles) leads to the battlefield of Platées (Plataea). Within the considerable remains of triple ramparts stand the ruins of Hera's temple and the Katagogion, a hostel built for the pilgrims after the destruction of the ancient town. Scene of the final expulsion of the Persian invaders in 479 B.C., Plataea was declared sacred, a quality conveniently ignored by its long-standing enemy Thebes at the outbreak of the Peloponnesian War in 431 B.C. A disgruntled political party opened a gate to the Theban vanguard, but the main army was delayed by rain. The 100 Thebans surrendered on a promise of personal safety and were promptly executed. When the Plataeans surrendered in turn four years later to the Spartans on the assurance of a fair trial, the judges asked each citizen what he had done to benefit Sparta. Obviously unable to produce a satisfactory reply, all men were killed and the women and children sold into slavery; only the temples were spared.

Boeotia is a great place for battlefields, even for Greece. To the northwest is Léfktra (Leuctra), where in 371 B.C. the Theban phalanx won its first great victory over the traditional hoplite army of the Spartans.

Thebes spreads out over a flattish hill 19 km. (12 miles) to the east. After the death of its two great statesmen and generals, Epaminondas and Pelopidas, Thebes lost its ephemeral pre-eminence and in 336 B.C. was razed to the ground by Alexander the Great, who spared only the temples and the house of the poet Pindar. Though regaining some prosperity in the later Middle Ages under Frankish dukes, the modern small town holds little interest. There are a large, frescoed Mycenaean tomb, some scanty remains of ancient gateways of the palace of Cadmus and a museum containing, among various archaic, classical and Roman fragments, three rather remarkable *steles* in black stone, with bas-reliefs, and paintings representing Boeotian warriors of the 5th century B.C. Close to the museum there is a squat Frankish tower: a reminder of the annexation of Thebes to the Duchy of Athens by the de la Roche family in the 13th century.

Beyond Thebes, both road and rail traverse what was once the Kopaïk lake: the insalubrious marshy plain was drained by a British company at the end of the 19th century to become a main cotton producing region. The antique geographer Strabo's assertion that the lake had been drained in his time is borne out by the existence of an intricate system of dykes and canals channeling their water into the sea.

The branch right (north) to Homer's "grassy Haliartos" may be passed with no great loss, though modern Alíartos still lies within "well-watered meadows." A few miles further on, to the left is the next battlefield. Beyond fields and olive groves, a Catalan tower marks the acropolis of Koroneia, where the religious festival of the Panboeotia was held in honor of Athena Itonika. Her temple stood on the plain, where the Boeotians overthrew the Athenians in 447 B.C. The foundations of the ancient town are an unidentifiable jumble and the road ends at the village of Korónia perched on a hill.

Some 45 km. (28 miles) west of Thebes lies Livadiá, whose chief industry consists of hand-made blankets, brightly colored examples of which may be seen drying on old Turkish bridges spanning the Hercyna, a legendary stream on whose banks the oracle of Trophonius, a Boeotian divinity, was situated.

The Hercyna emerges out of a gloomy gorge at the foot of the medieval castle built by a band of Catalan mercenaries who ravaged and occupied several parts of central Greece during the 14th century. Two springs have been identified as those of Lethe (Oblivion) and Mnemosyne (Remembrance). Niches for votive offering are hewn out of the rock above the springs, and in one of them—the largest—the Turkish governors of

Livadiá used to retire during the heat of the day to snooze and smoke their *narghilés*. Today the site is shaded by plane trees, with little cafes along the stream.

At Livadiá the road divides, the left prong leading to Delphi, the other skirting the base of Parnassós in a north-westerly direction. Twelve km. (eight miles) to the right (east) of the latter route is Orhomenós, according to Homer one of the oldest and wealthiest cities of prehistoric Greece. Enthusiasts might be tempted to the acropolis on the hilltop, but of greater interest and less painful is the Mycenaean bee-hive tomb of Minyas, excavated by Schliemann in the 1880s. Nearby a 5th-century B.C. theater was dug out in the early 1970s; across the road, there is a very fine Byzantine church (the Dormition of the Virgin), the earliest example of a church in the Greek cross plan in the country.

To the northwest the road traverses the site of the battle of Chaironeia (Heronía), where, in 338 B.C., Philip of Macedon defeated the armies of Athens and Thebes, which defended the antiquated concept of the city state against northern monarchy. A large marble statue of a lion, which originally rested on a monument dedicated to the Boeotians who fell in the battle, may be seen from the road. Odysseus Androutsos, a particularly rapacious leader in the War of Independence, hacked the statue to pieces, hoping to find it stuffed with treasures. Later excavations of the tumulus on which the fragments were lying revealed over 200 skeletons, of the Theban Sacred Band, the famous company of lovers wiped out by the better-armed Macedonian phalanx. The lion was put together at the beginning of the present century and now rests its haunches on a marble plinth.

To the east, a band of Catalan soldiers of fortune, to whom the Duke of Athens owed considerable arrears, in 1311 diverted the waters of the Kephisós to create a swamp covered by a carpet of grass. The Duke and his knights, clad in coats of mail, plunged their horses into the quagmire and became sitting targets for the arrows of their former foot soldiers. The massacre was sufficiently thorough to break the Frankish power in central Greece which fell to Catalan overlords.

Five kms. (three miles) beyond Heronía branch left to the village of Davlía: the ancient Daulis, where the wife of Tereus, the King of Thrace, revenged herself against her husband's violation of her sister by serving up the flesh of their own little son for him to eat. The ruins, in themselves unimpressive, are romantically situated on a spur of Parnassós which falls away in sheer precipices into a deep and luxuriant valley. The squat towers of the ramparts overhang a torrent above whose boulders is perched the brilliantly white Convent of Jerusalem.

At Brálos village, at the foot of the pass, a 63-km. (39-mile) branch left (south) leads through a spectacular gorge via Ámfissa to Delphi, making possible a circular tour of Parnassós.

The Sacred Way

The direct route to Delfí (Delphi) is the 45-km. (28-mile) stretch from Livadiá cutting out the hairpin bends of the Sacred Way of the ancients through the desolate uninhabited region between the massifs of Elikónas and Parnassós.

Almost exactly half way between Livadiá and Delphi is the famous junction of roads, the Triple Way, as it was known by the ancients, where the roads from Delphi, Daulis and Livadiá (and Thebes and Athens beyond) meet. It is a lonely spot, at the beginning of the long, narrow and deep valley leading to Delphi; and it is here, according to legend, and so described by Sophocles in *Oedipus Rex,* that Oedipus, returning on foot from Delphi, met his father, Laius, King of Thebes. The latter, having struck Oedipus with his whip in order to make room for his chariot to pass, was in turn attacked and accidentally killed by the enraged young man, who did not recognize his father. It was after this unintentional murder that Oedipus, who had been brought up in Corinth and had not seen his parents since his birth, returned to his native town of Thebes and answered the riddle of the deadly Sphinx that had held the Thebans in the grip of fear. He then ascended the throne of Thebes and unknowingly married his mother, Jocasta, thus fulfilling the prophecy that had caused his parents to abandon him at birth.

Close by, a side road leads into a fertile cup-shaped valley among the foothills of Elikónas, after passing through the village of Dístomo, the scene of a savage Nazi act of reprisal in 1943, when one male member of each family was taken out and publicly shot. On a flank of the hillside, amid orchards of almond trees, is situated the monastery of Óssios Loukás, one of the most important Byzantine monuments in the country. The monastery is open 8:30 to 3 daily except Mondays.

At first a hermitage, a shrine was subsequently founded on the spot by an orthodox ascetic, Luke the Stiriote (not to be confused with St. Luke) in the 10th century. Luke possessed prophetic powers, and his shrine gained such renown that, after his death, it became a place of pilgrimage and his disciples decided to construct a fitting monument to his memory. Architects and mosaic workers, under the patronage of the beautiful and notorious Empress Theophano, were despatched to this lonely spot from Constantinople. When the Emperor Romanus II died, however, and Theophano married his successor, Nicephorus Phocas, the project had to be abandoned for the new emperor was a dour and stingy soldier, little given to lavish expenditure in the furtherance of the arts. But, on the accession of the Emperor Basil II, an intelligent monarch and redoubtable general, known as the Bulgar-slayer, work on the church of Óssios Loukás was resumed in 1019, at the new emperor's express orders.

Of the two churches (there is also a crypt and monastic cells), the larger, dedicated to Blessed Luke himself, is now a museum. Of exquisite proportions, constructed in the classic Greek cross plan (cross-in-square), with multi-colored marble paving-stones and overhanging balconies, it constitutes one of the finest extant examples of a great Byzantine shrine of the 11th century. Its supreme glory rests, however, in its mosaics. Although none have the inspirational force or exquisite mastery of execution of the mosaics of Daphni, they possess an austerity and hieratic formality which makes a powerful impression. The subtle disposition of the apostles on the arches in the narthex concentrates the attention on the Pantocrator who was once depicted above the entrance to the inner church. The most striking portraits are those of St. Peter on the east wall, and St. Andrew opposite, with disproportionately large heads. Particularly impressive are the gaunt saints and warriors in the dome and the Nativity and Baptism in the pendentives. Some of the mosaics have been restored at different dates from the 16th century. The smaller church, dedicated to the Virgin, no longer bears any traces of mosaics or frescos; but it contains some fine stone carvings (see the capitals of the four columns supporting the dome and the cornice of the iconostasis). Outside the church, there is a large terrace, shady with plane trees, overlooking the cup-shaped valley. The simple tourist pavilion is situated here.

Beyond the fork to Óssios Loukás, the Sacred Way continues the long and lonely ascent towards Delphi. The air becomes more rarefied, the scenery more awesome. The road passes the narrow main street of dizzily perched Aráhova, noted for its woolen handicrafts and red wine. From this mountain village a comfortable crossing of Mount Parnassós through dense fir forests passes between the Fterólaka and Kellária ski centers, within easy climbing distance of the summit (2,450 meters, 8,040 ft.). After descending to the village of Eptálofos you can join the Livadiá–Lamía road at Amfíklia (42 km., 26 miles). Back on the Delphi road the gorge of Pleistos opens out into what seems to be a sea of olive trees below the great cliffs of the Phaedriades.

Delphi—Grandeur and Mystery

After the Acropolis of Athens, the site of Delphi leaves the most powerful and lasting impression. The scene, both from the ruins of the sanctuary and from any one of the hotels or terraced village houses, is of the greatest possible grandeur. Down below in the gorge, the bed of the Pleistos winds between a narrow strip of olive trees flanked by precipitous cliffs, opening out into the Sacred Plain where the sea of olives, probably the finest grove in all Greece, ends in the calm aquamarine waters of the seemingly landlocked Bay of Itéa. In the far horizon, across the Gulf of Corinth, to the south, tower the mountains of the Peloponnese—Zíria, Helmós and Panahaïkó—while in the west the massif of Vardóussia inclines gently towards the sea.

Above the ruined sanctuary rise the cliffs of the Phaedriades, cleft by a narrow but deep chasm, at the foot of which gushes the Kastalian Spring. At sunset the sides of the cliff glow red with the reflection of the sun's rays and the whole ravine of the Pleistos and the steep terraced vineyards round Aráhova are bathed in a warm deep purple light. Overhead, occasionally, an eagle soars.

The modern village of Delphi, overhanging the gorge of the Pleistos, is traversed by a single main street, lined with hotels, restaurants and souvenir shops, filled with postcards, thick woolen rugs and bags from Aráhova with bright-colored patterns, and other products of the local crafts. The entrance to the sanctuary can be reached from almost any point in the village, in anything from a five to ten minutes' walk. At night the street is alive with the strains of pop music, which the local inhabitants imagine tourists prefer to the melancholy folk music of the Parnassós country, from numerous radios and cassette-players in the cafes. Some of these have terraces overhanging the gorge, the plain and the gulf beyond.

For a millenium a village covered the site of the sanctuary and had to be completely expropriated and demolished in order to permit the excavations to be undertaken. The villagers were indemnified by the French Treasury and their houses rebuilt on the present site. The excavations by the French School of Archeology in Athens were begun in 1892 under the direction of Theophile Homolle and continued for over ten years. In a faint reflection of antique prestige, the Cultural Council of Europe holds congresses here in a modernistic building.

The ruins of Delphi can actually be seen in one day. This means, however, that the visit will be a hurried and very exhausting one, for the monu-

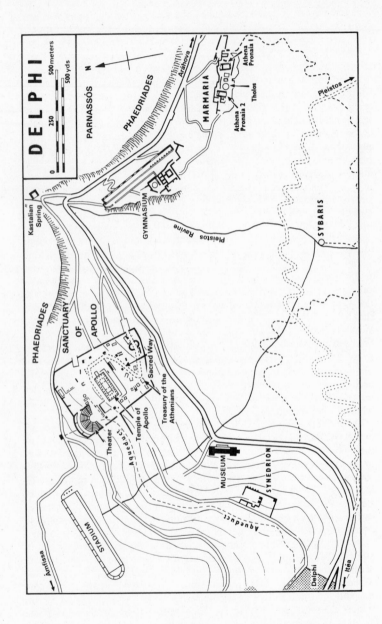

ments of the sanctuary and the temples of the Marmaria are built on steep terraces, involving a considerable amount of climbing. A stay of at least a day and a half is recommended in order to see the sights comfortably. Thus the first afternoon could be devoted to a visit to the sanctuary, the following morning (during the heat of the day) to the museum, which contains some of the glories of Greek sculpture, and the last afternoon to a tour of the Marmaria, below the Kastalian spring.

Hardly anyone would, however, regret a longer stay: not only to examine the ruins in detail and explore the surrounding Parnassós country, but even more to sense that extraordinary atmosphere of grandeur and mystery which haunts the place. At few other ancient sites do legend and reality, the monuments and the scenery harmonize so completely; few other places feel so completely isolated from the everyday world yet, at the same time, the very center of things that matter—the navel of the earth, as the ancients believed in a figurative as well as a metaphorical sense. The navel of Gaea, Mother Earth, was located when two eagles flying from the opposite ends of the earth met here midway. Rather surprisingly from a physiological angle, the navel turned out to be a conical stone, eventually placed in Apollo's temple, where it was daily anointed and adorned with flowers.

The Sanctuary of Apollo

The sanctuary, with its ruined temples, treasuries and foundations of various monuments, is contained in a trapezoid enclosure extending across the northern side of the slope below the cliffs of the Phaedriades. After the expropriation and demolition of the original village the entire site was systematically and scientifically excavated by the French archeologists. When first seen from the road, it would appear that little remains to attest to the splendors of antiquity. Only the treasury of the Athenians and a few other columns are left standing; but once within the precincts, the plan becomes clearer and the lay-out is revealed in such detail that it is not impossible to conjure up a vision of what the scene must have once been when Delphi was the holiest place in all Greece.

On entering the precincts from the main road, the visitor finds himself in a small rectangular paved space, on the north side of which there are the remains of a Roman portico. From this point the narrow Sacred Way to the Temple of Apollo commences a zigzag ascent, flanked on either side by the bases of statues, long since removed or destroyed, and of such buildings as the ex-votos of the Athenians, the Arcadians, the Argives and the Lacedaemonians. The first was ornamented with 16 statues, of which the earliest (those of Apollo, Athena and Miltiades, the victor of Marathon) were, according to Pausanias, executed by Pheidias.

Beyond the uniformly ruined foundations of the treasuries of Sykyon, Siphnos, Megara, Thebes and Boeotia, rises the exquisite little treasury of the Athenians. This small Doric temple was rebuilt in 1904 by the French School from funds supplied by the municipality of Athens. Reconstructed for the most part out of original blocks of marble lying on the spot, it stands out in the otherwise confused scene of trenches, foundations and masses of stone. It was originally erected after the battle of Márathon in 490 B.C., and on its walls is engraved the score of a hymn to Apollo. Original fragments of sculpture may also be seen on the pediment and metopes. Beyond the treasury rise three small slender Ionic columns once belonging to the portico of the Athenians, below a polygonal wall which served as a support to the temple of Apollo and which retains a superb patina to this day.

The podium and peristyle of the great temple, the seat of the oracle, in the very center and heart of the shrine, where Apollo slew the python and established the worship of his cult, are complete and several Doric columns have been replaced in their original position. From the platform of the temple, it is easy to understand the layout of the sanctuary.

Divine Doubletalk

It was from a deep subterranean fissure on the site of the temple that the mysterious exhalations originally emanated. Before each prophecy, the priestess, who was always a woman of over 50 (to ensure her chastity), would be purified with water from the adjacent Kastalian spring. In historical times, the subterranean gases had ceased, probably after an earthquake, and the priestess would chew equally poisonous laurel leaves and seat herself in full ceremonial robes on a tripod above the crevasse. Then followed the sacrifice of an animal, whose entrails were carefully examined. Questions relating to the fate of a war, journey, marriage or business enterprise would finally be put to the priestess, who, having now gone off into a trance, would make strange incoherent utterances which were interpreted to the anxious and puzzled consultant by a "prophet." Inscribed on the temple was the wisest and most famous of all Greek maxims: "Know thyself"—a maxim, alas, not always heeded by those who came, and still come, to Delphi.

Although ambiguity was, as often as not, the keynote of the prophecies, the effect nevertheless made on men's destinies by their interpretation cannot be exaggerated. For two millennia, mythology and history, states and individuals were guided by increasingly obscure pronouncements. Colonies and constitutions were established, war and peace were decided after consultations.

Megarian colonists, told to "settle opposite the city of the blind," dutifully emigrated to the coast facing Chalcedon, where the Chalcidians, "blinded" by the attractions of the fertile soil of the Asiatic shore of the Bosphorous, had established themselves. But the Megarians, led by Byzas and confident in the oracle's advice, built their city above the splendid harbor on the European shore and founded Byzantium.

Lykourgos and Solon sought the oracle's advice for the constitutions of Sparta and Athens. But insult seemed to be added to injury, when Croesus of Lydia, relying on "Crossing the River Halys, you will destroy a great empire," attacked Persia, was defeated and barely escaped with his life. On complaining, he was admonished for inadequate consultation, not having clarified which empire.

During the Persian Wars the oracle was alarmist, even defeatist. Basing its judgement on its far-flung intelligence service, the oracle for once departed from cautious reticence by telling the Athenians "Flee to the end of the earth." But Themistocles insisted on a second opinion, and though the oracle could not reverse itself completely, with the probable assistance of a bribe, it enigmatically declared that the "sons of men" would be "devoured" at sea. The Persians—"sons of men" indeed—suffered a crushing defeat in the naval battle of Salamis in 480 B.C., and the tide of conquest by the Asiatic hordes was halted.

In the subsequent war between the principal Hellenic city states the oracle's good name suffered as a result of its prophecies, many of which were inspired by obviously venal motives. The treasuries offered by the city states were frequently pillaged by victorious generals of the contending states, and earthquakes added to the destruction. But a masterly phrased oracle that with hindsight could be interpreted as having foretold the assassination of Philip of Macedonia restored Delphi to a vital factor in Greek life until growing religious indifference set in and undermined its hold over the popular imagination. Aristotle summed up the attitude of the Hellenistic intelligentsia: "It's hard to believe and harder still to deny." The Roman emperors favored the cult of the oracle, but Nero did not help by removing 500 statues from the sanctuary, then was outshone by Constantine the Great who beautified his capital with Greece's masterworks. Sceptical philosophers had undermined the sanctuary's prestige, bands of Goths and Visigoths wrought havoc, but the final blow came when paganism was proscribed throughout the Roman world by the Christian Emperor Theodosius I in A.D. 381. Apollo's temple was closed and pulled down by the Emperor Arcadius who built a church in honor of the new God.

Theater and Stadium

Above the temple rises the 4th-century B.C. theater restored during the Roman epoch. Although considerably smaller than the theater at Epidaurus, it remains in a good state of preservation, and its position, dominating the terrace of the temple of Apollo and the whole sanctuary, is extremely impressive. From a sun-warmed seat on the last tier, the visitor may obtain a panoramic bird's-eye view of the sanctuary and the convulsed landscape that encloses it. At sunset, when the Phaedriades glow coral pink and the soft blue light spreads over the valley and the mountains opposite, the silence, if a pullman car has not just disgorged a load of polyglot tourists, is almost complete. It is here that the feeling of isolation is at its most complete, and the circular configuration of the mountains seems best to justify the description of Delphi as the navel of the earth.

In this theater ancient tragedies are produced from time to time, performed in the late afternoon. Sophocles' *Oedipus Rex,* for instance, is so timed that when Oedipus gouges out his eyes with his own hands after being convinced of his crimes of parricide and incest, the glow fades from the Phaedriades and the warm blue, pink and mauve tints on the sides of the enclosing hills turn dun-gray.

Still higher up, on a final bastion of the cliff, as though perched midway between sky and earth, extend the well-preserved ruins of the Stadium, where the Pythian games were held. 201 meters (220 yards) long, its 12 tiers of seats still more or less intact, the stadium could hold 7,000 spectators. The decorative marbles ornamenting the judge's rostrum, the gift of Herodes Atticus, the famous Athenian benefactor of the 2nd century A.D., have, however, long since disappeared. Three columns of a Roman triumphal arch, through which the contestants entered the stadium, are still standing.

The Pythian games were held at the beginning of September of every fourth year, under the direction of the Amphyctionic Council, a religious body, including representatives of all the principal Greek states, which administered the affairs of the shrine and its oracle. The games also included the performance of a sacred drama describing Apollo's victory over the python, a musical competition and a chariot race held in the hippodrome down below in the Sacred Plain.

The Marmaria

The term Marmaria (the Marbles) is applied to a group of ruins situated below the main road, little more than five minutes' walk from the sanctuary of Apollo. These are actually the first vestiges of ancient Delphi seen by the traveler approaching from Aráhova.

Midway between the sanctuary and the Marmaria, the Kastalian spring gushes out of the narrow chasm between the twin Phaedriades. It was from the summit of these cliffs, where the eagles soared in the rarefied mountain air, that criminals were hurled headlong into the valley below by the Delphians: a fate reserved for Aesop, the fable-teller of the 6th century B.C., who, as ambassador of Croesus, had fallen out with Delphi's governing body over the distribution of certain monies donated by the Lydian king before the unfortunate misunderstanding about which empire was going to be destroyed.

A visit to the Kastalian spring, which was supposed to have purifying properties, was considered an essential preliminary to a pilgrim's visit to the oracle. The stream, clear and ice-cold, now trickles from a basin surrounded with niches into a modern cistern, where hot and exhausted passers-by may refresh themselves with deep draughts of water. Several cafes are situated under the large plane trees.

A path leads down among the olive trees to the terraced enclosure of the Marmaria, dedicated to the worship of Athena. The archaic temple of Athena was destroyed in the 5th century B.C. by several rocks crashing down on it from the top of the Phaedriades during a violent storm. The second temple of Athena, built to replace the earlier one, was constructed on a spot less exposed to the mercy of avalanches.

The treasury of Marseille, situated between the two temples of Athena, and of which little remains today, was one of the earliest examples of a building in the Ionic order (6th century B.C.). Elegant mouldings surround the base of the treasury, and its columns, none of which are any longer standing, are crowned with capitals ringed with a design of palm leaves. Close by, the Tholos, a round Doric temple, the exact purpose of which is unknown, is one of the purest and most exquisite monuments of antiquity still to be seen at Delphi. Theodoros, its architect, wrote a treatise on his work: an indication in itself of the exceptional architectural quality of the monument. The base of the temple is complete, and several columns have been judiciously restored.

On another terrace of the Marmaria, a little further to the west, extend the ruins of the Gymnasium. Built in the 4th century B.C. and considerably added to by the Romans, the gymnasium served as a training ground and meeting-place for the athletes participating in the Pythian games. Only mere traces of the large swimming-bath survive.

The setting of the Marmaria, among olive trees and tall bushes on terraced slopes, is more gentle and bucolic than that of the sanctuary, nor is the view so panoramic and awe-inspiring. Across the Pleistos gorge, the perpendicular sides of Mount Kirfis may be discerned, with a mule-track zigzagging up to a bare upland plateau.

Down below, among the olive groves is the ugly gash of the cement water duct from Lake Mórnos. On the northern flank of the gorge, the pit of the Sybaris lies not far from the riverbed of the Pleistos. A mule-track, starting at the eastern extremity of the village leads in a walk or ride of about an hour to the pit, where a spring, situated among a chaos of huge boulders, rises. The Sybaris was a terrible monster which lay concealed in a cavern, emerging only to devastate the surrounding countryside. The monster finally found its match in a local youth, Eurybatos, who hurled it down into the ravine. Thereupon a spring gushed forth where the monster struck the earth. More modern folklore, however, has it that a shepherdess, the wife of a *pappás* (priest), met her death here for having taken her flock to pasture by the spring on a Sunday. Hence the name Pappadiá is often applied to the spring and sometimes to the whole ravine.

The Museum

The museum, a partly-screened modern eyesore, is all too conspicuously placed on the main road between the village and the sanctuary. At the top of the staircase stands a copy of the conical *omphalos*, the navel of the earth, whose interlocking marble fillets symbolize the continuity of life. The most famous exhibit is the life-size bronze statue of a charioteer, effectively displayed on its own against a pale gray background. It was part of a quadriga that stood on a terrace wall above the temple of Apollo, near which it was found in 1896. It is not established who executed the work, although the donor was a well-known patron of chariot-racing, Gelon, the Tyrant of Syracuse. The statue commemorates a victory in the Pythian games at the beginning of the 5th century B.C. Most striking is the severe classical simplicity of the execution which does not detract from the intensely natural and life-like aspect of the young man holding the reins. Equally impressive are the eyes, which are inlaid with a white substance resembling enamel, the pupils consisting of two concentric onyx rings of different colors. The sculpture of the feet and of the hair clinging to the nape of the neck is perfect in detail.

The earliest example of ancient Greek sculpture in the museum is a pair of Caryatids from the treasury of Knidos (Asia Minor). Of a slightly later period are the Caryatids from the treasury of the island of Siphnos. Other fragments from the frieze of this treasury depict such scenes as the Judgement of Paris, the Battle of the Giants and the Contest of Greeks and Trojans before the gods. The admirable sculpture of the groups of horses deserves particular attention. A completely restored replica of the treasury of Siphnos gives the visitor an idea of what these elaborately adorned little temples flanking the Sacred Way of the sanctuary, must have looked like in the 5th century B.C. There are also fragments from the metopes of the treasury of Sicyon and of the temple of Apollo depicting the Rape of Europa, the Caledonian Boar, Castor and Pollux and the Sons of Aphareus, etc.

An impressive example of mid-6th-century B.C. sculpture is the heraldic Winged Sphinx of the Naxians, with scythe-shaped wings and a bosom draped with stylized feathers, seated on the Ionic capital of a marble column.

Fourth-century B.C. art is represented by the column of the Dancing Girls, held to be the work of an Athenian sculptor of the school of Praxiteles. It represents three dancing girls grouped round a support, and the ten-meter (33 ft.) high acanthus column on which it stood in front of the ex-voto of the Syracusans, was of Parian marble. The draperies of the figures are not only naturalistic but extremely graceful.

The greatest Hellenistic sculptor, Lysippus, is commemorated by a marble copy of his bronze nude athlete, the Thessalian Agas, who won 14 prizes at panhellenic festivals.

The Roman period is represented by a fine nude of the Greek youth, Antinous, the favorite of the Emperor Hadrian. The museum also contains numerous other sculptural fragments, statues, sherds, terracottas, vases, ceramics, etc. All the exhibits were found either in the sanctuary and the Marmaria or in the immediately adjacent neighborhood.

The Olive Country

From Delphi to Náfpaktos the distance is 125 km. (78 miles), 113 km. (70 miles) along the sea. The road climbs down the last bastions of Parnassós into the plain of huge gnarled olive trees, some of which are said to be centuries old, the olives which they produce—large, bluish and fleshy—known as "Ámfissa olives," being among the best in Greece. The branch left (south) leads six km. (four miles) south to Itéa, where cruise ships often call.

On the tapering western arm of the Bay of Itéa lies the quiet, relatively tourist-free port of Galaxídi, whose Byzantine Church of the Savior dates from the 13th century. The Archaeological and Naval Museum, with its exhibits of model ships, sea maps, weapons from the Revolution, and other memorabilia, evokes the old port's past glories and is worth a visit. From here the scenic coastal road skirts the Corinthian Gulf via Eratiní to Náfpaktos.

The narrower, winding inland road leads in a westerly direction to Ámfissa, 23 km. (14 miles) from Delphi, situated on the slope of a hill crowned with a medieval castle built by the Franks and Catalans in the 13th and 14th centuries, when the town was known as Salona. The ruins of the castle include some quadrangular and polygonal walls, two watch towers, two gateways, a cistern, a circular dungeon and the remains of a Frankish and a Byzantine church.

At Ámfissa one road leads through the gorge of Graviá and over the Bralos pass to Lamía or the motorway near Thermopylae. The east–west branch continues 109 km. (68 miles) to Náfpaktos; after Ámfissa there is a steep climb up the massif of Vardoussia in a series of hairpin bends. Magnificent views are obtained of Delphi, Parnassós, the gorge of the Pleistos and the olive groves of the Sacred Plain. After the village of Lidoriki, the road hugs the scenically magnificent vast artificial lake created by the damming up of the Mórnos River. On the walled acropolis of antique Kallion, on a rock still rising above the waters that cover the lower town, the largest collection of 4th-century B.C. clay seals was discovered. The lake supplies 2,000,000 cubic meters of water daily through pipelines to Lake Ylíki in Boeotia, thence to Lake Márathon, to quench the thirst of Athens 193 km. (120 miles) away. The road crosses the dam and follows the trickle of water in the original bed of the river between steep green banks until it reaches the sea near Náfpaktos.

From here, the road runs along a short flat coastal strip to Antírio, from where the ferry can be taken across the narrows of the Gulf of Corinth to Río and the northern shore of the Peloponnese. Westward the motorway bypasses Messolóngi and then turns north to Epirus.

A visit to Náfpaktos and even an overnight stay, is recommended despite the indifferent accommodation. Situated on a fertile coastal strip washed by tributary streams of the Mórnos, the lively little harbor faces the peaks of the Panahaïkó in the Peloponnese. The bathing beaches are adequate, and there is an air of friendliness about the little town. Luxuriant bushes of oleanders, bright in summer with red, pink and white blooms, line the banks of the streams, and the flowers and comparatively lush vegetation present a strong contrast to the austere grandeur of the Parnassós country.

The steep cone-shaped hill behind the town is dotted with blocks of masonry of a vast rambling Venetian castle. The road stops at the triple line of well-preserved fortifications, entered through a series of arched gateways overlooked by a crenelated bastion. The defenses were divided into five successive wards on different levels, now covered with a dense growth of pines mounting the bailey to the Chapel of Profitis Ilias (Prophet Elijah) built on the foundations of a pagan monastery. Trees and walls allow only occasional glimpses of the blue waters of the channel between the mainland and the Peloponnese. In the evening it is pleasant to sit at one of the cafes in the little semi-circular fortified harbor and watch the caiques chugging in and out between the two miniature medieval towers guarding the entrance into the port, while the lights begin to twinkle in the villages strung out along the opposite shore of the Peloponnese.

PRACTICAL INFORMATION FOR
DELPHI AND THE PARNASSÓS

WHEN TO COME. Most of the Parnassós country can be seen in the course of a visit to and from Delphi. The Boeotian plains are very hot and dusty in the summer months. A visit of the ruins involves much climbing which is exhausting during the middle of the day in the summer when the motorcoaches disgorge vast hoards of sightseers. In spring the countryside is comparatively green; a variety of wild flowers grow on the hillside, and the fields around Thebes are carpeted with red tulips.

So the best time of the year for a visit is April–May and October–November. But the grandeur of the scenery at Delphi is such, however, that a profound impression will be made on the visitor in all weathers. Dramatic storms are frequent in autumn.

Mountaineers will find the ascent of Parnassós most practicable in July, August and September. But you can also drive to the ski centers and walk from there, for 45 minutes, to the top.

For sun-seekers, Náfpaktos has pleasant beaches.

SPECIAL EVENTS. February. The Vláhikos Gámos is a mock-highland wedding which brings large crowds to Thebes on Shrove Monday. **April.** The Mikró Panegýri (Small Fair) is held at Aráhova on St. George's Day, April 23, with costumed dancing contests of the old men. **September.** The Pindaria Festival, named after the lyric poet Pindar, includes music, drama and dance performances.

HOTELS AND RESTAURANTS. Delphi offers a quality choice of hotels, but only a quantity choice of eating places. Elsewhere, accommodation is at best adequate, and food is better not discussed. However, try the large juicy olives from Ámfissia: they are among the best in the country. The red wine from Aráhova is rough but drinkable.

Amfíklia. *Leonidas* (I), tel. 2 2544. 14 rooms.

Ámfissa. *Amfissaeum* (I), tel. 2 2161. 40 rooms. Roofgarden, disco. AE, V. *Stallion* (I), tel. 2 8330. 24 rooms.

Antíkyra. *Antikyra Beach* (I), tel. 4 2156. 24 rooms.

Antírio. *Antirio* (I), tel. 3 1450. 11 rooms.

Aráhova. *Anemolia* (M), tel. 3 1640/4. 42 rooms. Airconditioned, disco; on slopes of Mount Parnassós. DC. *Xenia* (I), tel. 3 1230/2. 43 double rooms. Half board only. In the village but equally splendid view over the Pleistos Gorge. DC, MC, V.

Delphi. Hotels in the Expensive and Moderate price ranges insist on half board. Numerous Inexpensive modern hotels line the main street, called after King Paul and Queen Frederika: only those (I) hotels with restaurant terraces looking over the gorge down to the Gulf of Itéa are listed, but the view has to compensate for the largely uninteresting food.
   Amalia (E), tel. 8 2101/5. 185 rooms. Airconditioned; for once, large is best, though hardly beautiful. AE, DC, MC, V. *Castalia* (M), tel. 8 2205. 26 rooms. Roofgarden. *Europa* (M), tel. 8 2353/4. 46 double rooms. Next to the Cultural Center of Europe. *King Iniohos* (M), tel. 8 2701/3. 50 rooms. Airconditioned. AE, MC. *Pan* (M), tel. 8 2294. 30 rooms. Unpretentious and friendly; quiet location overlooking valley. *Vouzas* (M), tel. 8 2232/4. 60 rooms. Closest to the ruins, overhanging the Pleistos Gorge; food is unremarkable. AE, DC, MC, V. *Xenia* (M), tel 8 2151/2. 44 rooms. Higher up in the village, this hotel offers panoramic views from terraces. AE, DC. *Acropole* (I), tel. 8 2676. 35 rooms. *Hermes* (I), tel. 8 2318. 24 rooms. DC. *Iniohos* (I), tel. 8 2316. 15 rooms. AE, DC, V. *Parnassos* (I), tel. 8 2321. 23 rooms. *Pythia* (I), tel. 8 2328. 27 rooms. DC, MC.
   Restaurants. Though these are (M), they are better than some of the (E) hotel dining rooms. *Asteras* (M). For food and view. *Chalet Maniati* (M). Big garden opposite the Xenia hotel. *Symposium* (M). Reliable; tennis court. AE, MC.

Eratiní. *Delphi Beach* (M), tel. 3 1237/8. 177 rooms. Halfboard; air-conditioned, pool, tennis, disco. AE, DC.

Galaxídi. *Ganimede* (M), tel. 4 1328. 7 rooms. An Italian-run pension with charming furnishings and a delightful patio garden. Quiet, comfortable, and highly recommended. *Ta Adelfia* (I), tel. 4 1110. 5 rooms.

Itéa. *Galini* (M), tel. 3 2278. 30 double rooms. Roofgarden. AE, DC, MC, V. *Kalafati* (M), tel. 3 2294. 40 rooms. *Nafsika* (M), tel. 3 3300/4. 77 rooms. Airconditioned, roofgarden. *Panorama* (I), tel. 3 3161/2. 27 rooms. Closest to the muddy beach. MC.

Livadiá. *Livadia* (M), tel. 2 3611/5. 51 rooms. In the center of town. Cafeteria. *Philippos* (I), tel. 2 4931. 58 rooms.

Náfpaktos. *Akti* (I), tel. 2 8464. 60 rooms. At Gribovo. *Lido* (I), tel. 2 2501. 15 rooms. Airconditioned; disco. *Xenia* (I), tel. 2 2301/3. 48 double rooms. Located 30 yards from beach; restaurant.

Restaurant. *Fisherman's Boat* (M). An American-Greek couple serves good seafood.

Platanítis. Near Antirio. *Kalydon Beach* (I), tel. 3 1412. 76 rooms.

Thebes. *Dionyssion Melathron* (I), tel. 2 7855. 30 rooms, most with shower. *Meletiou* (I), tel. 2 7333. 34 rooms.

GETTING AROUND. By Train. Thebes and Livadiá are easily reached by rail from Athens. Livadiá can be used as a base for visiting Orhomenós, Chaironéia and Davlía.

By Car. The drive to Delphi is under 160 km. (100 miles), whether you take the old road or the national road, turning off at Thebes. A short detour can be made to Óssios Loukás, lying 13 km. (eight miles) off the main Livadiá to Delphi road. Continuing from Delphi via Ámfissa over the western shoulder, or crossing the main range of Parnassós from Aráhova between the ski centers of Fterólaka and Gerontovrahos to Eptálofos, both connecting over the Bralos pass with the motorway at either Thermopylae or Lamía, make possible a circular detour on the way from Athens to Thessaloníki.

Náfpaktos can be reached by car from Delphi by the spectacular coastal road via Itéa and Galaxídi (112 km., 70 miles) or inland via Ámfissa and the Mórnos valley (125 km., 78 miles); and from Athens on the toll motorway via Corinth and the northern shore of the Peloponnese.

By Bus. Buses go to Thebes and Livadiá from the Liossion terminal (Liossion 260), Athens. One-day and two-day coach tours to Delphi are operated daily by various coach companies in Athens. Longer coach tours lasting four or five days and visiting the main archaeological sites always take in Delphi.

By Boat. There is a car ferry five times daily from Égio to Ágios Nikólaos (eight km., five miles from Eratiní) and every 15 minutes across the narrows between Río and Antírio.

SKI CENTERS AND MOUNTAIN REFUGES. Fterólaka and Kellária on the Parnassós are Greece's largest ski centers. No hotel, but snack bar, self-service restaurant, and ski shop. 16 skilifts up to 2,200 meters (7,200 ft.); 30 runs. Reached by 27 km. (17 miles) paved road from Aráhova to parking at Kondókedro for 800 cars; for climbers, it is a good four-hour walk from here, past the ski lift pylons, to the Liakoura summit. Main refuge is at Sarantari, 1,900 meters (6200 ft.).

THE PELOPONNESE

Four Millennia of History

Hanging like a large leaf from the stem of the Corinthian Isthmus, the Pelopónissos (Peloponnese) has also been called Morea, which means mulberry leaf. This slight botanical variance is nothing compared to the bewildering variety of imposing ruins, situated in equally varied and beautiful scenery. 4,000 years of history are more fully and comprehensibly illustrated on this peninsula of a mere 21,463 square km. (8,287 square miles) than anywhere else in Europe. A gap of a 100 years in the stately cavalcade of temples, palaces, churches, Crusader castles and mosques is a rare exception, due to catastrophic barbarian invasions, like that of the Dorians in the 11th century B.C., or of the Turks in the 15th century A.D.

The Peloponnese, the isle of Pelops, is named after the son of Tantalus, whose intolerably tragic descendants dominate the half-legendary Mycenaean centuries. This was the area's golden age, but it was to intervene prominently in world affairs three further times: when Sparta contributed decisively to Persia's defeat in the 5th century B.C., and gained after the Peloponnesian War a brief ascendancy over the other Greek cities; when the Frankish principalities of the Morea formed the cornerstone of Latin power in the Levant in the 13th and 14th centuries; and when the bishop of Patras raised the standard of revolt against Turkish domination in 1821. But more important than that is the peaceful contest the Peloponnese has given mankind: the Olympic Games.

Exploring the Peloponnese

Unless landing off a cruise, Athens is the most likely start for a tour of the seven provinces: Corinthia, Ahaia, Elis, Arcadia, Messinia, Laconia and Argolis. The toll highway leading south from the capital roughly follows the coast for 80 km. (50 miles) to Corinth, over the same stretch of country along which Theseus met and defeated numerous robbers and giants.

The Canal of Corinth is 6,345 meters (6,939 yards) long and 23 meters (75 ft.) wide. Completed between 1882 and 1893, it is spanned by a road and a railway bridge, and can be crossed in two places by submersible bridges, the one at Isthmia connecting with the direct road to Epidaurus. The concept of connecting the Ionian with the Aegean sea originated with the tyrant Periander of Corinth, one of the Seven Wise Men of antiquity, in the 7th century B.C. and was toyed with by Alexander, Julius Caesar and Caligula. But only Nero proceeded actively with the tremendous task, the emperor himself striking the first blow with a golden pickaxe, thus setting a fashion for royalty. Vespasian, who had offended his imperial master by falling asleep during a song recital, supplied a labor force of 6,000 Jewish prisoners of war; work was far progressed when the rebellions of A.D. 68 stopped the excavations. But Periander had constructed a paved road and up to the 13th century ships were dragged on rollers across the Isthmus. The submersible bridge to Posidonía at the western entrance of the Canal is scheduled to be supplemented by another of this kind to Isthmía at the eastern end.

The remains of the Isthmian wall stretch across the narrow neck of land behind the bridges. The foundations of the original fortifications, which failed to keep out the Dorians in about 1200 B.C., have been unearthed by an American archeological team in continuing excavations. The wall was restored on the occasions of subsequent invasions, against the Persians in 480 B.C. and by the Emperor Justinian against the Avars in the 6th century. Rebuilt on a grand scale by the Emperor Manuel II in 1415, it proved incapable of withstanding the Turkish onslaught 43 years later.

Little remains of the Isthmian sanctuary to the south, at the head of the Saronikós Gulf, as it was pillaged for stone to build the wall. Celebrated in honor of Poseidon, the biennial games were second only to the Olympic festival, and the scene of important historic events. In 481 B.C. the Panhellenic League of 31 states decided on the defense against the Persians; in 338 Philip of Macedonia and in 336 B.C. Alexander the Great, forced their elections as *hegemons* (leaders) on the reluctant Greeks; and in the same Isthmian stadium the victorious Roman general Flaminius proclaimed the independence of Greece from Macedonian rule in 196 B.C., to swallow it up all the better 50 years later. An early Christian basilica has been partly restored. Among the local finds in the small museum are unique Egyptian glass mosaics, raised from a ship that foundered in the harbor about A.D. 400.

New Kórinthos (Corinth), built on the present site after a devastating earthquake in 1858, was in its turn destroyed in 1928 and again in 1981. The direct road to Epidaurus, the toll road to Pátra and the road to Árgos bypass the modern town, which, despite its lovely position, could at best be called innocuous.

Old Corinth, the Frivolous City

Along the Pátra road, which branches off to the left, the ruins of ancient Corinth are reached after an eight-km. (five-mile) drive through vineyards. One of the oldest towns of Greece, it underwent in antiquity the customary changes from subjection to the kings of Mycenae to government by the Dorian aristocracy, replaced by enlightened tyrants, a title which in the 7th century B.C. simply indicated rule by one man. Under Kypselus and Periander, Corinth became the leading commercial city in Greece, which it remained for a while after the restoration of oligarchy. But trade had dampened the belligerent spirit of old, and Corinth's main contribution to the Persian wars were the prayers for victory, offered piously by its celebrated courtesans.

The rising commercial power of Athens led to constant frictions, which finally culminated in the Peloponnesian War. Corinth regained supremacy and became the largest city in Greece. Its vast, luxury-loving wealth brought about pillage and total destruction by the Romans in 146 B.C. All men were killed, women and children sold into slavery, and the site remained uninhabited until the foundation of a Roman colony by order of Julius Caesar in 44 B.C. This explains why there is only one Greek ruin, the seven Doric columns of the 6th-century temple of Apollo, dominating the well-preserved remains of the Roman town. On both sides of the Lechaeon road, formerly the chief artery of the ancient city leading to the port, and on the market-place, the ruins of public and private buildings are adequate to give a comprehensive picture of the frivolous capital of Roman Greece, which soon regained its former prosperity, due to its position between Italy and Asia, besides controlling all trade between the mainland and the Peloponnese. The well-arranged museum contains finds from the whole of Corinthia, but because of the destruction, little of the Greek town, except a fine collection of pottery and the unique stoup of holy water from Poseidon's temple at Isthmía. Outstanding among the Roman statuary is the archaic sphinx, recently discovered in the antique cemetery. To the north of the building are the remains of a fountain hewn out of solid rock. Pausanius tells how Medea, deserted by Jason for Glauke, the daughter of King Creon, wreaked her revenge. Medea sent as a wedding present to Glauke a poisoned robe which burst into flames the moment the unsuspecting princess put it on. Glauke, saving herself, leaped into the fountain, later named after her. Both the site and the museum are open daily from 8 to 5.

In A.D.51, St. Paul fulminated against immorality, caused a riot, but was acquitted by the Roman proconsul Gallio. The earthquake of A.D. 375 and Alaric's Goths 20 years later, drove the survivors up to the top of Acrocorinth, behind the ancient town. On the highest point stood the temple of Aphrodite, with no less than 1,000 sacred prostitutes dedicated to the service of the goddess. An awesome proof of the ancients' lustfulness and vigor to satisfy the carnal and financial exigencies after such a climb. In the Middle Ages, deploying heroism in different ways, Acrocorinth became a fortress town. Strengthened and enlarged by Byzantines, Crusaders, Venetians and Turks in turn, the two miles of crenelated walls enclosing 60 acres of the summit are the most imposing medieval monument in Greece. Cars can drive up to the triple gate, and the superb view over the Saronikós and Corinthian Gulfs, framed by the mountains of the Peloponnese and the mainland, should on no account be missed.

It is 133 km. (83 miles) to Pátra, through a narrow, fertile plain, delightfully green with vineyards and olive trees even in the height of summer. Road and rail run close to the blue waters of the Corinthian Gulf, while the motorway higher up along the gentle pine- and cypress-clad Peloponnesian foothills bypasses the coastal villages of Lehéo, Corinth's ancient port Lecheion, Kokóni, Nerántza and Kiáto, from where a road leads to the ruins of Sikyon (Sikyóna), six km. (four miles) inland. The birthplace of Lysippus, probably the greatest Hellenistic sculptor and Alexander the Great's favorite for his sculptural portraits—as well as that of his brother Lysistratus, the first to model a likeness in plaster from a living object—the prosperous city was the scene of particularly bloody struggles between the Dorian aristocracy and non-Dorian tyrants. After destruction in 303 B.C. by Demetrius Poliorcetes, it was rebuilt and named Demetrias in his honor (one of several). The theater, the gymnasium, the council chamber and a lovely fountain all belong to that Hellenistic town. The museum is in a partly rebuilt Roman bath.

Forty km. (25 miles) of mountain road, turning inland after the Kiáto bridge, lead to Stymfalía (Stymphalia), where Heracles accomplished his sixth labor by killing the man-eating birds. Now there is only some less exciting duck-shooting on the reedy shores of the lake, graced by some uninspiring ruins of small temples and ramparts. A further 12 km. (eight miles) climb 920 meters (3,000 ft.) to the hotel at Kastaniá. Turning north round Mount Zíria, Tríkala can be reached through fir forests. Another road branches east below the lake into the heart of Arcadia, with a fork to Neméa.

Ahaïa (Achaea)—Origins Recalled

Rather than being the original settlement of the first authenticated Greek tribe to invade the Peloponnese in the 17th century B.C., this northwestern province was the refuge of the Achaeans after the collapse of their Bronze Age states and before the onslaught of their Iron Age Dorian cousins some 500 years later. Xylókastro, a popular weekend resort for Corinthians with a magnificent view over the Parnassós and Elikónas ranges from the pine-girt beach stands on the site of one of the 12 cities founded in the northwestern Peloponnese by the Achaeans after their expulsion from Árgos.

Another scenic road zigzags up the mountains to Tríkala, which belongs to Corinthia. Only 32 km. (20 miles) from the heat of the Mediterranean one finds relief in the cool freshness of three tiny villages strung out in a fine Alpine setting. The cave where Hermes was born is near the lower of the Hellenic Alpine Club's two refuges on Mount Zíria (2,400 meters, 7,900 ft.), snowcovered till June above the green valley. A skilift leads into this main skiing center of the south.

From Trápeza and the orange groves of the coast there is a 22 km. (14 miles) ascent up the verdant slopes affording a superb view over the sea and distant mountains framed by perpendicular cliffs, past the monastery of Méga Spíleo to Kalávryta 760 meters (2,500 ft.). Another approach is from Diakoftó, by the rack and pinion railway, undoubtedly the finest train journey in Greece, through the wild magnificence of the Vouraïkós gorge. The line precariously overhangs the madly churning stream, shaded by a profusion of trees and bushes. From Zahloróu station half-way up, the road mounts to the monastery of Méga Spíleo, a white elephant of the first magnitude. The old monastery burnt down in 1934, and as it happened to be one of the richest in Greece was rebuilt on a grandiose scale, though without reference to any recognizable style. Moreover, no account was taken of the constantly diminishing number of monks, who now huddle together in one wing during the long cold winter. Central heating was installed, but never functioned, because of the expense of bringing up the fuel. The electrical switches are likewise purely ornamental. Following a vision, St. Symeon and St. Theodore discovered the miraculous icon, painted by St. Luke, in the large cave behind the church, whence the name of Méga Spíleo. Despite repeated fires, there are still some lovely 10th-century illuminated gospels, relics, silver crosses and pretentious Russian jewelry, gifts of Catherine the Great.

Kalávryta was burnt by the Germans in 1943, and over 1,000 of its inhabitants massacred. The clock on the Metropolitan Church stands at 2:34, the hour of the massacre. The magnificent plane trees, the cool streams, and the ruined Frankish castle on a rock, lend some distinction. The Límnes Kastríon cave, formed by a subterranean stream connecting 13 pools by waterfalls, is only one mile away, but the excursion to the falls of the Styx, the mythological river of the underworld, is exhausting. The Agía Lávra Monastery, originally built in A.D. 961 and housing 961 monks, was also burned down by the Germans. It has been rebuilt on the same prominent hill, which overlooks the Kalávryta plain. It is commonly believed that Bishop Germanos of Pátra raised here the banner of revolt against the Turks on March 25, 1821 and the monastery has become a national Greek shrine. On the opposite hill, a monument to the heroes of the 1821 Revolution looks down over the monastery. The longer 77 km. (48 miles) road from Pátra to Kalávryta runs through superb mountain scenery and links up after 32 km. (20 miles) with the Pátra–Trípoli road. The branch right (west) 21 km. (13 miles) after Kalávryta goes via Tripótama to Olympia by the shortest, loveliest and most difficult (no signposts) route, 90 km. (56 miles) through the fastness of Mount Erýmanthos, where Heracles slew the Erymanthian boar, and remainders of the vast oak forests that once covered the entire interior.

Nikoleíka, Valimítika and Digeliótika are on the coastal road, 19 km. (12 miles) before Égio, which is prettily situated on three levels rising from the sea. Villages, not yet beach resorts, follow one another: Lóngos, Lambíri, Rodíni and Psathópyrgos. Río, the Castle of the Morea, was built by Sultan Bayazid II in 1499, and together with Antírio, the Castle of Róumeli on the opposite shore, guarded the narrow entrance to the Corinthian Gulf. On the main road between the two fortresses is the car ferry uniting the Peolponnese with Epirus and Central Greece. A bridge is now being built across.

Pátra is the third town of Greece and its main western port where currants, dried Corinth raisins—so much prized in Anglo-Saxon cakes—are dispatched by the shipload. There is a Roman theater and the usual Frankish castle, but more distinctive are the arcaded streets, equally beneficial in the hot summer and the rainy winter. St. Andrew was crucified here and became the city's patron saint. His relics, however, met with even greater adventures than the apostle in his lifetime. The Emperor Constantine had them conveyed to Constantinople, except for one shoulder, three fingers, a bone and sundry teeth, which St. Regulus, bishop of Pátra, spirited away to Scotland, where they were received with due respect. In the 9th century the head was returned to Pátra, later returned to Rome, and finally, in the present ecumenical spirit, Pope Paul VI returned the head once again in 1965, to, one hopes, permanent rest in the cathedral.

Halandrítsa, 23 km. (14 miles) south of Patras, is a delightful village lying deep in the hills with fine views over the coastal plains to Xante. Once a Frankish barony, the village is now a pleasant stopping village due to its partly ruined churches, stone houses, courtyards, narrow lanes, and, of course, the remains of a Frankish castle.

Ilída (Elis)—the Frankish Outpost

After Káto Ahaía the road turns into the plain of Elis, dominated by Castel Tornese rising above the village of Kástro. A circular branch right (west) either from Lehena or Andravida skirts the castle hill, descends to the largest beach hotel in the Peloponnese and rejoins the main road via Loutrá Kylínis, Greece's most up-to-date spa for respiratory diseases, at Gastóuni. From here a branch left (east) follows the Piniós River to Ilída, ancient Elis, where the Austrian Archeological School is bringing to light the agora and theater of Olympia's protecting power.

Built by Villehardouin in 1219, hexagonal Castel Tornese remains an outstanding example of Frankish medieval architecture in the Levant, the bailey, keep and vaulted gallery still intact. Originally called Clairmont, the castle's later name derived from the Tournois coined there by the Frankish mint. Despite the formidable walls Castel Tornese failed in its main task: to protect the main port of the Morea, Clarence, of which little remains after its destruction by Constantine Palaeologus, the last Byzantine emperor. His later misfortunes were believed to have originated in a curse he incurred for his treatment of Clarenza. Railway and road branches terminate at Kylíni (not to be confused with Loutrá Kylínis, about 19 km., 12 miles south), whence it is less than two hours by ferry boat to the island of Zákynthos.

Andréville, now Andravida, just off the main road, was the capital of the Frankish principality. The sad remains of the Gothic cathedral of St. Sophia are rather depressing. Pýrgos, a few miles from the fine Katákolo and Spiatza beaches, is the road and rail junction for Olympia. The railway south and the coastal road both pass Kaiáfas, another watering place, this time for skin diseases, on an island in a lake and near a splendid, lonely beach. There, according to local tradition, the High Priest Kaiaphas was shipwrecked on his way to Rome after the Crucifixion. Washing off the salt in the hot springs he transmitted to them his evil sulphurous smell, which has persisted ever since. The line continues along the gulf of Arcadia to Kyparissía, 64 km. (40 miles) through particularly beautiful scenery, which loses none of its charm all the way south to Methóni.

The first important branch road east leads to Krestena, where it is joined by the 11-km. (seven-mile) shortcut across the Alfiós River from Olýmpia. The 45 km. (28 miles) up through idyllic hills to Andrítsena make possible the inclusion of the temple of Bassae in the excursion to Olýmpia and a return inland via Karítena, Megalópoli and Trípoli. The second branch, 35 km. (22 miles), connects with the Megalópoli–Kalamáta road.

Olýmpia—Center of the Panhellenic Games

Nineteen km. (12 miles) east of Pýrgos (which can be bypassed by road) lies Olýmpia among over 5,000 acres of the *Grove of the Sacred Altis,* revived as a national park in 1976. Quadrennial games were held here from time immemorial, first in honor of Hera, then of Zeus. Greek chronology was based on the Olympiads beginning with the festival of 776 B.C. and until A.D. 393 athletes from as far apart as Sicily and Asia Minor competed under the protection of a sacred truce. Apollo and Heracles were reputed among the early winners, while Nero was certainly the most quixotic, falling twice off his chariot, as he had difficulties in controlling his team of ten horses (all other competitors had to content themselves with four), yet, not surprisingly, coming first. He likewise won the singing contest, specially introduced to display his talents, whereupon he helped himself, as he had in Delphi, to some 500 statues.

Women were excluded under penalty of death. One mother, however, accompanied her boy disguised as a trainer. Betraying herself in her joy over his victory, her life was spared because she was the sister and mother of Olympic victors. Increasing honors were heaped on the winners, their statues were erected in the Altis—which must have been a forest of statuary—as well as in their home towns, and great poets glorified their successes. There were usually 14 contests, extending over five days at the midsummer full moon, culminating in the prize-giving ceremony and a feast on the fifth.

The almost rectangular Altis sanctuary is bounded by the Alfiós and Kladéos rivers, which both changed their courses in the Middle Ages, and on the north side by steep pyramidical Mount Kronion, which contributed with repeated landslides to the sanctuary's obliteration by six meters (20 ft.) of mud and pebbles.

The chariot races took place in the hippodrome which, though largely washed away, was the first to be rediscovered in the 18th century. From 1875 on, systematic excavations were undertaken by Professor Curtius under the active patronage of the German Crown Prince Frederick. Quite likely, it was Hitler's wish to emulate the imperial family that was responsible for his personal order to the reluctant archeologists to dig up the stadium during the German occupation in World War II. Below the repeatedly raised earth embankments, which finally accommodated some 30,000 spectators, the largest of its kind, a great number of ex-votos was discovered, including Miltiades' helmet, dedicated after his victory at Márathon, now a prize exhibit in the museum.

The earthquake-proof museum below Mount Kronion, open during the week from 8 to 5 and on weekends from 8:30 to 3, has the two pediments of Zeus' temple, among the most brilliant examples of ancient sculpture. The front pediment commemorates Pelop's chariot race, with Zeus standing in the middle; the other, artistically even superior, depicts the favorite theme of the fight between the drunken Centaurs and the Lapiths with Apollo trying to restore order. His serene nobility is perhaps more moving than the flashy beauty of Praxiteles' Hermes, the famous statue found near Hera's temple, Olympia's oldest, of which two columns still stand in the shade of pine-clad Kronion. The metopes of the temple representing Heracles' Labors, the Victory by Paeonios flying down from the sky, the terracotta Zeus and Ganymede, a head of Hera and a head of Antinous are among the few masterpieces that remain from the wealth of beauty that once filled the Altis.

The ruins of the religious and secular monuments in the Altis are well marked. To the right of the entrance is the Portico of the Gymnasium, which was washed away by the Kladeos. Continuing anti-clockwise, the enclosure of the Palestra (wrestling school) is followed by a complex including the Theokoleon (priests' lodgings), the Heroon (Heroes' Memorial) and Pheidias' workshop overlaid by an early Christian basilica. The southwest corner is taken up by the huge quadrangle of the Leonidaion (probably a hostel) and the Bouleuterion (Council Chamber) in front of the south portico. In the southeast corner stood the house built for the Emperor Nero's visit in A.D. 67. The east side is taken up by the Echo Portico which extends to the arched passage leading to the Stadium. On the north side the Metroon (Temple of the Mother of the Gods) stood before the Terrace of the Twelve Treasuries backing on to Mount Kronion. The lavish Nymphaion, established by the 2nd-century banker, Herodes Atticus, adjoined the 7th-century B.C. Temple of Hera. The circuit ends at the Philippeion (erected by Philip of Macedonia) and the foundations of the Prytaneion (Residence of the Magistrates).

The great Doric temple of Zeus still dominates the sanctuary as it has since the 5th century B.C., though the broken columns lie scattered under the trees. The sacred flame burnt within a rough circle of stone about three meters (ten ft.) in diameter, where the Olympic oracle spoke through the crackling of the sacrificial bull's skin. The flame was relit every spring by a "spark from heaven," unfortunately no more to be relied upon when runners convey the flame to wherever the Games may be held. The god's ivory and gold statue by Pheidias, one of the Seven Wonders of Antiquity, was taken to Constantinople by the Emperor Theodosius the Great, and perished in a fire. The Pelopion Mound contained the altar to the first known Olympic cheat.

As often in Greece, the ruins owe their enchantment to the serenity of the setting. German archaeologists have made the Altis a grove again; the aging pines they planted are gradually being replaced by the olive trees of antiquity. The attempt to return the Olympics permanently to the original site has luckily been abandoned, so that the tranquil beauty of the valley is no longer threatened by the vast installations needed.

Arkadía (Arcadia)—Mistaken Identity

The road east passes the International Olympic Academy and the Museum of the Olympic Games to follow the Alfiós River through a valley charmingly Arcadian in the romantic 18th-century tradition, though actually still in Elis. The wild Arcadian mountains further on have nothing of the idyllic quality the word acquired for the Romantics. In antiquity Arcadia was renowned for its backwardness and cruelty, only imperfectly counterbalanced by compulsory musical instruction.

Along the Ládonas River the scenery changes from bucolic to Alpine. A bridge on the right after eight km. (five miles) leads to the rudimentary spa called just that, in Greek Loutrá. Nineteen km. (12 miles) further along the Ládonas a road forks left (north) to Trópea and a large, artificial lake created by damming the Ládonas. The water rushes underground for nearly ten km. (six miles) to the hydroelectric plant. The winding lake is enclosed by steep, pine-clad mountains, and is strangely reminiscent of a Norwegian Fjord. The road forking right 11 km. (seven miles) after the picturesque mountain village of Langadiá leads via Dimitsána to Karítena. Despite the hair-raising sheer drop of 300 meters (1,000 ft.) after Stemnítsa the road permits full enjoyment of the surrounding peaks and summits, snow-covered from November to May. At the same fork a lesser road goes southeast to Trípoli via Davía. Both roads are splendidly remote. The usual approach to Karítena is from Megalópoli through vast olive groves. The picturesque little town crowds up a precipitous rock to an imposing Frankish castle which was the fitting abode for its builder, Geoffrey de Bruyères, a model of chivalry, and one of the few feudal lords to try to reconcile his Greek subjects to Frankish domination. The main road from Olýmpia continues northeast, is joined by another from Pátra, and then turns south. At Levídi a road branches left to the sad remains of Orhomenós, where Orestes' bones were found in 570 B.C. as predicted by a Delphic oracle. The road continues through little-frequented mountains, dividing for Nemea and Kiato. South from Levídi the main road comes into the plain of Trípoli. This, the capital of Arcadia, where the main Peloponnese roads cross, can be bypassed, for it is an uninteresting market town, as it was razed to the ground by Ibrahim Pasha during the War of Independence.

Ten km. (six miles) south, off the road to Sparta, you come to the scattered remains of the Tegaea. This was a major Arcadian power until it began to lose out to Sparta in the 6th century B.C.; despite this, it still flourished till its destruction by Alaric's Goths in the 5th century A.D. The famous Parian sculptor Scopas rebuilt the temple of Athena Alea in the 4th century B.C.; its Doric columns still stand (as high as the second drum) opposite the village church of Tegéa. Some of Scopas's work is in the small museum; the better preserved of it is in Athens. Three km. (two miles) further east at Paleá Episkopí (Old Bishopric), a neo-Byzantine basilica replaced in 1888 the church of medieval Nicli, seat of the High Court of the Frankish Principality.

A branch road extends to the Tripolí–Astro road. Fifteen km. (ten miles) north of Trípoli is the battlefield of Mantinia, best known for Epaminondas' victory and death in 362 B.C. The town was greatly strengthened by the great Theban to contain Sparta. But here, unlike his two other strong points, Megalopolis and Messini, almost nothing remains of the theater or the ramparts with their ten gates and 126 towers.

Most important of Arcadian antiquities is the temple at Vásses, which is reached from Andrítsena, on the road between Pyrgos and Megalópoli via Créstena. Andrítsena is a well-shaded village clambering up a mountain slope and the final 11 km. (seven miles) to Vásses (Bassae) open up ever more grandiose vistas. On a narrow platform, 1,125 meters (3,700 ft.) above sea level, stands the second best preserved temple in Greece. Dedicated to Apollo Epikouros (the Succorer), the temple was designed by Iktinos, the architect of the Parthenon, and erected in about 418 B.C. by the Phygalians in gratitude for saving them from a pestilence. Unfortunately the local stone has not stood up to the ravages of time and, as some protection, the temple is now covered by an enormus grey-white plastic tent, which is unlikely to be removed in the near future. Although it detracts from the awe-inspiring and impressive sight of the long, unbroken Doric colonnades against the stark mountains, the splendor of the temple can still be appreciated.

South of Trípoli beyond the first mountain barrier, stretches a rolling, oak-grown plain round Epaminondas' most ambitious creation, Megalópolis. The walls were almost nine km. (five and a half miles) long, and the theater, cut into a hill, the largest in Greece. The ruins bear witness to the ancient greatness, but not the modern town, badly polluted by a large thermo-electric plant. Twenty-six km. (16 miles) further down the Kalamáta road a branch right connects with the west coast at Kaló Neró (32 km./19 miles), roughly following the railway line.

Messinía—Meritoriously Idyllic

The idyllic southwest has largely preserved its romantic appeal. Both coasts are like a huge park with olive and cypress groves, through which one catches glimpses of the sea. Shepherds tend their flocks, and the occasional villages do not detract from the serenity of a perfectly enchanting landscape.

Rail and road follow the coast south from Pýrgos. In the 4th century B.C., Epaminondas built Kyparissía as Messíni's harbor, but after a checkered career it is a sleepy little town, mainly distinguished by some dilapidated wooden houses climbing the rock to the Byzantine castle. The railroad turns here, but the road roughly keeps to the shore. A branch ascends to Gargaliáni, perched on a rock-shelf above the fertile coastal plain, and then to Hóra, where the museum contains the finds from Nestor's palace. The royal tombs are so poorly indicated that no one's conscience will be ruffled by missing out on this series of rock tombs, whose chronology is anywaydisputed (1500–1100 B.C.). The coastal road continues to Nestor's palace. A corrugated iron roof shelters walls still standing about three feet high over a considerable area, giving an excellent idea of the complex of palace, guardhouses, and storerooms. Ancient Pýlos provides a fascinating example of Mycenaean palace architecture, centered on the large open hearth in the throne room. The main curiosity is a 13th-century B.C. bathtub of painted clay. The most important find was in fact the first to be discovered, within two hours of the first day's dig in 1939. This was the uncovering of several hundreds of tablets inscribed with Linear B script, an early form of Greek, confirming for the first time the link between the Mycenean and Minoan civilizations. The bones in the sarcophagus found in the well-preserved beehive tomb 73 meters (80 yards) north are commonly believed to be those of Nestor, but are more likely to belong to an earlier king. Superfluous to say that the view is superb. This was the first consideration for the ancient Greeks before choosing the site for a temple or palace.

Modern Pýlos (Navarino to the Venetians) stands at the southern horn of the large, landlocked bay in which the allied fleets of Great Britain, France and Russia destroyed the Turco-Egyptian forces in 1827, and thus made Greek independence a reality. The rocky island of Sfaktiría (Sphacteria) which almost blocks the harbor, was the scene of another famous engagement. In 425 B.C. an Athenian expeditionary corps forced the Spartan garrison to surrender after a memorable siege lasting 72 days. The huge Venetian castle dominating Pýlos is well worth a visit, having been restored, and now equals the grandeur of Methóni in the south.

Methóni's fortifications are a perfect model of the military architecture of the period. Together with Koróni on the other side of the western prong of the Peloponnese it was the first Venetian foothold on the Greek mainland, and the two fortresses were called "the eyes of the Republic." Koróni is less impressive with the peaceful convent of St. John the Baptist within the castle walls. But it commands an incomparable view across the Messinian gulf to the Taygetos and the mountains of the Máni. Koróni is 29 km. (18 miles) south via the simple beaches of Ágios Avgoustínos, Petalídi and Ágios Andréas from the main Pýlos-Kalamáta road (53 km., 33 miles). Koróni is a picturesque town, still relatively undiscovered by tourists, retaining much of its Venetian charm and character. The direct, mainly coastal 29 km. (18 miles) from Methóni via Finikoúndas to Koróni, though lovely, are hard going in parts.

Dreary, modern Messíni bears no relation to its antique namesake and no comparison with its offspring in Sicily. The enormous walls of the ancient town, Epaminondas' third foundation, climb and descend the mountain, 17 km. (11 miles) north. The small museum is located at the village of Mavromáti. Near the restored Arcadian Gate the poignantly scenic road passes through the splendid masonry of the broken towers towards the Trípoli highway. Far below, among extensive olive groves, are the ruins of the theater, the temples and the agora; closer inspection necessitates a steep descent. Mount Ithómi, 807 meters (2,650 ft.) above the sea, was the last refuge of the earlier Messinians during their 300 years of war and rebellion against the Spartan invaders, to whom it fell at last in 459 B.C. The view from the deserted monastery on the top over the Messinian plain and gulf rewards the intrepid climber.

Kalamáta, constructed by the French in 1829 as capital of Messinía, was partly destroyed in 1986 by an earthquake which killed 20 , injured hundreds, and left 12,000 families homeless. A great many buildings were—and still are—flattened and the town's population has dropped by 50% in the years following the earthquake. The series of shocks up to 6.2 on the Richter scale felled the keep of the 13th-century Villehardouin castle, where some pines add a pleasantly romantic touch to the incomprehensible jumble of fallen masonry. Yet the drive or walk up the low hill is worthwhile for the view over the plain, sea and river, the Nédonas flowing through the ruined town.

International contributions have assisted in the rebuilding, beginning with the tiny Byzantine Agii Apóstoli (Church of the Twelve Apostles), remarkable more for the exterior brickwork than for the obscure interior. A new museum is needed, as the old one seems beyond repair, with some of the exhibits badly damaged. But on sale again are the astoundingly cheap products of the local Levi-Strauss factory, the tasty black olives, and silk handkerchiefs handmade and sold by the nuns in the convent off the cathedral square.

The small port of Kalamáta is about three km. (two miles) from the town. Along the coastal road east numerous minor hotels back on to lemon and orange orchards, while directly on the long sand beach is a string of restaurants where music and movement continue till a late hour in summer.

The Máni—Vanished Vendetta

The middle prong of the southern Peloponnese was for over a millennium Greece's, and perhaps even Europe's, wildest outpost. The last Spartans were pushed by successive waves of Slav settlers into these inaccessible mountains from the 7th century onward. Yet the present-day Maniates seem surprisingly swarthy for descendants of fair Dorians, obviously diluted by a forcible mixture with Arab pirates. Until the recent construction of a circular road, raids from the sea were much easier than by land; the Turks never bothered to occupy the poor inhospitable southern cape, contenting themselves with a nominal tribute, mainly goats, from the local feudatories.

The Máni adapted surprisingly quickly to the pattern imposed by tourism throughout the Mediterranean. Almyró and Mikrá Mantinía herald several small but increasingly popular beach resorts in the Outer Máni. The road turns inland to Kámpos, to rejoin the sea at Kardamýli (42 km., 26 miles). Stop on the bridge to enjoy a perfect landscape.

A little further on a road leads up into the Taygetus foothills, passes along a ridge with extensive views over the coast, and then descends to reach the sea again at Stóupa. Past Ágios Nikólaos, the road climbs and dips, conforming to the exigencies of the rocky coast. At one of the ups, at Plátsa, is the Folkloric Museum of the Máni; most visitors prefer the really splendid view over the Messiniakos Gulf. Soon the lush vegetation gives place to the lunar landscape of the Inner Máni, where the descendants of the Spartans, organized in clans, maintained their independence in fortified towerhouses, necessitated by the constant blood-feuds arising from quarrels over the scarce soil. Vendetta is now no more than a cherished memory; the Maniates are, on the whole, less surly than most "proud warriors turned into waiters." Despite their regrets, the unreformed elders do seem to enjoy the comparative comfort and luxury of the new houses built with the filthy lucre of the resented tourists.

Ítylo beach seems like an oasis before the climb to the rocky waste of Areópoli (82 km., 51 miles), the principal village, far from lively, though the main road junction. To the left of the road to Gýthio (26 km., 16 miles) rises the large fortress of Keléfa, the last Turkish outpost, occupied temporarily by the Venetian Morosini in 1685. The two large stalactite caves of Glyfáda and Alepótripa, commonly called the Díros Caverns, are ten km. (six miles) through Pýrgos Dírou on the west coast. The former, electrically lit and easily accessible by specially constructed motorboats might well turn out to be the largest seacave ever discovered, as so far only five km. (three miles) of splendid chambers and halls have been explored, with corridors and passages extending into a mysterious distance, in antiquity reputedly one of the entrances to the Underworld. In the latter, cave paintings, stone implements and even a primitive pottery workshop of paleolithic man have been found. *(Closed for further excavations.)*

Seventeen km. (11 miles) south is the small fishing port of Geroliménas. A road winds on to Vathiá, a small hilltop village, where several of the characteristic tower houses have been restored and a complex of traditional guest houses created. The settlement overlooks Cape Tenaro, where several of the characteristic towers have been restored as a traditional settlement, overlooking Cape Ténaro, the southernmost point of continental Europe except for Tarifa in Spain. Offshore, the Mediterranean descends to its greatest depth at the Inóusses Pit, 4,850 meters (15,900 ft.). The return along the solitary east coast is closer to the sea, 45 km. (28 miles) via Solotéri to Kotronás, then 15 km. (nine miles) to rejoin the main road at Areópoli. The circuit of the Máni requires a full day.

Lakonía—Laconic No More

No less spectacular, and much shorter, is the direct Kalamáta–Sparta road (59 km., 37 miles) following the Nedonas gorge, before climbing through fir forests to the Taygetos Pass at 1,000 meters (3,300 ft.).

The descent through the Langáda Gorge on a good but rather narrow road cut into the solid rock affords fine views over the sea of olive trees in the plain of surprisingly un-Spartan Spárti (Sparta), bisected by a wide, tree-lined avenue where 19th-century neo-classical houses maintain provincial respectability among recent cement blocks of manageable proportions. Water from the broad Évrotas (Eurotas) screened by pleasant orchards, flows into a swimming pool among the trees, and though icy, it offers welcome refreshment in the hot summer. Fortunately there is no need to emulate the luckless boys of antiquity who had to swim the Eurotas in winter in a desperate quest for physical fitness. Yet the hour of Sparta's greatness was shorter than that of cultured Athens, and pleasure-loving Corinth outlasted both. Except for the foundations of Artemis' sanctuary, of Athena's Brazen House, where two kings were starved to death, and the Menelaio to the east, the shrine of deified Menelaus and Helen, as well as some fragments of Apollo's temple at Amýkles, where hyacinths still bloom in spring from his lover Hyacinthus' drops of blood, nothing remains of ancient Sparta, which was a mere conglomeration of five villages. For hundreds of years it relied on the martial superiority of its warrior caste, and only in its decline were fortifications hurriedly constructed in 369 B.C. The Romans built a theater facing the temple of Artemis, the better to gloat over the scourging of the young Spartans before the goddess' statue. But times have changed: Sado-masochists need not queue for tickets, and Spartans today are no more spartan than Greeks in general.

Half-legendary Lykourgos organized Sparta on a warlike basis sometime between 900 and 600 B.C., his laws being interpreted ever more stringently with the passing of time. Its worst features were the oppression of the earlier Achaean inhabitants, once ruled by Menelaus and Helen of Troy, now serfs known as Helots, by an all-powerful secret police. But even membership of the Dorian aristocracy was a mixed blessing. Boys were taken at the age of seven from their parents and submitted to a training without parallel in history for ruthlessness, their only consolation being a lover undergoing similar sufferings. Stealing was encouraged as it sharpened the wit, but being caught out was cruelly punished. Wordiness was a disgrace, speech was reduced to laconic brevity and trade impeded by an iron coinage—not accepted outside Spartan territory—intended to enforce contempt of wealth and luxury. As a result Spartan kings and generals became notoriously rapacious, and increasingly open to bribes. In short, Sparta presented all the hateful characteristics of a totalitarian state. But Lykourgos received his punishment at long last: in front of the large, modern cathedral stands what might easily qualify as the most hideous statue in the Peloponnese. And to add insult to injury it bears only the sculptor's, but not the lawgiver's name.

Perhaps the paucity of sunshine contributed to Spartan austerity. The sun rises late over the Parnónas range and sets early behind Taygetos. Yet in Roman times life became more civilized, as witnessed by several mosaics, the finest presenting Europa and the Bull. The museum's showpiece is an archaic pyramidal *stele* depicting Agamemnon, his wife and in-laws.

Byzantine Mystrás

The prosperity of Byzantine Sparta continued under its first Frankish lord. But his son, William de Villehardouin, moved his chivalrous court in 1249 to Mystrás, a great castle on top of the steep hill, *Mezythra* (Goat-cheese), three miles west, at the foot of Taygetos. For ten years young nobles from the greatest kingdoms in Christendom were initiated into the art of chivalry in that splendid medieval setting, which Goethe chose for Faust's symbolic union with Helen, German mysticism and Greek Classicism. Taken prisoner by the Emperor Michael Palaeologus, at the battle of Pelagonia, William had to cede Mystrás as part of his ransom, and soon a town grew under the protection of the Byzantine fortress. Mystrás is thus essentially Byzantine, and for over 100 years was the capital of a despotate, governed by sons and brothers of the emperors. Constantine Palaeologus reigned here, from 1443 to 1449, before becoming the last emperor, and under his brothers the despotate survived the fall of Constantinople for seven years. Mystrás had then over 40,000 inhabitants and remained a populous town till the abortive revolt of 1770, when it was burnt by the Sultan's Albanian troops. Abandoned, in a reversal of fortune for Sparta, the empty shell of the city still stands as a great monument to the Byzantine Renaissance. Visiting the ruins of the Frankish castle on the summit necessitates a strenuous climb with few compensations. Yet, the winding road to the castle gate should be taken, as the easiest way to see the restored churches scattered throughout the town below. It is then all downhill, with the car ideally waiting at the main gate.

The monastery of the Perivleptos in the lower town is partly hollowed out of the rock, and possesses some fine frescos, particularly the Transfiguration, and the Divine Liturgy, celebrated by Christ, in the vestment of a Byzantine patriarch. Though a tiny museum occupies the bishop's palace attached to the 13th-century Metropolis, it is the view, opening north over the Eurotas valley, that holds the attention. The Aphendiko is architecturally the most interesting church, while the Pantanassa's frescos are considered the supreme manifestation of late Byzantine art. Particularly striking is the raising of Lazarus, where strawberry pink buildings blend with a honey-colored landscape under a navy-blue sky, in a singularly daring use of color in medieval religious painting. The nuns of the Pantanassa convent faithfully guard the deserted churches, and are the only inhabitants of this ghost town. The vast arched hall in the despot's palace, open to the sky, with crumbling walls and staring windows, still conveys its past grandeur.

Gýthio, Sparta's port, lies 45 km. (28 miles) south, on the Gulf of Lakonia. Squeezed between the sea and a steep hill crowned by a castle, this small ancient town is well worth a visit, mainly for the pleasant situation, bathing, and as a starting point for excursions into the Máni. A causeway leads to the island of Kranaí, where Paris and Helen spent the first night after their elopement in Aphrodite's sanctuary. Gýthio is the port of embarkation—in no way resembling Watteau's famous painting—for Kýthira (Cythera), a harsh, dry island and a curious choice for Aphrodite to make her first appearance.

Though historically joined to the Seven Ionian Islands, Kýthira belongs geographically to Lakonía. There is an air connection with Athens and sea connections with Piraeus. The hydrofoil calls at a number of eastern Peloponnesian ports including Monemvassía before ending up at the island's two harbors of Agía Pelagía, on a good beach, and Kapsáli (three km., two miles, from the capital), which rises like an amphitheater to the Venetian castle on an imposing cliff. Displayed in the castle museum are interesting finds from several archeological sites, mostly accessible by an adequate road network. More impressive than the ruins of Aphrodite's temple at Paleókastro is the monastery of the Panagía, whose ikon attracts large numbers of pilgrims on August 15.

Monemvassía is roughly 60 km. (37 miles) from Gýthio, 95 km. (59 miles) from Sparta and connected to Piraeus by hydrofoil and boat. Malvoisie to the Franks, Malmsey to the English, its vineyards were famous for centuries—until the arrival of the Turks. Legend has it that the Duke of Clarence was drowned by his brother, Richard Crookback, soon to be Richard III, in a butt of malmsey. The great rock with the impregnable Byzantine and Venetian fortifications, that for a while owed allegiance to the Pope, towers above the causeway leading to the walled but sadly diminished town, in which only the restored 12th-century churches retain something of the former splendor. The narrow lanes, crumbling churches, half-ruined stairways leading nowhere, and acres of ruins provide hours of frustrating and rather depressing exploration. Although most residents of Monemvassía live in the characterless, modern quarter of town, on the mainland, more and more of the 16th-century houses are being renovated and put to use as guest houses. In fact, one of the best hotels, the Malvasia, in the area can be found in several combined restored houses, in the old kastro.

For the scenically loveliest return, branch north via Ágios Dimítrios to Géraki, among whose medieval churches the best preserved is the 13th-century basilica of Ágios Georgios within the Bronze-Age walls, successively restored by Franks, Venetians and Turks. Continue northeast at the crossroads through fine mountain forests to the Elóna Monastery, seemingly suspended from the sky. The road descends through a dramatic gorge to Leonídio. A very scenic 80 km. (50 miles) road follows the Argolikós Gulf via the beaches of Paralía Ástros, Mýli, and Néa Kíos to Náfplio. From Ástros two roads climb northwest to Trípoli, one 45 km. (28 miles) via Doliána, the second a more adventurous 68 km. (42 miles) through the mountain villages of Meligóu, Ágios Pétros, and Kastrí. They meet near Tegéa.

Flanked by Taygetos and Parnónas, the 60 km. (37 miles) north from Sparta to Tripoli pass through a middling highland scenery, followed by cherry orchards. After Trípoli the descent to Árgos, 57 km. (35 miles), is made in hairpin bends which give a stunning view across the Argolikós Gulf to Náfplio and the mountains beyond that's among the finest in Greece, where views are innumerable.

Argolída (Argolis)—Unique Continuity

The first village on the gulf is Mýli, ancient Lerna, where Heracles killed the nine-headed serpent, Hydra; a team from Cincinnati University has unearthed a large terracotta-tiled Bronze Age building dating from 2200 B.C. Of more recent appeal is, of all unlikely places, the rail station, a graceful building surrounded by eucalyptus trees. Vines shade a tavern, of which there are more under huge plain trees on the quayside, facing the fortifications of Náfplio on the opposite shore from a different angle. Three rusting steam engines, 2–8–2's built in Boston, lie close to a crumbling domed mosque.

Nine km. (six miles) north through orange groves is Árgos, Hera's city, the most ancient continuously occupied site in Greece. Here the 50 daughters of Danaus killed their bridegrooms, except one, the ancestor of Perseus, founder of Mycenae. Another of their descendants was Heracles, the reputed ancestor of royalty in Greek antiquity, progenitor of the kings of Sparta as well as of Árgos. Emerging from the Dark Ages under a Dorian oligarchy, Argive ascendancy peaked under the tyrant Pheidon, but declined after the defeat by the Spartans in 520 B.C. Usually allied to Athens against the hereditary Spartan enemy, Árgos maintained a secondary position in Classical times. An important road junction close to the sea assured continuous commercial eminence, highlighted by occasional political revivals.

The modern town curves round the Lárissa, named after a daughter of Pelasgus, rising sheer from the plain. This 300-meter (984-ft.) high crag is crowned by the double ramparts of the Byzantine-Frankish citadel with Turkish additions. There is no road to the summit, only a steep path which passes the whitewashed chapel in a cypress grove less than halfway up. Cut into the crag's foot, the 81 tiers of the 4th-century B.C. theater are sufficiently ruined to preclude a festival—at least until extensive restoration. In front stand the crumbling brick walls of the 1st-century B.C. Roman baths, later converted into a monastery. Some interesting mosaics of the same period are across the street. The best, coming from the bath complex, are in the Museum in Vassilíssis Sofías, sumptuous 5th-century A.D. floors, depicting hunting scenes with surprisingly lifelike portraits. A Neolithic figurine from Lerna combines a beak-like mouth with stunted arms and sharply-pointed breasts. A head of Sophocles is more reassuring.

At nearby Kokla a 21-meter (23-yard) long passage leads to the unique wall-engravings on the facade of a beehive tomb of 1500 B.C.,accidentally discovered in 1981.

A little more than half the 13 km. (seven miles) to Náfplio is Tíryntha (Tiryns), Heracles' birthplace. To the left of the road rises a low mound, on which a palace stood as early as 3000 B.C. The Cyclopean walls were built with enormous blocks of stone in about 1800 B.C. and the impressive vaulted galleries were added some 300 years later. According to German archeologists, who are continuing excavations of a religious center with Mycenaean frescos among the houses of the settlement, the fortress was finally abandoned in the 13th century B.C. following an earthquake.

Náfplio (Nauplia) is an unusually well-preserved Venetian town, beautifully situated overlooking a lovely bay. It offers a choice of good hotels and taverns, besides being ideal for excursions. Nothing remains of the town founded by Nauplius, son of Poseidon and one of the Danaids. His son Palamedes invented dice, arithmetic, some of the letters of the Greek alphabet and gave his name to the higher hill, on which solid, yet graceful Venetian walls until recently enclosed the modest house where Otho, first king of Greece, held court from 1833 to 1834. The National Assembly ratified his election in the Church of the Annunciation after the first President, Capodistrias, had been assassinated at the steps of the Church of Ágios Spiridon by the Mavromichalis clan, lords of the Máni. Otho's unfortunate ministers and courtiers had to climb the 999 steps from the town. A road now winds up to the back entrance of the vast compound or, for the sound in wind and limb, a vertiginous flight of steps climbs up from the town park. Within the restored walls encircling the lower hill of Ákronafplio are two excellent hotels. Boúrdzi, a picturesque Venetian fort built on an islet in the bay, once the hangman's residence, now scheduled to become a tourist pavilion, merits the pleasant boat ride. The Venetian naval arsenal on the town square houses the museum, crowded with Mycenaean finds. The Peloponnesian Folkloric Foundation displays its collections in a neo-classical house on Vassiléos Alexandrou, while the new Folklore Museum for Children, run by the same foundation, is in the old municipal railway station. The larger of the two disaffected mosques, now a cinema, housed the first Greek parliament. The fountain in the garden of Agía Moni on the outskirts, founded in 1144, has been identified with ancient Kanathos, where Hera bathed once a year to regain her virginity.

The sanctuary of Asklepios is at Epídavros (Epidauros) 29 km. (18 miles) northwest. At this shrine of the god of healing revolting superstitions, like being licked by the sacred serpents, were slowly replaced by medical treatment, based on diet, fresh air, medicaments and even surgery. The health-giving smell of thyme and pines still lingers, but only foundations remain of the vast establishments, which included the earliest hospital ward. Models in the museum convey a picture of what Epídavros must have looked like at the height of its fame in the 5th and 4th centuries B.C. The theater is the best preserved in Greece and seats 14,000 spectators. The acoustics are so perfect that even from the last of the 55 tiers every word can be heard during the annual festival of Greek drama.

The very scenic 59-km. (37-mile) direct link to Corinth makes a one-day round trip through the Argolida from Athens possible, though regrettably hurried. Even the drive to a festival performance is not too formidable, though the special boat or hydrofoil from Piraeus is more restful. It lands at Paleá (Old) Epídavros, a short worthwhile detour on a car trip, through groves and orchards to a crescent-shaped bay divided by a spit near which the ruins of the antique town of 70,000 inhabitants can be discerned beneath the transparent sea in a skin-diver's paradise. At the north end of the bay the whitewashed houses of the present port are enlivened by scarlet hibiscus, yachts and caiques are moored along the mole, and on a hill are the foundations of an Early Christian basilica. To the left, above the coastal road north, is Néa Epídavros, a village hardly larger than it was in 1822, when a National Assembly granted modern Greece's first constitution, which proved even more ephemeral than its numerous successors.

The main road is joined inland, before the large two-storied peribolus of the 14th-century Monastery Agnóunda. The domed tri-apsidal Church of the Kimisis (Dormition of the Virgin) is a mixture of architectural styles following repeated reconstructions since the 11th century. The late-Byzantine interior wall-paintings have been restored. After approaching the scrub-covered cliffs of several inlets, the road passes the small post-Byzantine Church of the Odigítria (the Virgin Indicator of the Way) in an idyllic valley of vineyards, then descends to the beaches of Almyrí, Loutró Elénis, Paleó Kalamáki and Isthmía.

A lovely circuit can be made by continuing 61 km. (38 miles) from Epídavros to Galatás, opposite the island of Póros. The view from the height at Áno Fanári over the islands of the Saronikós Gulf is one of the finest in Greece. After descending into the orange and lemon groves of the coastal strip there is a choice of interesting places to visit: the spa of Méthana (12 km., eight miles to the left), the ruins of Trizina (three km., two miles right), Theseus' inheritance from his mother, and the setting of the tragedy of Phaedra, immortalized by Euripides and Racine. The road continues beyond Galatás through orange and lemon groves for 32 km., 20 miles, along the coast facing Ýdra island to the pleasant fishing village of Ermióni, where Roman mosaic pavements have been uncovered, beside an idyllic bay. Eleven km. (seven miles) southeast is the beach of Kósta, opposite Spétses island. Five km. (three miles) northeast, Portohéli has grown into the Peloponnese's largest beach resort, with the added attractions of the ruins of ancient Halieis submerged in the shallow sea; and bones and stone tools of the Mesolithic Period around 25,000 B.C. discovered in the nearby Franhthí cave, which was still inhabited in 8,000 B.C. as witnessed by chips of black volcanic glass imported from Mílos, the earliest evidence of maritime trade. Reading the region's history in its soil, archeologists from Stanford University found that over 50,000 years man has been consistently destructive to his environment. Only at the ephemeral peaks of the Mycenaean, Classical and Roman civilizations were attempts at soil conservation made by building dams and terraces to prevent erosion. The growth of the tourist industry at the expense of agriculture may finally sweep what little topsoil is left into the sea. The return inland via Kranídi leads back to Epídavros. Shortly before the road forks at Trahiá, a branch connects with the road along the northeastern shore of the Argolikós Gulf, linking Íria to the coastal village of Drépano and the fast-growing beach resort of Toló, as well as the prehistoric acropolis, Mycenaean cemetery and Hellenistic remains of Assíani, all easily accessible just south of Náf-plio.

In Agamemnon's Realm

The two hills concealing Mykínes (Mycenae) stand at the northwestern confines of the Argive plain. It is only five km. (three miles) from the Árgos-Corinth highway to the gloomy, gray ruins, hardly distinguishable from the rock beneath. In their uncompromising severity they provide a fitting background to the horrors perpetrated by three generations of the hateful family of Atreus.

History is difficult to disentangle from legend, but his belief in Homer was triumphantly vindicated by Schliemann, when he discovered the royal towns of Troy and Mycenae, where the great poet had indicated them. The astounding beehive tombs are outside the reconstructed walls. The largest is called Treasury of Atreus or Tomb of Agamemnon—though it was neither—belonging to an earlier period. A 36-meter (40-yard) long passage cut into the hill leads to a soaring, vaulted circular chamber of exquisite masonry, opening on to another, smaller burial chamber. The so-called Tomb of Clytemnestra is closer to the citadel.

(We advise that you carry a torch light when exploring the tombs on your own.)

The Acropolis of Mycenae is entered by the famous Lion Gate. A Cyclopean lintel supports a triangular slab, on which two lionesses are depicted standing on their legs, their forepaws resting on a column. Within the walls are the six shaft graves, the First Royal Grave Circle, where the gold masks and other treasures were found, which are now in the Mycenaean room in the Archeological Museum of Athens. In the 1950s, excavations by British archeologists brought to light a Second Royal Grave Circle, considerably older (c. 2000–1600 B.C.) than the one discovered by Schliemann. The quantity of jewelry and precious objects that was found with the skeletons again seems to justify the "Royal." Most original is a duck-shaped rock-crystal bowl, together with gold and silver clasps and necklaces, a gold rattle that accompanied a baby, and an assortment of bronze weapons.

The palace stood on a narrow platform on the top of the hill, commanding a sweeping view of the plain. A cistern was connected by terracotta ducts to a spring outside the citadel, assuring a water supply during a siege. The descent to the ravine opposite bleak scrub-covered Mount Zara ends at the small Postern Gate, a double door under a huge lintel, through which Orestes escaped after the murder of Clytemnestra. Along the walls to the Lion Gate are the remains of a Hellenistic town. It is worth finding time to take this site at a slower rate than the quick tours on which ever-increasing numbers are herded at break-neck pace through this haunted place, where even time has failed to weaken the palpable impact of doom.

The new Museum of Archaeological Research nearby will be unusual, if not unique, in offering lectures, tuition, and demonstrations of methods.

From the village of Mykínes, a badly indicated road branches south, into gentler valleys. Closer to Árgos, an ancient shrine of the Great Goddess was for once not usurped by a male god but devolved to Hera. At the Iréo, the Argive Heraion, Agamemnon was elected to lead the Achaeans against Troy at a shrine predating by 500 years the 8th-century B.C. temple on a terrace supported by Cyclopean walls, one of the oldest identifiable sanctuaries in Greece. It was burnt down through the carelessness of a priestess in 423 B.C. and replaced by another temple of which likewise only the foundations remain. Overgrown, neglected, hard to find and thus little visited, the site has preserved a serenity which explains why it was chosen in the first place.

Further north along the Corinth road, six km. (four miles) left (west) lead to the ruins of Neméa. Here that untiring young hero, Heracles, performed yet another of his labors by strangling the Nemean lion. Yet the Nemean Games, one of the four great Panhellenic competitions, were held bi-annually in memory of Prince Opheltes, put near a well by his nurse and bitten by a dragon. American archeologists have uncovered the baby's tomb, the foundations of the stadium, of the athletes' bathing installations and of an archaic temple burnt in the 5th century. Of the 4th-century Doric temple, dedicated to Zeus, three columns are still standing. The disproportionately large museum houses a rich collection of local coins, models of the finds, displays relating to the Games, and collections of photographs and 19th-century travelers' views of the site.

PRACTICAL INFORMATION FOR
THE PELOPONNESE

WHEN TO COME. The great variety of scenery makes a visit rewarding all the year round, with the possible exception of February, usually the worst month in Greece, though March too can be cold and rainy. The halcyon days of January are very suitable for sightseeing involving a fair amount of climbing, as at Mystrás or Messíni. But spring is the best season, when mountains and meadows are all covered with wild flowers. The sea breeze and bathing make the coast enjoyable in summer, but mountains and plains inland are baked dry. Flies and mosquitoes have reappeared on some beaches.

TOURIST OFFICE. There is a G.N.T.O. office at **Pátra,** Iroon Polytehniou, Glyfáda (tel. 42 0305).

SPECIAL EVENTS. March. Pátra attracts large crowds to the Carnival celebrations, far fewer to the Festival in the ancient theater in **August.**

May. The *Paleologia* celebrations at Mystrás in late May commemorate the Byzantine Renaissance.

July–August. The great event of the Peloponnese is the festival of Greek drama at Epidauros on weekends.

HOTELS AND RESTAURANTS. Modern hotels exist at all places of interest, while rooms in private houses, though not quite warranting the furnished apartment sign, are clean and cheap. Seaside taverns offer fresh fish, but display little imagination in its preparation. Young artichokes—anginares—from the Pátra region make a good entree. Corinth is known for its grapes and Kalamáta for its olives.

Ágios Andréas. *Akroyali* (I), tel. 3 1266. 15 double rooms. *Angelos* (I), tel. 3 1268. 13 double rooms. Like Akroyali, basic, on shingle beach, with very simple restaurant.

Ágios Avgoustínos. *San Agostino Beach* (M), tel. 2 2150/9. 330 rooms and bungalows on beach. Half board only. Pool, minigolf, tennis, disco.

Akráta. *Akrata Beach* (M), tel. 3 1813. 30 rooms.

Alagoniá. *Taýgetos* (I), tel. 7 6236. 14 rooms. Motel in the fir forest on the Sparta–Kalamáta road.

Almyrí. *Almyri Beach* (M), tel. 3 3301. 48 rooms. Tennis. *Orea Eleni* (M), tel. 3 3231. 22 rooms. Beach.

Almyró. *Messinian Bay* (M), tel. 4 1251/2. 45 rooms. Beach, minigolf. Halfboard. v.

Amaliáda. *Olympic Inn* (I), tel. 2 8632. 42 rooms. Airconditioned; roof-garden. v.

Andrítsena. Inadequate accommodations; book well ahead in summer. *Theoxenia* (M), tel. 2 2219. 33 rooms, half with bath. Fine view over the mountains. *Pan* (I), tel. 2 2213. 6 double rooms with showers.

Areópoli. Remote town in bleak landscape. *Pyrgos Kapetanaki* (M), tel. 5 1233. 6 rooms. In converted tower—quaint and beautifully decorated. Modern facilities in traditional setting. *Mani* (I), tel. 5 1269. 16 rooms, most with shower. Restaurant. MC.

Árgos. Only if nearby Náfplio is booked out. *Mycenae* (I), tel. 2 8569. 24 rooms, most with shower. *Telessila* (I), tel. 2 8351. 32 rooms, most with shower. Restaurant. MC.
Restaurants. The food in the restaurants on the main square ranges from dreary to awful.

Arkoudi. *Bratis* (I), tel. 9 6350. 40 rooms. Beach.

Ástros Paralía. *Chryssi Akti* (I), tel. 5 1294. 23 rooms, some with shower; good beach. *Georgakakis* (I), tel. 5 1412. 20 rooms. On good beach.

Corinth. *Acropolis* (M), tel. 2 6568. 27 rooms. DC. *Ephira* (I), tel. 2 2434. 45 rooms. Roofgarden. *Korinthos* (I), tel. 2 6701/3. 34 rooms.
Restaurants. Food in town is uniformly unsatisfactory.
At **ancient Corinth.** *Xenia* (M), tel. 3 1208. 3 rooms. DC.
At the **Canal.** *Isthmia* (I), tel. 2 3454. 76 rooms. Very noisy motel. AE, DC.

Diakoftó. *Chris-Paul* (I), tel. 4 1715. 26 rooms. Public rooms airconditioned.

Dimitsána. *Dimitsána* (I), tel. 3 1518/20. 27 rooms. Restaurant. Traditional settlement.

Drépano. *Danti's Beach* (M), tel. 9 2294. 64 airconditioned rooms, pool, tennis. *Plaka* (M), tel. 9 2020. 180 rooms. Beach, tennis, pool.
Restaurants. Several good fish tavernas along the waterfront.

Égio. *Galini* (I), tel. 2 6150/2. 31 rooms. DC, MC, V. *Telis* (I), tel. 2 3140. 30 rooms.

Epidauros. *Xenia* (M), tel. 2 2003. At the ruins. 24 bungalows, most with showers.
At **Lygóurio,** 5 km. (3 miles) from the ruins. *Avaton* (I), tel. 2 2059. 10 double rooms. No restaurant.
Restaurants and Shopping. Several simple eating places. Many more souvenir shops, amongst which the *Argo* offers the widest choice.
At **Paleo (Old) Epidauros,** 19 km. (12 miles) east, on the sea. *Apollon* (I), tel. 4 1295. 38 rooms. *Maik* (I), tel. 4 1213. 14 rooms. Disco. V. *Maronika* (I), tel. 4 1391. 18 rooms. *Paola Beach* (I), tel. 4 1397. 27 rooms. *Saronis* (I), tel. 4 1514. 39 rooms. Enchanting site, poor beach.

Ermióni. *Costa Perla* (M), tel. 3 1112/5. 191 rooms, bungalows. Pool, minigolf, tennis, disco. AE, DC, V. *Lena-Mary* (M), tel. 3 1450/1. 120 rooms. Airconditioned; nudist beach.
At **Petrothálassa,** 6 km. (4 miles) southwest. *Aquarius* (M), tel. 3 1430/4. 415 rooms. Pool, minigolf, disco, tennis.
At **Plepi,** 8 km. (5 miles) east. *Porto Hydra* (E), tel. 41112. 272 rooms. Airconditioned. AE, MC, V. *Kappa Club,* (M), tel. 4 1002. 272 rooms.
Self-contained holiday complexes; half or full board available, disco, tennis, minigolf.

Gargaliáni. *Ionian View* (I), tel. 2 2494. 6 double rooms. Splendid view over the coast. Restaurant, disco.

Gýthio. *Cavo Grosso* (M), tel. 2 3488. 27 bungalows. *Lakonis* (M), tel. 2 2666/7. 74 rooms. Pool; both on private beach near town. *Belle Hélène* (M), tel. 2 2867/9. 98 rooms. Tennis; on private beach 12 km. (7 miles) south. In town, *Laryssion* (I), tel. 2 2021/6. 78 rooms. *Pantheon* (I), tel. 2 2284. 53 rooms.

Isthmía. *King Saron* (M), tel. 3 7201/4. 161 rooms. Airconditioned; beach, pool, tennis, disco. AE.

Ítylo. *Ítylo* (I), tel. 5 1300. 19 rooms. Near tiny harbor of Karavostassi.

Kaiáfas. Several old hotels near sulfurous springs. *Jenny* (I), tel. 3 2252. 8 double rooms with showers.

Kalamáta. *Elite* (M), tel. 2 5015. 49 rooms. 5 km. (3 miles) from town. Tennis, disco. AE, DC, MC, V. *Filoxenia* (M), tel. 2 3166/8. 208 rooms. 2 km. (1 mile) from town. Tennis, disco. Both Elite and Filoxena are on the beach. AE, DC. *Rex* (M), tel. 2 2334. 51 rooms. *Flisvos* (I), tel. 8 2282. 41 rooms. V. *Galaxias* (I), tel. 2 8891. Both in town. On the seafront: *Haikos* (I), tel. 8 2886/8. 30 rooms. *Valassis* (I), tel. 2 3849. 37 rooms.

Kalávryta. *Helmos* (M), tel. 2 2217. 27 rooms, most with shower. MC.

Kardámyli. *Theano* (I), tel. 7 3222. 9 small apartments.

Kastaniá. *Xenia* (M), tel. 3 1283. 17 rooms. In fir forest. Half board only. MC.

Kastro. *Robinson Club Kyllini Beach* (M), tel. 9 5205/6. 332 rooms in four blocks on excellent beach. Airconditioned; pool, tennis, minigolf, disco. AE.

Kiáto. *Pappas* (M), tel. 2 2358. 44 rooms. MC. *Triton* (I), tel. 2 3421/3. 32 rooms. Airconditioned; restaurant, roofgarden. V.

Kokoni. *Kokoni Beach* (M), tel. 3 3108. 32 rooms. *Angela* (I), tel. 3 2486/7. 136 rooms. Pool, tennis, disco, restaurant.

Korfos. *Argo* (M), tel. 9 5258. 25 furnished apartments. Pool; 50 yards from beach. Cycladic-style buildings. Minimarket, pool. *Korfos* (I), tel. 9 5217. 14 rooms. Airconditioned. Near beach.

Koróni. *Auberge de la Plage* (I), tel. 2 2401. 28 rooms. Roofgarden, restaurant.

Kósta. *Cap d'Or* (M), tel. 5 1360/3. 146 rooms in main block and bungalows. Pool, tennis, minigolf, disco. *Lido* (M), tel. 5 1393. 40 rooms.

Kranídi. *Hermionida* (I), tel. 2 1750/1. 27 rooms.

Kylíni. *Glarentza* (I), tel. 9 2397. 30 rooms.

Kyparissía. *Artemis* (I), tel. 2 2145. 22 rooms. *Ionion* (I), tel. 2 2511. 33 rooms. Restaurant.

Kýthira. At **Agía Pelagía.** *Kytheria* (I), tel. 3 3321. 10 rooms. Beach.

Lakópetra (35 km., 22 miles, west of Pátra). *Lakópetra Beach* (E), tel. 5 1394. 199 rooms. Pool, tennis, beach, disco. AE. *Ionian Beach* (M), tel. 5 1300/1. 79 bungalows. Pool, tennis, minigolf, disco. AE.

Lehéo. *Corinthian Beach* (I), tel. 2 5666. 57 rooms. Beach, tennis, restaurant. *Symi* (I), tel. 2 6930. 106 rooms. Beach, pool, tennis, restaurant.

Leonídio. *Kamaria* (M), tel. 2 2757. 22 furnished apartments. On beach.

Lóngos. *Long Beach* (M), tel. 7 1296/8. 139 rooms. Beach. *Spey Beach* (I), tel. 7 1724. 39 rooms. Restaurant.
Accommodations are also available in private houses.

Loutró Elénis. *Politis* (I), tel. 3 3249/50. 26 rooms. Airconditioned; restaurant. *Seaview* (I), tel. 3 3551/2. 22 rooms. Both are near the hydrotherapy center and close to the beach.

Melíssi. *Xylokastron Beach* (I), tel. 6 1190. 80 rooms. Pool, disco, restaurant.

Messíni. *Messini* (I), tel. 2 3002/3. 21 rooms. v.

Méthana. *Avra* (I), tel. 9 2550/2. 55 rooms. Restaurant.

Methóni. *Methóni Beach* (M), tel. 3 1544. 12 rooms. Disco, restaurant. *Alex* (I), tel. 3 1239. 20 rooms. Airconditioned; restaurant.

Metóhi (35 km., 22 miles, southwest of Pátra). *Christina Beach* (M), tel. 3 1469. 45 rooms. Pool. *Kalogria Beach* (M), tel. 3 1276. 96 rooms. Central block and bungalows. Tennis, minigolf, disco.

Mikra Mantinía. *Taygetos Beach* (I), tel. 4 1294. 25 rooms. Restaurant.

Monemvassía. *Malvasia* (M), tel. 6 1323. 28 rooms. Adjoining mansions, beautifully restored; full of character. Airconditioned. *Castro* (I), tel. 6 1413/4. 12 rooms. Overlooking the beach. *Minoa* (I), tel. 6 1209. 16 rooms.
Restaurants. There are fish taverns on the waterfront.

Mycenae. *La Petite Planète* (M), tel. 6 6240. 29 rooms. Garden restaurant.

Mystrás. *Vyzantion* (I), tel. 9 3309. 22 rooms. At entrance of medieval town. Restaurant.

Náfplio. *Amalia* (E), tel. 2 4401. 175 rooms. Airconditioned neoclassical building; large pool, garden; 2 km. (1 mile) out of town, on the sea. AE, DC, V. *Xenia Palace* (E), 48 rooms, 3 suites; and *Xenia Palace Bungalows* (E), tel. 2 8981/3, 54 bungalows, pool. On Ákronafplio, fine view. DC. *Xenia* (M), tel. 2 8991/2. 58 rooms. Private beach. DC, MC.
Agamemnon (I), tel. 2 8021/2. 40 rooms. On waterfront; small roofgarden, pool. *Dioscouri* (I), tel. 2 8550. 51 rooms. Fine view. *Nafplia* (I), tel. 2 8167. 56 rooms. *Park* (I), tel. 2 7428. 70 rooms. Airconditioned. Restaurant. DC, V.
Restaurants. *Hellas* (M), on Syntagma, is the most popular town restaurant. *Kondogiorgis* (M), on the waterfront, is the most elegant cafe/sweetshop. *Savouras* (I), also on the waterfront, is the leading seafood taverna.

Neápoli. *Aivali* (I), tel. 4 1561. 26 rooms. Beach.

Nerántza. *Nerantza* (I), tel. 3 2329. 27 rooms. On beach.

Niforeíka. *Acheos* (M), tel. 2 2561. 39 rooms in bungalows. *White Castle* (M), tel. 2 3390/2. 34 rooms. Pool.

Nikoleíka (6 km., 4 miles, west from Égio). *Poseidon Beach* (I), tel. 8 1400/2. 90 rooms. Pool, tennis, restaurant.

Olýmpia. Most hotels and restaurants are closed Nov. through Mar., except for Christmas holidays. *Amalia* (E), tel. 2 2190/1. 147 rooms. Pool; well situated and comfortable. AE, DC, MC, V. *Europa* (E), tel. 2 2650. 42 rooms. Pool, tennis, riding. Modern facilities and superb view over archeological site. Open all year, and recommended for excellent service. AE, DC, MC, V. *Antonios* (M), tel. 2 2348/9. 80 rooms. Roofgarden, pool. V. *Apollon* (M), tel. 2 2522. 110 rooms. Pool. AE, DC. *Olympic Village* (M), tel. 2 2211/2. 51 rooms. Airconditioned; disco. AE, V. *Ilis* (I), tel. 2 2547. 57 rooms. Restaurant. V. *Kronion* (I), tel. 2 2502. 23 rooms. Restaurant. MC, V. *Pelops* (I), tel. 2 2543. Restaurant. *Xenia* (I), tel. 2 2510. 36 rooms. Restaurant. DC, V.

Paleó Kalamáki (6 km., 4 miles, southwest of Corinth). *Kalamáki Beach* (M), tel. 3 7331/4. 74 rooms. Minigolf, tennis; on beach.

Pátra. *Astir* (E), Agiou Andreou 16 (tel. 27 6311). 120 rooms. Roofgarden, pool. V. *Galaxy* (M), Agiou Nikolaou 9 (tel. 27 8815). 53 rooms. Airconditioned. AE, DC, MC, V. *Moreas* (M), Iroon Polytehniou 40 (tel. 42 5494). 105 rooms. AE, DC. *Rannia* (M), Riga Ferreou 53 (tel. 22 0114). 30 rooms. *Acropole* (I), Agiou Andreou 32 (tel. 27 9809/13). 33 rooms. Restaurant. DC, MC. *Adonis* (I), Kapsali 9 (tel. 22 4213). 56 rooms. AE, V. *Delfini* (I), Iroon Polytehniou 102 (tel. 42 1001/5). 71 rooms. Airconditioned; pool, restaurant; halfway to town beach.

At **Paralía Proastíou,** 3 km. (2 miles) west on the sea. *Achaïa Beach* (M), tel. 99 1801/4. 87 rooms. Halfboard; pool. V. *Tzaki* (M), tel. 42 8303. 38 rooms. AE, DC, V.

Restaurants. *Evangelatos* (M), Agiou Nikolaou 7. AE, DC, V. The restaurants (I) on the waterfront have a fine view, but little else.

Portohéli. *Hinitsa Beach* (E), tel. 5 1401/3. 222 rooms. On beach; pool, tennis, minigolf, disco. *Galaxy* (M), tel. 5 1271/5. 171 rooms. Airconditioned; roofgarden, pool, tennis, minigolf. MC. *Giouli* (M), tel. 5 1217/20. 163 rooms. Airconditioned; pool. *Cosmos Club Hotel* (M), tel. 5 1327. 151 rooms. Airconditioned; on beach; roofgarden, tennis, pool. AE, DC, MC, V. *Porto Heli* (M), tel. 5 1490/4. 218 rooms. Airconditioned; on beach; pool, tennis, minigolf, disco. DC, MC, V. *Thermissia* (M), tel. 5 1265. 88 rooms. On beach. *Ververoda Holiday Resort* (M), tel. 5 1342/5. 244 rooms in central block and bungalows. MC, V. *Alcyon* (I), tel. 5 1416. 89 rooms. Airconditioned; disco; 275 meters (300 yards) from beach. AE, MC.

Restaurant. *Papadias* (E). In the port near the church—good seafood.

Psathópyrgos. *Florida* (M), tel. 93 1279. 81 rooms. Beach, pool.

Pýlos. Insufficient accommodations. *Karalis Beach* (M), tel. 2 3021. 14 rooms. *Miramare* (M), tel. 2 2226. 16 rooms. *Galaxy* (I), tel. 2 2780. 34 rooms. Restaurant; 135 meters (150 yards) from the very small town beach. AE, DC, MC, V. *Karalis* (I), tel. 2 2960. 21 rooms. Restaurant. V.

Pýrgos. *Tsitsiris Castle* (M), tel. 5 4297. 19 rooms. A 200-year-old traditional settlement, carefully restored. All modern facilities. *Letrina* (I), tel. 2 3644. 68 rooms. Restaurant. V. *Olympos* (I), tel. 2 3650/2. 37 rooms. MC, V. *Pantheon* (I), tel. 2 9746. 47 rooms.

Río. *Porto Rio* (M), tel. 99 2124. 267 rooms in central block and bungalows. Airconditioned; pool, tennis, mingolf, disco. 35 meters (40 yards) from beach. 9 km. (6 miles) from Pátra. AE, DC, MC, V. *Rion Beach* (M), tel. 99 1421/2. 85 rooms. Disco. AE.

Rodíni (Halfway between Égio and Pátra). *Rodini* (M), tel. 93 1300. 43 apartments. Pool; near beach.

Sáladi (8 km., 5 miles, north of Kranídi). *Sáladi Beach* (M), tel. 7 1391/3. 404 rooms in central block and bungalows. Airconditioned; tennis, minigolf, disco, pool. One of the few nudist beaches.

Selianítika. All near beach. *Kanelli* (I), tel. 7 2442. 46 rooms. Restaurant. *Kyani Akti* (I), tel. 7 2202. 27 rooms. Restaurant. *Plage* (I), tel. 7 2206. 23 rooms.

Skafidía (11 km., 7 miles, northwest of Pyrgos). *Club Méditerranée Hotel and Bungalows* - see p. 13. Sometimes accommodation (E) is available.

Sparta. *Lida* (E), tel. 2 3601/2. 40 rooms. *Dioskouri* (M), tel. 2 8484. 35 rooms. *Sparta Inn* (M), tel. 2 5021. 80 rooms. *Apollo* (I), tel. 2 2491/3. 70 rooms. Restaurant. *Maniatis* (I), tel. 2 2665/9. 80 rooms. Airconditioned. *Menalaïon* (I), tel. 2 2161/5. 48 rooms. Restaurant. AE, DC, MC, V.

Stóupa. *Lefktron* (I), tel. 5 4322. 16 rooms.

Sýkia. *Paradissos* (I), tel. 2 8121. 26 double rooms. No restaurant; the name is rather an overstatement.

Toló. Of the large number of hotels on the excellent beach, we list only those which have restaurants. *Minoa* (M), tel. 5 9207. 44 rooms. The location is better than its food. AE, DC, MC, V. *Sofia* (M), tel. 5 9567/8. 52 rooms. *Solon* (M), tel. 5 9204. 28 rooms. *Aris* (I), tel. 5 9231. 30 rooms. *Electra* (I), tel. 5 9105. 18 rooms. *Epidavria* (I), tel. 5 9219. 39 rooms. DC, MC, V. *Possidonion* (I), tel. 5 9345. 36 rooms. *Tolo* (I), tel. 5 9248. 39 rooms.

Tríkala. *Trikala* (I), tel. 9 1260. 21 rooms. Restaurant.

Trípoli. *Arcadia* (I), tel. 22 5551/3. 45 rooms. Roofgarden, restaurant. MC. *Artemis* (I), tel. 22 5221/3. 60 rooms. *Galaxy* (I), tel. 22 5195/7. 80 rooms. AE, DC.

Týrou Paralia. *Blue Sea* (I), tel. 4 1369. 20 rooms. Near beach. *Kamvyssis* (I), tel. 4 1424. 22 rooms. Also near beach.

Valimítika (6 km., 4 miles, east of Égio). *Eliki* (I), tel. 9 1301/4. 144 rooms. Pool, disco, restaurant on beach.

Vathiá. Isolated hilltop hamlet. *Vathia* (M), tel. 5 4244. 14 rooms. Traditional features are retained in converted old gray-stone towers. Modern facilities including restaurant. Unusual, but comfortable.

Vytína. In the Arcadian mountains at 915 meters, 3,000 ft. *Villa Valos* (I), tel. 2 2210. 51 rooms. Fine setting; halfboard only. v. *Vytina* (I), tel. 2 2262. 12 double rooms. *Xenia Motel* (I), tel. 2 2218. 20 rooms. Half board only.

Xylókastro. *Arion* (M), tel. 2 2230. 64 double rooms. Halfboard; on beach. MC. *Fadira* (M), tel. 2 2648. 48 rooms. No restaurant; near beach. v. *Rallis* (M), tel. 2 2219. 74 rooms. Halfboard; near beach. *Periandros* (I), tel. 2 2272. 23 rooms. Restaurant.

CAMPING. The best equipped among some 30 organized camp sites are the following G.N.T.O. grounds. **Loutrá Kylínis:** *Kylini,* tel. 96 278; at Vartholomio, 6 km. (4 miles) east; accommodation for 500 persons; near beach. **Pátra:** *Agia Patron,* tel. 424 131; 5 km. (3 miles) from town; accommodation for 600; near beach.

MONASTERY HOSTELRIES. *Agia Lavra* and *Mega Spileo,* both modern with running water; near Kalavryta. Only men are allowed to stay overnight at these hostelries.

HOW TO GET AROUND. By Train. The diesel train follows the circular route described below for motorists (Athens–Corinth–Pátra–Pýrgos–Kalamáta–Trípoli–Náfplio–Mycenae–Corinth) not including the Messenian circle, and without touching at Sparta.

By Bus. There are organized tours to all the main archeological sites. Those not wishing to be tied to a schedule will find it easy enough to move about by the frequent, regular buses.

By Plane. There are daily planes from Athens to Kalamáta, and to the nearby island of Kýthira.

By Car. The Peloponnese is a region where a car will provide maximum enjoyment, as every few miles there is something to see and worth stopping for. The circular tour can be combined with an excursion to Delphi, by taking the summer ferry between Égio and Ágios Nikólaos (Eratiní) or the all-year-round half-hourly ferry from 6 A.M.–10 P.M. between Río and Antírio. The Athens–Corinth toll motorway continues along the coast to Pátra, and as a lesser but recently updated highway turns south for the 120 km. (74 miles) to Pýrgos and Olýmpia, for the first night. Returning to Pýrgos you follow the spectacular road to Kyparissía. Don't miss the Messenian circle including Pýlos, Methóni and Kalamáta, scenically very rewarding. The second night might be spent at Kalamáta, leaving for Sparta on the following day, with the third night at Trípoli. On the fourth day Náfplio, Epidauros, Mycenae and return to Corinth. A road along the coast links Epidauros directly with Corinth. Four days are an absolute minimum for the complete tour. For a shorter trip you can cut across the peninsula from Olýmpia via Andrítsena and the temple of Bassae in the Arcadian mountains to Megalópoli, Trípoli and Náfplio.

By Boat. The 160-seat hydrofoils connect Zéa harbor (Piraeus) via Póros and Spétses with all eastern Peloponnesian ports and Kýthira, also Pátra with Zákynthos and Náfpaktos. Most services operate all year round, and are more frequent in summer. There are ferry boats from Piraeus to most eastern ports, from Neapolis in the Peloponnese to Kýthira, and a ferry once a week between Gýthio and Kíssamos in Crete.

SKI CENTERS AND MOUNTAIN REFUGES. Two each on Panahaïkó and Zíria (Kilíni) the latter the most important skiing center in the Peloponnese; one each on Helmós, Ménalo, Parnónas and Taýgetos.

NORTHWESTERN GREECE

Epirus and Aetolia-Acarnania

Northwestern Greece, which stretches from the northern shore of the Gulf of Corinth to the Albanian frontier west of the Píndos range, has been aroused from its centuries-old slumber by the advent of the ferry-boats from Italy. Ípiros (Epirus) fully justifies its name, continent, by an overwhelming concentration of mountains, contrasting with the islands—Corfu, Paxí, Lefkáda—strung along the littoral. The abrupt changes from the delicately shaded green of the idyllic olive and orange groves on the coast to the tremendous solidity of the bare mountains have been faithfully depicted by that versatile Victorian, Edward Lear, of limerick fame. But few travelers would nowadays put up with the discomfort, hardship and very real danger from bandits that Lear seems to have enjoyed. The scenery has kept its grandeur, but has become easily accessible by a good road network, provided with plenty of hotels.

Mountainous provinces are often spared a surfeit of history, but in Greece the last 4,000 years have been so crammed with momentous events that Epirus received its fair share, though fair in this case refers to size rather than to pleasurable enjoyment by the inhabitants. Mountain barriers and the absence of anchorages kept the invasions of the 2nd millennium B.C. on a manageable scale, though not preventing one of Achilles' vaguely scattered sons from founding a kingdom in a remote vale. History started in deadly earnest in the 12th century B.C. with the Dorians spreading from this bastion all over Greece, while their rearguard, the Hellenes, imposed the worship of Zeus on the native population so successfully that all the various inhabitants of the mainland came to be known as Hellenes.

Oligarchical systems, which became fashionable in more sophisticated communities in the 8th century B.C., never penetrated into the mountain fastness. During the Classical period Epirus remained a stormy backwater of tribal warfare, highlighted by the traditional hospitality extended to the fugitive Themistocles by the king of the Molossians. That generous act must have brought them luck, as their tribe soon dominated the Epirotic confederation.

The Molossian Princess Olympias married her uncle Philip II of Macedonia in 357 B.C. How far that amiable lady was implicated in her husband's assassination has never been fully ascertained, but Alexander the Great would not permit his dangerous mother any part in the government. Her great hour came after Alexander's death in 323 B.C., when, as regent for her nephew in Epirus, and her grandson in Macedonia, she was free to intrigue to her heart's content. After her murder kings ascended and descended the shaky throne of Epirus at a bewildering speed with the system of co-kings greatly adding to the fun, until Pyrrhus reconquered the crown for a third time and entered the fray as sole ruler.

His fame, however, rests on his intervention in Italy, where he caused consternation and panic with his war-elephants. After defeating the Romans in two bloody battles in 279 B.C., he made his often quoted statement: "Another such victory and we are lost." Yet he continued to indulge indiscriminately in wars west and east, until an old woman made a lucky hit with a tile thrown from her rooftop, killing the king during an attack on Árgos.

For having changed sides at the wrong moment, Epirus was crushingly punished by the Roman Consul Aemilius Paulus in 167 B.C. One hundred and fifty thousand Epirotes were sold into slavery, while the 70 principal towns were razed to the ground, before history stopped for the blissful 400 years of the Pax Romana. The battle of Actium in 31 B.C. was a naval engagement, which for all its momentous consequences caused only moderate upheaval in the peaceful province.

Epirus shared the vicissitudes of the declining Byzantine Empire, falling briefly to the Sicilian Normans and after the Fourth Crusade to an illegitimate offspring of the Doukas family, great feudatories that occasionally and disastrously had occupied the imperial throne. Having served Bonifacio of Montferrat in defending Thessaloníki against the Bulgarians, Michael Doukas struck out on his own and in 1205 assumed the title of Despot of Epirus, adopting for good measure the names of the last two imperial dynasties, fancifully rather than rightfully. After his murder in 1215, his brother and successor Theodor Angelos-Komninos transferred the capital from Ioánina to Arta, then was crowned King of Thessaloníki in 1227 but was slain three years later by the Bulgarians. Briefly successful in a diminished station, the Angeli Despotate was incorporated in 1263 in the resuscitated empire of the Palaeologi.

Turkish Misrule

This incorporation lasted less than a century, as in 1358 Epirus was annexed to the Serbian Empire. The conquest of Ioanina in 1431 and of Arta in 1449 by the Turks was hardly an improvement. Pashas were appointed haphazardly from among the leading Moslem families, while the country was reduced to near anarchy by inherited feuds, frequent rebellions and constant brigandage. Christianity of a sort survived. In a popular poem

St. George was first bribed by a Christian maiden to hide her from a pursuing Turk, to whom the saint promptly betrayed her hiding place on receipt of a more lavish gift. But if things spiritual were in a bad way, they were at least housed in splendid bodies, dressed, according to Byron, in the most magnificent clothes in the world.

Against that colorful background there rose in the second half of the 18th century the most extraordinary figure in modern Greek history, Ali of Tepelen, who established his rule over the greater part of continental Greece and Albania, and then imposed the appointment of his sons to the governorship of the outlying provinces. But in the end Ali committed the one unforgivable sin in Turkish eyes: growing ever more avaricious with age he fell in arrears with his tribute. In 1820 a Turkish army invaded Ioánina where Ali Pasha had to rely on Christian support, because his Moslem subjects were unwilling to fight against the Sultan. Greek help was not intended to perpetuate Ali's despotism, but to keep the common enemy, the Turks, occupied. This facilitated the outbreak of the Greek revolution in 1821, which was heavily subsidized by Ali, but failed to save him. Epirus remained a Turkish province till the first Balkan war, when Ioánina was conquered by a Greek army under Crown Prince Constantine in 1913.

Etolia and Akarnania (Aetolia and Acarnania) played only a small part in antiquity, except between 332 and 189 B.C., when the Aetolian League became a dominant power. The capital of the League was at Thermon, east of the River Ahéloos, and that of Arcarnania at Stratos, west of it, were the ramparts and some other remains are still visible.

Exploring Northwestern Greece

The crossing from Corfu to Igoumenítsa (18 nautical miles) is enchanting, with the lush green of the island slowly receding and the stark outlines of the mainland dramatically ahead. The bay is at its best in the early morning, but sunset will do, when the gray rocks likewise flame with deep pinks and violets in an unforgettable welcome.

Igoumenítsa is the generally unappealing northwestern port of entry for motorists, but even without private transport there is no problem. The ubiquitous Greek buses shamble up the most improbable mountains, though heavily biased in favor of cruelly early morning hours. Peasant women and children are, moreover, very much given to being sick in public conveyances, while the radio is going full blast, indiscriminately and mercilessly for the entire program of religious service, self-congratulatory political speeches, learned discourse on handicraft and a fair share of bouzouki music.

Right at the start of the journey there is a tantalizing choice between the 100 km. (62 miles) northeast to Ioánina, on the first leg of the newly reconstituted Via Egnatia, once the main artery of the Roman Empire, linking Rome via Brindisi and Thessaloníki to Constantinople. (In antiquity, the eastern port on the Ionian Sea was at Dyrrhachium, in modern Albania, which sufficiently explains the shift further south.) Or the coastal highway to Préveza, taking in Párga (50 km., 31 miles), the main attraction on the coast. But this means bypassing the varied sites in and around Ioánina as well as the superb Alpine scenery of the Píndos range.

So northeast it is, climbing and descending mountains along the left bank of the Thíamis River. After 24 km. (15 miles) there is a branch road south to Paramythiá (13 km., eight miles), once the seat of a Turkish pasha.

Heroic Sóuli, Enchanting Párga

Paramythiá hardly justifies the detour, but the road continues south below Sóuli, celebrated in Greek folklore and by Byron. Twenty-two km. (14 miles) south, after crossing the Áheron a narrow track follows the torrent—one of antiquity's favorite entrances to the Underworld—up to Sóuli. Soon you catch the first glimpse of the main fortress—Koungi—guarding the entrance to the almost inaccessible highland.

Throughout the period of Ottoman rule the Christian Souliots maintained their independence. They were divided into clans like the Highland Scots, and their rivalry made it at last possible for Ali Pasha to subdue them in 1803 by a gruesome mixture of bribery, treachery and force. By the terms of surrender the Souliots were free to leave with their possessions, but the solemn promise was not worth the paper it was written on. A few hundred men succeeded in reaching Párga and eventually Corfu, to be enlisted in Byron's bodyguard in 1823; but most of the Souliots took shelter in the Zalongo Monastery, which was attacked and taken by Ali's army. Only 60 women escaped to the summit of the cliffs, where they began to sing the old Souliot songs, dancing in a circle with their babies in their arms, ever closer to the edge, working themselves into a frenzy of defiance before jumping one by one down the fearful precipice. The tragic ballad of Zalongo is a common theme of the *kalamatianós,* the most popular of Greek dances, performed in a circle, the leader waving a handkerchief, swirling and bounding, while the chain of dancers shuffles around in a basic step, accompanied by a lyre, drum, clarinet and scratchy violin.

The heroic episode is commemorated by a startlingly modernistic huge monument of the dancing women on the cliff above the monastery, now accommodating a few nuns. The monastery's painted church, dedicated to St. Michael and St. Gabriel and reputedly built in the 8th century, is interesting, but pales before the splendid view embracing the open sea, the land-locked Ambracian Gulf, at whose entrance the momentous battle of Actium was fought, the island of Lefkáda and the distant mountains of central Greece. Descending the six winding km. (four miles) to the main road, it is then only another 16 km. (ten miles) to Préveza.

The shortest route south from Igoumenítsa is also the loveliest, 91 km. (57 miles) to Préveza and the ferry to Áktio. After passing Platária and Sívota on the coastal road ("coastal" not to be taken too literally), turn right (west) for 15 km. (eight miles) to the most picturesque town on the west coast. The intimate square dominated by the Venetian castle high up on a rock, the smaller ruined fort on a wooded islet offshore, the dense olive groves covering the slopes down to the fine beaches, make Párga the outstanding holiday resort in the northwest.

Párga was founded in the 14th century, became Venetian in 1447 and remained a cherished possession of the Republic till the end of the Doges. After having been ceded by the British to Ali Pasha, the inhabitants, without exception, determined to leave. On Good Friday 1819 the bells were tolling, while the Pargiots disinterred the bones of their dead, burnt them and took the ashes together with the holy icons to Corfu. Ali's troops entered a town where all was solitude and silence, the only sign of former life being the smoke rising from the funeral pyres. Ali had a country house built on the promontory and settled the town with Mohammedans, who in turn were returned to Turkey in the general exchange of populations in 1924. The next branch right follows the Áheron four km. (two miles) to Amoudiá on the sea. At the confluence with the River Kókytos, Ephyra (Watch Tower) was antiquity's only necromanteion, an oracle of the dead, where Charon rowed them to Hades.

Ioánina—the Lair of Ali the Lion

The Via Egnatia, following the Thíamis upstream, does not lack scenic beauty. Stop above the village of Polýdrosso to enjoy the view over the mountains and river. A later branch road to the left (north) leads to Zítsa, a mountain hamlet a few miles off, where Byron stayed at the monastery of the Prophet Elias in 1809. He wrote enthusiastically of the situation, which he called "perhaps the finest in Greece." Zítsa, in addition to its literary associations, produces a very sweet sparkling wine.

The promontory of Ioánina juts into the melancholic lake that forms the center of a fertile valley hemmed in by ranges of imposing mountains: Mitsikéli in the north, snow-covered from December to May, links with the massif of Peristeri and Tsoumerka, Olitsika to the southwest overshadows the ruins of Dodona.

Ioánina was probably founded by the Emperor Justinian in about A.D. 540, as one of the forts in the defensive system stretching from the Ionian to the Black Sea. The impressive pentagonal citadel within 11th-century Norman walls, surrounded on three sides by the lake, dominates the town, which, in spite of the destruction during the epic siege of 1820–2 and modern progress, has retained a marked oriental character; the minarets and domes of the two mosques remain the most conspicuous feature. The mosque of Aslan Pasha, built in 1618, is now the Museum of Popular Art, housing a miscellaneous collection of weapons, icons and specimens of Epirote art. A refectory, library and baths flank the disused cemetery where Ali's body, minus the head, is buried next to his favorite wife, Umm Gulshun. The wrought-iron canopy and, inexplicably, even the marble tombstones were stolen during the German occupation in World War II. It was then that the Jewish community, which had so notably contributed to the city's prosperity, was almost exterminated.

Gone are the palaces of barbaric splendor, where Ali held his colorful court and received the ambassadors of the great powers. But his seraglio has been faithfully reconstructed and now accommodates cultural manifestations, next to the dilapidated Fethyé mosque on the citadel's second eminence. The fortress-palace of Ali's son, Muhtar Pasha, has likewise been partly rebuilt, rising above the main square. The small park atop is flanked on one side by a cafe affording a fine view, on the other by the Museum, whose exhibits range from antique finds to a well-meant collection of 19th-century paintings. Muhtar's betrayal of his father hastened the downfall of Ali who, after defeating the French forces, which had invaded his dominions from the Ionian islands, had become a factor in European politics. After becoming Vizier and Pasha of three tails, he described his methods in these simple terms: "I sent some heads to Constantinople to amuse the Sultan, and some money to his ministers, for envy never sleeps."

Yet when Ali stopped sending tribute, the Sultan was not amused and his army, led by the former Grand-Vizier Kurshit Pasha, pillaged and burnt Ioanina, then the biggest town in Greece and center of an early Hellenic revival.

The Lake and the Island

The rock of the citadel rose formerly straight from the lake, thus greatly facilitating the disposal of unwanted bodies sewn in sacks. A stately avenue of plane trees now encircles the grim walls to the landing-stage of Kyra Frossyni, named after the Greek mistress of Ali's eldest son. According to popular ballads she refused Ali's advances and was drowned together with 15 other ladies, erroneously referred to as maidens, one dark night in 1801. Possessed by a perverse desire to interfere in his children's love-life, Ali shortly afterwards raped the wife of his second son. Little wonder the sons were easily won over by the Turks, but instead of the promised high honors they were beheaded and their heads, together with that of Ali's eldest grandson, were displayed at the gates of the Constantinople Seraglio. The grandson's head led Sultan Mahmud II to make what must surely rank high among the truly perspicacious remarks in history: "I'm sorry now that I condemned him to death; I thought he was as old as his father."

To the left of the landing-stage are a number of cafes and restaurants, center of Ioánina's nightlife and scene of the traditional *volta,* the evening promenade of the younger set. Motorboats leave frequently for the far side of the island, where refugees from the Máni built in the 17th century a village sufficiently picturesque to be declared a traditional settlement. Six small Byzantine and post-Byzantine monasteries are scattered among the gardens. The most interesting are Philanthropinón (13th cent.), Dilíou (11th cent.) and Ágios Panteléimon. The first of these was founded by the great Byzantine family of the Philanthropinoi, whose last three members joined the monastery, and figure in the frescos of 1530 inside the porch of the church dedicated to St. Nicholas the Hairless. Also depicted among conventional saints are Plato and Socrates as proof of the tolerant acceptance of the most unlikely candidates in the Orthodox hagiarchy, a charming continuation of the ancient hospitality extended to foreign divinities by the Olympians.

Ágios Panteléimon was the scene of the dramatic death of Ali Pasha on January 24, 1822. It is ironic that Ali, who in all his 82 years had never kept a promise, should have trusted Kurshit's assurance of the Sultan's pardon. Ali, accompanied by his Greek wife and some faithful retainers, occupied the guest-house of the monastery, when the Turkish emissary, Mehmet Pasha, brought the *firman* ordering instant execution. Ali fired at Mehmet, wounding him in the hand, but was himself mortally wounded by a fusillade through the wood and plaster floor. Ali's head was cut off and exposed throughout his former domains. The monastery has been turned into a museum with interesting engravings of the period.

Swimming in the muddy lake is made no more attractive by the thought of Ali's countless victims lying at the bottom, than by the eels and watersnakes competing playfully with the bather.

Stalactites and Hospitality

A visit to the magnificent stalactite cave of Pérama, though attacked by mold because of ecological upset, is a must. After five km. (three miles) along the Métsovo road turn left to an undistinguished low hill, which covers a fantastic succession of lofty halls. Discovered in 1942 by a shepherd hiding from the Germans, a well-lit concrete path meanders now for over 900 meters (1,000 yards) through a weird growth of stalactites and stalagmites to the further end, making all the explored parts accessible without retracing one's steps. The late King Paul and his family were entertained by the Ioánina municipality in one of the halls, an entertainment remarkable for originality rather than intrinsic enjoyment, what with the cold and constant dripping.

The road to Métsovo (58 km., 36 miles) and Kalambáka (125 km., 78 miles) is not only the shortest east–west connection across the Píndos range to either Athens or Thessaloníki, but also the most spectacular, winding up Mount Mitsikéli to reveal splendid views over Ioanina and the lake. Snow-chains are required in winter for the drive through the fir forests to Métsovo (1,200 meters, 3,950 ft.), an attractive wintersports center. The village, strikingly situated on the steep sides of two converging mountains, is rapidly becoming a popular summer resort. Its Alpine charm, old wooden mansions, steep, cobbled pathways, and the delicious locally-made smoked cheeses have attracted visitors by the busloads. The central square is now a bus park and terminus, lined with shops selling handicraft items and other souvenirs, as well as the reknowned *tyropoleía* (cheese shops). A visit out of tourist season can be delightful. Métsovo held a unique place in the Turkish dominions thanks to a story of hospitality and gratitude which seems to be taken straight from the pages of the *Arabian Nights*. In the 16th century a Grand Vizier incurred the Sultan's disfavor and considering prudence to be the better part of valor he took refuge in the remote mountains of Epirus. For one year he was entertained by a Greek villager who remained ignorant of his visitor's identity. When at last restored to favor the Vizier promised his host anything he might desire. But instead of the expected request for money, the Greek begged freedom from Turkish rule for his home town. The demand was unprecedented, but the Vizier kept his word. Four *firmans* with golden seals in the Town Hall bear proof of the autonomy granted by successive sultans.

The inhabitants still wear the local costume on feast days or touristic occasions, the men in dark blue or black homespun wool and flat black hats and the women in colorfully embroidered bibs and aprons over long dark skirts. They also still speak Greek and also Vlach, a Latin dialect akin to Rumanian used by the villagers and nomad shepherds in the Píndos country. The Metropolis dates from 1511, but is in an exceptionally good state of repair, with its original roofing, Baroque arches and interesting modern Italian mosaics. The Tositsa mansion, rebuilt in 18th-century style, houses a collection of Epirote arts and crafts.

Further east, snow chains are required over the 1,700-meter (5,600-ft.) Katara Pass during most of the severe winter in this Alpine landscape. The branch left (north) at the Mourgani fork enters Macedonia via Grevená (61 km., 38 miles) to either Kastoriá (90 km., 56 miles) or Kozáni (53 km., 33 miles); straight on (east) leads to Kalambáka (ten km., six miles) and the Thessalian plain.

Zagória—Wild Gorges and Painted Churches

From the road junction three km. (two miles) north of Ioánina, an equally scenic 198 km. (123 miles) lead past the airfield north via Kónitsa

to Kastoriá. After 18 km. (11 miles) a branch turns right (northeast) into
the Zagória district, once the feudal domain of Ali Pasha's youngest son.
The road passes Kípi, the administrative center, on the 27 km. (17 miles)
to Negádes (1,030 meters, 3,400 ft.). The deep-green waters of a nameless
stream, locally known only as *parapotamos* (tributary of the Arahthos)
are spanned by a number of old stone bridges, veritable architectural gems
matched by the surprisingly large churches of the once prosperous 46 villages set among the flowering meadows, firs and pines. Little else grows,
so that the male inhabitants have always had to emigrate. Epirus provided
the skilled masons who built the great mosque in Constantinople; Epirote
merchants founded Greek colonies in Italy and Russia in the 17th and
18th centuries. On their return they built fine houses and proud churches
with their savings. Later emigrants went to the United States, but though
many were driven back by homesickness, they had not made good to the
same extent as their predecessors. The latest migration wave was directed
to Germany, but the returning workers settle in towns rather than in the
dying gray villages, where life continues without the modern distractions
they have become used to.

The Basilica at Negádes is unique, being three churches in one. The nave
and each aisle lead to three separate altars, dedicated respectively to the
Holy Trinity, Ágios Georgiós and Ágios Dimitrios. The pulpit and iconostasis are richly carved and gilded, while vivid frescos by local artists cover
every inch of space. Here Aristotle and Plutarch feature among the saints.
Particularly remarkable is the naïvely conceived stream of hell, sweeping
Judas, bishops and priests, followed at a distance by the lesser sinners, into
the devil's mouth. The church, surrounded on all sides by cloisters, is a
fine example of the highly original rustic architecture of Epirus, which
differs radically from the usual Byzantine ecclesiastical style.

The middle branch left (north) five km. (three miles) before Kípi leads
via Vitsa to the village of Monódendri, with the painted church of Ágios
Athanasios. From the village square, where you can have a meal as rustic
as the paintings, continue another half mile to the abandoned monastery
of Agía Paraskeví (a female St. Friday, 1412), from whose balcony you
have a stupendous view over the Vikos Gorge. Better still, climb the stairs
left of the church, and follow the path high up on the rocks a few hundred
dizzy yards to a cave.

Epirus' distinctive flora and fauna is preserved in the Vikos-Áoös National Park that covers most of the outstanding mountain scenery between
the gorge of the former and the canyon of the latter torrent. But in spite
of the varied beauty of Central Zagória, it would be rash to spend a night
there except in one of the converted traditional houses of Monódendri.
Other village guesthouses are of the simplest, and when the locals wish
"may you see the dawn" instead of the usual "sleep well," they know what
they are talking about.

The next branch, left from the mainroad, crosses at Kakavía into Albania, in the unlikely case that your visa application has been granted. The
wary traveler will content himself with the less esoteric 23 km. (14 miles)
right, into the West Zagória, to Áristi above the Monastery of the Spiliótis-
sa (Our Lady of the Cave), to Papíngo close to the mouth of the Vikos
gorge. The main road crosses the Voidomatis River, and skirting Albania's
forbidden and forbidding mountains goes on to Kónitsa (63 km., 39 miles
from Ioanina), which nestles picturesquely at the foot of the thickly-
wooded Mount Trapezítsa. The Aoös Gorge is entered by a new bridge,

alongside one of the finest old Turkish bridges in the Balkans. The foot-path on the right of the gorge continues for eight km. (five miles) to the monastery of Stómion.

Dodona, Birthplace of the Hellenes

Twenty-one km. (13 miles) south of Ioánina is Dodóni (Dodona), seat of an ancient oracle of the Great Goddess dating as far back as 2,000 B.C. Zeus worship was introduced in the 13th century B.C. and the new god manifested himself through the rustling of oak leaves or the sound of a metal whip blown by the wind against a brass basin. These sounds had to be interpreted by priests, the *Selloi* or *Helloi,* whose faithful followers, the Hellenes, spread the cult of Zeus, champion of male supremacy, over the lands once ruled by the Triple Goddess.

Zeus was victorious, but the oracle had its ups and downs. Consulted in the heroic age by Heracles, Achilles, Odysseus and all the best people, it went later into a gentle decline, because of its failure to equal the master-ly ambiguity of Delphi. Enduring for a time as the poor man's Delphi, Dodona became again fashionable under the Macedonian dynasty, which favored an oracle near the seat of government.

The temple was destroyed by the Aetolians in 221 B.C., rebuilt, sacked together with all Epirus by the rapacious Aemilius Paulus, restored once more to be converted into a church in the 4th century A.D. Bishops of Do-dona disputed at the great ecumenical councils, and it is interesting to speculate how far the political acumen and psychological insight gained by their *Helloi* predecessors proved useful. The Goths, more thorough than previous despoilers, succeeded in erasing the very memory of Dodo-na's location for over 1,000 years. Byron, the eager sightseer, complained angrily that all traces of the sanctuary had been obliterated.

It was only in 1876 that the Greek amateur archeologist Karpanos dis-covered the ruins below nine meters (30 ft.) of rubble and earth. Founda-tions of temples and the priests' houses, broken gray columns of severe Doric, and a large theater, recently restored for the performances of an-cient tragedies, are all that remain. Dodona ranks high among the minor festivals that have sprouted prolifically all over Greece, but it is astonish-ing how hard the stone benches seem after two hours of culture. So bring cushions to Dodona, to listen in comfort to the heart-rending woes of an-cient heroes, unless you prefer the tranquillity on off-nights, so much closer to the spirit of the sacred valley.

Nikopolis—City of Victory

After returning the 15 km. (nine miles) to the junction with the highway south, you drive through a narrowing plain, parched in summer, but green with corn in spring. Abundant winter rains make Epirus the wettest prov-ince, as the mountain barriers prevent the rain clouds that drift up from the Ionian Sea from penetrating further inland.

At the inn of Emin Agha, near the highest point of the Kanétta Gorge (600 meters, 2,000 ft.) Crown Prince Constantine received in 1913 the sur-render of the Turkish forces defending Ioánina. A bust of doubtful taste commemorates that event. The descent is alongside the Lóuros River, lined with plane trees and wild laurel. The Roman aqueduct once carried the clear water from the springs of Ágios Géorgios to Nikópoli

(Nikopolis), while the barrage one mile downstream now supplies Epirus with electricity. The most extensive orange groves in Greece begin at Filipiáda, and the fragrant perfume of the blossoms pervades the entire plain in spring. Sixty-six km. (41 miles) from Ioánina the road divides: left (southeast) to Arta (ten km., six miles), right (southwest) to Préveza (40 km., 25 miles) and the vast ruins of Nikopolis just outside.

Founded by Octavianus Augustus in 30 B.C., on a grand scale, Nikopolis immortalized the new emperor's resounding victory over Mark Antony's and Cleopatra's superior forces in the battle of Actium the previous year. There was a fatal flaw in Antony's strength, as the 60 biggest ships of his fleet were under the command of Cleopatra. Suddenly, inexplicably, in the thick of battle, with all the odds in their favor, Cleopatra's ships broke line and set course towards the Peloponnese. Plutarch dramatically describes what ensued: "No sooner did Antony see her ship sailing away, than, forgetting everything and deserting those who were fighting and dying in his cause, he got into a five-oared galley and followed after her who had already ruined him and was destined to complete his ruin." Antony's 120,000 infantry and 12,000 cavalry encamped near Apollo's temple at Actium (Áktio) across the narrow entrance to the gulf, hailed Octavian as master of the world without a blow being struck on land.

Nikopolis was built on the site of Octavian's camp, populated from the surrounding districts, exempted from taxes and adorned with splendid palaces and temples. Ubiquitous St. Paul did not fail to visit the most Roman town in Greece, to lay the seed of Christianity. In the 5th century Nikopolis became the seat of a bishop, and 100 years later Justinian was still adding churches and strengthening the walls.

What was left after the devastating Bulgarian raids of the 9th century was destroyed by an earthquake. Parts of the town sank into the Ambracian Gulf (Amvrakikós), where walls and columns are still visible in the clear water. Further out are the wrecks of Roman war galleys which an American-Greek venture is planning to raise. Above ground remain the impressive though broken line of the ramparts, two theaters, the larger with the inevitable performances of ancient drama in summer, an aqueduct, the stadium, temples of Ares and Poseidon. The ruins of the four early Byzantine churches are no less interesting, especially the lovely "universe" mosaic in the basilica of St. Dumetius (about A.D. 530).

Préveza, eight km. (five miles) south, at the tip of the long promontory between the Ionian Sea and the Ambracian Gulf, is a town of 13,000 inhabitants. Some minor Venetian fortifications bear witness to the century-long connection with the Ionian Islands, only broken by Ali Pasha's conquest. There are several good beaches on the Ionian coast, and a bridge to Áktio is under consideration; at the moment, a car ferry crosses the strait every half hour until 10P.M., then every hour until early morning.

Byzantine Arta

Arta has maintained a rare prosperity ever since its foundation as a Corinthian colony in the 7th century B.C. under the name of Ambracia. It became twice the capital of Epirus, first under Pyrrhus in 294 B.C. and again at the time of the Despotate of the Angeli in the 13th century.

Foundations of Classical and Hellenistic buildings cover a large area below the ancient acropolis; an equally ruined theater, a temple of Apollo and the huge blocks of ancient walls are scattered about. But some well-preserved monuments bear witness to Arta's medieval glory. First and foremost the church of the *Panagía Parigorótissa* (Our Lady of Consolation), built by the Despot Michael II and his consort Anna. It stands on a spacious square above the market. The mosaics in the cupola are interesting, but most remarkable are the projective pendentives above the pillars, a unique architectural device, supported by horizontal columns traversing the wall. The refectory nearby is now a small museum.

The churches of Ágios Vassílios, with exterior decorations, and Agía Theodóra, built by the consort of Michael II, belong to the same period. The convent of Káto Panagía is three km. (two miles) south of the town, while the monastery of Vlahérna, containing the tomb of Michael II, stands on a hill to the northeast. All have been expertly restored and are as easily accessible as the Byzantine fortress. You drive straight through the double gate in the crenelated ramparts, built with the stones of the ancient acropolis, to an incongruously modern hotel commanding a splendid view over the orange groves sloping down to the river, which runs through the fertile valley to the distant Tsoumérka mountains.

The beautiful bridge over the Arahthos, which was built in the 18th century, is celebrated in many old ballads. Legend has it that the masterbuilder sacrificed his wife by building her into the bridge, to placate the river which was destroying the foundations. Though the sacrifice worked, he committed suicide from remorse.

Aetolia-Acarnania

A scenically lovely road hugs the southern shore of the land-locked gulf for 38 km. (24 miles) to Vónitsa. From the road junction just beyond that pleasant fishing village below an imposing Venetian castle, the 16 km. (ten miles) northwest lead to the airport of Aktio, close to the site of the temple of Apollo Aktios, and the ferry to Préveza; 19 km. (12 miles) southwest take you past the romantic Santa Maura castle and good beaches to the island of Lefkáda, accessible over a long causeway and a drawbridge, a highly recommended excursion; the 116 km. (72 miles) south more or less follow the coast via Mýtikas to the attractive bay of Astakós—though this means crayfish, the local diet knows nothing of such delicacies—and then through occasional oak groves to Etolikó, thus providing the shortest link between Igoumenítsa and the Peloponnese or Delphi.

South of Amfilohía, the highway passes two lakes and crosses the Ahéloos near the very ruined ruins of Strátos, ancient capital of Acarnania, to the extensive tobacco plantations round Agrínio (41 km., 25 miles). One mile south of this prosperous town, bypassed at no great loss, is the branch left (north) to Karpeníssi (112 km., 70 miles) via the large artificial lake of Kremastá, formed by damming up the Ahéloos (see *Central Greece and Thessaly*). Another branch east after a further mile climbs 29 km. (18 miles) through the luxuriant olive and cypress groves on the northern shore of Lake Trihonída, past the pretty monastery of Mirtiá, to Thermon, the sanctuary of the Aetolian League. The temple of Apollo dates from the 6th century B.C., but there are also remains of a temple belonging to the geometric period, three stoas, the longest being no less than 169 meters (185 yards), and extensive walls. The curious painted heads in the museum are probably of the Mycenaean period. The wish to preserve self and car precludes an attempt on the atrocious 40 km. (25 miles) north over the Panetolikó to the Proussós Monastery, which is at present only accessible from Karpeníssi (see *Central Greece and Thessaly* below).

If you skirt the south shore of Trihonída to Makrinóu—but don't be too distracted by the delightful contrasting colors of the green shores, blue lake and snow-capped mountains; there are some gullies in the village streets that become torrents after heavy rain—it is possible to continue straight on (southeast) to Náfpaktos (34 km., 21 miles), crossing a mountain range with lovely views before descending to the Évinos river.

The highway south from Agrínio passes between the lakes Lissimahia and Trihonída, then cuts eight km. (five miles) off the scenically more rewarding narrower parallel road to the right (west) through the Klissóura Gorge, whose towering sides are the nesting place of eagles, hawks and kites. Emerging at a wide lagoon you see the houses of Etolikó mirrored in the surrounding shallow water. It all looks very picturesque from the mainland, but the island is somewhat disenchanting on closer acquaintance. Twelve km. (eight miles) west, across the Ahelöos, extensive walls enclose the ruins of the antique Aetolian port Oeniadae.

Messolóngi on the edge of the lagoon is famous for the heroic siege during the War of Independence (May 1825–April 1826) and for its romantic association with Lord Byron, who died there of fever, shortly after having been appointed commander-in-chief of the Greek forces.

The town was closely besieged by a Turco-Egyptian army. After hunger had reduced the inhabitants to the direst extremities, the defenders, escorting their women and children, attempted to break through the enemy lines on the night of April 22, 1826, but most of them perished in the attempt. This sortie, known as the exodus, is commemorated every year by a solemn celebration. At the memorial cemetery, the *Dafía* (Bastion), stand the monuments of the Philhellenes of all nations who died there during the siege fighting for the liberty of Greece. The fall of the town helped greatly to arouse European sympathy for the Greek cause.

If your visit coincides with the sunset, drive out to Tourlída, five km. (three miles) along the narrow strip extending into the lagoon. The islets scattered at its entrance were defended by the forts of Vassiládi and Kleissóura, which played an important part during the siege. Unfortunately, drainage and reclamation work is hastening the disappearance of the local fishing community and their small reed huts at the edge of the water.

PRACTICAL INFORMATION FOR
NORTHWESTERN GREECE

WHEN TO COME. Thanks to the protecting mountains the climate is delightful in spring and fall, while the heat is rarely oppressive in summer. Winters are cold in the interior and very wet on the coast.

TOURIST OFFICES. There are G.N.T.O. offices at **Ioánina,** Napoleon Zerva 2 (tel. 25 086); and in the port of **Igoumenítsa,** Limin Igoumenitsis (tel. 22 227). The latter operates summer only.

SPECIAL EVENTS. August. The *Nikópolia* Festival—ancient drama at Nikópolis. Also the *Epirótika* Festival—theatrical, musical, and folkloric performances at Ioánina. Ancient drama at Dodóna.

HOTELS AND RESTAURANTS. The hotel restaurants are on the whole the safest, though the *tavernas* certainly have more local color, sometimes too much. The Ioánina lake fish, carp, pike, eel, are palatable enough, especially the baked eel (*helí sto harti*). The cloyingly sweet sparkling wine from neighboring Zítsa is sacrilegiously referred to as Greek champagne. Ioánina has some good oriental pastry; besides the usual *baklavá, kataífi* and *galaktoboúreko,* try *raváni* and *bougátsa* (made with custard cream and cinnamon). Of regional dishes there are few. In Messolóngi ask for fish roe appetizer *ávgo táraho* (expensive); in Préveza for shrimps (*garídes*); shrimps with rice (*garídes piláffi*) are among the better fare in coastal region, but pies are the real Epirote specialty.

Agrínio. *Esperia* (M), tel. 2 3033. 26 rooms. *Alice* (I), tel. 2 3056. 34 rooms.*Galaxy* (I), tel. 2 3551/3. 36 rooms. DC, MC, V. *Leto* (I), tel. 2 3043. 36 rooms, most with shower. V. *Soumelis* (I), tel. 2 3473. 20 rooms. Motel on bypass, 2 km. (one mile) out; restaurant. V.

Ahéloos. *Filoxenia* (M), tel. 7 1201. 3 double rooms. Motel at the ruins of Stratos, near the Ahéloos bridge, 13 km. (8 miles) north of Agrínio.

Amfilohía. *Amvrakia* (I), tel. 2 2213. 39 rooms. Restaurant. *Mistral* (I), tel. 2 2287. 40 rooms. Restaurant. *Oscar* (I), tel. 2 2155. 33 rooms. All three have roofgardens.

Árta. *Xenia* (M), tel. 2 7413. 22 rooms. Lovely location within the Byzantine fortress; book well in advance in summer. Tennis. DC, MC, V. *Kronos* (I), tel. 2 2211/3. 55 rooms. Restaurant, disco.

Astakós. *Astakos Beach* (M), tel. 4 1096. 33 rooms, 4 suites.

Igoumenítsa. *Astoria* (M), tel. 2 2704. 14 rooms. MC, V. *Jolly* (M), tel. 2 3970/4. 27 rooms. Roofgarden.MC, V. *Oscar* (I), tel. 2 3338. 34 rooms. Airconditioned. V. *Xenia* (I), tel. 2 2282. 36 double rooms. Motel on the sea; half board. AE, DC, MC, V.

Ioánina. *Xenia* (M), Dodonis 33 (tel. 2 5087). 60 rooms. Far from lake. AE, DC, MC.*Alexios* (I), Poukevil 14 (tel. 2 4003). 92 rooms. *Dioni* (I), Tsirigoti 10 (tel. 2 7864). 44 rooms. *Egnatia* (I), Dagli 2 (tel. 2 5667). 52 rooms. *Olympic* (I), Melanidi 2 (tel. 2 5888). 44 rooms. V. *Vyzantion* (I), Leofóros Dodonis (tel. 2 3898). 104 rooms. The only (I) hotel with a restaurant. AE, V.
Restaurants. *Ta Litharitsia* (M). Cafe-restaurant and disco in the park. DC. Those on the lakeside and on the island close in winter.

Kastrossykiá. *Preveza Beach* (M), tel. 5 1481/4. 264 rooms in central block and bungalows. 16 km. (10 miles) north of Préveza. Airconditioned; pool, tennis, minigolf, disco. May be running as a Holiday Club.

Klidonia. *Farangi* (I), tel. 2 2054. 12 rooms, restaurant. At the Voidomatis River bridge.

Konitsa. *Bourazani* (I), tel. 2 2783. 9 rooms. Restaurant, pool.

Lia. The village described and made famous by Nicholas Gage, *New York Times* journalist, in his book *Eleni,* about his family and their involvement in the Greek civil war. *Lia* (I), tel. 3 1208. 9 rooms. New, with a good restaurant and wonderful views over village and mountains.

Messolóngi. *Theoxenia* (M), tel. 2 8098. 103 rooms. On the sea; roof garden, tennis, restaurant. MC. *Liberty* (I), tel. 2 8050. 122 rooms. Restaurant. MC.

Métsovo. *Egnatia* (M), tel. 4 1263. 36 rooms. On the main road in town center, this hotel has an Alpine atmosphere with carved wooden ceilings and paneled walls. *Victoria* (M), tel. 4 1771. 37 rooms. On the outskirts of town, overlooking the valley. Local handicraft decor. Disco. MC, V. *Bitounis* (I), tel. 4 1545. 24 rooms. V. *Galaxy* (I), tel. 4 1202. 10 rooms, only 5 with shower. Restaurant on tree-shaded terrace. Near funicular for winter sports. V. *Kassaros* (I), tel. 4 1662. 24 rooms. V.

Monódendri. Five converted traditional houses (M). An original accommodation.

Mýtikas. *Simos* (M), tel. 8 1380/2. 27 rooms. Restaurant.

Papíngo. Five converted traditional houses (I).

Párga. *Bacoli* (M), tel. 3 1200. 34 rooms. Restaurant. *Lichnos Beach* (M), tel. 3 1257. 84 rooms in central block and bungalows. Minigolf, tennis. AE, MC. *Parga Beach* (M), tel. 3 1293. 80 bungalows. Minigolf. AE, DC, MC, V. Further out, *Valtos Beach* (M), tel. 3 1005. 19 rooms. V.

Pérama. *Ziakas* (I), tel. 2 8611. 40 rooms. Next to the cave.

Platária. *Plataria Beach* (M), tel. 7 1287. 22 rooms. Other hotels under construction.

Préveza. *Margarona Royal* (M), tel. 2 4361/8. 117 rooms. Roofgarden, pool, disco. 3 km. (2 miles) outside. AE, DC, MC, V. *Zikas* (M), tel. 2 7505. 54 rooms. AE, V. *Dioni* (I), tel. 2 7381/4. 30 rooms. Restaurant. V. *Minos* (I), tel. 2 8424. 19 rooms. On waterfront. V. *Preveza City* (I), tel. 2 7370. 51 rooms. V.
Restaurants. There are several restaurants on the waterfront.

Sívota. *Robinson Club* (M), tel. 9 1461/3. 120 rooms. Beach, pool, tennis, disco. On Mourtos Bay.

Vónitsa. *Bel Mare* (M), tel. 2 2394. 33 rooms. *Kekrops* (I), tel. 2 2490. 20 rooms. Restaurant. *Vonitsa* (I), tel. 2 2594. 34 rooms.

GETTING AROUND. By Plane. There are twice daily flights between Athens and Ioánina (50 min.), as well as flights once daily between Athens and Áktio (1 hr. 5 min.) for Lefkáda, and Préveza.

By Car. The 100-km. (62-mile) stretch from Igoumenítsa to Ioánina is the beginning of the modern version of the antique Via Egnatia, under reconstruction to Thessaloníki. Ioánina is the hub of the system: 198 km. (123 miles) northeast to Kastoriá in west Macedonia; 64 km. (40 miles) south to Árta, another 45 km. (28 miles) to Amfilohía, thence bypassing Agrínio and Messolóngi to Antírio, thence by ferry (half-hourly) to Río, where it links with the toll motorway along the northern shore of the Peloponnese to Corinth and then to Athens.

But there are three shorter west–east crossings to the Athens–Thessaloníki motorway: the *first* from Ioánina along the lake and through the magnificent scenery of the Píndos range via Métsovo and Kalambáka (Meteóra) to Lárissa 206 km. (128 miles); the *second* from Agrínio across the Kremastá lake by the Tatarna bridge and through the foothills of the Panetoliko via Karpeníssi to Lamia 195 km. (121 miles); the *third* branches left (east) at the roadfork before Antírio to Náfpaktos ten km. (six miles) and then via Delphi to Thebes 209 km., (130 miles).

Párga is reached by branching 13 km. (eight miles) right (west) off the coastal highway from Igoumenítsa to Préveza, avoiding the mountains of the interior 92 km., (57 miles); a half-hourly ferry takes cars in ten minutes from Preveza to Áktio. Nineteen km. (12 miles) southwest is the 75 m. drawbridge over the narrow channel to Lefkáda, which can also be reached by skirting the Ambracian Gulf from Amfilohía 55 km., (34 miles); 14 km. (nine miles) east of Áktio is Vónitsa, whence the shortest road south connects via Mýtikas and Astakós at Etoliko 105 km., (65 miles) with the main artery.

By Bus. There are three buses a day between Athens (the terminal at Kifissou 100) and Igoumenítsa, taking about eight hours for the 418 km. (260 miles).

By Boat. The ferry-boats Brindisi–Corfu–Pátra call at Igoumenítsa, but there is also a local ferry service between Corfu and Igoumenítsa, ten times daily in summer, taking about two hours.

PLACES TO VISIT. Those with a special interest in archeology are recommended to visit—in addition to Dodóna—the following sites: **Amotopos,** ten km. (six miles) northeast of Filipiáda, ancient walls dating from the 4th–3rd century B.C. **Doliani,** near Riziani, to the right of the Ioánina–Igoumenítsa highway, with the ruins of a walled town of the 3rd–2nd century B.C. **Kassopi,** 26 km. (16 miles) north of Préveza on the Zalóngo road; the ruins of a 4th-century B.C. town.

SHOPPING. Ioánina used to be famous for its metalworkers and embroiderers. Metalwork (small silver boxes with enameled designs, brooches, buckles, ashtrays etc.) are still made in traditional designs, though the quality of the silver has somewhat deteriorated. These as well as some fine needlework, rugs and bags of good color and design, in the traditional Métsovo style, can be bought in numerous tourist shops.

SKI CENTER. With snow regularly from December to March. Métsovo, at 1000 m. (3280 ft.), is an expanding winter resort. There is one ski-lift to Karakoli at present; contact the *Metsovo Alpine Club,* tel. 4 1249, for further information.

THE IONIAN ISLANDS

In the Realm of Odysseus

There are seven islands, which accounts for the Greek name Heptanesa. Six—Kérkyra (Corfu) of which the neighboring islet of Paxí is a part, Lefkáda, Itháki (Ithaca), Kefaloniá (Cephallonia) and Zákynthos (Zante)— are strung in a chain off the western shores of Greece. The seventh, Kýthira (*see* The Peloponnese chapter, above) lies far to the south, close to the eastern promontory of the Peloponnese, and has more often than not followed a destiny apart, ever since Aphrodite chose it for her first sensational appearance.

Ruins and tombs on Lefkáda and Kefaloniá prove the existence of a flourishing Mycenaean civilization at the time of the Trojan War, in which Odysseus, King of Ithaca played such a decisive part. Leucadius, Penelope's brother, gave his name to one of the isles, while on Corfu, the land of the Phaeacians, was enacted the charming idyll between Princess Nausicaa and the shipwrecked Odysseus. These Homeric associations formed a common bond, which however was broken in Classical times. Though the northern islands were colonized from Corinth in the 8th and 7th centuries B.C., Corfu soon revolted and its conflict with the mother city led to the Peloponnesian War, when the colony appealed for help to Athens, while Corinth, allied to the other islands, turned to Sparta. After subjection to the tyrants of Syracuse, the kings of Epirus and of Macedonia, the islands passed in the 2nd century B.C., under Roman rule.

With the break up of the Byzantine empire each island again resumed a separate and stormy existence. Resisting Germanic and Saracen invasions with varying degrees of success, the old ties with Sicily were at last re-established in the 11th century, and for 300 years Norman and Angevin kings ruled either directly or through their vassals, of whom the counts of Cephallonia and Zante were the most powerful. Corfu was the first to place itself under Venetian protection in 1386, and in spite of the two momentous Turkish sieges in 1537 and 1716, has the distinction of being the only part of modern Greece never to have experienced Ottoman rule. The other islands suffered severely from the Turks, before being slowly gathered under the protective wings of the mighty maritime republic. The astute diplomats of San Marco won the loyal support of the leading Greek families by a liberal scattering of high-sounding titles, which, to the islanders' great regret, are not recognized by the Greek constitution. The life of the island aristocracy centered on their elegant country houses, and the general prosperity led to a flowering of arts and letters in happy contrast with the prevailing material and spiritual misery on the mainland. Italian became the official language till 1851, when a British governor reintroduced Greek, which had decayed into a peasant dialect.

The fall of Venice in 1797 started an unparalleled game of musical chairs among the great powers. Under the treaty of Campo Formio the French occupied all Venetian territories, but Russo-Turkish forces established in 1800 the Republic of the Seven Isles under the sultan's sovereignty. In 1802 the Russians took over, to be in their turn dispossessed by the French in 1807. Britain joined the game in 1810, but the French garrison in Corfu held out against the English blockade until 1814, when the treaty of Paris re-established the Ionian Republic under British protection.

The senate and legislative assembly had little real authority under the personal rule of the Lord High Commissioners, who were great individualists, to put it mildly. The first Commissioner, Sir Thomas Maitland, was notorious for his rudeness, especially to bearers of letters of introduction. He was known to have exposed an unmentionable part of his anatomy to unwanted visitors, yet his eccentricity was no greater than that of his successor. Sir Frederick Adam married an ambitious Corfiote, whose moustache, it was said, would not have shamed a dashing hussar. This peculiarity did not prevent the misguided second Commissioner from lavishing the revenue of the islands on the bearded lady.

Successive commissioners built roads, hospitals, asylums and prisons, reformed education, law and agriculture, but these benefices could not stem the rising tide of nationalism. Ruthless suppression failed, as also Gladstone's attempt at reconciliation by a liberal constitution. Britain acknowledged the trend by using the Ionian islands to secure the election of Prince William George of Holstein-Glücksburg, son of the King of Denmark, to the Greek throne, and after his accession as George I, the islands were ceded to Greece in 1864.

Earthquakes had been a fairly common calamity, especially in Zákynthos, but never as widespread and devastating as the series of shocks which in summer 1953 leveled the towns and villages on Itháki, Kefalonía and Zákynthos. By 1959 the reconstruction was completed, a remarkable feat in a poor country, largely due to the active help of the army and generous support from foreign welfare organizations. But the fine old houses of Venetian Zante are gone, replaced by modern buildings, perhaps pleasanter to live in, but infinitely less pleasing to the eye.

Exploring the Ionian Islands

The ferries from Italy or the Dalmatian coast call at Corfu, thus giving the best possible introduction to Greece. The unrivaled beauty of the island is enhanced by the inhabitants' famed courteousness, the happy result of centuries of unbroken civilization. Corfiotes have been accused of being overcivilized—as if that were possible. The 19th-century English painter and nonsense poet Edward Lear captured the unique quality of the lush and luxuriant island, whose capital he calls "a very small tittle-tattle place" against the background of Albanian mountains possessing "a certain clumsiness and want of refinement." The main contemporary objection is the touristic overdevelopment which has degraded numerous beauty spots.

Corfu

Boats coming from Italy and Yugoslavia pass through the narrow channel separating the northern bulge of the island from Albania, so the traveler from abroad is presented with the entire east coast on his way to Athens. But he should break the journey for a while, to enjoy the tranquil dignity of the tall 18th-century buildings lining the arcaded streets, little changed since Venetian times, though the Italian bombing of 1941 destroyed the opera house and other public buildings.

The road from the harbor ascends past the mansion where John Capodistrias, Greece's first President, was born in 1776, now a school for interpreters. The Cathedral (Metropolis), a little higher up, dates from 1577 but of greater interest is the Church of St. Spyridon (1589), the island's patron saint, which lies just off the main square and is easily recognizable by its red dome. Corfu's sensuous beauty seems to preclude sanctity, though a patron had to be found in saintlier parts. The embalmed body of Ágios Spiridon, Bishop of Cyprus in the 4th century, was smuggled out of Constantinople in a sack of straw after the Turkish conquest and after an adventurous journey, placed in a silver casket in the chapel to the right of the altar. Most efficacious in saving the town from the plague in 1630 and the Turks in 1716, his prestige was further enhanced when a bomb hit the church, but failed to explode in World War II during an air raid that destroyed a third of the town. No wonder his name is proudly borne by a good half of the male islanders.

British rule has left some unexpected marks, especially on the large central square, the Esplanade, where cricket is still played. The game has inevitably undergone certain local modifications, together with some English words and drinks, as for instance *tsintsibira,* no other than ginger beer. On the north side of the square rises the elegant colonnade of the former Royal Palace, built after the plans of Sir George Whitmore between 1816 and 1823. The attractive residence of the High Commissioners and seat of the Ionian Senate, known as the Palace of St. Michael and St. George, as it was also the headquarters of the newly-founded order, became a favorite residence of George I. The staterooms, with the stern portraits of the High Commissioners, are open to the public; the Museum of Asiatic Art contains the remarkable Sino-Japanese collection donated by a former Greek ambassador to those countries.

The British High Commissioners, a self-assured lot, scattered monuments all over the Esplanade, the most original being an Ionian rotunda to the memory of Sir Thomas Maitland, near the bandstand where the municipal orchestra performs on Sundays. Capodistrias' statue faces the empty shell of Lord Guilford's Ionian Academy on the upper Esplanade, bombed out but scheduled for reconstruction. According to contemporaries Lord Guilford was "a queer fish, but very pleasant; he goes about dressed up like Plato, with a gold band round his mad pate and flowing drapery of purple hue. The pretty dress of the students consists of a tunic and cloak, with buskins of red leather reaching to mid-leg. The professors bind fillets round their heads. Medicine wears the tunic citron and the cloak orange; Law light green and violet; Philosophy green and blue." In spite, or perhaps because, of the fancy dress, this nucleus of a university started Greece's literary revival round the poets Solomos and Mavilis.

The west side of the Esplanade was the exclusive reserve of the nobility till revolutionary France swept away feudal privileges and substituted a local adaptation of the Rue de Rivoli. The arcades below the tall houses, still called the Liston after the *Lista d'Oro* of the Venetian aristocracy, are now taken up by souvenir shops and cafes, overflowing into the square after sunset. During the evening, open-air concerts and dance performances are sometimes held in the lovely flower parks near the fortress.

The old fortress on the east is cut off by a deep canal. This artificial island was a suburb of the ancient town, but the center of the Byzantine settlement. The Venetians, recognizing its strategic importance, transformed it into a fortress, which decisively contributed to the successful resistance against the Turkish attacks in 1716. The hero of the siege, Count Schulenburg, is honored by a statue near the bridge. English barracks were built in the fortress area and the former Anglican Chapel of St. George, in the Doric style, has been converted to Orthodoxy. Since the 1980s the former military complex accommodates the Ionian University.

The massive walls of the new fortress, on a hill dominating the harbor, have also been restored. This fine example of solid Venetian military architecture now houses the town's archives. From the top there is a fine view over the town and the surrounding villages half hidden in cypress and olive groves, while the distant mountains of Epirus and Albania seem to merge with the island's highest peak, Mount Pantocrator.

On the south the square narrows to the shady Dimokratías Boulevard. A favorite evening stroll is along the bay past the 7th-century B.C. Cenotaph of Menecrates to the ruins of the Artemis temple, whose colossal Gorgon pediments are (together with the lioness of Menecrates) the pride of the museum behind the Corfu Palace Hotel. Above the Anemómilos suburb rise the cupolas of the 12th-century Church of Ágios Iason and Ágios Sosipater.

The Haunt of Royalty

Paleopolis, the antique capital, occupied most of the promontory where several sanctuaries have been excavated. Within the precincts of the large archaic temple stood two minute shrines, one dedicated to Hermes, the other to Aphroditos, patron of transvestites, judging from the clay statuettes depicting Aphrodite with moustache and beard, a curious anticipation of things to come in the shape of Lady Adam.

A Russian general was the first to rediscover the serenity of the wooded promontory, and instead of a gun emplacement he built himself a pavilion. It would be going too far to say that this aesthetic indulgence led to the loss of the island, but soon afterwards the second Lord High Commissioner outshone his Russian predecessor by building the villa of Mon Repos, surrounded by a beautiful park, for his bearded spouse. "Sir Frederick's Folly" became the summer residence of the Greek royal family; the Duke of Edinburgh was born there. The beach of Mon Repos is well provided with cabins and a cafe under huge plane trees; it is open to the public and within easy reach of the town, but the bathing is marred by the seaweed in the shallow water.

The road continues through gardens and parks to the suburb of Kanóni, one of the world's great beauty spots, made deservedly famous by countless pictures. The name derives from a French cannon that once stood there, no doubt utterly incongruous in that sublimely peaceful landscape. The open sea is separated by a long, narrow causeway from the lagoon of Halikiopóulou, with the intensely green slopes of Mount Agía Déka as a backdrop. A shorter breakwater leads to the white convent of Vlahérna on a tiny islet. Beyond, tall cypresses guard the chapel on Pontikonisi, the Mouse Island, a rock rising dramatically from the clear water, which mythology has identified with the Phaeacian ship turned to stone by enraged Poseidon for bringing Odysseus home to Ithaca. The sunset over the lagoon is one of those experiences that will not be forgotten in a lifetime.

The long causeway's main function is as an aqueduct, built by Sir Frederick, though pedestrians and even cyclists may pass. The road south skirts the lagoon, past the international airport. One branch of the road continues to the open sea, to be rejoined by the other branch shortly before the pretty village of Benítses. That other branch first climbs to the village of Gastóuri nestling among the trees, and then turns to the Achilleion, the palace of the Empress Elizabeth of Austria, at an altitude of 145 meters (476 ft.), 19 km. (12 miles) from Corfu.

This remarkable monument to bad taste is redeemed by the lovely garden stretching to the sea. Halfway down, in an open pavilion, stands the statue of the empress, her beauty marred by the impossibility of reproducing modern clothes in marble. The street façade of the palace is fairly inoffensive, but the interior is a preposterous hotch-potch of a pseudo-Byzantine chapel, a pseudo-Pompeian room and a pseudo-Renaissance dining hall, culminating in an hilariously vulgar fresco of "Achilles in his Chariot." It is astonishing that a woman as fastidious as the empress so entirely succumbed to the appalling taste of her period. Yet she was independent enough to choose for her retreat an island that until then had been unfashionably remote.

Worse is to come on the terrace which commands a superb view over Kanóni and the town. In what was seriously intended as an Ionic peristyle stand a bewildering number of statues (from the Muses down to somebody's Aunt Fanny), in various degrees of undress, but uniformly depressing or funny, according to the visitor's mood. Almost artistic is the marble "Achilles Wounded," Elizabeth's favorite hero, in whose honor the palace was named.

To prove that he could do everything bigger and better, the German emperor inscribed his colossal Achilles with the modest dedication: "to the greatest Greek from the greatest German." Always the Supreme War Lord, the Kaiser had a riding saddle fixed up as a chair for the writing desk; the imposing throne of the lavatory, complete with electric bell, witness that Wilhelm II insisted on his illustrious status even in his most intimate moments. He bought the Achilleion after the assassination of the Austrian empress, and resided there regularly till the outbreak of World War I. Before being turned into a casino the palace was completely renovated, but the historic monstrosities have been well preserved.

Paleokastrítsa

Lacking the comic touch, but scenically equally splendid is the longer excursion to Paleokastrítsa. The road, constructed by the Eleventh Regiment of Foot to a convalescent camp, but according to gossip, to Lady Adam's favorite picnic spot, crosses the island between orange and olive groves to the rugged bays and promontories of the west coast. On a rock towering over the crystal clear water of the creek stands the monastery facing the open Ionian Sea. The steep mountain behind the monastery rock is crowned by the grim ruins of Angelokastro, built in the 13th century by Michael I Angelos, Despot of Epirus, during his brief rule over Corfu. To enjoy the magnificent view over the wild coast drive up to the restaurant on the Bella Vista terrace, a favorite vantage point of Wilhelm II. The twin bays below are the traditional site of the Phaeacian capital ruled by Alcinous, when Odysseus was washed ashore and found by Nausicaa, playing ball with her maidens, at the mouth of the Ermónes river further south. Paleokastritsa is one of Corfu's most popular resorts, and the hillsides above the bays are covered with hotels, tavernas, bars, and shops, and the beaches swarm with hordes of day-trippers up from Corfu town. However, it is still undeniably a spectacular spot and certainly worth a visit.

Another monastery on the west coast that should be visited for the lovely site is the hermitage of the Myrtiótissa, an hour's walk from the village of Pélekas, lying below Mount Ágios Géorgios. Then there is the drive north to Kassiópi along the east coast, past the Castello, an early 20th-century Florentine-Renaissance confection; the splendid bay of Dassiá, Ypsós, Pyrgí and Nissáki, to return over mighty Mount Pantokrator.

Lefkáda and Itháki

The annual Festival of Art and Literature attracts, by its varied folkloric manifestations, large crowds in August and has put Lefkáda deservedly on the tourist map. But hotel accommodation is totally insufficient, though supplemented by B&B. Here, as on all Ionian islands with the exception of Kefalinía, the capital has given its name to the whole island. Lefkáda is easily reached; either by boat from Athens, calling at the lesser ports of northwestern Greece; or in about two hours by motorboat from Préveza, over the site of the naval battle of Actium, which Cleopatra's cowardice or treachery lost for Mark Antony; or by road from Amfilohiá 61 km. (38 miles) along the shores of the Ambracian Gulf and then across the Lefkáda Ship Canal that separates Lefkáda from the mainland. A "boatbridge" has replaced the old towrope ferry that used to run between the mainland and the island.

The canal through the marshy isthmus was originally dug by the Corinthians in 640 B.C., but silted up again. Augustus ordered a new excavation and also linked the town to the land, as he was interested in the island which lay so close to the scene of his greatest victory. The canal was sufficiently important to be kept open by successive conquerors, and in the

13th century the Franks built the Santa Maura Fortress to guard the entrance. An aqueduct of 260 arches brought water to the castle, which was
later occupied by the Venetians and Turks.

A strip of sand, 16 km. (ten miles) long, on which windmills and trees
seem to rise straight out of the water, separates the open sea from the lagoon on which the town stands, connected by a long causeway over the
salt marshes to the port. Lefkáda suffered severely in the earthquakes of
1867 and 1958, though it escaped the still greater devastation of 1953. The
damaged Venetian churches are undistinguished, but the 21 km. (13 miles)
to the Bay of Vlího, hugging the coast, are a sheer joy. Some Mycenaean
ruins at Nidrí, now the haunt of sailing yachts, led the German archaeologist Dörpfeld to elaborate an ingenious theory that there was the site of
ancient Ithaca. But without going into complicated archaeological argu-
ments the traveler will be able to appreciate the scenic beauty of the drive.
After Vlího the road climbs into the mountainous but fertile interior, to
rejoin the sea at the fishing village of Vassiliki in the south, halfway (43
km., 27 miles) on the island circuit. The island of Skorpiós, a few miles
off, now belongs to Christina Onassis' young daughter, Athina, following
Christina's death in 1989. Aristotle Onassis, his daughter, and his son are
all buried there. The return journey, on a pretty road high up in the cliffs
of the west coast, presents another facet of this lovely island, the laborious-
ly terraced mountain slopes and the beaches on the Ionian Sea.

To include the four northern islands in one tour, it is possible to proceed
from Vassiliki on Lefkáda to the port of Koliéri in the northern bay of
Itháki. The journey takes about four hours, for the first part in the shelter
of the Lefkatos, the White Cape, now Cape Doukáto, once crowned by
a temple of Apollo, near the modern lighthouse. From the cliff 72 meters
(236 ft.) high the Lefkadian leap was performed as a divine judgment for
certain crimes, but curiously enough also as a drastic cure for love-
sickness. It was indeed a case of kill or cure as the poetess Sappho experienced to her detriment. Disappointed lovers of the Roman period were
less reckless and equipped themselves with feathers to break the fall, while
boats were waiting to haul them out of the water. Apollo's priests performed the dive as a routine observance.

A steep scenic road crosses the island over the narrow waist below
Mount Aëtós (Eagle), on which Schliemann excavated a 7th-century B.C.
town. Enthusiastic as ever, the indefatigable archeologist named some Cyclopean walls Odysseus' Castle, one of his lesser anachronisms. From the
highest point of the road, without climbing the 380 meters (1,246 ft.) to
the summit, one enjoys a magnificent view: to the west Kefaloniá, separated only by a strip of water, and to the east the entrance to the Gulf of
Pátra, guarded by high mountain sentinels.

The capital is locally called Vathý (Deep), as it lies at the head of a deep
inlet, branching off from the big eastern bay. Vathý as well as Ithaka, the
Precipitous, are indeed singularly apposite and in perfect agreement with
Homer's description in the Odyssey.

This is the quietest of the Ionian island capitals, as lack of beaches has
prevented touristic development. The meager Mycenaean finds are in the
small Archaeological Museum.

Though the smallest of the four islands over which Odysseus ruled, it
was, owing to its strategical position and ports at every point of the compass, the obvious center of a maritime kingdom. Even now, the villages

on the coast, like Frikés and Kióni, are less deserted than those inland, among the cultivated terraced mountain slopes crumbling away.

Kefaloniá and Zákynthos

Kefaloniá is the largest of the Ionian islands, with its barren western mountain chain rising to the peak of Mount Áïnos (1,619 meters, 5,313 ft.). Though the plains are fertile and there are even forests of a local variety of fir, it is only at the lovely fishing villages of Ássos and Fiskárdo in the north that Kefaloniá rivals the enchantment of Corfu and Zákynthos. From Sámi opposite Itháki, near the extensive but dull ruins of ancient Samaea, it is 25 km. (16 miles) to Argostóli, the modern capital in a fjordlike bay in the south. The drive takes in the main sights: in the central plain the Monastery of Ágios Gerásimos, Kefaloniá's patron saint, who failed to protect his sanctuary in the terrible disaster of 1953; the 83 Mycenaean tombs at Mazarákata, partly of the beehive variety, partly hewn into the rocks, which have yielded numerous Bronze Age vases and implements; and about six km. (four miles) before Argostóli the ramparts of Kástro (Castle), the seat of the Norman Counts Palatine, captured by the Turks in 1483 and by the Venetians in 1500. As the latters' capital, San Giorgio, it flourished till the destructive earthquake in 1636 and was finally abandoned in favor of Argostóli in 1757. The empty shells of churches and houses straggle up to the solid ramparts of the castle, unscathed by repeated upheavals. Just behind the drawbridge are the ruined British barracks.

Argostóli, originally the port of San Giorgio, lies inside the branch of the long Linadi Bay. Razed to the ground in 1953, it has been rebuilt on occasionally startling modernistic lines, following utilitarian principles mitigated by wide, tree-lined avenues. The *Katovathres,* deep clefts in the coastal cliffs in subterranean communication with the sea, are a local attraction. The Melissani seacave can be explored by boat, while one of the green-colored chambers of the Drongorati caves has been transformed into a subterranean, stalactite-roofed concert hall, renowned for its acoustics. The fine sandy beach of Platýs Gialós is three km. (two miles) out of town. The second town, Lixóuri, across the bay, is fringed by good beaches.

Last, but certainly not least, comes Zákynthos, long known as *Zante, fiore di Levante.* Till 1953 the flower of the Levant rivaled Corfu in natural beauty as well as in the attractiveness of the arcaded town and of the country houses scattered over the plain. The architectural gems are all gone and the new box-like arcades, so indispensable in the torrential winter rains, are but a sad substitute for their rounded, elegant 18th-century predecessors. But at least the local patron saint, Ágios Dionýsios, proved here more efficacious, as only his church and the National Bank building survived the last great earthquake. This curious juxtaposition has been attributed by the faithless to good, solid masonry, a belief reinforced by the inevitable Venetian fortress, which on the hill dominating the town proved itself impervious to the successive violent upheavals afflicting the island during the last 150 years. But even here there is the proverbial silver lining in the richness and fertility of the volcanic soil, and the view from the castle over the wide, intensively cultivated plain between the two seas only presents the luxuriant vegetation of the flowering island.

Zante hospitably welcomed the artists who fled Crete after the Turkish conquest in the 17th century. The museum thus contains an outstanding collection of paintings belonging to the Ionian School, especially the superb *Christ as Highpriest,* by Nikolas Kallergis. The closest beach is at Argássi (five km., three miles); while Pórto Róma (11 km., seven miles) is an idyllic bay below a rocky promontory. The longest stretch of fine sand is can be found at Laganás (10 km.—six miles—south), where there is considerable tourist development; hotels, villas, local speedboat, jetski, and Windsurfer operations. This lovely beach, however, is also the home of the threatened loggerhead sea-turtles that come up to lay eggs in the sand on August evenings. Tourists and turtles are waging a battle and the turtles appear to be losing. The World Wildlife Fund and the Greek Sea Turtle Protection Society are attempting to protect the turtles whose numbers have dwindled rapidly over the past few years. Despite the Greek government's 1987 declaration of Laganás as a "marine zone of special protection," all the land around the bay is now scheduled for development. There is some good news, though. The lovely beach of Kalamáki, just north of Laganás, is also a sea turtle nesting place and, for the moment, further building of hotels has been halted here. The two mineral springs at Kerí, the southernmost point, where pitch bubbles up at the rate of three barrels a day to be used for the caulking of boats, were described by Herodotus in the 5th century B.C.

PRACTICAL INFORMATION FOR
THE IONIAN ISLANDS

WHEN TO COME. Decidedly not in winter. From November to March there are torrential rains, depressing in their persistency. The rains do, however, make the islands an earthly paradise in spring and summer.

TOURIST OFFICE. There is a G.N.T.O. office in the government building, Corfu, tel. 3 0298.

SPECIAL EVENTS. March–April. Processions in honor of Ágios Spiridon, patron saint of Corfu, on Palm Sunday and Easter Saturday. **May** through **September.** Sound and Light at the Old Fortress, Corfu, with traditional dancing. **June.** International Ionian Regatta. **August.** Procession in honor of Ágios Spiridon, patron of Corfu, on August 11. Performances by theater groups and folkloric dancers in Corfu, Itháki, Lefkáda and Zákynthos, continuing into early September. **December.** The feasts of Ágios Spiridon, patron of Corfu, and of Ágios Dionýsios of Zákynthos, fall respectively on December 12 and 17.

HOTELS AND RESTAURANTS. Hotels are crowded from May to September with package tours. Most hotels, except at Lefkáda, face the sea; many offer halfboard or fullboard only. On the islands, food at the usual waterfront taverns is uninteresting, in spite of the long connection with Italy. Some wine, on the other hand, is pleasant. *Theotoki,* produced by Corfu's leading family, is difficult to obtain. Kefaloniá produces the excellent *Robola* and *Calligas* and Lefkáda produces a very drinkable rough red wine, *Santa Maura,* that goes well with the local sausages. The

Corfu Barbecue and Wine Festival offers wine, folk dancing and cabaret combined with a folkloric museum and handicrafts in the making in the *Village* eight km. (five miles) north of town. A major tourist attraction.

Corfu

Distances (km./miles) from Corfu town are shown in brackets after the name of the town or resort.

Ágios Górdis (14/9 southwest). *Ágios Górdios* (M), tel. 3 6723. 209 rooms. Pool, tennis, disco; above the beach. *Chrysses Folies* (I), tel. 3 0407. 20 double rooms. Nothing to do with follies, but the Golden Nests, which is almost equally off the mark. Restaurant. 275 meters (300 yards) from beach.

Ágios Ioánnis (36/22 north). *Sidari Beach* (I), tel. 3 1115. 31 rooms. Near beach. Restaurant, tennis.

Alykés (3/2 north). *Kerkyra Golf* (E), tel. 3 1785/7. 240 rooms. Name is confusing because the golf course is near the west coast; not airconditioned; pool, roofgarden, tennis, disco; on beach. AE, MC. *Salina* (M), tel. 3 6782. 16 rooms. *Sunset* (M), tel 3 1203. 60 rooms, 3 suites. Pool.

Anaharávi (34/21 north). *Aharavi Beach* (M), tel. 9 3146. 43 rooms and 14 bungalows are available at beachside hotel. Pool, tennis. *Ionian Princess* (M), tel. 9 3110/1. 90 rooms. Pool, disco.

Anemómylos. Suburb opposite Mon Repos beach. *Arion* (M), tel. 3 7950. DC. 105 rooms. Disco, minigolf, pool, roofgarden. *Marina* (M), tel. 3 2783. 102 rooms. Airconditioned; pool, roofgarden; on the beach. Both half board only.

Aríllas (45/28 northwest). *Arilla Beach* (I), tel. 3 1401. 32 rooms.

Benítses (11/7 south). *Odyssey Apartments* (E), tel. 9 2227. 56 furnished apartments. *San Stefano* (E), tel. 9 2292. 250 rooms. Pool, tennis; 730 meters (800 yards) from beach. Romantic and isolated. AE, DC, MC, V. *Potamaki* (M), tel. 3 0889. 149 rooms. Beach, pool, roofgarden, disco which features Greek traditional dancing performances. AE, DC, V. *Corfu Maris* (I), tel. 9 2381. 25 rooms. On beach.

Corfu Town. *Corfu Palace* (L), tel. 3 9485/7. 106 rooms. Two pools, tennis. Guests are taken to bathe at Miramare Bungalows at Moraitika. AE, DC, MC, V. *Astron* (M), tel. 3 9505. 33 rooms. Tennis. *Olympic* (M), tel. 3 0532. 50 rooms. Tennis. DC. *Arcadion* (I), tel. 3 7670. 55 rooms. Well situated on the Esplanade. MC. *Atlantis* (I), tel. 3 5560. 58 rooms. Airconditioned; on seafront. *Ionion* (I), tel. 3 9915. 81 rooms. The last two are on the waterfront and all three in the (I) category have restaurants.

Restaurants. *Xenichtis* (E), at Mandouki (tel. 2 4911). *Averoff* (M), Alipiou 4 (tel. 3 1468). Near the old harbor, good choice of local dishes, *sofrito* (veal with garlic and vinegar sauce). AE, DC, V. *Bella Napoli* (M), Skaramanga 11, tel. 3 3338. Really good Italian pasta dishes; closed for lunch. AE, DC. *Quattro Stagioni* (M), tel. 4 2956. In the old Campiello quarter. There are Expensive fish restaurants in the Mandouki suburbs, and beyond at Kondokali, e.g. *Gkereko* (don't be put off by appearances). Numerous cafe-sweetshops in the Liston, crowded till late at night. AE, DC, V.

Entertainment. *Bouzoukia* in *Corfu by Night* (E), tel. 3 8123. Among the discos on the port road, *La Boom* (E), *Bora Bora* (M), and *Koukouvaya* (M).

Dafníla (13/8 north). Promontory with olive groves. *Eva Palace* (E), tel. 9 1286/7. 174 rooms. Pool, tennis, disco. DC. *Grecotel Dafnila Bay* (E), tel. 3 5836. 260 rooms in hotel and bungalows. Airconditioned; pool, tennis, disco; close to beach.

Dassía (11/7 north). *Corfu Chandris* (E), tel. 3 3871. 301 rooms in central block, bungalows and villas. AE, DC, MC, V. *Dassia Chandris* (E), tel. 3 3871/5. 251 rooms. Beach, pool, tennis, disco. AE, MC, V. *Elaea Beach* (E), tel. 9 3490. 198 rooms. Halfboard. On tree-lined beach, with sea sports. AE. *Margarona Palace Corfu* (E), tel. 9 3742/6. 118 rooms. Pool, tennis. *Dassia* (I), tel. 9 3224. 54 rooms. Beach. DC. *Paloma Bianca* (I), tel. 9 3575. 34 rooms. Airconditioned; pool, tennis.

Restaurant. *BP Grill* (M). tel. 9 3511. This place serves excellent *sofrito,* a special Corfiote dish.

Ermónes (14/9 west). *Ermónes Beach* (E), tel. 9 4241/2. 272 bungalows. Not airconditioned; pool, tennis. AE, DC, MC, V.

Gaéna (10/6 south). *Achilleus* (M), tel. 9 2425/6. 74 rooms.

Gastóuri (5/3 southwest). *El Greco* (I), tel. 3 1893. 14 rooms. The *Casino* has a good restaurant.

Glyfáda (16/10 west). *Grand Hotel Glyfáda* (E), tel. 9 4201/2. 242 rooms. Excellent beach; pool, tennis, disco. AE, MC, V. *Glyfáda Beach* (M), tel. 9 4257. 35 rooms.

Gouvia (8/5 north). *Grecotel Corcyra Beach* (E), tel. 3 0770/2. 252 rooms in central block and bungalows. Not airconditioned; pool, tennis, disco. *Park* (M), tel. 9 1310. 178 rooms. Public rooms airconditioned; pool. AE, V. *Pheakion* (I), tel. 9 1497. 36 rooms.

Kanóni (3/2 south). *Corfu Hilton* (L), tel. 3 6540. 274 rooms in hotel and bungalows above beach. Pool, tennis, nightclub, casino. Fine location with a marvelous view. DC, MC, V. *Corfu Divani Palace* (E), tel. 3 8996/8. 165 rooms; disco. AE, V. *Ariti* (M), tel. 3 3885. 171 rooms. DC, V. Both have pool but are over two km. (one mile) from beach. *Salvos* (M), tel. 3 1693/4. 92 rooms. Pool, disco; 180 meters (200 yards) from beach. MC, V. *Royal* (I), tel. 3 7512. 121 rooms. Pool, restaurant, disco; about 180 meters (200 yards) from beach.

Kávos (47/29 south). *Cavos* (M), tel. 2 2107. 21 rooms.
Restaurant. *O Naftis* (M), excellent fish cooked by the owner's American wife. Also 10 apartments.

Koméno (10/6 north). *Astir Palace Corfu* (L), tel. 9 1481/6. 308 rooms in central block and bungalows. Pool, tennis, nightclub; private beach. AE,

DC, MC, V. *Radovas* (M), tel. 9 1218. 115 airconditioned rooms and bungalows. Pool. AE.

Kontokáli (6/4 north). *Kontokáli Palace* (E), tel. 3 8736/9. 238 rooms. Beach, pool, tennis, nightclub. AE, DC, MC, V. *Pyrós* (I), tel. 9 1206. 26 rooms. **Restaurant.** *Pipilas* (M), tel. 9 1201. Typical and traditional dishes including delicious *bourtheto,* a spicy fish soup.

Liapádes (19/12 northwest). *Elly Beach* (M), tel. 2 2255. 40 bungalows. *Liapades Beach* (I), tel. 2 2115. 44 rooms. AE.

Messóngi (22/14 south). *Gemini* (M), tel. 5 5398. 40 rooms. *Melissa Beach* (I), tel. 5 5229. 32 rooms. Pool, restaurant. *Rossis* (I), tel. 55 352. 30 rooms. Airconditioned; beach, restaurant.

Moraítika (21/13 south). *Messongi Beach* (M), tel. 3 8684/6. 828 rooms. Beach, 2 pools, tennis, minigolf. AE, DC. *Miramare Beach* (E), tel. 3 0226/8. 149 bungalows. All rooms very close to sea and have verandas. Tennis, minigolf. AE, DC. *Delfinia* (M), tel. 3 0318. 83 rooms. Beach, pool. DC. *Margarita* (I), tel. 5 5267. 36 rooms. Restaurant.

Nissáki (23/14 north). *Nissaki Beach* (E), tel. 9 1232. 239 rooms. Half-board; pool, tennis, minigolf, disco. AE, DC, MC, V. *Asprochori* (M), tel. 9 1266. 43 furnished flats. Pool.

Paleokastrítsa (23/14 northwest). *Akrotiri Beach* (E), tel. 4 1275/6. 126 rooms. Not airconditioned; pool. AE, MC. *Oceanis* (M), tel. 4 1230. 71 rooms. Pool. AE, DC. *Apollon* (I), tel. 4 1211. 23 rooms. *Odysseus* (I), tel. 4 1209. 36 rooms. AE, V. *Paleokastrítsa* (I), tel. 4 1207. 163 rooms. 180 meters (200 yards) from beach; disco, pool. All those in (I) category have restaurants.
Restaurants. Renowned for salt-water crayfish (*astakos*), usually wrongly translated as lobster. Taste and price are similar.

Pérama (8/5 south). *Aeolos Beach* (M), tel. 3 3132/4. 324 bungalows. Pool, minigolf; on beach. AE. *Akti* (M), tel. 3 9445. 55 rooms. Pool; on beach. AE. *Alexandros* (M), tel. 3 6855/7. 91 rooms. Pool. *Aegli* (I), tel. 3 9812. 37 rooms. On beach; roofgarden. AE, MC. *Oassis* (I), tel. 3 8190. 66 rooms. Pool, disco; roofgarden; on beach. *Pontikonissi* (I), tel. 3 6871. 49 rooms. AE.
Restaurant. *Yannis* (M), for seafood. AE.

Pyrgí (14/9 north). *Anna-Liza* (E), tel. 9 3438. 36 apartments. *Pyrgi* (I), tel. 9 3209. 58 rooms. Airconditioned; beach, roofgarden, disco, restaurant.

Róda (35/22 north). *Roda Beach* (M), tel. 9 3202. 360 rooms. Airconditioned; beach, pool, tennis, minigolf, disco. AE, DC, MC. *Silver Beach* (I), tel. 9 3134. 33 rooms. Beach 275 meters (300 yards). Restaurant.

Sgómbou (11/7 northwest). Halfway to Paleokastritsa. *Lucciola Inn* (M), tel. 9 1419. 10 rooms in a genuine Corfiote setting.

Sidári (34/21 north). *Astoria* (I), tel. 3 1315. 19 rooms. *Mimosa* (I), tel. 3 1361. 35 rooms. Minigolf, restaurant. AE, DC, V. *Three Brothers* (I), tel. 3 1242. 36 rooms. Excellent restaurant.

Sinarádes (13/8 southwest). *Gyaliskari Palace* (M), tel. 3 1400. 227 rooms, 4 suites. Pool, tennis, disco.

Tsáki (13/8 south). *Regency* (E), tel. 9 2305/10. 185 rooms. Airconditioned; beach, pool, disco. DC.

Ypsós (13/8 north). *Sunrise* (M), tel. 9 3414. 36 furnished apartments. *Ypsos Beach* (M), tel. 9 3232. 60 rooms. Pool. *Mega* (I), tel. 9 3208. 32 rooms. Beach, restaurant; good value.

Itháki

Mentor (M), tel. 3 2433. Most of the 42 rooms with bath. On seafront.

Kefaloniá

Distances (km./miles) shown in brackets after the name of the town or resort are from Argostoli.

Agía Pelagía (10/6 south). *Irinna* (M), tel. 4 1285/7. 169 rooms. Half-board; beach, pool, tennis. AE, DC, MC, V.

Argostóli. *Xenia* (M) tel. 2 2233. 24 rooms. Located between the central square and the beach. *Aenos* (I), tel. 2 8013. 40 rooms. *Cephalonia Star* (I), tel. 2 3180. 36 rooms. V. *Mouikis* (I), tel. 2 3032. 36 rooms. AE, DC, MC, V.

Restaurants. *Aenos* (I), *Kephalos* (I), *Limenaki* (I), and *Lorentsatos* (I), all on waterfront and indistinguishably undistinguished.

Fiskárdo. Traditional settlement. Converted mid-19th-century houses (M), accommodating 6 to 18 guests.

Lássi (2/1 south). *Mediterranée* (E), tel. 2 8760/3. 227 rooms. Beach, pool, disco. AE, DC, V. *Lassi* (I), tel. 2 3126. 32 rooms. Near beach. AE.

Lixóuri. *Summery* (I), tel. 9 1771. 56 rooms. Near beach on town's outskirts. Roofgarden, restaurant. V.

Platýs Gialós. (3/2 south). *White Rocks* (E), tel. 2 8332/4. 115 rooms in central block and bungalows. Beach, disco. DC.

Póros (40/25 north). *Hercules* (I), tel. 7 2351. 6 rooms; beach, restaurant.

Lefkáda

Lefkas (M), tel. 2 3916. 93 rooms. One km. from fine beach. AE, DC, V. At **Aghia Mavra.** *Nirikos* (M), tel. 2 4132. 36 rooms. AE, DC, V. *Xenia* (M), tel. 2 4762. 64 rooms. One km. from fine beach. At **Nikiana.** *Alexandros*

(M), tel. 7 1376. 27 rooms. At **Vassiliki.** *Lefkatas* (M), tel. 3 1305. 33 rooms.

Paxí

Paxos Beach (I), tel. 3 1211. 37 simple bungalows close to beach. Disco, restaurant. DC.

Zákynthos

Distances (km./miles) shown in brackets after the name of the town or resort are from Zákynthos town.

Alykés (16/10 northwest). *Astoria* (M), tel. 8 3533. 31 rooms. *Montreal* (I), tel. 8 3241. 31 rooms. Beach restaurant, disco.

Argássi (5/3 southeast). *Captain* (M), tel. 2 2779. 37 rooms. Pool. *Chryssi Akti* (M), tel. 2 8679. 84 rooms. Tennis; on beach. AE, MC. *Mimosa Beach* (M), tel. 2 2588. 44 bungalows. On beach. V. *Levante* (I), tel. 2 3608. MC.

Kalamáki (5/3 southwest). *Crystal Beach* (M), tel. 2 2917. 54 rooms. AE. *Kalamaki Beach* (I), tel. 2 2575. 29 rooms. Private beach, restaurant.

Laganás (6/4 southwest). *Astir* (E), tel. 5 1730. 60 rooms. This new hotel on the beach has a pool. *Esperia* (M), tel. 5 1505/7. 35 rooms. *Galaxy* (M), tel. 5 1171. 80 rooms. Roofgarden; on beach. *Laganas* (M), tel. 5 1793. Simple, comfortable, and new (1987). Pool, snackbar. *Megas Alexandros* (M), tel. 5 1580. 42 rooms. *Zante Beach* (M), tel. 5 1130. 252 rooms in central block and bungalows. Tennis, disco; on beach. AE, DC. *Alkyonis* (I), tel. 5 1167. 19 rooms. Restaurant. V. *Ionis* (I), tel. 5 1141. 50 rooms. Among some 20 (I)s near the beach.

Plános (5/3 north). *Caravel* (2) (E), tel. 2 5261. 80 airconditioned rooms. Beach, pool. DC, V. *Orea Heleni* (I), tel. 2 8788. 22 rooms. Tennis. *Tsilivi* (I), tel. 2 3109. 55 rooms. Beach.

Zákynthos Town. *Bitzaro* (M), tel. 2 3644. 37 rooms. No restaurant. V. *Libro D'Oro* (M), tel. 2 3785. 47 rooms. Near beach. *Lina* (M), tel. 2 8531. 44 rooms. Pool, tennis, disco; 1 km. (½ mile) inland. *Strada Marina* (M), tel. 2 2761/3. 112 rooms. Roofgarden. AE, DC, MC. *Varres* (M), tel. 2 8352. 34 rooms. 2 km. (1 mile) inland. *Xenia* (M), tel. 2 2232. 39 double rooms. *Diana* (I), tel. 2 8547. 48 rooms. *Phoenix* (I), tel. 2 2719. 38 rooms. V.

Holiday Clubs and Villages. The *Club Méditerranée's* two on Corfu (see p. 13), the *Ilios* (E), tel. 2 2281, 240 rooms, at Nissáki, and the bamboo hut village at *Ypsos* (I), tel. 9 3272, sometimes have accommodation. The same applies to the now separate *Valtour Kerkyra* (L), tel. 3 9755, 296 rooms, at Agios Ioánnis.

GETTING AROUND. By Plane. Corfu's international airport is connected with several European cities. There are four flights daily from Athens. Kefaloniá and Zákynthos have daily flights from Athens, and there are charter flights to Zákynthos from some European capitals.

By Bus. There are daily bus services to the mainland ferry terminals opposite the respective islands from Athens, Kifissou 100. For a deluxe Pullman service, enquire at travel agencies. The islands have an extensive road network, with frequent bus services to all points of interest.

By Boat. Daily car ferries from Ancona, Bari, Brindisi, and Otranto to Corfu continue to Igoumenítsa and/or Pátra from April to October, and are less frequent in winter. Car ferries also sail from Brindisi via Corfu, Kefaloniá and Itháki to Pátra. There are also regular connections with Yugoslav ports.

Local ferry boats link Corfu many times a day to Igoumenítsa in Epirus, and there is a small ferry (no trucks) to Sagiada, directly opposite. There are boats to Paxi from Corfu. From Astakós there are ferries for Itháki and Kefaloniá, from Kylíni in the Peloponnese for Kefaloniá and Zákyn-thos, and from Pátra for Kefaloniá, Itháki, and Corfu. There are also nu-merous inter-island services.

SPORTS. Swimming is most enjoyable from the miles of lonely sand dunes that separate Límni Korissíon, Corfu's only lake, 26 km. (16 miles) southwest, from the sea. Corfu's north and west coast beaches are best. There are fine beaches at Platys Gialós on Kefaloniá, between lagoon and sea at Lefkáda, Laganás on Zákynthos.

Tennis can be played at most (E) and (L) hotels.

Golf. Corfu possesses an 18-hole golf course on a 175-acre sporting cen-ter at Livádi Rópa (Ropa's Meadow), 18 km. (11 miles) from town on the way to Ermónes.

Cricket can be played by visitors to Corfu at the Byron Cricket Club on the Esplanade—unique in Greece.

Casino. Baccarat, chemin de fer, roulette all year round in the Achilleon Palace and the Corfu Hilton on Corfu.

USEFUL ADDRESSES. *British Vice-Consulate,* Alexandras 11, Corfu (tel. 3 0055). G.N.T.O. office in the government building, Diikitirion Ker-kyras, Corfu (tel. 3 0298); and at Vallianou 3, Kefaloniá (tel. 2 2847).

CENTRAL GREECE
AND THESSALY

Home of Gods and Romans

Central Greece is officially called Stereá Elláda (mainland Greece), but usually referred to as the Róumeli, because the inhabitants proudly insist on their Roman heritage, if not descent. The Róumeli then is the land of Rome, bounded by Epirus, Thessaly and the Parnassós, rich in natural beauty, made easily accessible by an adequate road network.

Farther north, lies the province of Thessaly, once a vast inland sea, later divided into two fresh-water lakes, which ultimately forced an opening through the Gorge of Témpe. The surrounding mountains, the Píndos, Orthris, Pílio, Óssa and, above all, the great Ólympos range, now tower over a fertile plain.

This desirable land was the goal of a greater number of invaders than usual even in Greece, ever since the Pelasgians started the fashion in about 2000 B.C. In 1200 the Thessalians, a Doric tribe, made their appearance and divided the country into three principalities, which in Classical times formed a military league of particularly quarrelsome members.

In the 3rd century A.D., the invasions were resumed as of old. Goths, Huns, Bulgars, Serbs and Franks pillaged and burnt, sometimes incorporating Thessaly in their short-lived kingdoms. Ruled by the Turks from 1389 to 1881, it returned at last to Greek sovereignty in that year, thanks to Gladstone and Gambetta.

Exploring the Róumeli

The Athens–Thessaloníki highway sweeps from the Boeotian plain back to the coast and continues along the narrow sea, hemmed in by the island of Euboea. One branch right leads to the beach of Theológos, and another, left, inland to Atalánti, near which German archeologists are unearthing an important sanctuary of Artemis. After the small ports of Arkítsa and Ágios Konstantínos, the pleasant spa of Kamména Vóurla and the two huge dishes of the Earth Satellite Tracking Station, the road turns to historic Thermopylae, 29 km. (18 miles) southeast of Lamía. Hot Gates was indeed a fitting name, as the steaming sulphur springs of Thermopyles Spa, which now empty through an alluvial coastal strip into the sea, in antiquity further limited the narrow pass between the water and the towering rocks, where 300 Spartans under Leonidas offered a heroic resistance to the immense army of Xerxes in 480 B.C. Asked to surrender, because the Persian arrows would black out the sun, Leonidas gave his famous reply: "All the better, then we can fight in the shade." But the gallant defenders were overwhelmed when a Persian detachment, led over a mountain path by a local traitor, attacked them in the back. A simple inscription, beneath a modern statue of Leonidas, commemorates their sacrifice: "Stranger, tell the Lacedaemonians that we lie here, obedient to their command."

It is 214 km. (133 miles) on the toll motorway from Athens to Lamía, but this prosperous provincial town, bypassed by most drivers can also be reached by the old road from Livadiá, over the scenic Pournaraki Pass. The Catalan castle, on the antique acropolis hill, has been partly restored to house a minor museum. Karpeníssi is 82 km. (51 miles) from Lamía. Separate branch roads lead to the spas of Ğpati, up-to-date, Platýstomo and Smókovo, without modern accommodation.

The woodland hamlet of Gorgopótamos, 11 km. (seven miles) south of Lamía on a minor road, is worth the small detour. In one of the most celebrated exploits of Greek resistance during World War II, the bridge was blown up by the combined forces of Greek partisans and British parachutists, thus cutting off the Germans' supply route to North Africa. The present bridge was built by the U.S. army in 1948.

Past Ágios Georgios, the main road ascends through fir forests to the Ráhi ridge (1,066 meters, 3,500 ft.) and then descends the southern slopes of Mount Tímfristos, whence an adventurous branch left (south) leads via Domnísta to Náfpaktos. Karpeníssi, a small town in the heart of the Róumeli, is an excellent center for excursions by car and on foot. The site is pleasant under plane trees shading the fast-flowing Aspropotamos, the food less so, at Kefalóvrysi five km. (three miles) south. On the little island is a monument to Marko Botsaris, one of the Souliot leaders in the War of Independence, who died there valiantly fighting a superior Turkish force. The valley narrows at the Mikró Horió (Little Village, 13 km., eight miles), rebuilt after destruction by a gigantic landslide in 1963.

The next very rough 24 km. (15 miles) mostly follow the Aspropotamos through spectacular mountain scenery to the Próussos Monastery in a formidable gorge below Mount Panetolikó. Though possessing a miraculous picture of the Virgin attributed to St. Luke, Proussos is not only visited by pilgrims but also by those who really want to get away from it all.

The 112 km. (70 miles) from Karpeníssi to Agrínio are kept open in winter by snow ploughs (snow chains required). Several forest roads penetrate deep into the mountain fastness to isolated hamlets. A branch leads to the large dam and hydro-electric plant at the narrowest point of the impressive Ahéloos gorge. A diversion of the river's upper course to the Thessalian plain for hydro-electric and irrigation purposes is Greece's most ambitious undertaking of this kind. The last part of the journey is along the northern flanks of Mount Panetolikó to the fertile plain of Agrínio and the highway to Epirus.

Thessalian Battlefields

The inland road from Lamía to Lárissa (112 km., 70 miles) winds over the Fóurka Pass, where the Greek army under Crown Prince Constantine made a last stand against the superior Turkish forces in 1897. The first village in the Thessalian plain below is Fársala, famed for its sticky sweet *chalvas* (nougat).

The Romans were partial to Greece as a battlefield, as Pharsala was shortly followed by the equally decisive battles of Philippi and Actium. In 48 B.C., Pompey led his great army against the smaller forces of Julius Caesar and suffered a crushing defeat. But Pompey also lost his nerve and, abandoning his troops to their fate, fled to Témpe. Never stopping in his flight, he took ship to Egypt, where he was treacherously murdered, leaving Caesar master of Rome and the world.

In spite of these fascinating historical associations, it is pleasanter to enter Thessaly by the toll road which, after bypassing Lamía, more or less follows the coast via Stylída to Mikrothíves, where it turns inland to Lárissa (130 km., 81 miles). To visit Pílio, branch right (east) at Mikrothíves to Néa Anhíalos on the site of Byzantine Thebes and ancient Pyrasos, not so much for the remains of four basilicas and a small museum, but for the drive along the Pagasitic Gulf, with its superb views over the Pílio massif to Vólos. Another way of enjoying the magnificent scenery is by boat from Halkída to Vólos, a ten-hour trip, with stops on both sides of the narrow channel separating the mainland from the steep cliffs of Euboea, opening at last into the majestic sweep of the Pagassitikós. This vast, circular gulf seems entirely landlocked, its entrance masked by the foothills of the Pílio range, whose gentle slopes are covered with vineyards and olive groves almost to the summit.

The Pílio (Pelion) Country

Pagassés (Pagasae), the port of ancient Iolkos, stood on a promontory opposite Vólos. It was from here that Jason set out in the *Argo,* the first sizeable ship ever built by man, to make good a vague claim to the Golden Fleece. With the help of his formidable companions, the carefully chosen Argonauts, including such celebrities as Heracles, Theseus, Orpheus, the sons of the North Wind, and Asklepios as ship's doctor, he brought back not only the Golden Fleece from Colchis, but also the Witch-Princess Medea. She had stopped her father's pursuit by chopping up her brother and throwing the morsels overboard, forcing the fond parent to strike sail to collect the sad remains. Medea continued her happy family life by killing Jason's uncle, the former king of Iolkos, in a spurious rejuvenation operation. Exiled to Corinth, she murdered her two children before her husband's eyes and escaped to Athens in her dragon-car.

Pagasae was conquered by Demetrius Poliorcetes, who finally ended his adventurous career in the town that was renamed Demetrias in his honor.

Except for some sculptures, mostly funerary, in the museum, only a few walls remain of the favorite residence of successive Macedonian kings, who ruled Greece from behind the massive fortifications.

And little more remained of Vólos after the two devastating earthquakes of Easter 1955. It was rebuilt with commendable speed, but stark utility prevailed and has spread over the large industrial zone. Despite the bypass, the port is choked with the ferry traffic to Syria, making the lovely surroundings all the more enticing. A 5000 B.C. settlement has been unearthed, but a greater thrill awaits fans of the Neolithic at Dímini, four km. (two and a half miles) west, where six concentric rings of fortifications surrounded the chieftain's dwelling, while surprisingly artistic pottery sheds a favorable light on life in the 4th millennium B.C. And to top it all, another four km. west, mud-brick houses were built round the chief's larger residence in the Sesklo citadel, Europe's oldest fortified settlement.

In the suburb of Áno Vólos, straggling up the lower slopes of the 1,600-meter (5,252-ft.) high Pílio, a few 18th-century towerhouses still rise picturesquely above the orchards. Once they were considered the only possible habitation in a region rich enough to be pillaged by Turks, pirates and bandits alike. Here was the site of Iolkos, whose throne Jason claimed, after descending from the wise centaur Cheiron's cave near the summit. But Cheiron, the tutor of every self-respecting legendary hero, was an exception. The centaurs, those strange beings, half man and half horse, who haunted the dense forests of Pelion, were notorious for their lasciviousness and drunkenness.

The extraordinary frescos of the painter Theóphilos (1867–1934), one of the really original primitives, are displayed in a museum at Anakássia, harmoniously furnished in the style of the period. More of his work is in the Museum of Variá at Mytilíni.

On a cypress-clad hill overlooking Vólos and the calm waters of the gulf, stands the Episkopí, a charming small Byzantine church. This is the traditional site of the wedding banquet of Peleus, one of the Argonauts, and the sea-nymph Thetis. The Olympians honored the feast with their presence, but Eris, the uninvited goddess of discord, flung a golden apple among them, inscribed "For the fairest." Hera, Athena and Aphrodite all claimed it, and their bitter recriminations must have stood in tragic contrast to the serenely peaceful setting. At last Prince Paris of Troy was chosen as judge, and awarded the apple to Aphrodite, thus incurring the undying hatred of the other two goddesses. The fate of Troy was sealed.

Local Color

The slopes of Mount Pílio are dotted with 24 attractive villages, alive with rushing mountain streams among beech, chestnut, apple, and walnut groves. Gardens of roses, hydrangeas, and hollyhocks, reminiscent of English country gardens, envelop old stone houses with gray and green slate roofs and paved courtyards. Portariá, high above Vólos, is a popular summer resort, whose excellent *kokkinéli* (red wine) has to be consumed on the spot, as it does not stand up well to transport.

Separated by a deep ravine is Makrinítsa, less sophisticated, but richer in *couleur locale.* and now, because of its obvious attractions, being developed as a tourist center with the usual scattering of souvenir shops. The two frescoed 17th-century churches of an abandoned monastery contain the portraits of the most unheard-of saints. Several 18th-century mansions have been converted into hotels as parts of the Greek National Tourist Organization (G.N.T.O.) *Traditional Settlements* program. The village square would not be amiss in fairyland; a large, paved terrace, overhanging the town and gulf below, keeps its intimacy by a backdrop of huge plane trees, which shade a small Byzantine church and an exquisite fountain. On the numerous feast days there is dancing till late at night, and in their natural surroundings the national dances have none of the stiff artificiality they assume in town. Local custom prescribes that as a zebekiko dancer executes the intricate steps, he rewards his friend squatting at the edge of the dance floor with an occasional high kick over his head.

The Pílio is crossed steeply via Portaría and Hánia below the summit. Hánia has recently been developed as the first Pílio ski resort, with ski lifts and a refuge. Zagorá, the largest village, still retains an air of quiet 18th-century dignity, enhanced by the luxuriant vegetation, and the Church of the Savior, built in 1100, is well worth a visit. The gentler crossing from the eastern shores of the Pagassitikós Gulf passes Agria, then continues through the lush orchards on the Lehónia promontory and dense olive groves to Kalá Nerá. There, the road turns inland to Miliés (where there is a very interesting museum of local arts and crafts and a delightful old railway station) and to Vyzítsa (another traditional settlement with mansions converted into guest houses.) The road then goes over the low ridge of the Pílio to Tsangaráda, in the middle of a chestnut forest. Tsangaráda is an enchanting village and its old mansions, layered on the hillside, are interspersed with cobbled alleys and flag-stoned squares while surrounding a 1,000—year—old plane tree in the main square. From Móuresi, a steep branch road descends to the idyllic beach of Ágios Ioánnis, the Pílio's major resort, with 16 hotels but still retaining its charm, facing the open sea. The Pílio roundtrip is continued to Zagorá and Horeftó on the sea.

It is 59 km. (37 miles) from Vólos to Lárissa, mainly on the Lamía toll road parallel to the Kinoskefalé hills (dogs' heads), which divide the plain. Velestíno, in the midst of modern market gardens, is the ancient Pherae, where Apollo served King Admetus for a year to atone for his murderous attempt on the Cyclopes. Not only did he help his master to win the hand of Alcestis by yoking a lion and a boar to a chariot, but Apollo even prevailed on the Fates to let Alcestis die in place of her husband. This noble sacrifice was eagerly accepted by the far-from-gallant Admetus, but not by the gods, who sent Heracles to wrestle with Death. Victorious in this supreme contest, the hero returned triumphantly with the faithful wife.

By returning to the road junction at Mikrothíves and then turning west, battlefield addicts may still visit Fársala on the way to Kardítsa, a prosperous market town, the abode of numerous storks. Before rushing off on the treeshaded straight 26 km. (16 miles) to Trikala do not miss the excursion to the artificial Plastíras Lake (25 km., 15 miles), past the hydroelectric plant a few miles west, to which huge water pipes descend from the mountain ridge. The Monastery of Korona (21 km., 13 miles), burnt by the Germans in 1943, has been rebuilt with a comfortable guesthouse overlooking the vast Thessalian plain to Mount Ólympos. A little higher, but still in sight of that plain, you witness its sudden dramatic transformation into an idyllic alpine valley. Fields and fir forests slope gently to the shores of the blue lake, while the jagged summits of the Píndos range, snow-clad most of the year, tower in the background. The road round the lake passes the dam at the southern end.

In Trikala, on the banks of the Lítheos River, the Lethe of the ancients, the search is on for a presumed temple of Asklepìos following the excavation of an Hellenistic stoa and some Roman baths. A clocktower on a wooded eminence rises above the insignificant ruins of Justinian's fortress, later the palace of the 14th-century Serbian emperors. There is also a pretty but neglected mosque, shortly to be developed as a museum, on the Kardítsa road built by Sinan Pasha in 1550.

The Metéora

The next 21 km. (13 miles) approach the mighty Píndos range on the left (west), while on the right strange rock formations rise ever higher from the plain. Below a dramatic sheer cliff nestles Kalambáka, whose 14th-century Metropolis is decorated with frescos, providing a suitable introduction to one of the wonders of the later Middle Ages.

A circular road winds six km. (four miles) through an unearthly forest of gigantic pillars rising to 555 meters (1,820 ft.) above sea level. These rock-needles were believed to be meteors hurled by an angry god, though in fact they owe their fantastic shapes to river erosion.

These inaccessible pinnacles offered a safe refuge to pious hermits in the turbulent 14th century, when the Serbian emperors of Trikala were competing with Byzantium for the fertile valley, retreating before the incursions of soldiers and brigands to their impregnable rocks. Within a few years the monk Athanasius founded the Monastery of the Transfiguration on the Great Meteoron and imposed the austere rules of the Holy Mountain, rigorously excluding women. Other hermitages followed the example and expanded into monasteries, but the Meteoron retained a dominant position, counting among Athanasius' disciples members of the rival imperial houses of Constantinople and Serbia. A scion of the latter, the Hermit-King Joasaph, richly endowed the monastery; but it was the advent of John Cantacuzene, expelled by his joint emperor from the Byzantine throne, that gave the Meteoron imperial prestige. The abbots refused to recognize the overriding authority of the Superior of the Ascetics any longer, but instead sought to secure their own domination. The ensuing bitter struggle was sharpened by the contest for arable soil, and the violation of all the founder's precepts led inevitably to a rapid decline. Only six of the 24 imposing monasteries that once rose proudly on the black rocks remain today while snow and wind have swept away all vestiges of the others from the towering summits they crowned.

The expropriation of Church land for the settlement of refugees in the 1920s sealed the fate of the already decaying monasteries, which have become too poor to serve the traditional liqueur or coffee to the crowds of visitors. Loss of refreshment, however, is more than compensated for by less perilous access, through awesome, but perfectly safe, staircases. The monasteries may be visited daily. Although opening hours may vary from place to place, they are generally open in the mornings until 1 P.M., closed for siesta and re-open for a couple of hours in the afternoons. It is wise to check the closing times before setting off up the hundreds of steps. Leave sufficient time to climb them, or you may find the monastery door closed at the top once you get there.

Nearer to Heaven

The days of jointed ladders, pulled up in an emergency, are no more, and the nets are now strictly limited to hauling up supplies. Once, upon a time, the traveler was pulled up squeezed into an outsize stringbag, suspended from a rope, which, the story goes, wasn't changed until it broke.

The architecture of the monasteries is conditioned by the restricted space available, with buildings rising from different levels. Some are whitewashed, while others display the pretty Byzantine pattern of stone and brick, the multiple domes of the many churches dominating the wooden galleries and balconies, that hang precariously over frightening abysses.

Ágios Stéphanos is connected to the main cliff by a drawbridge. This ancient hermitage was transformed into a monastery by the munificence of the Emperor Andronicus III Palaeologus and still preserves some of its former treasures. There are fine wood carvings in the main church, a few old icons, but the votive offerings have been pillaged or sold, and the priceless manuscripts eaten by worms. From the windows one enjoys a sublime view over the vast plain to the sea, just discerned on the horizon. North and west rise the formidable barriers of Ólympos and Píndos, still snow-covered when the almond and peach trees below are in bloom, shading the green corn and the flaming red poppy fields. But the last monk has departed, and 20 nuns are kept busy preventing 30 orphans from falling into the awesome abyss.

A nunnery in the retreat of the Ascetics—what would Athanasius have said to that? Though even the severe Master might have considered the venerable age of the surviving handful of monks a certain guarantee for their impeccable behavior, with intervening precipices dampening any remaining sinful ardor. The small fortress-like Agía Roussáni was the first to be converted to a convent, while recently restored Ágios Nikólaos, on the lowest rock, is still untenanted. Agía Roussáni is worth the climb up the steep hillside, if only to see the tiny church dedicated to the Transfiguration and its particularly gruesome murals depicting the suffering of the Martyrs, still bright and vivid after 400 years.

Agía Triáda, on a particularly forbidding pinnacle, is reached by a flight of steps cut into the rock face. The reward for the steep climb lies more in the position of the monastery, perched perilously atop, than in any artistic merit of the Church of the Holy Trinity.

But it is different at fortress-like Ágios Várlaam, founded as late as the 16th century. The frescos in the Chapel of All Saints have been skillfully restored and retain some of their original freshness, and some manuscripts remain in the library.

The Great Meteóron is only a stone's throw away, yet only reached after a breathtaking climb. The path faces the tallest rock-needle, bearing the ruins of the deserted Monastery of the Manuscripts, which was renowned for its illuminated missals. Looking at the perpendicular rock, one easily credits the story about the original ascent being achieved by way of a rope fastened to an eagle's leg, whose nest lay on top of the peak. Just below are the traces of a large painting representing the Virgin and Child. Yet even the perils of painting in such an unpropitious place pale before the awe-inspiring prison cells, shallow caves situated at a dizzy height, where the trespassers against the monastic discipline had to crouch on a narrow ledge, exposed to the rigors of the climate for long periods.

At the top of galleries hollowed out of the rock, the massive gate of the Great Metéoron opens on a large, irregular courtyard. The cloister, the refectory, the churches and chapels are a moving monument to an extinct way of life, whose infinite pain and labor required a religious fervor incomprehensible to later generations.

The lovely Church of the Transfiguration has, until recently, borne the signs of continued neglect and the frescoes had been allowed to suffer by time and dampness. Now however, the frescoes have been almost completely restored to what must surely be a close approximation of their original, colorful, medieval splendor. They are now quite breathtaking and alone worth the exhausting climb up the hundreds of steps. Other restored treasures include a bishop's inlaid ivory throne.

The Ólympos Country

The road westwards crosses the Píndos range at the Katára Pass, in the magnificent alpine approach to Epirus, while the branch right (north) after ten km. (six miles) provides via Grevená the shortest approach to western Macedonia. Following the Pinios downstream, it is 82 km. (51 miles) from Kalambáka to Lárissa, in the heart of the fertile plain. This position assured Lárissa of a predominant place in Thessalian history. Reputedly founded by Acrisius, the luckless grandfather of Perseus, it fell later to the progeny of Heracles, at whose brilliant court Pindar and Hippocrates shone. Christianity was appropriately introduced by St. Achilles, the namesake of the great Homeric hero, who ruled somewhere in the vicinity. Under the Turks Lárissa gained new importance, the remains of the past providing building material for the extensive fortifications. Yet in 1985 an antique theater was unearthed opposite the Nymphs' Wood, beyond the Pinios bridge, a park with open-air restaurants and cafes.

Tírnavos is 16 km. (ten miles) along the inland road to Macedonia. Only in this large village has the old fertility symbol survived and been sanctioned by Orthodoxy. On Shrove Monday *ouzo* is served in outsize phallic vessels painted in gaudy colors.

The whole countryside rising slowly towards the Ólympos is a living museum of folklore. The conservative mountaineers have retained their traditions and customs intact over the centuries. The Church adopted most, with slight modifications, and the funeral rites and dirges, the beating of the ground with the forehead, the rhythmic calling of the departed.

The upper reaches of the Ólympos range were the favorite hideout of the *kléphtes,* terror of the Turks. These young Greeks, finding life under foreign rule intolerable, fled into the mountain fastnesses of the country, raiding Turkish posts and caravans. They were the nucleus of the 1821 revolutionary forces.

Elassóna, 40 km. (25 miles) from Lárissa, lies in the foothills of Ólympos, the highest in mountainous Greece. A paved road crosses the lower range from eight km. (five miles) north of Elassóna to Kateríni (61 km., 38 miles), reaching the highest point at the forlorn village of Ágios Dimítrios. On no account attempt the crossing by turning right at Kallithéa, the first road fork, to Olimbiáda and Kariá, surrounded by chestnut and fir forests, to join the toll road 61 km. (38 miles) north of Lárissa. Better is the branch to the Alpine Club Refuge B (1,980 meters, 6,500 ft.), within a three-hour easy climb to Skólio, an exciting ski-ascent in winter and the second highest of the peaks standing in a semi-circle round the wild, desolate Mavrólongos Valley. The highest summit, Mýtikas (Pántheon), 2,918 meters. 9,574 ft., was only scaled in 1913. In antiquity no mere mortal dared to climb the abode of the gods. The rebellious Titans were duly punished for their sacrilegious attempt to reach the Throne of Zeus, the third of the great peaks.

The toll-highway to Thessaloníki shortens the distance from Lárissa by 90 km. (56 miles) to 154 km. (96 miles), besides being scenically more interesting than the old inland route via Kozáni. The highway follows the railway to Gortyne, once ruled by Ixion, a kind of Greek Cain.

Vale of Témpe

The vale of Témpe, nine and a half km. (six miles) long, is entered at Bába, whose name and mosque recall the Turkish occupation. This gateway to ancient Greece has been fortified since time immemorial, yet the elaborate fortifications were turned by successive invaders, by Xerxes in 480 B.C., Alexander the Great, and most spectacularly by the Roman general Q. Marcius Philippus in 169 B.C. Hauling his war elephants over the mountains, he outflanked the strong fortress of Gamos, and the last Macedonian king, Perseus, withdrew in panic to final defeat.

Only once was successful resistance offered in this seemingly impregnable defensive position. The Emperor Alexius annihilated the Norman army during the first Crusade, thus postponing for over 100 years the dismemberment of Greece into feudal principalities. This was left to the shameful Fourth Crusade, when the Franks poured through the abandoned valley.

The varied history is fittingly illustrated by the ruins of fortresses belonging to all ages, culminating in the romantic medieval Castle of the Beauty, Kástro tís Oréas, on top of a precipitous rock. The orderly Romans even left an inscription, now barely legible, recording the fortification of Témpe by Caesar's legate Cassius.

For 3,000 years poets have extolled the beauties of Témpe, which provided the idyllic background to a host of myths centering on Apollo, from the time he was still in his mother's womb. Yet there is many a gorge in Greece, the Vouraïkós and Langada in the Peloponnese, Vikos and Aoos in Epirus, which surpasses Témpe in scenic grandeur. The beauty of the peaceful vale lies mainly in the delightfully refreshing contrast with the burning plain of Thessaly. A profusion of trees on both banks of the icy-cold Pinios provides welcome shade.

Through the trees arching over the river at the Fountain of the Nymphs one catches a glimpse of the sea, bounded by the Halkidikí peninsula. Here the mountain walls of the lower Ólympos and Óssa are most formidable, bearing witness to the tremendous convulsion, when the waters of the inland sea forced an outlet, an event that gave rise to the legend of Deucalion's flood.

The narrow valley opens out and the highway turns north, along the coast to Thessaloníki. The road to the right (southeast) leads to the pretty little port of Stómio, where the lovely long beach has become an international camping ground, and for good reasons: it ideally combines the attractions of sea and mountain, by being the natural center for excursions up the thickly wooded slopes of Óssa.

The return to Lárissa can be made by following the coast south to Agiókambos and then turning inland via Skíti and Agiá; a branch right (northeast) rises to Anatolí, from which the ascent of the 1,978-meter (6,490-ft.) Óssa is best undertaken. The easy climb is rewarded by the superb view over the sea to the distant shores of Asia Minor.

PRACTICAL INFORMATION FOR
CENTRAL GREECE AND THESSALY

WHEN TO COME. The Ólympos and Pílio regions are pleasantly cool even in summer, but the Thessalian plain bakes in the vast oven formed by the surrounding high mountains. June is harvest time, and the stubble fields are here no more attractive than anywhere else. Néa Anhíalos is sufficiently close to the sea to allow for a wine festival in mid-August. Maximum enjoyment will be obtained in spring, especially at the famed Meteóra monasteries, when the mountains are still snowcovered and blend harmoniously with the green fields, the red poppies and the white and pink fruit trees. The winter is cold, with snow and rain; February is the worst month.

TOURIST OFFICES. There are G.N.T.O. offices at: **Lárissa,** Koumoundourou 18 (tel. 25 0919); **Vólos,** Platía Riga Fereou (tel. 3 6233).

SPECIAL EVENTS. May. The *Karaískakia* folkloric celebrations include dancing, parades and pageantry. **August.** The *Balkan Crafts Fair* takes place in the Municipal Theatre, Vólos, with dancing and music from the Balkans.

HOTELS AND RESTAURANTS

Agiókambos. *Golden Beach* (I), tel. 5 1222/3. 25 rooms. Restaurant.

Ágios Konstantínos. *Motel Levendi* (M), tel. 3 1806. 28 double rooms. Beach. *Astir* (I), tel. 3 1625. 31 rooms. 45 meters (50 yards) from beach.

Arkítsa. *Kalypso Club* (M), tel. 9 1390/2. 250 bungalows. Pool, tennis, minigolf, disco. MC. *Helena* (I), tel. 9 1343. 34 rooms.

Atalánti. *Anessis* (I), tel. 22147. 15 rooms.

Drossiá. (Agios Minas.) (Opposite Halkis). *Pelagos* (E), tel. 9 8595. 95 rooms; on cliff top; pool, disco, tennis. *Saint Minas Beach* (M), tel. 9 8411/3. 80 rooms. Beach, pool, tennis, disco. *Drossia Beach* (I), tel. 9 8248. 28 rooms.

Glýfa. *Akroyali* (I), tel. 6 1204. 19 rooms. *Glýfa* (I), tel. 6 1247/9. 27 rooms.

Kalambáka. *Motel Divani* (E), tel. 2 3330. 165 rooms. Airconditioned, pool. AE, DC, MC, V. *Edelweiss* (M), tel. 2 3966. 50 rooms. Recently opened

(1989), this hotel is bright, clean, and comfortable. In the center of town, it offers an excellent view of the rocks. Pool. *Xenia* (M), tel. 2 2327. 22 double rooms. Airconditioned. *Atlantis* (I), tel. 2 2476. 28 rooms. *Galaxias* (I), tel. 2 3233. 24 rooms. *Rex* (I), tel. 2 2372. 32 rooms.

Kamména Vóurla. Large number of hotels along the seashore of this popular spa. *Galini* (E), tel. 2 2248/9. 131 rooms. Pool, tennis, disco, thermal installations. DC, MC. *Possidon* (M), tel. 2 2721/5. 93 rooms. Pool, tennis, minigolf, restaurant; directly on beach. AE, DC, MC, V. *Sissy* (M), tel. 2 2190/1. 102 rooms. Pool, tennis, minigolf, disco, restaurant; directly on beach. AE, DC. *Delfini* (I), tel. 2 2321. 22 rooms. The only one among some 40 (I)s with showers to all rooms, restaurant, and beach across the road. AE. *Radion* (I), tel. 2 2308. 62 rooms, most with bath. Thermal installations. DC, MC.

Karavómylos. *Stylis Beach* (I), tel. 4 1201/5. 154 rooms. Airconditioned; pool, tennis, disco; good value.

Kardítsa. *Astron* (I), tel. 2 3551/2. Most of the 47 rooms with showers.

Karpeníssi. *Anessis* (I), tel. 2 2840. 36 rooms. V. *Lecadin* (I), tel. 2 2131/5. 104 rooms. Above the town, commanding a fine view. Restaurant. *Mont Blanc* (I), tel. 2 2322. 37 rooms. Restaurant.

Lamía. All central. *Delta* (I), tel. 2 1600. 39 rooms. The only one with restaurant. *Elena* (I), tel. 2 5025. 51 rooms. DC. *Samaras* (I), tel. 2 8971. 64 rooms. Airconditioned.

Lárissa. *Divani Palace* (E), 25 2791/5. 77 rooms. AE, DC, MC, V. *Astoria* (M), tel. 25 2941/4. 84 rooms. Airconditioned; pool. V. *Metropole* (M), tel. 22 9911/5. 95 rooms. Airconditioned; roofgarden, pool. AE, DC, MC, V. *Ambassadeur* (I), tel. 25 0028. 89 rooms. Airconditioned; restaurant. V. *Motel Xenia* (I), tel. 23 8183. 30 double rooms. Airconditioned; restaurant. 3 km. (2 miles) out on motorway. AE, DC, MC.

Néa Anhíalos. *Protessilaos* (I), tel. 7 6310. 37 rooms.

Pílio Region. Distances in km./miles from Vólos are shown in brackets after the name of the town or resort.
Áfyssos (26/16). *Alexandros* (I), tel. 3 3246. 9 double rooms. *Katia* (I), tel. 3 3297. 22 double rooms.
Ágios Ioánnis (61/38). All on beach. *Aloe* (M), tel. 3 1241. 44 rooms. *Maro* (M), tel. 3 1477. 47 rooms. *Kentrikon* (I), tel. 3 1232. 20 rooms. Restaurant. V. *Zephyros* (I), tel. 3 1335. 12 double rooms. Both with restaurants.
Agriá (6/4). *Barbara* (I), tel. 9 2367. 9 rooms. *Foula Beach* (I), tel. 9 2336. 28 furnished apartments. Restaurant.
Hánia. *Manthos* (I), tel. 9 9541. 35 rooms.
Horeftó (47/29). *Dimitrios* (M), 2 2444. 38 furnished apartments. *Katerina* (I), tel. 2 2772. 26 double rooms.
Hórto. *Spalathra* (I), tel. 6 5326. 21 rooms; restaurant.
Kalá Nerá (13/8). *Alcyon* (I), tel. 2 2364. 11 double rooms. *Izela* (I), tel. 2 2379. 31 double rooms. *Roumeli* (I), tel. 2 2217. 27 rooms, most with showers. Has the only restaurant.

Makrynítsa (16/10). All are converted traditional mansions, run by the G.N.T.O. *Archontikon Mousli* (M), tel. 9 9228. 8 rooms. *Archontikon Sissilianon* (M), tel. 9 9556. 7 double rooms. *Archontikon Xiradakis* (M), tel. 9 9250. 7 double rooms. All are delightful, although the Archontikon Xiradakis is unsuitable for elderly or disabled visitors since it is at the bottom of a steep path. Excellent breakfasts and wonderful views down to Volos, the sea, and distant Euboea are available at each.

Restaurants. At the two Inexpensive restaurants on the village square, the splendid setting has to compensate for the very inadequate food, but the local red wine is drinkable.

Miliés. Traditional settlement. Two converted houses; *Despina* (I), tel. 8 6361. 4 rooms. *Zaira* (I), no telephone. 3 rooms.

Restaurant. *O Palios Stathmos* (I), below the village, at the old railway station among the trees. Excellent traditional fare is served here.

Portariá (13/8). *Xenia* (M), tel. 9 9158/9. 76 double rooms. MC. Openair dining terrace, disco. *Alkistis* (I), tel. 9 9178. 47 rooms. *Pelias* (I), tel. 9 9175. 28 rooms.

Tríkeri (Island). *Palio Trikeri* (I), tel. 9 1451. 21 double rooms. V.

Tsangaráda (50/31). *San Stefano* (I), tel. 4 9213. 37 rooms; restaurant; in chestnut forest 6 km. (4 miles) above a lovely beach. *Xenia* (I), tel. 4 9205. 46 rooms, not all with bath. Restaurant. AE, DC, MC.

Vyzítsa. (I), tel. 8 6373. These are eight old houses in a traditional settlement converted by G.N.T.O. Other restored houses are privately owned: *Archonitkon Kontou* (M), tel. 8 6793. 10 rooms. Dating from 1792, with modern facilities. *Archontikon Katsanaki* (M), tel. 8 6250. 5 rooms. *Archontikon Vergou* (I), tel. 8 6293. 7 rooms.

Stómio. *Vlassis* (I), tel. 9 1301. 50 furnished apartments. Near beach.

Theológos. *Economo's Silver Bay* (M), tel. 9 3291/5. 196 rooms in central block and bungalows. Airconditioned; pool, tennis, minigolf, disco. *Nafsika* (I), tel. 9 3204. 8 double rooms. Restaurant. Near beach.

Thermopýles. A hydrotherapy center including Moderate hotels is under construction at these hot sulphur springs, mentioned by Herodotus, for the treatment of rheumatism. *Aegli* (I), tel. 93304. 45 rooms, none with shower. Restaurant.

Trikala. *Achillion* (M), tel. 2 8291. 73 rooms, most with bath. AE, MC, V. *Divani* (M), tel. 2 7286. 66 rooms. AE, MC, V. *Dina* (I), tel. 2 7267. 57 rooms. *Lithaeon* (I), tel. 2 0690. 54 rooms.

Vólos. *Alexandros* (M), tel. 3 1221/4. 78 rooms. AE, DC, MC, V. *Electra* (M), tel. 3 2671/3. 38 rooms. Both are on Topali St., near the sea and yacht marina. AE, V. *Park* (M), tel. 3 6511/5. 119 rooms. Airconditioned. Half board only. AE, DC, MC. *Admitos* (I), tel. 2 1117/9. 31 rooms. *Galaxy* (I), tel. 2 0750/2. 54 rooms. *Sandi* (I), tel. 3 3341/3. 39 rooms. Also located on Topali.

At **Alykés Beach** (6 km., 4 miles, south). *Filoxenia* (I), tel. 9 8336. 17 double rooms.

Ypáti. *Xenia* (M), tel. 5 9509. 81 rooms. *Alfa* (I), tel. 5 9507. 27 rooms. *Astron* (I), tel. 5 9595. 27 rooms.

CAMPING. *Kamména Vóurla,* tel. 22 053. The best equipped among some 10 organized campsites; run by G.N.T.O.; accommodates 1,500.

MOUNTAIN REFUGES AND SKI CENTER. The *Greek Mountaineering Federation* organizes refuges on Íti (at Trapeza, alt. 1,800 m., 5,900 ft.), Grammeni Oxia (at Karvounolaka, alt. 1,700 m., 5,575 ft.), and Vardoússia (at Pitimaliko, alt. 1,750 m., 5,740 ft.). Contact Lamía, tel. 2 6786, for information. Also on Tímfristos (at Diavolopotos, alt. 1,840 m., 6,035 ft.) and Karpeníssi, tel. 2 4483.

At Hánia (1,200 m., 3,936 ft.) there is a winter sports center, with refuge, ski lifts, a slope for experienced skiers, and a separate area for beginners. Contact Hánia, tel. 9 9136. The ski center at Veloúhi has three ski refuges and a ski school; contact Karpeníssi, tel. 2 3506.

GETTING AROUND. By Car. The tollroad keeps closer to the coast, thus avoiding the mountains of the old interior road via Fársala. After bypassing Lamía and Almyros, the motorway turns at Mikrothives inland to Lárissa, hub of the road network. The branch to the right (east) skirts the Pagasitic Gulf to Vólos, then continues southeast to Tríkeri at the Gulf's entrance, with a branch to Platánia, opposite Skíathos. The circular road of the Pílio 109 km. (68 miles) leaves the coast 27 km. (17 miles) southeast of Vólos, turning north to Tsangaráda, returning via Zagorá over the summit at Haniá and down through Portariá. There are two lateral connections with the west coast: Lamía-Karpeníssi–Agrínio (195 km., 121 miles) and Lárissa–Kalambáka–Ioánina (206 km., 128 miles), both very mountainous but well-graded. The quickest approach to Metéora (Kalambáka) from Athens is along the inland road north from Lamía, turning left (northwest) 18 km. (11 miles) after the Domokós Pass on a treeshaded branch to Kardítsa and Trikala (61 km., 38 miles). The quickest way to western Macedonia is from the road junction five km. (three miles) northwest of Kalambáka via Grevená to Kastoriá (153 km., 95 miles). Of the two roads crossing the Ólympos range north of Elassóna, the southerly via Kariá has deteriorated into impassability, the northerly via Ágios Dimítrios to Kateríni is entirely paved.

By Plane. There are several flights weekly from Athens to Lárissa.

By Train. The railway traverses the province from south to north: Lamía, Lárissa, Témpe; with a branch from Lárissa to Vólos, the ferry port for Cyprus and Syria. 29 km. (18 miles) of the narrow gauge railway from Vólos to Miliés on the Pílio's south slope are to be reopened as a tourist attraction, using the wooden wagons of 1901.

By Boat. There are car ferries from Arkítsa, on the Athens–Lamía road, to Edipsós, and from Glýfa, a little way off the tollroad 55 km. (35 miles) east of Lamía, to Agiókambos, both on Euboea. Car ferry services are regular from Ágios Konstantínos and Vólos to the Sporades, and hydrofoils operate in summer.

MACEDONIA AND THRACE

The Drama of Contrast

Macedonia and Thrace, cut off by the vast mountain ranges of the Ólympos and Píndos, give the illusion of having more in common with the adjoining Balkans than with peninsular Greece. Only a part of what once was known by the name of these two provinces has been included in the modern Greek nation. The region has always been particularly desirable to its northern neighbors, as it is geographically the culmination of the fertile river valleys of Serbia and Bulgaria, and this has ensured an unsettled history. This is best documented in Thessaloníki, where stratum upon fascinating stratum from every era of the city's turbulent past can easily be traced.

The vegetation differs from the rest of the country, and the climate, too, is continental, with bitterly cold winters spiced by the local demon, *vardari*, the icy north wind. The Axiós River, flowing into the Thermaïkós Gulf west of Thessaloníki, divides Macedonia into two distinct regions— the western forest-clad mountains and the fertile eastern plains stretching inland from the sea, near which trees and buildings are mirrored in glassy lagoons. In both regions are large lakes and rivers that actually flow all the year round. Thrace, separated by the Nestos River and the Rodópi Mountains, is an extension of the eastern plains, with vast fields of maize, cotton and, above all, tobacco. The excellent beaches of the mountainous three-pronged peninsula of Halkidikí are attracting a rapidly increasing number of tourists.

The landscape of this northern region is varied and beautiful enough to warrant a prolonged visit, all the more as there is also a wealth of Hellenistic and Byzantine remains.

Historic Background

Though invasions from the north started in the 4th millennium B.C., it was only in the Mycenaean period that contacts were established with the rest of Greece, where the Macedonians and Thracians, to their chagrin, continued to be considered foreigners and barbarians, even after the glorious exploits of the Great Alexander.

In the 8th century B.C. Greek colonization began on a large scale, resulting in constant strife with the Macedonian kings, whose endeavor at unification finally succeeded in the 5th century with the foundation of a popular infantry based on free yeomanry as a check on the cavalry of the feudal nobles. During the Persian wars the north bore the brunt of the Asiatic invasions. The revenge came in the 4th century B.C., after Greece had been subjected first by Philip II of Macedon, then by his son Alexander the Great, who brilliantly carried out his father's plans and conquered the Persian empire with his invincible Macedonian phalanx.

After Alexander's death in 323 B.C. there followed 50 hectic years of undignified scramble for the succession, ephemeral empires and kingdoms fighting over the Macedonian homeland till Antigonos Gonatas firmly established his dynasty in 276 B.C. Antigonid Macedonia served as a useful shield against the outer barbarians, but after the final defeat in 168 B.C. of Perseus, the last king, Macedonia became a Roman and later a Byzantine province. Centuries of vicissitudes followed, invasions by Germanic tribes, Huns, Avars, Bulgarians, Petchenegs, Arabs, Crusaders, Serbs and finally Turks, who remained in possession until the Balkan War of 1912.

Liberation proved only a temporary solution, as Greeks, Serbs and Romanians now quarreled with their former ally Bulgaria over the spoils. The resulting Second Balkan War was no more successful in appeasing conflicting aspirations than World War I. The same regions were fought over in World War II and the Bulgarian occupation distinguished itself by exceptional cruelty, retarding all progress. But the efforts of recent years in such diverse fields as land reclamation, irrigation, hydro-electric plants and the industrial zone as well as the International Trade Fair have transformed the region.

Exploring Macedonia

The Lárissa–Thessaloníki toll road (151 km., 94 miles) runs parallel to the railway on entering Macedonia across the Piniós bridge at the northeastern end of the Vale of Témpe. It is a lovely drive along the shore of the Thermaïkós Gulf to Platamónas (12 km., eight miles) sprawling down the foothills of Ólympos to the sea, below the romantic ruins of a 14th-century Catalan castle.

Along the coast is a string of minor beach resorts Paralía Panteleïmona, Paralía Skotinás, Leptokaryá and Pláka. Then a branch left (west) leads five km. (three miles) to Litóhoro, whence a forest road continues for 17 km. (11 miles) to the parking place at Prionía in the National Park. An easy ascent leads in two and a half hours to the Alpine Refuge A and about the same time is required to make the much steeper, final climb to the highest peak, Mýtikas (2,918 meters, 9,574 ft.).

Fittingly, a much wider avenue branches likewise five km. (three miles) to Díon, Macedonia's main sanctuary ever since an earth goddess had been worshipped there in prehistoric times for the fertility assured by numerous springs. When the Olympians took over, she was superseded by Demeter, inevitable at the foot of the new gods' own home. The second patroness' two small archaic temples, c. 500 B.C., were replaced by a more splendid Hellenistic edifice, though in the meantime she had lost out to male superiority, albeit only temporarily. Her brother Zeus held sway in Classical times; his temple as well as a stadium and theater were built at the end of the 5th century B.C. by King Archelaos, who enlivened the religious ceremonies with athletic and theatrical competitions. Dionysos was, naturally, honored near the larger of the two theaters.

Díon was also a big military camp, where Philip II celebrated his victories, and where Alexander sacrificed before setting out to conquer Persia. From then on, inscriptions registering affairs of state and treaties were set up at the sanctuary for the information of pilgrims at the festivals. The eternal female reappeared in a new guise, Aphrodite Hypolympidia (Below Ólympos), whose cult statue still stands in a graceful small temple. Even greater care was lavished on Artemis, whom the Ptolemies Egyptianized as Isis in a successful politico-religious propaganda campaign. The rise in the water level after an earthquake submerged that Hellenistic shrine outside the southeast corner of the city wall in mud, which prevented pillage, made excavations difficult, but preserved one portrait statue and two cult statues among the Ionic columns.

Homeric graves, the sanctuaries, the stadium, the Greek theater and the Roman odeum, intended for the pilgrims rather than for the local residents, covered a large area outside the well-planned, strongly fortified town. The eastern ramparts, with square towers and a marble gate, can be followed over a considerable distance. Fourteen paved roads on the grid system have so far been uncovered, dividing the residential quarters, in which the huge complex of the Roman baths was prominent. In the north wing stood a unique group of statues, representing Asklepios' children. Excavation in 1987 revealed a very fine, huge 2nd-century A.D. floor mosaic of Dionysos, and four headless statues of seated philosophers. Still more mosaics are being uncovered and painstakingly reassembled; they look very much as they must originally have done. The Romans built in A.D. 375 a Christian basilica, some of whose floor mosaics are preserved. A final devastating earthquake finished all worship towards the end of antiquity.

Excavations started in earnest only in the 1970s and are continuing. The statues *in situ* are copies; the originals are in the museum, together with votive offerings and a good collection of Macedonian coins found in the mound that covered the theater, which now shares with the castle of Platamónas the performances of the Ólympos Festival in July and August. But Dion's main attraction lies in its splendid site at the foot of the Ólympos range, convincingly chosen as the abode of the gods. It is also possible here, unlike many of Greece's other sites, to find yourself alone among the ruined streets on a spring or autumn afternoon.

Kateríni is bypassed at no great loss, unless one is crossing the Ólympos to Elassóna by the only practicable road. The remaining 68 km. (42 miles) of the toll road keep close to the coast, past Korinós to Pydna, where the Macedonian kingdom finally succumbed to the Roman Consul Aemilius Paulus in 168 B.C.; tombs from that period have lately been discovered nearby. There is more beach development at Makrygialós and Methóni, the Athenian colony whose conquest gave Philip II his first port. The coast then becomes too marshy for tourism as the road crosses successively the Aliákmon—the only river left with its traditional name by officialdom, though it appears by its new name of Aliákmonas on maps—Loudiás, Axiós and Galikós near their mouths before entering Thessaloníki. Between the last two rivers a motorway branches north to Evzóni (62 km., 38 miles), the border station to Yugoslavia.

Vergína

Twelve km. (seven miles) before that branch, one of the few parts of the reconstituted Via Egnatia (see p. 351) worthy of that proud name more or less follows the north bank of the Aliákmon to Véria for a complete round trip of western Macedonia. But before entering the town, Greece's longest river course is better recrossed for a visit to one of the greatest archeological discoveries of recent times. To obtain a comprehensive picture, it might be as well to begin at the first Macedonian palace discovered in Europe—that of 3rd-century King Antigonus Gonatus (He of the Big Knee). In 1855, Leon Heuzey, a young French archeologist, was shown the ruins of an imposing but forgotten large building, remarkable not only for its size, but for its architecture and workmanship, on a terrace in the northern slope of the Pierian Mountains, southeast of Vergína. Having interested Emperor Napoleon III, Heuzey returned with an expedition and explored a subterranean vaulted chamber. The unusual features of style were acknowledged—the marble doors, the first of their kind, were taken to Paris—but the full significance of the discovery was not recognized. It was not until 1938 that a second Macedonian tomb on the northwest terrace was found: although pillaged, a marble throne indicated that this was a royal burial chamber, probably of the early 3rd century B.C.

The plain stretching to the village of Vergína, named after a mythological queen of Véria, is freckled with more than 300 small tumuli, mostly one and a half meters (five ft.) high. This tumuli cemetery was used from the Early Iron Age, about 1100 B.C., for some 800 years, with the oldest graves in distinct groups of clans. But burial practices radically changed dimensions, with the huge mound at the western edge, 12 meters (39 ft.) high over a diameter of 110 meters (120 yards), unique in the Greek world. Though the mound had been described by Heuzey, excavation of it was not begun until 1976; directed by Professor Andronikos of Thessaloníki University, it upset earlier concepts of Macedonia. It was found to contain three royal tombs of the 4th century B.C.: the uppermost had been thoroughly looted, but the first complete ancient Greek painting to be found, the Rape of Persephone by Hades, was perfectly preserved. Next, five meters (17 ft.) below ground level, a much larger tomb, in the form of a Doric temple with two chambers, was excavated and has been hailed as one of the outstanding finds of this century, as all antique European tombs of this caliber had been previously plundered. The painted frieze is a brilliant composition of a lion hunt. A marble sarcophagus enclosed a casket of solid gold weighing 11 kg. (24.2 pounds), whose lid, bearing the exploding star, symbol of Macedonian kings, opened on bones and teeth topped by a delicate diadem of oak leaves and acorns. Silver vessels and goblets, armor and helmet, a unique gold, bronze and ivory shield, another diadem and scepter, but above all five marble heads, which Professor Andronikos claimed to be those of Philip II and his family, supported the belief that this was the tomb of the great Macedonian king and the bones in a smaller gold casket those of his seventh wife, Cleopatra (Macedonian royalty being given to polygamy). These treasures are now in the Thessaloníki Archaeological Museum, together with those of the third tomb, dated by vases to 375–350 B.C., perhaps that of Philip's two brothers.

The excavations in the 1980s of the acropolis walls, a temple with votive offerings by Philip's mother Euridyce, but above all the remains of a theater near the even scantier vestiges of a palace, left little doubt that this was indeed Aigai, Macedonia's ancient capital, until then placed at Édessa in the northwestern foothills. Philip was murdered in the theater of Aigai by Pausanias, a former guardsman, who was himself felled by a spear before he could confess who had put him up to the deed. Philip's son Alexander was immediately acclaimed as king by the army, thus ending one of the great murder mysteries of history. In 1989 and 1990, further important discoveries were made by Professor Andronikos and his team at Vergína. Five tombs, dating from the 5th century B.C., were uncovered, most of them thought to be those of women. Although they had been plundered in antiquity, they still contained some exciting finds. The most important of these were gold soles from the shoes of the women, gold jewelry and buttons, and unusual life-sized clay heads, with the remnants of paint still on them. In another grave, white Attic funerary vases demonstrate close cultural and commercial ties between Ancient Macedonia and southern Greece.

At Véria, 21 km. (13 miles) beyond the Aliákmon, St. Paul was well received by the Jewish community, after his hasty exit from Thessaloníki, and was allowed to preach where a ruined mosque now stands. Houses have been built into the ramparts in an intriguing way, often using the old blocks. Several tiny Byzantine churches tucked away in courtyards were so built to escape the notice of the Turks: Ágios Nikólaos, with a fresco of the Sleeping Virgin; Ágios Christos, with many 14th-century frescos; Agía Fotiní, with a carved wooden door, capitals and more frescos; Ágios Georgios, again for woodwork and frescos; and Prophet Elias, which has a bishop's throne and a beautiful icon. The finest icons are in the small Byzantine museum. A Hellenistic cemetery with interesting Macedonian tombs was excavated in 1985.

If you are pressed for time, the abridged circuit still takes in the main sites: north to Náoussa (21 km., 13 miles), Édessa (40 km., 25 miles, further on), returning via Pélla to Thessaloníki. Náoussa is a prosperous little town on the slopes of Mount Vérmio. From the public gardens there is a splendid view over the vast orchards below.

For lovely mountain scenery, drive up Mount Vérmio to Kato Vérmio (21 km., 13 miles; 1,400 meters, 4,600 ft.) or Seli, the two main skiing resorts. Alternatively, take the narrow, winding road from Náoussa through woods and fields up to Tría Pigádia (16 km., 10 miles), another skiing center with several fairly steep tracks. Back in the plain, five km. (three miles) along the Édessa road, it is possible to indulge further in any newly-acquired passion for Macedonian tombs. Near the village of Lefkádia, in the orchards to the right (east), the 3rd-century B.C. tomb of a Macedonian general was accidentally unearthed by peasants in 1954. The hideous modern concrete structure is unfortunately necessary to preserve the paintings—the general himself, Hermes Conductor of Souls, two of the judges in Hades—on the half Doric, half Ionic façade of the small temple. Nearby a larger tomb fronted by three Ionic columns was discovered 20 years later. Across the road, unmarked and closed to the public, is the tomb of the Lyson and Kallikles families.

The 61 km. (38 miles) from Véria to Kozáni, on the wider circuit, wind along the southern flank of Mount Vérmio, below the new monastery of Panagía Sóumela, to which the miraculous icon of the Virgin was entrusted in 1931, having lain buried after the abandonment of the great motherhouse in Asia Minor in 1923. Between Kastaniá and the pass of Hantóva you have a wonderful view over valleys and mountains.

Kozáni has no intrinsic merit, but is the hub of western Macedonia: it lies roughly halfway between Lárissa, reached over Greece's longest bridge, almost a mile, across the artificial Lake Poliphiton created by damming up the Aliákmon for the country's largest hydro-electric plant, and Thessaloníki on the inland road (278 km., 173 miles); the road north leads to the big thermo-electric plant of Ptolemaída and then forks at Vevi left (west) to Flórina (80 km., 50 miles) and right to Edessa 109 km. (68 miles); the branch to the right, 22 km. (14 miles) west of Kozáni, leads to Siátista, with some well-preserved 18th-century houses, two of which can be visited, the painted Church of Agía Pareskeví (1611), modern Ágios Dimítrios and a Paleontological Museum full of skeletons. After a further three km. (two miles) the road forks left (south) across the Aliákmon to Grevená and over a lonely highland affording fine views of the Píndos range to the Mourgani junction (116 km., 72 miles from Kozáni) near Kalambáka on the Ioánina–Trikala road; right (northwest) following the upper course of the Aliákmon for 66 km. (41 miles) to Kastoriá.

Kastoriá, the Town in the Lake

Kastoriá's particular charm is largely due to its site on a promontory joined to the mainland by a narrow isthmus. The old town is thus almost surrounded by the lake, which is appropriately called Orestias, after the town's reputed founder, Orestes, son of Agamemnon. The Byzantine governors of this imperial frontier outpost left monuments to their piety in the multiplicity of miniature churches. Not all 72 are, however, medieval, as several were built as private chapels to the 17th- and 18th-century houses of the rich merchants. These *arhontiká* with painted upper stories projecting over the windowless lower floors, are being restored, and one, the Nerandzis house, has been converted into a folkloric museum. The important Byzantine museum is higher up.

The tiny churches are: the 11th-century Panagia Koubelidiki, named after its singular cylindrical dome, in the court of the high school; a little further down Mitropoleos street is the 12th-century Ágios Nikólaos, a tiny single-naved basilica with impressionist frescos; the 14th-century Taxiarches (Archangels) has interesting frescos, as also Ágios Athanasios (1385), still nearer the large modern Metropolis; the 11th-century Ágios Stephanos, a triple-naved basilica, is in the eastern quarter, not far from Ágii, and is probably the oldest. But these architectural gems are lost among large apartment blocks which have spread beyond the promontory, for Kastoriá's 400-year-old industry has once again brought prosperity to the town—the skillful piecing together of scraps of fur left over from cutting. The fur-on-a-roll, looking like a form of textile, is heavier than normal fur and makes up into cheaper garments.

A one-way anti-clockwise road, shaded by large plane trees, circles the promontory. Halfway, at the extreme point (one mile), stands the monastery of the Panagia Mavriotissa with two old churches. That of Agios Ioánis has well-preserved frescos; particularly interesting is the *Stilling of the Waters,* featuring the typical Kastorian fishing boats, flat-bottomed and blunt at both ends. To immerse yourself in local color you might punt to that lovely spot, which is an ideal camping site, although you might find the smell of stagnant water—which is overpowering in summer—offputting. Bathing is prohibited in the badly polluted water.

Kastoriá lies at 762 meters (2,400 ft.), but for the return journey you have to climb higher still, up Mount Vérno. Over the southern flank to the junction with the Kozáni–Édessa road (61 km., 38 miles) past the village of Klissóura (1,188 meters, 3,900 ft.), whose church of Ágios Dimítrios possesses an admirably carved 15th-century *iconostasis;* over the northern flank, even higher, on a worse but scenically more rewarding road across the Pisoderi Pass, allowing for a short side-trip to the bird sanctuary in the solitude of the Little and Big Préspa Lakes, the latter bordered by Greece, Yugoslavia and Albania, to Flórina (71 km., 44 miles) near the Yugoslav frontier post of Niki (19 km., 12 miles).

Capitals Fallen and Risen

Close to Flórina, archaic statues were unearthed in 1978 in what is believed to have been the first Macedonian capital, before the kings moved to Aigai, in about 800 B.C. Though it revived in the Middle Ages, nothing of interest remains.

The 67 km. (42 miles) to Édessa climb after the Vevi junction to an altitude of 960 meters (3,150 ft.). Mount Kaïmaktsalan (2,517 meters, 8,260 ft.), another favorite in innumerable Balkan skirmishes, on the left (north) forms the border with Yugoslavia; on the right is Lake Vergorítida, with the pretty village of Árnissa on a promontory. At Ágras is a hydro-electric station powered by the 25-meter (82-ft.) falls of the Voda River with important fish hatcheries down stream.

Édessa, till recently identified with antique Aigai, lies on a northwestern ledge of Mount Vérmio. It is a pleasant town crossed by several rivulets uniting into spectacular waterfalls hiding a small stalactite cave. The view over the sea of fruit trees in the valley below even surpasses that at Náoussa, in spite of the hydro-electric installations.

After descending into the orchards and passing near Skýdra (14 km., nine miles) the branch road to Náoussa and Véria, another Macedonian tomb built in 320 B.C. reveals a unique ground plan at Arhontiká Gianitsás. Five km (three miles) further east, an ancient reservoir on the left, the so-called "Bath of Alexander" heralds the extensive ruins of Pélla.

King Archelaos (413–399 B.C.) transferred the capital from Aigai to Pélla, to which he attracted the greatest artists of his time, as for instance Euripides. In the year of the 106th Olympic Games, 356 B.C., Queen Olympias gave birth in the royal palace to Alexander, deservedly called the Great. Pélla, protected by vast swamps and the island fortress of Phakos, remained the seat of the Macedonian kings till 168 B.C.

Intermittent excavations since 1958 have thus far brought to light several public buildings, whose peristyles surround open courtyards. Excellently preserved pebble mosaics, probably copies of Apelles' lost paintings, depict the story of Helen of Troy, Dionysos riding a prancing panther, Alexander being saved by Krateros at a lion hunt, each surrounded by a border design. Remarkable are the huge roof tiles, some of marble, others of clay, bearing the names of people or of the city. Kassandros' main gate opened on Philip V's huge agora, which has been uncovered: 400 square meters (478 square yards) in size and surrounded by Doric stoas. The remains of a theater and a small temple are less impressive. Archelaos commissioned the painter Zeuxis to decorate the palace and was severely criticized by his nobles for this un-Macedonian extravagance; it eventually became Europe's largest Hellenistic building, spreading over the acropolis, where excavations are progressing. Bisected by a broad avenue, Pélla's water supply and sewers are as good as in any modern Greek town. Tools in bone, iron and bronze have been found, besides clay vessels and figurines, also many coins ranging from the reign of Philip II to Roman times. The museum's chief glories are a superb vase decorated with the battle of the Amazons, and a bronze statuette of Poseidon.

Just beyond Géfyra (bridge) on the Axios River is the junction with the motorway north to Evzóni (47 km., 29 miles) on the Yugoslav border; continuing east, across yet another river, the Galikós, you reach Thessaloníki (89 km., 55 miles from Edessa).

The Halkidikí, Macedonia's Playground

All the beaches southeast of Thessaloníki have been appropriated by huge hotel and bungalow complexes. The mountainous, thickly-wooded Halkidikí Peninsula is bounded north by the two elongated lakes of Korónia and Volvi, west by the Thermaïkós Gulf, east by the Strymonikós, while in the south three prongs jut far into the Aegean. It offers infinite scenic (and on Mount Áthos, architectural) variety, easily accessible by an adequate road network. To avoid having to retrace your steps for any great distance, start with the westernmost prong, the Kassandras, named after the Great Alexander's general and not after Priam's sinister daughter.

At Mikrá, just after Thessaloníki's international airport, the road branches right (west) to the beaches of Peréa and Agía Triáda, southwest to the coast beyond Epanomí, and left (south) towards Néa Moudaniá. From the crossroads for Néa Kalikratía you can take the 12 km. (seven miles) sidetrip inland to the cave of Petrálona (open daily 9–5) where part of a Neanderthal woman's skull was found in 1960 and a full skeleton, in 1976. The stalactites give the cave a golden-red glow. The new museum, at the entrance to the cave, with its displays of primitive human habitation and remains of cave bears, lions and wolves, is certainly worth a look.

After Néa Moudaniá, 61 km. (38 miles), and the canal cut across the narrow isthmus, are the insignificant ruins of Potidea, whose revolt against Athens was one of the causes of the Peloponnesian War. Destroyed by Philip II, refounded by Kassander as Kassandría, it was finally razed by the Huns. As the promontory widens, the enchanting view over both coasts is limited to the eastern, studded with fishing villages. The coastal road passes through Néa Fokéa, Kalithéa and Kryopigí to Palioúri. After a last glance at the seemingly land-locked Gulf of Kassandras and the Sithonia prong topped by the unmistakable triangular summit of Mount Áthos, the road climbs into the hills and pine woods, with a branch extending to the headland. Again you view both gulfs before reaching the west coast at Ágia Paraskeví. Along the sea to Kálandra, where you turn inland to complete the circuit three km. (two miles) after Kassandría, the dull main village.

After this appetizer proceed to the even lovelier middle prong, Sithonia. Recrossing the isthmus turn right (northeast) to Ólynthos (six km., four miles), in 392 B.C. the capital of an important confederation. All that is left is a huge mound crowned by scattered foundations and broken sections of the ramparts. At the Gerakiní road fork (eight km., five miles) continue right (south) along a series of fine beaches below thickly wooded hills.

The next 58 km. (36 miles) skirt the tranquil pine forests past Metamór-fossi, a dull, characterless village, its narrow, pebbly beaches crowded with campers, to Nikíti. In the 14th century, this village was inhabited by work-ers of the Neakitou *metochi* (a small, independent community), part of the Xenofontos monastery on Mount Athos. Although destroyed by the Turks in 1821, it was rebuilt in 1827 and the village is now a pleasant mix-ture of the old, to the north of the main road, and the new, with fish tav-ernas stretched along the seafront. The road carries on to Néos Marmarás, a picturesque fishing town, with two natural harbors and two squares, both now smothered in souvenir shops and rooms to rent. Here, almond and olive trees as well as vineyards producing Greece's best wine, surround a luxurious tourist complex; comprising three very large, rather ugly, modern hotels, an 18-hole golf course, two theaters, an exhibition hall and a marina capable of accommodating luxury craft. After the beautiful natu-ral harbor of Pórto Koufó near the tip of the peninsula, the round trip of Sithonia continues up the east coast and ends at Ormós Panagías, a small fishing hamlet.

From Gerakiní it is 14 km. (nine miles) to Polýgyros (535 meters, 1,755 ft.), the attractive capital of the Halkidikí. The next 11 km. (seven miles) climb through densely-wooded mountains to the pass (913 meters, 2,996 ft.), whence there is another one of those fine views over the Kassandra Gulf and promontory. The inland road is joined after 58 km. (36 miles) from Thessaloníki, but the Halkidikí has still much to offer, so turn right (east) to Arnéa and the forest beyond.

Among the unremarkable ruins of Stágira stands the remarkably ugly statue of its greatest son, the philosopher Aristotle, tutor of Alexander the Great. Ierissós (116 km., 72 miles from Thessaloníki) has an excellent beach, a mediocre medieval castle and some ancient walls; Néa Roda has only the first. Crossing from the east to west coast along Xerxes' canal, long since filled in, the road hugs the shore to Ouranópoli (13 km., eight miles). This is the last village on the Áthos promontory at which women and children are allowed, and that only since 1923, when refugees from Asia Minor were settled on the confines of the monks' republic. The forti-fied tower at the end of the splendid beach was built by the Emperor An-dronicus II, and served later as a look-out against the pirates, who infested the four surrounding islands. Ouranópoli has sprouted a jungle of concrete boxes as it is the most convenient base for visiting the Holy Mountain.

A quick and scenic alternative for the return journey is provided by con-tinuing north from Stratóni through pinewoods to Olympiáda, then for 34 km. (21 miles) along the shore to Stavrós, a deservedly popular resort, whence it is three km. (two miles) to the Kavála highway.

This is the usual tourist route from Thessaloníki east to Komotiní in Thrace, mainly along the sea, but there is an inland alternative via Séres and Dráma, among fertile plains and mountains with a lesser road in be-tween. Along this rather dull middle road is Langadás (21 km., 13 miles northeast of Thessaloníki) where on the feast of St. Constantine and his British-born mother St. Helena—May 21—the firewalkers (*anastenárides*) brandish the saints' ikons above their heads and dance barefoot on glowing charcoal embers, and are none the worse for it. A similar event, reminiscent of ancient Dionysiac rituals including the sacrifice of a calf in whose ears lighted candles have previously been stuck, attracts large crowds to Agía Eleni near Séres.

Just before the Strymónas bridge, it is possible to join the shortest west–east road from Thessaloníki along Lake Korónia and then Lake Volvi, beside which is the spa of Apolonía. A picturesque fortress heralds the Rendína gorge, at whose other end is the branch to Stavrós.

The next 24 km. (15 miles) follow the sea to the bridge over the Strymónas, flowing down from Bulgaria. The huge stone lion, standing at the side of the road, was found in the river bed, probably washed down from the ruins of Amfípoli, less than a mile from the crossroad. Ancient Amphipolis was founded by Pericles on a spur of Mount Pangéo on the river's left bank; it was the object of constant dissent among the Thracians, Athenians, Persians and Macedonians before the advent of the Romans, owing to the rich mineral deposits in the area. Imposing ramparts strengthened by round towers, one of antiquity's most formidable fortifications, surrounded the acropolis where—between the remains of early-Christian basilicas—new finds are constantly coming to light. The more important, especially jewelry, are sent to the Kavála museum, the remains are exposed in the village museum over the hill. The 1,200 tree trunks buried in the sands of the river supported a wooden bridge, used for a thousand years after its construction in about 425 B.C., as witnessed by the remains of Byzantine towers. There is a wide view from the acropolis over the coastline across to Mount Áthos and the Halkidikí.

Continuing straight on (north) from Amfípoli you reach either Dráma or Séres if you are in hurry to return, while the first branch to the right (northeast) climbs to Rodólivos, starting point for climbing or skiing on Mount Pángeo. The Monastery of Ikossifiníssis, supposedly founded in 518, possesses rare old manuscripts, though the frescos in the Church of the Zoodóhos Pigí are modern.

"Thou Shalt See Me At Philíppi"

So says Caesar's ghost in Shakespeare's tragedy, and as this is eastern Macedonia's outstanding archeological site, to Filípi (Philíppi) it shall be.

Eleftheróupoli can be reached from Rodólivos along the road circling Mount Pangeo. The usual approach, however, is by the highway east from the Amfípoli junction through the southern foothills of the mountain. Five km. (three miles) before Kavála you meet the road from Dráma; if it happens to be summer afternoon this is the time to visit Philíppi, ten km. (six miles) along that road, as the heat haze will have lifted and the plain looks its best, when you drive along the tree-lined avenue.

Anxious to protect his newly acquired gold mines on Mount Pangeo, Philip II settled numerous Macedonians in 358 B.C. in the Thasian colony of Krinídes to which he graciously gave his name. Here it was that Brutus had his fatal rendezvous with Caesar's ghost, when he and Cassius were defeated by Mark Antony and Octavian in 42 B.C., the second of the three momentous encounters that decided the fate of Rome on Greek soil. Brutus and Cassius committed suicide, but the victors enriched and embellished Philíppi, which continued to prosper in the following centuries, thanks to its privileged position on the Via Egnatia, the empire's main artery. Standing at the edge of the plain, under the Thimodes Mountains, the town was a natural stopping place for cross-empire travelers. Here St. Paul preached his first sermon in Europe, extempore, to the women washing their clothes in the river, and baptised Lydia, the cloth merchant. After spending some time in prison, St. Paul departed for Thessaloníki by way of Amphipolis and Apollonia, only to make a hasty retreat to Veria, and yet another to Athens. In spite of this erratic course he made a great impression and laid the seeds of Christianity in Macedonia.

The extensive remains of the town lie mostly below the road on the left, entered through the restored propylaeum. The large *agora* contains the ruins of many Roman buildings; beyond stand the remains of a huge 5th-century basilica, two imposing pillars supporting an arch, which catch the eye from afar. Their large blocks and sculptures had been used in some previous edifice, while in the 6th century another basilica with a dome was superimposed on the earlier one. Further on were the Roman baths. Among the various scattered ruins on the rocky ledges on the right, above the road, is the so-called prison where St. Paul and St. Silas were thrown, with their feet "made fast in the stocks." The small cave hardly seems adequate for housing several prisoners.

In the rocks are niches of ancient shrines, with inscriptions and carved reliefs of deities. The climb up to the acropolis (which affords an excellent view) leads past the Egyptian shrine; the crumbling ramparts above are partly Macedonian and partly Byzantine, but the three towers, which stand out so well from a distance, are later additions. The gray stone theater backing on to the rocks dates from the time of Philip II, but it was actually converted into a gladiatorial arena (like the one on Thasos), supplementary tiers supported by arches as well as an underground entry for the wild beasts were then added. Returned to its original use, ancient tragedies are now again performed in summer.

Excavations have recently brought to light the foundations of the oldest known octagonal church, built by Constantine the Great and rebuilt by Justinian, the Propylaea on the Via Egnatia, a large bath establishment and mosaics.

By Rivers and Lagoons

Returning from Philíppi, stop at the height above Kavála to enjoy the great panorama of the town and of Thássos, the island which once held it in thrall; on a clear morning you might even be able to see the distant Dardanelles. Kavála, forming an amphitheater on the lower slopes of Mount Symvólon, is, with some 60,000 inhabitants, the fifth largest town of Greece, a big fish market and the center and port of the tobacco trade. The middle of the town is given over to warehouses. The coastal road after the Amfípoli junction via Loutrá Elefthéron, Néa Péramos, Néa Iraklitsa and Kalamítsa leading straight into the busy waterfront, is scenically lovelier.

Known as Neapolis by the Romans, Christopolis by the Franks, Kavála's present name—meaning on horseback—indicates its importance as a relay station for changing horses. It was here that Brutus stationed his fleet during the battle at Philíppi; and,here, too, that St. Paul landed, having sailed from Samothrace. The Roman aqueduct curving across the center of the town is still its distinguishing feature, while the decaying Byzantine fortifications are less interesting than the climb through the somewhat

Oriental eastern quarter of old Turkish houses and Mohammed Ali's badly neglected religious foundations. Mohammed Ali was the son of a rich tobacco merchant, and after a checkered career almost as colorful as that of his contemporary, Ali Pasha of Ioánina, became the founder of the Egyptian royal dynasty, whose last reigning member was the late King Farouk. The house where Mohammed Ali was born in 1769 stands on a promontory, behind his equestrian statue. Now a museum, it gives a good idea of Moslem family arrangements, with carved cupboards for storing the rugs and cushions, which would be brought out for sleeping, and wooden latticed screens, whence the women could look out of the harem quarter without being seen. The doors to the women's apartments are strongly bolted, and there is even a lift by which the food was sent to the exclusively male gatherings. On the opposite side of the waterfront crescent is the archaeological museum with most of the Amphipolis and Ávidra finds.

It is 178 km. (111 miles) from Kavála to Alexandróupoli. After 26 km. (16 miles) is the branch right (south) to Hrissóupoli airport and the port of Keramotí (21 km., 13 miles), the ferry terminal for Thássos (four nautical miles). The highway follows for a short distance the romantic Nestós Valley and then crosses the river into Thrace. This is still tobacco country, but the villages become markedly Oriental, as Thrace is the one province where the Moslem population was not exchanged after World War I; in return, Greeks were allowed to remain in Istanbul and other mainly Greek-inhabited Turkish towns. Although Greece has always stood by this agreement, there is some anti-Moslem, anti-Turkish feeling in parts of Thrace, on one occasion in 1990 erupting into violence, and many Thracian "Turks" feel discriminated against by the government. The Thracian Moslems are extremely traditional and, to all visible appearances, seem old-fashioned; houses, preserving their privacy, show blank, white-painted walls to the road. Slim minarets of mosques dominate the skyline, especially at Xánthi, which clings to the hilly sides of the Kósinthis Valley. The town of 30,000 inhabitants is the market for the Pomaks, descendants of Bulgarians who embraced Islam about 500 years ago. It is pleasant to sit on an evening in one of the numerous cafes or restaurants on the large central square. Visits to the Convent of the Panagía and the Monastery tón Taxiarhón, now a school, are justified by the magnificent view they command from their vantage points.

The coastal road to Komotiní (56 km., 35 miles) bypasses Xánthi by turning again towards the sea. The first branch to the right (southwest) leads to Ávdira (16 km., ten miles), near the walls and tombs of ancient Abdera founded by Heracles in memory of his friend Abderos. Birthplace of several philosophers, including Democritus who propounded the Atom Theory in the 5th century B.C., the foundations of a Byzantine church prove its continuing importance some 1,200 years later. Further excavations have uncovered two Hellenistic walled compounds, the ruins of terra cotta workshops, and Roman baths. Lágos lies on a narrow strip of sand between the sea and Lake Vistónia. It is an attractive landscape in its own melancholy way, rich in all sorts of water birds and extensive fisheries. The road runs on a dyke, along which bridges, trees and the Church of Ágios Nikólaos are perfectly mirrored in the still water of the lagoon. One of the best beaches of the north is only eight km. (five miles) to the right at Fanári. Signposts indicate a small Byzantine church, prehistoric tombs and the pavement of the Roman Via Egnatia.

Komotiní resembles Xánthi, but in a less attractive setting. A restored 18th-century mansion houses the Folkloric Museum.

Continuing southeast, the last branch west (right) shortly before reaching the sea leads to the excavations of Messimvría (Mesembria), a Hellenistic town dependent on the Kingdom of Samothrace. Ramparts climb three km. (two miles) from the sea up to the acropolis and back to the sea, enclosing a sanctuary of Demeter; rich finds are coming to light in the vast cemetery. Back on the mainroad, the Cyclopean sea cave of Mákri claims a rather doubtful place in the *Odyssey*. The road follows the coast via Néa Hilí to Alexandróupoli (64 km., 40 miles), which makes up for its surprising lack of historical remnants—considering it was founded by Alexander the Great and the first of some 20 towns to bear his name—by finds from the neighborhood in the Archeological Museum.

Close to the Turkish border, the road turns again inland, along the west bank of the Évros River, which divides Greece from Turkey, but has its source near the Bulgarian capital, Sofia. The wide fertile river valley is apt to be flooded in winter and springtime, especially the delta opposite the island of Samothrace. Important flood-prevention works are under execution on both banks, while the long bridge between Kípi (43 km., 27 miles) and Ypsála is the main border crossing to Istanbul.

Further up the valley is Souflí, renowned for its silks. In the Byzantine castle above Didymótiho the Emperor Ioannis Paleologus was born in 1349, and later the Sultan Bayazit. At Plthio the railway, which has previously run roughly parallel to the road, divides; the direct line to Istanbul crosses the Évros, while the line to Adrianople continues on the right bank to Orestiáda. The road bridge and frontier station is still further north, at Kastaniés (137 km., 85 miles from Alexandróupoli) within sight of Adrianople (Edirne).

As there is no alternative route back as far as Komotiní, few travelers, except those proceeding to Turkey, venture up the Évros Valley, in spite of its undoubted picturesqueness. From Komotiní, however, it is possible to take the shorter inland road to Xánthi (50 km., 31 miles), through the plain divided by a wall that extends at Amaxades from the foothills to Lake Vistónia, and has from time immemorial failed to keep out invaders from the east.

It is possible to drive north up the Kósinthos Valley where the Pomak shepherds graze their flocks, but there is no crossing over the formidable Rodópi Mountains into Bulgaria. The road west via Stavróupoli to Dráma is scenic, especially along the Nestós valley to Paranésti.

The Golden Plain

This was the name given by the Turks to the plain of Dráma, not only for its great fertility, but also for the diffused golden light in the late summer afternoons. For the sake of that light Philíppi was included in the outgoing journey, as that is the time the motorist from Thessaloníki is likely to arrive, after a swim at Stavrós and with the prospect of comfortable accommodation close at hand in Kavála.

Nobody will begrudge retracing the 14 km. (nine miles) to Philíppi, which, like the remaining 20 km. (12½ miles) to Dráma, are shaded by huge poplars. Trees—poplar, elm, lime and plane—line many of the Macedonian roads, and often form a roof, to the driver's delight. Dráma was the scene of an Athenian defeat by the Macedonians in the 5th century

B.C.; nothing remains of that period and neither some insignificant Roman ruins nor the Byzantine chapel near the walls warrant more than a cursory glance; you might, however, take a meal on the island at the Agía Varvára springs within the town.

Séres deserves much closer attention. About half way along the unexciting 71 km. (44 miles) from Dráma is the junction with the road from Amfípoli (29 km., 18 miles). Séres has seen much fighting since its foundation in pre-Hellenistic times. Xerxes stabled the sacred mares of the Sun Chariot in the rich plain, watered by the Strimon; while after bearing the brunt of repeated attacks by the Bulgars on their way to Thessaloníki, Séres was temporarily relieved when the Emperor Basil II, the Bulgar-slayer, defeated Tsar Samuel in the Strimon gorge. Ten thousand of the latter's troops were blinded by the emperor's orders, leaving only every hundredth man with one eye to lead his comrades home. The Turks stayed from 1368 to 1913, but liberty did not come gently to this old stronghold, for in the same year it was burnt down by the "liberating" Bulgars. During the last war it was to suffer yet again under Bulgarian occupation.

Little is left of the old Christian and Turkish quarters, which have been replaced by a busy, prosperous modern town. Close to the new, the old Metropolis Ágios Theodoros has been restored as a museum, containing some Roman sculptures. The triple-naved basilica possesses several unusual features, such as the raised *Synthronum* behind the aspe. In the large mosaic of the Last Supper, Our Lord is shown twice, offering the bread and wine to those on the left and right respectively. The small sunken side-chapel was used as a secret school under the Turks.

Brightly colored hand-woven rugs are on display in the mosque on the central square, but the two other mosques are left to decay as symbols of the hated Turkish domination. Yet, the mosque on the river, standing forlorn among the weeping willows, is one of the finest and most romantic buildings in Macedonia.

An easy climb from the town, or a short drive on the further side, along the nameless tributary of the Strymónas, past a swimming pool, cafes and taverns, brings you to the acropolis, crowned by the ruins of the 13th-century castle. Within the walls is the Byzantine Church of Ágios Nikólaos, which also has a crypt that was used secretly, entered between two rocks. From the height you have a wonderful view in all directions; the outlines of the town are softened and beyond the valley, in which the most varied architectural styles of churches can be discerned, are range after range of mountains. The 43 km. (27 miles) north ascend through that tempting landscape past the Vrondóu range to Promahonas, the only crossing into Bulgaria, via Sidirókastro, a picturesque township below a medieval castle. The less scenic but tree-lined 22 km. (14 miles) south to the spa of Nigríta—whose bottled water is drunk for digestive disorders—cross the Strymónas. The 90 km. (56 miles) southwest to Thessaloníki curve across the plain and over a mountain rising to 650 meters (2,130 ft.), whence you enjoy some spectacular views over Lakes Korónia and Volvi and the country beyond as far as the sea. 12 km. (seven and a half miles) before Thessaloníki is the junction with the road on which you set out for Kavála.

PRACTICAL INFORMATION FOR
MACEDONIA AND THRACE

WHEN TO COME. Late spring or early summer is the best time for traveling about, since snow and ice sometimes block the roads in winter. The summer is hot and dusty in the eastern plains, though not in the western mountains, and obviously best for the lovely beaches in the Halkidikí, at Pórto Lágos, Fanári and near Alexandróupoli.

TOURIST OFFICES. There are G.N.T.O. offices at **Kavála,** Filellinon 5 (tel. 22 8762); at the Yugoslav border, **Evzóni** (tel. 5 1223); and at the Bulgarian border, **Promáhonas** (tel. 4 1241).

SPECIAL EVENTS. February/March. Carnival is ebulliently celebrated in Náoussa, the Dionysian tradition being particularly strong in the Halkidikí villages and at Kozáni during the traditional three weeks before Orthodox Lent, rising to its gayest for the last two days. Kastoriá's Carnival is held at the unusual season of Epiphany, while Litóhoro extends the festivities for a week.

May. Among the most popular Saints' days is that of Saints Constantine and Heleni, on May 21. Crowds visit Langadás and Agía Eléni (Séres), to watch the *Anastenarides,* or Firewalkers. So great a draw is this ancient custom whose origins are pagan, that it is very difficult to get near enough to view the spectacle. On May 14, Komotiní presents Thracian folkloric customs.

June. Flower festival at Édessa, early in the month.

July. Strawberry festival at Flórina. Wine festival at Alexandróupoli, extending into August. Performances of ancient drama at Philílippi and the Ólympos festival in the castle of Platamónas and the ancient theater of Díon from July to August.

August. In the Kastaniá Pass between Kozáni and Véria, the miraculous icon of the monastery of the *Panagía* (Our Lady) *Sóumelas* attracts large crowds of pilgrims for the Feast of the Assumption on August 15.

September. International windsurfing competition in the Halkidikí at the end of the month. **December–January.** In midwinter, a Hunting Week is organized in the Évros delta and the Hellenic Alpine Club holds six races on Mount Vérmio.

HOTELS AND RESTAURANTS. The best accommodations are offered by the beach hotels and bungalows in the Halkidikí; most insist on halfboard.

Specialties here include *lagós* (hare) in walnut sauce or stewed in wine; quail, woodcock and wild duck in season; *saláta piperiés,* a salad of fried red peppers mostly found in Flórina; *mydia saganaki,* mussels in a hot, spicy soup, with cheese, wine and garlic; *manóuri* in western Macedonia, *telemes* in Thrace and the *graviera* (Gruyére) of Séres are good cheeses. Náoussa produces Greece's most popular red wine, while the Domaine Carras in the Halkidikí produces some of the country's best wines of any color.

Agía Triáda. *Galaxy* (M), tel. 2 2291/3. 80 rooms. Beach, roof garden, disco. Minigolf and tennis nearby. AE. *Sun Beach* (M), tel. 5 1221/4. 120 rooms. Airconditioned; 2 pools, disco; minigolf and tennis nearby. AE, MC, V.

Alexandróupoli. *Motel Astir* (M), tel. 2 6448. 53 rooms. Pool; on beach. AE, DC, MC. *Motel Egnatia* (I), tel. 2 8661. 96 rooms. On beach; tennis. Both on the town's outskirts. *Alex* (I), tel. 2 6302. 28 rooms. *Alkyon* (I), tel. 2 7465. 30 rooms. Restaurant. V. *Hera* (I), tel. 2 5995. 32 rooms. DC, V. 2 km. (one mile) west, *Alexander Beach* (M), tel. 2 9250. 102 rooms. Those overlooking the pool and sea are quieter; airconditioned, seawater pool.

Restaurant. *Klimataria* (I); One block inland from seafront. This typical taverna serves a wide range of cooked dishes including *gyro salma,* a local speciality rather like haggis, the traditional Scottish meat pudding.

Asproválta. *Strymonikon* (I), tel. 2 2209. 13 rooms.

Didymótiho. *Anessis* (I), tel. 2 2050. 13 rooms. *Plotini* (I), tel. 2 3400. 67 rooms; disco, restaurant. V.

Dispílio. 3 km. (2 miles) south of Kastoriá. *Tsamis* (M), tel. 4 3334. 81 rooms. Beach on the lake.

Dráma. *Xenia* (M), tel. 2 3195. 48 rooms. Airconditioned; disco. V. *Apollo* (I), tel. 2 5551. 40 rooms. *Marianna* (I), tel. 2 1520. 45 rooms. DC, V.

Édessa. *Katarraktis* (M), tel. 2 2300. 44 rooms. Restaurant, roofgarden. At the waterfall, fine view. AE, DC, V. *Alfa* (I), tel. 2 2221. 36 rooms. DC, MC. *Xenia* (I), tel. 2 2995. 20 rooms. Restaurant. MC, V.
Restaurant. *Tourist Pavilion* (M). At the waterfall.

Evzóni. *Evzoni* (M), tel. 5 1209. 25 rooms.

Flórina. *King Alexander* (M), tel. 2 3501. 59 rooms. On the outskirts; food above average. *Tottis* (M), tel. 2 2645. 48 rooms. V. *Antigone* (I), tel. 2 3180. 80 rooms. *Lyngos* (I), tel. 2 8322. 40 rooms. Restaurant, roofgarden. DC, MC, V.

Géfyra. *Géfyra* (I), tel. 5 1287. Motel; 12 rooms.

Halkidikí Áfytos. *Afytis* (M), tel. 9 1273. 31 rooms. V.
Agía Paraskeví. *Aphrodite* (M), tel. 7 1228. 24 rooms.
Gerakiní. *Gerakina Beach* (E), tel. 5 1118. Hotel and bungalows; 503 rooms. 2 pools, gym, tennis, minigolf, disco. AE, DC.
Haniótis. *Dionyssos Apartments* (M), tel. 5 1402. 47 suites. *Pella* (M), tel. 5 1679. 179 rooms. AE, DC, V. *Soussouras* (M), tel. 5 1251. 73 bungalows on beach. Tennis. V. *Ermis* (I), tel. 5 1245. 28 rooms. *Strand* (I), tel. 5 1261. 45 rooms. Disco; restaurant. DC.
Ierissós. *Villa Giouli* (M), tel. 2 2295. 8 apartments.
Kálandra. *Mendi* (E), tel. 4 1323/7. 172 rooms. Not airconditioned but on cool promontory. Beach, pool, tennis, minigolf, disco. AE, DC.

Kalithéa. *Athos Palace* (E), tel. 2 2100/10. 599 rooms. On beach; pool, tennis, minigolf, disco. AE, DC, MC, V. *Pallini Beach* (E), tel. 2 2480/10. 495 rooms in central block and bungalows. On beach; pool, minigolf, tennis, disco. AE, DC, MC, V. *Ammon Zeus* (M), tel. 2 2356. 112 rooms. Airconditioned; beach, disco. *Belvedere* (I), tel. 2 2352. 60 rooms. Near beach.

Kryopigí. *Alexander Beach* (E), tel. 2 2991. 164 rooms. Partially airconditioned. Tennis, pool. *Kassandra Palace* (E), tel. 5 1471/5. 192 rooms. Pool, tennis, disco. AE, DC.

Metamórfossi. *Danai Beachotel* (E), tel. 2 2310. 50 rooms. This hotel is located in an attractive, wooded setting, with its own private beach; tennis, pool. V. *Golden Beach* (I), tel. 2 2063. 41 rooms.

Néa Kalikratia. *Aegeon* (I), tel. 2 1554. 27 apartments.

Néa Moudaniá. *Kouvraki* (I), tel. 2 1292. 21 rooms. Near beach. V.

Restaurant. *To Psari* (M). One of several fish tavernas on the seafront serving delicious *barbounia* (red mullet).

Olympiáda. *Germany* (I), tel. 5 1255. 19 rooms.

Ormýlia. *Sermili* (M), tel. 5 1308/11. 123 rooms. Beach. MC, V.

Ouranópoli. *Eagle's Palace* (E), tel. 2 2747/8. 180 rooms in central block and 15 bungalows. Tastefully furnished and well-run, this is a pleasant hotel, although Ouranópoli itself is unattractive. On beach; pool, tennis, disco. AE, DC, MC. *Xenia Motel* (M), tel. 7 1202. 42 rooms. Beach, tennis. AE, DC. *Xenios Zeus* (I), tel. 7 1274. 20 rooms. Near beach.

Palióuri. *Xenia* (M), tel. 9 2277. 72 bungalows. On beach. AE, DC, MC.

Pórto Carrás. Greece's largest and most comprehensive holiday complex. 2 nightclubs, convention center, cinema theater; restaurants, pools, tennis, golf, marina with all facilities and 10 km. of private beach including 34 coves. *Meliton Beach* (L), tel. 7 1381. 445 rooms. DC, MC, V. *Sithonia Beach* (E), tel. 7 1381. 468 rooms. AE, DC, MC, V. *Village Inn* (E), tel. 7 1381. 85 rooms. Airconditioned; the only beach hotel to remain open Nov. through Mar. DC, MC, V.

Restaurants. *Harry's* (M), on the road from Pórto Carrás to Néos Marmarás. This is an excellent, if expensive, fish taverna, serving good *mydia saganáki* (mussels in spicy sauce). *Zorba* (M). Another taverna with good seafood. In Néos Marmarás, 4 km. (2 miles) from Pórto Carrás, overlooking sea.

Sáni. *Sáni Beach* (E), tel. 3 1231/2. 469 rooms. All sports facilities. V. *Robinson Club* (M), tel. 3 1221/3. 218 bungalows on beach. Pool, tennis, minigolf; wooded grounds; camping site.

Sárti. *Sárti Beach* (M), tel. 4 1450. 21 apartments.

Kalamítsa. *Lucy* (M), tel. 83 2600/5. 217 rooms. Airconditioned; beach, pool, disco. AE, DC.

Kastoriá. *Xenia du Lac* (M), tel. 2 2565. 26 rooms. Old-fashioned and in need of renovation, but this hotel offers a view over lake. *Europa* (I), tel. 2 3826. 36 rooms. V. *Keletron* (I), tel. 2 2676. 21 rooms.

Restaurants. Food is below the already low provincial standard.

Katerini. *Olympion* (I), tel. 2 9892/3. 56 rooms. In town.

Paralia Katerinis. The following are some of the 20 or so Inexpensive hotels on or near the beach. *Alkyon* (I), tel. 6 1613. 34 rooms. *Aktaeon* (I), tel. 6 1424. 36 rooms. *Dion* (I), tel. 6 1506. 15 rooms. *Muse's Beach* (I), tel. 6 1212. 60 rooms. All have restaurants, with the exception of *Dion*.

Kavála. *Egnatia* (M), (tel. 83 5841/5). 38 rooms. Roofgarden. AE, DC, V. *Galaxy* (M), (tel. 22 4521). 149 rooms. AE, DC, MC, V. *Oceanis* (M), (tel. 22 1981). 168 rooms. Airconditioned; roof garden, pool, disco. AE, DC, V. *Tosca Beach* (M), tel. 22 5003. 100 bungalows. Beach, pool. AE. *Esperia* (I), tel. 22 9621. 105 rooms. Airconditioned; 450 meters (500 yards) from beach. Restaurant. AE, V. *Nefeli* (I), tel. 22 7441. 94 rooms. Also about 450 meters from beach. Restaurant. V.

Kilkís. *Evridiki* (I), tel. 2 2304. 44 rooms.

Komotiní. *Orpheus* (M), tel. 2 6701/5. 79 rooms. Airconditioned; roofgarden, disco. AE, DC. *Xenia* (I), tel. 2 2139. 26 rooms. Restaurant. MC, V.

Korinós. *Europa* (I), tel. 4 1382. 17 rooms; 275 meters (300 yards) from beach; tennis, restaurant.

Kozáni. *Aliakmon* (I), tel. 3 6015. 85 rooms. *Helena* (I), tel. 2 6056. 39 rooms. *Xenia* (I), tel. 3 0484. 30 double rooms. Restaurant. DC.

Langadás. *Lido* (I), tel. 2 2653. 18 rooms.

Leptokaryá. *Olympian Bay* (M), tel. 3 1311/5. 228 rooms in central block and bungalows; beach; minigolf. Among some 15 (I)s, near the beach: *Galaxy* (I), tel. 3 1224. 26 rooms. Restaurant. *Matos* (I), tel. 3 1266. 29 rooms.

Litóhoro. *Aphroditi* (M), tel. 8 1415. 26 rooms. *Myrto* (I), tel. 8 1398. 31 rooms.
Pláka (5 km., 3 miles, west). *Olympios Zeus* (M), tel. 2 2115. 100 rooms. Bungalows and camping; tennis, beach. *Leto* (I), tel. 2 2122. 93 rooms. Pool, tennis, disco, beach; restaurant.

Makrygialós. *Achillion* (I), tel. 4 1210. 28 rooms. On beach; restaurant. *Panorama* (I), tel. 41 269. 42 rooms. Restaurant.

Methóni. *Arion* (I), tel. 4 1214. 39 rooms. *Ayannis* (I), tel. 4 1216. 28 rooms. Both with restaurants.

Naoussa. *Vermion* (M), tel. 2 3013. 32 rooms. At foot of Mount Vérmio, next to stream. Restaurant serves good trout; tennis. DC, V. *Hellas* (I), tel. 2 2006. 14 rooms.

Néa Halkidóna. Near Pélla. *Philippos* (I), tel. 2 2125. 32 rooms. Restaurant.

Néa Hilí. *Aphroditi* (I), tel. 2 6165. 20 rooms. Restaurant. *Dionyssos* (I), tel. 2 6845. 33 double rooms. Restaurant.

Néa Iraklitsa. *Blue Bay* (M), tel. 7 1777. 33 airconditioned rooms in central block and bungalows; beach, pool. *Vournelis* (I), tel. 7 1353. 12 rooms. Restaurant.

Néa Péramos. *Plage* (I), tel. 7 1401. 42 rooms. Restaurant; on beach.

Neápoli. *Galini* (I), tel. 2 2329. 35 rooms.

Neí Epiváte (near Thessaloníki airport). *Europa House* (I), tel. 2 2455. 28 rooms. Airconditioned; restaurant; 90 meters (100 yards) from polluted beach.

Oreókastro. *Haris* (I), tel. 69 6174. 29 rooms. Restaurant.

Orestiáda. *Selini* (I), tel. 2 2636. 41 rooms. v.

Peréa. *Xenia Ilios* (M), tel. 2 5551. 76 rooms; beach. *Aegli* (I), tel. 2 2243. 24 rooms. *Lena* (I), tel. 2 2755. 42 rooms. Both with restaurants.

Perivóli. In the Píndos range. *Perdika* (I), tel. 2 4110. 24 rooms.

Platamónas. *Maxim* (M), tel. 4 1305. 73 rooms. High up on the toll road. AE, DC, V. *Platamon Beach* (M), tel. 4 1212. 170 rooms. Half board only; pool, tennis, minigolf. DC. *Alkyonis* (I), tel. 4 1416. 33 rooms. By the sea. *Artemis* (I), tel. 4 1406. 16 rooms. On toll road. *Dias* (I), tel. 4 1267. 24 rooms. On the sea. All with restaurants.

Platanítis. *King Maron Beach* (M), tel. 2 2189. 56 rooms. Restaurant, beach, tennis.

Polýkastro. *Park* (I), tel. 2 2221. 12 rooms.

Ptolemaída. *Kostis* (I), tel. 2 6661. 27 rooms. Restaurant. *Ptolemaeos* (I), tel. 2 6217. 47 rooms. Outside the town.

Séres. *Xenia* (M), tel. 2 2931. 55 rooms. On river. DC. *Galaxy* (I), tel. 23 289. 49 rooms.

Siátista. *Arhontikon* (I), tel. 2 1298. 26 rooms. Disco, restaurant. MC.

Sidirókastro. *Olympic* (I), tel. 2 3811. 42 rooms. V.

Skotiná. *Lefkes* (I), tel. 9 1256. 9 rooms.

Skýdra. *Adonis* (I), tel. 8 9231. 30 rooms.

Souflí. *Orpheus* (I), tel. 2 2305. 18 rooms.

Stavrós. *Aristotelis* (I), tel. 6 1474. 15 rooms. Restaurant. *Athos* (I), tel. 6 1353. 24 double rooms. Several very simple taverns near the sea.

Véria. *Macedonia* (M), tel. 6 6902. 37 rooms. A former clinic and rather spartan, but good restaurant and roofgarden. *Aristidis* (I), tel. 2 6355. 50 rooms. *Polytimi* (I), tel. 6 4902. 32 rooms. *Veria* (I), tel. 2 1424. 62 rooms. Restaurant, pool, tennis, minigolf. Fine view of mountains but near unattractive industrial area. *Veroï* (I), tel. 2 2866. 48 rooms. MC.

Restaurant. *Kostalar* (M), next to waterfall in center of old town. Good grills and oven-cooked dishes are available.

Xánthi. *Motel Natassa* (M), tel. 2 1521. 70 rooms. DC, V. *Nestos* (M), tel. 2 7531. 82 rooms. Airconditioned; disco. AE, DC, V. *Democritus* (I), tel. 2 5111. 40 rooms. Restaurant. DC, V. *Xanthippion* (I), tel. 2 7933. 50 rooms.

CAMPING. The best equipped among some 40 organized campsites, mostly on the coast, are the G.N.T.O. and municipal camping grounds at: *Aktí Thermaïkóu,* Agía Triáda, tel. 51 360; *Aktí Aspróvalta,* tel. 31 249; *Aktí Kryopigí,* tel. 22 321; *Alexandróupoli,* tel. 28 735; *Bátis,* Kavála, tel. 227 151; *Epanomí,* tel. 41 378; *Fanári,* tel. 31 270; *Kálandra,* tel. 41 345; *Ólympos,* Skotiná, tel. 41 487; *Palióuri,* tel. 92 206.

MOUNTAIN REFUGES AND SKI CENTERS. Four on Ólympos as well as on Vérmio, half at road terminals; four on Falakró; two on Pángeo; one on Áskio, Meníkio, Píeria, and Vrondóu. Most open for skiing in winter. Information from *Hellenic Alpine Club,* Karolou Dil 15, Thessaloníki.

The region's biggest ski center is at Séli on Mount Vérmio (alt. 1,400 m., 4,590 ft.), with seven lifts, cafeteria, ski school, and rental service. Slopes for all levels. Contact Séli, tel. 7 1226, for information. Tría Pigádia ski center, near Naoussa (alt. 1,470 m, 4,820 ft.), with two lifts, ski school and rental, has two more difficult slopes. For information, contact Naoussa, tel. 2 8567.

YOUTH HOSTELS. At Agía Triáda and Litóhoro.

GETTING AROUND. By Plane. Thessaloníki can be reached by plane directly from several European cities, including London, Paris, Munich and Amsterdam; from Athens by at least six flights daily (50 min.); from Límnos and Mytilíni once daily; from Corfu, Ioánina, Iráklio, Rhodes, and Sámos at least four times weekly, and Skíathos several times a week. There are three flights daily from Athens to Alexandróupoli (55 min.), two daily to Kavála's international airport at Hrissóupoli (1 hour), once daily to Kastoriá (1 hour, 30 min.) and Kozáni (1 hour, 30 min.).

By Car. If you are entering Greece from the north, the road from Belgrade and Skopje crosses the Yugoslav border at Evzóni, while the road from Bitola crosses the border near Níki. The only road crossing from Bulgaria is at Promahónas. The two main frontier posts on the Turkish border are Kípi at the Évros bridge and north at Kastaniés, opposite Adrianople (Edirne). Thessaloníki lies roughly halfway on the reconstituted *Via Egnatia* between the port of Igoumenítsa in Epirus and the Turkish border, and is the obvious center for excursions, if not in actual mileage at least in time, as progress in the western mountains is necessarily so much slower than in the eastern plains.

By Bus. Thessaloníki is about eight hours by bus from Athens. Daily buses connect not only all towns, but also the outlying villages. The beaches on the Halkidikí peninsula are well served from Thessaloníki. It is advisable, when traveling by provincial buses to buy the ticket the evening before, or at least to go half an hour before departure time.

By Train. The journey from Athens to Thessaloníki takes about six and a half hours on the new express trains. The other, more frequent trains, are considerably slower, taking about eight hours. International trains cross the Yugoslav border at Evzóni and go on to Thessaloníki. From Turkey, the railroad crosses the border at Pýthio. From Thessaloníki there are trains to Flórina and to Alexandróupoli and intermediary stations. On the long distance trains it is essential to get a ticket beforehand (this also bears your seat number).

By Boat. Alexandróupoli, Kavála and Thessaloníki are connected by regular ferries with Límnos and Lésvos; Kavála with Thássos; and Alexandróupoli with Samothraki. Thessaloníki to Dafní, the port of Áthos, takes about eight hours; the frequency of sailings depends on the weather and the season.

THESSALONÍKI

The Byzantine City

Thessaloníki is not very old as towns go in Greece: the 2,300th anniversary was celebrated in 1985. Kassandros, one of Alexander the Great's generals, strengthened his precarious hold on the Macedonian throne by marrying the last surviving member of the ancient royal family, Alexander's step-sister, Thessaloníki. In her honor, he named the town built in the form of an amphitheater at the head of the Thermaïkós Gulf below the Hortiates Mountains, one of the few good harbors on this northern coast.

The origin of its founder was a definite handicap under the succeeding rival Antigonid dynasty, but after the Roman conquest in 168 B.C., it became the capital of the Macedonian province. The building of the Via Egnatia, the Empire's main east–west artery linking Rome and Byzantium, further enhanced the prosperity already assured by the trade route up the Axios Valley into the Balkans.

The historic nucleus of narrow winding lanes, where the picturesque, if flimsy, wooden houses with overhanging balconies are increasingly giving way to utilitarian concrete structures, has been engulfed by similar huge blocks of flats, partly saved from the dreary uniformity of their likes all over the world by neo-Byzantine features in many public buildings, the lavish use of pastel colors, but above all, by the lovely situation.

The population has undergone no less radical changes, first by the exchange of the Turkish minority against Greeks from Asia Minor in 1923, then by the extermination of almost all the 50,000 Sephardic Jews during the German occupation in World War II, so that there are at present only some 1,400 among the almost 1,000,000 inhabitants of Greece's second town.

Owing to the visits of St. Paul, it became an early center of Christianity. The Emperor Galerius, who made it an imperial capital after his victory nearby over the Goths, was responsible for the martyrdom in A.D. 306 of St. Dimítrios, the patron and protector of the city. As the result of a blood-thirsty demonstration during his absence, a later emperor, Theodosius the Great, inflicted upon the town a punishment as stark and horrible as any-thing in its history. The citizens appear to have been great racing enthusi-asts, and so furious were they at the imprisonment of a favorite charioteer for making improper advances to one of the Gothic commander's atten-dants, that they lynched the general, Botheric, and several of his men. It is held by some that this was really an excuse for demonstrating the resent-ment of the people against the Gothic officers and troops. Theodosius car-ried out his brutal revenge with great cunning. The townsfolk were invited to the Hippodrome to attend the Games in his honor. When they were all enclosed, the Gothic troops massacred them by the thousand.

After the loss of Egypt and Syria in the 7th century, Thessaloníki be-came the second city of the Byzantine Empire, not only an important com-mercial but also a spiritual center, sending forth the brothers Cyril and Methodius in the 9th century as the Apostles of the Slavs. A prosperity rare for the age and the region attracted a highly undesirable number of greedy contenders from near and far. Bulgars and Serbs were successfully repulsed, but in 904 a Saracen force managed to enter and plunder the town, making off with thousands of slaves. In 1185 the city was sacked by the Normans, and in 1204 it was made into a feudal kingdom under Marquis Bonifacio of Montferrat, as a consolation prize for having missed the Latin imperial crown of Constantinople. In 1246 it was re-united with the Byzantine Empire, later to be sold to Venice. In 1430 it was to suffer the worst siege of its history led by Murad II, after which it remained under Turkish domination for nearly 500 years.

During all the centuries of Byzantine rule, the building and decorating of numerous churches was pursued vigorously. In its heyday, a wealth of mosaics was produced, succeeded in poorer days by frescos. A period of renewed prosperity accompanied the arrival of 20,000 Jews, exiled from Spain in 1492, whose nucleus of cultured and energetic leaders made vast improvements to the city and its trade. But only a few who survived World War II still speak among themselves in medieval Spanish. Many of the Oriental buildings, including practically all the minarets, were destroyed by the Greeks when they recaptured the city in 1912. Then a great deal more was gutted in 1917 by the worst of the many fires the city has known, and some of the early churches were partially destroyed in the severe earthquake of June 1978.

Yet Thessaloníki offers something from almost every period of its 2,000 and more years of history. The Hellenistic walls were extended by the Ro-mans, who left their own remarkable monuments. Among the many early Christian edifices are the galaxy of Byzantine churches whose beauty of exterior design, or of interior decoration in mosaic or fresco, is the main interest of many visitors, and after which the Macedonian School of By-zantine Art is named. A Venetian tower and some sadly dilapidated Turk-ish mosques and baths remain from subsequent occupations, having sur-vived siege and sack, fire and fighting. The citadel still crowns the hill above.

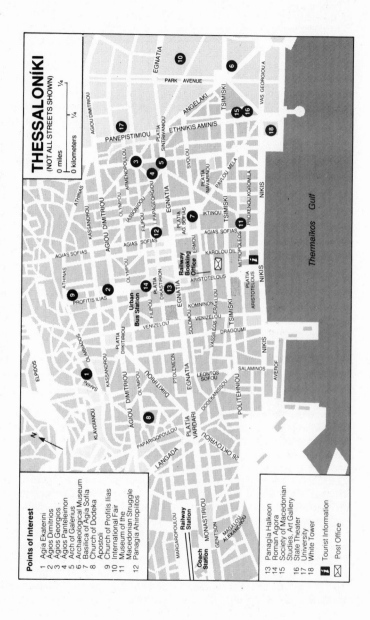

THESSALONÍKI
(NOT ALL STREETS SHOWN)

0 miles ¼
0 kilometers ¼

Points of Interest

1 Agía Ekaterini
2 Agios Dimítrios
3 Agios Georgios
4 Agios Panteleímon
5 Arch of Galerius
6 Archaeological Museum
7 Basilica of Agía Sofía
8 Church of Dodeka
  Apostoli
9 Church of Profitis Ilias
10 International Fair
11 Museum of the
  Macedonian Struggle
12 Panagía Ahiropiitos

13 Panagía Halkeon
14 Roman Agora
15 Society of Macedonian
  Studies, Art Gallery
16 State Theater
17 University
18 White Tower

ℹ Tourist Information
⊠ Post Office

Exploring Thessaloníki

The Thessaloníki bypass connects western with eastern Macedonia, but arrival in the city is fairly simple, not only by the less glamorous successors of the spy-thriller favorite, the Orient Express. The railway station is conveniently situated in Monastiriou which, after crossing Platía Várdari, becomes the Via Egnatía, now as for the last 2,000 years the town's main thoroughfare, lined by a wide choice of moderate and inexpensive hotels. The 21 km. (13 miles) from the junction of the toll motorway from the Yugoslav border to Athens with the road network to western Macedonia lead into Monastiriou, while the motorist from Athens arrives by 26 Oktovríou, from Séres or Kavála by Langada on Platía Várdari. The town terminal of Olympic Airways is situated at the corner of Komninon and Níkis along the sea. Nearby, in Triti Septemvriou, the foundations of Thessaloníki's oldest Christian church were discovered in 1981.

Níkis is not only the most favored spot for the *volta,* the traditional evening stroll, but also the most useful all-purpose waterfront; if you have, Heaven forbid, lost your passport or have to call at your consulate for less dramatic affairs; or are seized by the irrepressible desire to see some of the neo-Byzantine government offices from the inside, the National Tourist Organization, Post Office, Town Hall, all just around various corners; or simply want to enjoy the splendid view over the Thermaïkós Gulf from a sidewalk cafe after indulging in seafood in the adjoining restaurants; Níkis is the answer to the tourist's prayers, including the first dose of sightseeing.

At the eastern end rises the massive circular White Tower, the city's emblem, constructed by Venetian craftsmen probably working for Turkish masters and not for their own Serene Republic during an ephemeral occupation. This bastion, where land and sea walls met till the latter's destruction in 1866, is also known as the Bloody Tower, owing to the massacre of the Janissaries (elite troops, recruited from among forcibly converted Christian boys, who made and unmade sultans for centuries till Sultan Mahmoud II freed himself in 1826 from their somewhat oppressive protection). It is a strange irony of history that the same town where imperial authority over the army was re-established also witnessed the army uprising which led to the deposition of Turkey's last absolute ruler in 1909, while one of the conspiring officers, Kemal Atatürk, brought sultanate and caliphate to an end almost exactly 100 years after the massacre. The interior of the White Tower has been beautifully adapted as a museum.

Across the square is Macedonia's cultural center, the Society of Macedonian Studies with the Art Gallery, the State Theater, the military center and the Officers' Club. In the adjacent public gardens is a marble statue of Crown Prince Konstantine, who led the liberating army on Saint Dimítrios Day (1912) into the town, only a few hours ahead of the Bulgarians. A stone marks the spot nearby, where King George I was assassinated in 1913 while taking his morning stroll, unaccompanied as usual. The murderer was neither Bulgar nor Turk, as might have been expected in the middle of the Balkan Wars, but a Greek lunatic.

Beyond the gardens is the Archaeological Museum, where pride of place is held by the treasures found in the Hellenistic tombs at Derveni in 1961 and the magnificent finds from the 4th-century B.C. Macedonian royal tombs at Vergína, made during the excavations of 1977–78—gold caskets, wreaths and jewelry. Most of the richest items were found in the bigger of the two tombs, believed to be that of Philip II, father of Alexander the Great. The exquisitely delicate, gold oak wreath found in the chamber of the Great Tomb is the most impressive ancient wreath to be found to date. Not to be eclipsed, however, are the exhibits which range from the Geometric Age via the Archaic to the Classic, with many gold and silver objects from 5th-century B.C. tombs in ancient Sindos, now submerged in the industrial zone that pollutes air and sea; sarcophagi, glass vases and mosaic floors were unearthed in Thessaloníki, other important finds come from Ólynthos. The large collection of Roman sculpture from the 1st to the 5th century includes a rare likeness of the 14-year-old Emperor Alexander Severus.

Across the road the pagoda-like Telecommunication Tower (it has a revolving restaurant), even more incongruously far-eastern at night, dominates the extensive grounds of the International Fair. In addition to specialized exhibitions held every month, the ground hosts the General Fair, whose over 3,000 exhibitors from 20 countries attract a million visitors every September. Though started only in 1926, the fair is in fact a revival of the *Dimitria,* a popular annual occurrence attended by many foreign merchants, held at least as early as the 12th century in memory of St. Dimítrios. The cultural part of the *Dimitria,* under its old name, now comprises religious and artistic events in the Byzantine tradition, leading up to the celebration of St. Dimítrios Day, October 26, followed on the 28th by a big military parade before the president of the republic on Greece's second National Day, "Óchi" Day, commemorating the historic "No" to the Italian ultimatum in 1940.

In Vassilíssis Ólgas, running southeast, parallel to the gardens on the seafront of the elegant residential district, large blocks of flats overshadow the sham-Baroque of the Villa Alatini, in 1909 the home of the leading Jewish family and the town's most elegant building, where the deposed Sultan Abdul Hamid II was imprisoned by the Young Turks till he had divulged the whereabouts of his vast private fortune to the revolutionary officers. The Folkloric and Ethnological Museum is housed in the one-time Governor's Residence at No. 68.

The road leading inland from the White Tower, Ethnikís Aminis leads to the well-equipped university campus, the largest in Greece, named after Macedonia's greatest mind, the philosopher Aristotle. The large, well-equipped university town extends over what was till World War II the Jewish cemetery, beyond the intersection with Egnatia in which, to the left, rises the Triumphal Arch of Galerius. Built in A.D. 303, the worn bas-reliefs depict the Emperor's victories over the Persians. The arch spanning the remaining pillars is an unmistakably modern restoration in brick. Not far off the pink wooden house where Kemal Atatürk, the creator of modern Turkey, was born, looks rather forlorn among the uniformly uninspiring modern buildings.

Byzantine Monuments

Thessaloníki is constantly being likened to a museum of Byzantine Art, and as the most interesting churches are fairly well grouped together, it may be found convenient to arrange one's visit in the same way as a museum, chronologically. From the Arch it is a mere 90 meters (100 yards) up to the earliest church, Ágios Géorgios. This large Roman Rotunda, once connected by a gallery to Galerius' long-vanished palace, was intended to serve as the Emperor's mausoleum. His Christian successor Constantine the Great denied such magnificence to the body of the pagan persecutor, and used it as the palace church, the first of its kind in Europe. Theodosius the Great dedicated it to St. George and adorned it with the most splendid 5th-century church mosaics in existence; a striking ring of saints around the dome, set against a unique illustration of contemporary Roman architecture on the glittering golden background that was to become typical of such mosaics. In 1591 the Turks made it into a mosque, adding a minaret which is one of the only two remaining in Thessaloníki. There is also a Dervish's tomb of the early 19th century, besides the 15th-century ones on a lower level. Briefly restored as a Christian church in 1912, the Rotunda is now a museum, providing an unusual setting for occasional concerts of Byzantine and classical music. Unfortunately, it is temporarily closed while belated restoration takes place, following earthquake damage. To the left is Ágios Pantéleimon, another church of the 12th century.

To reach the next church, return to Egnatía. On the junction at your right with Agías Sofías is the Church of the Panagía Ahiropíitos, which means Our Lady Made Without Hands. This triple-naved basilica was built in the 5th century and was probably originally the Church of Agía Paraskeví (Friday), the principal church of the city. It was the first to be turned into a mosque by the Turks as a triumphant gesture and was named Eski Djouma (also meaning Friday). The arches are decorated with patterns in mosaic.

Agías Sofías ascends to Ágiou Dimítriou. On the left is apparently modern Ágios Dimítrios, the city's largest church, originally built in the 5th century, as a paleo-Christian basilica, with five naves. It was partially destroyed by a fire during the celebrations of Ágios Dimítrios in 538 and rebuilt, only to be burnt and again rebuilt in the 7th century. The present building was erected after a fire in 1917. Some of the 8th-century mosaics are still to be seen near the choir, one depicting Ágios Dimítrios as protector of children and another showing him with Leontius (who built the church) and a bishop. Two more show Our Lady and Ágios Sergios. Then there is an interesting painting on the south wall. Also there are some of the original pillars of colored marble with carved capitals. The side-chapel of Ágios Euthémios was built about 1303 in the time of the Emperor Andronicus II, by Michael, his Master of Horse. In the crypt, which is on the site of the martyrdom of Ágios Dimítrios by Galerius, and has recently been excellently restored, is the so-called Baptistry, near the saint's legendary tomb. From here flowed the sweet-smelling and miraculous healing oil which attracted pilgrims and gave Ágios Dimítrios the name *Myróvlitos* (Flowing with Myrrh). The relics of the saint were returned piecemeal from San Lorenzo in Italy in the oecumenical spirit prevailing between the Catholic and Orthodox Churches.

Going back down Agías Sofías it is easy to pick out the Basilica of Agía Sofía (Holy Wisdom) by its large green dome, similar to its namesake in Constantinople. This spacious building (dating from the 8th century) heralds a change in architecture; the basilica, besides being crowned with a dome, shows the first signs of what was to develop into the Greek Cross plan. Converted into a mosque, the mosaics were restored by the Turkish government at the beginning of the century, and in 1912 it became a church again. In spite of bomb damage and redecoration, the 8th and 11th century mosaics are very impressive. Besides the Madonna and Child in the apse, the great work is the Ascension in the cupola, showing Our Lord seated on a rainbow, surrounded by a ring of angels and apostles alternating decoratively with olive trees. Continue on down Agías Sophías, past the Museum of the Macedonian Struggle, dedicated to the fight before the Balkan Wars, to the seafront, turning right towards Aristotélous Square. This square, surrounded by benches and cafe tables under awnings, is the scene of vast political rallies during the run up to elections. Turn away from the sea and walk up Aristotélous into vast central Platía Dikastiríon, in whose upper part the Roman Agora is being excavated. Below stands a picturesque but dilapidated Turkish bath and in the other corner the only surviving medieval Guild church, the graceful *Panagía Halkéon* (Our Lady of the Coppersmiths). This church, built in 1042, is typical of the Byzantine Greek cross. Note the frescos of the Apocalypse and Last Supper; also the tomb of Christoforus, the founder.

The next two churches, also in the Greek Cross shape, date from the 13th and early 14th centuries and are close together. At Platía Vardári, turn right for the church of Dodeka Apostoli (the Twelve Apostles), with its ornamental brickwork and its high dome surrounded by four smaller ones. There are interesting frescos inside. Agía Ekaterini, right up Sahini, is very similar in shape and of a slightly earlier date. Unless you have someone to guide you to Profítis Ilías Church (which is quite close), it is easier to go down to Kassándrou, continue left till above Ágios Dimítrios Cathedral, then go left up Profítis Ilías. This 14th-century church, also domed, has the trefoil or triple-shell feature often seen on Mount Áthos. The buttresses were added when it became a mosque.

It is interesting to walk around the remains of the city walls. Only the northern one is still intact and it gives opportunities for wonderful views. It is best reached by Venizélou, which continues as Dragoúmi. On the way up Venizélou, you may notice the old Turkish baths with their cluster of domes, on the corner of what is now the Bezestini Market, while at the junction with Via Egnatia is an old mosque. A few of the old gates and towers (a short distance apart) are still standing, such as the 4th-century Eski-Delik Gate and the 14th-century Manuel Paleologos Tower. Near the junction with the Citadel Wall is a rock on which perches the monastery of Vlatádon. This is traditionally the place where St. Paul addressed the Thessalonians. Its small 14th-century church is cruciform, dwarfed by the Neo-Byzantine Institute of Patriarchal Studies. Below its terrace the whole town spreads down to the sea, beyond which are the lofty peaks of Ólympos and Óssa.

Still higher up rise the ramparts of the *Eptapýrgon* (Castle of the Seven Towers), that has been restored as a national monument and is now a prison. The city walls descend past a big tower to the university city, but it is not possible to go down that way. Below the monastery of Vlatádon, with its quiet, tree-shaded courtyard, 14th-century Óssios Davíd incorporates a 6th-century apse with a Christ mosaic.

PRACTICAL INFORMATION FOR THESSALONÍKI

WHEN TO COME. Spring and early fall are the best seasons, but the International Fair, lasting two weeks in September, attracts such large crowds that accommodations are difficult. Summer can be stifling, while late autumnal rains do not enhance the appearance of a city designed for sunshine, and in winter icy winds sweep down the Axios valley from the Balkans.

TOURIST OFFICE. The G.N.T.O. office is at Platía Aristotelous 8 (tel. 27 1888). The Tourist Police are at Egnatía 10 (tel. 52 2821).

SPECIAL EVENTS. March. Fur Fair. **April/May.** International Music Days, with performances of Greek and foreign compositions and artists. **September.** International Fair, International Film Festival and Greek Film Festival. **October.** *Dimitria,* a Festival of Music and Drama with a Byzantine slant. **November.** Jewelry Fair.

HOTELS. Thessaloníki is well equipped with hotels in all price ranges, but it is essential to book ahead during the International Fair in September when hotel prices are generally higher and a hotel may, for a short period, be in a higher price category than normally.

Deluxe

Makedonia Palace, Megalou Alexandrou (tel. 83 7520/10). 287 rooms, 15 suites. In quiet residential district with fine view over the bay, plus roofgarden, restaurants and garage. Luxurious but anonymous. AE, DC, MC, V.

Expensive

Capitol, Monastiriou 8 (tel. 51 6221/10). 194 rooms, 7 suites. Near the rail station; garage. AE, DC.

Electra Palace, Platía Aristotélous 5 (tel. 23 2221/30). 158 rooms, 7 suites. Comfortable and central. AE, DC, MC, V.

Nepheli, at Panorama, ten km. (six miles) away (tel. 94 2002). 70 rooms. Partially airconditioned; disco. Superb view over Thessaloniki to the sea.

Moderate

Astoria, Tsimiski 20 (tel. 52 7121/5). 88 rooms. Garage and roofgarden. AE, DC, MC.

Capsis, Monastiriou 28 (tel. 52 1421/10). 428 rooms. Roofgarden, pool, nightclub, garage; near rail station. Popular with tour groups. AE, DC, MC, V.

El Greco, Egnatia 22 (tel. 52 0620/10). 90 rooms. AE, DC, V.

Metropolitan, Vassilíssis Olgas 65 (tel. 82 4221/8). 118 rooms. Only public rooms are airconditioned. DC.

Olympia, Olympou 65 (tel. 23 5421/5). 111 rooms.

Pefka, also at Panorama (tel. 94 1153). 50 rooms. No airconditioning.

Queen Olga, Vassilissis Olgas 44 (tel. 82 4621/30). 148 rooms. Garage. AE, DC, MC, V.

Rotonda, Monastiriou 97 (tel. 51 7121/3). 79 rooms. Only public rooms are airconditioned. Roofgarden. MC.

Victoria, Langada 13 (tel. 52 2421/5). 68 rooms. Only public rooms are airconditioned. AE, DC, MC, V.

Inexpensive

All the following hotels are airconditioned, unless otherwise stated.

A.B.C., Angelaki 41 (tel. 26 5421/5). 112 rooms. Only public rooms are airconditioned. This hotel is located at the intersection of several busy streets; rooms overlooking traffic are very noisy. DC, MC, V.

Amalia, Ermou 33 (tel. 26 8321/5). 66 rooms.

Esperia, Olympou 58 (tel. 26 9321/5). 70 rooms. DC. Good value.

Park, Ionos Dragoumi 81 (tel. 52 4121/4). 56 rooms.

Pella, Ionos Dragoumi 61 (tel. 52 4221). 79 rooms.

Philippion, at Asvestohori, three km. (two miles) out in the hills (tel. 20 3320/4). 92 rooms. Only public rooms are airconditioned; pool, tennis, minigolf, nightclub. AE, DC, V.

Telioni, Agiou Dimitriou 16 (tel. 52 7825/6). 63 rooms. Not airconditioned; restaurant.

Vergina, Monastiriou 19 (tel. 51 6021). 133 rooms. Restaurant. DC.

Y.W.C.A. Hostel, Agias Sofias 11 (tel. 27 6144). Summer only.

RESTAURANTS. These are on the same level as those in Athens, if less varied, though the hotel dining rooms tend to be uniformly uninteresting. Numerous cafe/pastry shops line the waterfront. For inexpensive eating, look for *donér kebáb* turning on a spit outside any Psistariá.

Expensive

Capsis Piper Roofgarden, Capsis Hotel, Monastiriou 28 (tel. 52 1421/9). Lively orchestra. AE, DC.

Cyprus Corner, Komninon 16 Panorama (tel. 94 1220). Sophisticated restaurant in smart hill-top suburb. Pianist and singer. AE, DC, V.

Estiatorio, Kapodistriou 5 (tel. 53 2428). French cuisine is served in this bistro-style restaurant.

Grill House, Electra Palace Hotel, Platía Aristotelous 5 (tel. 23 2221/9). Serves excellent meat dishes. DC.

Nautical Club, Sophouli 82 (tel. 42 9945). Open to the public in spite of the name. A little way out, but worth the trouble.

Riva, Proxenou Koromila 10 (tel. 23 6561). With light music. DC.

Roof Garden, Makedonia Palace, Megalou Alexandrou (tel. 83 7520/9). Splendid view, but bland international food.

Tiffany's, Iktinou 3 (tel. 27 4022). Popular with businessmen at lunchtimes, this restaurant offers a long and varied menu.

Votsalo, Proxenou Koromila 17 (tel. 27 3557).

Moderate

Archipelagos, Kanari (tel. 43 5800). At Aretsóu. Good quality Greek food.

Krikelas, Gramou Vitsi 32 (tel. 41 4690). Pleasant tavern with guitar music; evenings only. AE, DC.

Olympos-Naoussa, Níkis15 (tel. 27 5715). Good waterfront restaurant. For *mídia tiganitá* (fried mussels), best washed down with white Macedonian *Korona* wine.

Paradisos, Plastira (tel. 43 6300). At Aretsóu. Specializes in tasty seafood. DC.

Stratis, Níkis 19 (tel. 23 4782). Waterfront restaurant also serving *mídia tiganitá.* AE, DC, MC, V.

Ta Delfinakia, Plastira (tel. 43 0380). At Aretsou. Seafood.

Ta Nissia, Proxenou Koromila 13 (tel. 28 5991). Tavern with pleasant atmosphere and excellent *mezedes;* open evenings only. DC.

Tottis, Platia Aristotelous 3 (tel. 27 5960) Italian-style food is served in this plush dining room, where fileto in walnut and cream sauce is a specialty. They also have an *ouzeri (a bar with snacks).* AE, DC, V.

Inexpensive

Kefallinia, Botsi 5 (phone reservations not accepted). Tavern for rough but tasty food and wine.

Klimatariá, Pavlou Mela 10 (tel. 27 7854). Casual grill *(psistario).*

Soutzoukakia, Venizélou 8 (tel. 27 7694). This old-established restaurant, with no less than 7 white-jacketed waiters, specializes in tasty meatballs.

Ta Koumbarakia, Egnatia 140 (no phone). Grills, seafood, and tasty salads are served at this restaurant, which is set off from busy Egnatía behind the small Church of the Transfiguration.

NIGHTLIFE. Thessaloniki has a very lively nightlife with something to suit most tastes. Recently, bars and pubs have sprung up all over the town, with the most popular strung out along the seafront and in the streets surrounding the White Tower. Among the quieter, more upmarket **wine bars** and **piano bars** are *Mandragore,* Mitropóleos 98, an elegant wine-and-mezedes bar; *Velerefondis,* Vass. Olgas 133, in a converted neoclassical mansion with wooden floorboards, shabbily smart; *De Facto,* Pávlou Melá 17, small and trendy and *Erodos,* Pávlou Melá 21, a basement bar with a grand piano and local modern art exhibitions. Among the many **discos** are *Golden Gate,* Aristotélous 11, and *UFO,* Egnatia 119, and several lively discos beyond the airport and at Aretsóu. All are moderate in price.

SHOPPING. The main shopping street is Tsimiski, and you should be able to find everything and anything you need here, and in the surrounding streets. There are one or two good department stores as well as antique shops, leather shops (leather is perhaps one of the very best things to be had in Greece, and the leather goods available can make excellent souvenirs), clothes shops, pharmacists and shoe shops (these are also very good value in Greece). Shoe shops particularly worth looking at are *Petridis,* Tsimiskí 40, *Forum,* Tsimiskí 31 and, for more fashionable styles, *Moccassino,* Tsimiskí 58, on the corner of Agías Sofías.

Other shopping streets include Mitropóleos, parallel to Tsimiski, with more expensive and exclusive shops, Agías Sofías with its younger, more fashionable boutiques, Egnatía, Ermou and Venizélou.

Shops selling hand-painted icons are mostly spread out along Egnatía, while good-value jewelry shops can be found along Venizélou and Egnatía (traditional styles in gold) and Navarínou (more modern, bold designs in silver).

Molho, Tsimiskí 10, has the city's largest stock of English-language magazines and books, including fiction, travel guides, art, and architecture and has a helpful, knowledgeable staff. *Malliaris,* Aristotélous 9, is another bookshop with English-language books.

GETTING AROUND. Information on how to reach Thessaloníki is under *Practical Information for Macedonia and Thrace.*

By Bus. The terminal for most overland buses is at the railway station; for the Halkidikí at the opposite end of town, at the corner of Egnatía and Karakassi. The urban bus terminal is at Platía Dikastiríon.

By Taxi. Taxis are blue and white.

By Boat. The east coast of the gulf is studded with small resorts and fishing villages with facilities for bathing and for meals. Many can be reached by boat from the White Tower as well as by bus. The beach of the Aretsóu suburb is closed because of pollution, so to have a swim it is necessary to cross the head of the gulf to Peréa, Néa Epiváte or Agía Triáda, about 26 km. (16 miles) by road or 11 km. (seven miles) by sea. Néa Mihaniona is 29 km. (18 miles) by road and 21 km. (13 miles) by sea.

On Foot. The main sites are all within easy walking distance. An archeological walk is mapped out at the White Tower. A popular excursion is to Panórama, some ten km. (six miles) away, on the slopes of Mount Hortiatis.

USEFUL ADDRESSES. Consulates. *American Consulate,* Níkis 59 (tel. 26 6121); *British Consulate,* Venizélou 8 (tel. 27 8006).

Airlines. *Olympic Airways,* Komninon 1 (tel. 26 0121); *British Airways,* Níkis 13 (tel. 23 8326); *Lufthansa,* Níkis 3 (tel. 23 5722).

Travel Agencies. For flights, hotels, and tours: *Doucas Tours,* Venizélou 8 (tel. 26 9984); *Oceanic World,* Níkis 21 (tel. 26 5400); *Wagons-Lits Tourisme,* Tsimiskí 21 (tel. 23 6293). For specialty tours (botanical, ornithological, etc.): *Charioteer Travel,* Agías Sophías 10 (tel. 28 4373).

Car Hire. *Avis,* Airport and Nikis 3; *Hellascars,* Venizelou 8; *Hertz,* Airport and Venizelou 4.

Touring. *Automobile and Touring Club of Greece,* Vassilíssis Olgas 228 (tel. 42 6386).

Post Office. Tsimiskí 45. *Telegraph Office,* Heraklion 56.

HOLY MOUNT ÁTHOS

A Visit to the Monks' Republic

Byzantine hierarchic and hieratic tradition has continued in splendid immutability on the 339 square km. (131 square miles) peninsula below the Holy Mountain of Áthos. For more than 1,000 years generation after generation of monks have dedicated at least one third of every 24 hours to the exacting service of the Eastern Church, which does not prevent them from retaining an absorbing interest in earthly matters.

Perhaps the greatest resemblance to paradise lies in the difficulty of entering the monks' republic. Access is only through Dafní, the mountain's port, by an occasional boat from Thessaloníki; or, more usually, first by road across the mountainous Halkidikí peninsula, 143 km. (89 miles) to Ierissós, a pleasant fishing village on an excellent beach. Then 24 more km. (15 miles) across the gently undulating narrow neck of the Áthos promontory, near the canal Xerxes cut in 480 B.C. to avoid the disaster his predecessor's fleet suffered off the stormy cape, and you reach Ouranópoli. In fair weather a motorboat leaves every morning for Dafní.

Non-Orthodox laymen are only allowed overnight on Mount Áthos when they can prove religious or scientific reasons. Their stay is limited to four days. Foreign visitors require a letter of introduction from their respective consulates to the Greek Ministry of Foreign Affairs in Athens, or the Ministry of Northern Greece in Thessaloníki, which then issue another letter to the Port Authorities of Ierissós and Ouranópoli, responsible for administering not more than ten permits per day. No women or children are allowed to visit Mount Áthos under any circumstances, and it should be noted that all regulations regarding visits to Mount Áthos are very strictly observed.

Áthos is organized on the lines of a theocratic republic, ruled by the Holy Community in Kariés, consisting of one representative from each of the 20 monasteries since 1920 under the benevolent supervision of a Greek governor. Though the number of monks has more than doubled from an all-time low in the 1970s to almost 2,000, with a concomitant lowering of the average age to a mere 40 years, it is still a dramatic decline from the 15th century, when the mountain rang with the prayers of 1,000 monks in each of 40 monasteries, not to count the host of hermits. Clever diplomacy succeeded in maintaining a large degree of autonomy and prosperity under Turkish rule, one of the sultans, Selim I, even paying a state visit. The lack of novices is a more serious problem than the infidels ever were, although in the last year or so there seems to have been an increase in interest and a corresponding increase in intake.

After Ouranópoli the pine-clad cliffs rise steeply from the sea. The first *skiti,* a community of semi-independent monks, is an agglomeration of surprisingly large houses, founded in the period of Russian preponderance in the 19th century. The czarist government cultivated this foothold in the Mediterranean, claiming that the Holy Mountain belonged to the whole of Orthodox Christianity. The revolution of 1917 put an end to the influx of Russian monks, until suddenly in 1958 the Patriarch of Moscow expressed a desire to replenish the dwindling contingent of his compatriots. The Greek government has long kept a wary eye on this unexpected religious zeal and only recently again admitted novices from Eastern Europe, as under the constitution every monk becomes a Greek citizen.

Further along the coast vast buildings of every conceivable architecture are separated by the dense forest coming down to the sea: impressive Dohiaríou, Zenophónta, with 16th-century frescos, and the Russian Agíou Panteleímona, where only a few old men remain of the former 1,500.

Nine Centuries without Women

For the 1,000-year celebrations in 1963 a road was constructed from Dafní to Kariés, and an incongruous bus shambles through the thickets of pink and white oleanders, while the bare triangular peak of Áthos towers above the tall trees. The guest-wing of Xiropotámou, on a hill overlooking the sea, has fallen to one of those periodical fires that are inseparable from wood stoves and candles; the valuable library suffered no loss. Placid bulls graze on lush meadows, but of course no cows, in deference to the edict of the Emperor Constantine IX in 1060, forbidding access: "To any woman, any female, to any eunuch, to any smooth Ávisage." The part excluding females is still strictly enforced, though it is no longer necessary to grow a beard. In 1976, the government showed an admirable sense of tradition, if little understanding for the eccentricities of modern life, by upholding this discriminatory regulation.

Stately buildings dot a well-watered valley, which slopes, lush and green, down to the sea. At Kariés, man has helped nature to perfect a Greek Shangri-la.

The 10th-century Church of the Protation is decorated with exquisite frescos by Panselinos, the leading representative of the Macedonian school of painting. The palace of the Holy Community faces the Athonian Academy, where the peasant monks receive a high-school education. The governor's pleasant residence is on the way to Agíou Andréa, which, like all Russian foundations on Áthos, relies more on size than artistic merit; damaged in a recent fire, it is now deserted. The few shops and the stuffy inn are run by monks, but it is preferable to stay at the Koutloumousíou Monastery, in the midst of lovely gardens. The building, badly damaged by fire in 1980, is the usual large rectangle, with wooden balconies along the upper floors. In the courtyard the domed cruciform church faces the refectory.

There are several monasteries on the west coast, south of Dafní, of which Símona Pétras, perched high on a cliff, spectacularly evokes Tibet. Perhaps the thrill of very real physical danger contributed to making it a center of Áthos' spiritual revival. On rounding the cape where the Persian fleet was wrecked, the wooded slopes give way to barren rocks rising steeply to the 10,730-meter (6,670 ft.) high summit, crowned by a chapel. In caves precariously connected with the world by ropes and ladders dwell hermits in all the primitive fervor of the early Christians. Yet, as a concession to Greek sociability, they usually live in pairs.

The community of monks at Kapsokalívia earn their livelihood by making rosaries, woodcarving and a variety of handicrafts, unfortunately less artistic than the pretty village itself.

The Oldest Monastery—Lavra

Megístis Lávras, Great Lavra, the oldest, richest and most powerful monastery, is not far off. Founded in the year 963 by St. Athanasius with the help of the Emperor Nikephorus Phocas, Lávras alone has never suffered from fire and retains its original aspect of a large, fortified hilltop village, the perfect Byzantine architecture not marred by later additions.

This vision of Byzantium becomes all the more real on the numerous feast days, when the abbot receives important visitors riding up on mules, with the immutable pomp and ceremony his predecessors must have shown to the imperial dignitaries of old. In late 1989, a piece of the True Cross, one of the monastery's most treasured possessions, was stolen by a visitor (an ex-monk, as it happens) and, as a result, the monks may be particularly cautious when admitting visitors for quite a while to come. White-bearded monks and boy novices prostrate themselves during the all-night service in the 1,000 year old church, under the eyes of the abbot seated in hieratic immobility on a gilded throne. The liturgy ends with a solemn procession at dawn, moving to the refectory, where clergy and pilgrims eat in silence at 1,000-year-old marble tables, under the menacing frescos of the Last Judgment, while a monk reads from the lives of the martyrs.

Ivíron, higher up the eastern coast, is another of those improbable immense constructions surrounded by virgin forest. Here the monastic peace is for once unbroken, as the persistent beating of an oak-board, the call to prayers, does not penetrate the thick walls of the deep-blue guest room.

Vatopedíou Monastery

That champion of progress comes suddenly and dramatically into sight, behind a promontory crowned by the ruins of the original Athonian Academy, later transferred by an exiled patriarch to Kariés. The gaunt ruin among olive trees, the tranquil bay with white houses submerged by creepers and hibiscus, compose the perfect romantic landscape down to the last detail of the mill's giant waterwheel. The stupendous rectangle of Vatopedíou stands on a slight eminence, the styles ranging from Byzantine to Renaissance, connected by incongruous wooden balconies. Besides the refectory and a fountain there are no less than three churches in the vast courtyard, dominated by a massive medieval tower. Yet somehow this incredible mixture achieves a serene harmony.

According to legend the Boy-Emperor Arcadius was traveling to Constantinople in A.D. 395, when a huge wave swept him overboard. He was mourned as lost, until hermits found him sleeping under a mulberry tree. In gratitude Arcadius later founded a monastery where he had been washed ashore, and named it Vatopédi, the Greek for mulberry and child. A pretty tale, but though several monasteries cherish their Roman origin, history does not bear them out.

The grim walls of Esphigmenou rising straight from the sea enclose some charmingly naive rustic wall paintings. A road, marvelous to relate—bearing the mark of a tractor donated by the Yugoslav faithful—leads inland to Hiliandaríou, founded in 1197 and richly endowed by successive Serbian princes. The church, an exceptionally good example of the Athonian triple style, displays its delicate pattern of colored bricks without the dark-red coating which protects and disfigures many architectural gems nearer the sea.

In spite of a multitude of ugly wires, the more congenial oil lamps and candles still light the long vigils, as another gift, an electrical installation, only rarely works. Or perhaps they considered it tactless to use this gift for the illumination of the late King Peter's numerous pictures.

Tucked away behind the library are the most beautiful icons on Áthos: a moving 13th-century Madonna and four large panels depicting the archangels, which testify to the beginning of the Renaissance in the studios of the 14th-century Constantinople. A portable mosaic of a rosy-cheeked Virgin is interesting rather than beautiful, and there is also a three-handed Virgin, nobody quite knows why.

One wing of Bulgarian Zográfou, in the center of the promontory, was burnt down in 1976. The remaining monasteries are no less richly endowed by nature and pious princes. But it is hardly possible to visit them all during one stay, without suffering from a surfeit of monastic Árt and especially of monastic food and beds. They may better be left for another dreamlike return in time, while the relative comfort of Ierissós is only five hours by boat from Esfigménou.

AEGEAN ISLAND MAGIC

Heart of the Greek World

by
ROBERT LIDDELL

*Robert Liddell is an authority on the eastern Mediterranean and author
of these chapters on the Aegean Islands. He has written travel books about
the eastern Mediterranean, including* Aegean Greece, Byzantium and Istanbul, The Thracian Ships, *as well as biographies of several English and
Greek writers.*

In mountainous Greece, it is the land that separates and the sea that divides. The 1,425 islands thickly scattered over the Aegean Sea have formed
stepping stones between East and West since the dawn of history. Only
130 have ever been inhabited, but their fishermen evolved into Europe's—
perhaps the world's—first society of seafarers who added art to navigation
and commerce. For 5,000 years the distinctive civilization of the Aegean
islands has been the envy of the three surrounding continents, fully justify-
ing Lord Byron's enthusiasm:

> The isles of Greece, the isles of Greece,
> Where grew the arts of war and peace.
> Where burning Sappho loved and sung,
> Where Delos rose, and Phoebus sprung.

Though most visitors now come for the sun and sea, few fail to respond to the age-old romantic associations of the archipelago, the appeal of great and varied beauty, to the exquisite outlines and superb colors of rock and sea. In this sea of many moods, the islands are sometimes grouped round a well-defined center, as the Cyclades are round Delos; they are sometimes dominated by the largest, as the Dodecanese are by Rhodes; simply form an archipelago with no bond except proximity, as the Spórades do; or, like Euboea or Sámos, lie so close to the mainland as to be, at least geographically, part of Europe or Asia; or, like Crete, lie in splendid isolation, equidistant from three continents.

Outstanding among the 39 Cyclades that form a rough circle—*kyklos* in Greek—round sacred Delos is Thíra, a vision of brilliant white houses perched precariously on the lip of a not-quite-extinct volcano. Mýkonos is a household word among more sophisticated vacationers, Náxos and Páros are appreciated by connoisseurs, while a few, like Folégandros, have preserved their age-old way of life.

Rhodes is the touristic capital of the Aegean, rightly so as its natural advantages have been enhanced by antique remains and medieval towns, by numerous hotels along excellent beaches. A good second in the Dodecanese is Kos, equally favored by nature and man.

The large eastern islands are proudly individualistic. Híos claims Homer, features a splendid Byzantine monastery, and in the highly original mastic villages produces a tasty gum and liqueur. No other Lesbian has equalled the fame of 6th-century B.C. Sappho; today Lésbos is a fertile island dotted with Genoese castles. Sámos, 19th-century capital of Sámos, is a pleasing introduction to delightful Pythagório, named after its greatest son, the 6th-century B.C. mathematician-philosopher Pythagoras.

Crete produced Europe's oldest fully-matured civilization and the world's first naval empire. Greece's biggest island accommodates the tourist crowds on its splendid beaches, separated by three tall mountain ranges. Here history is magnificently illustrated from the Minoans in 3,000 B.C. to union with Greece in 1913.

History and geography have created a widely different architecture. Medieval Rhodes is Gothic, the work of crusading knights; Venetian influence can be felt in Náxos and Thíra. Híos, Lésbos and Sámos have adopted Turkish features but the most widespread is the cubistic Cycladean style—which extends to the Spórades and the Dodecanese—with its characteristic houses and churches, all whitewashed. Nearly all the present port-capitals, often on antique sites, bear the name of the island, while the medieval inland capitals, now mostly insignificant villages or even totally abandoned, are with few exceptions called Hóra (the Place).

The main attractions on the islands are Classical antiquities, medieval monuments and some charming towns, scenery and beaches. Windmills have been restored throughout the Cyclades, on Mýkonos some actually work. One of the few welcome touches of modernity is the increasing use of solar energy on the remoter islands.

Masters of the Aegean

According to ancient legend and modern science, the Aegean islands are the tops of drowned mountains rising from the submerged land bridge between Europe and Asia. But mythology is silent on the means of propulsion by which King Aegeus—driven to suicide by the thoughtlessness of his son Theseus—flung himself from the Athens Acropolis eight km. (five miles) inland into the sea which has borne his name ever since. In about 1450 B.C. a tremendous volcanic eruption shattered Thíra and the Minoan empire. By then the primitive fishing communities had developed into a society of seafarers, most remaining Aoelian or Ionian, others being occupied by the Dorians during the Dark Ages.

When history began in earnest, the Asian offshore islands equalled the Greek cities on the mainland shore opposite in culture and trade, and maintained their superiority over their poorer European mainland cousins well into the 6th century B.C. Commercial decline merely shifted pre-eminence from the east to the center as religion proved a lucrative substitute. With the consolidation of the male Olympians' position, Apollo's birthplace—Delos—became the heart of the Ionian world, if not of the Greek. For its protection, the Cyclades formed an Amphyctyony, an alliance of the islands surrounding Delos, which more or less fulfilled its purpose. But this embryo United Nations failed to prevent war. After the briefest of Persian interludes, the Athenians used the prestige of Delos to impose their autocratic rule on the entire Aegean in the guise of the Delian League.

Not for long: independence meant war, which even Alexander the Great could not end. His successors gained and lost islands with remarkable speed, until the Ptolemies gained superiority as far north as Samothrace. Rhodes had its century of glory, Delos reverted from religion to commerce, while piracy flourished through most of the Pax Romana. The Byzantines had to relinquish mastery of the sea, first to the Arabs, then to the Italian maritime republics. To the Venetians "The Archipelago" was a potential military strongpoint or hostile base along their main shipping lanes. Mastery of the Aegean was the reason for the Doge's unscrupulous diversion of the Fourth Crusade against the Byzantines in 1203. The Most Serene Republic never lived up to Wordsworth's Romantic view:

> Once did she hold the gorgeous East in fee
> and was the safeguard of the West. . . .

But she imposed a lasting overlordship on the two biggest islands, Crete and Euboea, as well as on the Cyclades. Hated by the islanders for their religion and their part in the destruction of Byzantium, the Venetians derived small revenues from their possessions, but spent heavily on their preservation for over five centuries.

In 1205 the Cyclades were put up for privatization: any Venetian citizen might occupy an island under the sovereignty of the Republic. The first to grasp the opportunity was a nephew of the Doge, Marco Sanudo, who seized the Cyclades as Duke of the Archipelago. In theory the Cyclades were a fief of the Latin Empire, though in practice they were dependent on Venice and the Venetian dialect of Italian became the official language. Sanudo and his successors resided on Náxos, with minor islands allotted as sub-fiefs to influential Venetian families. Distant Kýthira fell to Marco Venier on the surprisingly pagan justification that his name denoted descent from the goddess Venus, who rose from the sea near that island.

Venice's supervision, though stern, often failed to restrain the bloody feuds of the tumultuous princelings. Aegean suzerainty must sometimes have seemed more trouble than it was worth. Duke Niccolo III actually attempted to appropriate Euboea, but was conveniently murdered by

Francesco Crespi, who was recognized as Francesco I by the grateful Serene Republic. At the end of the 15th century Giovanni III encouraged the pirates, taxed his subjects into misery and provoked the Turks, so that the Archbishop of Náxos appealed for his removal. Venice was saved the trouble by the Duke's assassination. Francesco III, the Mad Duke of the Archipelago, stabbed his wife, tried to murder his son and assaulted his aunt, the Lady of Nio, before he was whisked away to Crete. In 1564 the Duchy was bought by a Jewish financier, Joseph Nasi, who acknowledged the Sultan's dominance. But it was not until 1715 that the banner of St. Mark was lowered from the last island fortress, Exombourgo on Tínos.

The ineffective rule of the Turks was, on the whole, less hard on the islanders, until their prominent part in the War of Independence led to sanguinary reprisals. The struggle against foreign occupation came to an end only in 1948 with the liberation of the Dodecanese.

PRACTICAL INFORMATION FOR THE AEGEAN

WHEN TO COME. Crete and Rhodes strive for winter tourism, but on the whole, May to October is the season for the islands, though a fine April or a mellow November can be pleasant for a visit. Most of the island hotels open at Orthodox Easter (whenever that happens to fall), though outdoor restaurants or taverns hardly get going until June even if there is an early heat-wave. Greek families generally take their holidays between July 15 and late August, and the islands are therefore emptier and pleasanter before and after those dates, and there is more room on the boats. The Cyclades should be avoided round August 15 (Assumption of the Virgin) when some boats are diverted to take pilgrims to Tínos or Páros and the rest are packed. August is also the season of the *meltémi* (the prevailing north summer wind), and the sea is very rough. Ships returning to Piraeus are very crowded in the second half of August, and plane bookings are almost impossible to obtain.

GETTING AROUND. By Plane. Several islands have international airports which are served by charter flights, and most holidaymakers from abroad will arrive at these. Otherwise, the starting point is likely to be Athens from which there are several flights a day to most of the islands. From April through October there are regular flights at least once daily from Thessaloníki to Mytilíni and Rhodes. There are also many inter-island connections, especially with Mýkonos and Rhodes, and including Rhodes–Crete. Helicopters fly from the bigger islands to the smaller ones, at least in summer. Thus this unique island world has become easily accessible, which makes it unlikely that it will remain unique much longer.

Two standard excursions for those with little time to spare are: a flight to Rhodes, most popular of the Aegean islands, enabling one to see a great deal of the archipelago from the air en route; or a flight to Mýkonos and a visit to Delos, returning to Athens all within 27 hours.

By Car. Cars and motorcycles can be hired on all the bigger islands. On the smaller islands there is often only one road: from the port to the *Chora* (island capital).

By Boat. The starting point for island trips is likely to be Piraeus, Rafína, or Lavrion. From Zea, Piraeus, there are hydrofoils to the nearby Saronic islands, and also from Ágios Konstantínos and Volos to the Sporádes. Sea communication, often by hydrofoil, within each island group is easy, but is less easy between groups (sometimes making it necessary to return to Piraeus) although sailings are becoming more frequent in summer such as between Crete and Rhodes, Crete and the Cyclades. Double bookings still occur, and in summer it is essential to book in advance, especially for the return.

Greek island boats are a law unto themselves. The schedules warn that timings are subject to alterations without notice, which, in the case of inter-island boats, is the understatement of the century, so check with a local travel agent, especially for remoter islands.

To encourage visits to the remoter islands, third class passage is free from Rhodes to the lesser Dodacanese, as well as between some of the Cyclades, during April and May, September and October; all summer between Rhodes and Kastelórizo. Local *caiques* should be sternly refused except by the hardiest sailors.

By far the most comfortable, but also fairly expensive, way to explore the Aegean is on one of the numerous cruise ships, some of which are up to the highest standards.

A visitor who has time only for a day trip can take the hydrofoil from the Zéa Marína, Piraeus, for Aegina (35 minutes), take a taxi or bus to the temple, bathe at Agía Marína, and be back in Athens that night. Another hydrofoil leaves in the morning for Póros (1 hr. 5 min.) and Ýdra (1 hr. 40 min.), returning to Athens in the evening. There are, moreover, organized daily excursions to the offshore islands.

HOTELS AND RESTAURANTS. Despite the great number of hotels and bungalows which have opened in recent years, it is necessary to book well in advance for July and August. Deluxe and Expensive hotels are air-conditioned unless otherwise stated. Almost all the beach hotels close from November through March, but in the towns, especially on Crete, Rhodes, and at Halkída, some remain open all year. Villas are for rent in the larger resorts, but being expensive and modern does not necessarily mean that plumbing, electricity and other amenities work. They should all be tried *before* renting; similarly in the numerous furnished flats. The private rooms available are unpretentious, clean, inexpensive, but often very noisy. Again, check first, especially the number and age of the family's children.

All Deluxe, Expensive and Moderate hotels in our lists have restaurants unless otherwise stated. Inexpensive hotels have restaurants only when indicated, but they are uniformly uninspiring and sadly neglect seafood. If that's what you're after, walk along the seafront taverns guided by your eyes (and nose). Fish will be brought out for your inspection and you can go into the kitchens and look into the pots with no obligation. With luck and judgment, you shouldn't fare badly as a rule. But generally there are no restaurants that deserve special praise and only a very few could be singled out.

THE EUROPEAN OFFSHORE

ISLANDS

Euboea and the Argo-Saronikós

The five islands situated in the Saronikós Gulf and off the shores of the Argolid are the closest islands to Athens, and are easily accessible by frequent hydrofoils and ferry boats. The sea is rarely rough, and the close proximity of land makes voyages particularly interesting and beautiful.

Salamis and Aegina

The largest and most populated of the offshore islands is probably the best-known among those who have never visited Greece, the least among those who have. A very justifiable paradox, because in the narrow straits dividing it from Attica raged in 480 B.C. the famous naval battle in which the Greeks decisively defeated the numerically vastly superior Persian fleet. After watching the massacre of his troops on the islet of Psittalia from a marble throne on Mount Egaleo, King Xerxes hastily embarked and Europe was saved.

As for the scarcity of visitors, Salamína (Salamis) quite frankly does not live up to so glorious a name. The pretty white church of the Monastery Tís Faneroménis (Apparition of the Virgin), on the north shore facing the landlocked Gulf of Eleusis, is noteworthy for a 17th-century fresco of the Last Judgment. The domestic architecture of the capital and the smaller villages is pleasing; the Archeological Museum goes in for pots in a big way. At Eántio are the ruins of Homeric Telamon. The beaches are polluted, poor and overcrowded.

Égina (Aegina), which can be reached in half an hour, displays the most varied scenery. Its beautiful outline, with the pure peak of Oros, the extinct volcano (532 meters, 1,745 ft.), provides the fitting centerpiece for the Saronikós Gulf as seen from Athens.

Zeus abducted the nymph Aegina to the island, where their son Aeacus became king, before assuming a judgeship in the underworld. To provide him with subjects, Zeus changed the island's ants (*myrmex*) into the Myrmidons, a name still borne by the followers of his grandson, Achilles. The capital, named after the island, but locally known like every island capital as *Hóra* ("the place") has returned to the ancient site, continuously occupied from about 2500 B.C. to A.D. 1,000, as witnessed by rich ceramic finds now in the museum. From the middle of the 2nd millennium B.C. onward, Aegina sent its ships far afield and the discovery of silver mines in Spain enabled it to mint the first coins in Europe in 700 B.C., the famous Turtle Drachme eagerly coveted by collectors.

The 5th-century B.C. Doric temple of Apollo—its situation possibly superior to that of Poseidon's temple at Sounion—and the 2nd-century B.C. theater and stadium were built by the kings of Pergamon to whom the island had been sold for 30 talents. They were used as convenient quarries by too many conquerors to present any great interest today except to the ardent archeologist. Opposite the temple, the English shipping agent George Brown built a house in the 19th century over a Mycenaean tomb to extract the superb Minoan jewelry, probably hidden there by an antique grave robber. This Aegina Treasure was sold to the British Museum for £4,000 in 1892. Even Capodistrias' first Greek government used the temple for the construction of an orphanage, now a prison for capital offenders, and the first high school, now the museum. In a typical Greek return to square one, the first coins of modern Greece were minted in Aegina during its brief glory as capital in 1828. The port, partly neo-Classical, partly Cycladic, is protected by two long spits, one bearing the dazzling-white Church of Ágios Nikólaos, crowned by a pastel-blue cupola. On the sidewalks, below the multicolored houses, stand rows of porous clay jars of the type that has served since time immemorial as an efficient water cooler; of somewhat more contemporary usefulness are the sponges and delicious pistachio nuts for which the island is rightly famous. The view southward extends to the serrated ridge of the volcanic isthmus of Méthana, which is flanked by two satellite islands, Moni and Angistri; in the distance are the mountains of the Peloponnese.

The road traversing the island passes the Ómorfi Eklisía (Beautiful Church), built in 1289 but not as beautiful as all that, on the way to Paleohóra, the medieval capital on a conical hill, which was only abandoned in 1826, when the danger from corsairs had at last disappeared. The houses were removed stone by stone to the antique site of the capital, so that now only 27 crumbling Byzantine chapels cling to the bare cliff. But below, a huge modern church rises above the white convent, the goal of many a pilgrim, because it contains the embalmed body of Ágios Nektarios, though it is far from clear who canonized the latest Greek saint, who died in 1920. There is no recognized procedure for beatification in the Orthodox Church, as such occasions have become so exceedingly rare.

Thirteen km. (eight miles) further on is the great Doric Temple of Aphaia, probably a native deity, or perhaps a daughter of King Minos of Crete, or why not the nymph Aegina, with one being the priestess of the other? She was also known as Diktynna as she was fished up in a net (*diktyon*) after trying to commit suicide, which rather bears out the abduction theory. For good measure she was related to Britomartis, the Cretan Artemis, but was finally identified with Athena on the pediment depicting the struggle of Greeks and Trojans. Dominating the east coast from a beautiful mountain site surrounded by pine woods, the temple was built in the 5th century B.C. with the spoils of victory at Salamis, and is in a remarkably good state of preservation. No other Greek temple in the islands is so well preserved, and, on the mainland, its only rivals are the Theseion in Athens, and the temple of Bassae in the Peloponnese. Its fine sculptures were bought by Prince Louis of Bavaria, father of Greece's first king, Otto, in 1813 and are now in Munich.

The road descends to Agía Marína, where a popular, but fairly unappealing, summer resort has developed on the otherwise excellent bathing beach, which can also be reached by boat from Piraeus or the *Hóra*.

From Aegina, the boat coasts the Méthana Peninsula, and puts in, near the isthmus, at a spa locally called Vromolímni ("stinking lake," from the sulphur springs) but officially known as Méthana, which, beside its curative properties for rheumatism, is also a convenient center for excursions along the Peloponnesian east shore. The boat then enters a beautiful land-locked bay.

Póros

Póros consists of a largish limestone island, thickly wooded and joined by a low isthmus and bridge to a small volcanic projection on which the town is built. This peninsula was once the island of Sphaeria, named after Sphaeros, the charioteer of Pelops. The pink, white or yellow houses climb up the rock, and face another village—Galatás—on the mainland opposite, across a strait so narrow that it made Arthur Miller in his *The Colossus of Maroussi* feel that he was sailing among houses. Long before, it had seemed like a small-scale Bosphorus, hence its name. It has very great charm, particularly when the houses are shining in the afternoon sun. The view of the Peloponnesian mainland is most beautiful; the green plain of Trizína is backed by rugged mountains, of which a noble range is generally called—on account of its form—the Kimoméni or Sleeping Woman.

Póros is naturally very full of Athenians, especially at weekends in the summer. The bathing is not more than moderately good—best at the beach of the Neório, among pinewoods (reached by caique) or below the 18th-century Monastery of Zoodóchos Pigí which can be reached by the one road on the island. This road also leads to Askeli, with several good taverns, a fine beach and a watersports school. Water-taxis travel to most of the island's beaches as well as to those on the Peloponnesian coast and cost very little.

Delightful excursions may be made; on Póros, to the site of the Temple of Poseidon (few remains, but exquisite view), where Demosthenes, last champion of Greek independence, poisoned himself in 322 B.C. to avoid capture by the Macedonians, and on the mainland to the *Lemonodasos* (lemon grove), full of fragrance in the spring, or the beautifully situated ruins of ancient Trizína, a steep 30-minute climb above the village 13 km. (eight miles) from Galatás.

There is a naval school in Póros, and this, the good communications, and the proximity of Athens give the place a bustle and gaiety rarely met with in the islands.

From Póros the boat passes through the strait, follows the long mountain, Adera, and rounds the point where it ends in the sea as Cape Skylli, the southern end of the Saronikós Gulf.

Ýdra (Hydra) and Spétses

The first of these two is a long, bare, high rocky island. Little of the town can be made out until one is actually entering its narrow harbor. It is then seen to be something unique in Greece, being a homogeneous town, full of tall handsome houses, all built in the years round 1800.

Not long before that date, a number of mountaineers from Epirus moved here, to escape from Turkish oppression. The barrenness of the island forced them to turn to the sea for a living; they became adventurous merchants, and many of them made a large fortune by running the British blockade during the Napoleonic wars. They built these stately houses, one of which has been converted into a historical museum. Each was a self-contained world, and ready to resist a siege with bakery, store-rooms, and great cisterns for water (most essential on this waterless island). There are also beautiful smaller houses, generally white, but sometimes with brightly colored doorways or other features.

When the revolution against the Turks broke out, Ýdra mustered an important fleet, led by two brilliant naval men, Tombazis and Miaoulis. Because of the island's maritime superiority and substantial riches it helped considerably to win the War of Independence when gunrunning went out of fashion. Unable to compete in more peaceful trading, the far-from-gentle decline was halted only by tourism, though there are no roads or "modern" developments.

Ýdra is a natural center for artists and there is a sizeable foreign colony of writers and painters, more appreciated by their fellow residents than by the world at large. If they don't outstay their welcome—as occasionally happens—they can find accommodation in the Tombazis mansion, acquired by the Athens School of Fine Arts.

Though crowded in season, Ýdra is not altogether a suitable summer resort; most of the town is only approachable up ankle-breaking flights of steps, and, in the heat of summer, the place feels shut in. One has to go a long way for a good bathing beach, and excursions are very limited— the steep ascent to the three monasteries, Profítis Ilías, Agía Matróna and Agía Triáda, near the summit of the mountain ridge (392 meters, 1,285 ft.) can be made on a mule, and is to be recommended, on account of the beautiful view of the little town, which exudes great dignity.

After Ýdra the journey is again most attractive. Some boats enter the Bay of Ermióni, adorned by curiously shaped rocks and islands, and backed by the high twin peaks of Mount Dídyma.

Spétses is a low, wooded, undulating island, lying close to an eastern promontory of the Peloponnese. It is the setting for several successful novels, and is favored alike by international residents and Athenian families bringing their children for the summer holidays. It is more bracing than the other Argo-Saronikós islands, and generally cooled by the breezes. Motorboats cross frequently to the beach of Kósta and the resort of Porto-héli on the Peloponnese. Ágii Anárgyri, a fine beach on the other side of the island, with its development limited to a few villas, can be reached by road, but motor traffic, a few taxis and bikes, are banned after 6 P.M. Though the shores are not of great interest, there are fine distant views to the south of the great mountains on the other side of the Gulf of Náfplio.

The town of Spétses is white, clean and pretty, but lacks Ýdra's distinction in architecture or in situation. There are, however, a great number of small churches and chapels of a quality much superior to that often found in the islands. The mansion of Lascarina Bouboulina, heroine of the War of Independence and Admiral of the Fleet, has been preserved as a national monument, and the home of the first governor of the island, Hadjiyanni Mexis, accommodates the Naval Museum, coins, uniforms, weapons and models of boats. Excursions may well be made to the convent (with a charming view of the small satellite island, Spetsopóula, the property of the Niarchos family and once stocked by the famous shipping magnate with game for his hunting parties), or to the fine wood of Brellos. Unlike Ýdra, where there is no wheeled traffic, Spétses has a great number of horsedrawn cabs. The *plateía* is pleasant to sit in in the evening, and the view towards the islands of Dókos and Ýdra, and their attendant rocks is very fine. Spétses, though the least exciting of the Argo-Saronikós islands, is in many ways the best for a prolonged stay.

It might also be a center for excursions; the other islands are easily visited by boat, and those who have left their car at Kósta or Portohéli—connected by road to Corinth via Epidaurus as well as to Náfplio—can explore the mainland.

Euboea

A nymph, this time one favored by Poseidon, gave her name to Évia (Euboea), 175 km. (109 miles) long and up to 56 km. (35 miles) wide, the second largest Greek island after Crete. It is separated from the Boeotian mainland by the channel of the Evrípos, which narrows to a mere 40 meters (130 ft.) at the capital, Halkída (Chalkis). Thus barely an island, Euboea has been connected to the opposite shore since antiquity by a succession of bridges. The most famous predecessor of the present toll drawbridge—briefly open at dawn for the passage of ships—was the Venetian Negroponte, Black Bridge, which for centuries gave its name to the whole island.

The Catholic Patriarch of the defunct Latin Empire transferred his see here from Constantinople in 1261, as this was Venice's most important possession. His Cathedral of St. Mark has reverted to Orthodox Agía Paraskeví, in whose honor a fair is held in late July.

Nothing remains of the towers and turrets behind a moat, as painted by Theophilos in his conception of the Turkish siege in 1470, one of the principal pictures of the museum in Vólos. A tourist pavilion operates in the ruins of the Turkish fortress on the site of the antique acropolis on the mainland. A Byzantine Museum is located in a former Turkish mosque. No longer a great port, the southern roadstead is crowded with laid-up shipping. The northern seafront is pleasant, lined with excellent fish restaurants above the funnel of the Evrípos, through which an immensely powerful current rushes in alternate directions four times a day. This change remains the enigma that supposedly drove the philosopher Aristotle to drown himself in the torrent.

The spa of Edipsós, whose sulphur springs have brought relief to sufferers from rheumatism since Roman times, can be reached by frequent ferry boats from Arkítsa on the mainland opposite, or over 150 km. (93 miles) of road north from Halkída. After Néa Artáki the road turns inland, with a first branch left (west) to the sea at Polítika, then climbs through superb mountain and forest scenery with views over both coasts of the island. At Strofilía the branch left to Límni continues up the west coast, the main road goes up to the north end of the island, from which there is a ferry to the mainland, and the two routes meet at Edipsós. On the northwestern promontory, stands the self-contained resort complex of Gregolímano, more conveniently reached by its own launch from Ágios Konstantínos on the mainland.

The coastal road south passes Lefkánti, where a large 9th-century B.C. site, recently unearthed, vies with a similar excavation at Kommós in Crete for Archaic seniority. Erétria (23 km., 14 miles) was destroyed by the Persians before they sailed to their defeat at Márathon in 490 B.C., but the strategic position was quickly reoccupied—as witnessed by the ruins of the temples of Apollo and Dionysos, of a large theater, fortifications on the acropolis as well as the finds now in the Archeological Museum. The small beaches hardly justify the conglomeration of holiday complexes.

The road continues through Amárynthos to Alivéri, where a thermo-electric plant supplies Athens with electricity. Turning inland and up the island's mountainous spine, the road divides after 11 km. (seven miles). One branch continues south, offering spectacular views—at one point over both shores—before touching on the up-and-coming beaches of Néa Stýra, Marmári and Kárystos, all three connected by ferries with the Attic east coast.

The northern branch climbs the gentle slopes of Mount Dírfis (1,745 meters, 5,725 ft.) past Venetian towers and post-Byzantine chapels to Kými on the east coast, looking toward Skýros. Kými is finely situated on a plateau 260 meters (850 ft.) high, from which an olive grove descends the four km. (two miles) to the sea. The daily bus from Athens takes only four hours via the Oropós–Erétria car ferry, and from Kými's small port Skýros can be reached within two hours.

PRACTICAL INFORMATION FOR
THE EUROPEAN OFFSHORE ISLANDS

SPECIAL EVENTS. Easter. Ýdra, has a particularly moving Good Friday ceremony, the procession of the *Epitaphios,* or Christ's funeral. **June.** On Ýdra, the *Miaoulia Festival,* in honor of Miaoulis, hero of the War of Independence, commemorates victory over the Turkish navy. **September.** Another festival on Spétses celebrates the defeat of the Turkish fleet in 1822.

HOTELS AND RESTAURANTS

Aegina

Agía Marína. *Apollo* (M), tel. 3 2271/4. 107 rooms. Beach, pool, tennis. AE, MC, V. *Argo* (M), tel. 3 2471/3. 60 rooms. Halfboard, tennis; Greek night twice a week in summer. *Pantelaros* (M), tel. 3 2431/2. 55 rooms. AE. There are some 20 Inexpensive hotels on or near the beach. *Galini* (I), tel. 3 2203. 35 rooms. *Kyriakakis* (I), tel. 3 2588. 30 rooms. *Marina* (I), tel. 3 2301. 29 rooms. All with restaurants.

Angístri Island. There are about 10 simple Inexpensive hotels. *Alkyon* (I), tel. 9 1377. 14 rooms. *Kekryfalia* (I), tel. 9 1243. 8 double rooms. Both with restaurants.

Aegina Town. *Danaë* (M), tel. 2 2424/5. 52 rooms. Half board, pool. AE, DC, MC. *Nafsika Bungalows* (M), tel. 2 2333. 34 rooms. On a not particularly attractive beach just outside town. *Areti* (I), tel. 2 2806. 21 rooms. *Avra* (I), tel. 2 2303. 33 rooms. Airconditioned; restaurant, disco. *Klonos* (I), tel. 2 2640. 46 rooms.

Pérdika. *Aegina Maris* (M), tel. 2 5130/2. 164 rooms in central block and bungalows. Airconditioned; tennis, minigolf, disco; on beach. DC. *Moondy Bay* (M), tel. 2 5146/7. 72 bungalows. Pool, tennis, minigolf, disco; on beach.

Souvála. *Efi* (I), tel. 5 2214. 32 rooms. Restaurant.

Euboea

Amárynthos. *Olympic Star (Blue Beach)* (E), tel. 7 3613/18. 210 rooms. Airconditioned; pool, tennis, minigolf, disco; on beach. AE, DC. *Flisvos* (I), tel. 7 2385. 26 rooms. On beach. *Stefania* (I), tel. 7 2485. 80 rooms. Disco, restaurant; on beach.

Edipsós. *Aegli* (M), tel. 2 2215/6. 85 rooms. Thermal facilities. MC. *Avra* (M), tel. 2 2226. 71 rooms, half with bath. Modernized, with thermal facilities; on beach.
There are many Inexpensive hotels, mostly old. *Anessis* (I), tel. 2 2248. 55 rooms. *Capri* (I), tel. 2 2496. 45 rooms. Restaurant. V. *Galaxias* (I), tel. 2 2184. 36 rooms. Pool, near beach. *Hara* (I), tel. 2 2236. 37 rooms. *Irene* (I), tel. 2 2981. 30 rooms. *Mitho* (I), tel. 2 2780. 36 rooms. Restaurant. *Taenaron* (I), tel. 2 3250. 28 rooms.

Erétria. Large concentration of hotel and bungalow complexes, all on rather small beaches. *Golden Beach* (M), tel. 6 1012. 138 rooms in central block and bungalows. Airconditioned; pool, tennis, disco; on beach. AE, DC, V. *Holidays in Evia* (M), tel. 6 2611/4. 334 rooms. Pool, tennis, disco; on beach. AE, DC. *Malakonta Beach* (M), tel. 62 511. 155 rooms. Pool, tennis, disco; on beach. AE, DC. *Miramare* (M), tel. 6 1112. 34 rooms. Pool, tennis, disco; on beach. AE. *Perigiali* (M), tel. 6 2439. 42 rooms. Pool, tennis, disco; on beach. AE, MC. *Delfis* (I), tel. 6 2380. 88 rooms.

Gregolímano. *Gregolimano* (E), tel. 3 3282. The Club Méditerranée's hotel, bungalow and villa complex sometimes has accommodation available (see p. 13). AE, V.

Halkída. *Lucy* (M), tel. 2 3831/5. 92 rooms, not all with bath. Airconditioned; disco; excellent restaurant.AE, DC, MC, V. *Paliria* (M), tel. 2 8001/6. 110 rooms. Airconditioned. AE, DC, MC. *Hara* (I), tel. 2 5541/2. 47 rooms. DC. *John's* (I), tel. 2 4996/8. 57 rooms. Restaurant, roofgarden.
Restaurants. There are several excellent Moderate seafood taverns on the seafront.

Kárystos. *Aetos Beach* (M), tel. 2 3447. 36 rooms in bungalows. Opened in 1988; on beach. *Apollon Resort* (M), tel. 2 2045/9. 79 rooms. Beach, tennis. DC, MC. *Karystos Beach* (M), tel. 2 3141/4. 85 rooms. Airconditioned; pool, tennis, disco. AE, DC. *Galaxy* (I), tel. 2 2600/3. 72 rooms. Airconditioned. *Karystion* (I), tel. 2 2391. 39 rooms.

Kými. *Beis* (I), tel. 2 2604. 30 rooms. Beach; restaurant. V.

Lefkánti. *Lefkanti* (I), tel. 5 2853. 61 rooms. Restaurant.

Límni. *Limni* (I), tel. 3 1316. 47 rooms. Beach.

Marmári. *Marmari Bay* (I), tel. 3 1301/3. 114 rooms. Pool, disco, restaurant. *Michel-Marie* (I), tel. 3 1347. 30 rooms.

Néa Artáki. *Angela Beach* (M), tel. 4 2330. 60 rooms. *Bel Air* (I), tel. 4 2263/4. 44 rooms. Beach, pool, restaurant.

Néa Styra. *Venus Beach* (I), tel. 4 1226. 80 bungalows. Restaurant, tennis. *Delfini* (I), tel. 4 1210. 44 rooms. *Nektarios* (I), tel. 4 1544. 36 rooms. Restaurant.

Péfki. *Galaxias* (I), tel. 4 1325. 25 rooms. *Galini* (I), tel. 4 1208. 30 rooms. Restaurant.
Restaurants. There are some Inexpensive seafood taverns on the seafront.

Polítika. *Euboean Beach* (I), tel. 3 1121. 48 rooms.

Stení. *Stení Motel* (I), tel. 5 1221. 36 rooms. Restaurant.

Póros

Neon Aegli (M), tel. 2 2372. 72 rooms. On pine-fringed Askeli beach near village. AE, V. *Pavlou* (M), tel. 2 2734. 36 rooms. No restaurant; also on pine-fringed beach (Neorio) near village. *Póros* (M), tel. 2 2216/8. 98 rooms. Beach, disco; beyond the village. AE, DC. *Sirene* (M), tel. 2 2741/5. 120 rooms. Pool, disco; on nearby beach. AE, MC. *Angyra* (I), tel. 2 2432. 53 rooms. On beach; restaurant. *Saron* (I), tel. 2 2279. 24 rooms. On noisy waterfront.
Stella Maris Holiday Center (M), tel. 2 2562. Five km. (three miles) north on the **mainland,** across the narrow channel. 93 rooms in central block with bungalows on beach, plus pool, tennis, minigolf, disco. AE, V.

Restaurants. Many good value waterfront taverns, with good views, including *Caravella* (I). Also *Garden of the Hesperides* (M), near Canalia beach, *Galaxy* (I), on Monastiri beach and *Panorama* (I) at Askeli.

Spétses

Kasteli (E), tel. 7 2311/3. 79 rooms in central block and bungalows on beach outside village. Partially airconditioned; tennis. AE, DC. *Spétses* (E), tel. 7 2602/4. 77 rooms. Airconditioned; small beach. AE, DC. *Possidonian* (M), tel. 7 2208. 55 rooms. This in-town hotel was the sophisticated Edwardian setting for John Fowles' *The Magus. Ilios* (I), tel. 7 2488. 27 rooms. Airconditioned; near beach. *Roumanis* (I), tel. 7 2244. 35 rooms. v. *Star* (I), tel. 7 2214. 37 rooms. Airconditioned; near beach.

Restaurant. *Soulias* (E), and *Trehandiri* (M) in the old port. Both places are good for fish *Spetsiotika,* baked with tomato, onion, and garlic.

Ýdra

Accommodations are unsatisfactory and insufficient. Better are the large holiday complexes at Plepi and Petrothálassa on the mainland opposite. However, private lodging is also available.

Miranda (E), tel. 5 2230. 14 rooms. This smart converted 18th-century sea captain's mansion is delightfully furnished. Reservations essential.

Hydroussa (M), tel. 5 2217. 36 rooms. MC. *Kamini* (M), tel. 5 2335. 10 rooms; English owned. No restaurant. *Miramare* (M), tel. 5 2300/1. 28 rooms. On Mandráki beach, two km. (one mile) from town. AE, DC, MC. *Mistral* (M), tel. 5 2509. 18 rooms. Newly opened, the Mistral may be forbidding-looking, but its's comfortable. No restaurant. *Delfini* (I), tel. 5 2082. 11 rooms.

Restaurants. *Bajazzo* (E), rather pretentious. AE, v. *Xerí Eliá* (Drouscos) (M), on the square. There are also numerous waterfront restaurants.

GETTING THERE. By Boat. There are ferries from Arkítsa, which is on the Athens-Lamía motorway, to Edipsós; and from Glyfa, which is off the Lamía–Lárissa motorway, to Agiókambos in the north, as well as from Oropós to Erétria, from Agía Marína (northwest of Marathónas) to Néa Styra, from Rafína to Marmári and to Kárystos in the south of Euboea.

Sálamis, the closest of the Argo-Saronikós islands, can be reached by hourly ferry from the main harbor of Piraeus as well as by frequent car ferries from Pérama, a Piraeus suburb, and Néa Péramos on the Athens-Corinth motorway. There are many ferries daily from Piraeus to Aegina, some of which continue to Póros, Ýdra, and Spétses.

There are at least four hydrofoils every day from the Zea Marina in Piraeus calling at Aegina, Póros, Ýdra, Ermióni, Spétses and Portohéli. Póros can also be reached by car ferry from Galatás, which is connected by road to Epidauros, while there is also a car ferry to Spétses from Kósta.

By Car and Train. Halkída, on Euboea (Evia), is connected to Athens by road and rail. The new road bridge not only shortens the route but makes bypassing the center of Halkída possible.

THE CENTRAL ISLANDS

The Cyclades

The Cycladic civilization began to deserve this name in about 3000 B.C. and for the ensuing millennium developed concomitantly with the Helladic civilization on the mainland. The originality of its doll-like artefacts cannot be denied, though their appeal is mainly to 20th century abstract sculptors and their followers.

The sheer simplicity of life which was so attractive to earlier visitors has given way on many of the islands to prefabricated holidays in large international complexes, the sense of remoteness and individuality gone for ever. The grace and rhythms of scenes and places only recently still idyllic and very much apart are being mindlessly sacrificed to the exploitation of touristic developments. A few of the islands, by their isolation and lack of water have so far largely preserved their distinctive way of life, but they can be rapidly opened up.

Lying in the center of the shipping lanes criss-crossing the eastern Mediterranean between Europe and Asia, the islands have—naturally, but hardly fortunately—experienced to the full influences, occupations and raids from both continents, topped up by occasional forays from Africa. It started rather well during the Bronze Age, when most of the Cyclades were ruled by Cretan governors, who left everywhere vestiges of a sophisticated civilization, most remarkable at Thíra. After the collapse of the Minoan empire, obscure Minoan principalities mentioned by Homer emerged from the Dark Ages as commercial city-states, subjected for only ten years by the Persians.

The Delian League evolved into the Athenian empire, was forcibly usurped by the Spartans, then reconstituted on more liberal lines as the Athenian Alliance. The islands fell under the sway of the Ptolemies, were taken over by the Romans, after the Byzantines they passed from the hands of the Venetians to those of the Turks, were plundered by pirates, were partly occupied by the Russians and then, in this century, were the focus of violent conflict in the two world wars.

Delos

The Kyklades (Cyclades) are so called because the inner ring of this archipelago circles round the holy island of Delos. The safest anchorage within the circle of central islands, Delos was a natural half for vessels sailing between the Greek mainland and the shores of Asia, the geographical as well as the religious center of the Aegean. But the most important island in antiquity is now sadly deserted, receiving only two- and four-legged flocks from Mýkonos. Sheep stay the year round, tourists for the day, as there is no current accommodation. However, in its serene isolation, the sacred isle is still fascinating.

Dílos (Delos) is the birthplace of the twins Apollo and Artemis, whose mother, Leto, was relentlessly pursued by the serpent Python, by the order of Hera, the jealous wife of Zeus by whom she was pregnant. She could find nowhere to rest until Poseidon, moved with compassion, anchored the floating island of Delos with a diamond column, just in time for Artemis to be born; in truly divine, if somewhat precocious fashion, she helped her brother Apollo into the world the following day.

From at least the 8th century, Delos was a holy place for the Ionian Greeks; when Athens rose to power, and had aspirations to Ionian Leadership, she began to have eyes on Delos. In 540 B.C., the tyrant Peisistratus of Athens purified the island, removing all human remains buried there; another such purification was made by the Athenians in 425, and two years later they deported all living Delians to Asia Minor—the sacred island was held to be defiled if birth or death took place there.

After the defeat of the Persians, the Delian League was founded in 478 B.C. to defend the Greek states against Persia, and its funds were kept here, until in 454 they were transferred to the acropolis of Athens for safe keeping. In Hellenistic times an international merchant community settled on Delos, which flourished even more under the Romans, as witnessed not only by the impressive public buildings but also by the sumptuous private villas of that period. It is hardly imaginable that this small islet, five km. (three miles) long and only two km. (one mile) wide, supported in 88 B.C. a population of some 20,000, who were massacred to the last person by order of King Mithridates of Pontus, the ally of Athens; Roman attempts at revival ended in failure due to a raid by pirates 20 years later. Religion proved an insufficient substitute for commerce, and by the 2nd century B.C. tourism was the mainstay for the upkeep of the magnificent monuments. But in the Middle Ages, neighboring islanders, and even worse, the Venetians, helped themselves to what remained of marble and stone. The museum, open again after being closed for several years, contains most of the finds from the island, except the finest sculpture which is in the National Archaeological Museum in Athens.

The columns of the sanctuary are mostly broken off at a low level, as are those of Apollo's Archaic temple as well as of two Classical Athenian

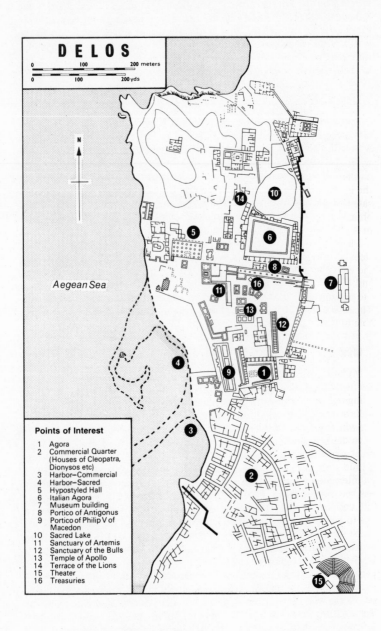

DELOS

0   100   200 meters
0   100   200 yds

Aegean Sea

N

Points of Interest

1   Agora
2   Commercial Quarter
     (Houses of Cleopatra,
     Dionysos etc)
3   Harbor–Commercial
4   Harbor–Sacred
5   Hypostyled Hall
6   Italian Agora
7   Museum building
8   Portico of Antigonus
9   Portico of Philip V of
     Macedon
10   Sacred Lake
11   Sanctuary of Artemis
12   Sanctuary of the Bulls
13   Temple of Apollo
14   Terrace of the Lions
15   Theater
16   Treasuries

shrines and, impartially, those of miscellaneous Greek, Egyptian and Syrian divinities; likewise those of Antigonus Gonatas' 125-meter (410-ft.)
long portico and the slightly smaller portico of Philip V of Macedon, facing the portico of Attalus II of Pergamon. For the Hellenistic kings vied
with each other in the construction of splendid monuments. But an earlier
protective power, Náxos, left the most impressive memorial, the Terrace
of the Lions, where five Archaic beasts (7th century), lean, vigilant, with
tapering waists, still crouch on their hind legs. The Venetians appreciated
these heraldic guardians, one of which has for centuries been standing sentinel before the arsenal in Venice.

Otherwise, the Hellenistic and Roman commercial city has most to offer
in the way of remains. Roman bankers as well as Egyptian and Phoenician
merchants settled in the elegant residential quarter round the theater. The
walls of several villas rise three meters (ten ft.) bright with painted stucco
on the restored colonnaded courts. The House of Cleopatra is named after
the imposing statue of an Athenian matron, but the others after the delicate floor mosaics. Outstanding are the Houses of the Trident, of the Dolphin, of Dionysos, where the handsome god is riding a tiger, changing over
to a panther in the House of the Masks.

The easy ascent of Mount Kýnthos (112 meters, 368 ft.) up a flight of
steps is recommended, particularly at sunset, for the wonderful view of
the encircling Cyclades—to Sýros, which inherited Delos' trade, Náxos
and Páros dominating the distant south, Tínos, the new holy island, to
the north, while nearby Mýkonos has obtained the heritage of tourism.
The nearer view, to be enjoyed on the way up the street, is also of remarkable beauty.

Mýkonos

Mýkonos was of little importance in ancient times and until the 1950s,
mainly visited for its proximity to Delos. But the sundrenched bare hills
rising from a deep blue sea and dotted with dazzling white chapels, windmills and dovecotes converging on the attractive port, whose cubic houses
are whitewashed twice a year, while the innumerable little churches introduce delicate pastel shades with their cupolas, were bound to make it a
great tourist resort, corresponding so exactly to what an Aegean island
should look like. During the peak tourist season. Mýkonos is alive with
an international mix of fairly liberated travelers and, over the last decade,
has become known as a "good-time" resort, with its nonstop nightlife, its
gay and nudist beaches, and its sophisticated bars and restaurants. It is
apt to be very crowded in August which is, for another reason also, the
worst summer month to visit it—the *meltémi* blows very strongly and can
make sea travel rather unpleasant.

The characteristic cubist, white architecture can be seen better only in
such remote islands as Sífnos and Folégandros. There is a good deal of
variety in the size and shapes of houses, but color is not admitted except
on doors or shutters, or on the pink or blue domes of the little churches.
The architectural gem is the Paraportianí, four chapels on different levels
forming one church on the site of the old fortress. The Athens School of
Fine Arts enjoys a superb view from the town's highest point. Visitors are
attracted by the round, white, thatched windmills with canvas sails, and
it is agreeable to wander at random, even to get lost, in the narrow winding
lanes. Particularly to be mentioned is Enetica (Venice), a row of old hous-

es, lashed by the sea. It is a pleasant drive to Áno-Méra, the one other village, to visit the pretty monastery, on a day when one wants a change from the sea.

The beaches of Ágios Stéfanos, Kalafáti, Megáli Ámos, Órnos and Platýs Gialós are accessible by road, and lonelier coves can be reached by boat or on foot.

Sýros and Tínos

Though only 86 square km. (33 square miles), Sýros with 19,000 inhabitants is the most populous of the Cyclades. Ermóupoli, built on the site of ancient Ermes, named after the god of commerce, is the administrative capital. After the Venetian conquest, and then under the protection of the French kings, the port of Ermóupoli dominated sea transport in Greece until 1870; afterwards Piraeus rose, and Sýros declined till the opening of shipyards and docks exactly 100 years later brought about a modest revival. The presence of industrial workers gives the town a different feeling from the peasant and fishing based communities of most other islands. A replica of Milan's opera house, the Apollon State Theatre, where, alas, no opera has been performed since 1914, large private houses, and handsome public buildings round the big, rectangular, inland plateia where there is no traffic, testify to the former wealth of the island. In the countryside are many villas built by rich Greeks from Egypt.

The harbor, full of Aegean craft of every kind, is always lively, and the square is amusing on a Sunday evening, when the band plays, and it is full of people strolling about. The hills behind the lower town—Áno-Sýros, covered with white houses, and predominantly Catholic, on account of the long Venetian dominance in the island; and the Orthodox hill, Vrontádo—look well from the sea. It is interesting to spend an hour or two in Ermóupoli, but if you stay on the island, go to the charming bays of Galýssas, Fínikas, Possidonía or Vári where there are good beaches. In antiquity, Europe's first observatory was here—the Heliotropion, connected with the worship of Poseidon.

Tínos has assumed Delos' position as the Aegean's religious center, an island of pilgrimage for many Orthodox Greeks. The pleasant capital contains some very pretty traces of Venetian architecture. Its great glory is the enormous Church of the Blessed Virgin, the Evangelistria, a modern church of no distinction, though its courtyard, with fine trees, is not unattractive. It was built as a shrine for an icon discovered at the time of the War of Independence, to which miraculous powers are attributed. It is crowded with pilgrims on August 15, the feast of the Virgin's Assumption. After the church service, the miraculous icon is borne aloft by sailors over the prostrate bodies of the sick and maimed. Thousands of ex votos witness frequent miracles. The second Marian feast, the Annunciation, is celebrated on March 25, but the faithful pray before the diamond- and pearl-encrusted *Megalohári* (Great and Gracious Lady) the year round. In the white marble stoas round the vast courtyard are a Byzantine Museum, a Picture Gallery and a Sculpture Museum. The Archaeological Museum is in the wider street leading up from the port; the narrower is lined with shops selling religious articles, souvenirs and wicker baskets, a local handicraft. The Orthodox Kehrovóuni Convent above the town was a favorite retreat of Princess Andrew of Greece, mother of the Duke of Edinburgh; the nuns sell embroideries.

Tínos is mountainous, unlike low-lying Sýros, and it is worth going into the interior for the sake of the wonderful view, and for the prettiness of the white Cycladic architecture. Towered dovecots are a special Cycladean feature; the 800 or so on Tínos date from the Venetian period. Like Sýros, this island also has a large Catholic population.

Ándros and Páros

Boats rarely call at Ándros' capital on the east side, and rarely pass through the narrow strait dividing Ándros from Tínos to the south—so narrow that it is said that people can converse across it. The usual access is from the Attic port of Rafína to Gávrio on Ándros' west coast. Further south is Batsí in a pretty bay, popular with Athenian vacationers.

The main road follows the western shore, below the ruins of antique Paleópoli, before crossing in a deep and wide valley to the capital—which is admirably situated on a long spit of rock. As in Euboea, the scenery is almost more continental than insular. The mountains are high, bare, and squarish; in their folds are several charming oases of greenness, and tall, white houses.

The capital looks fine from the sea, which almost surrounds it but is only to be seen down long and narrow lanes. The leading family has set up the Goulandris Museum of Contemporary Art, with some interesting Picassos and works of the island's sculptor, Michael Tombas. The mountain spa of Sáriza, with its iron spring, is beautifully situated. The best bathing is at Kórthi, in southern Ándros—cut off from the capital by high mountains—but here the landscape is much less impressive. At Ménites there are several churches and a fine monastery and on the promontory at Zágora, south of Paleópoli, there are remains of an abandoned 8th-century town. Its excavation by the University of Sydney has helped archaeologists understand how people lived before the arrival of classical Greece. Some boats continue via Tínos and Sýros to Páros, reached directly from Piraeus on the line to the southern Cyclades.

Páros and its white capital, Páros or Paríkia, on the west coast, are particularly attractive, the high central mountains are bare, but there are several areas of greenness, objects for delightful excursions.

The great glory of Páros town is the church of Ekatontapyliani (Our Lady of the Hundred Gates)—it has not, of course, a hundred gates, but if all the openings, arches, windows, etc., are counted, they may well come to a hundred or more. This is a rambling building, for it includes a great church of the Virgin, a small church of Ágios Nikólaos, and a baptistery; they may date from the reign of Justinian (6th century).

The interior is at first puzzling. In the seventeenth century the nave vault was replaced by another, resting on baroque piers and arches; at first one seems to have entered a large baroque church. It is then seen that an ancient triforium gallery with square-headed openings runs round three sides of the church (everywhere except at the east end). This should be ascended, and is the most beautiful feature of the church. It is a fascinating building, with cross-vistas, and many nooks and corners; apart from Néa Moní in Híos, it is architecturally the most important church in the Aegean. Only traces of the once-marvelous frescos remain, but the stonework itself, in bold patterns of white, red and green, is impressive; also note the "patriarchal" seats round the apse, behind the high altar, and the early cruciform font, with steps down to the water.

Prehistoric Minoa was obviously a Cretan possession until its name was changed after conquest by the Arcadian chief Páros. Wealth came early from the celebrated white marble, supposedly employed by Solomon for the Temple in Jerusalem, but certainly much used at Delos. The quarries are worth the short trip by car.

The most popular excursion is to the caves of Antí-Paros, a large satellite island connected by regular boats. At the village of Antí-Paros, mules may be hired. The ride to the entrance of the caves is most beautiful; in fine weather there is a marvelous view of the southern islands. The caves may now be visited with ease; a staircase has been constructed, and electric light is laid on. But the stalactites must have looked their weird best in the torchlight during the celebration of Christmas mass in 1673, organized by the French ambassador. The islets of Strongylí and Despotikó to the west are for the more adventurous.

Páros is an island that invites a lengthy stay. It accommodates the Aegean School of Fine Arts. There is fairly good bathing at Agía Ánna and in the bay, opposite the capital (reached by boat), though the finest beaches are around the lovely bay of Náoussa on the northeastern shore. The extensive walls of antique Asty have long supplied the building material for the Cycladic fishing village of Náoussa. Now concrete is the more common building material and Naoussa's picturesque charm has been spoiled over the last few years by the continuous building of ugly hotels and "rooms to rent." But recent excavations on the Acropolis hill have brought to light a Mycenaean palace complex, whose finely dressed huge blocks are blackened by the fire by which the Dorian invaders put an end to the Bronze Age civilization throughout Greece round 1200 B.C. Márpissa and Dryós, further south, are more simple beach resorts on the way up.

For men only, a short bus ride from Paríkia, the Monastery of Longovárda, where some of the monks paint icons, rises from the shore. An hour and a half by donkey, for the hardy only, to the southwest of Paríkia is the Garden of the Butterflies, where, on a smaller scale but in a quieter and more attractive place, the same moths can be seen as in the famous Valley of the Butterflies at Rhodes.

The wine of Páros, dark and sweet, will only please a few.

Náxos and Íos

The sea between Páros and mountainous Náxos is often rough. About 448 square km. (173 square miles) in size, Náxos is the biggest in this group, which accounts for its historical preponderance. The port is also the capital, largely the creation of the Venetian dukes of the archipelago, who made it their seat. Kástro, the fortified palace, forms the upper town, seen from afar. But only one of the seven towers built by Marco Sanudo in 1207 remains and is to become a Byzantine, Venetian and ethnographical museum. Antiquity is represented by finds ranging from Mycenaean to Roman times in the nearby excellent Archaeological Museum. The first Duke also built the Catholic Metropolis, which was repeatedly altered in subsequent centuries, and the mansion of the bishop who still attends a considerable Catholic flock. Slightly lower is the Capuchin Monastery of Ágios Antónios.

The Orthodox Metropolis dates only from the 1780s, and is situated above the remnants of the Archaic agora in the picturesque lower quarter, in which Venetian features blend with the characteristic architecture of the Cyclades.

On a tiny islet, connected by a short causeway to the northwestern angle of the seafront, rises the tall marble gateway of Apollo's temple built by the Tyrant Lygdamis (533–515 B.C.). This impressive symbol of Naxos is locally believed to have been the entrance to the palace of Ariadne, deserted by Theseus after she had saved him from the Labyrinth of Knossos. This is one of the very few mythological tales with a happy ending, as the Cretan princess was found by Dionysos on his triumphal progress propagating wine throughout the Aegean.

For once, there is sufficient water for the 14,000 or so islanders in the 41 villages, and for agriculture and tourism, activities which are facilitated by an extensive road network. The narrow lanes wind below the flowering balconies of the old mansions in the white town, which contrasts intriguingly with the surrounding green valleys, rising to high craggy mountains beyond. In the marble quarries of Flerio lies the large unfinished statue of a 6th-century B.C. *kouros* (youth). A second can be found some way up the hillside. The main axis crosses the island to Apóllonas (50 km., 31 miles) on the northeast coast, via Galanádo with a twin Catholic-Orthodox Church of Ágios Ioánnis. The three villages of Sagrí are the center of monuments and ruins from the Archaic to the Venetian periods; to the south, the 13th-century Monastery of the Kalorítissa and some Byzantine churches still display some fine frescos not far from the grim castle of Apáliros.

The central village of Halkí preserves its pure Cycladic aspect within medieval fortifications. There are more Venetian castles and Byzantine churches at Filóti, where three windmills have been restored. The pretty village of Apíranthos even possesses a small prehistoric museum that is usually open; here is the first branch to the east coast, the beach of Moutsóuna. But Apóllonas is better provided with accommodation; in the local quarries is another *kouros,* much larger and less sculpted than those at Flerio.

At Íos another halt is made in a large and beautiful bay cutting deeply into the olive-clad hills. The island capital can be seen, an attractive white town, on the hill above. In recent years Íos has been overrun by the knapsack set, which has made the hospitable islanders unfriendly and distrustful. If you want to get any impression of Cycladic atmosphere you have to decamp to the hilly interior of the island. A tumulus at Plakotó on the other side of the island is called "Homer's grave," and he has but this one, though seven cities claim the honor of being his birthplace. At Psáthi are the ruins of a temple of Apollo.

Thíra (Santoríni)

Thíra is undoubtedly the most extraordinary island in the Aegean. A volcano rose here from the sea in prehistoric times, deposited its lava on the flanks of a high rock already there, and an island was born. The hottest argument in archaeology centers at present on what remains several thousands of years and natural phenomena later. Egyptian papyri, describing Atlantis, the Happy Isle, submerged by the sea in an unparalleled catastrophe, were quoted by many ancient writers, among them Solon and Plato. The latter insisted that he was presenting neither a moral fable nor a man's eternal desire for a lost paradise, but recounting a true story. His descriptions singularly fit the last bloom of Bronze-Age Thíra, from the town built of red, white and black stone—the strange coloring of the island's cliffs—

where ritual bull dances played a major part in the cult, to the tragic end when Atlantis sank in a day and a night.

However, neither direction nor date tallied. The papyri indicated the west, and Solon claimed Atlantis had disappeared 9,000 years before his time. The late Professor Marinatos from the Athens Academy ingeniously explained that Solon had simply added one nought too many. Though one of the seven Wise Men of Antiquity, Solon was, after all, neither geographer nor mathematician, and 900 years corresponds miraculously to the fateful date of about 1450 B.C. when the volcano exploded, the middle of the island sank, the surrounding circle split and the sea poured in, only to be spewed out in an unprecedented tidal wave which swept across the Aegean and engulfed Crete, some 112 km. (70 miles) away. Devastating earthquakes caused by the upheaval completed the ruin of the Minoan empire.

That calamity has been followed by further, if less violent, eruptions. In 236 B.C. the islet of Thirassía was splintered off the northern rim of the circular gulf, 60 km. (37 miles) in circumference, surrounded by fragments of the broken crater; throughout the centuries islets have risen and sunk; and Néa and Paleá Kaméni (the New and the Old Burnt Islands), which appeared between 1573 and 1925 in the middle of the gulf, are still active.

In 1967 legend, though hardly the Atlantis version, was once again vindicated. A tunnel dug through the 49 meters (160 ft.) of pumice at Akrotíri, the southernmost promontory, almost immediately revealed a Bronze-Age town of some 30,000 inhabitants. Buildings standing two and three stories high, with traces of balconies on the 15-meter (50-ft.) street fronts, had been preserved by the ash that enveloped them before the final explosion. They were decorated with delightful frescos of men, plants, birds, antelopes and apes, the last never before depicted in Minoan paintings; those in the governor's palace seem to illustrate the story of the Argonauts. They surpass in artistic delicacy all other famed Mediterranean frescos, those of Crete as well as the later Roman variations at Pompeii, and, after having been painstakingly reassembled, some are at the Athens Archeological Museum, others at the museum at Akrotíri. No human skeletons have come to light, so evidently the islanders had been warned by some volcanic activity before the final disaster and took to boats in time, probably to be engulfed in the tidal waves. The small museum in the capital contains mainly finds from the Dorian and Hellenistic periods.

Called Kállisti (The Loveliest) when first settled, the island has now reverted to its subsequent name of Thíra, after the 9th-century B.C. Dorian colonizer Thiras, though it is also known as Santoríni, a name derived from its patroness, St. Irene of Thessaloníki. Sailing into the gulf, one sees gaunt and sheer cliffs rising all round; they seem to shut you in, for one islet or another blocks the view of the outlets. The amazing gamut of colors—black, pink, brown, white or pale green—changes in a rather sinister way according to the light, while the dead texture of the volcanic rock is a great contrast to the living, warm limestone of most Greek islands. In one place the bare peak of Profítis Ilías rises to 566 meters (1,856 ft.); otherwise nothing shows above the cliff-top but a string of white villages—like teeth on the lower jaw of some monster.

Visitors arrive at the new landing-place and go up by bus or taxi, or at the old one directly below the town and go up by cablecar. The incurably romantic might prefer to ascend the 588 steps of the zig-zag cliff path on foot or on a mule.

From below, on the sea, Thíra looks much as it was before the great earthquake of 1956: a line of whiteness above the cliffs. Most of the houses have been restored, though not always to the harmonious mixture of Cycladic architecture and Venetian elegance, which so greatly enhanced the amazing natural scenery of the island. The village has spread to the safer, gentler outer slopes, away from the cliff-top of the volcanic crater.

Every excursion reveals new facets of the unique scenery: by boat to the Burnt Islands to visit the active craters; a strange and infernal landscape, set against the backdrop of the multicolored 300-meter (1,000-ft.) cliff; by bus along the cliff top, dropping to the northern port of Ía, reborn as a traditional settlement; southwest to the ancient city of Thíra, in the south of the island, best by taxi to a point near the monastery on Profítis Ilías (from whose terraces the view ranges over many islands, to the Dodecanese and, on clear days, even to the mountains of Crete), thence over the mountain flank, covered with pumice stone or loose earth, to an altitude of 365 meters (1,200 ft.).

The remains of antique Thíra were thoroughly excavated and studied at the turn of the century by Hiller von Gärtringen. There are relics of a Dorian city, one of the pioneers of early Greek colonization, and the mother-city of Cyrene in North Africa. At the sanctuary of Apollo, graffiti dating back to the 8th century B.C. record the names of some of the boys who danced naked at the god's festival.

Later, the Ptolemies of Egypt kept a garrison here, to maintain their rule over the Aegean. They too have left their traces. The Romans, when they in turn came, restored a charming Ptolemaic portico, and built a very pretty little theater of their own. There is a wide view of encircling islands from the plateau where the ancient city was built. On the site of the antique port far below stands the village of Kamári, and further south the sweep of fine black sand at Perissa contrasts with the translucent sea. The dazzling white church of Ágios Stavrós (Holy Cross) owes its strange circular shape with flying buttresses partly to the exigencies of frequent earthquakes.

Thíra produces potent sweetish wine; the rich volcanic soil is friendly to viniculture, and to the growth of small sweet tomatoes.

Anáfi, Ámorgos, Sýkinos and Folégandros

Small southernmost Anáfi emerged from the sea at Apollo's command to shelter Jason and his Argonauts from a storm. A considerable layer of volcanic rock was added by the explosion of Thíra, brought by wind and tidal wave. Apollo and Artemis were the local deities, and the ruins of their temple mark the site of the ancient town, east of the present village. Further north is the better preserved castle of Gulglielmo Crispi, to whom his brother Giacomo, 12th Duke of Naxos, had enfeoffed the island. The fortifications failed to stop the pirate Haireddin Barbarossa, who doubled as commander-in-chief of the Turkish navy and Dey of Algeria, from enslaving the entire population in the middle of the 16th century. Settlers trickled back centuries later, maintaining old customs against the lure of progress. There is hardly any accommodation to speak of, a few rooms in private houses, with food an even greater problem. Just the place for a romantic but uncomfortable return in time.

Ámorgos, however, is struggling to overcome the reputation of splendid if primitive isolation. Separated from Náxos by an archipelago of islets,

Ámorgos is 33 km. (20 miles) long though never more than six km. (four miles) wide, rising abruptly to considerable altitudes. Its great eastern cliffs, in particular, are very grand; they have been called the natural defense wall of Europe—for the Dodecanese beyond is really Greece in Asia. In the splendid orange limestone cliffs, 300 meters (985 ft.) above the sea, nestles the 11th-century white Monastery of the Panagía Hozoviótissa, perhaps meaning Our Lady Saving Life—from shipwreck in these perilous seas—though the local version credits a woman from Chozova (wherever that may be) with throwing an ikon into the sea, to be miraculously washed up at the Church of Agía Ánna at the small bay below. The Panagía marked the exact emplacement for the monastery in which the ikon was to be housed with a nail, preserved in the treasury with other ikons, valuable manuscripts, sacred vessels and gold-embroidered vestments.

It is less than an hour of strenuous ups and downs to the capital, a typical white Cycladic town built at 367 meters (1,205 ft.) above sea level around a 13th-century Venetian castle. The main road then curves southwest through some fine mountain scenery past a Hellenistic watchtower at Agía Triáda to terminate at Arkessíni, site of one of the three ancient towns. Inscriptions give details of Classical and Hellenistic cults, constitutions and treaties, leading up to the prosperity of the 2nd century A.D. Parts of the city walls still rise six meters (20 ft.) high around the foundations of Roman public buildings and baths. The second town was in the northeast: Egialí flourished from Archaic to Roman times, and has remained a very secondary port.

The main harbor is in one of the Cyclades' most attractive bays, six km. (four miles) west from Ámorgos town through a fertile valley. Concrete and what passes for modern architecture have been particularly unkind to Katápola, which dates back to Cycladic beginnings. The first 3,000 B.C. idols were discovered in 1891 in graves on the waterfront of what was the Lower Town (Kátopolis) of yet another Minoa, now Mountouliá, on the eastern slopes of a mountain. Broken Hellenistic and Roman walls and gates enclose the foundations of a gymnasium, a stadium and a temple.

Sýkinos and Folégandros, which lie between Íos and Mílos, are so far seldom visited. And yet the ascent from the tiny harbors to the capitals is rewarding on both islands, especially on Folégandros, where a mosaic path climbs beside the only road from Karavostássis to the *Hóra,* a white Cycladic town built between the walls of an old fort, and on the edge of a beetling precipice. The cliffs of Folégandros (in which is the Golden grotto, very difficult of access, and not worth the trouble and hazard) are, with those of Ámorgos, the finest cliff scenery in the Cyclades.

The Western Cyclades

The six largest stretch in a chain from Mílos north to Kéa, and all are newcomers to the touristic scene. Yet the name of Mílos has long been widely known because it was where one of the most famous 4th-century B.C. statues, Scopas' Aphrodite, was found in the 19th century; forcibly carried away on a French ship, it is now known as the "Venus de Milo" and can be seen in the Louvre in Paris. Mílos is the southernmost of the western Cyclades, in form like a ring round a huge bay. There is a tall mountain, and the shape of the island is lovely, with views of small islets as one approaches. Mílos is less actively volcanic than Thíra, but not beyond the occasional tremor. The curative qualities of the warm sulphurous springs were appreciated in antiquity, while a geothermic unit is now producing 100 megawatts. The mixture of minerals has resulted in the strangely white soil fringed by purple-blossomed trees on the shores.

From Ádamas, the main port, it is five km. (three miles) to Mílos, capital since 1100 B.C. and today nestling below the inevitable medieval fortress. The catacombs, where early Christians sought refuge are closed because of the danger of cave-ins. The second port, Apolonía, is more frequented by tourists because of its proximity to Filakopí, where excavations are bringing to light three Minoan and Mycenaean towns, the oldest dating back to 2500 B.C.

Mílos gained unwanted fame by the cruel treatment it received at the hands of the Athenians in 416 B.C. during the Peloponnesian War, so poignantly related by Thucydides, whose "Melian Dialogues" is perhaps the most moving account in all literature of an aggression by a greater power.

An unreported catastrophe submerged the isthmus that joined Mílos to Kímolos in the north. An islet rises from the narrow strait, the acropolis of a town whose ramparts and ruins are visible in the shallow sea. Archeologists have decided that it was inhabited from the 1st millennium B.C. to the end of antiquity, but the nearby necropolis of Elliniká was already in use 1,000 years earlier. A medieval fortress stood at Paleókastro in the mountainous west; larger and more easily accessible on a hill, but likewise in ruins, is Venetian Kástro, around which the present capital has grown, 1 km. inland from the port Psathí.

Sífnos is more pleasing to the eye, and also to the limbs by providing better accommodation: in the west at Kamáres, the principal port with a fine beach; and at another Apolonía, the capital, which extends over the amphitheater of three hills overlooking the east coast. It is a smiling island, its bare hills terraced on their lower slopes for cultivation or for olive trees. It produces the best olive oil in the Cyclades, and in consequence Siphniac cooking is better than the average in this region. Another product of Sífnos is pottery; it is made at several places on the island, always by the sea, so that it may be shipped with ease.

It is on this island that the Cycladic cubic type of architecture, seen with small variations in so many islands, is found in its greatest perfection. Here a projecting ledge, over every door or window, adds to the interest of the exteriors (a feature also to be seen on Folégandros, where the houses are also very beautiful).

Most of the inhabitants live in a line of almost connecting white villages on the crest of a hill, but the finest architecture is to be seen in the old island capital, Kástro, down by the eastern shore, looking towards Páros; here one street passes over the roofs of one-storied buildings below, and it is joined by bridges to the upper stories of the opposite houses.

Ancient Sífnos enjoyed a brief period of great prosperity when gold was found there; the remains of the Siphnian treasury which was erected at Delphi are impressive. The Siphnians were supposed to give Apollo at Delphi a golden egg annually: once they tried to fob him off with a gilded stone, and in anger he sunk their gold mines. Indeed, in antiquity they had a name for sharp practice. Today they are singularly gentle and pleasant people, with the reserve that characterizes those islanders whose life is lived remote from their principal port.

The next island, northward, is Sérifos, where the boat enters the deep gulf of Livádi on the east coast. The capital is a labyrinth of steep lanes climbing a pyramidal hill topped by a formidable Venetian fortress. A rare kind of pink, indigenous to Sérifos, grows out of the walls in abundance. This is where the infant Perseus came to land in a chest, with his mother Danäe who later married the island's king, Polydectes; and it is here that, when he came to manhood, he petrified the ruthless king with the head of the Gorgon Medusa. A cave is shown as that of the Cyclops, whom Odysseus blinded, but the geography of the Odyssey is much in dispute, and other islands claim to be the scene of this event.

Kýthnos' port Meríhas also lies in a fine bay, but on the west coast, from which it is six km. (four miles) to the rather featureless capital inland. On the east coast, Loutrá in the north is the Cyclades' only operative spa, where two hot springs have relieved rheumatic sufferers since ancient times. The bigger ancient settlement was, however, in the south at Dryópis, named after the tribe led by Kýthnos that occupied the island during the Dark Ages. Some walls remain and there are several good beaches.

Kythnos is as yet little visited, but Kéa (locally known as Tzia), the closest to Attica, is increasingly appreciated for its splendid beaches, antique ruins, Venetian castle and the superb view over a wide sweep of the Aegean from the Monastery of the Panagía Kastrianí (Our Lady of the Castle), which possesses a miraculous ikon.

Koríssia, the port, is in the northwest, from which the road climbs southeast to the attractive capital, which curves like the letter S round a high hill, the acropolis of ancient Ióulis. On these foundations the Venetians built a castle and some handsome mansions, oddly contrasting with the remains of the Apollo temple. The lower town is distinguished by a great number of arches that cross its one long street. Some way beyond, in the hillside, is a huge antique lion, carved out of the rock, which has apparently fallen from its original position to the site that it now occupies under some olive trees.

PRACTICAL INFORMATION FOR
THE CENTRAL ISLANDS

TOURIST OFFICE. There is a G.N.T.O. office on **Sýros**, Laikis Kiriarchias, Ermóupolis, (tel. 2 6725).

HOTELS AND RESTAURANTS. Beach hotels are closed from November through March. The Moderate and Inexpensive hotels rarely have restaurants. As far as food is concerned, the Cyclades do not differ greatly from the mainland. If you happen to call in at Ámorgos, try the *fava,* a purée of chickpeas and oil; it's quite tasty. The only cheeses of distinction are *kopanisti,* pride of Mýkonos, and the so-called Gruyere (*graviera*) of Naxos.

The best Turkish Delight in Greece comes from Syros and the same can be said of Sífnos for honey-pies (*melópita)* and honey-cookies (*melomakárona).* The volcanic soil of these islands is favorable to the cultivation of grapes but their wines are mostly undistinguished except perhaps for the light white wine of Santorini. Kéa has chosen a promising French name: *Bouquet.* You can round off a meal with a lemon liqueur, *Kítro,* from Naxos.

Ámorgos

Egialí. *Mike* (I), tel. 7 1252. 10 rooms, some with shower. The island's only hotel; on beach.

Ándros

Ándros Town. *Paradissos* (M), tel. 2 2187/9. 41 rooms. *Xenia* (I), tel. 2 2270. 26 rooms. On a cliff above the beach. Restaurant.

Batsí. *Aneroussa Beach* (M), tel. 4 1444. 37 rooms. *Chryssi Akti* (I), tel. 4 1236/7. 61 rooms. Restaurant. *Karanassos* (I), tel. 4 1480. 22 rooms. *Skouna* (I), tel. 4 1240. 20 rooms. Restaurant; beach.

Gávrio. *Perrakis* (M), tel. 7 1456. 30 rooms. On the beach. *Gavrion Beach* (I), tel. 7 1312. 21 rooms.

Kórthi. *Korthion* (I), tel. 6 1218. 15 rooms. Beach, restaurant.

Delos

The only hotel, *Xenia* (I), tel. 2 2259, is likely to be closed in 1991. Visitors to the island should stay on nearby Mykonos and travel to and fro by boat (a half-hour trip).

Folégandros

Fani-Vevis (I), tel. 4 1237. 18 double rooms. Very simple.

Íos

Íos Town. *Mare-Monte* (M), tel. 9 1564. 27 rooms. AE. *Armadoros* (I), tel. 9 1201. 27 rooms. *Corali* (I), tel. 9 1272. 14 double rooms. Restaurant. AE. *Flisvos* (I), tel. 9 1315. 13 rooms. Restaurant. AE, DC. *Homer's Inn* (I), tel. 9 1365. 21 rooms. *Leto* (I), tel. 9 1357. 39 rooms. On the beach. *Sea Breeze* (I), tel. 9 1285. 14 rooms. DC, MC.

Manganári. *Manganari* (E), tel. 9 1395. 31 bungalows. Disco, private beach.

Mylopota. *Íos Palace* (E), tel. 9 1224. 44 rooms and bungalows. Pool; on wide sandy beach.

Kéa

Koríssia. *I Tzia Mas* (I), tel. 3 1305. 24 double rooms. On beach. *Karthea* (I), tel. 3 1222. 35 rooms. On the beach. MC. Both with restaurants.

Kóundouros. *Kea Beach* (M), tel. 2 2144. 80 rooms in central block and bungalows. Plus disco, pool, private beach. AE.

Kýthnos

Loutrá. *Xenia Anagenissis* (I), tel. 3 1217. 46 rooms. Thermal facilities, restaurant; near the beach. DC.

Meríhas. *Possidonion* (I), tel. 3 1244. 83 rooms.

Mílos

Adamás. *Aphrodite of Milos* (M), tel. 2 2020. 23 furnished apartments. *Venus Village* (M), tel. 2 2030. 91 rooms in central block and bungalows. Beach, tennis, pool and disco. AE, DC, V. *Chronis* (I), tel. 2 2226. 16 rooms. V. *Korali* (I), tel. 2 2204. 16 rooms. *Milos* (I), tel. 2 2087. 19 rooms.

Mýkonos

Ágios Stéfanos. *Alkistis* (M), tel. 2 2332/4. 102 rooms in bungalows. On beach. AE, DC, MC, V. *Artemis* (I), tel. 2 2345. 23 rooms. *Panorama* (I), tel. 2 2337. 27 rooms. Tennis, restaurant, minigolf and disco: good service.

Áno Méra. *Ano Mera* (E), tel. 7 1215. 67 rooms. Pool, disco. AE, DC, MC, V.

Kalafáti. *Aphrodite* (E), tel. 7 1367. 135 rooms in bungalows; pool, disco, tennis. AE, DC, MC.

Megáli Ámmos. *Mýkonos Beach* (M), tel. 2 2572/3. 27 bungalows.

Mýkonos Town. None of the Moderate hotels have restaurants. *Anastassios-Sevasti* (E), tel. 2 3550. 30 rooms. Airconditioned. In quiet area.V. *Cavo Tagoo* (E), tel. 2 3692. 24 rooms in pleasant island architecture; at present the best. Seawater pool. *Ilio Maris* (E), tel. 2 3755. 18 rooms and 4 suites. Almost in center of town; pool. *Leto* (E), tel. 2 2207. 25 rooms. Near beach, but few facilities for the price. AE, MC, V. *Calypso* (M), tel. 2 3429. 31 rooms. Between beach and town. *Despotiko* (M), tel. 2 2009. 36 rooms. Airconditioned; pool. *Kouneni* (M), tel. 2 2301. 19 rooms. *Les Moulins* (M), tel. 2 3244. 14 rooms. *Manoulas Beach* (M), tel. 2 2900. 30 rooms. V. *Petassos* (M), tel. 2 2608. 16 rooms. V. *Poseidon* (M), tel. 2 2437. 41 rooms. *Rohari* (M), tel. 2 3107/9. 53 rooms. MC, V. *Vencia* (M), tel. 2 3665. 32 rooms.

Aeolos (I), tel. 2 3535. 25 rooms. *Manto* (I), tel. 2 2330. 15 rooms. *Marianna* (I), tel. 2 2072. 23 rooms. *Pelecan* (I), tel. 2 3454. 23 rooms. *Thomas* (I), tel. 2 3148. 38 rooms. AE, MC, V. *Zannis* (I), tel. 2 2481. 19 rooms.

Órnos. *Órnos Beach* (M), tel. 2 2243. 24 rooms. Disco, water sports.AE, MC. *Yannaki* (M), tel. 2 3393. 29 rooms. V. *Paralos Beach* (I), tel. 2 2600. 40 rooms. AE.

Platýs Gialós. *Petassos Beach* (M), tel. 2 3437/8. 44 rooms. Pool. AE. *Petinos* (M), tel. 2 3680. 29 rooms. On beach. MC.

Tóurlos. *Rhenia* (M), tel. 2 2300. 37 rooms in bungalows. No restaurant. *Irene Beach* (I), tel. 2 2306. 14 rooms.

Vrýssi. *Konhyli* (M), tel. 2 2107. 29 rooms. AE. *Korali* (M), tel. 2 2929. 28 rooms. *Mangas* (I), tel. 2 2577. 19 rooms.

Restaurants. Prices are above the country's for the quality. *Nikos* (E), the most popular. *Katerini* (E). French cuisine. DC, MC. *Antonini* (M), on the square; the oldest. *El Greco* (M) and *Edem* (M) in a garden in the center of town, are both reasonable. Try *Spiro's* (M), for seafood.
Bars and Discos. Lively bars include *Remezzo* (E) and *Piero's* (E). Among the many discos, try *City Disco* (E), *Kookoo's Nest* (E), *Nine Muses* (E), and *The Yacht Club* (E).
Beaches. Very crowded near town. It's better to go a certain distance: by bus to *Psarou,* by boat to *Ilia, Paradise* and *Super Paradise.* The last two are nudist preserves, respectively hetero and gay. Least crowded is *Kalafati* across the island by bus.

Náxos

Mathiassos Village (M), tel. 2 3300. 108 bungalows, not on the sea. Pool, tennis. *Aegeon* (I), tel. 2 2852. 21 rooms. AE. *Aeolis* (I), tel. 2 2321. 17 rooms. *Barbouni* (I), tel. 2 2535. 14 rooms. *Iliovassilema* (I), tel. 2 2107. 21 rooms. MC. *Koronis* (I), tel. 2 2626. 32 rooms. AE, DC, MC, V. *Naxos Beach* (I), tel. 2 2928. 37 double rooms. *Sergis* (I), tel. 2 2355. 28 rooms. *Sphinx* (I), tel. 2 3811. 21 rooms.
Restaurants. *Florin* (M), *Nikos* (M), for fish, in behind the waterfront; the latter is very popular and has recently been expanded. *Kastro* taverna (I). *Vassilis* taverna (I), in the market.

Páros

Alýki. *Afroditi* (I), tel. 9 1249. 20 rooms.

Antíparos. *Chryssi Akti* (I), tel. 4 1366. 9 rooms.

Dryós. *Annezina* (I), tel. 4 1364. 13 double rooms. *Julia* (I), tel. 4 1494. 12 rooms.

Náoussa. All these hotels are on or near the island's best beaches. *Atlantis* (M), tel. 5 1209. 28 rooms. *Hippocambus* (M), tel. 5 1223/4. 49 rooms in bungalows. AE, MC, V. *Kouros* (M), tel. 5 1000. 55 rooms and bungalows in neo-classical style. *Aliprantis* (I), tel. 5 1571. 15 rooms. *Ambelas* (I), tel. 5 1324. 16 double rooms. Restaurant. *Kalypso* (I), tel. 5 1488. 24 rooms. Restaurant. *Mary* (I), tel. 5 1201. 15 rooms. *Minoa* (I), tel. 5 1309. 26 rooms. *Papadakis* (I), tel. 5 1269. 16 rooms.

Páros Town. None of the (I)s have restaurants. *Apollon* (M), tel. 2 2364. 23 rooms. On beach. V. *Paros Bay* (M), tel. 2 1140. 65 rooms. Pool. *Polos* (M), tel. 2 2173/4. 21 rooms. V. *Xenia* (M), tel. 2 1394. 23 rooms. This traditional place is on a hill overlooking the harbor. *Alkyon* (I), tel. 2 1506. 24 rooms. *Argo* (I), tel. 2 1367. 44 rooms. MC, V. *Argonaftis* (I), tel. 2 1440. 15 rooms. MC, V. *Asterias* (I), tel. 2 1797. 36 rooms. *Galinos*

(I), tel. 2 1480. 34 rooms. *Georgy* (I), tel. 2 1667. 33 rooms. *Nikolas* (I), tel. 2 2251. 43 rooms.

Restaurants. There are many (I) seafront taverns, but it's worth wandering round the back streets, where you'll find more variety and, on the whole, better quality. *To Tamarisko* (M), in quiet, trellissed garden off the marketplace, is particularly good.

Písso Livádi. *Andromachi* (I), tel. 4 1387. 12 rooms. Restaurant. *Leto* (I), tel. 4 1283. 14 rooms. *Písso Livádi* (I), tel. 4 1309. 12 rooms.

Púnta. *Holiday Sun* (E), tel. 9 1284/5. 53 rooms. Airconditioned; pool, tennis, good beach.MC, V.

Sérifos

Livádi. *Maïstrali* (I), tel. 5 1381. 20 double rooms. *Serifos Beach* (I), tel. 5 1209. 33 rooms. Restaurant. Both on beach.AE, DC, V.

Sífnos

Apolonía. *Sífnos* (I), tel. 3 1624. 9 rooms.
Restaurant. *Cyprus* (I), Cypriot specialties.

Artemónas. *Artemon* (I), tel. 3 1303. 28 rooms. Restaurant.V.

Kamáres. *Kamari* (I), tel. 3 1641. 18 rooms. V.

Platýs Gialós. *Platys Yalos* (M), tel. 3 1224. 22 rooms, most with bath. Beach. *Benakis* (I), tel. 3 1334. 14 rooms. Lovely sea view; near long, sandy beach.

Sýros

Ermóupoli. *Vourlis* (M), tel. 2 8440. 7 rooms, in neo-classical 19th-century mansion. Luxurious and elegant. No restaurant. AE, DC, MC, V. *Nissaki* (I), tel. 2 8200. 42 rooms. Near beach.
Fínikas. *Olympia* (I), tel. 4 2212. 40 rooms. Airconditioned; beach, restaurant.

Galýssas. *Françoise* (I), tel. 4 2024. 24 rooms. Beach.

Possidonía. *Eleana* (I), tel. 4 2644. 44 rooms. MC, V. *Poseidonion* (I), tel. 4 2100/1. 60 rooms. V. Both with restaurants.

Varý. All on beach. *Alexandra* (I), 4 2540. 30 rooms. *Domenica* (I), tel. 6 1216. 22 rooms. V. *Romantica* (I), tel. 6 1211. 30 rooms. All with restaurants.

Thíra

Akrotíri. *Akrotiri* (I), tel. 8 1375. 17 rooms. AE.

Embório. *Arhaea Elefsina* (I), tel. 8 1250. 15 rooms.

Exo Gonia. *Makarios* (M), tel. 3 1375. 28 rooms.

Ía. *Atlantis Villas* (E), tel. 7 1214. 14 furnished apartments in traditional houses. *Perivolas* (E), tel. 7 1308. Rooms in 12 modernized "Caves" or traditional settlements above black sand beach. Original rather than comfortable. Spectacular views over bay.

Kamári. *Artemis Beach* (M), tel. 3 1198. 29 rooms. *Kamari* (M), tel. 3 1243. 55 rooms. Beach, pool, tennis, disco. AE. *Sunshine* (M), tel. 3 1394. 35 rooms. *Blue Sea* (I), tel. 3 1481. 26 rooms.

Karterádos. *Santorini Tennis Club* (E), tel. 2 2122. 9 apartments. Tennis, pool. *Babis* (I), tel. 2 2314. 20 rooms. Restaurant. *Cyclades* (I), tel. 2 2948. 15 rooms. *Olympia* (I), tel. 2 2213. 25 rooms.

Messaría. *Santorini Image* (M), tel.3 1174. 130 rooms in bungalows set around a pool. Tennis. *Artemidoros* (I), tel. 2 2245. 16 rooms. AE, MC, V. *Loïzos* (I), tel. 2 2359. 12 rooms.

Perissa. *Christina* (I), tel. 2 2568. 8 rooms. Good restaurant. Near black volcanic sand beach.

Thíra Town. Reserve well in advance during the Music Festival Late Aug. through mid-Sept. *Atlantis* (E), tel. 2 2232. 27 rooms. Comfortable and spacious. Fine view. *Kallisti Thira* (M), tel. 2 2317. 33 rooms. AE, DC. *Panorama* (M), tel. 2 2481. 20 rooms. Disco. MC, V. *Pelican* (M), tel. 2 3113/4. 18 rooms. Next to bus station. *Theoxenia* (M), tel. 2 2740. 11 rooms and 7 villas, built into cliffs overlooking the volcano.AE, DC. *Santorini* (I), tel. 2 2593. 24 rooms. MC.
Restaurant. *Camile Stefani* (M). This is one of the island's best, for seafood and Greek specialities.

Vothonas. *Anny* (I), tel. 2 3102/3. 25 rooms.

Tínos

Tinos Beach (E), tel. 2 2626/8. 180 rooms in central block and bungalows. Pool, tennis, minigolf, disco; 2½ km. (1½ miles) from town. AE, DC, MC, V. *Aeolos Bay* (M), tel. 2 3339. 69 rooms. On beach.V. *Alonia* (M), tel. 2 3541/4. 34 rooms. V. *Asteria* (I), tel. 2 2132. 52 rooms. *Delfinia* (I), tel. 2 2289. 38 rooms. On seafront. *Meltemi* (I), tel. 2 2881/4. 43 rooms. Restaurant. *Oassis* (I), tel. 2 3055. 23 rooms. V. *Oceanis* (I), tel. 2 2452. 47 rooms. Restaurant; on seafront. MC. *Poseidonion* (I), tel. 2 2245. 39 rooms. Restaurant; on seafront. V.

GETTING THERE. By Plane. In summer there are daily flights from Athens to Mílos, Mýkonos, Páros and Thíra; from Iráklio and Rhodes to Mýkonos, Páros and Thíra; from Sámos and Híos to Mýkonos, and from Mýkonos to Thíra.

By Boat. There are usually two car ferries a day to Tínos and Mýkonos, and three or four to Sýros, Páros, Náxos, Iós, and Thíra. Sérifos, Sífnos, and Mílos have a boat most days. There are less frequent boats to Ámorgos, Folégandros and Sykinos.

From the Attic port of Rafína, there are daily car ferries to Ándros (Gávrio), Tínos, Mýkonos, and also to Sýros, Páros, Náxos; there is also a car ferry from Lávrio to Kéa and Kýthnos. Daily motorboats, usually part of an organized tour, run from Mýkonos Páros and Náxos to Delos (weather permitting) which, like Thíra, is included in most cruises. In summer there is a service between Iráklion and Thíra.

THE EASTERN ISLANDS

The Dodecanese, Sámos, Híos and Lésbos

The Dodecanese are islands scattered off the southwest coast of Asia Minor; though called the "12 islands" they come to more, on most of the varied enumerations. Travelers seldom visit others than Pátmos, Kós and Rhodes, though some of the lesser-known islands well repay exploration. This group of islands was taken from Turkey by Italy in 1912; the islanders believed that it was a step towards their immediate liberation, but the Italians established themselves there, and the Dodecanese achieved union with Greece only in 1948. Kos and Rhodes still have Turkish minorities, who enjoy full cultural and religious liberty, and live in friendship and harmony with the islanders—they even join in each other's feasts. The Italian occupation, at first benevolent, became in the later years of Fascism vain and tyrannical—a few buildings, beautiful gardens and good roads remain, otherwise it might never have been.

Exploring the Dodekánissa (Dodecanese)

Pátmos, the northernmost island, is a place of pilgrimage, because it was here that St. John the Divine wrote the Apocalypse, and because of the famous monastery the whole island was declared sacred by the Greek Parliament in 1980. There is indeed an atmosphere of unusual serenity, though hardly Biblical as touted in the tourist handouts. The southern part is famed for its charming white "cubist" architecture.

From the port, Skála, on a deep bay, the road ascends a hill on the south. Towards the top is the church of the Apocalypse, which enshrines the cave where St. John received the Revelations; the voice of God spoke through a threefold crack in the rock, and St. John (to whom alone it was audible) dictated to his disciple Prochorus. A slope in the rock wall is shown as the desk where Prochorus wrote, and silver haloes are set on the stone that was the apostle's pillow, and the grip by which he raised himself from his knees. Tradition says that St. John was sent here in A.D. 95 by the emperor Domitian for preaching Christ in Ephesus, but returned to Ephesus on Domitian's death the next year.

The pleasant small capital of Hóra, at the top of the hill, is dominated by the great fortified monastery of St. John the Theologian, on the site of an early Christian basilica that had replaced a sanctuary of Artemis. The prey of pirates, Pátmos had been completely deserted for centuries when in 1088 it was granted by Alexios I to Blessed Christodoulos, the founder of numerous ecclesiastic establishments in those parts. Alexios I's imperial bull—reverently preserved—was confirmed by successive emperors and patriarchs, so that the autonomous island remained a spiritual center rivalling Mount Áthos until the 18th century.

The church contains a wonderful array of beautiful treasures, never yet plundered, including a noble 11th-century ikon of St. John the Divine, the gift of Alexios, and the silver shrine of St. Christodoulos; there is also a fine carved screen of early 19th-century work, fine Byzantine jewels and embroidery, and an 11th-century mosaic ikon.

The well-arranged and spacious library of some 1,000 manuscripts is famous: its greatest treasure is the *Codex Porphyrius* of the Gospels, 33 leaves containing most of St. Mark's gospel. This beautiful book was written in silver, on purple-stained vellum, in the 5th century; other leaves from the same manuscript are preserved in Leningrad, the Vatican, the British Museum, Vienna, and the Byzantine Museum of Athens. Famous manuscripts from Pátmos (including an important text of Plato) were bought by the traveler Edward Daniel Clarke in 1808.

The terraced roofs and the bell towers are the most attractive feature of the monastery—which commands a superb view over the whole island with its many creeks. The visitor should also see the refectory, with its long stone tables.

There are many coves, mostly with pebble beaches; the best bathing is at lovely Gríkos, Méloï, Netía, and Lambi, noted for its many-colored pebbles, or more isolated at the island of Lípsi to the west, where simple taverns serve an honest local wine.

Léros and Kálymnos

Léros is, like Pátmos, an island of many creeks and promontories but, despite its orchards and vineyards, is less attractive. From Láki, in one of the Mediterranean's largest natural harbors, it is three km. (two miles) to the capital, Plátanos, built in tiers below the Byzantine fortress, which is kept in repair by the Knights of St. John and the Venetian Dukes of Náxos. Two old churches have been expertly restored. The closest beach is at Agía Marína, but Alínda deeper inside the northeastern bay has greater touristic ambitions. As the ancient commercial port, it features the ruins of an early Christian basilica.

The crossing to Kálymnos, the main port and capital of that mountainous island, is one of very great beauty. Prehistoric remains have been discovered in a cave, and Horió, the old inland capital, features the usual fortress (this time Byzantine), but it is for the splendid varied scenery that Kálymnos deserves a visit. Yet the port is impressive from the sea, with its blue, white or yellow houses piled on the reddish rock. The Kálymnians particularly delighted in painting their houses alternately blue and white—the Greek colors—to annoy their Italian keepers during their occupation. Until recent years, most of the active male population was absent, sponge-fishing during the summer months. Disease has destroyed many of the Mediterranean sponge beds, but despite attempts to encourage visitors, tourism has yet to overtake the old, more traditional way of earning a living. Of those Kalymnians who are not diving for ever-elusive sponges off the North Africa coast, many leave the capital for the lovely beaches of Linária, Massóuri, Myrtíes and Pánormos. The sea caves at Kéfala with their stalactites are accessible by boat, but the radioactive sources of Thérma, one km. (half a mile) south of the town, are yet to be exploited.

Kos

Kos is much better prepared for its hordes of summer visitors when the town is aglow with flowering oleanders and hibiscus. After the devastating earthquake of 1933, a low, white modern town was built to withstand earthquake shock. The catastrophe at least afforded opportunities for further excavations of the Greek and Roman antiquities.

Kos preserves traces of all the different civilizations that it has known: remains of Hellenistic and Byzantine sanctuaries, the castle of the Knights of Rhodes, and Turkish mosques and fountains. The pretty 18th-century mosque of the "Loggia" contains marble from a Byzantine basilica, which had in its turn been constructed out of the remains of an Hellenistic arcade.

By this mosque is an ancient plane tree, called after Hippocrates, the "father of medicine," who was born on the island. There is no reason for this ascription; a plane tree does not live above 500 years; nor is it likely that this is a remote descendant of a plane tree under which Hippocrates could have sat in the 5th century B.C. In his day the Koan capital was at the far, western end of the island—it was called Astypalaia, and Thucydides recounts its destruction by an earthquake.

The site of modern Kos was inhabited from 366 B.C., and it was in the century following that the island had its greatest period. It was in the Ptolemaic sphere, after the death of Alexander the Great, and it is here that Berenice, wife of Ptolemy I, gave birth to Ptolemy II Philadelphus—who earned that title by resuming the immemorial tradition of Pharaonic arrogance and marrying his sister Arsinöe II. At the beginning of the 3rd century B.C., a famous school of pastoral poetry flourished here. The greatest exponent of this type of poetry, Theocritus, probably came from Sicily, visited Kos and immortalized some Koan scenes.

From the town's shingle beach, lined by restaurants and cafes under shady trees, there is an exquisite view across to Bodrum on the Turkish mainland (Halicarnassus, the birthplace of Herodotus). Outstanding among the widely scattered Hellenistic and Roman remains are the noble statue of Hippocrates in the museum, and the exquisite 2nd century A.D. floor mosaic of fish, a very fine and delicate work, in the Casa Romana, an antique villa. At the partly restored Hellenistic Asklepeion (four km., two and a half miles to the southeast), a sanctuary and a medical school, terraced in the hillside, the Hippocratia, is held in August. This minor festival includes the revival of the Hippocratic oath, musical concerts, dancing, athletics, and a series of rural fairs.

The town of Kos is at the east end of a northern coastal plain, on the south of which is a great mountain range, whose principal peak is called Díkeos, or Christ the Just (685 meters, 2,250 ft.). On the northern slopes of this range are many charming villages, below which are the rapidly developing beaches of Mastihári and Tigáki. The largest resort is at Kardámena on the south coast close to the airport. Beyond the westward end of the mountain range there is a long tail to the island: wild volcanic country where the ancient city once stood near Kéfalos. The seaside near Kéfalos is developing into an important holiday area.

The Lesser Isles

The southern sea journey from Kos is most beautiful, passing several smaller islands. Níssyros is very much off the beaten track, a strange, square-shaped island a mere 48 square km. (18½ square miles) in size, rising on all sides towards a central ring of hills which surround a large volcanic depression in which there are two extinct craters, Aléxandros and Polyvótis. The villages of Émborios, below a ruined Byzantine fortress, and Níkia cling to the northern and southern lips respectively of the craters, while the outer slopes are planted with almond trees, an exquisitely beautiful sight in February. In the northwest, the acropolis of ancient Níssyros, surrounded by imposing Pelasgian walls of black trachyte, is only a short walk from the present capital and port Mandráki. The standard medieval castle encloses the Monastery of the Panagía Spilianí (Our Lady of the Cave), which attracts a large number of pilgrims for the feast of the Assumption on August 15.

Slightly less on the religious, a little more on the touristic itinerary, is arid, rocky yet attractive Sými, almost encircled by the mountains of the Turkish mainland. Its mountains are as impressive as those of Kálymnos and Kárpathos, and entitle it to rank with them as the finest in the Dodecanese. As one might expect, there are several myths of nymphs or princesses abandoned on the deserted island, but more original is the association with Prometheus: it was here that he fabricated the first human being from clay, whereupon Zeus turned him into an ape, hence the word simian. Homer calls Nereus, King of Sými, the best-looking man (after incomparable Achilles) in the Greek army, a reputation that seems to have waned.

Nor does Gialós quite live up to Plinius' Egialo among "the eight magnificent ports," but the neo-Classical architecture of the waterfront harmonizes with the colorful boats and caiques of the sponge fishers. It is a mere quarter of an hour's walk to the capital, really the port's upper town with steep narrow lanes. The Archaeological Museum is beyond the large Church of the Panagía. The best beach is in another bay, at Pédio to the north, but it requires a boat to circumnavigate Sými to its finest bay, Pánormos. The large Monastery of the Archangel Michael Panormítis, in heavy Greco-Russian Baroque, is a place of pilgrimage on the feasts of its patron.

Tílos is likewise mountainous and deeply indented by several bays. On the east shore lie the attractive arcaded houses of Livadiá, encircled by the ruins of four Genoese castles. Megálo Horió, the capital, is six km. (four miles) north, below yet another fortress, amidst vineyards and fig trees, which extend to the Monastery of Ágios Panteléimon farther west.

Hálki, closest to Rhodes, though the smallest in this group, displays the whole lot: Pelasgian walls, vestiges of no less than three temples of Apollo, two Byzantine monasteries, a castle and some fine beaches. For reasons known only to those in authority, it has been proclaimed "Island of Peace," assembling various manifestations during the milder seasons.

Ródos (Rhodes)

The great island of Rhodes, with its fine walled town, is Greece's biggest and most cosmopolitan resort, with some 25,000 beds in hotels of all categories accommodating over 800,000 visitors annually. Congresses extend the foreign influx, and there is some winter tourism, despite the abundant rainfall which favors the luxuriant vegetation, badly devastated in the great fires of 1987 and 1988.

The first town-planner in Europe, the Milesian architect Hippodamus, designed, in 408 B.C. the checker-work layout of Rhodes, named like the island after the nymph Rhodos, beloved by the sungod Helios, patron of the island. Succeeding Athens as the main commercial power in the Aegean, Rhodes introduced maritime law, while its wealth made possible the development of a new School of Sculpture tending towards the colossal, in the manner of Alexander the Great's court artist, Lysippus, who executed the famous bronze Quadriga of the sun. Rhodian sculptors created the superb Laocoon excavated by Michelangelo in Rome, the victory of Samothrace, now in the Louvre, and the original of the Farnese Bull in the Naples Museum. Allied to Rome, Rhodes suffered the common fate of these allies by being finally annexed. The decline in political and commercial eminence in the 1st century B.C. meant the end of expensive sculpture, but a new School soon flourished, that of Rhetoric, rivaling that of Athens.

In A.D. 43, the Apostle Paul brought Christianity; while, in 654, the Saracens started depredations which still left enough in 1191 for Richard Coeur de Lion to wonder at the mighty works of art. Rhodes made news when in 1306, the chief admiral of the Byzantine empire sold it to the military Order of Saint John of Jerusalem, which was then established in Cyprus, after the loss of the Holy Land. The Emperor Andronicus II objected to such a powerful vassal and it took four years of hard fighting before some knights were able to enter the town mixed with a flock of sheep on a dark misty night and to open the gates to their comrades. The Order was composed of Knights, Brothers (hospitalers) and Clerks; it was organized into eight national sub-divisions or "Languages": Provence, Auvergne, France, Italy, England, Germany, Castile and Aragon. It was ruled by a Grand Master, who was elected for life by the General Chapter. Nineteen Grand Masters ruled in Rhodes, 14 of French origin, which proves the preponderance of French knights.

Rhodes was made so firm a stronghold, that in 1480, the Grand Master Pierre d'Aubusson was able to resist the attacks of 70,000 Turks led by Mohammed II, the conqueror of Constantinople. In 1522, Villiers de l'Isle Adam was obliged to surrender to Suleiman the Magnificent's 200,000 men, but only after a six months' siege that captured the imagination of all western Europe. Thereafter the Order retired to Malta, where an equally heroic Grand Master, La Valetta, victoriously beat back the Sultan's final onslaught.

The modern port is a part of the Knights' fortifications, topped by an iron deer, Rhodes' emblem, on the harbor pillars. Walls encircle the old town and the five-km. (three-mile) circuit of the battlements affords a fine view over the Byzantine, Latin and Turkish architecture framed by luxuriant parks across the moat.

Apart from the Castellania (the Knights' market-building) the best of Gothic Rhodes may be seen by walking up the newly restored street of the Knights, which follows a steep, straight ancient road that once led from the acropolis of Rhodes to the port. On one corner is the Knights' hospital, now the museum, which contains a handsome court with cloisters. The exhibits in the beautifully proportioned refectory and spacious pillared infirmary range from the Mycenaean period to the Middle Ages, highlighted by two lovely Hellenistic statues of Aphrodite. On either side of the street are the restored inns of the different "Languages"; the fine battlemented French inn, with large square windows, and the cardinal's hat and arms of the Grand Master Pierre d'Aubusson should be noted, also the heavy round Aragonese door to the Spanish inn. A small church projects out of line, with a battered Madonna in a niche. The street is spanned by an arch, below the Provençal inn, and then comes the modern archway of the Grand Master's palace. Helion de Villeneuve (1319–1346) copied the papal palace of Avignon for this grandiose residence, which survived the sieges but was wrecked in an accidental explosion in 1856. The last, somewhat megalomaniac, Italian governor finished the reconstruction in 1940. It is commonly maligned, but though ostentatious, with much of the interior a monument of bad taste, it is a fairly convincing Gothic replica—especially in the flattering illumination of the Sound and Light performance from April through October. The interior should be visited, for it contains many mosaic pavements, which the Italians removed here from Kos.

The Knights' quarter adjoins within the walls the Turkish quarter with its narrow streets spanned by anti-seismic arches, further propped against shock by flying buttresses forming a charming labyrinth of round squares, where huge plane trees shade the fountains. Slim minarets rise over the cupolas of mosques and Byzantine churches, tiled eaves and overhanging wooden balconies. The fine dome of the Mosque of Regib Pasha tops a double portico and it is worth entering the Hammam of Suleiman to see the plasterwork in the great room.

The modern town centers on the small port of Mandráki, used by caiques and yachts. Three windmills stand on the breakwater which terminates at the Ágios Nikólaos lighthouse. Here was the ancient harbor, whose entry was bestridden by the largest of all Rhodian sculptures, the Colossus of Rhodes, one of the Seven Wonders of the World. Chares of Líndos' 30-meter (100-ft.) bronze statue of Helios was overthrown by the devastating earthquake of 227 B.C., having guarded the port for a mere 65 years. Despite generous donations by Hellenistic rulers, the technical difficulties of raising the statue could not be overcome. Broken up by the Saracens, the fragments were shipped to Syria, where 980 camels were loaded with the ponderous debris for the final purchaser at Édessa. This chief waterfront of the town is marked by pseudo-Venetian and massive pseudo-Roman buildings, the octagonal Italian market-building, which is pleasant enough, the Bishop's Palace and the Church of Evangelismou giving on to the same courtyard with a fountain, the rather lamentable Post Office, Theater and Municipality and the Venetian Gothic Prefecture, beside which the Mosque of Murad Reis looks all the more graceful.

Except for the Hydrobiological Institute with its well-stocked aquarium, the northern promontory is almost entirely taken up by modern hotels, from the sea to Mount Smith, from which Sir Sydney Smith, commander of the English fleet, kept an eye on the French during Napoleon's Egyptian campaign. Scattered over the eastern slopes are the remains of the 2nd-century B.C. acropolis, with the Temples of Zeus and Athena, the partially restored Temple of Apollo, gymnasium and stadium, and the small theater.

A waterlily pond reflects a ruined aqueduct and Ptolemaic tomb in the beautiful park of Rodini, two km. (one mile) along the east coast. It is pleasant to dine by the sea in the tavernas of the small port of Kóuva, just outside the city walls.

Three Ancient Cities

The Dorian invaders of the 11th century B.C. founded on Rhodes the cities of Ialyssós, Kámiros and Líndos, which were leagued with Kos, and with the Asiatic cities of Halicarnassus and Knidos, in a religious and political confederacy, called the Dorian Hexapolis. Such local leagues are found in other parts of Greece, and preceded larger systems of Hellenic unity. In 408 B.C. the three Rhodian cities founded Rhodes itself as their administrative and religious center.

Of the three ancient cities, not very much is to be seen of Ialyssós, eight km. (five miles) inland. On the acropolis stands the now derelict Franciscan monastery of Filerimo, and there are extensive views. More interesting than the antique foundations, the remains of an early Christian basilica and the 4th century B.C. Doric fountain on the hillside is the little Chapel of St. George with its Gothic wall-painting. Twenty-seven km. (17 miles) along the west coast, the extensive ruins of Kámiros, on the slopes of a hill that is crowned with a handsome colonnade, give a much better picture of a 3rd century B.C. town.

But the gem of the three is undoubtedly Líndos, a lovely 56-km. (35-mile) drive along the east coast. The entire town has been officially designated an archaeological site, thus ensuring its intact preservation. A small masterpiece of cubism, its architecture includes Byzantine and Arabic influences and all of it is ancient and impressive. This intriguing village with its imposing historical site and beautiful curved sandy bay attracts thousands of visitors every year. The small cobbled alleyways leading through the village up to the acropolis can be tremendously crowded in high season.

Its acropolis is on the top of a high headland, whose flank falls abruptly to the sea; from sea and land it is a grand sight, even finer than the site of the temple of Sounion, with which it may in some ways be compared. It is a very ancient foundation, attributed to Danaos and his 50 daughters, who came here from Egypt on their flight from Aegyptos and his 50 sons. There is a beautiful colonnade, and, on a high platform, the Temple of Athena Lindia; this is Greece's most restored Acropolis except for that of Athens, but has kept later additions, a Byzantine church (in ruins), a castle of the Knights, and Turkish fortification. Líndos thus contains a history of its island in miniature.

In a small gulf at one side of the cliff foot, St. Paul is believed to have landed, no doubt greatly vexed by the great veneration accorded to Athena Lindia, whose mantle Alexander the Great wore in battle and to whom he dedicated the shields taken at the battle of Issos that gave him the greater part of the Persian Empire. In the charming white town, the Church of Our Lady of Líndos was built by the Knights of Rhodes. It has a tunnel-like frescoed nave, with a black and white pebbled floor. Some of the pretty 17th-century houses have pebbled courtyards. In several of them collections of early "Rhodian" pottery may be seen. The legend that a Grand Master of the Order captured some Persian potters, and made them work for him, has no foundation. No fragments of this ware have ever been found on the island, and not until recent times has "Rhodian" pottery been manufactured in Rhodes. It has, however, now developed into a local industry, known especially for its ornamental tiles.

On the road from Rhodes to Líndos one may visit Kallithéa, where the medicinal springs of the seaside spa, specializing in the cure of digestive and kidney disorders are closed at present. At Faliráki there is another large concentration of hotels. Further along the coast are two villages in the white style of the Cyclades: Afándou with the interesting Church of the Panagía Í Katholikí in the hills above the golf course, and Archángelos below a medieval castle. From Haráki a beach extends to the Bay of Vlíha.

Beside the attraction of antique and medieval sites, as well as fine beaches, there is the heavily-wooded and pleasantly-cool mountain retreat of Profítis Ilías (Prophet Elias), 720 meters (2,360 ft.) above sea level, and 50 km. (31 miles) from the capital.

At only half that distance lies the famous Valley of the Butterflies, Petalóudes, a wooded gorge about one km. (half a mile) long and crossed by many rustic bridges. The golden tiger moths have not taken to the innumerable visitors, so an E.C. grant is employed to preserve them from ecological catastrophe. In summer swarms settle thickly on the leaves, and inside hollow *amber orientalis* trees. In repose, their protective coloring makes them look like dark leaves, with yellow veins. If stirred, they fill the air with a thick shower of reddish gold.

The Outlying Isles

The name Kárpathos is probably a derivation from Árpaktos, Robbery Island, as pirates once used the numerous gulfs for their bases. It is a mountainous and elongated island, with sufficient space for fertile plains on its 301 square km. (116 square miles). The broader southern part with the fine natural port opening eastwards, and the capital Kárpathos or Pigádia—ancient Poseidonion, which claimed to be the sea god's home town—conforms to the usual island pattern. But the narrow northern part is almost unique in two things: it preserves its forests, and local costume is still worn by the women as ordinary working dress.

In many islands women treasure the beautiful traditional clothes of their grandmothers. They will show them to interested visitors, and may sometimes wear them at Easter, at weddings, or on other festive occasions. But they are best dresses, and have nothing to do with everyday life. The women of northern Kárpathos wear long boots, into which they tuck their white Turkish breeches; their white skirts are looped up, when they work in the fields. Over all is worn a graceful cloak of night blue, and a black handkerchief patterned with colored flowers covers the head. The women here take a large part in the heavier work; "we will find a woman to carry your things," is a typical remark. This grand, if grim region, so little influenced by the outer world, preserves a life of its own. Ethnologists have studied the oldest settlement on the island, Olimbos, to learn more about the roots of contemporary Greek folk tradition. Many villagers still speak a dialect retaining Doric words and fit their houses with the kind of wooden locks described by Homer.

Among the orchards of Arkássa, south of the capital Kárpathos, are the remains of several 5th century Byzantine churches, their mosaic floors now in Rhodes museum. Southwest of Arkássa are more ruins, these of the ancient Classical town of Arkaseia.

North, across a narrow strait, is small Saría, once an island principality. The ruins of a second Nissyros are at Palátia, the main settlement. South is Kássos, closest to Crete. The capital, Fry, is a fishing port. Near the stalactite cave of Selai are Pelasgian walls.

Far to the east, barely a mile from the Turkish coast, Kastelórizo, though the smallest of the 12, is perversely also known as Megísti, the Biggest, which it is of its own group of tiny islets. The houses of the present 270 inhabitants cluster below the reddish Venetian fortress from which the island's name derives. The oblong harbor is so perfectly sheltered that it once provided a safe landing-ground for hydroplanes from Paris; it forms a vast pool where the bathers glimpse ancient amphorae through the crystal clear water, hardly ruffled by some fishing smacks; though few, these provide an abundance of seafood, comprising delicious sea snails and crabs. All the other food is brought from Rhodes, either by the twice-weekly boat or the twice-weekly airplane, landing at the new inland airport.

At the western periphery of the archipelago, Astypaléa is the nearest to the Cyclades, and is clearly seen from Thíra and Ámorgos; it is connected with the latter as well as with Kos and Rhodes, towards which its main harbor is turned. While Astypalea is politically one of the Dodecanese, its culture is Cycladic, remote and isolated. Until 1980 there was only one ship a week from Piraeus, and no jetty. Remoteness, however, is not the only charm of this island. Its great bay, Maltezána, with its rocks and satellite islets is of great beauty.

The Asian Offshore Islands

Sámos, Híos and Lésbos, these great islands so near the coast of Asia Minor (of which they are geographically a part) should be called "Greece in Asia." They are all that is left to Greece of the glorious Greek civilization which flourised on the Asiatic coast at a very early period, long before the rise of Athens as an important state and city. Few parts of the Aegean have greater variety and beauty of landscape.

Sámos

Sámos, the southernmost, is connected with the other two by regular communications. Boats from Piraeus and Mýkonos first call at Ágios Kírykos, the port of Ikaría, a large rocky island with Europe's most radioactive springs. Sámos' highest mountain Kérkis (1,301 meters, 4,720 ft.) is seen from miles away. It is near the western tip of the island, and seems to float above the sea, like a mountain in a Japanese print. On a nearer approach its great bald head is seen, rising out of surrounding forest. Early travelers saw a mysterious light shining out of this mountain; superstitions and scientific conjectures were made about its origin, but it has never been explained.

During the century that followed the fall of Constantinople (1453), Sámos was completely depopulated, except for a few people who hid on this mountain, and perhaps continued the line of aboriginal Samians till the next century, when the Turkish admiral, Kilidj Ali Pasha, fell in love with the island (where he had gone hunting) and obtained permission from the sultan to repopulate it with Greeks from other parts and grant them autonomy. From 1834 onwards Sámos was a Christian principality under Turkish dominion until its union with Greece in 1912.

Sámos is an island in which the mountains are disposed in a singularly fortunate way; after Kérkis there is a pass, and then the chain of Ámbelos (1,140 meters, 3,740 ft.) forms the backbone. Ámbelos sends out a number of spurs towards the sea in all directions, and they enclose many well-shaped small coastal plains. Every good view in Sámos, and there are so many, includes one or other of these mountains, and sometimes the grand peak of Mycale in Asia Minor, separated by a narrow strait. The island is almost everywhere well-wooded, and extremely fertile, growing some of the best grapes in Greece.

In 1854 the Christian prince moved from Chóra; a pleasant village that had been the capital from 1560, to Vathý (Deep), now Sámos, on a long, narrow gulf on the north coast. Pythagora Square is the center of modern Sámos; the princely Council Chamber is now the Town Hall, next to the recently-reopened Vathý Archaeological Museum. The partly wooden houses in the attractive upper town, still called Vathý, rise on terraces in the redtiled Turkish style; a great contrast to the cubist, white houses of the woodless Cyclades. There are pretty excursions to be made particularly above the town, to the Monastery of Zoödochos Pigi, with its wonderful view towards Asia, or a longer excursion (by bus or taxi) to the village of Vourliótis, on the northern slopes of Ámbelos. This village is in itself attractive (its plateia would make an exquisite stagesetting) and it is a short walk to the Monastery of Vrondianí, below a medieval castle.

Much better bathing can be enjoyed below the formidable walls of Sámos' ancient capital, now the attractive port of Pythagório, 14 km. (nine miles) south, named after the famous 6th-century B.C. philosopher and mathematician, Pythagoras. In 1989, the 30-foot-high (9 meters) bronze statue of Pythagoras was erected next to the harbor, the work funded by the Orthodox Patriarchate of North and South America, by Samian organizations in Canada and Australia, and by a local committee. Framed by two good beaches, it commands an exquisite view of Mycale and Asia Minor, but occupies only an insignificant part of the vast rectangle enclosed by well-preserved ramparts stretching ten km. (six miles) up and across the Astypalean hill. These fortifications were constructed by the political prisoners of the tyrant Polycrates, whose corsairs were, from 535 to 527 B.C., the terror of these seas, plundering friend and foe alike "for he argued," Herodotus tells us, "that a friend was better pleased if you gave him back what you had taken from him, than if you spared him at the first"; Herodotus, who had a warm partiality for this island, was especially interested in "the mighty works of the Samians" in which Polycrates showed his power. One of these was a harbor mole (part of which can be seen under the water), while another was a tunnel to bring water through the mountain, an astonishing feat of 6th-century B.C. engineering by Eupalinos. Although the central portion of the tunnel has collapsed, it is still possible (between April and October; mornings only) to explore its entrances and part of the aqueduct. The third "mighty work" was the temple of Hera, patroness of Sámos, of which one column is still standing, six km. (four miles) west of Pythagório, amid the extensive ruins in the coastal marsh past the airport. Hera, born nearby according to ancient beliefs, replaced the Great Goddess, who had been worshipped here from earliest times. The statue of the largest antique *Kouros,* a four-and-a-half-meter (15-ft.) high colossus, dating from 570–560 B.C., unearthed at the Iréo (Heraeon), is the pride of the museum in Vathý, which contains a very important collection of the art of Ionia.

A road more or less encircles the island, and the round trip is a highly desirable excursion, because of the great variety and beauty of the scenery. The old houses of Karlóvassi, the second town and port, extend to the 10th-century Monastery of the Panagía tóu Potamóu (Our Lady of the River).

The ferry boat south to the Dodecanese passes through the narrow strait, a mere two km. (one mile and a half) wide, that separates Sámos from the Turkish mainland, with beautiful views.

Híos (Chios)—Birthplace of Homer?

The scenery ranges from barren rocks and wooded mountains to four small fertile plains. The capital on the east coast features a ruined mosque, and the tiny prison where Bishop Platanos and 75 leading citizens were held before being hanged in 1822 as part of the massacre of 30,000 islanders by the Turks, as depicted in Delacroix's famous painting and described in Victor Hugo's poem. Another mosque on the main square is surrounded by cafes and pastry shops. Nor can much enthusiasm be raised by the museum of antiquities and a medieval castle—Genoese this time.

Híos is one of the seven traditional birthplaces of Homer, and the author of an Homeric hymn describes himself as "the blind old man of rocky Chios." Modern scholars, who tend to believe that he was a single individual, and not a company, are disposed to think it possible that he did indeed live and work here. The village of Kardámyla in the northeast is his traditional birthplace, and he is said to have lived and worked at Vólissos in the west; there is no evidence to support either of these traditions. The *Pétra Omírou* (The Rock of Homer), six km. (four miles) north of the town, was a rupestral shrine of the Asian goddess Cybele, represented with two lions, though it was once believed that the great bard had sat on a knob on the flattened top, and that rhapsodes sat round the edge, listening to him. The taverns under the plane trees are pleasant on a summer evening, and the stony beach is much frequented. Another six km. (four miles) on, at Vrondádos, is the seat of the International Society of Homeric Studies.

The town beach is inadequate, but possesses tremendous snob value for Híos society, as it extends to the house of one of the richest of the fabulous Greek shipping magnates. If bathing is the object, better take a bus six km. (four miles) south to Karfás, with its long bay of fine sand.

Starting from the capital, scenic roundtrips are possible in the mountainous north as well as in the flatter south. But a must is the excursion— 17 km. (11 miles)—to Néa Moní, high up on the mountain, where in the first half of the 11th century three holy hermits found a miraculous ikon of the Virgin; they were commanded in a vision to go to Lesbos and seek

Constantine Monomachos, then living there in exile, and to get him to promise to build a church for the ikon if ever he became emperor. When the eccentric empress Zoë, by a third marriage, raised him to the throne as Constantine IX in 1042, the hermits went to Constantinople, and exacted the fulfillment of the promise. He sent them back to Híos with masons and artists. On his death, the work was completed with the aid of Zoë's sister, the empress Theodora.

At one time this was a vast monastery, inhabited by 600 monks; for lack of novices a few nuns have now taken over. Turkish vandalism, earthquakes and neglect have done great harm to the church, but there is a most interesting cycle of excellent, brilliantly-colored mosaics depicting the life of Christ.

Of other monastic buildings, the refectory, on the south of the church, is an uninteresting 17th-century building, but should be visited on account of the fine stone table, which runs the length of the room. There are niches in it for knives and forks and napkins, and there are remains of ornaments in *opus Alexandrinum* on the top. Northwest of the church, you may look through a door down into a vaulted cistern; this 11th-century structure is reminiscent of the subterranean cistern of Constantinople.

South of the town is Kámpos, the fertile plain where high mud-brick walls hide the country houses of the older Híos families—and Híos, under the Genoese Trading Company that was its ruler until 1566 was almost unique among Aegean islands in fostering the growth of a local aristocracy. A Dutch traveler of the 18th century gives a description of these dwellings that is still true today: "These houses are walled round, and from the outer gate is a walk of trellis-work covered with vines, and supported with stone pillars from an adjacent quarry. At the end of this walk is a garden of about an acre of land, planted with orange and other trees."

In the southwest lie the mastic villages, prosperous from the gum exuded from the terebinth lentisk, a round bushy tree with dark green leaves. It is gathered, in the form of crystals, in the fall and late summer. In its natural state, it is a scented chewing gum of extreme adhesiveness. It is made into a liqueur, into chewing gum, and into a white sticky jam, served in Greek cafes as a "sweet of the spoon"—a spoonful in a glass of water, and it is called *ypovrýhio* (submarine). In Turkish times mastic was a strict monopoly of the sultans; it was much valued in Constantinople, where the ladies of the Serail liked to chew it, to lessen the boredom of their lives, and to sweeten their breath.

Of the mastic villages, Pýrgi is most frequently visited. It is built within medieval walls, and near the middle is a ruined *pyrgos* (tower), once the keep. The town is a labyrinth of narrow lanes, overshaded by vines or other creepers, and often spanned by arches, as a protection against earthquake shock. The houses are decorated with motifs known locally as *ksista*, geometric patterns in gray and white, rather like the Italian *sgraffito* technique. The women of Pýrgi are unique in the island in wearing a native costume; the big kerchief on the head—fringed at the side—is colored for a married woman, black for one recently widowed, and white for a widow of long standing. They are of a strange, unmediterranean type, and are probably descendants of Saracen marauders. It is worth returning via Mésta, a perfect example of the island's fortified villages, restored as a traditional settlement.

At Emborío, on a promontory along the southeast coast, a Bronze Age settlement has been unearthed, which had four stages of existence, and was destroyed in a great fire. It is thought to have been a rival to Troy. A Greek city of the 8th century B.C. was discovered on the higher hill, Profitis Ilias, although the only visible remains are of a megaron, a temple of Athena and an Early Christian baptistery south of the harbor. The black-stone beach below the scanty ruins is magnificent.

Lésvos (Lesbos)—Where Sappho Lived and Loved

Pittacus, the 7th-century B.C tyrant, and one of the Seven Wise Men of antiquity, unified the island and made his capital Mytilíni the center of the Aeolian Greeks and of a famous school of poetry. When "Burning Sappho" practised what she preached in about 600 B.C., Mytilíni was Greece's most advanced and civilized city; it was prosperous, possessed a considerable sea-power, and a remarkable intellectual life. Aesop, the great storyteller, was a native of Lesbos. Another great lyric poet, Alcaeus, was Sappho's exact contemporary. It is she, however, who has captured the imagination of posterity: the first and the greatest of women poets. Her erotic poems addressed to girls, in which the physical effects of love on the human frame are described as no other writer has described them, earned her the reputation which has clung to her ever since, and were the reason for the burning of those poems by the Church in Constantinople in 1073; fortunately many fragments survive. The biographical tradition about her is apocryphal, and there is no reason to credit the tale that she died as a result of a leap from a cliff at Lefkáda in the Ionian islands, on account of her unsuccessful love for a young boatman called Phaon. Legendary inhabitants of Mytilíni (at a much later date) were Daphnis and Chloë, the hero and heroine of the romance by Longinus.

In 802 the Byzantine Empress Irene was banished to the island, only shortly after her marriage to Charlemagne had been contemplated, a union which might have reunited the Eastern and Western Roman Empires as well as Christendom. She died on Lesbos the following year and, although she had blinded her own son in order to prolong her regency, became an Orthodox saint, as she had restored the worship of ikons at the Seventh Ecumenical Council.

Modern Mytilíni is built over the ancient city. The castle is sufficiently preserved to house relics from the 14th-century marriage of the Emperor John Palaeologus' sister into the Genoese Gateluzzi family that ruled until the Turkish conquest in 1462. The Hellenistic theater above the town, next to the Chapel of Agía Kyriakí, is too ruined to support the belief that it inspired the great Pompey to copy it in Rome. Several Roman floor mosaics at nearby excavations prove the Romans' appreciation of the fine view: they built their most sumptuous villas at the height of the hills that form a half-circle round the bay.

There are more museums than strictly necessary. The Byzantine and the Popular Art may be skipped without a crisis of conscience, but the Archaeological Museum has a rich collection of *Tanagra* figures, and of ancient lamps, beside some good mosaic pavement found at Eressós, and two beautiful 7th-century B.C. capitals of the rare Aeolic style. The Stratis Eleftheriadis-Teriant Museum-Library displays Chagall, Matisse and Picasso as well as illustrations by the post-impressionist art critic after whom the museum is named. Local color is strong in the pictures in the Theophilos Museum at Variá, four km. (two miles) south.

On the waterfront, you can enjoy the specialties of Lesbos, olives, ouzo from Plomári, and the excellent fresh sardines from the gulf of Kallóni.

Bathing in town is poor, but 13 km. (eight miles) north is the good beach of Paralía Thérmis, close to Thérmi, a small thermal establishment for rheumatic conditions.

Southeastern Lesbos—very much the best part of the island—is a country of high mountains and olive groves. Excursions are greatly to be recommended, particularly round the lovely Gulf of Géras, an inland sea in a sea of olives. At the head of the gulf the road divides, south (left) along the gulf's western shore, then up through a dense chestnut forest, with unusually fine views even for an Aegean island, then westwards down to the lovely, though pebbly, beach of Ágios Isidóros and the small port of Plomári, with its ouzo distilleries.

Barely three km. (two miles) further along the island's east-west axis, another roadfork diverges southwest (left) to Assómatos, thence south (left again) to Agiássos, a traditional settlement whose cobbled lanes and square are surrounded by birch, oak and pine trees, rising from deep ravines to the bald peak of the Lesbian Ólympos (967 meters, 3,170 ft.). St. Luke's ikon of the Panagía Vrefokratóusa (Our Lady and Child), brought by the monk Agathon the Ephesian from Jerusalem in 803, attracts large crowds of pilgrims on August 15. West of Assómatos, at aptly named Vassílika (Royal) the Empress Irene spent the last year of her agitated life, one hopes, praying at the small Church of Ágios Pávlos. Políhnitos, 45 km. (28 miles) from Mytilíni, is another traditional settlement, here enhanced by curative hot springs. To the north is the port of Skála Polihnítou and the popular beach of Nifída, both near the entrance of the vast, landlocked Gulf of Kallonís. South, the eight-km. (five-mile) long beach of Vatéra on the open sea is one of the Aegean's finest. On the Ágios Fokás promontory are the ruins of a Dionysos Temple.

The next branch from the main axis leads northeast (right) four km. (two miles) to the 16th-century monastery of Ágios Ignátios and the village of Agía Paraskeví where, late in May, the pagan Feast of the Bulls, complete with bull sacrifice, is celebrated as a Christian pageant. Not surprisingly, there are the foundations of several temples in the neighborhood. Forty km. (25 miles) from Mytilíni, at Kalloní, the main road forks north (right) to the pleasant fishing village of Pétra, where the beach is dominated by the Church of Panagía Glykophilóusa (Sweet-kissing Virgin) perched on a rock. Here is another Women's Agricultural Co-operative, offering rooms in local members' homes. Seven km. (four miles) north, Mithýmna (Mólyvos) has been chosen by the International Academy of Engraving for annual summer courses.

Mithýmna stands on the site of ancient Methymna, second most important city after Mytilíni, and its constant rival. Arion, the musician who was shipwrecked and saved on a dolphin's back, was a citizen of Methymna, and it is here that the current bore the head of the singer Orpheus, after it had been torn off by the Maenads (the bacchantes whose advances he disdained), and thrown into the River Évros in Thrace.

Mithýmna is the island's most attractive town, built on a high headland, under a fine Genoese castle—this was saved from a Turkish assault in the 15th century by the "Lady of Lesbos" Onetta d'Oria, wife of the ruling Genoese prince, who astonished the townsfolk by appearing in full armor, and leading them to victory. The bay below is lined by a pebbly beach, and the view of the Trojan mountains across the sea is admirable. The 17 km. (ten miles) east through varied scenery below the Lepetýmnos

Mountain are fairly rough, but allow a complete roundtrip, returning along the east coast via Mistégna and Thermí to Mytilíni.

Eressós, in the southwest, is by some accounts the birthplace of Sappho (the ancient city put her head upon its coins), and of the philosopher Theophrastos. The village lies in a valley, fine rocks rising above it. The Archeological Museum fills only a small part of the site once occupied by the early Christian basilica of Ágios Andréas. Four km. (two miles) south is the vast sandy beach of Skála Eressóu, with all the potential of a summer resort, stretching below the hill which was the acropolis of the ancient city.

Northwest at Sígri, lava covered huge trees, supposedly a million years ago. Fossilized tree trunks are dotted over the barren countryside, called locally and grandiloquently the Petrified Forest.

PRACTICAL INFORMATION FOR
THE EASTERN ISLANDS

TOURIST OFFICE. There is a G.N.T.O. office on **Rhodes,** Arhcbishop Makarios and Papagou 5 (tel. 2 3655).

SPECIAL EVENTS. April through **October.** Sound and Light performances at the Palace of the Knights, Rhodes town. **May** through **October.** Greek folk dance performances by the Nelly Dimoglou Group at the Rodinii Theatre.

HOTELS AND RESTAURANTS. Rhodes has plentiful modern accommodations in all categories. A number of hotels are open all year round. Except in the luxury hotels, the food is remarkably indifferent, with no trace of any seafood, which would certainly be welcome.

Híos is famous for its fruit preserves *(glykó)* and its aperitifs *(mastíka* and *óuzo*). Though Byron praised the Samian *Moscháto* in his *Isles of Greece,* it is almost too sweet to drink even as a dessert wine, but there is also a pleasant white table wine, *Samaina.* The light white Rhodian wines, especially *Lindos,* go well with fish, but Rhodes is better known for the full-bodied red wines of Cair.

Astypaléa

Aegeon (I), tel. 6 1236. 20 rooms. *Astynea* (I), tel. 6 1209. 20 rooms.
Restaurant. *Albatross* (M), on the waterfront. Excellent baked crab and grilled octopus.

Híos

Híos Town. *Chandris Chios* (M), tel. 2 5761/8. 156 rooms. Airconditioned; halfboard, pool, looking on to the port, disco. AE, DC, MC, V. *Kyma* (M), tel. 2 5551. 59 rooms. *Diana* (I), tel. 2 5993. 51 rooms. Roofgarden. DC, V.

Kámpos. *Villa Argentikon* (L), tel. 3 1599. 4 suites in 3 buildings. This is the former 16th-century home of a Chian-Genoese family, lovingly restored by the descendant and present owner. It is luxurious and civilized, with impeccable service and excellent food.

Kardámyla. *Kardámyla* (M), tel. 2 2378. 42 rooms. Airconditioned; beach, tennis, disco.

Mésta. *Traditional Settlement* (M), tel. 2 7908. 45 rooms in 20 modernized old houses in a very original setting.
Pyrgi. *The Women's Agricultural-Tourism Co-operative* (tel. 7 2496) offers accommodations (44 rooms) in local village homes.

Ikaría

Ágios Kírykos. *Toula* (M), tel. 2 2298. 246 rooms and bungalows. Beach, thermal facilities, pool, tennis, disco; 2 km. (1 mile) from town.

Thérma. *Apollon* (I), tel. 2 2477. 39 rooms, some with showers.

Kálymnos

Kálymnos Town. *Olympic* (I), tel. 2 8801. 42 rooms. MC. *Thermae* (I), tel. 2 9425. 18 rooms. Restaurant. AE, MC.

Massóuri. *Armeos Beach* (M), tel. 4 7488. 34 rooms. Pool, tennis. *Massouri Beach* (I), tel. 4 7555. 36 rooms.

Myrtiés. *Delfini* (I), tel. 4 7514. 18 rooms. Beach, restaurant. MC. *Zephyros* (I), tel. 4 7500. 28 rooms.

Pánormos. *Drossos* (I), tel. 4 7301. 51 rooms. Restaurant, minigolf.

Póthea. *Evanik* (I), tel. 2 2057. 21 rooms.

Kárpathos

Kárpathos Town. (Pigadia). *Seven Stars* (M), tel. 2 2101. 34 rooms. Pool. *Atlantis* (I), tel. 2 2777. 38 rooms. *Panorama* (I), tel. 2 2739. 23 rooms. *Porfyris* (I), tel. 2 2294. 22 rooms.

Kássos

Anagenissis (I), tel. 4 1323. 10 rooms, 5 with shower.

Kastelórizo

Xenon Dimou Megistis (I), tel. 2 9072. 17 rooms.

Kos

Kardámena. *Carda Beach* (M), tel. 9 1222. 67 bungalows. Tennis, pool, disco. *Norida Beach* (M), tel. 9 1220. 426 rooms. Pool, tennis, disco. Management has been a bit wanting recently. DC. *Valinakis* (I), tel. 9 1358. 73 rooms. Restaurant.

Kefálos. *Hellas* (I), tel. 2 3017/8. 17 rooms. *Kokalakis Beach* (I), tel. 7 1466. 23 rooms. The *Club Mediterranée's* big hotel and bungalows (E), tel. 7 1311/3, sometimes has accommodations available.

Kos Town. All (E) hotels are on beaches near town and have pool and tennis. *Caravia Beach* (E), tel. 4 1291. 297 rooms in central blocks and bungalows; disco. AE, DC. *Continental Palace* (E), tel. 2 2737. 210 rooms. AE, DC, V. *Dimitra Beach* (E), tel. 2 8581. 134 rooms. Not airconditioned. AE, DC, MC, V.

Agios Konstantinos (M), tel. 2 3301. 125 rooms. Pool. AE, V. *Alexandra* (M), tel. 2 8301. 88 rooms. Disco, roofgarden.AE, V. *Astron* (M), tel. 2 3704. 75 rooms. Roofgarden. *Atlanta Beach* (M), tel. 2 8889. 44 rooms. AE, MC. *Kos* (M), tel. 2 2480. 137 rooms. Pool. *Theodorou Beach* (M), tel. 2 2280. 54 rooms. V. *Theoxenia* (M), tel. 2 2310. 42 rooms.

Anastasia (I), tel. 2 8598. 43 rooms. V. *Captain's* (I), tel. 2 2961. 28 rooms. *Elli* (I), tel. 2 8401. 78 rooms. *Elma* (I), tel. 2 2920. 49 rooms. *Maritina* (I), tel. 2 3241. 68 rooms. AE, DC, MC. *Oscar* (I), tel. 2 8090. 160 rooms. The only (I) with restaurant. Large pool. AE, DC, V. *Zephyros* (I), tel. 2 2245. 52 rooms. V.

Lámbi. *Atlantis* (E), tel. 2 8731. 297 rooms in central block and bungalows. Half board; pool, tennis. DC. *Atlantis 2* (M), tel. 2 3755. 85 rooms. *Columbia Beach* (M), tel. 2 8440. 58 rooms. *Cosmopolitan* (M), tel. 2 3411. 580 rooms. Pool, tennis. V. *Argo* (I), tel. 2 4375. 55 rooms. *Irene* (I), tel. 2 8186. 55 rooms. *Laura* (I), tel. 2 8981. 23 rooms.

Psalídi. *Hippocrates Palace* (E), tel. 2 4401/8. 241 rooms and suites; huge swimming pool, sauna, tennis, disco. AE, DC, V. *Oceanis* (E), tel. 2 3728. 352 rooms. Pool, tennis. AE. *Ramira Beach* (E), tel. 2 2891/4. 250 rooms, 3 suites. Pool, tennis, disco. AE, DC. *Sun Palace* (E), tel. 2 4391. 145 rooms and suites. Pool, tennis. AE.

Tigáki. *Tigaki Beach* (E), tel. 2 9447. 167 rooms. Pool, tennis. *Ilios* (I), tel. 2 9411/2. 48 rooms. *Sunset* (I), tel. 2 9428/9. 52 rooms.

Léros

Alínda. *Maleas Beach* (I), tel. 2 3306. 48 rooms. Restaurant.

Láki. *Leros* (I), tel. 2 2940. 19 rooms, about half with shower. Restaurant.

Lésbos

Agiássos. *Agiassion* (I), tel. 2 2242. 12 rooms.

Ányfanta. *Silver Bay* (M), tel. 2 0952. 80 rooms. Pool.

Kratigós. *Katia* (M), tel. 6 1403. 38 bungalows. Thermal facilities, pool, tennis.

Mistegna. *Petalidi* (I), tel. 9 4220/1. 19 rooms.

Mithýmna. *Delfinia* (M), tel. 7 1315. On pebble beach. 82 rooms, most with bath. Pool, tennis. AE, MC. *Molyvos* (M), tel. 7 1386. 30 rooms. On beach. *Alkeos* (I), tel. 7 1002. 56 rooms. Pool, tennis.

Mytilíni. *Argo* (E), tel. 2 3693. 30 apartments. *Blue Sea* (M), tel. 2 3994. 61 rooms. Disco. *Mytilana Village* (M), tel. 2 0653. Six km. (four miles) out. 52 rooms; beach, pool. *Xenia* (M), tel. 2 2713/5. 74 double rooms. Pool, minigolf; two km. (1½ miles) out of town. AE, DC.

Néapoli. *Lesvos Beach* (M), tel. 6 1531/2. 37 apartments.

Pétra. *Petra* (I), tel. 4 1257. 18 rooms.
The Women's Co-operative (tel. 4 1238) has rooms in local houses, offering nontouristic accommodations for those who wish to share local life of villagers.

Plomári. *Oceanis* (I), tel. 3 2469. 42 rooms.

Thérmi. *Votsala* (M), tel. 7 1231. 47 double rooms with cooker and refrigerator. Beach, tennis. AE.

Pátmos

Gríkos. *Xenia* (M), tel. 3 1219. 35 double rooms. Beach. AE, DC. *Artemis* (I), tel. 3 1555. 24 rooms.

Skála. *Skála* (M), tel. 3 1343. 48 double rooms. Roofgarden. AE, DC, MC, v. *Astoria* (I), tel. 3 1205. 14 rooms. On the waterfront. *Chris* (I), tel. 3 1001. 26 rooms.
Restaurants. The Moderate seafood taverns on the waterfront at Hóra occasionally serve excellent crayfish. The aptly named *Fish Taverna* (I) and *Aristo's Acrogiali* (I) are justifiably popular.

Rhodes

Distances (km./miles) from Rhodes town are shown in brackets after the name of the town or resort.

Afándou (19/12). *Oasis Holidays* (M), tel. 5 1771/5. 37 rooms. Pool. *Xenia Golf* (I), tel. 5 1121/9. 26 rooms. Pool, beach and 18-hole golf course. DC, MC.

Faliráki (12/7). All (E) hotels are on or near beach, and have pool and tennis; most have disco. *Apollo Beach* (E), tel. 8 5251. 293 rooms. AE, DC, v. *Blue Sea* (E), tel. 2 9271. 296 rooms. *Calypso* (E), tel. 8 5455. 259 rooms. AE. *Colossos Beach* (E), tel. 8 5502. 733 rooms. Not airconditioned. AE. *Columbia* (E), tel. 8 5610. 114 rooms. v. *Esperides* (E), tel. 8 5267. 550 rooms. Public rooms only airconditioned. AE, DC, v. *Faliráki Beach* (E), tel. 8 5403. 316 rooms. AE, DC, MC, v. *Rodos Beach* (E), tel. 8 5471. 280 rooms in central block and bungalows. AE, DC. *Sun Palace* (E), tel. 8 5652. 166 rooms. AE, v.
Edelweiss (M), tel. 8 5442. 51 rooms. *Erato* (M), tel. 8 5414. 37 rooms. Airconditioned; pool. *Evi* (M), tel. 8 5586. 57 rooms. AE. *Lido* (I), tel. 8 5226. 20 rooms. Restaurant.

Ialyssós (8/5). *Blue Horizon* (E), tel. 9 3481/5. 211 rooms. Airconditioned. Pool, tennis, beach. AE, V. *Ialyssos Bay* (E), tel. 9 1841/5. 153 rooms. On beach below ruins. *Green View* (I), tel. 9 2484. 32 rooms.

Ixiá. Leofóros Ialyssóu, the avenue along the west coast, is lined throughout its 8 km. (5 miles) from Kritika past Ixiá with huge hotels. *Olympic Palace* (L), tel. 2 8775. 333 rooms. Nightclub, pool, tennis, minigolf. AE, V. *Rodos Palace* (L), tel. 2 5222. 610 rooms in an 18-story block and airconditioned chalets. Pool, tennis, minigolf, nightclub. Both have (E) accommodation also. AE, DC, MC, V.

All (E) hotels have pool; most have tennis and disco. *Avra Beach* (E), tel. 2 5284. 186 rooms in central block and bungalows. AE. *Bel Air* (E), tel. 2 3731/4. 237 rooms. AE. *Dionyssos* (E), tel. 2 3021/5. Slightly off the coastal road and thus quieter. 281 rooms. Large gardens. AE, DC. *Electra Palace* (E), tel. 9 2521/5. 216 rooms. AE, DC, MC, V. *Elina* (E), tel. 9 2466. 150 rooms. AE. *Elisabeth* (E), tel. 9 2656. 91 apartments. *Golden Beach* (E), tel. 9 2411/5. 225 bungalows directly on the beach. Only public rooms are airconditioned. AE, DC, MC, V. *Metropolitan Capsis* (E), tel. 2 5015/25. 694 rooms, 44 suites. The largest of them all, ten stories high. AE, DC, MC, V. *Oceanis* (E), tel. 2 4881/6. 229 rooms. Only public rooms are airconditioned. DC. *Rodos Bay* (E), tel. 2 3662. 330 rooms and bungalows. DC, MC.

Leto (M), tel. 2 3511. 97 rooms. Pool. *Solemar* (M), tel. 2 2941. 102 rooms. Pool. AE. *Velloïs* (I), tel. 2 4615. 51 rooms. Restaurant.

Kallithéa (4/2). *Sunwing* (E), tel. 2 8600. 389 rooms, 48 suites in hotel and "village." Nightclub, pool, tennis. AE, DC, MC, V.

Kritiká (3/1). *Sirene Beach* (E), tel. 3 0638. 92 rooms. Two pools. AE, DC, MC. *Poseidon* (M), tel. 2 4541. 35 rooms.

Líndos (42/26). *Steps of Lindos* (E), tel. 4 2262/7. 156 rooms. All expected facilities, friendly service, excellent setting. Beach, pool, tennis. AE. *Lindos Bay* (M), tel. 4 2211. 192 rooms. Beach, pool, tennis, disco. AE.

Neohóri (1/½). *Athina* (M), tel. 2 2631/4. 142 rooms. Pool, beach. AE, DC.

Remi Koskínou (6/4). *Eden Roc* (E), tel. 2 3851/3. 413 rooms in central block and bungalows. Pool, tennis, minigolf. AE, MC. *Paradise* (E), tel. 2 9220. 495 rooms. Also with nightclub, pool, tennis and minigolf. AE, DC, MC, V. *Kallithea Sun* (M) and *Kalithea Sky* (M), tel. 6 2492. 113 rooms and 53 bungalows respectively. Pool, tennis. AE, DC, V.

Rhodes Town. Most hotels are in the new quarter on the north promontory. *Grand Hotel Astir Palace* (L), tel. 2 6284/9. 377 rooms. Pool, disappointing beach, tennis, sauna, nightclub; houses the casino at present. AE, DC, MC, V.

The (E) hotels listed are near the bottom of the (E) price range. *Belvedere* (E), tel. 2 4471/4. 212 rooms. Only public rooms are airconditioned, beach across the road, pool, tennis. AE, DC, MC, V. *Chevaliers Palace* (E), tel. 2 2781/4. 188 rooms. Pool, minigolf, disco. AE, DC, MC, V. *Continental* (E), tel. 3 0873. 113 rooms. Pool. *Helios* (E), tel. 3 0033. 34 suites. *Ibiscus* (E), tel. 2 4421/3. 205 rooms. Not airconditioned. AE, DC. *Mediterranean*

(E), tel. 2 4661/5. 154 rooms. Only public rooms airconditioned, beach across the road. AE, DC, MC, V. *Park* (E), tel. 2 4190. 84 rooms. Not airconditioned, pool, disco. AE, DC. *Siravast* (E), tel. 2 3551/7, 29 2154. 92 rooms. Not airconditioned. AE, DC.

Rhodes town has a very wide choice of Moderate hotels, but fewer in the Inexpensive category. *Acandia* (M), tel. 2 2251. 82 rooms. *Als* (M), tel. 2 2481. 52 rooms. No restaurant. *Arion* (M), tel. 2 0006. 47 rooms. No restaurant. *Blue Sky* (M), tel. 2 4091/3. 182 rooms. Pool, disco. AE, V. *Cactus* (M), tel. 2 6100. 177 rooms. Beach across the road. AE. *Esperia* (M), tel. 2 3941/3. 191 rooms. AE, V. *Konstantinos* (M), tel. 2 2971. 133 rooms. AE, MC, V. *Manoussos* (M), tel. 2 2741/5. 124 rooms. Roofgarden, pool. AE, DC, MC, V. *Plaza* (M), tel. 2 2501/5. 128 rooms. Pool. AE, DC, MC, V. *Regina* (M), tel. 2 2171. 82 rooms. *Semiramis* (M), tel. 2 0741/2. 120 rooms. *Spartalis* (M), tel. 2 4371/2. 79 rooms; near harbor. AE, DC, MC.

Alexia (I), tel. 2 4061. 135 rooms. *Amaryllis* (I), tel. 2 4522. 39 rooms. *Astron* (I), tel. 2 4651. 43 rooms. *Diana* (I), tel. 2 4677. 42 rooms. *El Greco* (I), tel. 2 4071/2. DC. *Elite* (I), tel. 2 2391. 45 rooms. *Flora* (I), tel. 2 4538. 98 rooms. *Galaxy* (I), tel. 2 2401. 38 rooms. Restaurant. *Isabella* (I), tel. 2 2651. 42 rooms. *Majestic* (I), tel. 2 2031/3. 79 rooms. *Minos* (I), tel. 2 4041. 72 rooms. *Parthenon* (I), tel. 2 2351/2. 79 rooms. Roofgarden.

Restaurants. The string of Moderate establishments with open-air terraces along the Mandráki port are sadly lacking in everything but a fine situation. The hotel food lacks even that. *Captain's House* (E), Zervou 5 (tel. 2 1275). In a converted mansion; dinner only. Greek and international cuisine. AE, DC. *Casa Castelana* (E), Aristotelous 3 (tel. 2 8803). In a 15th-century Inn of the Knights; everything from snacks to full-course meals. AE, DC, V. *Kon Tiki* (E), Limin Mandrakiou (tel. 2 2477). On a boat in the old port; dinner only; seafood specialties. AE, DC, MC, V. *Kabo n' Toro* (M), corner of Ormilou and Parado streets, tel. 3 6182. One of the smallest but one of the best in Rhodes. *Neorion* (M), Platia Neoriou (tel. 2 4644). Cafe-restaurant. AE, DC, MC.

Shopping. The best handicrafts shops and some jewelers are in Sokratous in the old town. Branches in Deluxe and Expensive hotels are more expensive.

Tholós (20/12). *Doretta Beach* (E), tel. 4 1441/3. 295 rooms. Pool, tennis, disco. AE, DC.

Sámos

Iréo. Close to Heraeon and beach. *Adamantia* (I), tel. 5 1319. 32 rooms.

Kalámi. *Anthemis* (E), tel. 2 8050. 24 furnished apartments. *Kirki Beach* (M), tel. 2 3030/1. 22 rooms. *Myrini* (M), tel. 2 7762. 35 rooms. *Andromeda* (I), tel. 2 2925. 34 rooms. *Pythagoras* (I), tel. 2 8422. 16 rooms.

Karlóvassi. *Aspasia* (M), tel. 3 2363. 45 rooms. Pool, roofgarden.DC. *Aegeon* (I), tel. 3 3466. 57 rooms. DC. Both at beach. *Merope* (I), tel. 3 2650. 80 rooms. MC. All with restaurant.

Kokkári. *Kokkári Beach* (I), tel. 9 2263. 45 rooms. Restaurant. *Venus* (I), tel. 9 2330. 42 rooms. Restaurant. AE, DC, MC.

Marathókambos. *Kerkis Bay* (I), tel. 3 7202. 29 rooms. Restaurant. *Klimataria* (I), tel. 3 7256. 12 rooms. Restaurant.

Pefkákia. *Sun Waves* (I), tel. 2 8861/2. 31 rooms. Beach. *Samos Bay* (I), tel. 2 2101. 40 rooms. Beach, restaurant.

Potokaki. *Hydrele Beach* (M), tel. 6 1541. 45 rooms. Airconditioned. Beach across road.v.

Pythagório. *Doryssa Bay* (M), tel. 6 1360. 240 rooms in hotel and bungalows. Airconditioned. On the beach, just outside the town, near airport. Pool, tennis, disco. *Phito* (M), tel. 6 1314. 75 bungalows on beach. *Glicoriza Beach* (I), tel. 6 1321. 62 rooms. Restaurant. *Ilios* (I), tel. 6 1365. 33 rooms. *Polyxeni* (I), tel. 6 1359. 23 rooms. *Pythagoras* (I), tel. 6 1352. 30 rooms.

Sámos Town. *Aeolis* (M), tel. 2 8904/7. 51 rooms. Airconditioned. AE, DC, MC, V. *Galaxy* (M), tel. 2 2666. 32 rooms. *Xenia* (M), tel. 2 7463. 31 rooms. Airconditioned; in upper town. AE, DC, MC. *Eleana* (I), tel. 2 8665. 15 rooms. AE. *Samos* (I), tel. 2 8377. 105 rooms. AE, DC.

Sými

Aliki (M), tel. 7 1665. 15 rooms. Neo-classical mansion on harbor front. Roofgarden with good views.

Tílos

Livadia (I), tel. 5 3202. 20 double rooms, 10 with shower.

GETTING THERE. By Plane. Rhodes' international airport is linked by direct flights with several foreign countries. From Athens there are several flights daily to Rhodes, Kos, Sámos, Híos, Mytilíni and Léros; from Thessaloníki daily to Rhodes and Mytilíni. Inter-island connections: Rhodes/Kos and Mytilíni, Kos/Léros, Sámos/Híos and Mytilíni, Híos/Mytilíni. Kastellórizo, Kárpathos and Kássos are reached from Rhodes, the latter two are also connected with Sitía, Crete. In addition there are flights between Rhodes and Sitía, Iráklion, Santoríni, Páros and Mýkonos; and Sámos and Híos/Mýkonos.

By Boat. There are daily ferries from Piraeus to Híos and Lésbos; to Ikaría and Sámos; to Pátmos (included in most cruises), Léros, Kálymnos, Kos and Rhodes; ferries to the smaller Dodecanese islands are less frequent. There is a weekly ferry from Kavála to Rhodes, via Lésvos, Híos, Sámos and Kos; another from Thessaloníki to Lésvos and Híos, and a twice-weekly service links Santoríni, Crete and Rhodes. Daily ferries to Turkey go from Híos to Cesme; from Mytilíni to Dikeli; and from Sámos to Kusadasi.

THE NORTHERN ISLANDS

The Spórades, Límnos, Thássos and Samothrace

Little mentioned in mythology or in history—except, inevitably, as a base for pirates—the Spórades confidently rely on their great natural beauty to attract visitors. From each one of them, there are tempting views of other islands and their tiny satellites, and it is a constant pleasure to sail between them, in good weather. They are a delight for yachtsmen, while from the air, this thick sprinkling of islets gives an amazing beauty to the sea, when flying to or from Kavála.

Exploring the Spórades

The Spórades, the Scattered Isles, are the handful of colored pebbles the gods were left with after creating the world and, as an afterthought, they flung them over the northwestern Aegean. Skýros, the southernmost and largest, consists of two very different regions; the southern part is bare and Cycladic, while the north is forested.

From Linária the port on the east coast, to Skýros town above the west coast, the road passes through a Cycladic country of brown, terraced hills and fig trees. Skýros town is chiefly distinguished by the dramatically abrupt rock which supports the Venetian castle. It is a particularly attractive white village, in the cubist style of the Cyclades. The main route up to the rock is narrow and cobbled and all traffic stops at the square at the entrance to the main village. From here, it is a fairly steep walk up the curved lanes, with their white-painted ramp-like steps, to the Kastro; it is then a much steeper climb to the very top and the more ancient ruins of an old castle. The views over the gray and white flat-roofed houses of the town to the west and the sparkling sea and expanse of Magazia beach to the east are worth the effort. The hospitable people will gladly show visitors their houses, and one or two interiors should be seen; the carved woodwork, when it takes the form of a balustrade to the upper room in a house is often old and attractive. The contemporary arts and crafts are, on the other hand, sometimes a little depressing. As the locals are of average height, it is far from clear why the furniture is best suited to dwarves. The pottery is prettily painted with birds, fish, and geometric designs, in delightful, garish colors. The Faltaits Museum, on the edge of Skyros town overlooking Magaziá, is a personal collection of island folk art, embroidery, woodcarving, clothing, books, and paintings, proudly displayed by the owner and organizer, Costas Faltaits, in his home. Pleasant beaches and coves include the long, gray sandy beach of Magaziá beneath Skýros town, secluded Pefkos, on the other side of the island, with its single taverna, and Atsítsa, a pine-fringed bay with the remains of old mining operations and a "New Age" center, frequented by northern Europeans wishing to "rejuvenate mind, body and spirit" in the peaceful setting.

This is the one island where mythology is not lacking. As one heroic cycle ended, another started. Theseus was pushed to his death from the high castle cliff by his treacherous host. Some 900 years later, in 472 B.C., after the great Athenian general Kimon had put an end to the Dolopian pirates operating profitably from the island, the bones of a rather large man were unearthed. Lo and behold, the Delphic oracle had just pronounced that whoever returned Theseus' mortal remains would bring great glory to Athens. So Theseus' bones they were, laying a solid base to Kimon's political career.

Achilles was hidden on Skýros by his mother Thetis to keep him out of the Trojan War; it had been prophesied that his participation in it was essential to the success of the Greeks, but that he himself would be killed. During World War I the English poet Rupert Brooke died of septicaemia off the south coast and was buried in a beautiful olive grove at Tris Bóukes (an excursion by land or water from Linária). He is commemorated by a statue of Immortal Poetry, by the Greek sculptor Tombros, erected outside Skýros town.

Less Scattered

The other inhabited Spórades are strung at regular intervals east of the Pílio Peninsula, and are equally spectacular whether approached from Ágios Konstantínos through the North Euboean Channel or from Vólos through the Pagasitikós Gulf.

The first is Skíathos (shadow of Áthos), a low-hilled, thickly wooded island, with idyllic beauty. It has an impressive harbor, protected and adorned by a great many little islets. This island has no ancient history; its most interesting son was Alexandros Papadiamandis (1855–1911), whose short stories are based on island life and tradition.

The town dates from 1830; it is prettily built on two hills, overlooking the great harbor and smaller lagoon, crowded with colorful craft. When the Turks occupied the island in the 16th century, the inhabitants retired to an almost impregnable rock in the north, a village called Kástro, whose crumbling remains are dominated by the Church of Christ.

Skíathos has recently become a very busy tourist island, vying with Corfu, Mykonos, and Rhodes in populartiy, with over half a million visitors every year. Much of the island's appeal lies in its 60 beaches, scattered along its coasts. Outstanding among the tranquil bays is the wonderful beach of Koukounariés (the stonepines), one of the best in the Aegean, although it has become rather less tranquil since the building of several hotels. A magnificent grove of pine trees fringes a long sweep of sand; behind there is a charming inland lagoon, backed by maize fields and olive groves. During the height of the tourist season, the beach may become very crowded and there is a more isolated beach further along the coast, at Agia Eleni facing Pelion, which may be worth seeking out.

Equally enjoyable is a visit to the next island, Skópelos. This is also a green island, but its name means "rock," and rocky it is; when approached from Skíathos, its high uneven ridge makes it appear a different world.

The first port, Glóssa, is on the western side of the island; here the vegetation is very luxurious, and through the groves of olives and of fruit trees there are exquisite views of Skíathos, of the many scattered islets that lie in between, and of distant Euboea.

The exceptionally attractive island capital, Hóra, rises from a semicircular bay, which faces north and thus provides little shelter. The houses, roofed in a beautiful soft gray slate, are built in a modified form of the style prevalent on the Pílio peninsula, but a very rich use of color is made on the walls, which are washed over in white or blue or red or ocher; the ridges and eaves of the roofs are picked out in white.

Several small monasteries or convents, hiding among olive trees or shining out on the hillside round the gulf are pleasant objects for a short walk. Evangelístra, 4 km. (2½ miles) south of Hóra, belonging to the Xyropotamon monastery on Mount Athos, has some beautiful 14th-century icons. The silver-green olives shade a soil more vividly colored than any other in the Aegean, of a fine reddish purple.

The specialty of Skópelos is plums, and in the season (August) you may watch them being home-dried in slow ovens, and sample them at various stages of the process. A final polish is put on with finger and thumb.

Alónissos, though no less fertile, is only sparsely populated. The idyllic peace and solitude of its many sandy beaches make it ideal for underwater fishing among the ruins of sunken cities and to the caves of surrounding islets. A center for the protection of the rare Mediterranean seal was established in 1985.

The hilltop Byzantine capital, old Alónissos, 300 meters high and overlooking the harbor, was largely abandoned following a severe earthquake in 1965. It is now being painstakingly restored by locals and northern Europeans, using traditional methods and materials and in the past year or so several craft shops, artists's studios, tavernas, and bars have sprouted from the rubble.

The Islands of the Thracian Sea—Límnos

These three islands, though briefly united in the late Middle Ages under the Genoese Gateluzzi princes, whose main seat was in Lesbos, present all the astounding natural and cultural variety of the Aegean.

Límnos, the largest, with the best beaches, figures prominently in mythology. When hurled by his irate parent Zeus from Olympos, Hephaestos landed with both his legs broken, lame ever after, but still able to open the world's first foundry in unusually attractive surroundings. He became the patron god of this island, and when the Limnian women offended his wife, Aphrodite, she afflicted them with halitosis. Their husbands neglected them, were all massacred, but luckily were replaced by the crew of the *Argo,* en route for the Golden fleece. They stayed two years in Límnos, and fathered a new generation. Límnos is also the scene of the legend of Philoctetes, who was marooned here by the Greeks on their way to Troy, left in a cave with an invincible bow, and an incurable wound whose stench made his proximity unendurable. Sophocles' play describes how he was found ten years later by Odysseus, and taken to Troy, where he killed King Priam's son, Paris, in combat.

In prehistory, Límnos had a Tyrrheno-Pelasgian population, of which interesting traces remain; in history it was, in the 5th century, almost a colony of Athens. Later it went through many changes of ownership. The big, almost land-locked bay of Móudros in the south was an allied base in the Gallipoli campaign in World War I.

The island capital, Mýrina, known as Kastro among islanders, is a small town on the west side. There is a Genoese castle on a great rock, in whose face are also cut the outlines and streets of a prehistoric Pelasgian city. The Archeological Museum in the former residence of the Turkish Pasha is noteworthy for its prehistoric exhibits. Few trees can withstand the fierce winter gales, but this low-hilled island with its fine beaches is pleasant enough in the summer, for the climate is particularly dry and cool. In the evening, Mount Áthos stands up against the sunset, a superb outline, and one of the most striking views in the Aegean. Its shadow is said to touch Límnos twice a year.

The shallow northern bay is supposedly where Hephaestos landed, and the theater and agora of the ancient capital, Hephaestia, can be made out. To the northeast the Kabririon, best reached by boat, was the sanctuary of the gods of Samothrace. Philoctetes' cave was here, while further northeast, at Cape Platéa, a town sank into the sea after an earthquake. For prehistory, visit Políohni on the east coast, where Italian archeologists have uncovered four layers of settlements, the oldest dating from around 3500 B.C. A large Bronze Age city of about 2300 B.C. was connected with Troy, which is only some 97 km. (60 miles) east.

Samothráki (Samothrace)

This mountainous island possesses a very distinctive beauty and interest; its high central massif, rising to the peak of Fengári (Mountain of the Moon: 1,676 m./5,500 ft.) makes it a landmark from far away. It is perhaps the finest of all Greek islands as seen from the sea.

The Sanctuary of the Great Gods in the north of the island attracted pilgrims from prehistoric times to the 4th century A.D. The discovery in 1863 of the *Winged Victory,* one of the greatest Hellenistic sculptures, ascribed to the genius of either Lysippus or Leochares, and now in the Louvre in Paris, started systematic excavations by French and Austrian teams. The work was continued after World War II by New York University, under Dr. Karl Lehmann. The museum here, though small, houses some important finds. There is also a hostel for archaeologists and visitors, a simple but beautifully situated bungalow.

The Great Gods of Samothrace, the Kabiri, were Thracian deities whom the Greeks, when they colonized the island, adapted to their own mythology. The Kabiri were gods of the underworld in a cult that centered on the least attractive aspect of the Great Goddess, as Hekate, goddess of the night and witchcraft, joined by Hades and Persephone. There was a public festival of the Great Gods every summer, and in addition there were mysteries into which candidates could be initiated at any time of the year; there were two stages of initiation, and those who sought the higher degree are believed to have been obliged to confess their major sins—a unique feature in ancient Greek worship.

The sanctuary lies in a peaceful valley, between dry streams, and under the rugged peak of Ágios Géorgios. The lower flanks of the mountain are gray-green with olives and above, the 7th-century B.C. Cyclopean wall of the ancient city of Samothrace can be seen running up the slope till it reaches an outcrop of rock, under the peak. Paleópolis can be reached in some ten minutes from the hostel; from the jetty below, cruise passengers can visit the ruins with ease, if weather allows them to disembark (this is not always the case: the Thracian sea can be very stormy).

In the sanctuary the temples and other buildings are carefully labeled by notices. The buildings were of two sorts, those belonging to the public festival of the Great Gods, and those which were used for the mysteries. The former include the base of the rotunda of Arsinoë: this was a room for the reception of representatives of various Greek states who attended the festival. It was erected by that remarkable queen of Macedon, who later married her brother, Ptolemy II, Philadelphus, and ruled Egypt with him as Arsinöe II, until her death in 270 B.C. It is the largest round building known in Greek architecture; a reconstruction showing its elegant pilastered gallery is to be seen in the museum. Of the buildings pertaining to the mysteries, the Hieron, the holy of holies, most strikes the eye, as five Doric columns have been re-erected, composing the site into a more comprehensible and photogenic picture. The museum, with its useful models of buildings, displays of religious objects, bronze, glasswork, and pottery, together with portions of detailed freizes, is helpfully designed and instructive.

At the fountain, above the general level of the temples, Champoiseau, the French Consul in Adrianople, found the Winged Victory, dedicated to Antigonus II of Macedon after the naval battle of Kos in 258 B.C., in which he and his allies defeated Ptolemy II.

Samothrace is a cool and refreshing place to stay in the summer; unfortunately the bathing at the port, Kamariótissa, is not good. Those who are energetic will climb Fengári, if the weather is clear enough to promise a view. Poseidon sat on that peak to watch the Trojan War, and a mortal climber can see the Trojan Ida mountains and Áthos, if the day is clear. Less enterprising walkers may follow the walls of the ancient city of Samothrace, and they will also wish to visit the towers of a Genoese fortress, on a small high rocky acropolis, overlooking the Thracian sea. On a clear day the mountains behind Alexandróupoli are seen, and you can catch a glimpse of Áthos.

Modern Samothráki, six km. (four miles) inland from Kamariótissa, is a strikingly situated village, with a Genoese fort on a fine sugar-loaf rock. From the port an unpaved road hugs the north and west coasts. More interesting, but only in calm weather, is a boat trip along the wild rocky southern shore as far as the cascade that falls into the sea from high up on a cliff face. Halfway, a swim on the beautiful and deserted beach of Ammos, fine sand as the name promises, is recommended. Only very calm weather is good enough for this whole day's outing.

Thássos

Greece's first off-shore oil and gas field, providing ten percent of consumption, has not interfered with the beauty and variety of Thássos or diminished the appeal of its fascinating antiquities and beautiful bathing beaches. Repeated summer fires have, however, destroyed some areas of the forested island in recent years. Fire precaution signs request care and safety while traveling through the island.

The capital is a pleasant village, built on the site of the ancient city, whose agora and other buildings lie among the houses. The circular memorial to the Parian colonizer Telesikles was restored in 200 B.C., when the agora was framed by marble porticos; the propylaea faced the Hellenistic altar and temple of Zeus Agoraios (Of the Market); two choragic monuments were added to the temple of Dionysos; and Heracles' 5th-century B.C. Ionic temple was enlarged with a ritual hall. But the most important vestige of the past is the grand enclosure of walls rising behind the village, up to a ridge of rock that at one point provided a natural fortification. Performances of ancient drama are once more given in summer in the Hellenistic theater, which the Romans converted into a gladiatorial arena in the 2nd century B.C. Much of the ancient *bas relief* sculpture has been allowed to remain *in situ*. Particularly noteworthy is the large statue of Silenus near the restored walls of the modern village.

Thássos was a prosperous ancient state, owning gold mines both on the island, and on the mainland. Thasian marble (to be seen both here, and in the Sanctuary of the Great Gods in Samothrace) was an important article of export, and Thasian wine was in high repute all over the eastern Mediterranean; jars in which it was exported have been found as far afield as Egypt and the shores of the Black Sea. Viniculture has dramatically deteriorated, and the present product is better avoided.

The museum contains a wealth of local finds, but the masterpieces are in the Louvre. The works of Polygnotus—perhaps the Classical period's greatest painter—are known only by the description of Pausanias, antiquity's great guidebook writer. Born on Thássos in about 500 B.C., Polygnotus broke with the traditional arrangement of figures on a level base, distributing them freely in his monumental wallpaintings at Delphi and in the idealized pictures hung at the Pinakotheke in Athens. He died in Athens in about 440 B.C.

Makrýammos (the long sand) is the finest bathing beach. It may be reached by a pleasant walk of half an hour, by bus, or (best) by motor boat—one sails under the ancient walls and acropolis of Thássos. As Makrýammos has become the preserve of the Xenia guests, Glyfáda, a pleasantly shady place on the west coast, is now more frequented. Beach follows beach along that coast, with organized camping at Skála Rahoníou. More idyllic are Hrissí Amoudiá and Skála Potamiás on the east coast. The circular road above passes through the forest burnt in the devastating fires of recent years to the village of Panagía whose white houses are in the same style as those of the Pílio, one or two built across a running brook.

Thássos tends to fill up in the summer months because it is the weekend resort for eastern Macedonia. The circumnavigation of the island is as rewarding as a round trip by car, mostly along the shore. The road hugs the west coast to Limenária (37 km., 23 miles) and the infinite variety of scenery makes it worthwhile to bring over a car by ferryboat. Limenária can also be reached by direct boat from Kavála. In spite of some mining activity, Limenária has an attractive setting, with good bathing (both on the spot, and at the sandy beach of Pefkári, five km., three miles, south), and in the evening there is a noble view of the whole peninsula of Áthos, ending in the Holy Mountain. The longer return trip (55 km., 34 miles) along the east coast, passes near the marble quarries of Alýki where two ancient temples, two early Christian basilicas and numerous tombs have been unearthed, then turns north to Potamia and Panagia.

PRACTICAL INFORMATION FOR
THE NORTHERN ISLANDS

HOTELS AND RESTAURANTS. Book well in advance, unless you are happy to make do with a clean but very simple room in a private house. A pleasant diet can be based on a cheese called *graviéra,* seafood, and the excellent green figs (*sýka*) of Skýros.

Alónissos

Marpounta (M), tel. 6 5219. 104 rooms in bungalows on beach. Disco, tennis. DC. *Alonissos Beach* (I), tel. 6 5281. 45 rooms. *Galaxy* (I), tel. 6 5251. 52 rooms. Restaurant. AE.

Límnos

Myrína. *Akti Myrína* (L), tel. 2 2681/5. 125 bungalows, each with patio or small garden. Unpretentious, comfortable, and efficiently-run. There is good, if expensive, food in its four restaurants. Pool, tennis, minigolf, private beach. DC, V. *Kastro Beach* (M), tel. 2 2772. 72 rooms. V. *Lemnos* (I), tel. 2 2153. 29 rooms, most with shower. V.
Restaurants. There are several Inexpensive seafood taverns on the waterfront.

Samothrace

Kamariotissa. *Niki Beach* (M), tel. 4 1561. 38 rooms.

Skíathos

Ahladiés. *Esperides* (E), tel. 2 2245/6. 165 rooms. Pool, tennis, disco. AE, MC, V. *Belvedere* (M), tel. 2 2475/6. 50 bungalows. AE, V.

Koukounariés. *Skíathos Palace* (E), tel. 2 2242/3. 220 rooms. Pool, tennis, sauna. nightclub. AE, MC, V. *Mandraki* (M), tel. 2 1170. 32 bungalows. *Xenia* (I), tel. 2 7042/3. 32 double rooms. Restaurant. MC.

Skíathos Town. *Alkyon* (E), tel. 2 2981/5. 80 rooms. Disco. DC. *Koukounaries* (I), tel. 2 2215. 17 rooms. *Meltemi* (M), tel. 2 2493. 18 rooms. DC.

Tróulos. *Korali* (M), tel. 4 9212. 50 apartments.

Tzanería. *Nostos* (E), tel. 2 2420. 146 rooms in bungalows. Not air-conditioned; pool, tennis, disco. On beach, 3 km. (2 mi.) from Skiathos town. AE, DC, MC, V.

Skópelos

Glóssa. *Avra* (I), tel. 3 3550. 28 rooms. Beach, restaurant.

Livádi. *Prince Stafylos* (E), tel. 2 2775. 48 rooms. Pool. Pleasant, clean, and modern. V. *Sporades* (M), tel. 2 2146/7. 24 apartments.

Pánormos. *Panormos Beach* (M), tel. 2 2711. 30 rooms.

Skópelos Town. *Skópelos Village* (E), tel. 2 2517. 25 apartments. Pool. *Amalia* (M), tel. 2 2688. 50 rooms. V. *Aeolos* (I), tel. 2 2233. 41 rooms. *Denise* (I), tel. 2 2678. 22 rooms. Last three all near the town beach.

Stáfylos. *Rigas* (M), tel. 2 2618. 38 rooms.

Skyros

Xenia (M), tel. 9 1209. 22 rooms. Quiet and relaxed, this hotel features a shaded patio and open lawns overlooking one of the finest of the island beaches; 2 km. (1 mile) from the town. AE, DC, MC.

Thássos

Glyfáda. *Glyfáda* (I), tel. 2 2164. 52 rooms. Beach, restaurant.

Limenária. *Sgouridis* (I), tel. 5 1241. 14 rooms. Near beach. *Thalassies* (I), tel. 5 1163. 21 rooms.

Makryámmos. *Makryámmos* (E), tel. 2 2101. 206 bungalows on lovely beach. Pool, tennis, disco. AE, DC.

Panagía. *Golden Sand* (I), tel. 6 1471. 11 rooms.

Pefkári. *Thassos* (I), tel. 5 1596. 35 rooms.

Skála Potamiás. *Miramare* (M), tel. 6 1040. 25 rooms. Pool. *Blue Sea* (I), tel. 6 1482. 12 rooms. *Kamelia* (I), tel. 6 1463. 15 rooms.

Skála Prínou. *Krystal* (I), tel. 7 1272. 13 rooms.

Skála Rahoníou. *Argyro* (I), tel. 8 1263. 29 rooms. Restaurant.

Thássos Town. *Amfipolis* (E), tel. 2 3101. 42 rooms in converted traditional settlement. Pool, sauna. *Timoleon* (M), tel. 2 2177. 30 rooms. No restaurant; near the inadequate beach. AE, DC, MC, V. *Villa Nisteri* (M), tel. 2 2055. 10 rooms. Near beach. V. *Angelika* (I), tel. 2 2387. 26 rooms. On

beach. *Laïos* (I), tel. 2 2309. 27 rooms. *Possidon* (I), tel. 2 2690. 16 rooms.
AE, DC, MC.

GETTING THERE. By Plane. There are daily flights from Athens,
Mytilíni and Thessaloníki to Límnos. In summer, there are seven or more
flights a day from Athens to Skíathos, and three a week from Thessaloníki.
There are daily flights from Athens to Skýros.

By Boat. There are many ferries every day from Kavála to Thássos
town, and at least nine ferries daily from Keramotí.

Alexandróupoli is connected at least once a day with Samothrace, Kavála less often. From Kavála there are three to four sailings a week to Límnos. Daily buses link Athens with the Euboean port of Kými, from which
there is a car ferry service daily to Linária (Skýros) and less frequently
to Alónissos and Skópelos; also to Límnos.

There are buses from Athens to Ágios Konstantínos (153 km., 95 miles,
north of Athens) connecting with the daily ferry to Skíathos and Skópelos
calling some days at Alónissos. Ferries for the Sporádes depart also from
Vólos, both supplemented by hydrofoils in summer. There are also hydrofoils and car ferries from Thessaloníki to the Sporades.

CRETE

Europe's Oldest Civilization

About 1600 B.C., while the rest of Europe was still in the grip of primitive barbarity, one of the most brilliant and amazing civilizations the world was ever to know approached its final climax. The sophisticated elegance of King Minos' court on the island of Crete (Kríti) was an appropriate manifestation of imperial power patiently built up over centuries.

Legendary Minos, son of Zeus, in the shape of a bull, and Europa, won fame for his incorruptible justice, which earned him, after his death, a place on the high court in the underworld. His name seems to have been adopted as a sacred title by his successors, ruling as priest-kings of a strange religion, over which bulls held a frightening, though ill-defined sway. If the original Minos led his Neolithic people between 4000 and 3000 B.C. from Syria to Crete, if he founded the preeminent dynasty of Knossós in about 2000 B.C., or if he only united the island politically in about 1600 B.C., remains a matter for conjecture; though the latter theory is now most widely accepted. The Minoans were dark, almost certainly Asiatic; but their culture, though Egyptian-inspired, evolved in a uniquely original direction and produced a truly great civilization in the 600 years of the middle and late Minoan periods. Five palaces were the centers of government, while about 20 manor houses, on a smaller scale but in the same style, provided the feudal focus of an economy and society held together by religion. Shrines adjoined counting houses and storerooms.

From Knossós, the grandest palace, Minos ruled a maritime empire including the Cyclades, the Peloponnese and parts of Sicily. These conquests were made by the first organized royal navy in history, as distinct from

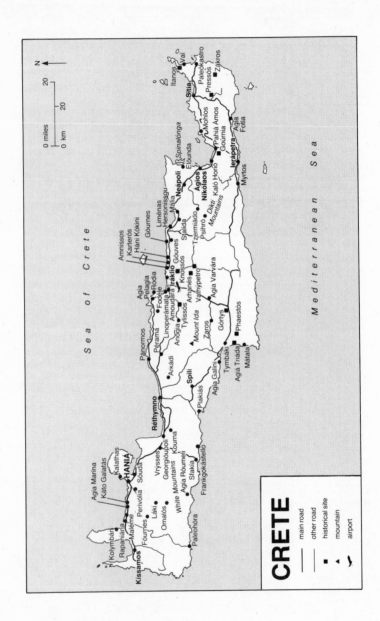

Sea of Crete

Mediterranean Sea

N

20
20
0 miles
0 km

Vaï
Itanos
Paleókastro
Pressós
Zákros
Sitía
Móhlos
Pahiá Amos
Gournia
Agía
Folía
Spinalónga
Eloúnda
Neápoli
Agios
Nikólaos
Kaló Horió
Ierápetra
Díkti
Mountains
Psihró
Mýrtos
Limenás
Hersonissou
Mália
Amnissós
Karterós
Háni Kokíni
Goúves
Sisália
Tzermiádo
Goúrnes
Agía
Pelagía
Fódele
Iráklio
Goúves
Rodiá
Amoudára
Knossós
Arhánes
Linoperámata
Pérama
Pánormos
Anógia
Tylissos
Vathýpetro
Agía Varvára
Mount Ida
Zarós
Górtys
Phaestos
Arkádi
Agía Galíni
Agía Triáda
Mátala
Tymbáki
Spíli
Plakiás
Frankokástello
Réthymno
Soúda
Vrýsses
Georgioúpoli
Kournás
Agía Rouméli
Sfakiá
Agía Marína
Káto Galatás
Kalathás
HANIÁ
Perivólia
Láki
White Mountains
Omalós
Fournés
Maléme
Rapaniána
Kolymbári
Kissámos
Paleohóra

CRETE

— main road
— other road
■ historical site
◄ mountain
〉 airport

earlier, individual trading ventures. The government of the islands was entrusted to royal princes, while heavy tributes were exacted from the Achaean principalities on the mainland. Onerous human tributes might have been the cause for a disastrous invasion of Crete by the subject peoples. But it might well have been a tidal wave and earthquakes caused by the explosion of the Thira volcano in 1450 B.C., even more devastating than the calamity which brought down the first palaces in about 1700 B.C., that led to the downfall of Knossós.

The last Minos was plagued with a nymphomaniac wife, Pasiphae, who, in the best family tradition, had fallen desperately in love with a gorgeous white bull. Daedalus, an Athenian craftsman of wondrous skill, undertook to satisfy the queen's desire. He built a hollow wooden cow, upholstered with a cow's hide, and concealing Pasiphae in the lifelike dummy brought about the union which she craved. The fruit of this union was the Minotaur, a monster who was born with a bull's head on a human body.

To avoid scandal Daedalus constructed a labyrinth, where Pasiphae's disgrace was concealed, entertained—one wonders how—by a yearly tribute of seven youths and seven maidens from Athens. Prince Theseus insisted on being included among the victims and, supplied with a sufficient length of thread by Minos' daughter, Ariadne, returned safe from the labyrinth after slaying the unlovable cross-breed.

Ariadne, who seems to have taken all the initiative in the courtship in accordance with the hereditary strain, prevailed on Theseus to take her along. However, by the time the couple reached Naxos, Theseus was eager to effect a second escape, this time from his recent savior, only to succumb finally to Ariadne's sister Phaedra. Ariadne had the best of both worlds, as abandoned by her hero she found favor with a god, Dionysos.

Daedalus had become involved in the Theseus affair, as it was he who had thought of the silken thread by which the hero made good his escape from the labyrinth. Imprisoned with his son Icarus in the now empty maze, Daedalus' ingenuity proved equal to the occasion. He made two pairs of wings, attached them with wax to the shoulders and rose with his son skywards. In spite of his father's warning, Icarus could not resist the temptation of soaring higher and higher, till the sun melted the wax. He fell and was drowned near the island which is called Icaria in his memory. Daedalus succeeded in reaching the haven of King Cocalus' court in Sicily, where Minos, arriving in hot pursuit, was done to death by the king's daughters. The Cretan fleet was destroyed by the Sicilians, and the whole legend of Theseus culminating in Minos' inglorious end lends credit to the invasion theory.

The golden Minoan days were followed by the not entirely inglorious twilight of Mycenaean rule. King Idomeneus led a Cretan contingent against Troy, but by 1200 B.C. the island was again divided into primitive city-states, constantly at war. With the arrival of the Dorians in the following century, the long night of the Iron Age descended and even the subsequent flowering of classical culture on the Greek mainland found only a weak reflection on Crete. In 66 B.C. it was occupied by the Romans, as it had become a pirates' nest. But the piratic tradition was revived by the Arabs in the 9th and 10th centuries, when the swift Moslem galleys dominated the eastern Mediterranean up to the Byzantine reconquest in 961.

The Fourth Crusade allotted Crete to Boniface of Montferrat, King of Thessaloníki, until the Venetians bought it as the centerpiece of their empire in 1210. It was governed by a Duke, assisted by a Grand Council.

The Cretan School of painters flourished in the 15th and 16th centuries, and Kornaros wrote the epic romance *Erotokritos,* but cultural and political integration were made impossible by the religious schism.

After centuries of local rebellions, the Turks attacked and in 1669 occupied the island, except for three off-shore islet fortresses, which remained Venetian until 1715. 19th-century insurrections were suppressed with increasing ferocity by the sultans, who were at last forced to grant home rule under a Greek prince. But not till 1913 was Crete definitely incorporated into Greece and the exchange of population in 1923 removed the Moslem minority from the island. The undaunted resistance of Greek, British and Anzac forces against the German airborne invasion in World War II was worthy of the long heroic Cretan history. The island is the first recipient of the E.E.C.'s Integrated Mediterranean Program.

Exploring Crete

The Mediterranean's fourth and Greece's largest island is equidistant from Europe, Asia and Africa. The envied junction of three continents was fought over and occupied by all three, often, and disastrously, at the same time. Though all the 8,617 square km. (3,327 square miles) are scenically rewarding, touristic overdevelopment has blighted the north coast. Iráklio, with a population of over 100,000 the biggest town, port and airfield, is the usual starting point for beach holidays as well as for an exploration of the fabulous Minoan palaces.

Yet the first impressions belong to a more recent past, measured in centuries and not millennia. The 13th-century church of San Marco, used for exhibitions, and the restored Renaissance Loggia overlook the baroque Lion Fountain on Iráklio's central Platía Venizelou. The Metropolis of Ágios Minás is garishly 19th-century, but *Agía Katerina* contains six large icons by Damaskinos, the Cretan School's outstanding representative and teacher of El Greco. Impressive ramparts (where Greece's best-known modern writer, Nikos Kazantzakis, is buried under a wooden cross bearing a quotation from his *Zorba the Greek*) and the Koulé fortress guarding the Venetian port and facing the barren island of Día, now a hunting area, bear testimony to the 24-year siege before the Venetians under Morosini finally surrendered to the Turkish Vizier Achmed Köprülü in 1669. But the waterfront is unusually forbidding, with hardly any taverns or cafes. The Historical Museum contains a variety of Roman and Byzantine finds.

When the foundations of the Cretan University's medical school were laid alongside the Knossós road, the British Archaeological School unearthed a wealth of interesting objects from an antique cemetery used from 1400 B.C. to A.D. 500. A jumble of human bones with fine knife marks like butcher's cuts seems to indicate that the Minoans were not averse to occasional cannibalism, though subsequent finds at Aharnes and Knossós allow the more charitable interpretation of human sacrifices.

Minoan Splendor

The Archaeological Museum stands in a class of its own, guarding practically all the Minoan treasures brought to light by the various excavations. The civilization of 2,000 years is superbly illustrated by an unique collection of pottery and jewelry, including the famous seal-stones with Linear B script, which first attracted Sir Arthus Evans to Knossós. The discovery by another Englishman, Michael Ventris, that Linear B is Greek, and the decipherment of hundreds of clay tablets found in the Minoan palaces as well as on Mycenaean sites on the mainland, alas exclusively store inventories, might indicate that the Minos who united Crete in about 1600 B.C. was an Achaean who usurped the throne. The hieroglyphic inscription winding spiralwise on both sides of the famous terracotta Phaestos disc seems likewise Achaean Greek, a prayer to the gods for help (deciphering was further confused in 1980, when Linear A was claimed to be an unknown Indo-Germanic language). The frescos most catch the eye: delightfully sophisticated representations of broad-shouldered, slim-waisted youths; ritual processions; scenes from the bull ring, far more dangerous than any toreador would dare, as the youth or girl took the bull by the horn when he lowered his head to toss, and somersaulted over his back; and groups of bare-breasted court ladies, whose puffed sleeves and flounced skirts led a French archaeologist to exclaim in surprise "des Parisiennes"—a name still applied to the fresco.

This introduction to a brilliant culture is climaxed by a visit to the palace of Knossós, five km. (three miles) inland. Only the intuition of Schliemann would have suspected that the huge mound hemmed in by low hills covered one of the most amazing archeological sites. Troy and Mycenae, Tiryns and Knossós, what a record of sensational finds, yet Turkish obstruction prevented Schliemann from exploring his last discovery. Cretan independence made it possible for Evans to start excavations in 1900 and find a forgotten civilization.

The original palace built about 2000 B.C. was destroyed some 300 years later and replaced by a more magnificent group of buildings, now partly reconstructed. Evans has been attacked for these reconstructions, paid for out of his own pocket to the tune of £250,000 in the days when pounds came as golden sovereigns and were worth a great deal more than they are today. But besides giving the layman an approximate idea of Minoan architecture, which relied largely on color effects, the much abused reinforced concrete restoration was essential to preserve the wonderfully theatrical great staircase and the throne room, where the oldest throne in Europe still stands unguarded.

Ruins in Crete tend to be particularly ruinous, not only because of their venerable age, but also because of the poorness of the building materials. The gaudily painted, downward-tapering wooden columns and beams supporting the fragile gypsum and stucco facades had been charred in the devastating fire of 1450 B.C. and only falling rubble sustained the delicate fabric. The rubble had to be replaced in the course of excavation, and reinforced concrete was used.

Minoan manor houses have come to light at Tylissós, four km. (two miles) southwest, at Arhanés, an attractive village 15 km. (nine miles) south, where a grape festival is held in September, and at Vathýpetro, four km. (two and a half miles) further on, all surrounded by vineyards and olive groves.

How much is owed to Sir Arthur Evans becomes apparent in the incomparably more splendid setting of Festós (Phaestós). Near the southern shores a conglomeration of buildings rose on a solitary hill dominating the lovely plain of Messara. Only the foundations remain, and much of the site is now fenced off, yet with the memories of Knossós fresh in mind it is possible to conjure up a picture of what the palace must have looked like. Still closer to the sea, near the beach of Tymbáki, lies the royal villa of Agía Triáda, the elegant country house of a Minoan prince, that contained some of the finest objects now in the Archaeological Museum.

Geography determined the choice of Knossós and Phaestós at the beginning and end of the only relatively easy north-south passage in the island's center. Crete is 257 km. (160 miles) from east to west, dissected by an unbroken range rising to almost 2,500 meters (8,000 ft.) in the western White Mountains, the central Mount Ídi (Ida) and the eastern Dikti Mountains. Yet the island is never more than 61 meters (38 miles) wide, narrowing to 13 km. (eight miles) on the isthmus of Ierápetra.

From Agía Varvára, on the highway connecting the two palaces, a branch right (west) opens up the spectacular southern slopes of Mount Ídi. The frescos of the Vrondísi Monastery and of Ágios Fanourios at Valsamonéro are attributed to El Greco but were most likely painted in an earlier century. High above is the Spíleon Kamáron, the cave in which the loveliest Minoan pottery, the *Kamáres*, were found.

Górtys, between the northern vineyards and the fertile plain of Messara, was the Roman capital of Crete. Ruins of an Egyptian sanctuary, a temple of Apollo and a Christian basilica are scattered among the olive groves. Embedded in the wall of the Roman Odeon is the famous 5th-century law code of Górtys, the fountainhead of Greek justice. The port of Phaestós, Mátala, was taken over by Górtys and lately by a nudist colony, which appropriated the caves carved as refuge against pirates into the cliff towering over the fine beach. To the north, at Kommós, American and Canadian archeologists are bringing to light the Minoan port, connected by a wide paved road with Phaestós. Flourishing from 2000 to 1300 B.C., it revived as a sanctuary with a unique proto-geometric temple, succeeded by an archaic and a Hellenistic shrine, to be finally abandoned in about A.D. 125.

To the west, Agía Galíni (St. Serenity) lives up to its name as the South's safest harbor. The quickest drive back to the north coast is via Spilí to Réthymno; the finer scenery, however, is along the Platiés River, passing a unique medieval bridge and a minor Minoan palace at Monastiráki, to Platánes.

The Hidden Highland

It is 56 km. (35 miles) from Iráklio to Ágios Nikólaos, a deservedly popular summer resort between the sea and a theatrical lagoon. The road follows the coast east past the beaches of Háni Kókini, Górnes, Góuves, Liménas Hersoníssou and Stalída to the golden sands of Maliá (35 km., 22 miles), where foundations of another, less elaborate Minoan palace crown a headland; then passes through a 247-meter (270-yard) tunnel to Neápoli. At Hersónissos a 32-km. (20-mile) long branch road climbs to the Lassithi plateau. A row of picturesque Venetian windmills—disused for centuries, but restored as a backdrop for the film of Kazantzakis' *Christ Recrucified*—guards the ridge of a dramatically barren mountain. Behind that some 39 square km. (15 square miles) of an idyllic tabletop plateau open up at an altitude of 732 meters (2,400 ft.) with thousands of old windmills, formerly used to draw water from wells to irrigate the rich plateau and allow potatoes, apples, figs, and olives to flourish. Most of these windmills have been replaced over the last few years by more efficient motor-driven irrigation and the remainder are operated for limited periods only during the summer months. The road skirts the plain linking Tzermiádo with most of the other 17 villages, to Psihró (The Cold), named after the icy spring beneath the huge plane tree in the village square. You can drive almost to the entrance of the perpendicular cave (guide required) on Mount Díkti which disputes with one on Mount Ídi the honor of being the birthplace of Zeus. The numerous votive offerings (now at the Iráklio museum) that were found at the bottom of the frightening chasm bear witness to the importance of the sanctuary in antiquity. The eastern descent from the highland to Ágios Nikólaos is a few miles longer.

Opposite Elóunda, 11 km. (seven miles) north of Ágios Nikólaos, is the island of Spinalónga, protected by an imposing Venetian fortress for 100 years after all Crete had fallen to the Turks. The grim ramparts enclosed a leper colony till 1958.

The same distance southeast is Goúrnia, the best-preserved ruins of a Minoan town as distinct from the palaces. The most striking feature is the narrowness of the streets and the smallness of the domestic quarters. Turning right (south) at Pahiá Ámos you reach the south coast at the excellent beach of Ierapetra after only 18 km. (11 miles). Carnations and gladioli are cultivated for export in Greece's largest flower fields. The road east follows the coast via Agía Fotiá, where next to an Early-Minoan cemetery a most unusual 37-room building has been excavated, then turns inland via the ruins of Pressós to Sitía. At Koutsounári an experiment to increase the villagers' livelihood from tourism has been made by doing up some genuine cottages.

The north coast highway follows the magnificent gulf of Mirabéllo to Sitía, the easternmost port, featuring a museum, a good beach and pleasant seaside taverns. Though Toplóu Monastery contains a magnificent icon painted by Kornaros in 1770, the fortified Cretan monasteries cannot rival the splendor of their mainland counterparts. The road continues to Paleókastro on the east coast. The branch north ends at the ruins of antique Itanos after passing the palm grove of Vaï on a beautiful sandy bay. The branch south leads to the remains of a 17th-century B.C. palace, near the beach of Káto Zákros. The palace conforms to the traditional plan, but the bathtubs were supplemented by a small swimming pool in what seems to have been the main Minoan naval base. The site had never been plundered, but huge lumps of volcanic debris had been flung across the 130 km. (80 miles) from Thíra, which greatly strengthens the theory that the fall of the Minoan Empire was primarily due to the aftermath of the Thíra eruption and not a Mycenaean invasion.

Arkádi and the White Mountains

The 145 km. (90 miles) west from Iráklio to Haniá fully display the varied beauty of the Cretan landscape. From the inland road you may branch left to Anogia and then a spectacular 23 km. (14 miles) under towering peaks to the Idéon Ándron, Zeus' alternative birthplace, continue westwards to the village of Melidóoni, where a large cave has now been opened to the public.

Bypassing the beach of Agía Pelagía, the coastal highway rejoins the sea at Fodéle, where Domenikos Theotokopoulos, the famed El Greco, was born in 1541. After passing Pánormos, a branch leads 18 km. (11 miles) inland (southeast) to the monastery of Arkádi, an interesting example of Greek-Venetian rococo. Believed to have been founded by the Emperor Heraclius in the 7th century, the monastery played a prominent part in the successive risings of the 19th century. On November 7, 1866, the

Turks were on the point of taking it by storm, when the Abbot Gabriel ordered the refectory to be blown up, killing the defenders together with 3,000 assailants. This heroic sacrifice is commemorated every year as the national Cretan holiday.

Réthymno, halfway to Haniá, has the liveliest waterfront below the arcades of 16th-century houses. St. Nicholas and the Rector's Palace have been restored within the ramparts of the huge Venetian fortress, part of U.N.E.S.C.O.'s European Heritage, on the acropolis of ancient Rithymna. A recently discovered Post-Minoan cemetery proves continuous occupation. There is a small archeological museum in the Venetian Loggia.

The foothills of the White Mountains straggle closer to the sea than those of Mount Ídi, and the road follows the coast till Georgióupoli. Georgióupoli is still a village rather than a tourist town, and boasts a beautiful, wide bay, a charming village square with towering eucalyptus trees, and several good cafes and bars.

At Vrýsses (Springs) huge plane trees shade the roadfork to Sfakiá, where the tall blond descendants of the Doric invaders of 1000 B.C. have preserved their racial purity and characteristics in a way unique in much-conquered Greece. Sfakiá is often likened to the Máni in the Peloponnese, and there are indeed many points of resemblance in these two wild and inaccessible regions, where the way of life has hardly changed over the centuries, where vendetta exterminated whole families and put the women into perpetual mourning for some relative killed.

On the whole both districts were little bothered by the foreign overlords, but successive waves of refugees diluted the ancient Hellenic stock in the Máni, and the continuous savage feuds there were not relieved by the homeric carousing and feasting of Sfakiá. Enormous quantities of a fierce liquor have to be consumed, this *tsipouro* often even taking the place of morning coffee.

The road ascends through increasingly barren and desolate country by a steep gorge, snowbound for many weeks each winter. Remote, inaccessible hamlets can be barely distinguished on the precipitous slopes. At Sfakiá, a fairly large village on the southern sea, the road turns east to follow the rugged coast which abounds in lonely coves and sandy beaches, to link up with the south axis near the fishing village of Plakiás.

Close to the shore stand the ruins of Frankgokástello, sole reminder of a vain Venetian attempt at ruling the ungovernable mountains. Scene of particularly heavy fighting, culminating in a wholesale massacre of the local population by the Turks in 1828, the castle has been haunted for over a century. At dawn during May knights in shining armor have been observed by many people manning the crumbling walls and towers.

After a visit to this land where time has stood still, it needs a violent wrench to return to modernity at Sóuda, the important naval base in the large northern bay. Atop a hill lie the ruins of ancient Áptera, Apollo's Doric and Demeter's Hellenistic temple, a Roman theater and vast underground cistern, still partly encircled by ramparts. A Minoan tomb, found intact with clay figures and tablets, dates from 1400 B.C. Sóuda is now the harbor of Haniá, as the Venetian port round which the town was built cannot accommodate modern steamers. The old port is now given to caiques and smaller craft, which makes an evening in the taverns encircling the harbor-basin, or in the cafe in the former mosque, all the more picturesque. The Cretan capital's tall 18th-century houses lend it a befitting dignity, which extends to the well-planned modern suburbs. The secularized

Venetian Church of San Francisco deserves a visit, as does the archeological museum. The historical museum is dedicated to mementos of Venizelos, and the naval museum in the Old Port displays ships' models from the triremes of antiquity onwards. In the small zoo in the Public Gardens are some kri-kri, the wild goats of Crete.

From the vast government building a shady avenue leads to the Halépa suburb facing the open sea, a favorite stroll of young and old in the evening. The road continues up the rocky promontory of Akrotiri, separating Haniá from Sóuda Bay. Among the pine trees lie the tombs of the illustrious Cretan statesmen Eleutherios Venizelos and his son Sophocles, likewise prime minister. Higher up you get some breathtaking views of Haniá before turning inland to the monastery of Agía Triáda, or crossing over to the airport.

The coastal road continues west via Agía Marína, Plataniás and Maléme, which saw some of the heaviest fighting in 1941, to Kolymbári, where the Orthodox Academy's huge congress hall near the 15th-century Gonias Monastery is used for international conferences. An ancient temple and theater stand in the 16th-century Venetian castle above the long but shadeless beach at Kíssamos in the western bay. A 3rd-century-A.D. Roman villa with multicolored mosaics and frescos stood above a large artificial Minoan port.

Several scenic roads lead from the north coast into the mountainous interior and to the splendid beach of Paleohóra on the south coast. Even the great White Mountains are easily accessible by a road that climbs via Fóurnes and Láki to Omalós, where a zigzag path descends steeply 760 meters (2,500 ft.) to the tremendous Samaría Gorge—closed November through March—that splits the cliffs for 13 km. (eight miles) down to Agía Róumeli on the Libyan Sea, where Greece's first sun-thermal station provides electricity. Boats convey the weary walker to Sfakía.

PRACTICAL INFORMATION FOR CRETE

WHEN TO COME. Crete is big enough to offer a variety of attractions all the year round. Winters are mild and hotels in the bigger towns are equipped with central heating, so that there is no obstacle to exploring the Minoan sites undisturbed by the crowds of the tourist season. Though snow lies on the high mountains till May, it practically never snows on the coast. Spring is the best time: it comes about the end of March.

TOURIST OFFICES. There are G.N.T.O. offices at **Haniá,** Kriari 40 (tel. 2 6426); and at **Iráklio,** Xanthoudidou 1 (tel. 22 8203).

SPECIAL EVENTS. July. Wine Festival at Dafnés, near Iráklio, mid-month. Wine Festival at Haniá, held in Municipal Park, second half of July. **July** and **August.** The *Krítsa* Festival; various cultural events held in Kritsa, near Ágios Nikólaos. **October.** The village of Elos, in the province of Kissamos, holds a Chestnut Festival, with old traditional songs and sweets made of chestnuts offered to visitors. **November.** The *Tsikoudiá* Festival offers the opportunity to taste the strong, Cretan liqueur in the village of Voukolios.

HOTELS AND RESTAURANTS. Crete has a large number of modern hotels and bungalows. Some hotels in the towns stay open during the winter, offering reductions of between 10 and 40%. Package tours dominate the scene at all times. There are also furnished flats and rooms in private houses.

Except in the luxury hotels, food varies from the uninteresting to the downright unappetizing. But seaside taverns provide fresh fish, grilled or fried. In season, *lagós* (hare) will often be on the menu. If you like goat's cheese, try *manouri;* *myzíthra* is a creamy sheep's cheese. Both are eaten with honey by the locals. *Anthótyro* and *graviéra* should also be sampled. Of the local wines, *Mirabello* and *Minos,* red or white, are best. But beware topping up too liberally with *tsikoudiá,* a Cretan *raki* with a kick.

Agía Fotia. *Eva Mare* (M), tel. 6 1225. 50 rooms. Pool, but far from beach.

Agía Galíni. *Astoria* (I), tel. 9 1253. 22 rooms. Restaurant; near beach. *Galini Mare* (I), tel. 9 1358. 27 rooms. The largest of some 30 (I)s.

Agía Marína. *Amalthia* (M), tel. 6 8542. 40 rooms. *Santa Marina* (M), tel. 6 8570. 66 rooms. Beach. V.

Agía Pelagía. *Capsis Beach* (E), tel. 81 1212. 554 rooms in central block and bungalows on rocky peninsula. Pool, tennis, minigolf, disco, small beach.AE, DC, MC, V. *Peninsula* (M), tel. 81 1313. 245 rooms in central block and bungalows. Comfortable and well-run with all expected facilities with disco set well away from main buildings; colorful gardens and fine views. Pool and swimming from small beach and rocks. DC. *Panorama* (I), tel. 81 1002. 56 rooms. Pool, tennis.

Agía Roumeli. *Agía Roumeli* (I), tel. 9 1293. 9 rooms.

Ágios Nikólaos. *Minos Beach* (L), tel. 2 2345/9. 132 bungalows. Not airconditioned. Minigolf, pool, tennis; on small beach. AE, DC, MC, V.
Minos Palace (E), tel. 2 3801/9. 151 rooms. On headland facing town, with pool and small beach. AE, DC, MC, V. *Mirabello Village* (E), 2 8806/10. 131 rooms in central block and bungalows set among attractive gardens. Partially airconditioned. Pool, tennis, disco, and minigolf. *Hera Village* (E), tel. 2 8971/3. 44 apartments. *Hermes* (E), tel. 2 8253/6. 204 rooms. Minigolf and disco. On the town seafront. AE, DC, MC, V. *Mirabello* (E), tel. 2 8401/5. 174 rooms. Pool, tennis and disco. AE, DC, MC, V.
Coral (M), tel. 2 8363/7. 170 rooms. On seafront, with roofgarden pool. AE, DC, MC, V. *Dimitra* (M), tel. 2 3290. 12 apartments. *El Greco* (M), tel. 2 8894. 38 rooms. *Miramare* (M), tel. 2 2962. 53 rooms. *Rhea* (M), tel. 28 321/3. 118 rooms. Disco on 10th floor.
Akratos (I), tel. 2 2721/5. 31 rooms. *Alfa* (I), tel. 2 3701. 40 rooms. V. *Almyros Beach* (I), tel. 2 2865. 47 rooms. *Apollon* (I), tel. 2 3023/5. 60 rooms. *Ariadni Beach* (I), tel. 2 2741/3. 76 bungalows. Restaurant. DC. *Creta* (I), 2 8893/4. 27 rooms. *Du Lac* (I), tel. 2 2711/2. 40 rooms. On the lagoon connected by a canal to the sea. *Nikos* (I), tel. 2 4464. 37 rooms. The largest among some 40 (I)s.

Restaurants. *Ariadni* (M), Iosif Koundourou 18. AE, DC, MC, V. *Avra* (M), Akti Koundourou. AE, DC, MC, V. *Cretan* (M), Iosif Koundourou 10. AE, DC.

CRETE 333

Rififi (M), Akti Koundourou. AE, DC, MC, V. *Vassilis* (M), Iosif Koundourou 16. AE, DC, MC. All serve good fish.

Amoudára. *Agapi Village* (E), tel. 25 0502. 276 rooms. Beach, pool, disco, tennis. AE, MC. *Creta Beach* (E), tel. 25 2302. 160 rooms. Pool, disco. AE, DC, MC, V. *Dolphin Bay* (E), tel. 82 1276/7. 269 rooms in central block and bungalows. Pool, tennis. AE, DC. *Tsangarakis Beach* (E), tel. 25 1768. 43 rooms. AE.

Anógia. Traditional settlement with several converted old houses.

Arhanés. *Dias* (I), tel. 75 1810. 31 rooms.

Dáratso. *Althea Village* (M), tel. 3 1320. 38 bungalows. Pool.

Elóunda. *Astir Palace Elounda* (L), tel. 4 1580/4. 297 rooms, 3 suites. On beach with pool, tennis, minigolf and nightclub, set in 20 acres of gardens. AE, DC, MC, V. *Elóunda Beach* (L), tel. 4 1412/3. 301 rooms. Beach, pool, tennis, minigolf and nightclub; attractively set in carob-tree garden. Ranked one of the best hotels in Greece. AE, DC, MC, V. *Elóunda Mare* (L), tel. 4 1512. 81 rooms in central block and bungalows. Pool, tennis. AE, DC, MC, V. *Elóunda Marmin* (E), tel. 4 1003. 133 rooms. AE. *Selena Village* (M), tel. 4 1525. 43 rooms.
The following are at **Shisma**, 1 km. (½ mile) south and are all near a beach. *Akti Olous* (M), tel. 4 1921. 49 rooms. *Aristea* (I), tel. 4 1300/5. 37 rooms. Restaurant, tennis and minigolf. AE, DC, V. *Kalypso* (I), tel. 4 1316. AE, DC, MC. Restaurant.

Férma. *Coriva Village* (E), tel. 6 1263. 35 bungalows on mediocre beach; nearby coves are better. Pool, minigolf, beautiful gardens. *Férma Beach* (E), tel. 2 8418. 166 rooms and bungalows. Pool, tennis. AE. *Porto Belissario* (M), tel. 6 1360. 35 rooms. Pool, beach.

Galatás. *Dolphin* (I), tel. 4 8507. 18 rooms.

Georgióupoli. *Gorgona* (I), tel. 2 2378. 38 rooms. Disco; restaurant. *Happy Days* (M), tel. 6 1220. 80 rooms. On beach.

Góurnes. *Royal* (M), tel. 76 1231. 66 rooms. Near beach.

Góuves. *Aphrodite Beach* (E), tel. 4 1102. 242 rooms. Pool, disco, tennis. AE, DC, V. *Creta Sun* (E), tel. 4 1103. 350 rooms. Only public rooms are airconditioned. On beach, with pool, tennis, minigolf and disco. Renovated 1987. *Marina* (E), tel. 4 1361/5. 310 rooms. On beach, with pool, tennis, minigolf and disco. AE, DC, V. *Christi Apartments* (M), tel. 4 1278. 36 apartments. *Villa Kalypso* (M), tel. 4 1390. 36 rooms. *Mon Repos* (I), tel. 4 1280/5. 37 rooms. DC, V.

Haniá. *Arkadi* (M), tel. 2 8724. 61 rooms. Airconditioned. V. *Contessa* (M), tel. 2 3966. 6 rooms. This pension is in a grand old family house overlooking Venetian harbor. No restaurant. *Doma* (M), tel. 21 772. 29 rooms. *Kriti* (M), tel. 2 1881/5. 88 rooms. Only public rooms airconditioned. V. *Kydon* (M), tel. 2 6190/4. 105 rooms, 8 suites. Roofgarden, disco. AE, DC,

MC. *Porto del Colombo* (M), tel. 5 0975. 6 rooms. Well-restored Turkish house in traffic-free quarter, near waterfront; roofgarden. *Porto Veneziano* (M), tel. 2 9311/3. 63 rooms. In a converted Venetian mansion on the old port; airconditioned. AE, DC, V. *Samaria* (M), tel. 5 1551/5. 58 rooms. Airconditioned; no restaurant. AE, DC, MC, V. *Xenia* (M), tel. 2 4561/2. 44 double rooms. In the Venetian fortress; closest to the town beach. AE, DC, MC, V. *Canea* (I), tel. 2 4673/5. 49 rooms. *Aptera Beach* (I), tel. 2 2636. 46 bungalows. Restaurant. Three km. (two miles) west.

Restaurants. The setting of the openair taverns (M) round the old port is more pleasing than the fare; *Amphora* (M) is one of the better restaurants. The same is true for *Aposperida* (M), an original tavern-cum-cafe on several floors in a 17th-century soap factory.

Háni Kókini. *Arina Sand* (M), tel. 76 1293. 233 rooms in central block and bungalows. Tennis. Partly airconditioned. AE, DC. *Knossos Beach* (M), tel. 76 1204. 106 rooms in central block and bungalows on the seafront. Partly airconditioned. AE, DC. *Themis Beach* (M), tel. 76 1374. 124 rooms. All with pool, minigolf and disco. AE, DC, V. *Danae* (I), tel. 76 1375. 18 rooms. Small pool, restaurant.

Ierápetra. *Lyktos Beach and Tennis Club* (L), tel. 6 1280. 250 rooms. Opened in 1989 to much acclaim, this lush place features a beach, pool, tennis, nightclub, sauna, cinema, and library. *Petra Mare* (E), tel. 2 3341/9. 214 rooms, 7 suites. Beach, pool, nightclub. AE, DC. *Atlantis* (I), tel. 2 8555. 69 rooms. Airconditioned. AE, DC. *Zakros* (I), tel. 2 4101. Largest of some 20 (I)s. Airconditioned; restaurant. AE, V.

Iráklio. *Astoria* (E), tel. 22 9002. 141 rooms. Pool, disco. Partially airconditioned. AE, DC, MC, V. *Atrion* (M), tel. 24 2830. 65 airconditioned rooms. *Galaxy* (M), tel. 23 8812. 140 rooms. Pool, disco. AE, DC, V. *Mediterranean* (M), tel. 28 9331/5. 55 rooms. Roofgarden. AE, DC, MC, V. *Asterion* (I), tel. 22 7913. 60 rooms. Restaurant. *Athinaïkon* (I), tel. 22 9312. 40 rooms. *Castello* (I), tel. 25 1212. 64 rooms. Restaurant. DC, V. *Daedalos* (I), tel. 22 4391. 60 rooms. Airconditioned. AE, V. *Gloria* (I), tel. 22 8334. 52 rooms. Restaurant. One km. (half a mile) along the sea at Poros, but without beach. *Grabelles* (I), tel. 23 5086/9. 42 rooms. Airconditioned; restaurant. *Olympic* (I), tel. 288 861. 73 rooms. Roofgarden. V.

Restaurants. Platia Venizelou is a prettier setting than Daedalou in the same central pedestrian zone, but the food is equally poor in all the openair Inexpensive establishments. *Caprice* (M). Closest to the lovely Morosini fountain. AE, DC. *Klimataria* (M), Daedalou. Efficient service, but the less said about the food the better. AE, V. *Maxim Fish Tavern* (M), Koroneou 5 beside the Park Hotel. Fresh fish. AE, DC. *Ta Psaria* (M), opposite the sea fortress. As the name suggests, more fresh fish.

Kandra Kitchen of San Francisco organizes badly-needed 6-day cooking classes Apr.-Oct.

Kalathás. *Tzanakaki Beach* (I), tel. 6 4363/5. 35 rooms. Restaurant.

Kaló Horió. *Istron Bay* (E), tel. 6 1303. 112 rooms. Pool, tennis, nightclub. Splendid location above private beach. MC, V. *Elpida* (M), tel. 6 1403. 68 rooms. Pool. *Golden Bay* (I), tel. 6 1202. 49 rooms. Restaurant. AE.

Karterós. *Minoa Palace* (E), tel. 22 7802. 124 rooms. Pool, tennis; private sandy beach. AE, DC. *Karterós* (M), tel. 22 8802. 54 rooms. DC, V. *Motel Xenia* (I), tel. 28 1841/3. 42 double rooms. Restaurant. AE, DC, MC.

Káto Galatás. *Panorama* (E), tel. 5 4200/5. 150 rooms, 17 suites. Partly airconditioned; pool and disco. AE, MC.

Kíssamos. *Helena Beach* (M), tel. 2 3300/5. 40 rooms. *Kastron* (I), tel. 2 2140/1. 11 rooms. Restaurant. *Kíssamos* (I), tel. 2 2086. 16 rooms. V.

Kolymbári. *Rose Marie* (I), tel. 2 2220. 9 rooms. Restaurant.

Kournas. *Manos Beach* (M), tel. 6 1221. 15 rooms.

Koutsounári. Traditional settlement with several converted old houses.

Liménas Hersoníssou. *Creta Maris* (L), tel. 2 2115/30. 516 rooms in hotel and bungalows. Pool, tennis, nightclub; on beach. AE, DC, MC, V. *Belvedere* (E), tel. 2 2371. 320 rooms in central block and bungalows. Pool, tennis, disco. AE, MC, V. *Glaros* (E), tel. 2 2106. 141 rooms. *Robinson Club Lyttos Beach* (E), tel. 2 2575/8. 326 rooms. Beach, pool, tennis, disco. DC, V. *Nana Beach* (E), tel. 2 2706. 153 rooms in hotel and bungalows. Pool, tennis, sauna. *Cretan Village* (M), tel. 2 2996/7. 272 rooms. Pool, tennis, disco. *Nora* (M), tel. 2 2271/5. 181 rooms. Pool, disco. AE, MC, V. *Albatros* (I), tel. 2 2144. 74 rooms. *Eva* (I), tel. 2 2090/2. 33 rooms. Airconditioned; disco, restaurant. *Heronissos* (I), tel. 2 2501. 145 rooms. Restaurant, pool, sauna. AE. *Ilios* (I), tel. 2 2500. 72 rooms. *Iro* (I), tel. 2 2136. 51 rooms. *Palmera* (I), tel. 2 2481/3. 72 rooms. *Sergios* (I), tel. 2 2583/5. 75 rooms. *Zorbas* (I), tel. 2 2075. 22 rooms. Restaurant. The best equipped of some 30 (I) hotels on or near the beach.

Linoperámata. *Apollonia Beach* (E), tel. 82 1602. 310 rooms in central block and bungalows. Disco, pool, tennis, minigolf; on beach. AE, DC, V. *Zeus Beach* (E), tel. 82 1503. MC, V. 378 rooms. Also on beach with pool, disco, tennis, minigolf. AE.

Maléme. *Crete Chandris* (E), tel. 6 2221/5. 414 rooms in central block and bungalows. Pool, tennis, disco. AE, DC, MC, V.

Mália. *Ikaros Village* (E), tel. 3 1267/9. 179 rooms in a German designed "typical" Greek village. Beach, pool, tennis. AE. *Kernos Beach* (E), tel. 3 1421/5. 280 rooms in central block and bungalows. Beach, pool, tennis. AE. *Sirens Beach* (E), tel. 3 1321/5. 275 rooms. Beach, pool, tennis, disco. AE, DC, MC, V. *Kostas* (M), tel. 3 1485/8. 34 rooms. *Malia Beach* (M), tel. 3 1301/3. 186 rooms. Pool. *Phaedra Beach* (M), tel. 3 1560/1. 71 rooms. Staff sometimes unhelpful. *Malia Holidays* (I), tel. 3 1206. 81 rooms. About 30 other (I) hotels near the beach.

Mátala. *Matala Bay* (I), tel. 4 2300/1. 55 rooms. Disco; 450 meters (500 yards) from beach. V.

Mohlós. *Aldiana Club* (I), tel. 9 4211/2. 138 rooms. Restaurant, disco, beach, pool.

Myrtós. *Esperides* (I), tel. 5 1207. 58 rooms. v.

Pahiá Ámos. *Golden Beach* (I), tel. 9 3278. 12 rooms. Beach, restaurant, and pool.

Paleohóra. *Elman* (M), tel. 4 1412/4. 23 apartments. Beach, disco. *Polydoros* (M), tel. 4 1068. 13 rooms. Basic but pretty and the best in town.

Paleokastro. *Marina Village* (I), tel. 6 1284/5. 28 rooms. Restaurant. v.

Pánormos. *Lavris* (M), tel. 5 1226/7. 28 rooms. Pool, tennis, minigolf. *Panormos Beach* (I), tel. 5 1321/3. 31 rooms.

Pérama. *Marelina* (M), tel. 9 3231/5. 201 rooms. Airconditioned; disco, pool, tennis.

Perivólia. *Minos* (I), tel. 2 4173/6. 74 rooms. Pool.

Plakiás. *Alianthos Beach* (M), tel. 3 1227. 124 rooms. Airconditioned; beach, disco. v. *Kalypso Cretan Village* (M), tel. 3 1210. 102 bungalows on beach. Pool. *Lamon* (I), tel. 3 1205. 23 rooms. Restaurant; on beach. AE, DC, MC. *Sophia Beach* (I), tel. 3 1251/2. 25 rooms.

Rapaniána. *Olympic* (I), tel. 2 2483. 34 rooms. 275 meters (300 yards) from beach; restaurant.

Réthymno. *Artemis Palace* (E), tel. 2 1991. 175 rooms. Pool, tennis, sauna.*Braskos* (M), tel. 2 3721/3. 82 rooms. Disco. AE, DC, MC, v. *Eleonora* (M), tel. 2 5121/2. 28 apartments. DC, v. *Ideon* (M), tel. 2 8667/8. 75 rooms. Pool. AE, DC, MC, v. *Jo-An* (M), tel. 2 4241/4. 50 rooms. Airconditioned. *Olympic* (M), tel. 2 4761/4. 59 rooms. Airconditioned. AE. *Xenia* (M), tel. 2 9111/2. 25 rooms. The only one directly on the excellent town beach. AE, DC.

There are some 20 adequate Inexpensive hotels, mostly without restaurants, and we give the largest. *Astali* (I), tel. 2 4721/2. 36 rooms. AE. *Golden Sun* (I), tel. 7 1284. 38 rooms. v. *Steris Beach* (I), tel. 2 8303. 45 rooms. Restaurant. *Valari* (I), tel. 2 2236. 29 rooms.

Out of Town. The following hotels are on beaches east of the town. *Creta Star* (E), tel. 9 3300. 308 rooms and 14 suites. Pool, disco, tennis, cinema, sauna.*El Greco* (E), tel. 7 1102. 307 rooms. With central block and bungalows, pool, tennis, minigolf and disco. AE, DC, MC, v. *Rithymna Beach* (E), tel. 2 9491. 556 rooms. Same facilities as El Greco. Some accommodation is (L). AE, DC, MC, v. *Adele Beach* (M), tel. 7 1081. 60 bungalows. Disco, pool. AE. *Orion* (M), tel. 7 1471/4. 73 rooms. Pool, disco; on beach. AE, DC. *Golden Beach* (I), tel. 7 1012. 72 rooms. Pool, restaurant. AE, MC, v.

Restaurants. Fish taverns—Moderate and Inexpensive—in the arcades along the waterfront serve fresh seafood; eat in the open at night. *Aghía*

Piano (M) is a sophisticated, Continental restaurant with a difference; dine under orange trees in the courtyard.

Ródia. *Rogdia* (I), tel. 82 1373. 22 rooms.

Sitía. *Kappa Club* (E), tel. 2 8821/4. 162 rooms. Only public rooms airconditioned; pool, tennis, disco. On beach, *Sunwing* (E), tel. 5 1621/4. 250 airconditioned rooms; pool, tennis. Some moderate accommodation here, too. MC, V. *Maresol* (M), tel. 2 8933. 27 bungalows. Pool, tennis. *Itanos* (I), tel. 2 2146. 72 rooms. Airconditioned; the only hotel with restaurant and largest among some 20 Inexpensive establishments. AE, DC.

Stalída. *Anthoussa Beach* (E), tel. 3 1380/2. 167 rooms. Pool, tennis, disco. AE, DC. *Amazones Villas* (M), tel. 3 1488. 51 apartments. *Arminda* (M), tel. 2 2486. 64 apartments. *Blue Sea* (M), tel. 3 1371/3. 197 rooms in bungalows. Beach, pool, disco. AE, DC. *Cactus Beach* (M), tel. 3 1319. 61 rooms. Pool. *Zephyros Beach* (M), tel. 3 1566. 76 rooms; pool. On remote beach. *Heliotrope* (I), tel. 3 1515/7. 81 rooms. Pool. *Stalis* (I), tel. 3 1246. 44 rooms. Restaurant, pool.

Tymbáki. *Ágios Geórgios* (I), tel. 5 1678. 10 rooms. MC.

Tzermiádo. *Kourites* (I), tel. 2 2194. 7 rooms. Restaurant.

Zákros. *Zákros* (I), tel. 2 8479. 16 rooms.

Zarós. *Idi* (I), tel. 3 1302. 22 rooms. V.

YOUTH HOSTELS. These are at: *Ágios Nikólaos,* 60 beds; (tel. 2 2823); *Iráklio,* 120 beds; (tel. 22 2947); *Mália,* 35 beds; (tel. 3 1338); *Sitía,* 30 beds (tel. 2 2693). Also at Haniá (tel. 5 3565) and Réthymnon (tel. 2 2848).

MOUNTAIN REFUGES. Two in the White Mountains, one on Mount Idi.

GETTING AROUND. By Plane. Iráklio international airport is connected to several European towns. There are seven flights daily from Athens, one from Rhodes and Thessaloníki; also flights from Mýkonos, Paros, and Thíra in summer. There are five flights daily between Athens and Haniá; and flights to Sitía from Rhodes, Kárpathos and Kassos.

By Boat. The daily ferries from Piraeus to both Iráklio and Haniá take about 11 hours. There is a service several times a week in summer from Santoríni to Iráklion, and from Thessaloníki once a week to Iráklion, once to Haniá. There is also a connection between Rhodes and Sitía.

By Car and Bus. On the island itself, there are excellent roads along both the north and the south coasts. These are linked by a number of good north/south roads. Buses are cheap and frequent, but car hire is expensive.

THE LANGUAGE

English presents no problem in the better hotels and restaurants; even in modest establishments, someone is usually able to cope. Yet it is useful to possess a smattering of everyday phrases and words—some of which are given in the Tourist Vocabulary below. The ancient Greek alphabet of 24 letters has survived unchanged. Although demotic (*dimotiki,* vernacular Greek) was officially imposed in 1977, most educated people, several authors and newspapers still speak and write in *kathomilouméni,* which is more akin to ancient Greek; but both follow the same rules of pronunciation, which differ considerably from the Erasmic—the Greek taught in classics' classes in American and British schools and universities. Biblical *(koiné)* Greek, yet another variation, is still read in church.

PRONUNCIATION

In romanized Greek, A/a, E/e, I/i, K/k, M/m, N/n, O/o, T/t, Y/y and Z/z present no difficulty.

Greek *vita* (B/β), when romanized, is written and pronounced as V/v.
English C and H sounds do not exist in Greek.

Ita (H/η) in Greek is pronounced as I/i.

Délta (Δ/δ) is pronounced as a soft TH, but it is written in romanized Greek as D/d.

Thíta (Θ/θ) is a strong TH/th.

Lámda (Λ/λ) is L/l.

Sigma (Σ/σ) is S/s.

Both *oméga* (Ω/ω) and *ómikron* (O/o) are written and pronounced as O/o.

More difficult sounds are the sounds that do not exist in English. The slightly guttural *gamma* (Γ/γ) used to be rendered as GH, but now is simply G/g.

The strongly guttural *hi* (X/χ) used to be CH or KH but is now H/h, except after S/s where, for clarity's sake, it remains KH/kh; it is no less guttural than before.

Fi (Φ/ϕ), formerly PH, is now F/f.

Ro (P/ρ) should be rendered R/r.

Pi (Π/π) is P/p.

Xi (Ξ/ξ) is X/x, and should not be confused with *hi.*

Psi (Ψ/ψ) is PS/ps.

MII/uh (MII/$\mu\pi$) is pronounced B.

The dipthongs AE/ and AI/ are written and pronounced as E/e (as in Elizabeth). EI/ and OI/ are as I/i (as in give); OY/ as U/u (pronounced -oo-); AY/ is pronounced -af-; EY/ is pronounced -ev-. When the first letter of a dipthong carries an accent, the two letters are pronounced separately.

PLACE NAMES. The real problem for the tourist is, however, the confusion over the naming of places, with bewildering variations on tourist folders, maps and signposts. To make these comprehensible to visitors from all nations, indications are given in Greek as well as Latin characters, but phonetically according to the modern Greek pronunciation, which differs not only from the ancient Greek, but even more from the latinized forms mainly used in English, French and German.

As if it were not enough that many villages, mountains and rivers are called differently by the locals from the Classical names favored by officialdom, *dimotiki* has changed most endings of names. Hence the confusing (how often we find ourselves using that word!) variety of indications, about evenly divided between the old and the new, even for the capital itself; thus Athina (new) as well as Athine (old). Names that reverberated through history for millenia have been deprived of their final "n" or "s." Pólis (town) has not been spared and has been reduced to póli, yet an "s" has often been added to the endings of the names of mountains and rivers. We give the new demotic form first in the text under the main entry, with the generally-used anglicized name in brackets, and then employ the generally-used name throughout the text for such familiar places as Athens and Corinth. But consistency is not a strong point: Achaia has become Ahaïa, Aegina is Égina, Chios is Híos, Heraklion is Iráklio, Phaestós is Festós, and Rhodes is Ródos, while Mikonos has more often than not reverted to Mykonos. The "Y" is creeping back again, for some inexplicable reason more in the islands, while Olympia and Ólympos have always remained sacrosanct.

Though neither the Greek capital letters nor the Latin characters are accented, we have stressed the relevant syllable, otherwise you might not be understood.

STREET NAMES in most towns and resorts are likewise indicated in both alphabets, but following the Greek habit, only in the possessive case of the name, omitting *odós* (street), but not necessarily *leofóros* (avenue) or *platía* (square); 3 Stadium Street thus becomes "Stadiou 3." Renaming streets is a favorite pastime of Greek municipalities, especially following elections.

TOURIST VOCABULARY

The phonetic spelling used in English differs somewhat from the internationalized form of Greek place names. There are no long and short vowels in Greek; the pronunciation never changes. For the sake of uniformity, the official "gi" has been adopted over the "y" or "yi." Note, also, that the accent is a stress mark, showing where the stress is placed in pronunciation.

GENERALITIES

Do you speak English?	Miláte angliká?
Yes—no	Málista or Né—óchi
Impossible	Adínato
Good morning—Good day	Kaliméra
Good evening—Good night	Kalispéra—Kaliníchta
Goodbye—*Au revoir*	Kalí andámosi

Mister—Madam—Miss	Kírie—kiría—despinis
Please	Parakaló
Excuse me	Me sinchórite *or* signómi
How are you?	Ti kánete *or* pós íste
How do you do (Pleased to meet you)	Chéro polí
I don't understand	Dén katalavéno
To your health!	Giá sas!
Thank you	Efcharistó

NUMBERS

1	éna	9	enéa	80	ogdónda
2	dío	10	déka	90	enenínda
3	tría	20	íkossi	100	ekató
4	téssera	30	triánda	200	diakóssia
5	pénde	40	saránda	300	triakóssia etc.
6	éxi	50	penínda	1000	chília
7	epta	60	exinda	2000	dió chiliádes
8	októ	70	evdomínda	3000	trís chiliádes etc.

DAYS OF THE WEEK

Monday	Deftéra	Friday	Paraskeví
Tuesday	Tríti	Saturday	Sávato
Wednesday	Tetárti	Sunday	Kyriakí
Thursday	Pémpti		

MONTHS

January	Ianouários
February	Fevrouários
March	Mátios
April	Aprílios
May	Maíios
June	Ióounios
July	Ióulios
August	Ávgoustos
September	Septémvrios
October	Októvrios
November	Noémvrios
December	Dekémvrios

TRAVELING

I am traveling by car . . . train . . . plane . . . boat	Taxidévo mé aftokínito . . . me tréno . . . me aeropláno . . . me vapóri
Taxi, to the station . . . harbor . . . airport	Taxi, stó stathmó . . . limani . . . aerodromio . . .
Porter, take the baggage/luggage	Akthofóre, pare aftá tá prámata
Where is the filling-station?	Pou íne tó pratirío vensínis (vensinádiko)

When does the train leave for . . . ?	Tí óra thá fíyi to tréno giá tin . . .?
Which is the train for . . . ?	Pío íne to tréno gía . . . ?
Which is the road to . . . ?	Piós íne o drómos giá %. . . ?
A first-class ticket	Éna isitírio prótis táxis
No smoking (compartment)	Apagorévete to kapnízin
Where is the toilet?	Póu íne í toaléta?
Ladies—Men	Ginekón—Andrón
Where?—When?	Póu?—Póte?
Sleeping-car—Dining-car	Wagonlí—wagonrestorán
Compartment	Diamérisma
Entrance—Exit	Íssodos—éxodos
Nothing to declare	Den écho tipota na dilósso
I am coming for my holidays	Érchome giá tis diakopés mou
Nothing	Tíota
Personal use	Prossopikí chríssi
How much?	Pósso?

ON THE ROAD

Straight ahead	Kat efthían
To the right—to the left	Dexiá—aristerá
Show me the way to . . . please	Díxte mou to drómo . . . parakaló
Where is . . . ?	Pou íne . . . ?
Crossroad	Stavrodrómi
Danger	Kíndinos
Drive slowly!	Sigá
Look out for the train (railroad crossing)	Prósseche to tréno

IN TOWN

Will you lead me? take me?	Thélete na me odigíste? Me pérnete mazí sas?
Street—Square	Drómos—plateia
Where is the bank?	Pou íne i trápeza?
Far	Makriá
Police station	Asstinomikó tmíma
Consulate (American, British)	Proxenío (Amerikániko, Anglikó)
Theater—Cinema	Théatro—Kinimatografos
At what time does the film start?	Tí óra archizi to film?
Where is the travel office?	Pou íne to touristikó grafío?
Where is the tourist information office? . . . tourist police?	Pou íne o tourismós . . . i touristiki astinomía?

SHOPPING

I would like to buy	Tha íthela na agorásso
Show me, please	Díxte mou, parakaló
May I look around?	Boró na tho lígo?
How much is it?	Pósso káni? (*or* kostízi)

It is too expensive	Íne polí akrivó
Have you any sandals?	Échete pédila?
Have you foreign newspapers?	Échete xénes efimerídés?
Show me that blouse, please	Díxte mou aftí tí blouza
Show me that bag	Díxte mou aftí tívalítza
Envelopes—Writing paper	Fakélous—grafikí íli
Roll of film	Film
Map of the city	Hárti tis póleos
Something handmade	Hiropíito
Wrap it up, please	Tilíxeto parakaló
Cigarettes, matches, please	Tsigára, spírta parakaló
Ham	Zambon
Sausage—salami	Loukánika—salami
Sugar—salt	Záchari—aláti
Grapes—cherries	Stafília—Kerássia
Apple—Pear—Orange	Mílo—achládi—portokáli
Bread—Butter	Psomí—voútiro
Peach—Figs	Rodákino—síka

AT THE HOTEL

A good hotel	Éna kaló xenodochio
Have you a room available?	Échete eléfthero domátio?
Where can I find a furnished room?	Pou boró na vró epiploméno domátio?
A room with one bed, with two beds	Éna monó domátio, éna dipló domátio
With bathroom	Me bánio
How much is it per day?	Pósso kostízi tin iméra?
A room overlooking the sea	Éna domátio prós ti thálassa
For one day, for two days	Giá miá méra, giá dió méres
For a week	Giá miá vdomáda
My name is	Onomázome
My passport	Tó diavatirió mou
What is the number of my room?	Piós íne o arithmós tou domatíou mou?
The key, please	To klidí parakaló
Breakfast, lunch, supper	Proínó messimergianó vradinó
The bill, please	To logariasmó, parakaló
I am leaving tomorrow	Févgo (or anachoró) ávrio

AT THE RESTAURANT

Waiter	Garsón
Where is the restaurant?	Pou íne to estiatório?
I would like to eat	Tha íthela na fáo
The menu, please	Dós mou ton katálogo
Fixed price menu	Menú
Soup	Soúpa
Bread	Psomí
Hors d'oeuvre	Orektiká
Ham omelette	Omelétta zambón
Chicken	Kotópoulo

Roast pork	Psitó chirinó
Veal	Moschári
Potatoes (fried)	Patátes (tiganités)
Tomato salad	Domatosaláta
Vegetables	Lachaniká
Watermelon—melon	Karpoúzi—pepóni
Cakes	Gliká *or* pástes
Fruit—Cheese—ice-cream	Fróuta—tirí—pagotó
Fish—Eggs	Psári—Avgá
Serve me on the terrace	Servírisse me sti tarátza
Where can I wash my hands?	Pou boró na plíno ta chéria mou?
Red wine—white wine	Mávro krasí—áspro krasí
Unresinated wine	Krasí aretsínato
Beer—soda water—water	Bíra—soda—neró
Greek (formerly Turkish) coffee	Ellenikó Kafé
Coffee with milk—milk	Kafé evropaiko—gála

(For the names of Greek specialties see our *Food and Drink* chapter).

AT THE BANK—AT THE POST OFFICE

Where is the bank? . . . post office?	Pou íne i trápeza? . . . to tachidromío?
I would like to cash a check	Thélo ná isspráxo éna tséki
I would like to change some money	Thelóna alaxo chrímata
Stamps	Grammatóssima
By airmail	Aëroporikos
Postcard—letter	Kárta—grámma
Letterbox	Grammatokivótio
I would like to telephone	Thélo na tilephonisso

AT THE GARAGE

Garage—gas (petrol)	Garáz—veníni
Oil	Ládi
Change the oil	Alaksete to ládi
Look at the tires—a tire	Rixe mia matiá sta lástika - ene lástiko
Wash the car	Plíne to aftokínito
Breakdown	Vlávi
Tow the car	Rimulkisse tó aftokínito
Spark plugs	Busí
The brakes	Fréno
Gearbox	Kivótio tachíton
Carburetor	Karbiratér
Headlight (headlamp)	Prowoléfs
Starter	Mísa
Axle	Áksonas
Spring	Sústa
Spare part	Antalaktikó

MOUNTAIN CLIMBING—SAILING

Guide	Odigós
Horse—Mule	Álogo—moulári
Food	Fagitó
I want to eat, to drink, to sleep	Thélo na fáo, na pió, na kimithó
Hut or refuge	Katafíyio
Do you want to guide us?	Thés na mas odigíssis?
How much do you want per day?	Pósso thélis tin iméra?
Sunrise—sunset	Anatolí—díssi
Sun—moon	Ilios—fengári
Day—night	Iméra—níchta
Morning—afternoon	Proi—apóyevma
Skipper—engineer	Kapetános—michanikos
Port—Port commandant	Limáni—Limenárchis
Port—starboard	Aristerá—dexiá
Boat—sail	Várka—paní
North wind	Meltémi
Course of the yacht	Poría
Speed	Tachítita
Creek—beach—rocks	Órmos—ammoudiá—vráchia
Engine breakdown	Zimía michanís
We are touching port	Fthánome stó limáni
We are sailing for . . .	Apopléome . . .
The weather is good—bad	Ó kerós ine kalós—kakós
The sea is calm—rough	I thálassa íne kalí—kakí

Index

The following abbreviations are used in this index: E-Entertainment; H-Hotels; R-Restaurants; YH-Youth Hostels

See also Practical Information at the end of each chapter for local information on camping, shopping, special events, sports, transportation.

Facts at Your Fingertips

Geographical

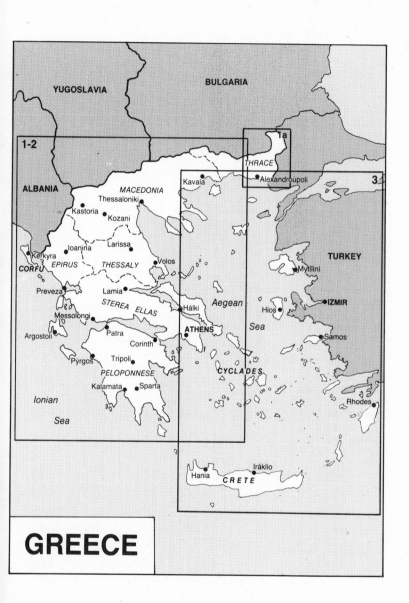

GREECE

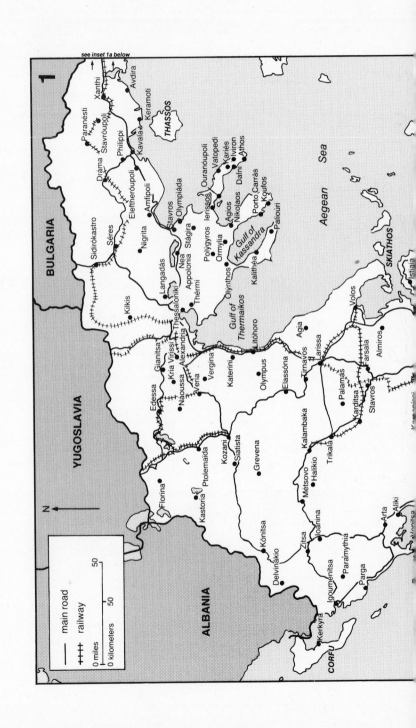

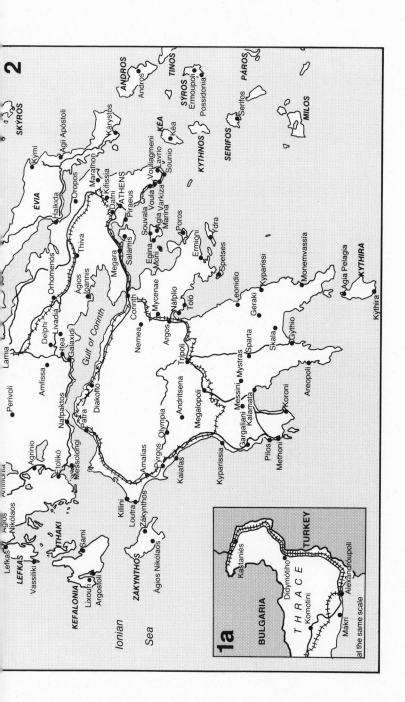

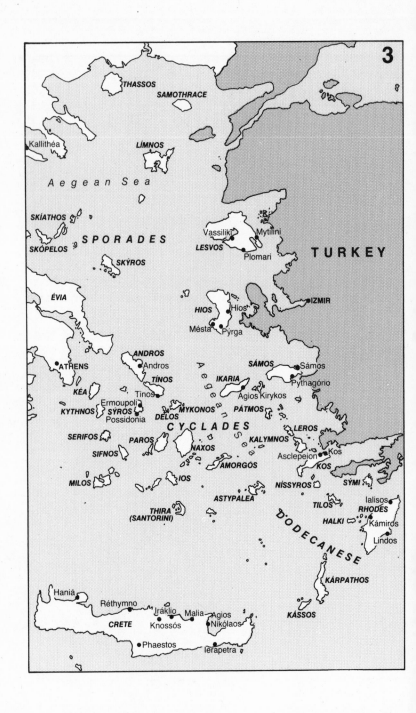

Fodor's Travel Guides

U.S. Guides

Alaska
Arizona
Boston
California
Cape Cod
The Carolinas & the
  Georgia Coast
The Chesapeake
  Region
Chicago
Colorado
Disney World & the
  Orlando Area

Florida
Hawaii
The Jersey Shore
Las Vegas
Los Angeles
Maui
Miami & the Keys
New England
New Mexico
New Orleans
New York City
New York City
  (Pocket Guide)

New York State
Pacific North Coast
Philadelphia
The Rockies
San Diego
San Francisco
San Francisco
  (Pocket Guide)
The South
Texas
USA
The Upper Great
  Lakes Region

Virgin Islands
Virginia & Maryland
Waikiki
Washington, D.C.

Foreign Guides

Acapulco
Amsterdam
Australia
Austria
The Bahamas
The Bahamas
  (Pocket Guide)
Baja & the Pacific
  Coast Resorts
Barbados
Belgium &
  Luxembourg
Bermuda
Brazil
Budget Europe
Canada
Canada's Atlantic
  Provinces
Cancun, Cozumel,
  Yucatan Peninsula
Caribbean
Central America
China

Eastern Europe
Egypt
Europe
Europe's Great
  Cities
France
Germany
Great Britain
Greece
The Himalayan
  Countries
Holland
Hong Kong
India
Ireland
Israel
Italy
Italy's Great Cities
Jamaica
Japan
Kenya, Tanzania,
  Seychelles
Korea

Lisbon
London
London Companion
London
  (Pocket Guide)
Madrid & Barcelona
Mexico
Mexico City
Montreal &
  Quebec City
Morocco
Munich
New Zealand
Paris
Paris (Pocket Guide)
Portugal
Puerto Rico
  (Pocket Guide)
Rio de Janeiro
Rome
Saint Martin/
  Sint Maarten
Scandinavia

Scandinavian Cities
Scotland
Singapore
South America
South Pacific
Southeast Asia
Soviet Union
Spain
Sweden
Switzerland
Sydney
Thailand
Tokyo
Toronto
Turkey
Vienna
Yugoslavia

Special-Interest Guides

Bed & Breakfast
  Guide to the Mid-
  Atlantic States

Bed & Breakfast
  Guide to New
  England
Cruises & Ports
  of Call

A Shopper's Guide
  to London
Health & Fitness
  Vacations
Shopping in Europe

Skiing in North
  America
Sunday in New York
Touring Europe